LITERACY
in the
MIDDLE GRADES

LITERACY
in the
MIDDLE GRADES

Teaching Reading and Writing
to Fourth Through Eighth Graders

SECOND EDITION

Gail E. Tompkins

California State University, Fresno

Boston • Columbus • Indianapolis • New York • San Francisco • Upper Saddle River
Amsterdam • Cape Town • Dubai • London • Madrid • Milan • Munich • Paris
Montreal • Toronto • Delhi • Mexico City • São Paulo • Sydney • Hong Kong • Seoul
Singapore • Taipei • Tokyo

Vice President, Editor-in-Chief:
  Aurora Martínez Ramos
Editorial Assistant: Amy Foley
Senior Development Editor: Hope Madden
Vice President, Marketing and Sales Strategies:
  Emily Williams Knight
Vice President, Director of Marketing:
  Quinn Perkson
Executive Marketing Manager: Krista Clark

Production Editor: Janet Domingo
Editorial Production Service: Nesbitt Graphics, Inc.
Composition Buyer: Linda Cox
Manufacturing Buyer: Megan Cochran
Electronic Composition: Nesbitt Graphics, Inc.
Interior Design: Carol Somberg
Photo Researcher: Annie Pickert
Cover Designer: Susan Swan
Cover Administrator: Linda Knowles

For related titles and support materials, visit our online catalog at www.pearsonhighered.com.

Between the time website information is gathered and then published, it is not unusual for some sites to have closed. Also, the transcription of URLs can result in typographical errors. The publisher would appreciate notification where these errors occur so that they may be corrected in subsequent editions.

Printed in the United States of America

Photo Credits: p 2 (Middle): Comstock Images/Getty Images; p 3 (Middle): Hero Images/Corbis; p 29 (Middle): Jamie Grill/Blend Images/Alamy; p 56 Robin Sachs/PhotoEdit, Inc.; p 114 Iofoto/Shutterstock; p 138 Spencer Grant/Art Directors & TRIP/Alamy; p 228 Monkey Business Images/Shutterstock; p 259 (Middle): Comstock/Getty Images; p 259 (Right): Contrastwerkstatt/Fotolia All other photos Gail Tompkins.

9

www.pearsonhighered.com

ISBN-10: 0-132-34849-7
ISBN-13: 978-0-132-34849-2

ABOUT THE AUTHOR

Gail E. Tompkins is Professor *Emerita* at California State University, Fresno. She currently spends her time writing and working with teachers and students in fourth- through eighth-grade classrooms. Dr. Tompkins was inducted into the California Reading Association's Reading Hall of Fame in recognition of her publications and other accomplishments in the field of reading, and she's received the prestigious Provost's Award for Excellence in Teaching at California State University, Fresno. Previously, Dr. Tompkins taught at the University of Oklahoma in Norman, where she received the Regents' Award for Superior Teaching, and at Miami University in Ohio, where she taught at the McGuffey Laboratory School and worked with preservice teachers. She was also a school teacher in Virginia for eight years.

Dr. Tompkins is the author of six other books published by Pearson: *Literacy for the 21st Century: A Balanced Approach*, 5th ed. (2010), *Literacy for the 21st Century: Teaching Reading and Writing in Pre-Kindergarten Through Grade 4*, 2nd ed. (2007), *Language Arts: Patterns of Practice*, 7th ed. (2009), *Language Arts Essentials* (2006), *Teaching Writing: Balancing Process and Product*, 5th ed. (2008), and *50 Literacy Strategies*, 3rd ed. (2009).

Dr. Tompkins has also worked with elementary- through college-level writing teachers at two National Writing Project sites during the last three decades. She directed the Oklahoma Writing Project when she taught at the University of Oklahoma, and more recently she was the director of the San Joaquin Valley Writing Project in California, where she initiated a program to encourage teachers to write for publication. Pearson has published three collections of classroom-tested teaching strategies and lessons written by teachers in the San Joaquin Valley Writing Project: *Teaching Vocabulary: 50 Creative Strategies, Grades 6–12*, 2nd ed. (2008), edited by Gail E. Tompkins and Cathy L. Blanchfield; *50 Ways to Develop Strategic Writers* (2005), also edited by Gail E. Tompkins and Cathy L. Blanchfield; and *Sharing the Pen: Interactive Writing With Young Children* (2004), edited by Gail E. Tompkins and Stephanie Collom.

BRIEF CONTENTS

CONTENTS

CHAPTER 2
Examining the Reading and Writing Processes 32

CHAPTER 3
Assessing Literacy Learning 56

CHAPTER 4
Differentiating Instruction 86

PART 2: *Powerful Teaching*   112

CHAPTER 5
Eliminating Obstacles to Fluency 114

CHAPTER 8
Promoting Comprehension: Text Factors 200

CHAPTER 9
Teaching Writing 228

PART 3: *Effective Instructional Programs* 258

CHAPTER 10
Teaching With Trade Books 260

CHAPTER 11
Teaching With Textbooks 290

CHAPTER 12
Using Literacy in the Content Areas   312

Compendium of Instructional Procedures   345

SPECIAL FEATURES

Assessment Tools

Minilesson

New Literacies

Be Strategic!

STRUGGLING READERS AND WRITERS

Spotlight on . . .

Welcome to *Literacy in the Middle Grades*! I invite you to step into my vision for reading and writing instruction in grades 4 through 8.

First and foremost, I've written this text for you. *Literacy in the Middle Grades* is meant to serve as a valuable resource that you can take into the classroom. As I address the topic of each chapter, I've linked theory and research with classroom practice so that you'll know what's important to teach, why it's important, and how to teach it effectively. I've featured real teachers throughout the text so you can envision yourself using the classroom practices I recommend. Also, I've compiled step-by-step directions for the best instructional and assessment activities in the Compendium of Instructional Procedures, placed at the end of the text for easy access.

Literacy does look different with middle-grade students, and classroom teachers face tremendous challenges today. Annual high-stakes tests measure student learning as well as teacher effectiveness. The rapid expansion of technology, especially the Internet, requires a rethinking of what it means to be literate. Teachers in grades 4 through 8 also need to keep in mind the specific instructional needs of young adolescent learners.

Effective literacy instruction must focus on developing strategic readers and writers, scaffolding English learners, and incorporating new literacies that support students' use of technology. Successful teachers create a classroom climate where literacy flourishes, and they differentiate instruction by adjusting their lessons and providing multiple options for learning so that every student can be successful.

With this new edition, I aim to answer the questions you might have about teaching reading and writing with middle graders—about instructional approaches, about scaffolding English learners, about guiding students who struggle, about using technology to teach reading and writing—and in the process, to create the most relevant and valuable teacher resource possible.

How does this book help teachers meet the diverse needs of middle graders?

It's crucial that teachers recognize the diversity of learners in 21st-century classrooms. Because students' achievement levels differ and their interests and preferred ways of learning vary, teachers modify instruction so that all students can be successful. I kept this idea in mind as I revised this text, and I offer rich and varied options for meeting diverse student learning needs.

■ *New!* In Chapter 4, Differentiating Instruction, I offer suggestions for adapting instruction for struggling students and identify ways to address students' reading and writing problems. This new material helps you understand how to vary instruction while meeting grade-level standards and provides instructional procedures to ensure that all students can be successful.

■ *New!* **Spotlight** features highlight three students—one at grade level, one struggling, and one advanced—to give you a good look at the individual needs of young adolescents, and to provide you with insights to help them become more successful readers and writers.

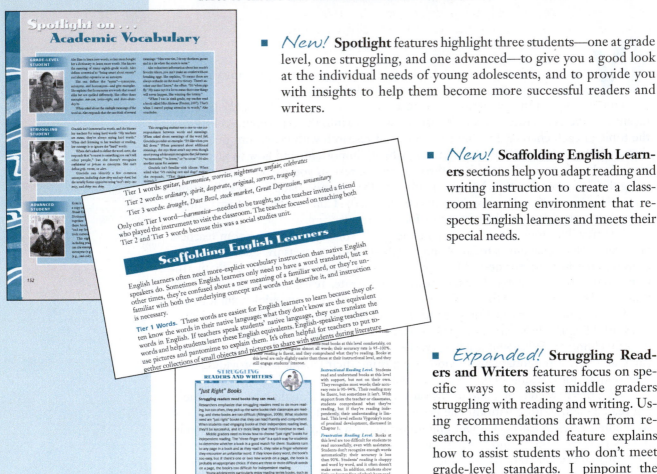

■ *New!* **Scaffolding English Learners** sections help you adapt reading and writing instruction to create a classroom learning environment that respects English learners and meets their special needs.

■ *Expanded!* **Struggling Readers and Writers** features focus on specific ways to assist middle graders struggling with reading and writing. Using recommendations drawn from research, this expanded feature explains how to assist students who don't meet grade-level standards. I pinpoint the ways in which readers and writers may struggle with each chapter's concepts, and provide answers to guide struggling students toward developing the reading and writing strategies they need to succeed.

How does this book help teachers address curricular demands?

Federal, state, and school district requirements often constrain classroom time and resources; high-stakes testing, national and state standards, and mandated curriculum materials complicate things even more. How can teachers be accountable to all these directives and still provide effective literacy instruction? I've revised this text to provide the guidance you'll need to navigate this maze of mandates while ensuring your students' academic success.

Assessment

Assessment must drive instruction, a principle I emphasize in this new edition. A full chapter, placed early in the text, lays the groundwork for assessing students' achievement and for using the results to inform instruction. You'll learn how to determine students' reading levels and use informal assessment tools and classroom tests to screen students at the beginning of the school year, monitor their progress, diagnose reading and writing difficulties, and document students' learning. This chapter also provides essential information about preparing students for high-stakes achievement tests.

- ■ *New!* Chapter-by-chapter **Assessment Tools** features provide detailed information about tests teachers use to survey, monitor, diagnose, and evaluate students' literacy learning. Focusing on everything from comprehension to motivation, this integrated treatment helps teachers understand how assessment figures into every lesson they teach.

New Chapter Coverage

In this revision, I've paid close attention to the changing demands on middle-grade teachers and provided more in-depth information on writing genres and on teaching and assessing writing in grades 4 through 8. I also devote two chapters to organizing class time to incorporate trade book and textbook approaches effectively and another chapter to using reading and writing as tools for learning and demonstrating learning in the content areas.

- ■ *New!* Chapter 9, Teaching Writing, presents information on responding to literature, writing essays, and doing workplace writing, as well as information on how to prepare students for high-stakes district, state, and national writing tests.

- ■ *New!* Chapter 10, Teaching With Trade Books, addresses how to implement literacy programs using authentic literature within the time constraints in middle-grade classrooms.

- ■ *New!* Chapter 11, Teaching With Textbooks, helps middle-grade teachers exploit required basal readers and language arts textbooks more effectively.

- ■ *New!* Chapter 12, Using Literacy in the Content Areas, guides teachers toward the most effective ways to help readers navigate content-area texts.

Modeling Effective Literacy Teaching

Authentic classroom artifacts, real stories from master teachers, and ideas for helping students develop cognitive and metacognitive strategies that will better prepare them for the literacy demands of the middle grades—these are all opportunities for me to show you what successful literacy classrooms look like so you can envision yourself in this context.

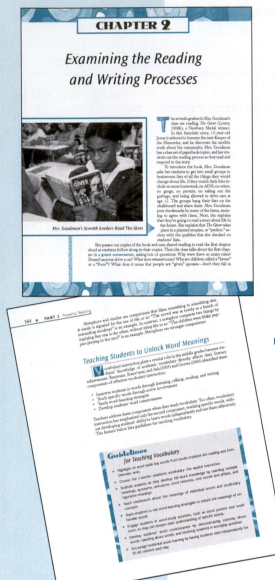

Chapter-opening vignettes, the signature feature of this text, provide true classroom stories that illustrate how effective teachers integrate reading and writing to maximize students' literacy learning, modeling the ways successful middle-grade teachers address curricular demands.

New! **Be Strategic!** features highlight the literacy strategies your students need to develop to be successful readers and writers.

Guidelines features list the most important points teachers need to know when teaching vocabulary, comprehension, and writing.

How does this book help teachers prepare themselves to teach in contemporary middle-grade literacy classrooms?

It's not enough to give teachers the foundational knowledge about literacy—the theories, the principles, the content knowledge. Although this is valuable information, my job wouldn't be complete if that were all I offered. You need strategies to take directly into the classroom, and you need the know-how to use them. That's why I've always filled my texts with application, from assessment tools to minilessons to the Compendium of Instructional Procedures in the back of the text. I want you to have the necessary materials to carry right into your classroom.

- The **Compendium of Instructional Procedures** provides a valuable bank of 35 step-by-step procedures. Look for highlighted terms throughout the text that connect chapter content with the matching fully crafted strategy in the Compendium—including powerful content-area instructional procedures.

- *New!* **New Literacies** features address 21st-century technology opportunities available to young adolescents, highlighting the ways that teachers prepare their students to read and write online, use e-portfolios, do webquests, and much more.

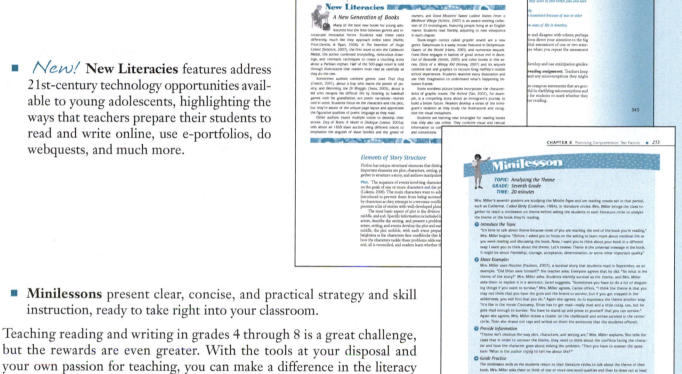

- **Minilessons** present clear, concise, and practical strategy and skill instruction, ready to take right into your classroom.

Teaching reading and writing in grades 4 through 8 is a great challenge, but the rewards are even greater. With the tools at your disposal and your own passion for teaching, you can make a difference in the literacy development—and in the lives—of young adolescents.

Supplements

The **Instructor Resource Center** at **www.pearsonhighered.com** has a variety of print and media resources available in downloadable, digital format—all in one location. As a registered faculty member, you can access and download pass code–protected resource files, course-management content, and other premium online content directly to your computer.

These digital resources are available for *Literacy in the Middle Grades*, 2e:

- A test bank of multiple-choice and essay tests

- PowerPoint presentations specifically designed for each chapter

- Chapter-by-chapter materials, including objectives, suggested readings, discussion questions, and in-class activities, as well as guidance on how to use the vignettes meaningfully in your instruction

To access these items online, go to www.pearsonhighered.com and click on the Instructor option. You'll find an Instructor Resource Center option in the top navigation bar; there you'll be able to log in or complete a one-time registration for a user name and password. If you have any questions regarding this process or the materials available online, please contact your local Pearson sales representative.

Acknowledgments

Many people encouraged me as I developed and revised this text. My heartfelt thanks go to the teachers who welcomed me into their classrooms, showed me how they work with young adolescents, and allowed me to learn from them and their students. In particular, I want to express my appreciation to the teachers and students who appear in the vignettes: Rich Abrams, Eileen Boland, Kimberly Clark, Whitney Donnelly, Laurie Goodman, Inez Jackson, Nicki Paniccia McNeal, Kacey Sanom, Marissa Sarkissian, Stacy Shasky, Paulette Simmons, and Darcy Williams. Thanks to the professors who reviewed this text for their insightful comments:

Shirley B. Ernst,
Eastern Connecticut State University
Carol J. Fuhler,
Iowa State University
Hollis Lowery-Moore,
Lamar University
Laura Pardo,
Hope College
Thomas C. Potter,
California State University, Northridge

Recently the Higher Ed division of Pearson was reorganized, and I've become an Allyn & Bacon author. I'm adjusting to these changes. Linda Bishop, who was my editor for nearly a decade, provided the vision and oversaw the planning for this edition. You're amazing! Thank you, Linda, for guiding my books so expertly year after year. My new editor, Aurora Martínez Ramos, took over this project and supervised the production; now I look to you, Aurora, for guidance. I'm very grateful to Hope Madden, my developmental editor. In this text, I've written about the importance of teachers scaffolding their students; that's what you've done for me—provided the scaffolding I needed to complete this revision. Once again I want to express my sincere appreciation to Janet Domingo, my most accommodating production editor, who has skillfully supervised the production of this book and deftly juggled the last-minute details, and to Melissa Gruzs, who expertly copyedited the manuscript and proofread the pages; you've taught me to be a more precise writer. It's because of this team's expertise and dedication that this new edition has been published.

LITERACY
in the
MIDDLE GRADES

PART 1

Literacy in the 21st Century

Effective teachers create a nurturing classroom environment and provide high quality and engaging literacy instruction. They strive to make a real difference in the lives of their students. It's likely that you'll notice that teaching is different today than when you were a young adolescent. Our society has changed, and teachers face new challenges today that reflect these changes.

Student Diversity

Middle-grade classrooms are culturally, linguistically, and academically diverse. Some students are learning to speak English at the same time they're learning to read and write. Some struggle with literacy, and others exceed grade-level standards. Teachers create culturally responsive and inclusive classrooms where all students are respected and everyone succeeds.

State and Federal Mandates

Teachers tailor their instructional programs to emphasize grade-level standards while differentiating instruction to meet individual students' needs. They also juggle federal mandates that are designed to assist underachievers and eliminate the achievement gap.

High-Stakes Tests

Teachers teach test-taking strategies and prepare students for annual standardized achievement tests that measure students' literacy learning against grade-level standards. These assessments are controversial because of the time test preparation and administration takes away from teaching and because the results are used to make educational decisions about students and to evaluate teachers' effectiveness.

Technology

New information and communication technologies, including Web browsers, word processors, presentation software, blogs, video cams, and social networking sites, affect our understanding of what it means to be literate and require that students learn new ways of communicating through reading and writing. Teachers teach the strategies and skills that students need to successfully use and adapt to rapidly expanding digital technology.

WHAT'S AHEAD

In Part 1, you'll read these chapters:

Chapter 1: Becoming an Effective Literacy Teacher

Chapter 2: Examining the Reading and Writing Processes

Chapter 3: Assessing Literacy Learning

Chapter 4: Differentiating Instruction

These chapters lay the foundation for teaching reading and writing to young adolescents and preparing them to become productive citizens in the 21st century. You'll learn about how effective literacy teachers teach and assess students' learning and how to accelerate students' academic achievement.

Becoming an Effective Literacy Teacher

Literacy is the ability to use both reading and writing for a variety of tasks at school and outside of school. Reading is a complex process of understanding written text. Readers interpret meaning in a way that's appropriate to the type of text they're reading and to their purpose. Similarly, writing is a complex process of producing text; writers create meaning in a way that's appropriate to the genre and their purpose. Peter Afflerbach (2007b) describes reading as a dynamic, strategic, and goal-oriented process. The same is true of writing. *Dynamic* means that readers and writers are actively involved in reading and writing. *Strategic* means that readers and writers consciously monitor their learning. *Goal-oriented* means that reading and writing are purposeful; readers and writers have a plan in mind.

Our concept of what it means to be literate is changing. Traditional definitions of literacy focused on the ability to read words, but now literacy is considered a tool, a means to participate more fully in the 21st century's digital society. Kist (2005) talks about *new literacies*—sophisticated technological ways to read and write multimodal texts incorporating words, images, and sounds—which provide opportunities for students to create innovative spaces for making meaning, exploring the world, and voicing their lives. These texts often combine varied forms of representation, including computer graphics, video clips, blogs, and digital photos, which students read and write differently than they do traditional books (Karchmer, Mallette, Kara-Soteriou, & Leu, 2005).

New Literacies

The Internet

The Internet is rapidly changing what it means to be literate. It's becoming common to see students involved in these online activities:

- Posting blogs on the class website
- Completing webquests
- Participating in virtual book clubs
- Researching informational topics

These activities foster students' engagement with reading and writing.

Some students learn to surf the Web, locate and read information, and communicate using e-mail, instant messaging, and blogs outside of school; others, however, haven't had many digital experiences. Teaching students how to read and write online has become a priority so that they become fully literate in today's "flat" world.

Internet texts are different than books (Castek, Bevans-Mangelson, & Goldstone, 2006). They're a unique genre with these characteristics:

Nonlinearity. Hypertext lacks the familiar linear organization of books; instead, it's dynamic. Readers impose a structure to fit their needs and reconfigure the organization, if necessary.

Multiple Modalities. Online texts integrate words, images, and sound to create meaning. Readers need to know how to interpret each mode and how it contributes to the overall meaning.

Intertextuality. Many related texts are available online, and they influence each other. As students read, they prioritize, evaluate, and synthesize the information.

Interactivity. Webpages often include interactive features to engage readers and allow them to customize their searches, link to other websites, and play games.

Reading and writing on the Internet require students to become proficient in new ways of accessing, comprehending, and communicating information. Students navigate the Internet to search for information; coauthor online texts as they impose an organization; evaluate the information's accuracy, relevance, and quality; and synthesize information from multiple texts (Leu, Kinzer, Coiro, & Cammack, 2004).

Writing online differs from using paper and pencil, too. It's more informal, although most texts should be grammatically acceptable and use conventional spelling. Immediacy is another difference: Writers post their writing within seconds. Third, writers create multimodal texts with digital photos, video clips, and website links. The fourth difference is audience: Writers send e-mail messages to people in distant locations, including military parents serving in Iraq and Afghanistan, and their postings are read by people worldwide.

Literacy in the 21st century involves more than teaching students to read books and write using pen and paper; it's essential that teachers prepare students to use the Internet and other information-communication technologies successfully (Karchmer, Mallette, Kara-Soteriou, & Leu, 2005).

This text focuses on teaching reading and writing in the middle grades. Students at this level—fourth through eighth grades—are called *young adolescents*; they're beginning the transition to adulthood that's marked by significant physical, social, and intellectual changes. The National Middle School Association's *This We Believe* (2003) document explains that students in the middle grades are "forming the attitudes, values, and habits of mind that will largely direct their behavior as adults" (p. 1). Effective teachers use their knowledge about young adolescents to plan a relevant and challenging curriculum, design instruction that engages students and addresses their needs, and ensure students' success through ongoing assessment.

Teachers teach a diverse group of students in middle-grade classrooms. It's not unusual to have students reading at five or six grade levels, from second to seventh or eighth grade in a fifth-grade classroom, for example. Today, too many students read significantly below grade level, and they can't access information in grade-level textbooks or learn independently by reading. Many are English learners or from minority and low socioeconomic groups. These students are in real danger of never being able to fully access information that will be crucial to their success in school and in the workplace. It's essential that teachers close the achievement gap so that all students can reach their potential.

Gambrell, Malloy, and Mazzoni (2007) recommend that teachers develop a vision of what they hope to achieve with the students they teach and then work to accomplish their plans. The goal of literacy instruction is to ensure that all students achieve their full literacy potential, and in that light, this chapter introduces eight principles of effective literacy instruction, and they provide the foundation for the chapters that follow.

PRINCIPLE 1: Effective Teachers Appreciate the Uniqueness of Young Adolescents

Young adolescents undergo a significant transition from childhood to adolescence. You've probably noticed kids aged 10 to 14 undergoing tremendous growth spurts, experiencing turbulent emotions, exhibiting distasteful public behavior, or demonstrating idealism through community projects. These behaviors are typical. Some students begin the transition as early as fourth and fifth grades, and by sixth, seventh, and eighth grades, the progression is obvious. It's crucial that teachers understand these changes so that they can provide developmentally appropriate instruction (Brown & Knowles, 2007).

Characteristics of Young Adolescents

Young adolescents experience dramatic physical, social, and intellectual changes during their transition to adolescence, and these changes directly affect their academic achievement.

Physical Development. Young adolescents undergo tremendous biological changes as their bodies mature, including growth spurts and the onset of puberty:

Growth Spurts. Boys and girls experience steady growth in height and weight before puberty; then physical development accelerates. This rapid growth increases students' nutrition and sleep needs.

Puberty. Girls, on average, reach puberty at age 11 and boys 2 years later. The onset of puberty causes observable changes in physical appearance, including breast growth in girls and voice change and facial hair in boys. These changes often make students self-conscious about their appearance.

The physical changes occurring during young adolescence are greater than in any other stage except the one from birth to age 3.

Social Development. Young adolescents strive toward independence during this stage. They broaden their social affiliations, search for identity, and address issues of social justice:

Peer Groups. Young adolescents yearn to belong to a group, and peer approval becomes as important as adult approval. They're extremely concerned about fitting in and overreact to ridicule and rejection. Same-sex friendships flourish; girls look for emotional support through their friendships, and boys seek friends who will lend support in times of trouble. Some kids join gangs to be part of a group and ensure their physical safety.

Search for Identity. Students begin the search to find out who they are and where they're going in life. They struggle with issues of gender, ethnicity, culture, sexuality, and spirituality, especially when they're confronting views that differ from those of their family. Many kids are bullied verbally or physically, and this harassment threatens their emerging identity.

Social Justice. Young adolescents are idealistic. They're interested in what's "fair," and as they become increasingly aware of the world, kids become passionate about social issues such as peace, homelessness, and the environment.

During the transition from dependence and independence, students learn to socialize, begin to define their lifestyle, and experiment with new viewpoints.

Intellectual Development. Young adolescents' brains undergo significant changes that affect their cognitive capabilities:

Reasoning Ability. Most young adolescents think concretely. They think logically about objects for which they've had personal experience, classify objects into hierarchical relationships, and conceptually combine objects to form categories (Elkind, 1970). By age 14, however, students' thinking begins a gradual shift toward abstract reasoning.

Metacognition. Students grow in their ability to think metacognitively or reflect on their thoughts. They become more proficient in using cognitive strategies and monitoring their learning. They recognize that they can control their attitudes toward learning and assume more responsibility for their academic achievement.

Intellectual Curiosity. Young adolescents are inquisitive about the world and interested in learning about real-life situations. As they increasingly recognize what's meaningful, they're less willing to study topics that don't matter to them.

Young adolescents refine their ability to think conceptually and reflect on their thinking during the middle grades.

Between fourth and eighth grades, students are on an emotional rollercoaster as they adjust to their developing bodies, expanding social roles, and enhanced thinking abilities. Their development in the three domains occurs concurrently, but individual students' growth rates vary widely. Figure 1–1 presents excerpts from seventh and eighth graders' "I Am . . ." poems that exemplify characteristics of this transition.

Instructional Implications

The dynamic changes that young adolescents undergo have important implications for literacy instruction (National Middle School Association, 2003). Literacy instruction should be developmentally appropriate and should embody these elements:

Active Learning. Students prefer activities where they're actively involved in using the information they're learning. For instance, they participate in student-led discussions, create graphic organizers, work in collaborative groups, and play games.

CLF

FIGURE 1–1   ◆   *Excerpts From "I Am . . ." Poems*

I am a proud seventh grader.
I pretend to be cool, but I'm not.
I worry about what people think of me.
I hope I'll survive middle school.
I am a proud seventh grader.
                    —Savannah

I am a Pacific Islander from Tonga.
I dream of going back home, but
I understand it costs a lot of money.
I worry that I might never get there.
I am a Pacific Islander from Tonga.
                    —Kolei

I am just a kid.
I touch my armpits to see if I have hair there.
I worry that I'll never be an adult.
I am just a kid.
                    —Lucas

I am a child with divorced parents struggling to survive.
I feel my heart and it is shattered.
I touch the chair where my father used to be.
I wish my family was whole again.
I am a child with divorced parents struggling to survive.
                    —Jenny

I am lost in the sorry of my heart.
I wonder if I'll ever be found.
I feel like I'm all alone.
I cry out to God, and I am found.
Now my heart sings with love.
                    —Marta

Social Interaction. Young adolescents value opportunities to interact with peers, and teachers teach students how to develop respectful group relationships and work together to complete assignments. Then they regularly provide opportunities for students to read and write with partners and in small groups.

Authentic Activities. Reading real trade books, writing compositions to share with genuine audiences, and creating projects to address actual social problems are authentic activities. It's up to teachers to design instruction that meets state expectations or standards while appealing to students' interests.

Strategy Instruction. Because middle-grade students can reflect on their thinking, they can use cognitive and metacognitive strategies to comprehend fiction and non-fiction books and content-area textbooks. Teaching these strategies is crucial because beginning in fourth grade, students are expected to read and understand books with increasingly complex ideas and vocabulary.

Individualization. Middle graders exhibit a wide range of learning, cultural, and linguistic differences that affect their reading and writing achievement. Within any classroom, students' reading levels vary up to five or six grades, and their writing runs the gamut from basic to advanced, so teachers differentiate instruction to meet students' needs.

Inquiry Learning. Young adolescents are curious about the world and want to find answers to solve problems. As they read literature, students can research social issues they're reading about and take action to address them in their community, and in content-area units, students find answers to their own questions and create projects to share what they've learned.

When middle-grade teachers understand the developmental characteristics of their students and provide appropriate instruction incorporating these recommendations, they'll be more effective (Wormeli, 2001). Figure 1–2 describes the characteristics of effective middle-grade teachers, based on the recommendations for teaching young adolescents.

PRINCIPLE 2: Effective Teachers Understand How Students Learn

Understanding how young adolescents learn influences how teachers teach. Until the 1960s, behaviorism, a teacher-centered theory, was the dominant view; since then, student-centered theories that advocate students' active engagement in authentic literacy activities have become more influential. The three most important theories are constructivism, sociolinguistics, and information processing. In the last few years, however, behaviorism has begun a resurgence as evidenced by the federal No Child Left Behind Act, renewed popularity of textbook programs, current emphasis on curriculum standards, and mandated high-stakes testing. Tracey and Morrow (2006) argue that incorporating multiple theoretical perspectives improves the quality of literacy instruction; accordingly, the stance presented in this text is that instruction should represent a realistic balance between teacher- and student-centered theories.

Constructivism

Constructivist theorists describe students as active and engaged learners who construct their own knowledge. Learning occurs when students integrate new information with their existing knowledge. This theory is student centered because teachers engage students with experiences so that they construct their own knowledge.

Schema Theory. Knowledge is organized into cognitive structures called *schemas*, and schema theory describes how students learn. Piaget (1969) explained that learning is the modification of schemas as students actively interact with their environment.

FIGURE 1–2 ◆ *Characteristics of Effective Middle-Grade Teachers*		
Characteristic	*Description*	*Instructional Recommendations*
Professional Commitment	Teachers are passionate about working with young adolescents.	• Understand the physical, social, and intellectual characteristics of young adolescents. • Engage students in learning experiences that reflect these characteristics.
Classroom Community	Teachers create a nurturing classroom community that's inviting, safe, and supportive.	• Build strong relationships with students. • Respect and value cultural diversity. • Create a classroom culture where learning flourishes.
Literacy Curriculum	Teachers create a literacy curriculum that's relevant, challenging, integrative, and exploratory. It includes reading and writing fiction and nonfiction and using reading and writing as tools for content-area study.	• Choose literature that deals with diverse cultures and social issues. • Teach students how to read nonfiction and content-area textbooks. • Expand students' ability to express ideas through writing. • Use reading and writing as tools for content-area learning. • Encourage lifelong literacy habits.
Meaningful Instruction	Teachers ensure that instruction is relevant and authentic, and they share their enthusiasm for reading and writing.	• Engage students in active and authentic reading and writing activities. • Have students work in groups. • Differentiate instruction. • Incorporate online literacy experiences. • Use multiple approaches to instruction. • Provide explicit instruction on literacy strategies.
High Expectations	Teachers set high expectations and believe all students will succeed.	• Communicate instructional goals clearly. • Link assessment and instruction. • Use a variety of assessment tools. • Teach students to self-assess their learning.

Imagine that the brain is a mental filing cabinet, and that new information is organized with existing knowledge in the filing system. When students are already familiar with a topic, the new information is added to a mental file, or schema, in a revision process called *assimilation*, but when students study a new topic, they create a mental file and place the information in it; this more-difficult construction process is *accommodation*. Everyone's cognitive structure is different, reflecting their knowledge and past experiences.

Inquiry Learning. Dewey (1997) advocated an inquiry approach to develop citizens who could participate fully in democracy. He theorized that learners are innately curious and actively create their own knowledge, and he concluded that collaboration, not competition, is more conducive to learning. Students collaborate to conduct investigations in which they ask questions, seek information, and create new knowledge to solve problems.

Engagement Theory. Theorists examine students' interest in reading and writing because engaged students are intrinsically motivated; they do more reading and writing, enjoy these activities, and reach higher levels of achievement (Guthrie & Wigfield, 2000). Engaged students have self-efficacy or confidence that they will reach their goals (Bandura, 1997). Young adolescents with high self-efficacy are resilient and persistent, despite obstacles that get in the way of their success. These theorists believe that students are more engaged when they participate in authentic literacy activities with classmates in a nurturing classroom community.

Figure 1–3 summarizes constructivism and the other theories you're reading about.

FIGURE 1–3 ◆ *Learning Theories*			
Orientation	**Theory**	**Characteristics**	**Applications**
Student-Centered	Constructivism	• Describes learning as the active construction of knowledge • Recognizes the importance of background knowledge • Advocates collaboration, not competition • Suggests ways to engage students so they can be successful	• Literature focus units • K-W-L charts • Reading logs • Thematic units
	Sociolinguistics	• Views reading and writing as social and cultural activities • Explains that students learn best through authentic activities • Advocates culturally responsive teaching • Challenges students to confront injustices and inequities in society	• Literature circles • Partner reading • Reading and writing workshop • Author's chair
	Information Processing	• Recommends integrating reading and writing • Views reading and writing as meaning-making processes • Explains that readers' interpretations are individualized • Describes students as strategic readers and writers	• Guided reading • Graphic organizers • Grand conversations • Reading logs
Teacher-Centered	Behaviorism	• Focuses on observable changes in behavior • Views the teacher's role as providing information and supervising practice • Describes learning as the result of stimulus–response actions • Uses incentives and rewards for motivation	• Basal readers • Textbooks • Workbooks • Whole-class instruction

Sociolinguistics

Vygotsky (1978, 1986) theorized that language organizes thought and is a learning tool. He recommended that teachers incorporate opportunities for students to talk with peers as part of the learning process. Vygotsky realized that students can accomplish more-challenging tasks in collaboration with adults than on their own but learn very little by performing easy tasks that they can already do independently, so he recommended that teachers focus instruction on students' *zone of proximal development*, the level between their actual development and their potential development. As students learn, teachers gradually withdraw their support so that students eventually perform the task independently. Then the cycle begins again.

Sociocultural Theory. Reading and writing are viewed as social activities that reflect the culture and community in which students live (Moll & Gonzales, 2004). Sociocultural theorists explain that students from varied cultures have different expectations about literacy and preferred ways of learning. Teachers apply this theory as they create culturally responsive classrooms that empower all students, including those from marginalized groups, to become successful readers and writers (Gay, 2000). Teachers are respectful of all students and confident in their ability to learn.

Teachers often use books of multicultural literature to develop students' cross-cultural awareness, including *Feathers* (Woodson, 2007), which examines the issue of race when a white boy is placed in an all-black sixth-grade classroom; *The Circuit* (Jiménez, 1999), which tells the moving story of a Mexican American boy and his migrant farming family; and *Project Mulberry* (Park, 2007), which portrays the conflict a Korean American girl feels as she tries to "fit in."

Culturally responsive teaching acknowledges the legitimacy of all students' cultures and social customs and teaches students to appreciate their peers' cultural heritages. This theory emphasizes that teachers are responsive to their students' instructional needs. When students aren't successful, teachers examine their instructional practices and make changes so that all students become capable readers and writers.

Situated Learning Theory. Learning is a function of the activity, context, and culture in which it occurs (Lave & Wenger, 1991). Situated learning theory rejects the notion of separating learning to do something from actually doing it and emphasizes the concept of apprenticeship, where beginners move from the edge of a learning community to its center as they develop expertise (Brown, Collins, & Duguid, 1989). For example, to become a chef, you could go to cooking school or learn as you work in a restaurant; situated learning theory suggests that working in a restaurant is more effective. For literacy learning, students learn through authentic and meaningful activities. They join a community of learners and become more-expert readers and writers through social interaction with peers. The teacher serves as an expert model, much like a chef does.

Critical Literacy. Freire (2000) called for sweeping educational change so that students examine fundamental questions about justice and equity. Critical literacy theorists view language as a means for social action and advocate that students become agents of social change (Johnson & Freedman, 2005). This theory has a political agenda, and the increasing social and cultural diversity in American society adds urgency to resolving inequities and injustices.

One way that students examine social issues is by reading books such as *The Bread-winner* (Ellis, 2001), the story of a girl in Taliban-controlled Afghanistan who pretends

FIGURE 1–4 ◆ *Books That Foster Critical Literacy*

Avi. (2003). *Nothing but the truth*. New York: Avon. (grades 6–8)

Bruchac, J. (2004). *The winter people*. New York: Puffin Books. (6–8)

Bunting, E. (1999). *Smoky night*. San Diego: Voyager. (4–5)

Curtis, C. P. (2000). *The Watsons go to Birmingham—1963*. New York: Laurel Leaf. (5–7)

Ellis, D. (2001). *The breadwinner*. Toronto: Groundwood Books. (4–6)

Fleischman, P. (2004). *Seedfolks*. New York: Harper-Trophy. (4–6)

Frank, A. (1993). *Anne Frank: The diary of a young girl*. New York: Bantam. (7–8)

Haddix, M. P. (1998). *Among the hidden*. New York: Simon & Schuster. (6–8)

Hesse, K. (2001). *Witness*. New York: Scholastic. (6–8)

Hiaasen, C. (2006). *Hoot*. New York: Yearling. (5–6)

Houston, J. W., & Houston, J. D. (2002). *Farewell to Manzanar*. Boston: Houghton Mifflin. (7–8)

Levine, E. (2007). *Henry's freedom box*. New York: Scholastic. (4–5)

Lowry, L. (2006). *The giver*. New York: Delacorte. (6–8)

Ryan, P. M. (2002). *Esperanza rising*. New York: Blue Sky Press. (4–5)

Winter, J. (2008). *Wangari's trees of peace: A true story from Africa*. San Diego: Harcourt. (4–5)

to be a boy to support her family, and *Homeless Bird* (Whelan, 2000), the story of an Indian girl who has no future when she is widowed shortly after her marriage. These stories and others listed in Figure 1–4 describe injustices that students can understand and discuss. In fact, teachers report that students become more engaged in reading about social issues and that their interaction patterns change after reading these stories (Lewison, Leland, & Harste, 2008).

Critical literacy emphasizes young adolescents' potential to become thoughtful, active citizens. The reason that injustice persists in society, Shannon (1995) hypothesizes, is because people don't "ask why things are the way they are, who benefits from these conditions, and how can we make them more equitable" (p. 123).

Information-Processing Theory

The information-processing theory compares the mind to a computer and describes how information moves through a series of processing units—sensory register, short-term memory, and long-term memory—as it's stored (Tracey & Morrow, 2006). There's a control mechanism, too, that oversees learning. Theorists create models of the reading and writing processes to describe the complicated, interactive workings of the mind (Hayes, 2004; Kintsch, 2004; Rumelhart, 2004). They believe that reading and writing are related, and their models describe a two-way flow of information between what readers and writers know and the words written on the page.

Interactive Model. Reading and writing are interactive processes of making meaning. The interactive model of reading emphasizes that readers focus on comprehension and construct meaning using a combination of reader-based and text-based information. This model also includes an executive monitor that oversees students' attention, determines whether what they're reading makes sense, and takes action when problems arise (Ruddell & Unrau, 2004).

Hayes's (2004) model of writing describes what writers do as they write. It emphasizes that writing is also an interactive, meaning-making process. Students move through a series of stages as they plan, draft, revise, and edit their writing to ensure that readers will understand what they've written. Writers use the same control mechanism that readers do to make plans, select strategies, and solve problems.

Transactive Theory.　Rosenblatt's transactive theory (2004) explains how readers create meaning. She describes comprehension, which she calls *interpretation*, as the result of a two-way transaction between the reader and the text. Instead of trying to figure out the author's meaning, students negotiate an interpretation based on the text and their knowledge about literature and the world. Their interpretations are individualized because each student brings different knowledge and experiences to the reading event. Even though interpretations vary, they can always be substantiated by the text.

Strategic Behaviors.　Young adolescents use strategic or goal-oriented behaviors to direct their thinking. They apply cognitive strategies to achieve a goal and metacognitive strategies to determine whether the goal is reached (Dean, 2006; Pressley, 2002b). Visualizing and drawing inferences are cognitive strategies that readers use, and organizing and revising are strategies for writers. Metacognitive strategies, such as monitoring and repairing, regulate students' thinking and help them solve problems. The word *metacognition* is often defined as "thinking about your own thinking," but more accurately, it refers to a sophisticated level of thought that students use to control their thinking (Baker, 2002). Metacognition is a control mechanism; it involves both students' active control of thinking and their awareness of their thinking.

Behaviorism

Behaviorists focus on the observable and measurable aspects of students' behavior. They believe that behavior can be learned or unlearned as the result of stimulus-and-response actions (O'Donohue & Kitchener, 1998). Reading is viewed as a conditioned response. This theory is described as teacher centered because it focuses on the teacher's role as a dispenser of knowledge. Skinner (1974) explained that students learn to read by mastering a series of discrete skills and subskills in a planned sequence. Teachers use explicit instruction to present information in small steps and reinforce it through practice activities until students achieve mastery because each step is built on the previous one. Students practice skills by completing fill-in-the-blank worksheets. They usually work individually, not in small groups or with peers. Behavior modification is another key feature: Behaviorists believe that teachers control and motivate students through a combination of rewards and punishments.

PRINCIPLE 3: Effective Teachers Create a Nurturing Classroom Culture

Classrooms are social settings. Together, students and their teacher create a classroom community, and the environment strongly influences the learning that takes place (Angelillo, 2008). The classroom community should be inviting, supportive, and safe so young adolescents will be motivated to participate in reading and writing activities. Perhaps the most striking quality is the partnership that the teacher and students create: They become a "family" in which all members respect one another and support each other's learning. Students value culturally and linguistically diverse classmates and recognize that everyone makes important contributions.

Think about the differences between renting and owning a home. In a classroom community, students and the teacher are joint "owners" where students assume responsibility for their own behavior and learning, work collaboratively with peers, complete assignments, and care for the classroom. This doesn't mean that teachers abdicate their responsibility; on the contrary, teachers are the guide, instructor, monitor, coach, mentor, and grader. Sometimes they share these roles with students, but the ultimate responsibility remains with the teacher.

Characteristics of a Classroom Community

A successful classroom community has specific, identifiable characteristics that are conducive to academic achievement:

Safety. The classroom is a safe place that promotes in-depth learning and nurtures students' physical and emotional well-being.

Respect. Students and the teacher interact respectfully with each other. Harassment, bullying, and verbal abuse aren't tolerated. Students' cultural, linguistic, and learning differences are honored so that everyone feels comfortable and valued in the classroom learning environment.

High Expectations. Teachers set high expectations and emphasize that they believe that all students can be successful. Their high expectations promote a positive classroom environment where students behave appropriately and develop self-confidence. In addition, teachers design activities to challenge and support students' learning.

Risk-Taking. Teachers encourage students to take intellectual risks and to develop higher-level thinking skills. They also challenge students to explore new topics and to try unfamiliar activities.

Collaboration. Students work with peers on reading and writing activities and other projects. Because young adolescents value opportunities for social interaction and belonging to a group, working together often increases students' motivation and enhances their achievement.

Choice. Students make choices about books they read, the topics they write about, and the projects they pursue within parameters set by the teacher. When students have opportunities to make choices, they're more motivated to succeed, and they value the activity.

Responsibility. Students are valued members of the classroom community who are responsible for their learning, behavior, and the contributions they make. Teachers and students share learning and teaching responsibilities, and students assume leadership roles in small-group activities.

Family and Community Involvement. Teachers involve parents and community members in classroom activities and develop home–school bonds through special programs and regular communication. Researchers have found again and again that when parents and other adults in the community are involved in classroom activities, student achievement soars (Edwards, 2004).

FIGURE 1–5 ◆ *Interest Inventory Questions*

Personal Questions	Reading Questions	Writing Questions
What are your favorite things to do? hobbies?	What kinds of books do you like to read?	What kinds of writing do you do at school?
What sports do you play?	Who are your favorite authors?	What are your favorite writing genres?
What do you know a lot about?	What are your favorite genres?	What makes writing good?
What music do you like? movies?	What do you read besides books (e.g., comics, magazines)?	What do you do well as a writer?
What do you want to be when you grow up?	Where and when do you like to read?	What is hardest for you as a writer?
Who's in your family?	Where do you get reading materials?	What writing strategies do you use?
What do you do with your family?	What do you do well as a reader?	What are you doing to become a better writer?
What languages do you speak? read? write?	What is hardest for you as a reader?	What's your writing process?
What books and other reading materials do you have at home?	What reading strategies do you use?	How often do you write at home?
Where do you study at home?	What are you doing to become a better reader?	What do you write at home?
How do you use computers? the Internet?	How often do you read at home?	Do you use a dictionary and thesaurus? Why?
What 3 words best describe you?	Do you like to read?	Do you like to write?

These characteristics emphasize the teacher's role in creating an inviting, supportive, and safe classroom climate for students (National Middle School Association, 2003).

How to Create the Classroom Culture

Teachers are more effective when they take the first 2 weeks of the school year to establish the classroom climate, learn about their students, and lay out their expectations. To get acquainted, teachers often have their students complete interest inventories. Students respond to a set of questions about their family life, personal interests and extracurricular activities, attitudes about literacy, and prior reading and writing experiences. Figure 1–5 lists questions that teachers can draw on to develop an interest inventory. Students can orally respond to the questions one-on-one with the teacher, answer the questions as a homework assignment, write an autobiographical essay, or create an autobiography box with photos and artifacts that they share in class. It's important that teachers also respond to the questions in the interest inventory to share information about themselves to establish rapport with their students.

Teachers explicitly explain classroom routines, such as how to work collaboratively with peers in a small group, and they set the expectation that students will adhere to them. They demonstrate literacy procedures, including how to use a **rubric** and how to participate in a **grand conversation**. Third, teachers model ways of interacting with classmates and solving problems that might develop.

Check the Compendium of Instructional Procedures, which follows Chapter 12, for more information on the highlighted terms.

Teachers are the classroom managers: They set expectations and clearly explain what's expected of students and what's valued in the classroom. The rules are specific and consistent, and teachers also set limits; students can talk quietly with peers when they're working together, for example, but they're not allowed to shout across the classroom or talk when the teacher's talking or when classmates are presenting to the class. Teachers also model classroom rules themselves as they interact with students. This process of socialization at the beginning of the school year is crucial to the success of the literacy program.

Not everything can be accomplished during the first 2 weeks, however; teachers continue to reinforce classroom routines and literacy procedures. One way is to have student leaders model the desired routines and behaviors; this way, peers are likely to follow the lead. Teachers also teach additional literacy procedures as students become involved in new types of activities. The classroom community evolves during the school year, but the foundation is laid during those first 2 weeks.

The classroom environment is predictable, with familiar routines and literacy procedures. Students feel comfortable, safe, and more willing to take risks in a predictable classroom environment. This is especially true for students from varied cultures, English learners, and struggling readers and writers (Fay & Whaley, 2004).

STRUGGLING READERS AND WRITERS

More Reading and Writing

Struggling students need to spend more time reading and writing.

Struggling students need to increase their volume of reading and writing. Allington (2006) recommends that teachers dramatically increase the amount of time struggling readers spend reading each day so that they can become more-capable and confident readers and develop greater interest in reading. Reading volume matters; better readers typically read three times as much as struggling readers do. This recommendation for increased volume applies to writing, too: Struggling writers need to spend more time writing.

In addition to explicit instruction and guided practice, students need large blocks of uninterrupted time for authentic reading and writing, and one of the best ways to provide this opportunity is reading and writing workshop. During reading workshop, students read self-selected books at their own reading level, and during writing workshop, they draft and refine compositions on self-selected topics. Practice is just as important for reading and writing as it is when you're learning to ride a bike or play the piano.

How much classroom time should students spend reading and writing? Although there's no hard-and-fast rule, Allington (2006) recommends that each day students spend at least 90 minutes reading and 45 minutes writing. Researchers have found that the most effective teachers provide more time for reading and writing than less effective teachers do (Allington & Johnston, 2002). It's often difficult for struggling students to sustain reading and writing activities for as long as their classmates do, but with teacher support, they can increase the time they spend reading and writing.

PRINCIPLE 4: Effective Teachers Adopt a Balanced Approach to Instruction

The balanced approach to instruction is based on a comprehensive view of literacy that combines explicit instruction, guided practice, collaborative learning, and independent reading and writing. It's grown out of the so-called "reading wars" of the late 20th century in which teachers and researchers argued for either teacher-centered or student-centered instruction. Cunningham and Allington (2007) compare the balanced approach to a multivitamin, suggesting that it brings together the best of teacher- and student-centered learning theories. Even though balanced programs vary, they usually embody these characteristics:

Reading. Teachers develop students' ability to comprehend fiction, nonfiction, functional texts (e.g., directions and nutritional labels), and Internet texts.

Writing. Teachers teach students to use the writing process to communicate effectively through writing. They also teach writing genres and the six traits of effective writing.

Explicit Instruction. Teachers provide explicit instruction that addresses the state's literacy standards for their grade level, with the goal that all students achieve those expectations.

Learning Tools. Teachers teach students to use reading, talk, and writing as tools for learning online and in the content areas.

Motivation. Teachers use authentic and meaningful activities to engage students' interest.

Pearson, Raphael, Benson, and Madda (2007) explain that "achieving balance is a complex process that requires flexibility and artful orchestration of literacy's various contextual and conceptual aspects" (p. 33). The characteristics of the balanced approach are embodied in an instructional program that consists of these components:

◆ Reading literature
◆ Reading nonfiction
◆ New literacies
◆ Literacy strategies and skills
◆ Oral language

◆ Vocabulary
◆ Comprehension
◆ Writing
◆ Spelling

FIGURE 1–6 ◆ *Components of the Balanced Literacy Approach*

Component	Description
Reading Literature	Students read and respond to fiction and poetry and learn about genres, text structures, and literary features.
Reading Nonfiction	Students read nonfiction books, textbooks, and magazines and learn about genres, text structures, and nonfiction features.
New Literacies	Students use the Internet and other information-communication technologies to learn and communicate with others.
Literacy Strategies and Skills	Students use problem-solving behaviors called *strategies* and automatic actions called *skills* as they read and write.
Oral Language	Students use talk as they work with peers, participate in grand conversations, and give oral presentations.
Vocabulary	Students learn the meaning of words through wide reading and listening to books read aloud, and they apply word-learning strategies to figure out the meaning of unfamiliar words.
Comprehension	Students use reader factors, including comprehension strategies, and text factors, including text structures, to understand what they're reading.
Writing	Students use the writing process and their knowledge about genres and the six traits to draft and refine reports, essays, poems, and other compositions.
Spelling	Students apply what they're learning about English orthography to spell words, and their spellings become more conventional.

These components are described in Figure 1–6. Creating a balance is essential because when one component is overemphasized, the development of the others suffers.

A balanced literacy program integrating these components is recommended for all students in fourth through eighth grades, including struggling students, on-grade-level students, advanced students, and English learners (Braunger & Lewis, 2006).

PRINCIPLE 5: Effective Teachers Scaffold Students' Reading and Writing

Supporting them until where they are and they can go further by themselves.

Teachers scaffold students' literacy development as they demonstrate, guide, and teach, and they vary the amount of support they provide according to the instructional purpose and students' needs. Sometimes teachers model how experienced readers read or guide students when they're revising their writing. Teachers use four levels of support, moving from more to less as students assume responsibility (Fountas & Pinnell, 2001). Figure 1–7 summarizes the levels of support—modeled, shared, guided, and independent—for literacy activities.

Modeled Reading and Writing

Teachers provide the greatest amount of support when they model how expert readers read and expert writers write. When teachers read aloud, they're modeling: They read fluently and with expression, and they talk about their thoughts and the strategies they're using. When they model writing, teachers write a composition on chart paper or on an interactive whiteboard so that everyone can see what they're doing and how the text is being written. Teachers use this support level to demonstrate procedures, such as choosing a book to read or doing a word sort, and to introduce

FIGURE 1–7 ◆ A Continuum of Literacy Instruction		
Level of Support	**Reading**	**Writing**
High **Modeled**	Teacher reads aloud, modeling how good readers read fluently and with expression. Books too difficult for students to read themselves are used.	Teacher writes in front of students, creating the text, doing the writing, and thinking aloud about writing strategies and skills.
Shared	Teacher and students read books together, with students following as the teacher reads. Books students can't read by themselves are used.	Teacher and students create the text together; then the teacher does the actual writing. Students may assist by spelling familiar words.
Guided	Teacher plans and teaches reading lessons to small, homogeneous groups using instructional-level books. Focus is on supporting students' use of strategies.	Teacher plans and teaches lessons on a writing procedure, strategy, or skill, and students participate in supervised practice activities.
Independent **Low**	Students choose and read self-selected books independently. Teacher conferences with students to monitor their progress.	Students use the writing process to write stories, essays, and other compositions. Teacher monitors students' progress.

new writing genres, such as writing an essay. Teachers often do a **think-aloud** to share what they're thinking as they read or write and the decisions they make and the strategies they use. Modeling has these purposes:

- Demonstrate fluent reading and writing
- Explain how to use reading and writing strategies, such as predicting, using context clues, and revising
- Teach the steps in a procedure for a literacy activity
- Show how reading and writing conventions and other skills work

Shared Reading and Writing

Students assume partial responsibility for doing the work in shared reading and writing. Classmates work together, and teachers provide assistance when it's needed. Probably the best-known example is shared reading in which teachers read big books with young children. The teacher does most of the reading, but children join in to read familiar words and phrases. Teachers who work with older students also use shared reading (Allen, 2002). When a novel is too difficult for students to read independently, for example, teachers often read it aloud while students follow along, reading silently when they can in their own copies. Another shared activity is **readers theatre**, in which students assume the roles of characters and read the lines in a script together.

Teachers use shared writing in a variety of ways, such as when they write text that students dictate. Sometimes it makes sense for teachers to do the writing during a lesson because they can write more legibly and quickly. Teachers also use shared writing to make **K-W-L charts** and draw graphic organizers.

Teachers assist struggling students with activities at this level. To develop reading fluency, for example, teachers have students use **choral reading** to practice reading the lines of a poem. To teach writing, teachers use **interactive writing**. In this procedure, students compose a group text and then take turns writing it sentence by sentence on chart paper. Teachers provide assistance with spelling, Standard English grammar, and other conventions.

Students also use shared reading and writing when they work with partners or in small groups. Two students can often read a book together that neither one could read independently; similarly, several students can craft a better composition together than on their own.

This level differs from modeled reading and writing in that students actually participate in the activity rather than simply observing the teacher. In shared reading, students read along with the teacher, and in shared writing, they work together with classmates or the teacher. Shared reading and writing have these purposes:

- Involve students in literacy activities they can't do independently
- Have students share their literacy expertise with classmates
- Provide practice before students work independently

Guided Reading and Writing

Teachers continue to support students during guided reading and writing, but students do the actual reading and writing themselves. In **guided reading**, small, homogeneous groups of students meet with the teacher to read a book at their instructional level. The teacher introduces the book and guides students as they read. Then students continue reading on their own while the teacher supervises. Afterward, they discuss the book, review vocabulary words, and practice skills. Later, students often reread the entire book, or parts of it, independently.

Teachers plan structured writing activities and then supervise students as they write. For example, when students make pages for a collaborative book, it's guided writing because the teacher organizes the activity and supervises students as they work. Teachers also provide guidance as they conference with students about their writing.

Minilessons are another type of guided reading and writing. As teachers teach about strategies, skills, and genres and other text factors, they support students as they learn. They also provide practice activities and supervise as students apply what they're learning.

Teachers use guided reading and writing to provide instruction and assistance as students are actually reading and writing. Guided reading and writing have these purposes:

- Support students' reading in appropriate instructional-level materials
- Teach literacy strategies and skills
- Involve students in collaborative writing projects
- Teach students to use the writing process—in particular, how to revise and edit

Independent Reading and Writing

Students apply the strategies and skills they've learned in authentic literacy activities. During independent reading, students usually choose their own books and work at their own pace as they read and respond to books. Similarly, during independent writing, students usually choose their own topics and move at their own pace as they develop and refine their writing. It would be wrong to suggest, however, that teachers play no role in independent-level activities; they continue to monitor students, but they provide much less guidance at this level.

Through independent reading, students learn how pleasurable reading is and, teachers hope, become lifelong readers. In addition, as they write, students come to see themselves as authors. Independent reading and writing have these purposes:

- Provide authentic and meaningful literacy experiences
- Create opportunities for students to apply the strategies and skills they've learned
- Develop lifelong readers and writers

Teachers working with fourth through eighth graders use all four levels. When teachers introduce a reading strategy, for instance, they model how to apply it. And, when teachers want students to practice a strategy they've already introduced, they guide students through a reading activity, slowly releasing responsibility to them. Once students can apply the strategy easily, they're encouraged to use it independently. The purpose of the activity, not the activity itself, determines the level of support. Teachers are less actively involved during independent reading and writing, but the quality of instruction that students have received is clearest because they're applying what they've learned.

PRINCIPLE 6: Effective Teachers Organize for Literacy Instruction

There's no one instructional program that best represents the balanced approach to literacy; instead, teachers organize for instruction by creating a program that fits their students' needs, their state's grade-level standards, and the school's curricular guidelines. The instructional programs teachers create should reflect these principles:

- Teachers create a community of learners in their classrooms.
- Teachers implement the components of the balanced approach.
- Teachers scaffold students' reading and writing experiences.

Teachers choose among a variety of instructional programs, combine parts of two or more programs, alternate programs, or add other components to meet their students' needs. Some of the programs are based on authentic literacy activities using trade books, and others are textbook based.

Literature Focus Units

Teachers create literature focus units featuring high-quality novels and other trade books. The books are usually found in a district- or state-approved list of books that young adolescents are expected to read. They include *Charlotte's Web* (White, 2006), *To Kill a Mockingbird* (Lee, 2006), and other classics and award winners such as *Holes* (Sachar, 2008) and *The Tale of Despereaux* (DiCamillo, 2003). Everyone in the class reads and responds to the same book, and the teacher supports students' learning through a combination of explicit instruction and reading and writing activities. Through these units, teachers teach about genres, authors, and literary analysis, and in the process, they nurture students' interest in literature.

Literature Circles

Students form small-group literature circles or book clubs to authentically read and respond to a novel or other trade book. Teachers select five or six books at varying reading levels that reflect the interests and reading levels of their students. Often, the books are related in some way—representing the same genre or the same topic, or written by the same author, for instance. Teachers collect multiple copies of the books and give **book talks** to introduce them. Then students choose a book and form a group to read and respond to it. They set a 5- to 10-day reading and discussion schedule and work autonomously, although teachers sometimes sit in on the discussions. Through the experience of reading and discussing a book together, students learn more about how to respond to books and develop responsibility for completing assignments.

Reading Workshop

Students independently read books that they've chosen themselves and that are appropriate for their reading level (Atwell, 2007). Everyone reads while teachers conference with individual students. After finishing a book, students share it with the class and offer it to another student. Teachers also teach **minilessons** on reading strategies and skills. This workshop program is authentic; students read more like adults do, making choices, working independently, and developing responsibility. Teachers report that fourth through eighth graders particularly value the opportunity to make choices and read independently.

Writing Workshop

Students do authentic writing on self-selected topics. They follow the writing process as they draft and refine their writing and conference with the teacher. Students spend

Literature Circles
These eighth graders are participating in a discussion during a literature circle featuring Rodman Philbrick's *Freak the Mighty* (2001), the memorable story of two unlikely friends. The students talk about events in the story, returning to the book to read sentences aloud. They also check the meaning of several words in a dictionary that one student keeps on his desk. They've read half of the book so far, and their conversation focuses on the friendship Max and Kevin have formed. They talk about their own friends and what it means to be a friend, and they make predictions about how the story will end.

most of writing workshop involved in their own writing activities, but teachers also read high-quality literature aloud to the class and use these books as a model when they present **minilessons** on reading and writing strategies and skills. Reading and writing workshop are literacy apprenticeships that situated learning theorists recommend, and teachers have repeatedly reported that literacy workshops are more motivational than other literacy programs (Atwell, 1998).

Basal Reading Programs

Commercially produced reading programs for fourth through sixth grades are known as *basal reading programs* or *basal readers*. These programs feature a textbook containing reading selections with accompanying workbooks, supplemental books, and related instructional materials at each grade level. Vocabulary, comprehension, grammar, writing, and spelling instruction is coordinated with the reading selections and aligned with grade-level standards. The teacher's guide provides detailed procedures for teaching the selections. Testing materials are also included so that teachers can monitor students' progress. Publishers tout basal readers as a complete literacy program, but effective teachers realize that they aren't.

Language Arts Textbooks

Commercial literacy programs for sixth through eighth grades are often referred to as *language arts textbooks* or *literature anthologies*, and they're very similar to basal reading programs. These programs feature a textbook with a mix of classic and contemporary multicultural literature that includes short stories, feature articles, poems, and functional selections, such as directions, product information, and diagrams. Teachers follow detailed instructions in teachers' guides for reading the selections and teaching literary analysis. Students write answers to questions included in the textbook, complete assignments in consumable workbooks, or take quizzes at the textbook's website. Detailed information about grammar, spelling, writing, and test-taking strategies is included in a special section at the back of the textbook or in a supplemental handbook.

Specialty Textbooks

Some teachers use grammar, spelling, and writing textbooks and other commercial programs to provide instruction in these areas. The Write Source's collection of writing textbooks is probably the best known. Many grammar textbooks are available today that are little more than workbooks for identifying parts of speech and parts of sentences. Kiester's *Giggles in the Middle: Caught'ya! Grammar With a Giggle for Middle School* (2006b) is a far more creative approach, and Killgallon's (1997, 2000) sentence-composing texts effectively link grammar and writing.

These instructional approaches can be divided into authentic and textbook programs. Literature focus units, literature circles, and reading and writing workshop are classified as authentic programs because they use trade books and involve students in meaningful activities. Basal readers, language arts textbooks, and other specialty textbooks, not surprisingly, are textbook programs that reflect behaviorist theories. Teachers generally combine these authentic and textbook programs because students learn best through a variety of reading and writing experiences. Sometimes the books that students read are more difficult or teachers are introducing a new writing genre that requires more teacher support and guidance. Some teachers alternate literature focus units or literature circles with reading and writing workshop and a textbook program, and others use some components from each approach throughout the school year. Figure 1–8 reviews these instructional programs.

PRINCIPLE 7: Effective Teachers Differentiate Instruction

Because young adolescents vary in reading level, academic achievement, and English language proficiency, effective teachers differentiate instruction by adjusting their instruction and assignments so all students can be successful. The National Middle School Association's *This We Believe* (2003) document states that "teaching approaches should enhance and accommodate the diverse skills, abilities, and prior knowledge of young adolescents" (p. 25).

Tomlinson (2004) explains that the one-size-fits-all instructional model is obsolete, and that teachers respect students by honoring both their similarities and their differences. Differentiation is based on Vygotsky's idea of a zone of proximal development. If instruction is either too difficult or too easy, it won't be effective; instead, teachers provide instruction that addresses students' instructional needs.

How to Differentiate Instruction

Teachers use varied instructional arrangements, instructional materials at students' reading levels, interest inventories to determine students' interests, and different assignments as they differentiate instruction. They monitor students' learning and make adjustments,

FIGURE 1–8 ◆ Instructional Programs

Type	Program	Instructional Emphases
Authentic Programs	**Literature Focus Units** Teachers and students read and respond to a book of grade-appropriate high-quality literature together as a class.	• Experiencing high-quality literature • Examining genres • Modeling reading strategies • Learning vocabulary
	Literature Circles Students form literature circles or "book clubs" to read and respond to a self-selected trade book.	• Working in small groups • Reading interesting books • Learning how respond to a book • Using discussion to deepen comprehension
	Reading Workshop Students choose interesting trade books at their reading level and read them independently.	• Doing authentic reading • Teaching strategies and skills in minilessons • Having students read books at their reading level • Reading aloud to students
	Writing Workshop Students use the writing process to write books and other compositions on self-selected topics.	• Doing authentic writing • Practicing the writing process • Teaching strategies and skills in minilessons • Having students share their writing with classmates
Textbook Programs	**Basal Reading Programs** Students in grades 4–6 read selections in grade-level textbooks and participate in teacher-directed lessons and practice activities.	• Reading short stories, excerpts from novels, and nonfiction articles • Teaching strategies and skills sequentially • Providing grade-level instruction for all students • Using workbooks for practice activities
	Language Arts Textbooks Students in grades 6–8 read selections in grade-level textbooks and participate in teacher-directed lessons and practice activities.	• Reading short stories, poems, and nonfiction texts • Providing grade-level instruction for all students • Teaching grammar, spelling, and writing skills • Teaching literary analysis
	Specialty Textbooks Students use textbooks for teacher-directed lessons and practice activities to learn grammar, spelling, and writing strategies and skills.	• Providing grade-level instruction on grammar, spelling, and writing • Completing practice activities • Using the textbook as a resource guide

when necessary, and they assess learning in multiple ways, not just using paper-and-pencil tests. Differentiation involves adjusting the content, the process, and the products:

Differentiating the Content. Teachers identify the information that students need to learn to meet grade-level standards so that every student can be successful. They differentiate the content in these ways:

- Choose instructional materials at students' reading levels
- Consider students' developmental levels as well as their current grade placement in deciding what to teach
- Use assessment tools to determine students' instructional needs

Differentiating the Process. Teachers vary instruction and application activities to meet their students' needs. They differentiate the process in these ways:

- Provide instruction to individuals, small groups, and the whole class
- Scaffold struggling students with more-explicit instruction
- Challenge advanced students with activities requiring higher-level thinking
- Adjust instruction when students aren't successful

Differentiating the Products. Teachers vary how students demonstrate what they've learned. Demonstrations include both the projects that students create and the tests teachers use to measure students' learning. Teachers differentiate the products in these ways:

- Have students create projects individually, with partners, or in small groups
- Design projects that engage students with literacy in meaningful ways
- Assess students using a combination of visual, oral, and written formats

These three ways to differentiate instruction are reviewed in Figure 1–9.

Student Diversity

America's public schools are becoming increasingly diverse. More than a third of students come from minority backgrounds. Many large school districts have students from more than 150 countries who speak 130 or more languages at home; smaller districts are reporting similar changes. Teaching diverse learners is both exciting and challenging. Teachers' goal is to assist all students to meet or exceed grade-level standards.

Grade-Level Students. Grade-level students are capable readers and writers. They can read grade-level trade books and textbooks and use comprehension strategies, including drawing inferences, to understand what they read. They're effective writers who use the writing process; develop and elaborate their ideas; choose appropriate language and style conventions; and eliminate most spelling, grammar, capitalization, and punctuation errors. They will achieve most grade-level literacy standards with high-quality instruction in a balanced literacy program and a nurturing classroom culture.

Grade-level instruction is appropriate for these students. Their background knowledge, academic vocabulary, and prior schooling have prepared them for success. Even so, many grade-level students face challenges such as reading content-area textbooks, learning spelling words, writing persuasive essays, or completing grammar exercises. Some are more-fluent readers, some prefer writing to reading, and some are more motivated than others. Teachers monitor these students' achievement to ensure that they're making expected progress.

FIGURE 1–9 ◆ Ways to Differentiate Instruction

Component	Description	Instructional Procedures
Content	The information students need to learn to meet grade-level standards, and the instructional materials that teachers use to ensure that all students are successful.	• Choose instructional materials at students' reading levels. • Consider students' developmental levels as well as their current grade placement in deciding what to teach. • Use assessment tools to determine students' instructional needs.
Process	Teachers vary instruction and application activities to address students' developmental levels and learning needs.	• Provide instruction to individuals, small groups, and the whole class. • Scaffold struggling students with more-explicit instruction. • Challenge advanced students with activities that require higher-level thinking.
Products	Teachers vary the ways that students demonstrate what they've learned.	• Have students create projects individually, with partners, or in small groups. • Design projects that engage students in authentic and meaningful ways. • Assess students using visual, oral, and written formats.

Struggling Students. Struggling students perform below grade-level standards; it's not unusual for these students to score 2 or more years below their grade-level placement on achievement tests. It's essential that teachers intervene by assessing students to determine their areas of weakness and then providing intensive and accelerated literacy instruction; if they don't, struggling students will fall farther and farther behind. The best intensive and accelerated instruction includes these components:

- Explicit instruction of reading and writing strategies and skills
- Guided reading lessons using texts at students' instructional reading level
- Lessons to build background knowledge and teach academic vocabulary
- Multiple daily opportunities to read and write
- Reading aloud to students from grade-level-appropriate fiction and nonfiction books

In the middle grades, time is the critical factor for helping struggling students because those who are more than 2 years below grade level rarely catch up with their grade-level peers quickly. It often takes several years to close the gap.

Advanced Students. Advanced students' academic achievement in reading and writing exceeds grade-level expectations, and they outperform their peers. Teachers focus instruction on expanding students' literacy knowledge so they remain engaged in learning. They allow students to design many of their literacy projects, and they challenge advanced learners through activities such as these:

- Reading and responding to more-sophisticated literature individually and in literature circles
- Integrating technology into writing projects
- Pursuing community-based projects related to issues of social justice

The Spotlight feature on the next page introduces three eighth graders; one is a capable student who meets grade-level standards, one really struggles with reading and writing, and the third is a high-achieving student. Learning about these students helps to put a face on each type of learner, and in upcoming chapters, you'll learn more about these students' literacy development.

Scaffolding English Learners

Students who come from language backgrounds other than English and aren't yet proficient in English are known as English learners (ELs). Many can converse in English but struggle with abstract academic language. These students benefit from participating in the same instructional programs that mainstream students do, but teachers make adaptations to create learning contexts that respect minority students and meet their instructional needs (Shanahan & Beck, 2006). Learning to read and write is more challenging because ELs are learning to speak English at the same time. Teachers scaffold ELs' oral language acquisition and literacy development in these ways:

Explicit Instruction. Teachers present more-explicit instruction on literacy strategies and skills because ELs are more at risk than other students (Genesee & Riches, 2006). They also spend more time teaching unfamiliar academic vocabulary (e.g., *homonym, paragraph, index, revise, summarize*).

Oral Language. Teachers provide many opportunities for students to practice speaking English comfortably and informally with partners and in small groups. Through conversations about topics they're learning, ELs develop both conversational and academic language, which in turn supports their literacy development.

Small-Group Work. Teachers provide opportunities for students to work in small groups because peers' social interaction supports their learning. As English learners talk with classmates, they're learning the culture of literacy.

Reading Aloud to Students. Teachers read aloud a variety of fiction and nonfiction books, including some that represent students' home cultures. As they read, teachers model fluent reading, and students build background knowledge and become more familiar with English vocabulary and written language structures.

Background Knowledge. Teachers organize instruction into units to build students' world knowledge about grade-level-appropriate concepts, and they develop ELs' literary knowledge through minilessons and a variety of reading and writing activities.

Authentic Literacy Activities. Teachers provide daily opportunities for students to apply the strategies and skills they're learning as they read and write for authentic purposes. English learners participate in meaningful literacy activities through literature circles and reading and writing workshop.

These recommendations promote English learners' academic success.

Spotlight on . . .
Young Adolescents

GRADE-LEVEL STUDENT

Almost-14-year-old Ales is a capable student. Her favorite color is pink, and she loves Hip Hop music. She's very knowledgeable about caring for animals because she helps her mother take care of their tropical fish tanks.

She's on the girls' basketball team at her school. Ales plays wing because she's strong and an excellent shooter.

Ales is part of a large blended family. She lives with her mother, stepdad, two sisters, two step-sisters, and a stepbrother. Her dad lives in Nevada, and she visits him every summer. Everyone in her family speaks English, but Ales wants to learn Spanish because so many people in her commu-

nity speak Spanish, and she wants to know what they're saying.

There's a computer with Internet access in a quiet part of her living room. Ales uses it for homework, and on weekends, she plays games and downloads the lyrics to new Hip Hop songs.

She reads a lot because her mom insists that she read for 30 minutes every night after finishing her homework.

Ales hopes to attend college in New York. She wants to become either a vet, because she loves animals, or a crime scene investigator, because it's an interesting career that she learned about by watching CSI on TV.

STRUGGLING STUDENT

Eighth-grade Graciela is a struggling reader and writer. She's a native Spanish speaker who's lived in the United States all her life. This attractive 13-year-old is soft spoken and has a quick smile. She has big brown eyes and loves to wear black nail polish.

Graciela is an athlete. Last week, she ran an 8:32-minute mile in PE. She loves to play soccer and flag football with her girl-friends.

Troublemaker! That's what Graciela calls herself. Her mother had to attend school with her in first and second grades. She remembers being angry, pulling girls' hair, and hitting classmates. She doesn't know why she did it, but her behavior im-

proved in third grade once she learned English. She still gets in trouble when a teacher is grouchy or a classmate bothers her, and she overreacts.

She lives with her mom and her younger brother, who's a fifth grader. They speak Spanish at home and watch the Telemundo and Univision channels on TV. She says she doesn't do much homework or reading, but her mom buys Hispanic magazines for her.

Graciela likes to go to the movies with her friends. Scary movies are her favorite. She dreams of becoming a model, but her mother says she should be a doctor.

ADVANCED STUDENT

14-year-old Kolei is a high-achieving student. His family came to the United States from the South Pacific island country of Tonga when his father was a child. Kolei has visited Tonga twice and wants to live there someday.

Kolei is poised and articulate. He describes himself as "a deep thinker." He's a native English speaker; he and his family speak English at home, and his grandmother taught him to speak and read Tongan and a bit of Tahitian.

There are six other people in Kolei's family: his mother, father, grandmother, and three siblings. He has an older brother and two younger sisters.

He's an integral part of his family's Polynesian catering and dancing business: He plays traditional Tahitian drums, has received awards for his dancing, and often helps out by lugging heavy trays of food.

Kolei's interested in fashion design and thinks it would be cool to be a supermodel. He watches Project Runway and Stylista, two fashion-themed reality-TV shows.

Kolei studies for more than 3 hours each night. He has a computer but rarely uses it because he's so busy doing homework. He wants to earn a doctorate and become a psychologist.

Teachers' attitudes about minority students and their understanding of how people learn a second language play a critical role in the effectiveness of instruction (Gay, 2000). It's important that teachers understand that ELs have different cultural and linguistic backgrounds and plan instruction accordingly. Most classrooms reflect the European American middle-class culture, which differs significantly from minority students' backgrounds. Brock and Raphael (2005) point out that "mismatches between teachers' and students' cultural and linguistic backgrounds matter because such mismatches can impact negatively on students' opportunities for academic success" (p. 5). Teachers and students use language differently. For example, some students are reluctant to volunteer answers to teachers' questions, and others may not answer if the questions are different than those their parents ask (Peregoy & Boyle, 2008). Teachers who learn about their students' home language and culture and embed what they learn into their instruction are likely to be more successful.

PRINCIPLE 8: Effective Teachers Link Instruction and Assessment

Assessment is an integral and ongoing part of both learning and teaching (Mariotti & Homan, 2005). Sometimes standardized high-stakes achievement tests are equated with assessment, but classroom assessment is much more than a once-a-year test. It's a daily part of classroom life: Teachers collect and analyze data from observations, conferences, and classroom tests, and then use the results to make decisions about students' academic achievement (Cunningham & Allington, 2007).

Purposes of Classroom Assessment

Teachers use assessment for these purposes:

Determining Reading Levels. Because students within a classroom typically read at a wide range of levels, teachers determine students' reading levels so that they can plan appropriate instruction and match students with books.

Monitoring Progress. Teachers regularly assess students to ensure that they're making expected progress in reading and writing, and when students aren't progressing, teachers take action to get them back on track.

Diagnosing Strengths and Weaknesses. Teachers examine students' progress in specific literacy components, including fluency, comprehension, and spelling, to identify their strengths and weaknesses. Diagnosis is especially important when students are struggling or aren't making expected progress.

Documenting Learning. Teachers use a combination of test results and collections of students' work to provide evidence of their academic achievement and document that they've met grade-level standards.

These four purposes emphasize that teachers in fourth through eighth grades use assessment tools every day to make instructional decisions.

Assessment is linked to instruction; teachers use results of assessment to inform their teaching (National Middle School Association, 2003). As they plan appropriate instruction, teachers use their knowledge about students' reading levels, background knowledge, and strategy and skill competencies. Teachers monitor instruction that's in progress as they observe students, conference with them, and check their work to ensure that the instruction is effective, and they make modifications, including reteaching when necessary, to meet students' needs. Teachers also judge the effectiveness of their instruction after it's completed. It's easy to blame students when learning isn't occurring, but teachers must consider how they can improve their teaching so that their students will be successful.

Classroom Assessment Tools

Teachers use a variety of informal assessment tools that they create themselves to monitor students' learning. These assessment tools include the following:

Observation of students as they participate in instructional activities
Examination of students' work
Conferences with individual students
Checklists to monitor students' progress
Rubrics to assess students' writing and other activities

These assessment tools support instruction, and teachers choose which one to use according to the kind of information they need. Teachers also administer commercial tests to individual students or the entire class to determine their overall reading achievement or their proficiency in a particular component—comprehension, for example. In upcoming chapters, you'll learn how to assess students' reading and writing and which assessment tools to use.

High-Stakes Tests

The results of yearly high-stakes standardized tests also provide evidence of students' literacy achievement. The usefulness of these data is limited, however, because the tests generally are administered in the spring and the results aren't released until after the school year ends. At the beginning of the next school year, teachers do examine the results and use what they learn in planning for their new class, but the impact isn't as great as it would be for the teachers who worked with those students during the previous year. Administrators also use the results to evaluate teacher effectiveness by determining whether students met grade-level expectations.

CHAPTER 1
Review

How Effective Teachers Teach Reading and Writing

▶ Teachers understand how the characteristics of young adolescents affect instruction.

▶ Teachers understand how learning theories influence literacy instruction.

▶ Teachers create a nurturing learning community in their classrooms.

▶ Teachers adopt a balanced approach to literacy instruction.

▶ Teachers link instruction and assessment.

CHAPTER 2

Examining the Reading and Writing Processes

Mrs. Goodman's Seventh Graders Read The Giver

The seventh graders in Mrs. Goodman's class are reading *The Giver* (Lowry, 2006b), a Newbery Medal winner. In this futuristic story, 12-year-old Jonas is selected to become the next Keeper of the Memories, and he discovers the terrible truth about his community. Mrs. Goodman has a class set of paperback copies, and her students use the reading process as they read and respond to the story.

To introduce the book, Mrs. Goodman asks her students to get into small groups to brainstorm lists of all the things they would change about life, if they could; their lists include no more homework, no AIDS, no crime, no gangs, no parents, no taking out the garbage, and being allowed to drive cars at age 12. The groups hang their lists on the chalkboard and share them. Mrs. Goodman puts checkmarks by many of the items, seeming to agree with them. Next, she explains that they're going to read a story about life in the future. She explains that *The Giver* takes place in a planned utopian, or "perfect," society with the qualities that she checked on students' lists.

She passes out copies of the book and uses shared reading to read the first chapter aloud as students follow along in their copies. Then the class talks about the first chapter in a **grand conversation**, asking lots of questions: Why were there so many rules? Doesn't anyone drive a car? What does *released* mean? Why are children called a "Seven" or a "Four"? What does it mean that people are "given" spouses—don't they fall in love and get married? Why does Jonas have to tell his feelings? Classmates share their ideas and are eager to continue reading. Mrs. Goodman's reading aloud of the first chapter and the questions that the students raised generate interest in the story. The power of this story quickly grabs them all.

They set a schedule for reading and discussion. Every 3 days, they'll come together to talk about the chapters they've read, and over 2 weeks, the class will complete the book. They'll also write in **reading logs** after reading the first chapter and then five more times as they're reading. In these logs, students write reactions to the story. Maria wrote this journal entry after finishing the book:

> *Jonas had to do it. He had to save Gabriel's life because the next day Jonas's father was going to release (kill) him. He had it all planned out. That was important. He was very brave to leave his parents and his home. But I guess they weren't his parents really and his home wasn't all that good. I don't know if I could have done it but he did the right thing. He had to get out. He saved himself and he saved little Gabe. I'm glad he took Gabriel. That community was supposed to be safe but it really was dangerous. It was weird to not have colors. I guess that things that at first seem to be good are really bad.*

Ron explored some of the themes of the story:

> *Starving. He has memories of food. He's still hungry. But he's free. Food is safe. Freedom is surprises. Never saw a bird before. Same-same-same. Before he was starved for colors, memories and choice. Choice. To do what you want. To be who you can be. He won't starve.*

Alicia thought about a lesson her mother taught her as she wrote:

> *As Jonas fled from the community he lost his memories so that they would go back to the people there. Would they learn from them? Would they remember them? Or would life go on just the same? I think you have to do it yourself if you are going to learn. That's what my mom says. Somebody else can't do it for you. But Jonas did it. He got out with Gabe.*

Tomas wrote about the Christmas connection at the end of the story:

> *Jonas and Gabe came to the town at Christmas. Why did Lois Lowry do that? Gabe is like the baby Jesus, I think. It is like a rebirth—being born again. Jonas and his old community didn't go to church. Maybe they didn't believe in God. Now Jonas will be a Christian and the people in the church will welcome them. Gabe won't be released. I think Gabe is like Jesus because people tried to release Jesus.*

During their grand conversations, students talk about many of the same points they raise in their journal entries. The story fascinates them—at first they think about how simple and safe life would be, but then they think about all the things they take for granted that they'd have to give up to live in Jonas's ordered society. They talk about bravery and making choices, and they applaud Jonas's decision to flee with Gabriel. They also wonder if Jonas and Gabe survive.

The students collect "important" words from the story for the classroom **word wall**. After reading Chapters 4, 5, and 6, they add these words to the word wall:

relinquish	*bikeports*	*regulated*	*infraction*
invariably	*gravitating*	*rehabilitation*	*stirrings*
serene	*chastisement*	*assignment*	*reprieve*

A Square for a Quilt on The Giver

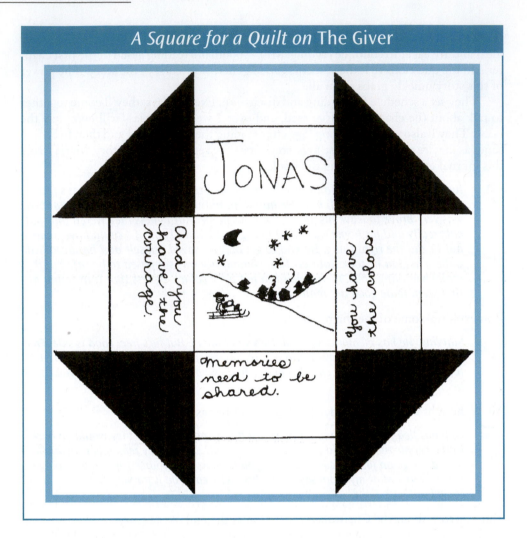

Sometimes students choose unfamiliar or long words, but they also choose familiar words such as *assignment* that are important to the story. Students refer to the word wall for words and their spellings when they're writing. Later, Mrs. Goodman teaches a minilesson about root words using some of these words.

As students read the book, Mrs. Goodman teaches a series of **minilessons** about reading strategies. For example, after students read about colors in the story, she teaches a minilesson on visualizing. She begins by rereading excerpts about Jonas being selected to be the next Receiver and asks students to "draw" a mental picture of the scene. She talks about how important it is for readers to bring a story to life in their minds. Then students draw pictures of their visualizations and share them with partners.

Another minilesson is about literary opposites. Mrs. Goodman explains that authors often introduce conflict and develop themes using contrasts or opposites. She asks students to think of opposites in *The Giver*; one example she suggests is *safe* and *free*. The students suggest these opposites:

alive—released
choice—no choice
rules—anarchy
families—family units

color—black and white
conform—do your own thing
stirrings—the pill
memories—no memories

Mrs. Goodman asks students to think about how the opposites relate to the story and how Lois Lowry made them explicit in *The Giver*. Students talk about how the community seemed safe at the beginning, but chapter by chapter, Lowry uncovered the community's shortcomings. They also talk about themes reflected in these opposites.

After they finish reading the book, the students make a quilt to probe the themes in the story: Each student prepares a paper quilt square with an illustration and several sentences of text. One quilt square is shown on the preceding page. The students decide to use white, gray, and black to represent the sameness of Jonas's community, add red for the first color Jonas saw, and include more colors in the center to represent Elsewhere.

Students also choose projects to work on individually or in small groups. One student makes a book box with objects related to the story, and two others read *Hailstones and Halibut Bones* (O'Neill, 1990), a collection of color poetry, and then write their own poems. One student makes an **open-mind portrait** of Jonas to show his thoughts the night he escaped with Gabe. Two groups form literature circles to read *Gathering Blue* (2006a) and *The Messenger* (2006c), two related books by Lois Lowry. Others write about their own memories, using the writing process to draft, refine, and publish their writing.

The reading process that Mrs. Goodman uses represents a significant shift in thinking about what students do as they read. Mrs. Goodman understands that readers construct meaning as they negotiate the texts they're reading. She knows that it's quite common for two students to read the same book and come away with different interpretations because meaning doesn't exist on the pages of a book; instead, comprehension is created through the interaction between readers and the texts they're reading. This individualized view of readers' interpretations reflects Rosenblatt's transactive theory (2004).

The reading process involves a series of stages during which readers comprehend the text. The term *text* refers to all reading materials—stories, maps, newspapers, cereal boxes, e-mail, and so on; it's not limited to basal readers and other textbooks. The writing process is a similar recursive process involving a variety of activities as students gather and organize ideas, draft their compositions, revise and edit their drafts, and, finally, publish their writings. Students learn to apply the writing process to craft and refine their compositions—autobiographies, reports, poems, and essays.

The Reading Process

Reading is a constructive process of creating meaning that involves the reader, the text, and the purpose within social and cultural contexts. The goal is comprehension, understanding the text and being able to use it for the intended purpose. Readers don't simply look at the words on a page and grasp the meaning; rather, reading is a complex process involving these essential components:

Fluency. Students become fluent readers once they recognize most words automatically and read quickly and expressively. This is a milestone because students have limited cognitive resources to devote to reading, and beginning readers use most of this energy to decode unfamiliar words. In contrast, most students in fourth through eighth grades are fluent readers who devote most of their cognitive resources to comprehension.

Vocabulary. Students think about the meaning of words they're reading, choosing appropriate meanings, recognizing figurative uses, and connecting them to their background knowledge. Knowing the meaning of words influences comprehension because it's difficult to understand when the words being read don't make sense.

Comprehension. Students use a combination of reader and text factors to understand what they're reading: They predict, connect, monitor, repair, and use other comprehension strategies as well as their knowledge of genres, organizational patterns, and literary devices to create meaning.

These components are supported by scientifically based reading research (National Reading Panel, 2000). As you continue reading, you'll learn how to teach and assess each one.

Teachers use the reading process to involve students in activities to teach, practice, and apply these components. The reading process is organized into five stages: prereading, reading, responding, exploring, and applying. This process is used no matter which instructional program teachers have chosen, even though some of the activities at each stage differ. Figure 2–1 summarizes the reading process.

Stage 1: Prereading

The reading process begins before readers open a book: The first stage, prereading, occurs as readers get ready to read. In the vignette, Mrs. Goodman built her students' background knowledge and stimulated their interest in *The Giver* as they talked about how wonderful life would be in a "perfect" world. As readers prepare to read, they activate background knowledge, set purposes, and make plans for reading.

Activating Background Knowledge. Students have both general and literary background knowledge (Braunger & Lewis, 2006). General knowledge is world knowledge, what students have acquired through life experiences and learning in their

---

FIGURE 2–1 ◆ *Key Features of the Reading Process*

Stage 1: Prereading
- Activate or build background knowledge and related vocabulary.
- Set purposes.
- Make predictions.
- Introduce key vocabulary words.
- Preview the text.

Stage 2: Reading
- Read independently or with a partner.
- Read with classmates and the teacher using shared or guided reading.
- Listen to the teacher read aloud.
- Apply reading strategies and skills.

Stage 3: Responding
- Write in reading logs.
- Participate in grand conversations or other discussions.

Stage 4: Exploring
- Study vocabulary words.
- Collect sentences.
- Examine genre and other text factors.
- Learn about the author.
- Participate in minilessons.

Stage 5: Applying
- Construct projects.
- Read related books.
- Evaluate the reading experience.

home communities and at school, and literary knowledge is what students need to read and comprehend a text, including information about reading, genres, and text structures. Students activate their world and literary background knowledge in this stage. They think about the title of the book, look at the book's cover and inside illustrations, and read the first paragraph to trigger this activation.

When students don't have adequate background knowledge to read a text, teachers build their knowledge base. They do this by teaching reading strategies and skills, providing information about genres and explaining how reading varies according to genre, enriching students' knowledge about a topic, and introducing key vocabulary words. It's not enough just to build students' knowledge about the topic; literary knowledge is also essential!

Setting Purposes. The purpose guides students' reading. It provides motivation and direction for reading, as well as a mechanism for students to monitor their reading to see if they're fulfilling their purpose. Sustaining a single purpose while students read the text is more effective than presenting students with a series of purposes (Blanton, Wood, & Moorman, 1990). Sometimes teachers set purposes for reading, and sometimes students set their own purposes. In literature focus units and basal reading textbooks, teachers usually explain how students are expected to read and what they'll do after reading. In contrast, students set their own purposes for reading during literature circles and reading workshop; they choose texts that are intrinsically interesting or that explain something they want to learn more about. As students develop as readers, they become more effective at choosing books and setting their own purposes.

Planning for Reading. Once students activate their background knowledge and identify their purpose, they take a first look at the text and plan for reading. Their plans vary according to the type of selection they're preparing to read. For stories, they make predictions, often basing them on the book's title or cover illustration. If they've read other stories by the same author or in the same genre, students use this information in making predictions. Sometimes students share their predictions orally, and at other times, they write them in reading logs.

When students are preparing to read nonfiction books and content-area textbook chapters, they preview the selection by flipping through the pages and noting section headings, illustrations, and diagrams. Sometimes they examine the table of contents to see how the book is organized, or they consult the index to locate specific information to read. They also notice highlighted terminology that's unfamiliar to them. To help students plan, teachers often use anticipation guides and prereading plans.

> Check the Compendium of Instructional Procedures, which follows Chapter 12, for more information on the highlighted terms.

Stage 2: Reading

Students read the book, textbook chapter, or other selection during the reading stage. Outside of school, most people usually read silently and independently, but in the classroom, teachers and students use five types of reading:

- ◆ Independent reading
- ◆ Partner reading
- ◆ Guided reading
- ◆ Shared reading
- ◆ Reading aloud to students

These types vary in the degree of scaffolding teachers provide: Teachers provide little or no support during independent reading, and the most support when they're reading aloud. Teachers consider the purpose for reading, students' reading levels, and the number of available copies of the text as they decide which type of reading to use.

Independent Reading. Students read silently by themselves, for their own purposes, and at their own pace. It's essential that the books students read independently are appropriate for their reading level; otherwise, they won't be successful. Independent reading is authentic; it's the way students develop a love of reading and come to think of themselves as readers. When the reading selection is too difficult for students to read independently, teachers use another type of reading to scaffold students so they'll be more successful.

Partner Reading. Students share the reading task with a classmate, and they can often read selections together that neither one could read independently (Friedland & Truesdell, 2004). Students either take turns reading to each other or read in unison. They help each other identify unfamiliar words, and they take a minute or two at the end of each page or section to talk about what they've read. When the book's too difficult for students to read independently, this social activity is a good alternative.

Partner reading is also an effective way to work with English learners and struggling readers who need more reading practice; however, unless students know how to work collaboratively, the activity often deteriorates into the stronger of the two readers reading to the other.

Guided Reading. Teachers use guided reading lessons to teach small groups of students who read at the same level (Allen, 2000; Fountas & Pinnell, 1996). They choose books at students' instructional level. Teachers introduce the book and support students' reading. Students do the actual reading themselves, and they stop after reading each chapter or so to talk about what they've read and the strategies they're using to comprehend. Teachers also direct students' attention to important vocabulary words, the book's genre or text structure, or another topic. It often takes several days to a week or two to finish the book. These lessons usually last 25 to 30 minutes and are held every day or every other day.

Shared Reading. Teachers use shared reading to read books that students can't read independently (Allen, 2002). Teachers distribute copies of the book to students, and students follow along as the teacher reads aloud. Sometimes students who are fluent and entertaining readers take turns reading sections aloud, but the goal isn't for everyone to have a turn reading. Often the teacher begins reading, and when a student wants to take over the reading, he or she begins reading aloud with the teacher; then the teacher drops off and the student continues reading. After a paragraph or two, the teacher or another student joins in and the first student drops off. Many teachers call this technique "popcorn reading." Shared reading differs from reading aloud because students follow along in their copies as the teacher reads.

Reading Aloud to Students. Teachers use the interactive read-aloud procedure to read aloud books that are developmentally appropriate but written above students' reading levels (Fisher, Flood, Lapp, & Frey, 2004). As they read, teachers actively engage students in making predictions, asking questions, identifying big ideas, and making

FIGURE 2–2   ◆   *Types of Reading*

Type	Strengths	Limitations
Independent Reading Students read a text on their own without teacher scaffolding.	• Students develop responsibility. • Students learn to select texts. • Students participate in an authentic experience.	• Students may not choose texts at their reading levels. • Teacher has little involvement or control.
Partner Reading Two students take turns as they read a text together.	• Students collaborate and assist each other. • Students become more-fluent readers. • Students talk to develop comprehension.	• One student may simply read to the other. • Teacher has little involvement and control.
Guided Reading Teacher supports students as they apply reading strategies and skills to read a text.	• Teacher teaches reading strategies and skills. • Students read books at their reading level. • Teacher monitors students' reading.	• Multiple copies of texts at the appropriate reading level are needed. • Teacher controls the reading experience.
Shared Reading Teacher reads aloud while students follow along in individual copies.	• Teacher models how to use reading strategies. • Teacher emphasizes in-depth comprehension. • The classroom culture is enhanced.	• A class set of books is needed. • Text may be too difficult or too easy for some students.
Reading Aloud to Students Teacher reads aloud and actively involves students in the experience.	• Students have access to books they can't read themselves. • Teacher models fluent reading and how to use reading strategies. • Students build background knowledge and vocabulary.	• Students have no opportunity to read. • Students may not be interested in the text.

connections. In addition, teachers model their use of reading strategies with **think-alouds** (Cappellini, 2005). There are many benefits of reading aloud, including introducing vocabulary, modeling comprehension strategies, and increasing students' motivation (Rasinski, 2003).

The five types of reading are compared in Figure 2–2. In the vignette at the beginning of this chapter, Mrs. Goodman used a combination of these approaches. She used shared reading as she read the first chapter aloud, with students following in their own copies of *The Giver*. Later, students read together in small groups, with a partner, or independently. As teachers plan their instructional programs, they include reading aloud, teacher-led student reading, and independent reading each day.

Stage 3: Responding

Students respond to what they've read and continue to negotiate their understanding after reading; this stage reflects Rosenblatt's (2005) transactive theory. Two ways that students make tentative and exploratory comments immediately after reading are by writing in reading logs and participating in grand conversations or other discussions.

Writing in Reading Logs. Young adolescents record their thoughts and deepen their understanding of what they've read in **reading logs**. As they write, students unravel their thinking and, at the same time, elaborate on and clarify their responses. These journals are called *reading logs* when students are writing about stories and poems, but when they're writing about nonfiction articles and books and content-area textbooks during thematic units, the journals are known as **learning logs**.

Students construct reading logs by stapling together 10 to 12 sheets of paper. They decorate the covers, keeping with the theme of the book, and they write entries after reading. Sometimes students choose topics for their entries; at other times, teachers pose questions to guide students' thinking. Teachers monitor students' entries by reading and responding to them. Because these journals are learning tools, teachers rarely correct students' spellings; instead, they focus their responses on the students' ideas, but they expect students to spell the book's title, characters' names, and common words correctly.

Participating in Discussions. Students talk with peers as they respond to books. Discussions about stories are called **grand conversations**. Peterson and Eeds (2007) explain that in grand conversations, students share their personal responses and tell what they liked about the text. After sharing personal reactions, they shift the focus to "puzzle over what the author has written and . . . share what it is they find revealed" (p. 61). Although the talk is primarily among the students, teachers participate by asking questions to stimulate students' thinking and by sharing information in response to questions that students ask. Too often, discussions become "gentle inquisitions" during which students recite answers to factual questions; however, the focus in grand conversations is on deepening students' comprehension.

Students also talk about nonfiction books and chapters in content-area textbooks. They share what interested them, but teachers also focus students' attention on the big ideas and the relationships among them.

Discussions can be held in small groups or as a class. When students meet in small groups, they have more opportunities to talk, but fewer viewpoints are expressed in each group; and when they meet as a class, there's a feeling of community, and the teacher can be part of the group. Teachers often compromise by having students begin in small groups and then come together as a class so that the groups can share what they discussed.

Stage 4: Exploring

This stage focuses on instruction: Middle graders delve into the selection to study academic vocabulary, collect sentences, examine the genre, and learn about the author. Teachers also teach minilessons on reading strategies and skills. When the reading selections are brief, students often reread them during the exploring stage.

Studying Academic Vocabulary. Teachers and students add key vocabulary to the **word wall** posted in the classroom and use the words for word-study activities, including drawing word maps, doing **word sorts**, completing a **semantic feature analysis**, and playing word games.

Collecting Sentences. Students also locate "important" sentences in the selection that are worthy of examination because they contain figurative language, employ an interesting sentence structure, express a theme, or illustrate a character trait. Students often copy the sentences onto sentence strips to display in the classroom, and sometimes they use them in **double-entry journal** entries.

Examining Genre and Other Text Factors. Students learn about genre, text structure, and literary devices using the selection they're reading as an example. They often create posters with genre information, make graphic organizers to highlight the selection's structure, and search through the text for examples of literary devices.

Learning About the Author. Teachers share information about the author of the featured selection and encourage students to view the author's website or read a biography or autobiography about him or her, if there's one available. They also introduce other books the author has written and invite students to read them.

Teaching Minilessons. Teachers present **minilessons** on procedures, concepts, strategies, and skills (Angelillo, 2008). They introduce the topic, provide information, and make connections between the topic and examples in the featured selection. In the vignette, Mrs. Goodman presented minilessons on visualizing and root words using examples from *The Giver*.

Stage 5: Applying

Readers move beyond the text in this final stage, creating projects to apply what they've learned. These projects take many forms, including creating a mural about the book's theme, designing a webquest, writing and performing a script based on the book, reading other books by the author, or getting involved in a community project related to an issue raised in the book. Figure 2–3 presents a list of application projects. Usually students choose the project they want to do and work on it independently, with a partner, or in a small group, but sometimes the class decides to work together. In Mrs. Goodman's classroom, for example, some students wrote color poems while classmates read other books by Lois Lowry or wrote about memories. During this stage, students often conference with the teacher to reflect on their understanding and value the reading experience.

Reading Strategies and Skills

Students use reading strategies and skills. Strategies represent the thinking that readers do as they read, and skills are quick, automatic behaviors that don't require any thought. For example, readers use the connecting strategy to compare the story they're reading to their own lives, the world around them, and other books they've read. They're actively thinking as they make connections. On the other hand, noticing quotation marks that signal a character's dialogue is a skill; students don't have to think about what these punctuation marks are signaling because they recognize their meaning automatically. The terms *strategy* and *skill* can be confusing; sometimes they're considered synonymous, but they're not.

Strategies are deliberate, goal-directed actions (Afflerbach, Pearson, & Paris, 2008). Readers exercise control in choosing appropriate strategies, using them flexibly, and monitoring their effectiveness. Strategies are linked with motivation. Afflerbach and his colleagues explain that "strategic readers feel confident that they can monitor and improve their own reading so they have both knowledge and motivation to succeed" (p. 370). Strategies reflect the information-processing theory. In contrast, skills

FIGURE 2–3 ◆ Application Projects

Visual Projects
- Design a graphic organizer or model about a book.
- Create a collage to represent the theme or big ideas in a book.
- Make a book box and fill it with objects and pictures representing the book.
- Construct a paper quilt about a book.
- Create an open-mind portrait to probe the thoughts of one character.

Writing Projects
- Rewrite a story from a different point of view.
- Write another episode, a prequel, or a sequel.
- Write simulated letters from one character to another.
- Create a found poem using words and phrases from a book.
- Write a poem on a topic related to a book.
- Keep a simulated journal from one character's viewpoint.
- Write an essay to examine the book's theme or a controversial issue.
- Create a multigenre project about a book.

Reading Projects
- Read other books from the text set.
- Read another book by the same author.
- Research a question related to a book.

Talk and Drama Projects
- Perform a readers theatre presentation of an excerpt from a book.
- Create a choral reading using an excerpt from a book and have classmates read it.
- Write a script and present it.
- Dress as a book character and sit on the "hot seat" to answer classmates' questions.
- Present a rap, song, or poem about a book.

Internet Projects
- Write a book review and post it online.
- Investigate an author's website and share information from it with classmates.
- Create or complete a webquest about the book.
- Create a multimodal project about the book using text, images, and sounds.
- Research online for information on a topic related to the book.

Social Action Projects
- Write a letter to the editor of the local newspaper on a topic related to a book.
- Get involved in a community project related to a book.

are automatic actions that occur without conscious awareness; the emphasis is on their effortless and accurate use. Skills are associated with behaviorism. They're used in the same way, no matter the reading situation. It's crucial that students become both strategic and skilled readers.

Reading Strategies. Readers use strategies for different purposes during the reading process:

Word-Identification Strategies. Students thoughtfully apply phonic, syllabic, and morphemic analysis to identify unfamiliar words.

Word-Learning Strategies. Students analyze word parts and use context clues to figure out the meaning of unfamiliar words.

Comprehension Strategies. Students predict, draw inferences, monitor, and use other strategies to understand what they're reading.

Study Strategies. Students take notes and use text features to identify big ideas when they're reading content-area textbooks.

Test-Taking Strategies. Students choose the best answer for multiple-choice questions on standardized tests and respond to prompts on writing tests.

You'll learn more about these types of strategies in upcoming chapters.

Reading Skills. Readers also use skills. Phonics skills are probably the best known, but, like strategies, students apply their knowledge of skills throughout the reading process:

Word-Identification Skills. Students use phonics rules, divide words into syllables, and separate root words and affixes to identify unfamiliar words.

Word-Learning Skills. Students identify synonyms, recognize metaphors, notice capital letters signaling proper nouns and adjectives, and use other word-learning skills.

Comprehension Skills. Students recognize details and connect them to big ideas, separate fact and opinion, and use other comprehension skills.

Study Skills. Students consult an index and notice boldface terms in the text to help them locate and remember information.

Students often use these skills in connection with strategies; the big difference is that strategies are used thoughtfully and skills are automatic, once they've been learned.

Minilessons. Teachers provide explicit instruction about reading strategies because students don't acquire the knowledge simply by reading (Pressley, 2000). They need to learn three types of information about a strategy:

- Declarative knowledge—what the strategy does
- Procedural knowledge—how to use the strategy
- Conditional knowledge—when to use the strategy (Baker & Brown, 1984)

Let's examine the declarative, procedural, and conditional knowledge for the questioning strategy, which is a comprehension strategy that students use to ask themselves questions while they're reading. They use it direct their reading, monitor whether they're understanding, and construct meaning (declarative knowledge). They ask themselves questions such as "What's going to happen next?" "How does this relate to what I know about . . . ?" and "Does this make sense?" (procedural knowledge). Students use this strategy while they're reading to activate background knowledge, monitor their reading, and signal the repair strategy, if they run into problems (conditional knowledge).

Teachers present **minilessons** to teach students about strategies. They explain the strategy and demonstrate how to use it; then students practice using it with teacher guidance and supervision before applying it independently. Through this instruction, students develop metacognitive awareness, the ability to think about their strategy use (Paris, Wasik, & Turner, 1991). The feature on page 44 presents a list of guidelines for strategy instruction.

Teachers demonstrate readers' thought processes using **think-alouds** (Wilhelm, 2001). Teachers explain what they're thinking while they're reading so that students become more aware of how capable readers think; they set a purpose for reading, make

Guidelines
for Strategy Instruction

▶ Teach strategies in minilessons using explanations, demonstrations, think-alouds, and practice activities.

▶ Provide step-by-step explanations and modeling so that students understand what the strategy does, and how and when to use it.

▶ Provide both guided and independent practice opportunities so that students can apply the strategy in new situations.

▶ Have students apply the strategy in content-area activities as well as in literacy activities.

▶ Teach groups of strategies in routines so that students learn to orchestrate the use of multiple strategies.

▶ Ask students to reflect on their use of single strategies and strategy routines.

▶ Hang charts of strategies and strategy routines students are learning, and encourage students to refer to the charts when they're reading and writing.

▶ Differentiate between strategies and skills so that students understand that strategies are problem-solving tactics and skills are automatic behaviors.

connections, ask questions, summarize what's happened so far, draw inferences, evaluate the text, and make other comments that reflect their thinking. Next, students practice thinking aloud to become more-strategic readers and improve their ability to monitor their comprehension.

Students record their strategy use on small self-stick notes. Teachers distribute pads of notes and explain how to use them. Students can focus on a single strategy or a group of strategies. They write comments about the strategies on these notes while they're reading and place them in the margin of the pages so they can locate them later. Afterward, students share their notes and talk about their strategy use in a class discussion or a conference with the teacher.

The Writing Process

The writing process is a series of five stages that describe what students think and do as they write; the stages are prewriting, drafting, revising, editing, and publishing. The labeling of the stages doesn't mean that the writing process is a linear series of neatly packaged categories; rather, research has shown that the process involves recurring cycles, and labeling is simply an aid to identifying writing activities. In the classroom, the stages merge and recur as students write. The key features of each stage are shown in Figure 2–4.

Stage 1: Prewriting

Prewriting is the "getting ready to write" stage. The traditional notion that writers have a topic completely thought out and ready to flow onto the page is ridiculous: If writers wait for ideas to fully develop, they may wait forever. Instead, writers begin

FIGURE 2–4 ◆ Key Features of the Writing Process

Stage 1: Prewriting
- Choose a topic.
- Consider the purpose.
- Identify the genre the writing will take.
- Engage in rehearsal activities to gather ideas.
- Use a graphic organizer to organize ideas.

Stage 2: Drafting
- Write a rough draft.
- Use wide spacing to leave room for revising and editing.
- Emphasize ideas rather than mechanical correctness.
- Mark the writing as a "rough draft."

Stage 3: Revising
- Reread the rough draft.
- Participate in writing groups.
- Make substantive changes that reflect peers' feedback.
- Conference with the teacher.

Stage 4: Editing
- Proofread the revised draft.
- Correct mechanical errors.
- Conference with the teacher.

Stage 5: Publishing
- Make the final copy.
- Share the writing with an appropriate audience.

tentatively—talking, reading, brainstorming—to see what they know and in what direction they want to go. Prewriting has probably been the most neglected stage in the writing process; however, it's as crucial to writers as a warm-up is to athletes. Murray (1982) believes that at least 70% of writing time should be spent in prewriting. During prewriting, students choose a topic, consider purpose and form, and gather and organize ideas for writing.

Choosing a Topic. Students should choose their own topics for writing—topics that they're interested in and know about—so that they'll be more engaged, but that isn't always possible. Sometimes teachers provide the topics, but it's best when teacher-selected topics are broad so students can narrow them in the way that's best for them.

Considering Purpose and Form. As students prepare to write, they need to think about the purpose of their writing: Are they writing to entertain? to inform? to persuade? Setting the purpose for writing is just as important as setting the purpose for reading, because purpose influences the decisions students make about form or genre. Young adolescents refine their knowledge of narrative and poetic genres, and they learn to use new forms, including essays.

STRUGGLING READERS AND WRITERS

The Writing Process

Struggling writers need to use the writing process.

Many struggling students don't like to write, and they avoid it whenever possible because they don't know what to do (Christenson, 2002). Teachers need to review the writing process with these students. Interactive writing, a procedure normally used with young children, is a good way to demonstrate the activities at each stage and the strategies writers use, including organizing and revising. Because it's a group activity, students are more willing to participate.

Once they're familiar with the stages in the writing process, students apply what they've learned to write collaborative compositions. Each student drafts a paragraph or short section and then moves through the writing process; this way, the workload is manageable for both students and their teachers. Once students know how to use the writing process, they're better prepared to write independently.

Struggling writers who don't understand the writing process often think they're finished once they write a rough draft; they don't realize that they have to revise and edit their writing to communicate more effectively. The key to enticing struggling writers to revise and edit is to help them develop a sense of audience. Many novice writers write primarily for themselves, but when they want their classmates or another audience to understand their message, they begin to recognize the importance of refining their writing. Teachers emphasize audience by encouraging students to share their writing from the author's chair. Lots of writing and sharing are necessary before students learn to appreciate the writing process.

Gathering and Organizing Ideas. Students engage in prewriting activities to gather and organize ideas for writing. To gather ideas, they brainstorm lists of words, do Internet research, read books, and talk about ideas with peers. Students often make graphic organizers to visually display their ideas and the relationships among them. Their choice of graphic organizer varies with the writing genre; to write a persuasive essay, for example, students use a diagram with sections to develop ideas for each argument.

Stage 2: Drafting

Students write the first draft, beginning tentatively with the ideas they've developed through prewriting activities. Their drafts are usually messy, reflecting the outpouring of thoughts with cross-outs, lines, and arrows as they think of better ways to express ideas. Students write quickly, with little concern about legible handwriting, spelling correctness, or careful use of capitalization and punctuation.

When they write rough drafts, students skip every other line to leave space to make revisions. They use arrows to move sections of text, cross-outs to delete sections, and scissors and tape to cut apart and rearrange text, just as adult writers do. Wide spacing is crucial. Some students make small *x*'s on every other line of their papers as a reminder to skip lines. They write only on one side of a page so their rough drafts can be revised more easily.

Students label their drafts by writing *rough draft* in ink at the top or by using a ROUGH DRAFT stamp. This label indicates to the writer, peers, parents, and administrators that the composition is a draft in which the emphasis is on content, not mechanics; it also explains why the teacher hasn't marked errors or graded the paper.

Instead of writing drafts by hand, many students use word processing to compose rough drafts and polish their writing. There are many benefits of word processing: Students are often more motivated when they use computers, they tend to write longer pieces, and it's easier to make revisions. Their writing looks neater, and they use spell-check programs to identify and correct misspelled words.

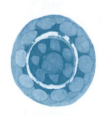

Stage 3: Revising

Writers refine the ideas in their compositions. Students often break the writing process cycle as soon as they complete a rough draft, believing that once they've jotted down their ideas, the writing task is complete. Experienced writers, however, know they must turn to others for reactions and revise on the basis of these comments. Revision isn't just polishing; it's meeting the needs of readers by adding, substituting, deleting, and rearranging material. *Revision* means "seeing again," and in this stage, writers see their compositions again with the help of classmates and the teacher. Revising consists of three activities: Students reread their rough drafts, get feedback on their writing, and make revisions based on the feedback they've received.

Rereading the Rough Draft. After finishing their rough drafts, writers wait a day or two, then reread them from a fresh perspective, as a reader might. As they reread, students make some changes right away and place question marks by sections that need work; it's these trouble spots that students ask for help with in their writing groups.

Getting Feedback. Middle graders meet in **writing groups** to share their rough drafts with classmates, who respond to the rough draft and suggest possible revisions. Writing groups provide a scaffold in which teachers and classmates talk about plans and strategies for writing and revising.

In some classrooms, writing groups form whenever four or five students finish writing their rough drafts; they gather around a conference table or in a corner of the classroom and take turns reading their drafts aloud. Classmates listen and respond, offering compliments and suggestions for revision. Sometimes the teacher joins the writing group, but if he or she is involved in something else, students work independently.

In other classrooms, teachers organize the writing groups. Students get together when everyone in the group is ready to participate. Sometimes the teacher joins these groups, responding along with students, or the groups can function independently. Lists of groups and their members are posted in the classroom. One student in each group is designated as the leader, and that role typically changes each quarter.

Making Revisions. Students make four types of changes to their rough drafts: additions, substitutions, deletions, and moves (Faigley & Witte, 1981). They often use a blue pen to cross out, draw arrows, and write in the space left between the double-spaced lines of their rough drafts so that revisions will show clearly; that way, teachers can see the types of revisions students make by examining their revised rough drafts. Revisions are an important gauge of students' growth as writers.

Many teachers set up revising centers to give students revision options: They can talk with a classmate about the ideas in their draft, examine the organization of their writing, consider their word choice, or check that they have included all required components in the composition. A list of revising centers is shown in Figure 2–5. Teachers introduce these centers as they teach writing, and then students work at a couple of them either before or after participating in a writing group. Teachers usually provide a checklist of center options that students put in their writing folders, and then they check off the centers that they complete. Through these center activities, students develop a repertoire of revising strategies and personalize their own writing process.

Stage 4: Editing

Editing is putting the piece of writing into its final form. During the first three stages, the focus has been on the content of students' writing; now it changes to mechanics, the commonly accepted conventions of written Standard English. They consist of capitalization, punctuation, spelling, sentence structure, usage, and formatting considerations specific to poems, scripts, letters, and other writing genres. The use of these commonly accepted conventions is a courtesy to those who will read the composition.

Students are more efficient editors if they set the composition aside for a few days before beginning to edit. After working so closely with a piece of writing during drafting and revising, they're too familiar with it to notice many mechanical errors; with some distance, students are better able to approach editing with a fresh perspective and gather the enthusiasm necessary to finish the writing process. Then students proofread to locate errors and then correct them.

Proofreading. Students proofread their rough drafts to locate and mark possible errors. Proofreading is a unique type of reading in which students read slowly, word by word, hunting for errors rather than reading quickly for meaning. Concentrating on mechanics is difficult because of our natural inclination to read for meaning; even experienced proofreaders often find themselves focusing on meaning and thus overlook errors that don't inhibit comprehension. It's important, therefore, to take time to explain proofreading and to demonstrate how it differs from regular reading. Teachers display a revised draft on an overhead projector and read it several times, each time hunting for a particular type of error. During each reading, they read slowly, pronouncing each

FIGURE 2–5 ◆ *Revising and Editing Centers*

Type	Center	Activities
Revising	Rereading	Students reread their rough drafts with a partner, who offers compliments and asks questions.
	Word Choice	Students choose 5–10 words in their rough drafts and consult a thesaurus for more-specific or more-powerful synonyms.
	Graphic Organizer	Students draw a diagram to illustrate the organization of their compositions, and they make revisions if their organization isn't effective or their writing isn't complete.
	Highlighting	Students use highlighter pens to mark topic sentences or sensory details in their rough drafts, depending on the teacher's direction.
	Sentence Combining	Students combine short sentences to improve the flow of their writing.
Editing	Spelling	Students work with a partner to proofread their writing. They locate misspelled words and consult a dictionary to correct them. Students may also check for specific errors in their use of recently taught skills.
	Homonyms	Students check their rough drafts for homonym errors (e.g., *there–their–they're*), and after consulting a chart posted in the center, they correct the errors.
	Punctuation	Students proofread their writing to check for punctuation marks. They make corrections as needed, and then highlight the punctuation marks in their compositions.
	Capitalization	Students check that each sentence begins with a capital letter, the word *I* is capitalized, and proper nouns and adjectives are capitalized. Afterward, students highlight all capitalized letters in their compositions.
	Sentences	Students analyze the sentences in their rough drafts and categorize them as simple, compound, complex, or fragment on a chart. Then they make any necessary changes.

word and touching it with a red pen to direct their attention, and they mark possible errors as they're noticed.

Editing checklists help students focus on particular types of errors. Teachers can develop checklists with 8 to 10 items appropriate for the grade level; for example, a fifth-grade checklist might contain items such as using commas in a series, indenting paragraphs, capitalizing proper nouns and adjectives, and spelling homonyms correctly. Teachers revise the checklist during the school year to focus on skills that have recently been taught.

A seventh-grade editing checklist is presented in the Assessment Tools feature on the next page. Pairs work together to edit their rough drafts. First, students proofread their own drafts, searching for errors in each category listed on the checklist. After completing the checklist, students sign their names and then trade checklists and drafts: Now they become editors and complete each other's checklist. Having both writer and editor sign the checklist helps them take the activity seriously.

Correcting Errors. After students proofread their drafts and locate as many errors as they can, they correct the errors independently or with an editor's assistance. Some errors are easy to correct, some require use of a dictionary, and others involve instruction from the teacher. It's unrealistic to expect students to locate and correct every mechanical error in their compositions; not even published books are always error-free!

Assessment Tools

Seventh-Grade Editing Checklist

Title: _____

Author   Editor

☐   ☐   **END PUNCTUATION**

Check that each sentence has end punctuation.

☐   ☐   **COMMAS**

Check that commas are used for these purposes:
• before a conjunction to create a compound sentence
• after a subordinate clause in a complex sentence
• in a list of items
• after an introductory word or phrase
• setting off interruptions
• separating adjectives
• in dates

☐   ☐   **APOSTROPHES**

Check that apostrophes are used for these purposes:
• in contractions
• to show ownership

☐   ☐   **SEMICOLONS**

Check that semicolons are used to connect sentences without conjunctions in a compound sentence.

Author: _____   Editor: _____

Once in a while, students may change a correct spelling or punctuation mark and make it incorrect, but they correct far more errors than they create.

Students also work at editing centers to identify and correct specific types of errors; a list of editing centers is also shown in Figure 2–5. Teachers often vary the activities at the center to reflect the types of errors students are making. Students who continue to misspell common words can check for these words on a chart posted in the center. Or, after a series of lessons on capitalizing proper nouns and adjectives, for example, teachers will organize one center to focus on applying the newly taught skill.

Editing can end after students and their editors correct as many mechanical errors as possible, or after students meet with the teacher for a final editing conference. When mechanical correctness matters, this conference is important. Teachers proofread the rough draft with the student, and they identify and make the remaining corrections together, or the teacher makes checkmarks in the margin to note errors for the student to locate and correct independently.

Stage 5: Publishing

Students bring their compositions to life by making final copies and by sharing them with an appropriate audience. When they share their writing with real audiences of classmates, parents, and the community, students come to think of themselves as authors. Publication is powerful: Students are motivated not only to continue writing but also to improve the quality of their rough drafts through revising and editing (Weber, 2002).

One of the most popular ways for students to publish their writing is by making books. Students construct booklets by stapling or sewing sheets of writing paper together and adding covers made of cardboard covered with fabric, contact paper, or wallpaper.

The best way for students to share their writing is to sit in a special chair called the *author's chair* and read their writing aloud. Afterward, classmates ask questions, offer compliments, and celebrate the completion of the writing project. Sharing writing is a social activity that helps writers develop sensitivity to audiences and confidence in themselves as authors. Beyond just providing the opportunity for students to share writing, teachers need to teach students how to make appropriate comments as they respond

Author's Chair
These fifth graders take turns sitting in the special author's chair to read their published writings aloud to classmates. It's a celebratory activity, and after reading, students ask questions and offer compliments. These students have learned to show interest in their classmates' writing and to think about the writing so that they can participate in the discussion that follows the reading. Afterward, another student is chosen to share, and the process is repeated. As students are sharing their writing from the author's chair, they learn to think of themselves as writers and consider their audience more carefully when they revise and edit their writing.

to their peers' writing. Teachers also participate, and they serve as a model, demonstrating how to respond to students' writing.

Here are some other ways for students to share their writing:

Read it to parents and siblings

Share it at a back-to-school event

Place it in the classroom library

Read it to students in other classes

Display it as a mobile or on a poster

Contribute it to a class anthology

Post it on the class website

Submit it to the school's literary magazine

Display it at a school or community event

Submit it to a literary magazine or an e-zine (online literary magazine)

The best literary magazines are *Stone Soup* and *Skipping Stones*. *Stone Soup* contains writing and artwork by kids ages 8–13. At its website (www.stonesoup.com), you can download a sample issue and listen to students reading their own works.

New Literacies

Online Publication Sites

The Internet offers unlimited opportunities for students to display their writing online, share it with a global audience, and receive authentic feedback from readers (McNabb, 2006). When students create multimodal compositions that incorporate audio, video, animation, or graphics, electronic publication is essential so that readers can fully experience them. Students are using new literacies when they implement multimodal technologies to express their ideas and engage in online communication (Labbo, 2005).

Here's a list of the best online publication sites:

Cyber Kids, at www.cyberkids.com
This site publishes original writing by 10- to 14-year-olds, including multimodal stories.

Kids' Space, at www.kids-space.org
This website posts students' art, writing, and music from around the world. In the writing category, young adolescents' stories, play scripts, and poems are invited.

KidsWWwrite, at www.kalwriters.com/kidswwwrite
Students' stories and poems are published in this e-zine.

Poetry Zone, at www.poetryzone.ndirect.co.uk
This British website posts students' poetry in the Poetry Gallery.

Stories From the Web, at www.storiesfromtheweb.org
This website accepts submissions of students' stories, play scripts, poems, raps, and songs.

Students can use Internet search engines to locate new e-zines. It's inevitable that some online publication sites will shut down, but others will spring up to take their place.

Each electronic magazine posts its own submission information that students should read and follow. Most e-zines specify that students' submissions must be original, and that writing dealing with violent or offensive topics or employing inappropriate language won't be published. Submissions must be ready for posting; it's naïve to assume that an editor will format students' writing or correct mechanical errors. Students usually complete an online information sheet and e-mail their writing to the e-zine's website, and parents must submit a permission statement.

Students can also display their writing on the class website for others to read and respond to in guest books, blogs, and e-mail messages (Weber, 2002). If the teacher doesn't have a class website, students can work with their teacher to create one and post their writing there.

Subscription information is available there as well as directions for submitting students' writing. *Skipping Stones* is an international magazine for kids ages 8–16 that accepts stories, articles, photos, cartoons, letters, and drawings. This award-winning publication focuses on global interdependence, celebrates cultural and environmental richness, and provides a forum for kids from around the world to share ideas and experiences. To read excerpts from the current issue and to get information about subscribing and submitting writing to *Skipping Stones*, visit the magazine's website at www. skippingstones.org. Many teachers subscribe to these magazines and use the compositions as mentor texts or models when they're teaching writing. Other literary magazines worth considering are *Magic Dragon* (www.magicdragonmagazine.com) and *New Moon: The Magazine for Girls and Their Dreams* (www.newmoon.org). Too often, literary magazines are labors of love rather than viable financial ventures, so even highly esteemed and popular magazines go out of business. Students should always check that a literary magazine is still accepting submissions before sending their writing.

Writing Strategies and Skills

Young adolescents augment their repertoire of writing strategies and knowledge about writing skills during the middle grades. They learn to regulate their use of writing strategies effectively and expand their knowledge about sentence and paragraph structure and writing mechanics.

Writing Strategies. Writing strategies are like reading strategies; they're tools students use deliberately to craft effective compositions. Students apply many of the same strategies for both reading and writing, such as activating background knowledge, questioning, repairing, and evaluating, and they also use some strategies that are specific to writing. Dean (2006) explains that using the writing process makes writers more strategic, and writers use a variety of strategies at each stage:

Prewriting Strategies. Students use generating ideas, organizing ideas, and other strategies before beginning to write.

Drafting Strategies. Students use strategies such as narrowing the topic to focus on ideas while writing the first draft.

Revising Strategies. Students use rereading, elaborating ideas, choosing precise words, and other strategies to communicate their ideas more effectively.

Editing Strategies. Students use strategies including proofreading and checking the dictionary to identify and correct spelling and other mechanical errors.

Publishing Strategies. Students use strategies such as designing the layout to prepare the final drafts of their compositions and share them with classmates and other authentic audiences.

Students apply these writing strategies purposefully as they draft and refine their writing.

Writing Skills. Writing skills are automatic actions that students learn to use quickly and accurately during the writing process. Students learn these five types of skills:

Content Skills. Students use their knowledge about main ideas and details to organize information into paragraphs and longer compositions. These skills are most important during the drafting and revising stages.

Word Skills. Students use their knowledge about precise words and vivid verbs during drafting and revising to make their writing clearer and more lively.

Sentence Skills. Students use their knowledge about types of sentences to make their writing more interesting to read. These skills are most useful during drafting and revising.

Grammar Skills. Students use grammar skills to correct any nonstandard English errors during editing.

Mechanical Skills. Students apply spelling, capitalization, and punctuation skills to make their compositions more readable, especially during the editing stage.

Writers use strategies thoughtfully and skills automatically as they develop and refine compositions. Through a combination of instruction and opportunities to practice the writing strategies and skills, young adolescents become more-effective writers.

Minilessons. Teachers use **minilessons** with demonstrations and **think-alouds** to teach writing strategies and skills, and then students apply what they're learning during guided practice and independent writing projects. These strategies and skills are often reflected in **rubrics** that teachers and students use to assess students' writing.

Reading and Writing Are Reciprocal Processes

Reading and writing are reciprocal; they're both constructive, meaning-making processes. Researchers have found that reading leads to better writing, and that writing has the same effect on reading (Spivey, 1997). Not surprisingly, they've also learned that integrating instruction improves both reading and writing (Braunger & Lewis, 2006; Tierney & Shanahan, 1996). It's possible that students use the same type of thinking for both reading and writing.

Comparing the Two Processes

The reading and writing processes have comparable activities at each stage (Butler & Turbill, 1984). A comparison of the two processes is shown in Figure 2–6. For example, notice the similarities between the activities in the third stage of reading and writing—responding and revising, respectively. Fitzgerald (1989) analyzed these two activities and concluded that they draw on similar author-reader-text interactions. Similar analyses can be made for other stages as well.

Tierney (1983) explains that reading and writing involve concurrent, complex transactions between writers as readers and readers as writers. It seems natural that writers read other authors' books for ideas and to learn about organizing their writing, and they also read and reread their own writing as they revise to communicate more effectively. The quality of these reading experiences seems closely tied to success in writing. Thinking of readers as writers may be more difficult, but readers participate in many of the same activities that writers use—activating background knowledge, setting purposes, determining importance, monitoring, repairing, and evaluating.

Classroom Connections

Classroom activities often involve both reading and writing, and making connections between reading and writing is a natural part of literacy instruction. Students read and

FIGURE 2–6 ◆ *A Comparison of the Reading and Writing Processes*

	What Readers Do	*What Writers Do*
Stage 1	**Prereading** Readers use knowledge about • the topic • reading • genres and other text factors	**Prewriting** Writers use knowledge about • the topic • writing • genres and other text factors
Stage 2	**Reading** Readers • use word-identification strategies • use comprehension strategies • monitor reading • create meaning	**Drafting** Writers • use spelling strategies • use writing strategies • monitor writing • create meaning
Stage 3	**Responding** Readers • respond to the text • deepen meaning • clarify misunderstandings • expand ideas	**Revising** Writers • respond to the text • deepen meaning • clarify misunderstandings • expand ideas
Stage 4	**Exploring** Readers • examine the impact of words and literary language • explore structural elements • compare the text to others	**Editing** Writers • identify and correct mechanical errors • review paragraph and sentence structure
Stage 5	**Applying** Readers • create projects • share projects with classmates • reflect on the reading process • feel success • want to read again	**Publishing** Writers • make the final copy • share their writing with genuine audiences • reflect on the writing process • feel success • want to write again

then write or write and then read: They write reading log entries after reading to deepen their understanding of what they've read, for example, or they make a semantic feature analysis to organize the information they're reading in a content-area textbook. Similarly, students read rough drafts aloud to make sure they flow and then read them to classmates to get feedback on how well they're communicating, or they use a structural pattern from a poem they've read in one they're writing. Shanahan (1988) offered these recommendations for connecting reading and writing so that students develop a clearer understanding of literacy:

• Involve students in daily reading and writing experiences.
• Make the reading–writing connection explicit to students.
• Emphasize both the processes and the products of reading and writing.
• Set clear purposes for reading and writing.
• Teach reading and writing through authentic literacy experiences.

It's not enough, however, for students to see themselves as readers and writers; they need to grasp the relationships between the two roles and move flexibly between them. Readers think like writers to understand the author's purpose and viewpoint, for instance, and writers assume alternative viewpoints as potential readers.

CHAPTER 2
Review

How Effective Teachers Use the Reading and Writing Processes

▶ Teachers use the reading process—prereading, reading, responding, exploring, and applying—to ensure that students comprehend the texts they read.

▶ Teachers use independent reading, partner reading, guided reading, shared reading, and interactive read-alouds to share fiction and nonfiction books with students.

▶ Teachers teach students how to use the writing process—prewriting, drafting, revising, editing, and publishing—to write and refine their compositions.

▶ Teachers understand that reading and writing are reciprocal meaning-making processes.

CHAPTER 3

Assessing Literacy Learning

Teachers Diagnose a Struggling Student

Mrs. Sarkissian is a seventh-grade "core" (combined language arts/social studies) teacher whose students are reading 2 or more years below grade level and who scored "far below basic" on last year's statewide standards-based achievement test. The class is capped at 20 students, but currently there are 23 in the class because of overcrowding. She asks Mrs. Jackson, the school's literacy coach, to assess Raquel, a well-behaved 13-year-old who participates actively in class but isn't making adequate progress.

Mrs. Jackson begins by visiting Mrs. Sarkissian's classroom to observe Raquel. First the students do Daily Language Practice, a 10-minute editing activity to reinforce capitalization, punctuation, and grammar skills. Students read a passage that's projected onto a whiteboard to locate and the correct the errors in it. Mrs. Jackson observes Raquel's group as they hunt for errors. Raquel quickly catches the capitalization errors but doesn't notice the punctuation errors involving quotation marks and commas. Everyone in the group struggles with the grammar, so Mrs. Jackson helps them identify verb, pronoun, and sentence fragment errors.

Next, students participate in integrated literacy/social studies activities. The class is currently involved in a monthlong unit on the Renaissance, and they're reading *Shakespeare's Secret* (Broach, 2007), a mystery about a lost diamond that may have belonged to Anne Boleyn. The book's reading level is sixth grade, too difficult for students to read on their own, so Mrs. Sarkissian does shared reading. She focuses on drawing inferences as she reads because her students have difficulty with inferential thinking. Raquel follows along as her teacher reads, and she participates in the discussion even though most of her comments indicate that she doesn't comprehend the book.

Writing workshop is next. Mrs. Sarkissian has taught students about persuasive writing, and they've read and analyzed sample essays before writing one together as a class. Now they're writing persuasive essays on topics they've chosen themselves. Raquel and her friend Etta's topic is "breakfast is the most important meal of the day"; it was Etta's idea, and she's more passionate about the topic than Raquel is. Today they're participating in a **writing group** to revise their rough draft. They share their draft and get advice about how to add a counterargument, and a classmate encourages to them to make sure every sentence makes sense.

During the last 15 minutes of class, students read independently in books at their reading level while Mrs. Sarkissian circulates around the classroom, listening to students read aloud and talking quietly with them about their reading. Raquel is reading *P.S. I Really Like You* (Krulik, 2008), the sixth book in the How I Survived Middle School series about Jenny and her girlfriends at Joyce Kilmer Middle School. Mrs. Jackson squats down beside Raquel and listens to her read aloud in this third-grade-level book. Raquel's reading is fairly fluent, but not very expressive. Mrs. Jackson asks, "So, who do you think Jenny's secret admirer is?" but Raquel doesn't have any ideas.

After the observation, Mrs. Jackson checks Raquel's permanent record to learn more about her: Raquel is Hispanic, her primary language is Spanish, and her English Language Development level is 3 (of 5 levels); her limited reading achievement keeps her from advancing to the next level. She's attended six schools since kindergarten. She was in a Spanish language program in the primary grades and transitioned to English in fourth grade. Her mother speaks only Spanish and didn't graduate from high school. There's no information about Raquel's father except that he's not living in the home.

Raquel attends school regularly. Her GPA for the first quarter of seventh grade is 3.3, and she received *A*s in both language arts and social studies. Her report cards for kindergarten through third grade indicate that she wasn't making adequate progress in reading and writing, and each year her teachers requested that Raquel's mother assist by reading and writing with her. Notes on her third-grade report card show that she was reading at first-grade level. In fifth grade, she read at second-grade level, and in sixth grade, she read at third-grade level. She began taking standardized achievement tests in third grade and has consistently ranked at the lowest proficiency level, "far below basic," in reading.

Mrs. Jackson decides to use these three assessments to learn more about Raquel and diagnose her literacy problems:

- Interest inventories to learn about Raquel and her perception of herself as a reader and writer
- An informal reading inventory to determine Raquel's reading level and examine her ability to identify words, read fluently, understand academic vocabulary, and answer comprehension questions
- Pieces of writing to investigate Raquel's ability to use the writing process, the six traits, and conventions (spelling, capitalization, punctuation, and grammar)

Mrs. Jackson already suspects that Raquel reads at the third-grade level and has comprehension problems that may be related to being an English learner.

The Interest Inventories. Mrs. Jackson asked Raquel questions about her home life, interests, and reading and writing achievement. Raquel is a Hispanic seventh grader who's tall for her age and has long, curly, dark hair. She seems confident and outgoing during the interview. She's adamant that she's a native English speaker, even though her school records indicate otherwise. She has four siblings, one sister and three brothers who are all older, and she emphasizes that everyone in her family speaks English. She's interested in becoming a fashion designer because her aunt taught her how to draw clothing and she likes to watch Project Runway on TV. She joined the drama club this year because she likes Mrs. Sarkissian, who sponsors it, and now she's thinking of becoming an actor.

Raquel explained that she tries hard because she wants to be a good student. She does homework at the kitchen table, but her siblings often distract her so she doesn't get it completed. Her family has a computer with Internet access, and she loves to play online games—her favorite website is Multiplication.com (www.multiplication.com). She doesn't have any books, but she regularly reads *Tiger Beat*, a teenagers' magazine about music and celebrities.

Raquel described herself as a good reader, but she doesn't use reading strategies. She said she's good at learning new words because she knows how to break them into syllables. Raquel admitted that she doesn't do much reading and couldn't think of a book she'd read recently. She likes to write but acknowledged that she's not a good writer. She stated that writing paragraphs is the hardest part for her. She couldn't recall any writing she'd done lately.

Informal Reading Inventory. Mrs. Jackson used the Qualitative Reading Inventory-4 (QRI) (Leslie & Caldwell, 2006), an informal reading inventory, to assess Raquel's reading performance. In particular, she wanted to determine Raquel's reading level, check the adequacy of her background knowledge, examine her oral reading fluency, and diagnose comprehension problems.

She began by asking Raquel to read graded word lists, beginning at first-grade level, to examine her ability to identify words and determine the starting point for the second part of the test, reading graded passages. As Raquel read the words, Mrs. Jackson marked a scoring sheet and at the end of each list, counted the errors to identify the reading level. Raquel read the first- through fifth-grade lists with these results:

First grade: independent reading level

Second grade: independent reading level

Third grade: independent reading level

Fourth grade: instructional reading level

Fifth grade: frustration reading level

Mrs. Jackson will begin the second part of the QRI at third grade because it's Raquel's highest independent word-reading level.

Mrs. Jackson noticed that Raquel made two types of word-identification errors. For one- and two-syllable words, she quickly substituted real words with the same beginning and ending sounds: *lock* for *look*, *plot* for *pilot*, *frame* for *fame*, *invited* for *invented*, *silvery* for *slavery*, and *punch* for *pouch*. She also tried without success to sound out these words: *environment*, *adaptation*, *guarded*, *irrigated*, *bulletin*, *adventurer*, *pioneers*, and *curious*. To examine her vocabulary knowledge, Mrs. Jackson pronounced some of the words that Raquel missed and asked her if she'd heard them before, but she didn't recognize any.

Next, Mrs. Jackson asked Raquel to read some passages aloud. Before she read each one, Mrs. Jackson asked several questions to investigate her background knowledge about the topic of the passage, and after the reading, she asked Raquel to retell what she'd read and answer some comprehension questions. Raquel first read a third-grade narrative passage about a field trip to the zoo; she read it smoothly, retold it accurately, and answered all questions correctly. Mrs. Jackson scored it as independent level. Next, Raquel read a third-grade expository passage on cats, but her retelling was incomplete, and she didn't answer any implicit comprehension questions correctly; Mrs. Jackson scored it as instructional level. Last, Raquel easily read a second-grade expository passage on whales, and Mrs. Jackson scored it as independent level.

The testing continued until Mrs. Jackson identified Raquel's independent, instructional, and frustration levels for narrative and expository texts; the results are presented in the box below. As passages became more difficult, Raquel demonstrated more strength in word identification than in comprehension. Her answers to before-reading questions indicated that she lacked adequate background knowledge about the topics, her retellings were increasingly incomplete and confused, and her answers to explicit comprehension questions were better than to implicit ones.

Raquel's QRI Results		
Reading Level	**Narrative Texts**	**Expository Texts**
Independent	3	2
Instructional	4	3
Frustration	5	4
Listening Capacity	6	5

Mrs. Jackson also tested Raquel's listening capacity level to determine whether she could understand orally presented information and books when they're read aloud; she calls listening capacity her "comprehension potential." Raquel's listening capacity score for narrative texts is sixth grade, and fifth grade for expository texts. Seventh-grade passages are too difficult for her to comprehend successfully.

Mrs. Jackson concluded that Raquel reads at the third–fourth grade level, depending on the topic and genre, and she comprehends sixth-grade-level fiction texts and fifth-grade-level content-area textbooks when they're read aloud. The teacher noted problems in these areas:

Word Identification. Raquel's word identification is stronger than her comprehension; nonetheless, she exhibited difficulty identifying words, including *settlers*, *guarded*, *lodge*, *canals*, and *beasts*. The word-identification errors seem to reflect her limited background knowledge.

Fluency. Raquel's reading speed averaged 109 words read per minute (wpm), which exceeds the 100-wpm threshold for fluency but is very slow for seventh grade. She read word by word and without expressiveness.

Vocabulary. Raquel's academic vocabulary knowledge is very limited; for example, she described a beaver as a "thing" and didn't know the meaning of *courage* or recognize the related word *courageous*.

Comprehension. Raquel has limited background knowledge about topics typically studied in the elementary grades, including Johnny Appleseed, Abraham Lincoln, beavers, and whales. She struggled to make predictions even after talking about a topic and reading the title of the passage. She was unable to draw inferences and answer implicit comprehension questions in narrative and expository passages. In addition, she didn't respond to humor even through Mrs. Jackson laughed as Raquel read a funny passage aloud.

Oral Language.   Raquel's speech reflects her status as an English learner. She confuses pronouns (*he/she/they*), and her sentence structure is often awkward. For example, as she retold the passage about Johnny Appleseed, Raquel said, "He was grateful from everyone because he planted them" when she was talking about the apple seeds people gave him.

Raquel exhibited problems in all areas, but comprehension presents her greatest challenge.

Writing Sample.   Mrs. Sarkissian didn't have a collection of Raquel's writings to share with Mrs. Jackson, so she reviewed Raquel's composition from the last district quarterly writing assessment. It's a response to literature, written after listening to a short story read aloud, and it received the lowest rating:

> *In the story was a boy name was Jerry and he lie a lost [lot] to he friend. He lie that he will buy some glab [gloves]. Then he want home and he said to he self were [where] will I get the glab. Then he lie to her mother that he will get the glub.*
>
> *Then after time past he said why do you care [carry] milk into the fost [forest]. Then a gril said my fish [fingers] are red. I need glab. Then the gril said last time said you buy a glab and verybody [everybody] said ooo yes. yes. Then they say were are your glab. Then he said at home in my clother [closet]. And they said bring we can us them. And then he said no. no.*
>
> *Fanily the boy tell the true that he not have glub because he lie. Then he friend said I want [won't] be your friend because lie to us that you got glab. Then he said I lie to my mom. And they say that it sad because not to lie to your mom.*

Students were instructed to write an essay, developing their interpretation of the story, and to support their ideas with evidence from the text. Raquel's composition is typical of middle-grade struggling writers. She wrote a three-paragraph summary, not an interpretation. Her writing is difficult to read and understand because of serious errors in spelling, sentence construction, and use of pronouns.

Recommendations.   After she completed the testing, Mrs. Jackson reviewed the data she collected. She concluded that Raquel's literacy problems affect her potential to meet grade-level standards. Her instructional reading level is 3–4 years below grade level, and her listening capacity is 1–2 years below grade level. Comprehension is her most serious problem area; she has limited background knowledge and academic vocabulary, she's unfamiliar with comprehension strategies, and she rarely thinks inferentially. Here are Mrs. Jackson's recommendations, beginning with the most important ones:

Comprehension.   Increasing Raquel's comprehension is the top priority. First, she needs to learn and apply comprehension strategies, including predicting, connecting, monitoring, and repairing. Small-group **guided reading** lessons are a good way to teach comprehension strategies. Second, Mrs. Sarkissian should continue to focus on inferential thinking during read-alouds.

Reading and Writing Practice.   Raquel needs to increase reading and writing volume. The 15-minute daily independent reading time is beneficial so Raquel can continue to read books at her independent reading level. She needs more writing practice, including writing about social studies topics in **quickwrites** and **learning logs**.

Vocabulary. Mrs. Sarkissian should emphasize academic vocabulary by posting a word wall in the classroom and involving students in more vocabulary activities, including word sorts, exclusion brainstorming, and semantic feature analysis.

Word Identification. Raquel should be taught to examine letter sequences in an entire word, not just make a guess based on the first and last letters. Classroom instruction on root words and affixes would also expand her vocabulary knowledge and provide a useful tool for identifying words.

She shares information about Raquel's independent, instructional, and frustration levels and these four recommendations with Mrs. Sarkissian. They talk about ways to implement the recommendations, and the conflict between addressing seventh-grade standards and providing more time for reading and writing practice. Mrs. Jackson agrees to come into the classroom to work with Mrs. Sarkissian as she begins guided reading groups, posts a word wall, and makes other changes to support Raquel and the other struggling readers and writers in her classroom.

A ssessment has become a priority in 21st-century schools. School districts and state and federal education agencies have increased their demands for accountability, and today, most students take annual high-stakes tests to judge their achievement. Teachers are collecting more assessment data now and doing it more frequently than in the past. They're using the information to make instructional decisions, as Mrs. Jackson demonstrated in the vignette. Researchers explain that "a system of frequent assessment, coupled with strong content standards and effective reading instruction, helps ensure that teachers' . . . approaches are appropriate to each student's needs" (Kame'enui, Simmons, & Cornachione, 2000, p. 10). By linking assessment and instruction, teachers improve students' learning and their teaching.

As you continue reading, you'll notice that the term *assessment* is used much more often than *evaluation*. These terms are often considered interchangeable, but they're not. Assessment is formative; it's ongoing and provides immediate feedback to improve teaching and learning. It's usually authentic, based on the literacy activities in which students are engaged. Observations, conferences, and student work samples are examples of authentic assessment. In contrast, evaluation is summative; it's final, generally administered at the end of a unit or a school year, and used to judge quality. Tests are the most common type of evaluation, and they're used to compare one student's achievement against that of other students or against grade-level standards.

Classroom-Based Assessment

T he purpose of classroom assessment is to collect meaningful information about what students know and do, and it takes many forms (Afflerbach, 2007a). Teachers use these four types of assessment to monitor and examine students' learning:

- Kits of leveled books and tests to determine students' reading levels
- Informal procedures, such as observations and conferences, to monitor student progress
- Tests to diagnose students' strengths and weaknesses in specific components of reading and writing
- Collections of work samples to document students' achievement

Each type of assessment serves a different purpose, so it's important that teachers choose assessment tools carefully. Researchers recommend that teachers use a combination of informal and formal assessments to improve the fairness and effectiveness of classroom literacy assessment (Kuhs, Johnson, Agruso, & Monrad, 2001).

Determining Reading Levels

Teachers match students with books at appropriate levels of difficulty because students are more likely to be successful when they're reading books that aren't too easy or too difficult; books that are too easy don't provide enough challenge, and those that are too difficult frustrate students. Researchers have identified three reading levels that take into account students' ability to recognize words automatically, read fluently, and comprehend what they're reading:

Independent Reading Level. Students read books at this level comfortably, on their own. They recognize almost all words; their accuracy rate is 95–100%. Their reading is fluent, and they comprehend what they're reading. Books at this level are only slightly easier than those at their instructional level, and they still engage students' interest.

Instructional Reading Level. Students read and understand books at this level with support, but not on their own. They recognize most words; their accuracy rate is 90–94%. Their reading may be fluent, but sometimes it isn't. With support from the teacher or classmates, students comprehend what they're reading, but if they're reading independently, their understanding is limited. This level reflects Vygotsky's zone of proximal development, discussed in Chapter 1.

Frustration Reading Level. Books at this level are too difficult for students to read successfully, even with assistance. Students don't recognize enough words automatically; their accuracy is less than 90%. Students' reading is choppy and word by word, and it often doesn't make sense. In addition, students show little understanding of what's been read.

Students should be assessed regularly to determine their reading levels and to monitor their progress.

These reading levels have important implications for instruction: Students read independent-level books when they're reading for pleasure and instructional-level books when they're participating in

STRUGGLING READERS AND WRITERS

"Just Right" Books

Struggling readers need books they can read.

Researchers emphasize that struggling readers need to do more reading, but too often, they pick up the same books their classmates are reading, and these books are too difficult (Allington, 2006). What students need are "just right" books that they can read fluently and comprehend. When students read engaging books at their independent reading level, they'll be successful, and it's more likely that they'll continue to read.

Middle graders need to know how to choose "just right" books for independent reading. The "three-finger rule" is a quick way for students to determine whether a book is a good match for them: Students turn to any page in a book and as they read it, they raise a finger whenever they encounter an unfamiliar word. If they know every word, the book's too easy, but if there's one or two new words on a page, the book is probably an appropriate choice. If there are three or more difficult words on a page, the book's too difficult for independent reading.

Young adolescents particularly enjoy reading series books, such as Lemony Snicket and Harry Potter, but these books are written at sixth- through ninth-grade reading levels, well beyond the reach of struggling readers. Luckily, many popular series available today are written at second- through fifth-grade reading levels, including A–Z Mysteries, Hank the Cowdog, Time Warp Trio, and Secrets of Droon. These books are "just right" for struggling readers. It's essential that teachers have books in these popular series in their classroom libraries so struggling readers have engaging "just right" books to read.

guided reading or another scaffolded lesson. They shouldn't be expected to read books at their frustration level; when it's essential that struggling students experience grade-appropriate literature or learn content-area information, teachers should read the text aloud to them.

Check the Compendium of Instructional Procedures, which follows Chapter 12, for more information on the highlighted terms.

Readability Formulas. For nearly a century, readability formulas have been used to estimate the ease with which reading materials, both trade books and textbooks, can be read. Readability scores serve as rough gauges of text difficulty and are traditionally reported as grade-level scores. If a book has a readability score of fifth grade, for example, teachers assume that average fifth graders will be able to read it. Sometimes readability scores are marked on books, with RL for *reading level* and a grade level, such as *RL 5*.

Readability scores are determined by correlating semantic and syntactic features in a text. Several passages from a text are identified for analysis, and then vocabulary sophistication is measured by counting the number of syllables in each word, and sentence complexity by the number of words in each sentence. The syllable and word counts from each passage are averaged, and the readability score is calculated by plotting the averages on a graph. It seems reasonable to expect that texts with shorter words and sentences would be easier to read than others with longer words and sentences. Readability formulas, however, take into account only two text factors; they can't account for reader factors, including the experience and knowledge that readers bring to reading, their cognitive and linguistic backgrounds, or their motivation for reading.

One fairly quick and simple readability formula is the Fry Readability Graph, developed by Edward Fry (1968); it's presented in the Assessment Tools feature on page 64. This graph is used to predict the grade-level score for texts, ranging from first grade through college level. Teachers use a readability formula as an aid in evaluating textbook and trade-book selections for classroom use; however, they can't assume that materials rated as appropriate for a particular level will be appropriate for all students because students' achievement within a class typically varies three grade levels or more.

Just looking at a book isn't enough to determine its readability, because books that seem quite different sometimes score at the same level. For example, these five books are rated at the sixth-grade level:

Every Living Thing (Rylant, 1988), a collection of short stories about people whose lives are altered by their interactions with animals

The Cay (Taylor, 2003), an award-winning novel about prejudice, love, and survival

Nightmares: Poems to Trouble Your Sleep (Prelutsky, 1993), a collection of spooky poems by a prolific poet

Rosie the Riveter: Women Working on the Home Front During World War II (Colman, 1998), a nonfiction book about the millions of women who served in the wartime labor force

Under the Royal Palms: A Childhood in Cuba (Ada, 1998), an autobiography by author Alma Flor Ada

You may be surprised that these books are all rated at the sixth-grade level because their topics, genres, and page lengths differ significantly.

Assessment Tools

The Fry Readability Graph

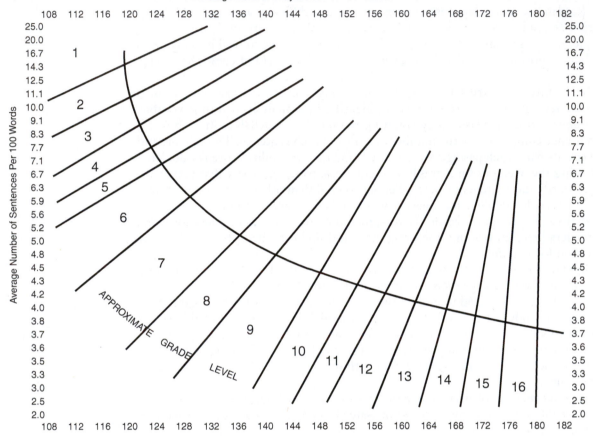

Average Number of Syllables Per 100 Words

DIRECTIONS:
1. Select three 100-word passages from the book or other reading material.
2. Count the number of syllables in each 100-word passage and average them.
3. Count the number of sentences in each 100-word passage and average them.
4. Plot the averages on the graph to determine the difficulty level. If the score falls outside the lined area, it isn't valid.

From "A Readability Formula That Saves Time," by E. Fry, 1968, p. 587.

Leveled Books. Basal readers have traditionally been leveled according to grade levels, but grade-level designations, especially in kindergarten and first grade, are too broad. Fountas and Pinnell (2006b) developed a text gradient, or classification system that arranges books along a continuum from easiest to hardest, to match students to books in grades K–8. Their system is based on these 10 variables that influence reading difficulty:

- Genre and format of the book
- Organization and use of text structures
- Familiarity with and interest in the topic
- Complexity of ideas and themes
- Language and literary features
- Sentence length and complexity
- Sophistication of the vocabulary
- Word length and ease of decoding
- Relationship of illustrations to the text
- Length of the book, its layout, and other print features

Fountas and Pinnell used these criteria to identify 26 levels, labeled A through Z, for their text gradient, which teachers can use to level books in their classrooms. More than 18,000 books have been leveled according to this text gradient. A sample trade book for each level is shown in Figure 3–1; other leveled books are listed in *The Fountas and Pinnell Leveled Book List, K–8* (Fountas & Pinnell, 2006a) and online at www.fountasandpinnellleveledbooks.com.

FIGURE 3–1 ◆ *Books Leveled Using Fountas and Pinnell's Text Gradient*

Level	Grade	Book
A	K	Burningham, J. (1985). *Colors*. New York: Crown.
B	K–1	Carle, E. (1997). *Have you seen my cat?* New York: Aladdin Books.
C	K–1	Martin, B., Jr. (2008). *Brown bear, brown bear, what do you see?* New York: Henry Holt.
D	1	Peek, M. (2006). *Mary wore her red dress*. New York: Clarion Books.
E	1	Hill, E. (2005). *Where's Spot?* New York: Putnam.
F	1	Hutchins, P. (2005). *Rosie's walk*. New York: Aladdin Books.
G	1	Shaw, N. (2006). *Sheep in a jeep*. Boston: Houghton Mifflin.
H	1–2	Kraus, R. (2005). *Whose mouse are you?* New York: Aladdin Books.
I	1–2	Wood, A. (2005). *The napping house*. San Diego: Harcourt.
J	2	Rylant, C. (1996). *Henry and Mudge and the bedtime thumps*. New York: Simon & Schuster.
K	2	Heller, R. (1999). *Chickens aren't the only ones*. New York: Putnam.
L	2–3	Marshall, J. (2000). *The three little pigs*. New York: Grosset & Dunlap.
M	2–3	Park, B. (2007). *Junie B. Jones and the stupid smelly bus*. New York: Random House.
N	3	Danziger, P. (2006). *Amber Brown is not a crayon*. New York: Puffin Books.
O	3–4	Cleary, B. (1992). *Ramona Quimby, age 8*. New York: HarperTrophy.
P	3–4	Mathis, S. B. (2006). *The hundred penny box*. New York: Puffin Books.
Q	4	Howe, D., & Howe, J. (2006). *Bunnicula: A rabbit-tale of mystery*. New York: Aladdin Books.
R	4	Paulsen, G. (2007). *Hatchet*. New York: Simon & Schuster.
S	4–5	Norton, M. (2003). *The borrowers*. San Diego: Odyssey Classics.
T	4–5	Curtis, C. P. (2004). *Bud, not Buddy*. New York: Laurel Leaf.
U	5	Lowry, L. (1998). *Number the stars*. New York: Yearling.
V	5–6	Sachar, L. (2008). *Holes*. New York: Farrar, Straus & Giroux.
W	5–6	Choi, S. N. (1993). *Year of impossible goodbyes*. New York: Yearling.
X	6–8	Hesse, K. (1999). *Out of the dust*. New York: Scholastic.
Y	6–8	Lowry, L. (2006). *The giver*. New York: Delacorte.
Z	7–8	Hinton, S. E. (2006). *The outsiders*. New York: Puffin Books.

Fountas & Pinnell, 2006a.

FIGURE 3–2 ◆ Books Ranked According to the Lexile Framework

Level	Grade	Book
100–149	K	Willems, M. (2003). *Don't let the pigeon drive the bus!* New York: Hyperion Books.
150–199	K–1	Marshall, E. (1999). *Fox all week*. New York: Puffin Books.
200–249	1	Bridwell, N. (2002). *Clifford the big red dog*. New York: Scholastic.
250–299	1	Kellogg, S. (2002). *Pinkerton, behave!* New York: Dial Books.
300–349	1–2	Allard, H. (1985). *Miss Nelson is missing!* Boston: Houghton Mifflin.
350–399	2	Bourgeois, P. (1997). *Franklin's bad day*. New York: Scholastic.
400–449	2	Coerr, E. (1989). *The Josefina story quilt*. New York: HarperTrophy.
450–499	2–3	Bunting, E. (1998). *Going home*. New York: HarperTrophy.
500–549	3	Rathmann, P. (1995). *Officer Buckle and Gloria*. New York: Putnam.
550–599	3–4	Sobol, D. (2008). *Encyclopedia Brown saves the day*. New York: Puffin Books.
600–649	3–4	Cole, J. (1994). *The magic school bus on the ocean floor*. New York: Scholastic.
650–699	4	Lowry, L. (1998). *Number the stars*. New York: Yearling.
700–749	4	Howe, D., & Howe, J. (2006). *Bunnicula: A rabbit-tale of mystery*. New York: Aladdin Books.
750–799	4–5	Creech, S. (2005). *Walk two moons*. New York: HarperTrophy.
800–849	5	Dahl, R. (2007). *Charlie and the chocolate factory*. New York: Puffin Books.
850–899	5–6	Naylor, P. (2000). *Shiloh*. New York: Aladdin Books.
900–949	6–7	Lewis, C. S. (2005). *The lion, the witch and the wardrobe*. New York: HarperCollins.
950–999	7	O'Dell, S. (2006). *The black pearl*. Boston: Houghton Mifflin.
1000–1049	8	Philbrick, R. (2001). *Freak the mighty*. New York: Scholastic.
1050–1099	9–10	Tolkien, J. R. R. (2007). *The hobbit*. Boston: Houghton Mifflin.
1100–1149	10–11	Freedman, R. (2006). *Freedom walkers: The story of the Montgomery bus boycott*. New York: Holiday House.
1150–1199	11–12	Brooks, B. (1995). *The moves make the man*. New York: HarperTrophy.
1200–1300	12	Alcott, L. M. (2004). *Little women*. New York: Signet Classics.

The Lexile Framework. The newest approach to matching books to readers is the Lexile Framework, developed by MetaMetrics. This approach is different because it's used to measure both students' reading levels and the difficulty level of books. Word familiarity and sentence complexity are the two factors used to determine the difficulty level of books. Lexile scores range from 100 to 1300, representing kindergarten through 12th-grade reading levels. Figure 3–2 presents a list of books ranked according to the Lexile Framework.

Students' results on high-stakes tests are often linked to the Lexile Framework. Standardized achievement tests, including the Iowa Test of Basic Skills and the Stanford Achievement Test, report test results as Lexile scores, as do a number of standards-based state reading tests, such as the California English-Language Arts Standards Test, the North Carolina End-of-Grade Tests, and the Texas Assessment of Knowledge and Skills. With this information, students, parents, and teachers can match students to books by searching the online Lexile database to locate books at each student's reading level.

The Lexile Framework is a promising program, because the wide range of scores allows teachers to more closely match students and books. The availability of the online database listing more than 44,000 leveled book titles that students, parents, and teachers can access makes it a very useful assessment tool; however, matching students to books is more complicated than determining a numerical score!

The Assessment Tools feature below describes three tests that teachers use to determine students' reading levels. These screening instruments use leveled texts that students read.

Assessment Tools

Determining Students' Reading Levels

Teachers use these screening instruments to determine students' instructional reading levels, monitor their progress, and document their achievement through a school year and across grade levels:

◆ **Developmental Reading Assessment (2nd ed.) (DRA2)** (Beaver & Carter, 2005)

The DRA2 kit for grades 4–8 assesses students' reading performance using leveled fiction and nonfiction books. The leveled books range from second- to eighth-grade reading levels. Teachers use an online system to manage students' scores and group students for instruction. A handheld version of the DRA2 is also available.

◆ **Fountas and Pinnell Benchmark Assessment System** (Fountas & Pinnell, 2007)

The Fountas and Pinnell Benchmark Assessment System kit for grades 3–8 contains 30 leveled fiction and nonfiction books written specifically for the kit and CDs with assessment forms to manage students' scores. Teachers use the books in the kit to match students' reading levels to the Fountas and Pinnell 26-level text gradient.

For both of these assessments, teachers test students individually. The teacher selects an appropriate book for the student to read and introduces it; the student reads the book while the teacher takes a running record. Then the student retells the text and answers comprehension questions. The teacher scores and analyzes the results, and testing continues until the teacher determines the student's instructional level.

◆ **Scholastic Reading Inventory (SRI)**

The SRI is a unique computer-adaptive assessment program that reports students' reading levels using Lexile scores. Students take a 20-minute computerized test individually. The student reads a narrative or informational passage on the computer screen and answers multiple-choice comprehension questions. This test is computer-adaptive because if the student answers a question correctly, the next one will be more difficult, and if the answer is wrong, the next one will be easier. Students read passages and answer questions until their reading level is determined. Afterward, students receive a customized take-home letter with their Lexile score and a personalized list of recommended books.

These assessments are usually administered at the beginning of the school year and periodically during the year to monitor students' progress. The results are also used to group students for guided reading and to identify students who need diagnostic testing.

Monitoring Progress

Monitoring is vital to student success (Braunger & Lewis, 2006). Teachers supervise students' learning every day and use the results to make instructional decisions (Winograd & Arrington, 1999). As they monitor students' progress, teachers learn about their students, about themselves as teachers, and about the impact of their instructional program. Teachers use a variety of informal, formative procedures to monitor students' progress.

Observations.   Effective teachers are *kid watchers*, a term Yetta Goodman (1978) coined to describe the "direct and informal observation of students" (p. 37). The focus is on what students do as they read or write, not on whether they're behaving properly or working quietly. Of course, little learning can occur in disruptive situations, but during these observations, the focus is on literacy, not behavior. Observations should be planned. Teachers usually observe specific students each day so that over the course of a week, they watch everyone in the class.

Anecdotal Notes.   Teachers write brief notes in notebooks or on self-stick notes as they observe students (Boyd-Batstone, 2004). The most useful notes describe specific events, report rather than evaluate, and relate the events to other information about the student. Teachers make notes about students' reading and writing activities, the questions students ask, and the strategies and skills they use fluently and those they don't understand. These records monitor and document students' growth and pinpoint problem areas to address in future minilessons or conferences. A teacher's anecdotal notes about sixth-grade students participating in a literature circle on *Bunnicula: A Rabbit-Tale of Mystery* (Howe & Howe, 2006) appear in Figure 3–3.

Conferences.   Teachers talk with students to monitor their progress in reading and writing activities as well as to set goals and help them solve problems. Here are six types of conferences that teachers have with students:

On-the-Spot Conferences.   The teacher visits with students at their desks to monitor some aspect of the students' work or to check on progress. These conferences are brief, with the teacher often spending less than a minute with each student.

Planning Conferences.   The teacher and the student make plans for reading or writing at the conference. At a prereading conference, they may talk about information or difficult concepts related to the book, or about the **reading log** the student will keep. At a prewriting conference, they may discuss possible writing topics or how to narrow a broad topic.

Revising Conferences.   A small group of students meets with the teacher to share rough drafts and get specific suggestions about how to revise them.

Book Discussion Conferences.   Students meet with the teacher to discuss the book they've read. They may share reading log entries, discuss plot or characters, or compare the story to others they've read.

Editing Conferences.   The teacher reviews students' proofread compositions and helps them correct spelling, punctuation, capitalization, and other mechanical errors.

FIGURE 3–3 ◆ *Anecdotal Notes About a Literature Circle*

March 7

Met with the *Bunnicula* literature circle as they started reading the book. They have their reading, writing, and discussion schedule set. Sari questioned how a dog could write the book. We reread the Editor's Note. She asked if Harold really wrote the book. She's the only one confused in the group. Is she always so literal? Mario pointed out that you have to know that Harold supposedly wrote the book to understand the first-person viewpoint of the book. Talked to Sari about fantasy. Told her she'll be laughing out loud as she reads this book. She doubts it.

March 8

Returned to *Bunnicula* literature circle for first grand conversation, especially to check on Sari. Annie, Mario, Ted, Rod, Laurie, and Belinda talked about their pets and imagined them taking over their homes. Sari is not getting into the book. She doesn't have any pets and can't imagine the pets doing these things. I asked if she wanted to change groups. Perhaps a realistic book would be better. She says no. Is that because Ted is in the group?

March 10

The group is reading chapters 4 and 5 today. Laurie asks questions about white vegetables and vampires. Rod goes to get an encyclopedia to find out about vampires. Mario asks about DDT. Everyone—even Sari—involved in reading.

March 13

During a grand conversation, students compare the characters Harold and Chester. The group plans to make a Venn diagram comparing the characters for the sharing on Friday. Students decide that character is the most important element, but Ted argues that humor is the most important element in the story. Other students say humor isn't an element. I asked what humor is a reaction to—characters or plot? I checked journals and all are up to date.

March 15

The group has finished reading the book. I share sequels from the class library. Sari grabs one to read. She's glad she stayed with the book. Ted wants to write his own sequel in writing workshop. Mario plans to write a letter to James Howe.

March 17

Ted and Sari talk about *Bunnicula* and share related books. Rod and Mario share the Venn diagram of characters. Annie reads her favorite part, and Laurie shows her collection of rabbits. Belinda hangs back. I wonder if she has been involved. I need to talk to her.

Evaluation Conferences. The teacher meets with students after they've completed an assignment or project to talk about their growth as readers and writers. Students reflect on their accomplishments and set goals.

Often these conferences are brief and impromptu, held at students' desks as the teacher moves around the classroom; at other times, however, the conferences are planned, and students meet with the teacher at a designated conference table.

Checklists. Checklists simplify assessment and enhance students' learning (Kuhs, Johnson, Agruso, & Monrad, 2001). Teachers identify the evaluation criteria in advance so students understand what's expected of them before they begin working. Grading is easier because teachers have already set the evaluation criteria, and it's fairer,

Assessment Tools

Book Talk Checklist

Name _Jaime_   Date _November 12_

Title _Cockroach Cooties_

Author _Laurence Yep_

___✓___ Hold up the book to show to classmates.

___✓___ State the title and author's name.

___✓___ Interest classmates in the book by asking a question, reading an excerpt, or sharing some information.

_____ Summarize the book, without giving away the ending.

___✓___ Talk loud enough for everyone to hear you.

___✓___ Look at the audience.

_____ Limit the book talk to 3 minutes.

too, because teachers use the same criteria to grade all students' work. The Assessment Tools feature above shows a fourth-grade checklist for giving book talks. At the beginning of the school year, the teacher introduced book talks, modeled how to do one, and developed the checklist with the students. Students use the checklist whenever they're preparing to give a book talk, and the teacher uses it to evaluate the effectiveness of their book talks.

Rubrics. Scoring guides called rubrics evaluate student performance in reading and writing according to specific criteria and levels of achievement (Afflerbach, 2007b). They're similar to checklists because they specify what students are expected to be able to do, but they go beyond checklists because they describe levels of achievement. A 4-level rubric for assessing sixth graders' independent reading during reading workshop is shown in the Assessment Tools feature on the next page. Students complete the rubric at the end of each quarter. The quality levels, ranging from Outstanding (highest) to Beginning (lowest), are shown in the column on the far left, and the achievement categories are listed across the top: number of books read during the quarter, reading level of the books, genres represented by the books, and students' interpretations. The Interpretation category assesses students' comprehension.

Students' Work Samples. Teachers have students collect their work in folders to document their learning. Work samples might include reading logs, audiotapes of students' reading, photos of projects, videotapes of puppet shows and oral presentations, and books students have written. Students often choose some of these work samples to place in their portfolios.

Diagnosing Strengths and Weaknesses

Teachers use diagnostic reading assessments to identify students' strengths and weaknesses, examine any area of difficulty in more detail, and decide how to modify instruction to meet students' needs. They use a variety of diagnostic tests to examine students' achievement in word identification, vocabulary, comprehension, and other components of reading and writing. The Assessment Tools feature on page 72 lists the diagnostic tests recommended in this text and directs you to the chapter where you can learn more about them.

Two of the assessments that teachers commonly use are running records and informal reading inventories. They're used to determine students' reading levels as well as to diagnose difficulties in word identification, vocabulary, and comprehension and to monitor students' growth as readers.

Running Records. Teachers take **running records** to assess students' oral reading. The teacher listens as a student reads aloud and makes a series of checkmarks on a sheet of paper for words that the student reads correctly and other marks to indicate words that the student substitutes, repeats, mispronounces, or doesn't know. Although running records can be taken on a blank sheet of paper, it's much easier to make a copy of the page or pages the student will read and take the running record next to or above the actual text. Using a copy of the text is especially important when assessing older students who read more-complex texts and who read more quickly than beginning readers do.

Shea (2006) developed a modified procedure for using running records with young adolescents who are struggling readers. Instead of having students read a complete text as younger children do, Shea recommends using a 1-minute probe: The student reads aloud for 1 minute from a text that's being used in class, and the teacher marks a copy of the text as the student reads. Afterward, the student retells what he or she has just read, and the teacher prompts the student about any ideas that aren't mentioned. Shea also suggests making an audio- or videotape of the student's reading and reviewing it to gain additional insights.

Assessment Tools

Independent Reading Rubric

Level	Books Read	Difficulty Level	Genres	Interpretation
Outstanding	Finishes 5 or more books.	Reads "just right" books and tries "too hard" books sometimes.	Reads books from 3 or more genres.	Makes insightful interpretation with evidence from the book, author's style, and genre.
Proficient	Finishes 3 or 4 books.	Reads mostly "just right" books.	Reads books from 2 genres.	Shares accurate interpretation using a summary, inferences, and story structure.
Developing	Finishes 2 books.	Reads mostly "too easy" books.	Tries a different genre once in a while.	Provides literal interpretation by summarizing events and making personal connections.
Beginning	Finishes 1 book.	Always reads "too easy" books.	Sticks with 1 genre.	Offers an incomplete or inaccurate response.

Assessment Tools

Diagnostic Reading and Writing Assessments

Component	Tests	Where to Learn More
Fluency	High-frequency word lists The Names Test Developmental Reading Assessment Fluency checks Informal reading inventories Running records 3-Minute Reading Assessments	Chapter 5, Overcoming Obstacles to Fluency, p. 121
Comprehension	Comprehension Thinking Strategies Assessment Developmental Reading Assessment Informal reading inventories Running records	Chapter 7, Promoting Comprehension: Reader Factors, p. 194
Motivation	Elementary Reading Attitude Survey Motivation to Read Profile Reader Self-Perception Scale Writing Attitude Survey Writer Self-Perception Scale	Chapter 7, Promoting Comprehension: Reader Factors, p. 198
Writing	Rubrics	Chapter 9, Teaching Writing, p. 246
Spelling	Developmental Spelling Analysis Qualitative Spelling Inventory Writing samples	Chapter 9, Teaching Writing, p. 257

Informal Reading Inventories. Teachers use commercial tests called *informal reading inventories* (IRIs) to evaluate students' reading performance. These popular reading tests are often used as a screening instrument to determine whether students are reading at grade level, but they're also a valuable diagnostic tool (Nilsson, 2008). Teachers use IRIs to identify struggling students' instructional needs, particularly in the areas of word identification, oral reading fluency, and comprehension, as Mrs. Jackson did in the vignette at the beginning of the chapter.

These individualized tests consist of two parts: graded word lists and passages ranging from first- to at least eighth-grade levels. The word lists contain 10 to 20 words at each level, and students read the words until they become too difficult; this indicates an approximate level for students to begin reading the passages. Because students who can't read the words on their grade-level list may have a word-identification problem, teachers analyze the words students read incorrectly, looking for error patterns.

The graded reading passages include both narrative and expository texts, presented in order of difficulty. Students read these passages orally or silently and then answer a series of comprehension questions; some questions ask students to recall specific information, some ask them to draw inferences, and others ask for the meaning of vocabulary words. When students read the passage orally, teachers assess their fluency. Teachers also examine students' comprehension. If students can't answer the questions after reading a passage, they may have a vocabulary or comprehension problem, and teachers check to see if there's a pattern to the types of questions that students miss.

Teachers record students' performance data on scoring sheets, and calculate students' independent, instructional, and frustration reading levels. When students' reading level is below their grade-level placement, teachers also check their listening capacity; that is, their ability to understand passages that are read aloud. Knowing whether students can understand and learn from grade-level texts that are read aloud is crucial because it's a common way that teachers support struggling readers.

Scaffolding English Learners

Teachers assess English learners' developing language proficiency as well as their progress in learning to read and write. It's more challenging to assess ELs than native English speakers, because when students aren't proficient in English, their scores don't accurately reflect what they know (Peregoy & Boyle, 2008). Their cultural and experiential backgrounds also contribute to making it more difficult to assure that assessment tools being used aren't biased.

Oral Language Assessment. Teachers assess students who speak a language other than English at home to determine their English language proficiency. They typically use commercial oral language tests to determine if students are proficient in English. If they're not, teachers place them in appropriate English language development programs and monitor their progress toward English language proficiency. Two widely used tests are the Language Assessment Scales, published by CTB/Mc-Graw-Hill, and the IDEA Language Proficiency Test, published by Ballard and Tighe; both tests assess students' oral and written language (listening, speaking, reading, and writing) proficiency in English. Individual states have developed language assessments that are aligned with their English language proficiency standards; for example, the New York State English as a Second Language Achievement Test and the California English Language Development Test.

An authentic assessment tool that many teachers use is the Student Oral Language Observation Matrix (SOLOM), developed by the San Jose (CA) Area Bilingual Consortium. It's not a test per se; rather, the SOLOM is a rating scale that teachers use to assess students' command of English as they observe them talking and listening in real, day-to-day classroom activities. The SOLOM addresses five components of oral language:

Listening. Teachers score students along a continuum from unable to comprehend simple statements to understanding everyday conversations.

Fluency. Teachers score students along a continuum from halting, fragmentary speech to fluent speech, approximating that of native speakers.

Vocabulary. Teachers score students along a continuum from extremely limited word knowledge to using words and idioms skillfully.

Pronunciation. Teachers score students along a continuum from virtually unintelligible speech to using pronunciation and intonation proficiently, similar to native speakers.

Grammar. Teachers score students along a continuum from excessive errors that make speech unintelligible to applying word order, grammar, and usage rules effectively.

Each component has a five-point range that's scored 1 to 5; the total score on the matrix is 25, and a score of 20 or higher indicates that students are fluent speakers of English. The SOLOM is available free of charge online at www.cal.org, at other websites, and in many professional books.

Reading Assessment. English learners face two challenges: learning to speak English at the same time they're learning to read. They learn to read the same way that native English speakers do, but they face additional hurdles because their knowledge of English is limited and their background knowledge is different (Peregoy & Boyle, 2008). Some English learners are fluent readers in their home language (Garcia, 2000); these students already have substantial funds of knowledge about how written language works and about the reading process that they build on as they learn to read in English (Moll, 1994). Having this knowledge gives them a head start, but students also have to learn what transfers to English reading and what doesn't.

Teachers use the same assessments that they use for native English speakers to identify English learners' reading levels, monitor their growth, and document their learning. Peregoy and Boyle (2008) recommend using data from running records or informal reading inventories along with classroom-based informal assessments, such as observing and conferencing with students.

Because many English learners have less background knowledge about topics in books they're reading, it's important that teachers assess ELs' background knowledge before instruction so they can modify their teaching to meet students' needs. One of the best ways to accomplish this is with a **K-W-L chart**. As they work with students to complete the first two sections of the chart, teachers learn what students know about a topic and have an opportunity to build additional background knowledge and introduce related vocabulary. Later, when students complete the K-W-L chart, teachers get a clear picture of what they've learned and which vocabulary words they can use.

Another way teachers learn about ELs' development is by asking them to assess themselves as readers (Peregoy & Boyle, 2008). Teachers ask students, for example, what they do when they come to an unfamiliar word, what differences they've noticed between narrative and expository texts, which reading strategies they use, and what types of books they prefer. These quick assessments, commonly done during conferences at the end of a grading period, shed light on students' growth in a way that other assessments can't.

Writing Assessment. English learners' writing develops as their oral language grows and as they become more-fluent readers (Riches & Genesee, 2006). For beginning writers, fluency is the first priority: They move from writing strings of familiar words to grouping words into short sentences that often follow a pattern, much like young native English speakers do. As they develop some writing fluency, ELs begin to stick to a single focus, often repeating words and sentences to make their writing longer. Once they become fluent writers, ELs are usually able to organize their ideas more effectively and group them into paragraphs. They incorporate more-specific vocabulary and expand the length and variety of sentences. Their mechanical errors become less serious, and their writing is much easier to read. At this point, teachers begin teaching the qualities of good writing and choosing writing strategies and skills to teach based on the errors that students make.

Peregoy and Boyle (2008) explain that ELs' writing involves fluency, form, and correctness, and that teachers' assessment of students' writing should reflect these components:

Fluency. Teachers monitor students' ability to write quickly, easily, and comfortably.

Form. Teachers assess students' ability to apply writing genres, develop their topic, organize the presentation of ideas, and use sophisticated vocabulary and a variety of sentence structures.

Correctness. Teachers check that students control Standard English grammar and usage, spell most words correctly, and use capitalization and punctuation conventions appropriately.

Teachers use **rubrics** to assess ELs' writing, and the rubrics address fluency, form, and correctness as well as the qualities of good writing that teachers have taught. They also conference with students about their writing and provide quick **minilessons**, as needed. To learn about students as writers, teachers observe them as they write, noticing how they move through the writing process, interact in **writing groups**, and share their writing from the author's chair. In addition, students document writing development by placing their best writing in portfolios.

Alternative Assessments. Because of the difficulties inherent in assessing English learners, it's important to use varied types of assessment that involve different language and literacy tasks and ways of demonstrating proficiency (Huerta-Macías, 1995). In addition to commercial tests, O'Malley and Pierce (1996) urge teachers to use authentic assessment tools, including oral performances, story retellings, oral interviews with students, writing samples, illustrations, diagrams, posters, and projects.

Assessment is especially important for students who are learning to speak English at the same time they're learning to read and write in English. Teachers use many of the same assessment tools that they use for their native English speakers but they also depend on alternative, more-authentic assessments because it's difficult to accurately measure these students' growth. Assessment results must be valid because teachers use them to make placement decisions, modify instruction, and document learning.

Documenting Learning

Teachers routinely collect students' work samples, including cassette tapes of them reading aloud, lists of books they've read, reading logs, writing samples with rubrics, and photos of projects. They also keep students' test results and the anecdotal notes they make as they observe students and meet with them in conferences. Teachers use these data to document students' progress toward meeting grade-level standards as well as to evaluate the effectiveness of their teaching. Students also collect their best work in portfolios to document their own learning and accomplishments.

Portfolio Assessment

Portfolios are systematic and meaningful collections of artifacts documenting students' literacy development over a period of time (Hebert, 2001). These collections are dynamic, and they reflect students' day-to-day reading and writing activities as well as content-area activities. Students' work samples provide "windows" on the strategies they use as readers and writers. Not only do students select pieces to be placed in their portfolios, they also learn to establish criteria for their selections. Because of students' involvement in selecting pieces for their portfolios and reflecting on them, portfolio assessment respects students and their abilities. Portfolios help students, teachers, and parents see patterns of growth from one literacy milestone to another in ways that aren't possible with other types of assessment.

New Literacies

E-Portfolios

Instead of collecting writing samples, photos of projects, videotapes of oral presentations, and other artifacts in bulky folders that take up lots of space, students can create electronic portfolios, or webfolios, to showcase their best work and document their learning. They scan their writing samples, photograph their artifacts with a digital camera, and have classmates videotape their oral presentations to add them to their e-portfolios. In addition, copies of collaborative projects can be saved in each student's portfolio. Students add text boxes and video clips to provide context for their samples, reflect on their learning, and explain how their work demonstrates that they've met grade-level standards. They also insert hyperlinks to connect sections and enhance their e-portfolios with music and graphics.

Teachers create a template that lays out the design, including a title, table of contents, and collections of artifacts, and students use the template to organize their portfolios. Sometimes rubrics are included to show how the artifacts were assessed. Collections from each grade are saved in separate files within students' portfolios. When they're creating the template, teachers often browse electronic portfolios that have been posted on the Web for ideas about how to organize their students' collections of work samples.

E-portfolios are versatile assessment tools: They accept a variety of multimodal items, incorporate a hierarchical organization, and make searching for and retrieving items easy to do. They're practical, too, especially if teachers and students know how to use computer software and if they're willing to devote the time needed to start up the portfolio system. E-portfolios are quick and easy for students to access because they're stored on CDs or zip drives or at the school's website.

The KEEP Toolkit, developed by the Carnegie Foundation for the Advancement of Teaching, is an exciting online tool for creating portfolios. Its purpose is to provide an economical way for teachers and students to design engaging Web-based representations of teaching and learning. The toolkit is used to enter information, upload files, create snapshots, and design single webpages or a linked series of webpages. A collection of young adolescents' e-portfolios is displayed in the Gallery of Teaching and Learning section of the Carnegie Foundation's website (www.cfkeep.org).

The 21st century has a knowledge-based economy, and middle graders who document their learning in e-portfolios are more likely to continue to use digital tools to showcase their knowledge and accomplishments as adults.

Collecting Work in Portfolios

Portfolios are folders, large envelopes, or boxes that hold students' work. Teachers often have students label and decorate large folders and then store them in plastic crates or cardboard boxes. Students date and label items as they place them in their portfolios, and they often attach notes to the items to explain the context for the activity and why they selected a particular item. Students' portfolios should be stored in the classroom in a place where they are readily accessible; students like to review their portfolios periodically and add new pieces to them.

Students usually choose the items to place in their portfolios within the guidelines the teacher provides. Some students submit the original piece of work; others want to keep the original, so they place a copy in the portfolio instead. In addition to the reading and writing samples that go directly into portfolios, students can record oral language and drama samples on audiotapes, videotapes, and CDs, and digital products on flash drives to place in their portfolios. Large-size art and writing projects can be photographed, and the photographs can be placed in the portfolio. Student products might include books, **choral readings** on audiotapes, **reading logs** and **learning logs**, graphic organizers, multigenre projects, lists of books read, and compositions. This variety of work samples reflects the students' literacy programs. Samples from literature focus units, literature circles, reading and writing workshop, textbook programs, and content-area units can be included.

Many teachers collect students' work in folders, and they assume that portfolios are basically the same as work folders; however, the two types of collections differ in several important ways. Perhaps the most important difference is that portfolios are student oriented and work folders are usually teachers' collections—students choose which samples will be placed in portfolios, but teachers often place all completed assignments in work folders. Next, portfolios focus on students' strengths, not their weaknesses. Because students decide what goes into portfolios, they choose samples that best represent their achievements. Another difference is that portfolios involve reflection (D'Aoust, 1992); through reflection, students pause and become aware of their strengths as readers and writers. They also use their work samples to identify the literacy procedures, strategies, and skills they already know and the ones they need to focus on.

Involving Students in Self-Assessment

Portfolios are a useful tool for engaging students in self-assessment and goal setting. Students learn to reflect on and assess their own reading and writing activities and their development as readers and writers (Stires, 1991). Teachers begin by asking students to think about their reading and writing in terms of contrasts. For reading, students identify the books they've read that they liked most and least, and they ask themselves what these choices suggest about themselves as readers. They also identify what they do well in reading and what they need to improve. In writing, students make similar contrasts: They identify their best compositions and others that weren't as good, and they think about what they do well when they write and what to improve. By making these comparisons, students begin to reflect on their literacy development.

Teachers use **minilessons** and conferences to teach about the characteristics of good readers and writers. In particular, they discuss these topics:

What fluent reading is

Which reading strategies and skills students use

How students demonstrate their comprehension

How students value books they've read

What makes a good project to apply reading knowledge

What makes an effective piece of writing

Which writing strategies are most effective

How to use writing rubrics

How proofreading and correcting mechanical errors are a courtesy to readers

As students learn about what it means to be effective readers and writers, they acquire the tools they need to reflect on and evaluate their own reading and writing. They learn how to think about themselves as readers and writers and acquire the vocabulary to use in their reflections, such as *goal*, *strategy*, and *rubric*.

Students write notes on items they choose to put into their portfolios. In these self-assessments, students explain the reasons for their choices and identify strengths and accomplishments in their work. In some classrooms, students write their reflections and other comments on index cards, and in other classrooms, they design special comment sheets that they attach to the items in their portfolios.

Teachers usually collect baseline reading and writing samples at the beginning of the school year and then conduct portfolio review conferences with students at the end of each grading period. At these conferences, the teacher and the student talk about the items being placed in the portfolio and the student's self-assessments. Students also talk about what they want to improve or accomplish during the next grading period, and these points become their goals.

Conferences
This fourth grader meets with his teacher for 15 to 20 minutes to talk about his achievement at the end of the second grading period. Even though it's time-consuming, this teacher meets with each student at the end of every grading period to talk about the student's progress, identify standards-based accomplishments, select pieces to add to the portfolio, determine grades, and set goals for the next quarter. Through this process, teachers involve students in assessment, and students become more responsible for their own learning as they self-assess their progress and set goals for themselves.

Showcasing Portfolios

At the end of the school year, many teachers organize "Portfolio Share Days" to celebrate students' accomplishments and to provide an opportunity for students to share their portfolios with classmates and the wider community (Porter & Cleland, 1995). Often family members, local businesspeople, school administrators, local politicians, college students, and others are invited to attend. Students and community members form small groups, and students share their portfolios, pointing out their accomplishments and strengths. This activity is especially useful in involving community members in the school and showing them the types of literacy activities in which students are involved as well as how students are becoming effective readers and writers.

These sharing days also help students accept responsibility for their own learning—especially those students who have not been as motivated as their classmates. When less motivated students listen to their classmates talk about their work and how they have grown as readers and writers, they often decide to work harder the next year.

Why Portfolios Are Worthwhile

Portfolios are used to document students' work, evaluate their progress, and showcase their achievements (Afflerbach, 2007b). Collections of work samples add context to students' learning, and students become more reflective about the quality of their reading and writing. There are other benefits, for both students and teachers:

- Students feel ownership of their work.
- Students become more responsible about their work.
- Students set goals and are motivated to work toward accomplishing them.
- Students make connections between learning and assessing.
- Students' self-esteem is enhanced.
- Portfolios eliminate the need to grade all student work.
- Portfolios are used in student and parent conferences.
- Portfolios complement the information provided on report cards.

In schools where portfolios are used schoolwide, students overwhelmingly report that by using portfolios, they're better able to show their parents what they're learning and also better able to set goals for themselves (Kuhs, Johnson, Agruso, & Monrad, 2001). Teachers also find that portfolios enable them to assess their students more thoroughly, and students are better able to see their own progress.

High-Stakes Testing

Annual high-stakes testing is emphasized in American schools with the goal of improving the quality of reading instruction. These tests are designed to objectively measure students' knowledge according to grade-level standards. The current emphasis on testing and on state-level standards are reform efforts that began in response to The National Commission on Education report *A Nation at Risk* (1983), which argued that American schools were failing miserably. The report stated that American students' test scores were dropping, comparing unfavorably with students' scores in other industrialized countries, and it concluded that the United States was in jeopardy of losing its global superiority. The No Child Left Behind Act, which promoted an increased focus on reading instruction to improve students' reading performance and narrow the racial and ethnic gaps in achievement, reinforced the call for annual standardized testing.

Researchers have repeatedly refuted these arguments (Bracey, 2004; McQuillan, 1998). Allington (2006) explained that average test scores have remained stable for 30 years despite the dramatic increases in federal funding over the past decade. He goes on to explain that reporting average scores obscures important findings, and it's necessary to examine subgroup data to discover that most students from middle-class families read well even though many students from low-income families lag behind. Allington also notes that despite a gap, significant progress has been made in closing the achievement gap between white and minority students at the same time the number of minority students has grown tremendously. Finally, he points out that grade-level standards of achievement have increased in the last 50 years, so that what was considered fifth-grade level is now fourth-grade level, and older readability formulas have been renormed to reflect today's higher grade-level standards. Nonetheless, the public's perception that schools are failing persists.

High-stakes testing is different than classroom assessment. The test scores typically provide little information for making day-to-day instructional decisions, but students, teachers, administrators, and schools are judged and held accountable by the results. The scores are used to make important educational decisions for students—to determine school placement and high school graduation, for example. These scores influence administrators' evaluations of teachers' effectiveness and even their salaries in some states, and they are used to reward or sanction administrators, schools, and school districts.

Standardized tests are comprehensive, with batteries of subtests covering vocabulary, comprehension, writing mechanics, and spelling. Figure 3–4 presents an overview of the most commonly used tests. Most tests have multiple-choice items, although a few are introducing open-ended questions that require students to write responses. Classroom teachers administer the tests to their students each year, typically in the spring.

Problems With High-Stakes Testing

A number of problems are associated with high-stakes testing (IRA, 1999). Students feel the pressure of these tests, and researchers have confirmed what many teachers have noticed: Students don't try harder because of them (Hoffman, Assaf, & Paris, 2005). Struggling students, in particular, get discouraged and feel defeated, and over time, test pressure destroys their motivation and actually harms their achievement. In addition, student dropout rates are rising.

Teachers complain that they feel compelled to improve students' test scores at any price, and they lose valuable instructional time for practice sessions and the administration of the test itself (Hollingworth, 2007). Overemphasizing the test often leads teachers to abandon a balanced approach to instruction: Sometimes students spend more time completing practice tests than reading books and writing compositions. One of the most insidious side effects is that teachers are often directed to focus on certain groups of students, especially those scoring just below a cutoff point, in hopes of improving test scores.

FIGURE 3–4 ◆ *Standardized Achievement Tests*				
Test	*Description*	*Components*	*Special Features*	*Publisher*
Iowa Test of Basic Skills (ITBS)	The ITBS provides information to improve instruction.	Vocabulary Comprehension Oral language Mechanics Spelling	The ITBS is the oldest statewide assessment program. It can be administered in the fall or spring.	Iowa schools are served by the Iowa Testing Program; outside Iowa, the test is available from Riverside.
Metropolitan Achievement Test (MAT)	The MAT measures students' learning using real-world content. Some items are multiple choice; others are performance based.	Vocabulary Comprehension Mechanics Writing Spelling	Test items are aligned with the IRA/NCTE Language Arts Standards. The MAT also provides Lexile scores.	The MAT can be ordered from Pearson.
Stanford Achievement Test (SAT)	The SAT measures students' learning according to state standards.	Vocabulary Comprehension Mechanics Writing Spelling	The SAT also estimates students' reading levels using Lexile scores.	The SAT is published by Pearson.
TerraNova Test (TNT)	This innovative test uses both multiple-choice and constructed-response items that allow students to write responses.	Vocabulary Comprehension Mechanics Spelling	Lexile scores are reported. Also, one version of the test is available online.	The TNT is published by CTB/McGraw-Hill.

Preparing for Standardized Tests

Standardized tests are a unique text genre, and they require readers and writers to do different things than they would normally, so teachers can't assume that students already know how to take tests. It's essential that teachers prepare students to take high-stakes tests without abandoning a balanced approach to instruction that's aligned to state standards (Calkins, Montgomery, & Santman, 1998). Greene and Melton (2007) agree; they maintain that teachers must prepare students for high-stakes tests without sacrificing their instructional program. Unfortunately, with the pressure to raise test scores, some teachers are having students take more multiple-choice tests while writing fewer essays and creating fewer projects.

Hollingworth (2007) recommends these five ways to prepare students for high-stakes tests without sacrificing the instructional program:

- Teachers check that their state's literacy standards align with their instructional program and make any needed adjustments to ensure that they're teaching what's going to be on the test.
- Teachers set goals with students and use informal assessments to regularly monitor their progress.

- Teachers actively engage students in authentic literacy activities so that they become capable readers and writers.
- Teachers explain the purpose of the tests and how the results will be used, without making students anxious.
- Teachers stick with a balanced approach that combines explicit instruction and authentic application.

Other researchers advise that in addition to these recommendations, teachers prepare students to take standardized tests by teaching them how to read and answer test items and having them take practice tests to hone their test-taking strategies (McCabe, 2003). Preparing for tests involves explaining their purpose, examining the genre and format of multiple-choice tests, teaching the formal language of tests and test-taking strategies, and providing opportunities for students to take practice tests; and these lessons should be folded into the existing instructional program, not replace it. Greene and Melton (2007) organized test preparation into **minilessons** that they taught as part of reading workshop.

The Genre of Standardized Tests. Students need opportunities to examine old test forms to learn about the genre of standardized tests and how test questions are formatted. They'll notice that tests look different than other texts they've read; they're typically printed in black and white, the text is dense, and few illustrations are included. Sometimes words, phrases, and lines in the text are numbered, bolded, or underlined. Through this exploration, students begin to think about what makes one type of text harder to read than others, and with practice, they get used to how tests are formatted so that they're better able to read them.

The Language of Testing. Standardized reading tests use formal language that's unfamiliar to many students. For example, some tests use the word *passage* instead of *text* and *author's intent* instead of *main idea*. Test makers also use *locate, except, theme, reveal, inform, reason, in order to, provide suspense*, and other words that students may not understand. Greene and Melton (2007) call the language of testing "test talk" and explain that "students are helpless on standardized reading tests if they can't decipher test talk" (p. 8). Students need help understanding test talk so that high-stakes tests really measure what they know.

Test-Taking Strategies. Students vary the test-taking strategies they use according to the type of test they're taking. Most standardized tests employ multiple-choice questions. Here's a list of test-taking strategies that students use to answer multiple-choice questions:

Read the Entire Question First. Students read the entire question before answering to make sure they understand what it's asking. For questions about a reading passage, students read the questions first to guide their reading.

Look for Key Words in the Question. Students identify key words in the question, such as *compare, except,* and *author's intent*, that will guide them to choose the correct answer.

Read All Answer Choices Before Choosing the Correct One. After students read the question, they stop and think about the answer before reading all possible answers. Then they eliminate the unlikely choices and identify the correct answer.

Answer Easier Questions First. Students answer the questions they know, skipping the difficult ones, and then they go back and answer the questions they skipped.

Make Smart Guesses. When students don't know the answer, they should make a smart guess, unless there's a penalty for guessing. To make a smart guess, students eliminate the answer choices they're sure are wrong, think about what they know about the topic, and then pick the best remaining choice. The correct answer also is often the longest one.

Stick With Your First Answer. Students shouldn't second-guess themselves; their first answer is probably right. They shouldn't change answers unless they're certain that their first answer was wrong.

Pace Yourself. Students budget their time wisely so they'll be able to finish the test. They don't spend too much time on any one question.

Check Your Work Carefully. Students check that they've answered every question, if they finish early.

Students use these test-taking strategies along with reading strategies, including determining importance, questioning, and rereading, when they're taking standardized tests. Teaching students about **Question-Answer-Relationships** helps them to understand that sometimes answers to test questions can be found in a passage they've just read, or they have to use their own knowledge.

Preparing for tests should be embedded in literacy activities and not take up a great deal of instructional time. Teachers often teach test-taking strategies through **minilessons** where they explain the strategy, model its use, and provide opportunities for guided practice and discussion. Greene and Melton (2007) recommend teaching minilessons on test-taking strategies as well as the genre of tests, test formats, and the language of tests as part of reading workshop. They reported that their students, many of whom are English learners and struggling readers and writers, became more confident and empowered test takers through test-preparation minilessons, and their test scores improved.

Be Strategic!
Test-Taking Strategies

Students use these test-taking strategies to answer multiple-choice questions on standardized tests:

► Read the entire question first
► Look for key words in the question
► Read all answer choices before choosing the correct one
► Answer easier questions first
► Make smart guesses
► Stick with your first answer
► Pace yourself
► Check your work carefully

Students learn to use these strategies through test-prep lessons and practice tests.

Practice Tests. Teachers design practice tests with the same types of items used on the standardized tests students will take. They use easy-to read materials for practice tests so students can focus on practicing test-taking strategies without being challenged by the difficulty level of the text or the questions. They include a combination of unrelated narrative, poetic, and expository passages on the tests because all three types of texts are found on high-stakes tests. Teachers also provide answer sheets similar to those used on the standardized test so that students gain experience with them. So that students will be familiar with the testing conditions, teachers simulate them in the classroom or take students to where the test will be administered for practice sessions. Through these practice tests, students develop both confidence in their test-taking abilities and the stamina to persist through long tests.

Preparation for reading tests is especially important because when students aren't familiar with multiple-choice tests, they'll score lower than they otherwise would. Don't confuse preparation with teaching to the test: Preparing for a test involves teaching students how to take a test, but teaching to the test is the unethical practice of drilling students on actual questions from old tests. The term "teaching to the test" is also used in a less pejorative way to describe when teachers tailor instruction to meet state standards.

Scaffolding English Learners

Researchers question the use of standardized achievement tests with English learners because these tests are often invalid, underestimating students' achievement (Peregoy & Boyle, 2008). It seems obvious that when students have limited English proficiency, their test performance would be affected; however, even students who do well in the classroom often score poorly on standardized achievement tests (Lindholm-Leary & Borsato, 2006). There are several reasons for this dichotomy. First, students are less familiar with test-taking procedures, and it's likely that ELs are more stressed by their unfamiliarity than native English speakers are. A second reason is that the language used in directions and test items is often complex, making comprehension more difficult for ELs. Another reason is cultural differences: English learners often lack background knowledge about the topics addressed in the reading passages and test questions.

Researchers believe that the best way to assess English learners more fairly is to provide accommodations, by modifying either the test or the testing procedure (Lindholm-Leary & Borsato, 2006). They've experimented with modifying tests by simplifying the language, translating the test into students' home language, or adding visual supports, and modifying the testing procedure by providing additional time, allowing students to use bilingual dictionaries, or translating or explaining the directions. Unfortunately, data are inconclusive about the effectiveness of these accommodations. Currently, there's renewed interest in rewriting test questions on high-stakes tests to avoid unnecessarily complex English syntactic structures and academic vocabulary so that ELs can actually demonstrate their knowledge.

Probably the best way to ameliorate the effects of ELs' potentially invalid test results is to use multiple measures, including some authentic assessments to document English learners' language proficiency and literacy achievement. This accommodation, however, is unlikely to be implemented in today's educational climate where both students and teachers are being held accountable using the results from a single test.

The Politics of High-Stakes Testing

High-stakes testing is a politically charged issue (Casbarro, 2005). Test scores are being used as a means to reform schools, and although improving the quality of instruction and ensuring that all students have equal access to educational opportunities are essential goals, there are unwanted consequences for both students and teachers. Proponents claim that schools are being reformed; however, although some gains in test scores for minority groups have been reported, many teachers feel that the improvement is the result of "teaching to the test." So far, no results indicate that students have actually become better readers and writers because of standardized achievement tests.

CHAPTER 3

How Effective Teachers Assess Literacy Learning

▶ Teachers determine students' independent, instructional, and frustration reading levels.

▶ Teachers informally monitor students' progress in reading and writing.

▶ Teachers use diagnostic assessments to identify struggling students' strengths and weaknesses and then provide instruction to address problem areas.

▶ Teachers have students document their literacy learning in portfolios.

▶ Teachers prepare students for high-stakes tests without sacrificing their instructional programs.

CHAPTER 4

Differentiating Instruction

Mrs. Shasky Differentiates Instruction

The students in Mrs. Shasky's sixth-grade class are reading *The Breadwinner* (Ellis, 2001), about a girl who disguises herself as a boy to support her family during the Taliban era in Afghanistan. Before students began reading the novel, they completed a webquest about Afghan culture and listened to an online interview with the novel's author. Today, some students are sitting on a sofa and lounging on floor pillows in the reading area as they read independently. Others are clustered around Mrs. Shasky, listening as she reads the book aloud; she reads softly to avoid distracting the other students. Some students close to Mrs. Shasky follow along in their copies, but others watch their teacher, listening intently.

Mrs. Shasky provides two ways to read the novel because her students' reading levels vary from third through seventh grade. Those who read at fifth- through seventh-grade levels can read the book independently, but her 10 students who read at third- and fourth-grade levels need extra support; that's why she reads the book aloud to them.

After reading the chapter, the class comes together for a **grand conversation**. Because the students have many questions about life under Taliban rule, Mrs. Shasky takes more discussion time than she would like to answer their questions, but gradually they're developing the background knowledge to understand the story. Mrs. Shasky teaches comprehension as they discuss the novel. She asks inferential questions that require students to go beyond literal information, for example: "Why did the Taliban arrest Parvana's father?" Hector quickly answers, "Because he went to college in another country, and they don't want teachers to do that." Mrs. Shasky persists, "Why doesn't the Taliban want teachers to study in another country?" No one has an idea, so Mrs. Shasky asks the question another way: "Lots of teachers in America go to other countries to study. You know that I visited schools in China last summer. Why is that a good idea?" The students offer several reasons—to meet different people, to learn new things, and to study new ways of teaching. "Wouldn't the Taliban want teachers to do these things, too?" Mrs. Shasky asks. Marisela replies, "The Taliban closed the schools because they want to control everyone. They don't like teachers who have new ideas because they could make trouble." "How could they make trouble?" Mrs. Shasky continues. Jared suggests, "Parvana's father and the other teachers could tell people that there is a better way to live, and then they might fight the Taliban." As they talk, students add *burqa*, *hospitable*, *turban*, *chador*, *nan*, *exhaustion*, and other new words to the word wall posted on a nearby wall.

Literature study is only one part of Mrs. Shasky's literacy block; her schedule is shown here. She differentiates instruction to ensure that her students are successful. Mrs. Shasky begins each morning with Accelerated Reader™. All students read independently in leveled books for 30 minutes, using books at their reading level, and complete online comprehension checks. Mrs. Shasky supervises students as they read, and she also monitors their progress. A chart is posted in the classroom so students can track their reading growth.

Ways Mrs. Shasky Differentiates Instruction

Schedule	Grade-Level Students	Struggling Students
8:30–9:00 Accelerated Reader	Students read books at their reading level and check their comprehension online.	Students read books at their reading level and check their comprehension online.
9:00–10:00 Literature Study	Students read the featured novel independently and participate in grand conversations.	Students listen to the teacher read the featured novel aloud and participate in grand conversations.
10:00–10:15 Minilesson	Mrs. Shasky presents whole-class minilessons on grade-level literacy topics.	Mrs. Shasky presents whole-class minilessons on grade-level literacy topics and others for small groups as needed.
10:15–11:15 Activities/ Guided Reading	Students are involved in activities related to the featured novel.	Students participate in guided reading groups and work in small groups on activities related to the featured novel.
11:15–11:45 Word Study	Students participate in whole-class and small-group word-study activities and lessons. They use an individualized approach to spelling.	Students participate in whole-class and small-group word-study activities and lessons. They use an individualized approach to spelling.

Next, students participate in a literature study. Books are usually chosen from the district's recommended reading list for sixth grade, and Mrs. Shasky supplements with other books such as *The Breadwinner* that are timely or that she thinks would appeal to her students. The novel becomes a vehicle for teaching reading strategies and literary analysis.

The third activity is a **minilesson**. Mrs. Shasky teaches minilessons on comprehension strategies, literary analysis, and other grade-level topics. Sometimes the whole class participates, and at other times, the lesson is designed for a specific group. She ties lessons to the novel they're reading; her focus for this novel is on how authors develop theme. Right now, the students are overwhelmed by the devastating effects of war, but later during the unit, Mrs. Shasky redirects the focus to human rights. Today, she reviews character development and explains how authors develop characters. She asks students to think about Parvana, the main character in *The Breadwinner*, and how the author developed her. As students share ideas, Mrs. Shasky draws a cluster, a weblike diagram, on chart paper and writes Parvana's name in the center circle. She divides the diagram into four sections and writes *appearance*, *actions*, *talking*, and *thinking* in the sections. Next, she writes a sentence or two that students have suggested in each section. Mrs. Shasky rereads the chart and asks, "Which of the four ways of character development is most important in *The Breadwinner*? What is the author trying to tell us?" The students are torn between "appearance" and "actions." Nita says, "It's her clothes. She has to dress like a boy." Javier disagrees, "No, it's what she's doing. She is pretending to be a boy to help her family. That's what matters." With more discussion, most students agree with Javier. The diagram is shown on the next page.

Most of the students return to their desks to work on various activities, but Mrs. Shasky keeps a group of struggling readers who need more practice writing summaries with her to write a summary statement about character development. She takes the students' dictation quickly as they develop this summary statement, which they'll share with the whole class:

> *Deborah Ellis tells us about Parvana in four ways: appearance, actions, talking, and thinking. The most important way we learn about Parvana is by her actions. She pretends she is a boy to make money so her family doesn't starve.*

Next week, Mrs. Shasky will introduce human rights with this scenario: Imagine that when you wake up tomorrow morning, life as you know it is totally different—it's like Parvana's life. What will be different? What will you do? What won't you be able to do? Students will talk and write about the ways their lives would change. Mrs. Shasky will explain what human rights are, talk about the rights guaranteed in the Constitution's Bill of Rights, and have students play an online game about human rights. Later, they'll participate in differentiated activities to think more deeply about the human rights they enjoy and those denied to Parvana.

While students are working on activities, Mrs. Shasky meets with small groups of struggling readers for **guided reading** lessons. One group is reading at early third-grade level (Level M), the second group is reading at late third-grade/early fourth-grade level (Level P), and the third group is reading at fourth-grade level (Level R). She usually meets with two groups a day for 25 minutes to read short chapter books at their reading levels; they read and discuss one or two chapters a day and then reread the chapters independently.

The group at the early third-grade level is reading Greenburg's wacky series, *The Zack Files*, about a fifth grader named Zack. In the book they've just finished reading, *How I Went From Bad to Verse* (Greenburg, 2000), Zack is bitten by an insect and catches Rhyme Disease. He speaks only in rhyme, and worse yet, he floats above the ground and turns blue. Finally, his teacher cures him and his life returns to normal—at least until the next book. The students reread the last two chapters and talk again about Zack's weird symptoms and his teacher's unusual cures.

These students also ceremoniously list the book on a chart of the books they've read; *How I Went From Bad to Verse* is number 28 on the list, and the students are amazed! "I've never read so many books before in my life," Ana comments. "I told my Tio Roberto that I'm a good reader now," Mark says. The students will take the book home tonight to read to their parents, a sibling, a grandparent, or a neighbor.

After conducting another guided reading group, Mrs. Shasky begins word study. Students do vocabulary and spelling activities during word study. On Monday, Mrs. Shasky takes the entire 30 minutes for spelling. She administers the pretest, and students check it themselves. Then they choose the words they'll study and make two copies of their word list, one for themselves and one for Mrs. Shasky. Because she's implemented an individualized spelling program, students study different words, depending on their developmental levels. The students practice their spelling words each day and take the final test on Friday.

On Tuesday, Wednesday, and Thursday, students participate in vocabulary lessons to study the meanings of specific words, examine root words, and learn to use

A Character Diagram About Parvana

When she was a girl she kept her face covered and tried to be envisible. She cut her hair and pretended to be a boy.

Appearance

She dressed as a boy to go to the markut and buy food.
She was a reader and writer.
She dug up graves.

Actions

Parvana

Talking

"I can do this".

"I am working to get my family back".

Thinking

She dident like the hard work but she did it to heep her family.
She was very lonely.

a dictionary and a thesaurus. They use words from the **word wall** for most activities. Over the past 5 weeks, Mrs. Shasky has taught lessons on these root words:

ann/enn (*year*): *annual, anniversary, millennium*

graph (*write*): *paragraph, autobiography, photograph*

mar/mer (*sea*): *mermaid, submarine, marsh*

tele (*far*): *telecast, telephone, telethon*

volv (*roll*): *revolution, evolution, revolver*

The students made posters about these root words, and they're displayed around the classroom. Today, students are examining words on the word wall to identify other root words.

Because Mrs. Shasky wants to do more to help her struggling readers, she developed Shasky's Reading Club, a twice-a-week after-school intervention. She invited the 10 struggling readers to stay after school on Tuesdays and Thursdays to participate. She began the club after parent conferences in early October. All parents agreed to pick up their children after the club and to provide 30 minutes of independent reading time at home 4 days a week.

During the 45-minute reading club meeting, students read self-selected books independently and participate in guided reading groups. Mrs. Shasky is pleased to see these students' growth over the 4 months the club has been operating. She's noticed that her struggling students behave like her grade-level readers do during the school day: Instead of being reticent and unsure of themselves as they sometimes are during the school day, they participate willingly in discussions and confidently assume leadership roles.

As the club meeting begins, the students have picked up books they're reading and settled on the sofa and on floor pillows to read. Mrs. Shasky checks that everyone has an appropriate book, and then she calls a group of four students reading at Level P; they're reading Jon Scieszka's The Time Warp Trio series about three modern-day friends who warp back into history. These students have already read *Your Mother Was a Neanderthal* (2004c) and *Tut Tut* (2004b).

Now they're reading *Knights of the Kitchen Table* (2004a), in which the boys find themselves at King Arthur's court. A giant and a dragon threaten Camelot, and the boys help King Arthur and his knights. The first few chapters were difficult because the students didn't know the King Arthur stories, but Mrs. Shasky told the stories to build their background knowledge. The vocabulary was unfamiliar, too—*vile knaves, methinks*, and *foul-mouthed enchanters*, for example—but now the group is really into the story. They begin by rereading Chapter 5 and doing a read-around, where they take turns randomly reading aloud their favorite sentences from the chapter. Then Mrs. Shasky takes them on a text walk of Chapter 6, and they examine a full-page illustration of the giant. Hector predicts, "I think Sir Joe the Magnificent will kill the giant and the dragon." "You should say he will *slay* them. *Slay* means to kill," explains Jesus. Mrs. Shasky asks how the knight might slay the giant and the dragon, and the boys quickly suggest using swords or guns, but the illustrations don't provide any clues.

Mrs. Shasky explains that this riddle is going to be important in the chapter: *Why did the giant wear red suspenders?* The students aren't familiar with suspenders, so Mrs. Shasky shows them a pair of her husband's. She models them and explains that sometimes her husband wears suspenders instead of a belt to hold his pants up. Marisela, who has been listening quietly while the boys eagerly talked about slaying dragons, asks, "So, why did the giant wear suspenders?" The teacher explains that they'll learn the answer as they read the chapter, and then Marisela predicts, "You have to be smart to answer a riddle, so I think those boys will use their brains to save Camelot." Mrs. Shasky smiles in agreement and says, "Let's read Chapter 6 to see if Marisela's prediction is right."

The students read the short chapter quickly, and while they're reading, Mrs. Shasky helps them decode several unfamiliar words and explains a confusing section when two boys ask about it. The group now knows the riddle's answer: *Why did the giant wear red suspenders? To hold his pants up.* They like the riddle and show interest in reading more riddles. Mrs. Shasky promises to get some riddle books tomorrow. They discuss the chapter, and Jesus sums up the group's feelings by saying, "Bleob [the giant] should be dead and gone by now. I just want to keep reading and find out what happens." Because the giant and the dragon do destroy themselves in the next chapter, Mrs. Shasky lets them continue reading.

Mrs. Shasky teaches a second guided reading lesson while the other students read independently. They finish when only several minutes remain before the reading club ends, so Mrs. Shasky joins the group in the back of the classroom and asks each student to briefly tell what he or she has been reading.

Teachers know that their students vary—in their interests and motivation, their background knowledge and prior experiences, and their culture and language proficiency as well as their literacy achievement—so it's important to take these individual differences into account as they plan for instruction. Differentiated instruction is based on this understanding that students differ in important ways. According to Tomlinson (2001), differentiated instruction "means 'shaking up' what goes on in the classroom so that students have multiple options for taking in information, making sense of ideas, and expressing what they learn" (p. 1). Customizing instruction is especially important for struggling readers and writers who can't access grade-level textbooks and other reading materials.

In the vignette, for example, Mrs. Shasky modified instruction to meet her students' needs. She provided additional support for struggling students by reading aloud to those who couldn't read the featured novel and taught **guided reading lessons**. In addition, Mrs. Shasky created an after-school intervention program for her struggling readers and got these students' parents to commit to providing time for independent reading at home.

> Check the Compendium of Instructional Procedures, which follows Chapter 12, for more information on the highlighted terms.

Ways to Differentiate Instruction

The expectation that all students will meet the same literacy standards at each grade level implies that everyone should receive the same instructional program, but teachers know that some students are working at grade level but others are struggling or advanced. Because students' achievement levels differ and their interests and preferred ways of learning vary, teachers modify their instructional programs so that all students can be more successful. Tomlinson (2001) explains that in differentiated classrooms, "teachers provide specific ways for students to learn as deeply as possible and as quickly as possible without assuming one student's road map for learning is identical to anyone else's" (p. 2). Heacox (2002) characterizes differentiated instruction as rigorous, relevant, flexible, and complex:

FIGURE 4–1 ◆ *Characteristics of Differentiated Instruction*

High Standards
Teachers maintain a commitment to meeting grade-level standards for all students.

Assessment–Instruction Link
Teachers use assessment procedures to diagnose students' needs and plan instruction to address those needs.

Flexible Grouping
Teachers have students work individually, in small groups, and as a class, and they change grouping arrangements to reflect students' achievement levels and interests.

Reading Materials
Teachers teach with collections of books and other reading materials at varying difficulty levels.

Varied Instructional Activities
Teachers design activities with multiple options to meet students' instructional levels.

Instructional Modifications
Teachers modify instruction to respond to students' specific learning needs and continue to make adjustments during instruction to ensure that all students are successful.

Respect
Teachers respect students and value their work.

Academic Achievement
Teachers focus on individual students' academic achievement and success.

Adapted from Heacox, 2002; Robb, 2008; Tomlinson, 2001.

Rigorous means that teachers provide challenging instruction that encourages students' active engagement in learning.

Relevant means that teachers address literacy standards to assure that students learn essential knowledge, strategies, and skills.

Flexible means that teachers use a variety of instructional procedures and grouping techniques to support students.

Complex means that teachers engage students in thinking deeply about books they're reading, compositions they're writing, and concepts they're learning.

It's crucial that teachers recognize the diversity of learners in 21st-century classrooms and understand that students don't need to participate in the same learning activities or work in whole-class groups all day long. The characteristics of differentiated instruction are summarized in Figure 4–1.

Teachers modify instruction in three ways: They modify the *content* that students learn, the *process* used for instruction, and the *products* students create to demonstrate their learning (Heacox, 2002; Tomlinson, 2001):

Differentiating the Content. The content is the "what" of teaching, the literacy knowledge, strategies, and skills that students learn at each grade level. The content reflects state-mandated grade-level standards. Teachers concentrate on teaching the essential content, and to meet students' needs, they provide more instruction and practice for some students and less for others. For those who are already familiar with the content, they increase the complexity of instructional activities. Teachers decide how to differentiate the content by assessing students' knowledge before they begin teaching, and then they match students with appropriate activities.

Differentiating the Process.   The process is the "how" of teaching, the instruction that teachers provide, the instructional materials they use, and the activities in which students are involved to ensure that they're successful. Teachers group students for instruction and choose reading materials at appropriate levels of difficulty. They also make decisions about involving students in activities that allow them to process what they're learning through oral, written, or visual means.

Differentiating the Product.   The product is the end result of learning; it demonstrates what students understand and how well they can apply what they've learned. Students usually create projects, such as posters, oral reports, board games, websites, and collections of poems. Teachers vary the complexity of the projects they ask students to create by changing the level of thinking that's required to complete them.

New Literacies

Computer-Based Reading Programs

Scholastic's Reading Counts! and Renaissance Learning's Accelerated Reader™ are two popular K–12 computer-based supplemental reading programs. They're consistent with differentiated instruction because students choose books to read independently from a leveled collection. More than half of American schools use one of these programs.

Both programs provide students with daily opportunities for reading practice, and students who do more reading are better readers (Topping & Paul, 1999). The programs are predicated on these principles:

- Students read authentic books at their reading levels.
- Quizzes provide frequent monitoring of students' comprehension.
- Students' motivation grows as they score well on the accompanying quizzes.
- Teachers use test results to quickly intervene with struggling students.

These principles reflect the balanced approach to reading instruction.

More than 100,000 leveled books are included in the Accelerated Reader collection and half that many in Reading Counts! One potential problem, however, is that a limited number of appropriate books are available for older struggling readers. Sometimes the book collections are housed in the school library, or teachers set out smaller collections in their classrooms.

Students take computer-generated quizzes to check their comprehension after reading each book, and the questions focus on literal comprehension. Students receive the results immediately afterward so they can learn from their errors. Teachers track students' progress using computer-generated reports with information about students' comprehension, their reading rates, and the amount of reading they've done.

Students participating in these programs score higher on standardized tests than students who don't use them; nonetheless, the programs are controversial (Holmes & Brown, 2003; Schmidt, 2008). One complaint is that the quizzes focus on literal comprehension, but proponents counter that the purpose is to determine whether students have read a book, not to assess higher-level comprehension. Next, detractors argue that students have limited choices because they can read only books that match their reading level, but proponents say that students can read other books at other times. Another complaint is that students often read the book with the goal of passing the quiz, rather than for enjoyment or to learn about a topic, but proponents point out that students need to learn to read for a variety of purposes. Many teachers report liking the program because they can effectively manage students' independent reading and monitor their progress.

Teachers create a classroom culture that promotes acceptance of individual differences and is conducive to matching instruction to students. Having a classroom community where students respect their classmates and can work collaboratively is vital. They learn that students don't always do the same activity or read the same book, and they focus on their own work rather than on what their peers are doing.

Grouping for Instruction

Teachers use three grouping patterns: Sometimes students work together as a whole class, and at other times, they work in small groups or individually. Deciding which type of grouping to use depends on the teacher's purpose, the complexity of the activity, and students' learning needs. Small groups should be used flexibly to provide a better instructional match between students and their achievement levels. In differentiated classrooms, students are grouped and regrouped often; they aren't always grouped according to achievement levels or with the same classmates.

Teachers use a combination of the three grouping patterns in each instructional program, but literature focus units and textbook programs use primarily whole-class groups, literature circles are predominantly small-group programs, and reading and writing workshop feature mostly individual reading and writing activities. Nonetheless, each instructional program incorporates all three grouping patterns. The activities involved in each instructional program are categorized in Figure 4–2.

Teachers use the three grouping patterns for a variety of activities. Whole-class activities typically include **hot seat** and **interactive read-alouds**. **Guided reading** and **writing groups** are small-group activities. Other activities, such as **open-mind portraits** and **quick-writing**, are done individually. Some activities, such as **minilessons** and **making words**, are used with more than one grouping pattern. In addition, when teachers introduce an activity, they have students work together as a class to learn the steps involved; then, once students understand the procedure, they work in small groups or individually.

Guided Reading. Teachers use **guided reading** lessons to teach reading to small groups of students who read at the same instructional level (Fountas & Pinnell, 2001). Teachers choose books according to students' reading levels and their ability to use reading strategies. They read the book in preparation for the lesson and plan how they'll teach it, considering how to develop students' background knowledge and which concepts and vocabulary to teach before students begin reading. Next, students do the actual reading themselves, although the teacher may read the first page or two aloud with students to get them started. After discussing the book, they teach a reading strategy and involve students in word-study activities. Guided reading lessons usually last approximately 20–30 minutes, and teachers meet with several groups each day.

Guided reading was developed to use with beginning readers, but teachers also use it with older students, especially English learners and struggling readers who need more support to decode and comprehend books they're reading. Sometimes guided reading is confused with round-robin reading and literature circles, but these three small-group instructional activities are different. In round-robin reading, an approach that's no longer recommended, students take turns reading aloud rather than doing their own reading, and in literature circles, students read and discuss books in small groups with limited teacher guidance.

Text Sets of Reading Materials

Teachers create text sets of books and other reading materials for students to read during literature focus units and thematic units. These collections include reading

FIGURE 4–2 ◆ *Grouping Patterns in the Literacy Programs*			
Program	**Whole Class**	**Small Groups**	**Individuals**
Literature Focus Units	Teachers: • introduce and read the book • teach minilessons Students: • participate in discussions • learn about author and genre • create projects	Teachers: • teach minilessons Students: • participate in discussions • do word-study activities • work at centers • create projects	Students: • respond in reading logs • do word-study activities • read related books • create projects
Literature Circles	Teachers: • introduce books	Students: • read and discuss the book • conference with the teacher	Students: • choose and read the book • prepare for discussions
Reading Workshop	Teachers: • read aloud to students • teach minilessons	Students: • share books with classmates Teachers: • teach minilessons	Students: • read self-selected books • conference with the teacher
Writing Workshop	Teachers: • read aloud to students • teach minilessons Students: • share writing with classmates	Teachers: • teach minilessons Students: • participate in writing groups • revise and edit at centers • edit with a partner	Students: • write on self-selected topics • conference with the teacher
Basal Reading Programs	Teachers: • introduce the selection • teach vocabulary • teach strategies and skills Students: • read and discuss the selection	Students: • reread the selection • practice skills • work at centers • complete workbook assignments	Students: • reread the selection • complete workbook assignments
Language Arts Textbooks	Teachers: • introduce the selection • teach literary analysis, vocabulary, and grammar Students: • read and discuss the selection	Students: • analyze the genre and literary devices • complete assignments	Students: • read the selection • complete assignments

materials representing different genres, bookmarked Internet resources, and books that vary in difficulty level. Figure 4–3 presents Mrs. Shasky's text set of books and Internet resources related to *The Breadwinner* (Ellis, 2001). The list includes all three books in Deborah Ellis's trilogy of novels about Parvana and two books of poetry by Naomi Shihab Nye (2002a, 2002b), an esteemed Arab American poet. Teachers use

FIGURE 4–3 ◆ *A Text Set for* The Breadwinner

Stories

Bunting, E. (2006). *One green apple*. New York: Clarion Books.

Ellis, D. (2001). *The breadwinner*. Toronto: Groundwood Books.

Ellis, D. (2003). *Parvana's journey*. Toronto: Groundwood Books.

Ellis, D. (2004). *Mud city*. Toronto: Groundwood Books.

Khan, R. (2004). *The roses in my carpets*. Markham, ON: Fitzhenry & Whiteside.

Nonfiction

Banting, E. (2003). *Afghanistan: The culture*. Minneapolis, MN: Crabtree.

Banting, E. (2003). *Afghanistan: The land*. Minneapolis, MN: Crabtree.

Banting, E. (2003). *Afghanistan: The people*. Minneapolis, MN: Crabtree.

Haskins, J., & Benson, K. (2006). *Count your way through Afghanistan*. Minneapolis, MN: Millbrook Press.

Whitfield, S. (2008). *National Geographic countries of the world: Afghanistan*. Washington, DC: National Geographic Children's Books.

Wolf, B. (2003). *Coming to America: A Muslim family's story*. New York: Lee & Low.

Zucker, J. (2004). *Fasting and dates: A Ramadan and Eid-ul-Fitr story*. New York: Barron's.

Poetry

Nye, N. S. (Compiler). (2002). *The flag of childhood: Poems from the Middle East*. New York: Aladdin Books.

Nye, N. S. (2002). *19 varieties of gazelle: Poems of the Middle East*. New York: Greenwillow.

Websites and Webquests

Afghanistan for Kids, http://www.public.asu.edu/ ~apnilsen/afghanistan4kids/index2.html

The Breadwinner: A Prereading Webquest Activity for Grades 4–7, www.literacynet.org/cortez/

Kids in Afghanistan Scavenger Hunt, http:// teacher.scholastic.com/scholasticnews/indepth/ afghanistan/

No Music, no TV, http://www.timeforkids.com/ TFK/kids/wr/article/0,28391,94545,00.html

Understanding Afghanistan: Land in Crisis, http:// www.nationalgeographic.com/landincrisis/

book talks to introduce books at the beginning of the unit and then display them on a special shelf in the classroom library. They often read some of the books aloud, have students read others in literature circles, and encourage students to read additional books independently.

Text sets are only a small part of well-stocked classroom libraries. Teachers set out collections of picture-book stories, novels, nonfiction books, magazines, and books of poetry written at a range of levels for students to read independently. They also provide plenty of other books that are grade appropriate but easy enough for struggling students to read on their own, including some books they read the previous year.

Tiered Activities

To match students' needs, teachers create several tiered or related activities that focus on the same essential knowledge but vary in complexity (Robb, 2008). These activities are alternative ways of reaching the same goal because "one-size-fits-all" activities can't benefit on-grade-level students, support struggling readers, and challenge advanced students. Creating tiered lessons, according to Tomlinson (2001), increases the likelihood that all students will be successful. Even though the activities are different, they should be interesting and engaging and require the same amount of effort.

Teachers vary activities in several ways. First, they vary them by complexity of thinking. In recall-level activities, students identify, retell, or summarize; in analysis-level activities, they compare and categorize; and in synthesis-level activities, students evaluate, draw conclusions, and invent. Second, teachers vary activities according to the level of reading materials. They use books and online materials written at students' reading level, or they vary the way the materials are shared with students. Third, teachers vary activities by the form of expression: Students are involved in visual, oral, and written expression as they complete an activity. Examples of visual expression are charts, posters, and dioramas; examples of oral expression are dramatizations, oral reports, and choral readings; and examples of written expression are stories, poems, and reports. Some activities require a combination of forms of expression; for example, students might write a poem from the viewpoint of a book character (written) and dress up as the character (visual) to read the poem aloud to the class (oral). Creating tiered activities doesn't mean that some students do more work and others do less; each activity must be equally interesting and challenging to the students.

Tomlinson (2001) suggests that teachers follow these steps to develop a tiered activity:

1. **Design an activity.** Teachers design an engaging activity that focuses on elemental knowledge and requires high-level thinking.

2. **Visualize a ladder.** Teachers imagine a ladder where the top rung represents advanced students, the middle rung on-grade-level students, and the bottom rung struggling students, and then decide where the activity they've created fits on the ladder.

3. **Create other versions of the activity.** Teachers create one, two, or three versions of the activity at different levels of difficulty to meet their students' needs. Versions can vary according to the difficulty level of reading materials they use, thinking levels, or forms of expression.

4. **Match activities to students.** Teachers decide which students will complete each version of the activity.

Tiered Activities
Teachers use tiered activities to maximize students' learning. These fourth graders are working on a tiered activity—a poster report about stagecoaches—based on Pam Muñoz Ryan's *Riding Freedom* (1998), the story of Charlotte Parkhurst, a legendary stagecoach driver during the California Gold Rush. The students have researched the vehicles and downloaded pictures from the Internet for their report. Today, they're revising their captions to include more facts. Later, they'll print out a "clean" copy, cut the captions apart, and attach them next to the pictures they've already glued on a poster.

To make tiering invisible, Heacox (2002) recommends that teachers alternate the order in which activities are introduced to students, show equal enthusiasm for each one, and use neutral ways of identifying groups of students who will pursue each activity.

One of the literacy standards that Mrs. Shasky addressed as her sixth graders read and responded to *The Breadwinner* (Ellis, 2001) was to analyze the theme through the characters and the plot. She decided to explore the theme of human rights and, in particular, what happens when they're denied. She began by talking about human rights during a **grand conversation** as the class discussed the book, and students looked for examples of human rights that the Taliban denied to Parvana and her family. Later, students worked in small groups to create lists of human rights, including religious freedom, the right to safe food and drinking water, freedom of speech, the right to education, freedom to earn a living, civil rights, and equal rights. They played the interactive game "Save the Bill of Rights" at the National Constitution Center's website to learn more about the rights that Americans are guaranteed.

Once students understood what human rights are and could find examples of these rights and freedoms being denied in *The Breadwinner*, Mrs. Shasky designed this activity:

> **Information, please!** *Create a Venn diagram on chart paper to compare the human rights we have in America to those Parvana and her family had in Taliban-controlled Afghanistan. Then create a statement to summarize the information presented in the Venn diagram and write it underneath the diagram.*

Mrs. Shasky decided that this graphic activity was appropriate for her on-grade-level students. Here's the version she developed for her struggling students:

> **A celebration of human rights!** *Choose the human right that you value most and create a quilt square using color, images, and words to describe it. Then we'll connect the squares and create a human rights quilt.*

Finally, Mrs. Shasky designed this version for her advanced students:

> **Get involved!** *Students in our class are passionate about human rights and want to help people like Parvana and her family. Find a way for us to get involved, and create a brochure about your idea to share with everyone.*

The advanced students researched organizations that aid refugees and promote human rights, including UNICEF, Habitat for Humanity, Heifer International, and Doctors Without Borders, before they heard about Greg Mortenson's work building schools in Afghanistan that's described in *Three Cups of Tea: One Man's Mission to Promote Peace . . . One School at a Time* (Mortenson & Relin, 2007). The group proposed that that their class raise money to build a school through the Pennies for Peace program, and before long, the class had gotten the entire school and their local community involved!

Literacy Centers

Literacy centers contain meaningful, purposeful literacy activities that students can work at in small groups; for example, students sort word cards at the vocabulary center, or listen to an author interview related to a book they're reading at the listening center. Literacy centers are described in Figure 4–4. Centers are usually organized in special places in the classroom or at groups of tables. Although literacy centers are associated with primary classrooms, they can be used effectively to differentiate instruction in the middle grades. In most classrooms, the teacher works with a small group of students while the others work at centers, but sometimes all students work at centers at the same time.

The activities in these literacy centers relate to concepts, strategies, and skills that the teacher recently taught in minilessons, and they vary from simple to complex. Other

FIGURE 4–4 ◆ Literacy Centers

Center	Description
Author	Students read online materials, books, and magazine articles about an author they're studying.
Computer	Students do word processing, perform webquests, search the Internet, create PowerPoint presentations, and complete other activities.
Grammar	Students practice grammar concepts that have been introduced in minilessons.
Graphic Organizers	Students complete graphic organizers and other diagrams related to books they're reading and other literacy activities.
Library	Students browse in the classroom library, select books to read, and read independently.
Listening	Students use a tape player or CD player to listen to books read aloud.
Poetry	Students read and write poems and participate in activities to manipulate lines of poetry and locate examples of poetic devices.
Proofreading	Students proofread with partners and then use spellcheckers and dictionaries to correct mechanical errors in their writing.
Research	Students conduct research using nonfiction books and other resources on a topic related to a book or a thematic unit.
Revising	Students participate in a variety of activities with partners to refine their rough drafts.
Spelling	Students practice spelling words, do word sorts to review spelling concepts, do word-making activities, and play spelling games.
Story Boards	Students create story board posters for each chapter of a novel the class is reading.
Vocabulary	Students practice recently taught vocabulary concepts, draw word clusters, and do word sorts.
Word Wall	Students participate in word-study activities using words posted on the word wall.

center activities relate to books students are reading and to thematic units. Students manipulate objects, sort word cards, reread books, complete graphic organizers related to books, and practice skills in centers. Some literacy centers are permanent, but others change according to the books students are reading and the literacy topics being taught. Teachers provide clear directions at the center so students know what to do. In some classrooms, students flow freely from one center to another according to their interests; in others, students are assigned to centers or are required to work at some "assigned" centers and then choose among other "choice" centers.

The Assessment Tools feature below shows a checklist that eighth graders used as they worked at centers as part of a thematic unit on the Constitution. Some centers are required; they're marked with an asterisk. Students are expected to complete the "required" centers and two others of their choice. When they finish work at a center, they put a checkmark in the "Student's Check" column. Students keep their checklists in their unit folders, and they add any worksheets or papers they do at a center. Having a checklist or another approach to monitor students' progress helps them develop responsibility for completing their assignments.

Differentiated Projects

Students often create projects to apply what they've learned and bring closure to a unit. Possible projects include charts, murals, and other visual representations; poems, essays,

Assessment Tools

U.S. Constitution Centers Checklist

Center	Activity	Student's Check	Teacher's Check
Word Wall	Choose three words from the word wall and make word-study cards for each word.		
Puzzle Center	Complete the "Branches of Government" puzzle.		
Library Center	Use nonfiction books at the center to complete the Constitution time line.		
Internet Center	Research the Constitution on the Internet and complete the study guide.		
Writing Center	Study Howard Christy's painting "The Signing of the Constitution" and write about it.		
*Legislative Branch Center	Complete activities at this student-developed center.		
*Executive Branch Center	Complete activities at this student-developed center.		
*Judicial Branch Center	Complete activities at this student-developed center.		
*The Bill of Rights Center	Complete activities at this student-developed center.		
*Alphabet Book Center	Choose a letter and create a page for the Class Constitution Alphabet Book.		

and other compositions; PowerPoint reports, **readers theatre** productions, and other oral presentations; websites and other Internet products; and community-based projects that reflect students' synthesis of the big ideas and high-quality workmanship. Projects are an important part of differentiated instruction because students follow their interests, demonstrate what they've learned in authentic ways, and feel successful (Yatvin, 2004).

At the end of some units, students work together on a class project. When fifth graders are studying idioms, for example, they often create a collaborative book about idioms. Most of the time, however, students choose their own projects. Some students work independently or with a partner, and others work in small groups.

Projects are especially valuable for advanced students and struggling students (Yatvin, 2004). When advanced students create projects, they have opportunities to pursue special interests and extend their learning beyond the classroom. For example, they often choose to get involved in community and social issues that they're passionate about, such as homelessness, global warming, and disaster relief, through the projects they do. Similarly, struggling students are often more successful in demonstrating their learning when they work with classmates in small, collaborative groups and use their special talents and expertise, such as drawing, making oral presentations, and using computers, to create a high-quality project.

Struggling Readers and Writers

Today, 6 million adolescents in the United States are struggling readers and writers (Joftus & Maddox-Dolan, 2003), and only 30% of fourth through eighth graders read at grade level and score at the proficient level on standardized achievement tests (National Governors Association, 2005; Ysseldyke & Taylor, 2007). These are startling statistics because underachieving students drop out of school more often than their peers, and even if they do graduate from high school, they're less likely to be successful in college or in the workforce.

Researchers point out innate, environmental, and instructional factors to explain why so many students don't meet grade-level standards (Ysseldyke & Taylor, 2007). Innate factors that affect academic success include students' processing deficits and other intellectual and learning disabilities. Environmental factors include students' prior experiences, their families, language and literacy characteristics, and their early educational experiences. Students who have a rich background of experiences, those whose parents are better educated and who value education, those who participated in home and preschool literacy experiences, those who are fluent English speakers, and those who complete homework assignments are more likely to be successful. Instructional factors include the components of literacy instruction and the quality of teaching. Effective teachers differentiate instruction, present explicit lessons on word identification, vocabulary, comprehension, and writing, and provide teacher-supervised and independent application activities with authentic texts. Teachers also use intervention programs to prevent reading failure in the primary grades and to accelerate the progress of older struggling readers. Young adolescents who read 2 or more years below grade level need both high-quality classroom instruction and an effective intervention program that addresses their specific reading and writing difficulties, or they have little chance of catching up with their peers.

Struggling Readers

Although many struggling readers are identified in the primary grades, other students who have been successful begin to exhibit reading problems in fourth or fifth grade. This phenomenon is known as the "fourth-grade slump" (Chall & Jacobs, 2003). Many teachers attribute this problem to the growing use of nonfiction books and content-area textbooks that present unfamiliar topics using academic vocabulary.

Struggling readers exhibit a variety of difficulties. Some don't read fluently, and others have insufficient vocabulary knowledge or difficulty understanding and remembering the author's message. Still others struggle because they're unfamiliar with English language structures. Figure 4–5 identifies some of the problems that struggling readers face and suggests ways to solve each one. When teachers suspect that

FIGURE 4–5 ◆ *Ways to Address Struggling Readers' Problems*

Component	Problem	Solutions
Word Identification	Student can't identify high-frequency words.	Make a personal word wall with words the student recognizes. Use a routine to teach and practice high-frequency words. Have the student look for high-frequency words in familiar books. Have the student write words on a whiteboard.
	Student can't identify consonant and vowel sounds.	Have the student sort objects or picture cards according to sounds. Have the student play phonics games, including those online. Do interactive writing with the student.
	Student can't decode one-syllable words.	Involve the student in making words activities and word ladder games. Have the student spell words using magnetic letters or on a whiteboard. Teach the student about vowel patterns. Have the student sort word cards according to vowel patterns. Do interactive writing with the student.
	Student can't identify multisyllabic words.	Teach a procedure for identifying multisyllabic words. Have the student remove affixes to identify the root word. Brainstorm lists of words from a single root word. Have the student write words with affixes on a whiteboard. Do interactive writing with the student.
Fluency	Student omits, substitutes, or repeats words when reading.	Teach high-frequency words that the student doesn't know. Ensure that the level of reading materials is appropriate for the student. Have the student read the text quietly before reading it aloud. Have the student reread familiar books or excerpts from books. Use choral reading in small groups.
Vocabulary	Student doesn't understand the meanings of words.	Create a K-W-L chart or do an anticipation guide before reading. Teach key vocabulary before reading. Have the student sort words from a book being read or a thematic unit. Have the student make diagrams and posters about key words. Read books aloud every day to build the student's vocabulary. Teach idioms, synonyms and antonyms, and word-learning strategies. Use tea party and semantic feature analysis to learn about words.
Comprehension	Student can't retell or answer questions after reading.	Build the student's background knowledge before reading. Ensure that the book is appropriate for the student. Read the book aloud before the student reads it. Have the student sequence big idea cards and use them to summarize a nonfiction article. Set a purpose for reading by having the student read a very brief text to find the answer to one question.

	Student can't draw inferences or do higher-level thinking.	Read the book aloud instead of having the student read it. Do think-alouds to model drawing inferences and higher-level thinking. Teach comprehension strategies. Teach the student about text structure. Use the Questioning the Author procedure. Use QARs to teach the student about types of questions. Involve the student in small-group grand conversations and literature circles.
	Student is a passive reader.	Use the interactive read-aloud procedure. Teach the student to self-select appropriate books. Teach the comprehension strategies. Have the student read a book with a partner or in a literature circle. Have the student view the movie version before reading a novel. Involve the student in hot seat, grand conversations, and other participatory activities. Use the Questioning the Author procedure.
Study Skills	Student can't locate information in reference materials.	Teach the student to use an index to locate information. Have the student practice locating information in TV guides, dictionaries, almanacs, and other reference materials. Teach the student to skim and scan to find information in a text. Teach the student to navigate the Web to locate information online .
	Student can't take notes.	Demonstrate how to take notes using a graphic organizer or small self-stick notes. Make a copy of a text and have the student mark the big ideas with a highlighter pen. Have the student identify big ideas and create a graphic organizer to represent them. Have the student work with a partner to take notes on small self-stick notes.

Adapted from McKenna, 2002; Shanker & Cockrum, 2009.

a student is struggling, they take action and assess him or her to diagnose problems, and they intervene if problems are present because expert instruction helps overcome reading difficulties.

Struggling Writers

Many students struggle with writing. It's easy to notice some problems when you examine their writing: Some students have difficulty developing and organizing ideas, some struggle with word choice and writing complete sentences and effective transitions, and others have problems with spelling, capitalization, punctuation, and grammar skills. Other students struggle with the writing process and using writing strategies effectively; they may be unsure about what writers do as they develop and refine their writing (Christenson, 2002). There are some students, too, who complain that their hands and arms hurt when they write, some who show little interest and do the bare minimum, and others who are so frustrated with writing that they refuse to write at all. Figure 4–6 lists some of the problems that struggling writers face and suggests ways to address each one.

Struggling students need to learn more about writing and have more opportunities to practice writing in order to build their confidence and become more successful.

FIGURE 4–6 ◆ *Ways to Address Struggling Writers' Problems*

Component	Problem	Solutions
Ideas	Student doesn't have any ideas.	Have the student brainstorm a list of ideas and pick the most promising one. Have the student talk with classmates to get ideas. Have the student draw a picture to develop an idea.
	Composition lacks focus.	After writing a draft, have the student highlight sentences that pertain to the focus, cut the other parts, and elaborate the highlighted ideas. Give the student a very focused assignment. Share samples of unfocused writing for the student to revise.
	Composition lacks interesting details.	Have the student brainstorm descriptive words to add to the composition. Have the student draw a picture about the writing topic and then add details reflected in the picture to the composition. Teach the student to use vivid verbs and adjectives.
Organization	Composition lacks organization.	Help the student decide on paragraph organization before beginning to write. Teach the concept of "big idea" using many types of texts. Have the student examine the structure of sample compositions.
	Composition is organized, but some sentences in a paragraph don't belong.	Have the student read each paragraph, checking that every sentence belongs. Have the student and a partner check sentences in each paragraph. Teach paragraph structure. Have the student examine sample paragraphs to locate sentences that don't belong.
	Composition lacks an exciting lead.	Have the student try several leads with an experience, a question, a quotation, or a comparison. Have the student get feedback about the effectiveness of the lead in a writing group. Have the student examine the leads in stories and nonfiction books.
	Ideas aren't sequenced.	Write the sentences on sentence strips for the student to sequence. Teach sequence words, such as *first*, *next*, *last*, and *finally*.
	Composition follows a circular pattern.	Have the student create a graphic organizer before beginning to write. Help the student identify the big idea for each paragraph before beginning to write. Teach sequence of ideas.
Word Choice	Composition lacks interesting vocabulary.	Have the student refer to classroom word walls for vocabulary. Have the student focus on adding more-interesting vocabulary words during revising. Have the student revise sample compositions.
Writing Process	Student doesn't revise.	Model revision with sample compositions. Compare the quality of unrevised and revised compositions. Include revision as a requirement in the assessment rubric.
	Revisions aren't constructive.	Use writing groups. Conference with the student to examine the revisions. Include substantive revision as a requirement on the rubric. Teach and model the types of revision.
	Student plagiarizes.	Use the writing process. Make the student accountable for graphic organizers or note cards. Have the student do the research and writing in class, not at home. Teach the student how to take notes and develop a composition.

Mechanics	Composition is riddled with misspelled words.	Have the student refer to a list of high-frequency words during writing. Have the student edit with a partner. Conference with the student to correct remaining errors. Teach the student to proofread. Have the student correct errors in sample compositions.
	Composition has many capitalization and punctuation errors.	Have editing partners identify and correct errors. Conference with the student to correct remaining errors during editing. Teach capitalization and punctuation skills. Have the student correct errors in sample compositions.
	Grammar errors interfere with meaning.	Have editing partners identify and correct grammar errors during editing. Conference with the student to correct remaining errors during editing. Teach grammar concepts. Have the student correct errors in sample compositions.
	Sentence structure is weak.	Have editing partners address sentence structure during the editing stage. Teach sentence structure. Teach sentence combining and then have the student practice it.
	Composition is illegible because of poor handwriting.	Have the student use word processing. Have the student use manuscript rather than cursive handwriting. Have the student try various types of paper and writing instruments. Take the student's dictation, if necessary.
Motivation	Student lacks engagement.	Conference with the student to determine why he/she is hesitant. Brainstorm ideas with the student during prewriting. Model how to expand a sentence into a paragraph. Have the student practice expanding a brief composition into a better-developed one.
	Student is dependent on teacher approval.	Have the student check with a classmate before coming to the teacher. Have the student sign up for conferences with the teacher. Make sure the student understands expectations and procedures.
	Student refuses to write.	Conference with the student to determine and address the problem. Try interactive writing. Have the student write a collaborative composition with a small group. Keep first writing assignments very short to ensure success.

Teachers address students' specific problem areas in their instruction, but high-quality instruction usually includes these components:

Minilessons. Teachers teach students about the writing process, writing strategies and skills, qualities of good writing, and writing genres through **minilessons**. Students often examine anonymous student samples saved from previous years as part of their lessons, use **rubrics** to score these samples, and revise and edit weaker papers to apply what they're learning in the lesson. As part of minilessons, teachers also model how they write and think aloud about how to use writing strategies.

Daily Opportunities to Write. Students need opportunities to apply what they're learning about writers and writing and to develop the stamina to see a composition from beginning to end. They also use writing as a learning tool as they write in **reading logs** about books they're reading and in **learning logs** as part of thematic units.

Conferences. Teachers meet with individual students to talk about their writing, the writing process they use, and how they view themselves as writers. They ask questions such as these:

- What's one important thing you've learned about writing?
- What part of writing is easy for you? hard for you?
- How do you decide what changes to make in your writing?
- What would you like to learn next?
- Do you think of yourself as a good writer? Why? Why not?

Through these conversations, students learn to think metacognitively and reflect on the progress they've made.

Daily Opportunities to Read. Students need time to read books at their reading level, and opportunities to listen to the teacher read aloud high-quality fiction and nonfiction that they can't read independently to develop background knowledge, examine genres, become more strategic, and deepen their knowledge of vocabulary words.

Through a combination of instruction and practice, struggling students become more-confident writers, develop stamina, and learn to craft well-organized and interesting compositions that are more mechanically correct.

Teaching Struggling Students

Struggling students have significant difficulty learning to read and write. Some students are at risk for reading and writing problems in first grade, but others develop difficulties in fourth or fifth grade or even later. The best way to help these students is to prevent their difficulties in the first place by providing high-quality classroom instruction and adding an intervention, if it's needed (Cooper, Chard, & Kiger, 2006). Unfortunately, there's no quick fix for low-achieving students. Helping struggling students requires both high-quality classroom instruction and "a comprehensive and sustained intervention effort" (Allington, 2006, p. 141).

High-Quality Classroom Instruction. Teachers use a balanced approach to literacy that combines explicit instruction in word identification, vocabulary, comprehension, and writing along with daily opportunities for students to apply what they're learning in authentic literacy activities (Allington, 2006). It's standards driven and incorporates research-based procedures and activities. Teachers address these four components to enhance the literacy development of all students, including struggling readers and writers:

Differentiate Instruction. Teachers adjust their instructional programs to match student needs using flexible grouping, tiered activities, and respectful tasks (Opitz & Ford, 2008). Results of ongoing assessment are used to vary instructional content, process, and assignments according to students' developmental levels, interests, and learning styles.

Use Appropriate Instructional Materials. Most of the time, students read interesting books written at their reading levels in small groups or individually. Teachers usually have plenty of books available for on- and above-grade-level readers, but finding appropriate books for struggling readers can be difficult. Figure 4–7 presents a list of easy-to-read paperback series for struggling students. Teachers also choose award-winning books for literature focus units, but even though these "teaching-texts" are important, Allington (2006) recommends using a single text with the whole class only 25% of the time because students need more opportunities to read books at their reading levels.

FIGURE 4–7 ◆ Easy-to-Read Paperback Series

Level	Series	Genre
2	A to Z Mysteries by Ron Roy	Mystery
	Andrew Lost by J. C. Greenburg	Informational
	Cam Jansen by David A. Adler	Adventure
	Henry and Mudge by Cynthia Rylant	Adventure
	Jigsaw Jones Mysteries by James Preller	Mystery
	Magic Tree House by Mary Pope Osborne	Adventure
	Marvin Redpost by Louis Sachar	Adventure
	Ricky Ricotta's Mighty Robots by Dav Pilkey	Science Fiction
	Scooby-Do Mysteries by James Golsey	Mystery
	Stink by Megan McDonald	Humor
	The Zack Files by Dan Greenburg	Fantasy
3	Abracadabra! by Peter Lerangis	Mystery
	The Adventures of the Bailey School Kids by Debbie Dadey	Adventure
	The Boxcar Children by Gertrude Chandler Warner	Mystery
	Captain Underpants by Dav Pilkey	Humor
	Geronimo Stilton by Scholastic Books	Adventure
	Hank the Cowdog by John R. Erickson	Fantasy
	Horrible Harry by Suzy Kline	Adventure
	Judy Moody by Megan McDonald	Humor
	The Magic School Bus Chapter Books by Joanna Cole	Informational
	Melvin Beederman, Superhero by Tony Abbott	Fantasy
	The Secrets of Droon by Tony Abbott	Fantasy
	Sports by Matt Christopher	Sports
	The Unicorn's Secret by Kathleen Duey	Fantasy
	The Zack Files by Dan Greenburg	Fantasy
4	Animal Ark by Ben M. Baglio	Animals
	The Babysitters Club by Ann M. Martin	Adventure
	Deltora Quest by Emily Rodda	Fantasy
	Dolphin Diaries by Ben M. Baglio	Animals
	Encyclopedia Brown by Donald J. Sobol	Mystery
	Goosebumps by R. L. Stine	Horror
	Guardians of Ga'hoole by Kathryn Lasky	Fantasy
	Island/Everest/Dive Series by Gordon Korman	Adventure
	Pyrates by Chris Archer	Adventure
	The Time Warp Trio by Jon Scieszka	Fantasy
5	The Amazing Days of Abby Hayes by Anne Mazer	Girls
	Animorphs by K. A. Applegate	Science Fiction
	The Black Stallion by Walter Farley	Animals
	Dinotopia by Peter David	Science Fiction
	From the Files of Madison Finn by Laura Dower	Girls
	Heartland by Lauren Brooke	Animals
	The Saddle Club by Bonnie Bryant	Animals
	Thoroughbred by Joanna Campbell	Animals

Expand Teachers' Expertise. Teachers continue to grow professionally during their careers (Allington, 2006): They join professional organizations, participate in professional book clubs, attend workshops and conferences, and find answers to questions that puzzle them through teacher-inquiry projects. Figure 4–8 outlines some ways that teachers stretch their knowledge and teaching expertise.

Collaborate With Literacy Coaches. Literacy coaches are experienced teachers with special expertise in working with struggling readers and writers who support teachers (Casey, 2006). They work alongside teachers in their classrooms, demonstrating instructional procedures and evaluation techniques, and they collaborate with teachers to design instruction to address students' needs. Toll (2005) explains that "literacy coaching is not about telling others what to do, but rather bringing out the best in others" (p. 6). Through their efforts, teachers are becoming more expert, and schools are becoming better learning environments.

FIGURE 4–8 ◆ *Ways to Develop Professional Knowledge and Expertise*

Professional Organizations

International Reading Association (IRA) (www.reading.org)

National Council of Teachers of English (NCTE) (www.ncte.org)

Teachers of English to Speakers of Other Languages (TESOL) (www.tesol.org)

Journals

Journal of Adolescent and Adult Literacy (IRA)

Reading Online (www.readingonline.org) (IRA)

The Reading Teacher (IRA)

Language Arts (NCTE)

Voices From the Middle (NCTE)

Essential Teacher (TESOL)

The Internet TESOL Journal (iteslj.org) (TESOL)

Professional Books

Teachers read books about research-based instructional strategies, current issues, and innovative practices published by IRA, NCTE, TESOL, Heinemann, Scholastic, Stenhouse, and other publishers.

Literacy Workshops and Conferences

Teachers attend local, state, and national conferences sponsored by IRA, NCTE, and TESOL to learn more about teaching reading and writing, and they also attend workshops sponsored by local sites affiliated with the National Writing Project (NWP).

Collaboration

Teachers at one grade level or in one discipline can participate in teacher book clubs, view videos about classroom practices, and discuss ways to improve teaching and differentiate instruction to meet the needs of their students.

Teacher-Inquiry Projects

Teachers conduct teacher research in their classrooms to solve literacy problems. For information about teacher inquiry, consult one of these books: *The Art of Classroom Inquiry: A Handbook for Teacher-Researchers* (Hubbard & Power, 2003), *The Power of Questions: A Guide to Teacher and Student Research* (Falk & Blumenreich, 2005), and *What Works? A Practical Guide for Teacher Research* (Chiseri-Strater & Sunstein, 2006).

National Writing Project

Teachers attend programs at local NWP sites and apply to participate at invitational summer institutes. To locate the nearest NWP site, check their website at www.nwp.org.

The quality of classroom instruction has a tremendous impact on how well students learn to read and write, and studies of exemplary teachers indicate that teaching expertise is the critical factor (Block, Oakar, & Hurt, 2002).

Interventions. Schools use intervention programs to address low-achieving students' reading and writing difficulties and accelerate their learning (Cooper, Chard, & Kiger, 2006). In elementary school settings, intervention programs are provided in addition to regular classroom instruction, and in middle school settings, they're used to replace regular instruction. The classroom teacher or a specially trained reading teacher diagnoses students' areas of difficulty and focuses instruction on these areas; using paraprofessionals isn't recommended because they aren't as effective as certified teachers (Allington, 2006). Interventions take various forms in the middle grades: They can be provided by adding a second lesson during the regular school day, substituting a comprehensive intervention program for students, offering extra instruction in an after-school program, as Mrs. Shasky did in the vignette at the beginning of the chapter, or holding extended-school-year programs during the summer. Figure 4–9 summarizes the recommendations for effective intervention programs.

One well-known intervention program is America's Choice Ramp-Up Literacy™; it's a yearlong, standards-based intervention program designed to boost the achievement of middle school students who read 2 or more years below grade level. The 90-minute daily program has these components:

◆ Explicit instruction
◆ Intensive writing
◆ Teacher read-alouds
◆ Independent reading

Ramp-Up Literacy helps teachers create a community of learners and promotes classroom practices that engage struggling readers, provides more instructional time, and uses differentiated instruction. Teachers learn to determine students' reading levels so they can match students with appropriate books and group students for instruction. Focused lessons on comprehension, vocabulary, and writing and working with students in small groups are key parts of the intervention program. Teachers use assessment tools to create individual profiles for students, tailor instruction to students' needs, and monitor their progress. Teachers also receive support through regular staff-development programs on how to differentiate instruction and accelerate learning. America's Choice cites its 10-year track record of improving student achievement and raising students' scores on high-stakes tests at schools in New York, Arkansas, Florida, and across the United States; however, Slavin, Cheung, Groff, and Lake (2008) didn't find any rigorous evaluation studies of Ramp-Up Literacy for their review of effective reading intervention programs.

Scholastic's READ 180® is another daily intervention program that provides differentiated instruction using instructional software, leveled trade books, and explicit instruction in reading, writing, vocabulary, and grammar skills. Technology and professional development are integral components. Technology resources include videos to build students' background knowledge before reading, audiobooks for shared reading, and interactive software for skills practice. Ongoing professional development provides teachers with background knowledge about how to intervene with struggling readers and instructional support to ensure that they use research-based teaching practices in the classroom. The 90-minute READ 180 program has three parts:

• Whole-class instruction in reading, writing, and vocabulary (20 minutes)

FIGURE 4–9 ◆ *High-Quality Interventions*

Scheduling
Interventions take place daily for 30–45 minutes, depending on students' instructional needs. Classroom teachers often provide the interventions as second reading lessons in the classroom or during after-school programs, but at other times, specially trained reading teachers provide the interventions.

Grouping
Teachers work with students individually or in very small groups; larger groups of students, even when they exhibit the same reading or writing problems, aren't as effective.

Reading Materials
Teachers match students to books at their instructional level for lessons and at their independent level for voluntary reading. The reading materials should engage students and provide some challenge without frustrating them.

Instruction
Teachers provide lessons that generally include rereading familiar books, reading new books, teaching reading strategies and skills, and writing activities. The lessons vary according to students' identified areas of difficulty.

Reading and Writing Practice
Teachers provide additional opportunities for students to spend time reading and writing to practice and apply what they're learning.

Assessment
Teachers monitor progress by observing students and collecting work samples. They also use diagnostic tests to document students' learning according to grade-level standards.

Professional Development
Teachers continue their professional development to improve teaching expertise, and they ensure that the aides and volunteers who work in their classroom are well trained.

Home–School Partnerships
Teachers keep parents informed about students' progress and involve them in supporting independent reading and writing at home.

- Small-group rotations where students divide into small groups for explicit instruction, independent and shared reading, and skills practice using interactive software (60 minutes)
- Whole-class wrap-up (10 minutes)

Assessment tools are included for assessing students' achievement, and teachers use the data to differentiate instruction. Scholastic touts the effectiveness of READ 180; in one study, for example, students tripled their gains in reading proficiency compared to students not enrolled in READ 180. In their evaluation of intervention programs, Slavin, Cheung, Groff, and Lake (2008) concluded that it is effective.

Response to Intervention (RTI) is another promising schoolwide initiative to identify struggling students quickly, promote effective classroom instruction, provide interventions, and increase the likelihood that students will be successful (Allington, 2009b; Mellard & Johnson, 2008). It involves three tiers:

Tier 1: Screening and Prevention. Teachers provide high-quality instruction that's supported by scientifically based research, screen students to identify those at risk for academic failure, and monitor their progress. If students don't make adequate progress toward meeting grade-level standards, they move to Tier 2.

Tier 2: Early Intervention. Trained reading teachers provide enhanced, individualized instruction targeting students' specific areas of difficulty. If the intervention is successful and students' reading problems are resolved, they return to Tier 1; if they make some progress but need additional instruction, they remain in Tier 2; and if they don't show improvement, they move to Tier 3, where the intensity of intervention increases.

Tier 3: Intensive Intervention. Special education teachers provide more-intensive intervention to individual students and small groups and more-frequent progress monitoring. They focus on remedying students' problem areas and teaching compensatory strategies.

This schoolwide instruction and assessment program incorporates data-driven decision making, and special education teachers are optimistic that it will be a better way to diagnose learning-disabled students (Bender & Shores, 2007).

Improving classroom instruction, diagnosing students' specific reading and writing difficulties, and implementing intensive intervention programs to remedy students' literacy problems are three important ways that teachers work more effectively with struggling students.

CHAPTER 4

Review

How Effective Teachers Differentiate Instruction

▶ Teachers differentiate instruction to meet the needs of all students, including those who struggle.

▶ Teachers understand that struggling readers have difficulties in fluency, vocabulary, and/or comprehension.

▶ Teachers understand that struggling writers lack knowledge about the qualities of good writing and the process that writers use.

▶ Teachers use a balanced approach to teach struggling students that incorporates explicit instruction, materials at students' reading levels, and more time for reading and writing.

▶ Teachers understand that interventions are additional instructional programs to remedy students' reading and writing difficulties.

PART 2

Powerful Teaching

Literacy instruction in the middle grades focuses on developing students' ability to comprehend and compose narrative, expository, and digital texts. Reading instruction expands students' academic vocabulary and promotes their comprehension. Writing instruction develops strategic writers. Teachers create a student-centered learning environment, develop a standards-based instructional program, differentiate instruction, and use assessment to inform instruction. Powerful teaching is balanced; it involves explicit instruction coupled with authentic application activities.

Explicit Instruction

Teachers use explicit instruction to teach reading and writing strategies and skills, often in minilessons. They follow these steps:

- Introduce the topic
- Provide information and examples
- Demonstrate how and when to use the topic
- Guide students as they practice what they're learning
- Monitor students' learning

Sometimes instruction is presented to the class; at other times, teachers adapt lessons and provide different instruction to small groups. Topics for instruction are chosen according to students' needs and grade-level literacy standards.

Authentic Application

Students apply what they're learning in meaningful ways through authentic activities. The word *authentic* means that readers and writers use real-life materials for genuine purposes. These *authentic* activities replicate those that people engage in outside of school:

- Reading and responding to real books
- Talking about novels in grand conversations
- Doing authentic writing using the writing process
- Sharing writing with classmates and other audiences
- Participating in collaborative real-world projects
- Pursuing individual projects on topics of special interest

Authentic application is engaging and relevant to students; it boosts their motivation and stimulates their continued interest in reading and writing.

WHAT'S AHEAD

The five chapters in Part 2 explain the components of literacy instruction in grades 4–8 and present research-based ways to extend students' reading and writing achievement:

Chapter 5: Eliminating Obstacles to Fluency

Chapter 6: Expanding Academic Vocabulary

Chapter 7: Promoting Comprehension: Reader Factors

Chapter 8: Promoting Comprehension: Text Factors

Chapter 9: Teaching Writing

These chapters explain how teachers provide powerful literacy instruction to ensure that all middle graders reach their potential, become effective literacy users, and are prepared to deal with more-challenging literacy demands of high school and beyond.

CHAPTER 5

Eliminating Obstacles to Fluency

Ms. Simmons Intervenes With Dysfluent Readers and Writers

Ms. Simmons is a reading teacher who works with students who aren't making adequate yearly progress. Usually she works in primary-grade classrooms, but at the request of the fifth- and sixth-grade teachers, she began working with their struggling readers. She began with three fifth graders and a sixth grader who were reading at the second-grade level; these students weren't fluent readers, and their insufficient knowledge of common words severely limited their reading achievement. During a 45-minute daily intervention, she taught high-frequency words, and the students generated sentences using the words that they wrote on whiteboards. She also conducted **guided reading** lessons using books at students' instructional level. After 8 weeks, the students still weren't fluent, but they'd reached the early third-grade level.

Seven additional fifth and sixth graders who read at the third-grade level joined the group, and Ms. Simmons expanded the intervention session to 60 minutes. She assessed the students to identify their strengths and weaknesses. She found that even though all 11 students read at approximately the same level, their strengths and weaknesses varied:

Word Identification. The students recognized between 91 and 147 of in the 300 high-frequency words; seven could sound out phonetically regular short- and long-vowel words, such as *chin, fly, stone,* and *soap,* but everyone had difficulty identifying one-syllable words with more-complex vowel patterns and multisyllabic words.

Reading Speed. Five students met the fluency threshold of reading aloud 100 words per minute; nonetheless, they read much slower than most fifth and sixth graders do. The remaining six students read from 75 to 92 words per minute.

Expressiveness. Most students read in a monotone, sometimes pointing at words as they read, but Jett, Darik, Dulce, and Andres read more expressively than the others.

Writing. The students were weaker writers than readers, and their writing was hard to decipher because of spelling, handwriting, and sentence structure problems. They wrote slowly and had difficulty thinking of ideas for writing and spelling high-frequency words.

Based on these results, Ms. Simmons designed an intervention program that included these activities:

- **Word wall** activities for reading and spelling high-frequency words to improve students' reading and spelling accuracy
- **Minilessons** on decoding one-syllable and longer words to improve students' ability to identify unfamiliar words
- **Guided reading** lessons with books at students' instructional levels to teach word identification, vocabulary, and comprehension
- **Sustained Silent Reading** of books at students' independent reading levels to develop their reading speed and motivation
- **Choral reading** of poems to emphasize chunking of words into phrases, reading speed, and expressive reading
- **Quickwriting** to develop spelling accuracy, writing speed, and writer's voice

Ms. Simmons's schedule for the fast-paced 60-minute intervention schedule is shown here.

Ms. Simmons's 60-Minute Intervention Schedule		
Time	**Activity**	**Description**
10 minutes	Word Wall	The 100 highest-frequency words are posted on the word wall, and 5 or 6 new words are added each week. Students practice reading and spelling the words.
15 minutes	Guided Reading/ Sustained Silent Reading	One group participates in a guided reading lesson while the other students do independent reading.
10 minutes	Minilesson	Ms. Simmons teaches minilessons on word-identification and spelling strategies, and students participate in hands-on activities.
15 minutes	Guided Reading/ Sustained Silent Reading	The second group participates in a guided reading lesson while the other students do independent reading.
10 minutes	Choral Reading/Writing	Students alternate doing choral reading and quickwrites.

Today, the students begin the intervention session at the word wall, which now displays 156 words. They spend 10 minutes practicing reading and spelling high-frequency words; Garon points at the words on the word wall and the group reads them in unison. They read the list twice, once from A to Z and the second time from Z back to A. Next, Paz passes out whiteboards for spelling practice. Ms. Simmons begins by calling out the words she introduced this week, and students write them, referring to the word wall, if necessary. They hold up their boards for Ms. Simmons to check.

Next, the students spend 15 minutes reading books. One group participates in **guided reading** with Ms. Simmons while the other group reads independently. She introduces J. R. Erickson's Hank the Cowdog series of chapter books to the guided reading group. Hank is the hardworking head of security on a west Texas ranch who barks up the sun and defends the ranch against coyotes and other marauders. She passes out copies of *The Original Adventures of Hank the Cowdog* (Erickson, 1998) and explains, "I know you're going to like this book. It's so funny. Hank is a cowdog and he's always in trouble. In this book, he's framed for murdering a chicken, and forced to leave the ranch. He's forced to become an outlaw, and things get even worse." They talk about cowboy stories and what *framed* and *outlaw* mean. The book's reading level is 3.5; it's the fourth book at this level that the group has read, but it's more challenging because it's longer—144 pages. The other books ranged from 96 to 120 pages in length. Ms. Simmons reads the first three pages of the first chapter aloud while the students follow along; then they finish reading it themselves.

While one group participates in guided reading, the other students do **Sustained Silent Reading** for 15 minutes. They reread books they've read during guided reading and read other books from popular paperback series written at second- and third-grade levels, including the following:

A to Z Mysteries by Ron Roy

Geronimo Stilton by Scholastic

Give Yourself Goosebumps by R. L. Stine

Time Warp Trio by Jon Scieszka

The Zack Files by Dan Greenburg

Ms. Simmons has a large collection of these series books in the classroom library, and the students pick the ones they want to read. They check that a book is suitable by reading a random page and holding up a finger for each word they don't recognize; if there are more than two words they don't know, the book is too difficult, so they choose a different one.

Ms. Simmons knows the importance of increasing students' reading volume, and she recognizes that these dysfluent students don't like to read because they've never been successful. To spur them on, she gives rewards. She bought them ice cream cones when they'd read 2 books and pizza to celebrate when they'd read 5 books. Each student received a book from a series he or she liked after reading 10 books, and another one after reading 15 books. Ms. Simmons plans to invite parents and siblings to an evening of reading to celebrate when students finish 20 books; she expects that they'll reach that point in 2 more weeks. In the spring, football players from a local college have agreed to visit the class to celebrate when they've read 25 books. They'll read books together and then go outside to toss a football around.

Today's 10-minute minilesson is on syllabication. The students are learning to break apart two-syllable words between the first and second consonants with words that end in *le*, such as *cattle* and *nimble*. Ms. Simmons reviews the syllabication rule and passes out cards with these words: *riddle, battle, puddle, little, sizzle, cuddle, puzzle, turtle, crumble, handle,* and *mumble*. The students break the words into syllables to read them and then place the cards in a pocket chart. They need lots of practice identifying the words, so they repeat the activity several times. Raymone and Deval read all of the words without a single error! Then they use magnetic letters to spell *middle, huddle, candle, crumble,* and *jumble*.

Next, the students are back to reading books. The second guided reading group is reading *The Get Rich Quick Club* (Gutman, 2006), the story of five kids who start a club to make lots of money fast. The 11-year-old narrator, Gina Tumolo, loves money and wants to become a millionaire before she turns 13. In this middle-grade satire, the kids cook up a scheme about aliens landing in their community to sell to a tabloid. The reading level of this 128-page book is 3.4. Today the students reread Chapter 5, "A Million-Dollar Idea," and Ms. Simmons briefly stands behind each student and listens as he or she reads softly to check students' reading. She notices that Jordynn is struggling more than the others. Afterward, they talk about the kids' scheme and make predictions about the likelihood of it succeeding. Dulce says, "I think it will work. At the grocery store, I see pictures of UFOs and aliens in all the magazines." Deval disagrees, "That stuff is fake. I think they'll get caught." The group is evenly split: Ayla, Darik, and Kat think the club members will be successful; the others don't. Chapter 6 is only four pages long, and the students read it before the group ends.

For the last 10 minutes of the session, students alternate choral reading and quick-writing. This month, Ms. Simmons selects poems for choral reading from Prelutsky's *A Pizza the Size of the Sun* (1996), and at the end of the month, students will take home a booklet with copies of the poems they've been practicing. They spend two or three sessions reading each poem using the **choral reading** procedure. They began with the title poem, and yesterday they were reading "Rat for Lunch!" for the second day. On the first day, Ms. Simmons read the entire poem aloud and talked about its meaning. Then they focused on reading it expressively. Yesterday, Ms. Simmons began by having the students repeat the chorus while she read the other stanzas. Next, she used echo reading for the students to practice the stanzas that she'd read. She divided the students into four groups, and each group practiced reading one stanza. Then the students came back together to read the poem as a class: Ms. Simmons read the chorus stanzas while the small groups of students took turns reading the stanzas they'd practiced. Tomorrow, they'll practice reading the poem again, and Ms. Simmons will tape-record their performance.

Today, the students are **quickwriting**. They write for 5 minutes, and Ms. Simmons's goal is for them to fill a half sheet of lined paper. She wants them to write 50 words to achieve a rate of 10 words per minute, write legibly, and spell most words correctly. She encourages them to check the spelling of words on the word wall. Students have begun looking in dictionaries to choose quickwriting topics. Each day, they suggest three topics and brainstorm words and phrases related to each one. Today's topics are *sand*, *circus*, and *teeth*. For *teeth*, they brainstorm these words: *tooth/teeth*, *toothbrush*, *decay*, *cavity/cavities*, *fillings*, *Crest toothpaste*, *dentist*, *check-up*, *smile*, and *twice a day*. Here is Kat's quickwrite about "teeth":

> *I used to have lots of cavitys and I did't brush my teeth ever. I got 9 fillings from the dentist. Now I say "brush your teeth to my little borther." I brush my teeth twice a day and I use Crest toothpaste. You sud see my smile!*

Kat wrote 48 words, and misspelled only 4! She's quickly approaching writing fluency and has learned to get ideas from the brainstormed words and refer to the word wall sometimes to spell high-frequency words correctly.

Today marks 8 weeks that the 11 fifth and sixth graders have participated in this intervention program, and Ms. Simmons plans to assess their reading and writing fluency next week. Although it's obvious that the students have become more-confident and engaged readers and writers, she wants to monitor their progress and adapt the intervention, if needed, to accelerate their achievement.

By the time they reach fourth grade, most students have become fluent readers and writers. They've moved from word-by-word reading into fluent reading; Allington (2009a) estimates, however, that 10–15% of young adolescents have difficulty recognizing words, and their reading achievement is slowed. In some classrooms, the problem is more widespread: More than half of the students read 2 or more years below grade level, and they have difficulty decoding words, reading at an appropriate speed, or reading expressively. At the same time they develop reading fluency, students usually become fluent writers. These students' writing flows easily, but others continue to struggle to get their ideas down on paper, form letters legibly, and spell common words.

It's crucial that teachers intervene to help students overcome these obstacles to reading and writing fluency because they must be able to focus their attention on meaning, not on decoding and spelling words. Researchers have found that fluent readers comprehend what they're reading better than less fluent readers (National Reading Panel, 2000). The same conclusion can be drawn about writers: Fluent writers are more successful in creating effective compositions than less fluent writers.

What Is Fluency?

Fluency is the ability to read and write effortlessly and efficiently. Too often, teachers focus on reading fluency, but both reading and writing fluency are essential for young adolescents' continued literacy development. Students who aren't fluent are slow and hesitant readers and writers; they devote most of their mental energy to decoding and spelling words, leaving few cognitive resources available for creating meaning.

Reading Fluency

Reading fluency is the ability to read quickly, accurately, and with expression, and to read fluently, students recognize most words automatically and identify unfamiliar words easily (Caldwell & Leslie, 2005). Pikulski and Chard (2005) explain that reading fluency is a bridge between decoding and comprehension. Fluent readers are better able to comprehend what they're reading because they automatically recognize most of the words and apply word-identification strategies to read unfamiliar words. Their reading is faster and more expressive (Kuhn & Rasinski, 2007). It involves these three components:

Accuracy. Accuracy is the ability to recognize familiar words automatically, without conscious thought, and to identify unfamiliar words almost as quickly. It's crucial that students know most of the words they're reading because when they have to stop to decode words in every sentence, their reading isn't fluent. The conventional wisdom is that students can read a text successfully when they know at least 95% of the words; that's 19 of every 20 words or 95 of every 100 words. Allington (2009a) challenges this notion, suggesting that students need to know 98 or 99% of the words to read a selection fluently; otherwise, they're stopping too often to figure out unfamiliar words, and this places a severe burden on readers.

Reading Speed. To read fluently, students must orally read at least 100 words per minute. Most readers reach this speed by fourth grade, and their reading rate continues to grow. Eighth graders read approximately 200 words per minute, and many adults read 250 words per minute or more. Of course, students' reading speed varies, depending on the difficulty of the text being read and their purpose, but excessively slow oral reading is typical of dysfluent readers.

Prosody. The ability to read sentences expressively, with appropriate phrasing and intonation, is called *prosody*. Dowhower (1991) describes prosody as "the ability to read in expressive rhythmic and melodic patterns" (p. 166). Beginning readers read word by word with little or no expression, but with experience, they chunk words into phrases, attend to punctuation, and apply appropriate syntactic emphases. Once students become fluent readers, their oral reading approximates speech.

Too often, reading quickly is equated with fluency, and some assessment tools use speed as the only measure of fluency, but accurately identifying words and reading expressively are also critical components.

Dysfluent Readers. Young adolescents who aren't fluent readers are dysfluent. They read hesitantly and without expression. They often try to sound out phonetically irregular words, such as *what* and *their*, and they complain that what they're reading doesn't make sense. Figure 5–1 summarizes the characteristics of dysfluent readers.

FIGURE 5–1 ◆ *Characteristics of Dysfluent Readers and Writers*

Mode	Component	Characteristics
Reading	Accuracy	• Students don't recognize many high-frequency words. • Students guess at words based on the beginning sound. • Students don't break multisyllabic words into syllables to decode them. • Students don't peel off affixes to decode multisyllabic words. • Students don't remember a word the second or third time it's used.
	Speed	• Students point at words as they read. • Students repeat words and phrases. • Students read slowly or too quickly.
	Prosody	• Students read in a word-by-word manner. • Students ignore punctuation marks. • Students read without expression.
	Other	• Students misbehave to avoid reading.
Writing	Accuracy	• Students misspell many words, including high-frequency ones. • Students leave out words.
	Speed and Legibility	• Students write slowly. • Students write laboriously, shaking their arms, rubbing their fingers, or complaining of pain. • Students write illegibly. • Students lack keyboarding skills to word process quickly.
	Voice	• Students don't insert punctuation marks. • Students don't make their writing distinctive.
	Other	• Students write very little. • Students misbehave to avoid writing.

Many struggling readers don't read fluently, and their labored reading affects their comprehension. Allington (2006) examined the research about dysfluent readers and found that there's no single common problem; some readers have difficulty decoding words, but others read very slowly or in a monotone, ignoring phrasing and punctuation cues. Because struggling readers exhibit different fluency problems, it's essential to diagnose students and to plan instruction that's tailored to their instructional needs.

Diagnosing Dysfluent Readers. By the time students reach fourth grade, they should be fluent readers. Teachers identify struggling readers, students whose instructional reading levels are more than a year below their grade-level placement, and screen them for fluency problems. They begin by listening to the struggling readers read aloud in instructional-level texts and considering these questions:

- Do students read most words automatically, or do they stop to decode many common words?
- Are students able to identify most grade-level-appropriate multisyllabic words?
- Do students read quickly enough to understand what they're reading, or do they read too slowly or too fast?
- Do students chunk words into phrases when they're reading, or do they read word by word?
- Do students read grade-level texts expressively, or do they read in a monotone?

Any of the fluency components—accuracy, reading speed, or prosody—can pose obstacles for dysfluent readers, and these questions help teachers quickly identify struggling readers with fluency problems.

If their observation suggests that students have difficulty with any of these components, teachers conduct additional testing to pinpoint fluency problems:

Accuracy. Teachers assess students' knowledge of high-frequency words and their ability to identify unfamiliar words. First, students read a list of high-frequency words, and teachers mark the words they read correctly. Second, students read a list of words taken from instructional-level texts, and teachers check whether they use their knowledge of phonics, analogies, syllabication, and root words and affixes to identify them.

Reading Speed. Teachers assess students' reading speed by timing them as they read an instructional-level passage aloud and determining how many words they read per minute. To be considered fluent, students need to read at least 100 words per minute.

Prosody. The best way to gauge prosody is to listen to students read aloud. Teachers choose excerpts from both familiar and unfamiliar instructional-level texts for students to read. As they listen, teachers judge whether students read with appropriate expression.

Middle-grade teachers generally use informal assessment tools to diagnose struggling students' fluency problems, but they can also use classroom tests, especially the graded word lists and passages in informal reading inventories to analyze students' fluency according to grade-level expectations. The Assessment Tools feature on the next page lists the tests that teachers use to evaluate reading fluency.

Assessment Tools

Reading Fluency

Teachers use these assessment tools as well as informal observation and teacher-made word lists to diagnose struggling readers' accuracy, reading speed, and prosody problems:

◆ **The Names Test: A Quick Assessment of Decoding Ability** (Cunningham, 1990; Duffelmeyer et al., 1994; Mather, Sammons, & Schwartz, 2006)

The Names Test measures young adolescents' ability to decode phonetically regular words. The test is a list of names that students read aloud. To plan for instruction, teachers record students' errors and then analyze them to determine which phonics concepts students know and which they don't. This free assessment is available online.

◆ **Fluency Checks** (Johns & Berglund, 2006)

Teachers use these graded passages to assess students' fluent reading. They listen to students read aloud a narrative or expository passage for one minute and mark errors on a scoring sheet. They also ask comprehension questions. Afterward, teachers calculate students' reading speed and score it against grade-level standards, and they rate their prosody (phrasing, expression, and attention to punctuation marks).

◆ **Developmental Reading Assessment (2nd ed.)(DRA2)** (Beaver & Carter, 2005)

The DRA2 kit for grades 4–8 contains a collection of leveled books that teachers use to assess students' reading fluency. Students read aloud books at their instructional levels while teachers take running records to examine their accuracy, speed, and prosody.

◆ **Informal Reading Inventories (IRIs)**

Teachers listen to students read aloud grade-level passages in an IRI and mark accuracy and prosody errors on scoring sheets. Accuracy errors include substituted, mispronounced, and skipped words; prosody errors include pauses, phrasing, and expressiveness. In addition, teachers use a stopwatch to record the time it takes students to read the passage and then calculate their reading rate (words read correctly per minute). They also examine students' accuracy errors to determine their knowledge of high-frequency words and their use of word-identification strategies. IRIs are recommended for students who read at the second-grade level or higher; running records provide more useful information for students reading below second-grade level.

◆ **Running Records** (Clay, 2007)

Teachers use running records to examine students' oral reading of authentic texts. Although they're more commonly used with children in the primary grades, running records can be used with older dysfluent readers, too (Lapp & Flood, 2003). As students read a passage orally, teachers time their reading, mark errors on a copy of the text, and evaluate their prosody. Afterward, students retell what they've read to provide a measure of their comprehension.

◆ **3-Minute Reading Assessments** (Rasinski & Padak, 2005a, 2005b)

This quick tool measures students' oral reading fluency using 200- to 400-word passages. Students read the passage aloud and teachers time the reading and mark uncorrected word-identification errors; then students retell what they've read. Two versions of the 3-Minute Reading Assessments are available from Scholastic; one is for grades 1–4 and the other is for grades 5–8.

Teachers use these tests to diagnose struggling readers' fluency problems and regularly monitor students' developing accuracy, reading speed, and prosody until they become fluent.

Writing Fluency

Fluent writers spell words automatically and write quickly so that they can focus on developing their ideas. Their writing seems to flow effortlessly, and it's distinctive. Fluent writing sounds like conversation—it has "voice." Fluency is as crucial for writers as it is for readers, and the components are similar:

Accuracy. Fluent writers write most words automatically, without having to stop to think about how to spell them. Students must know how to spell the most common words, and for other words, they must use strategies to spell words so they can reread them; otherwise, they get so bogged down in spelling a word that they forget the sentence they're writing or the one that comes next.

Writing Speed. Speed is as important to writers as it is to readers. Students need to write quickly to keep pace with their thinking. Researchers have examined the number of words students write per minute and compared their speed to the quality of their compositions, and they've concluded that to be fluent, writers need to write at least 10 words per minute (Graham, Weintraub, & Berninger, 1998). The average fourth grader writes 10 words per minute, and the average eighth grader writes 13.5 words per minute. Girls usually do more writing than boys, so it isn't surprising that they write one or two more words per minute than boys do.

Legibility. Legibility is a concern because students can't sacrifice neatness for speed: It doesn't do any good to write quickly if students can't decipher what they've written. Girls usually prefer cursive handwriting, and boys use the manuscript form more often, but most students use a combination of manuscript and cursive handwriting forms. Neither handwriting form is faster; students gain speed through experience. Word processing can be a faster and more legible alternative to handwriting, but students need strong keyboarding skills to write fluently. Otherwise, they have to stop to hunt for letter keys.

Voice. Writers develop distinctive voices that reflect their individuality (Spandel, 2009). Voice, which is similar to prosody, is the tone or emotional feeling of a piece of writing. Writers develop their voices through the words they choose and how they string words together into phrases and sentences. Each student's voice is unique, and teachers can usually identify which student wrote a composition according to its voice, just as many of us can identify books written by our favorite authors by their voice.

The characteristics of dysfluent writers are also summarized in Figure 5–1.

Diagnosing Dysfluent Writers. It's easy to spot dysfluent writers in the classroom because these students write slowly and accomplish very little. They often complain that their hands and arms hurt. Their slow, laborious handwriting interferes with their expression of ideas, and they may not be able to reread what they've written or describe what they're planning to write next. Teachers assess writing fluency as they watch students write and examine their compositions. They consider these questions:

- Do students spell most words automatically, or do they stop to sound out the spellings of many words?
- Do students write quickly enough to complete the assignment, or do they write slowly or try to avoid writing?
- Is students' writing legible?
- Do students write easily or laboriously, complaining that their hands hurt?

These questions help teachers quickly identify students who may not be fluent writers.

If their observation suggests that students are struggling writers, teachers conduct additional testing to diagnose fluency problems:

Accuracy. Teachers assess struggling writers' ability to spell high-frequency words and use strategies to spell other words with spelling tests or by examining their writing samples. Fluent writers spell most words correctly, so it's essential that students know how to spell high-frequency words automatically and efficiently figure out the spelling of most other words they write.

Speed and Legibility. Teachers time students as they write a composition, at least one or two paragraphs in length, to assess their writing speed. To be considered fluent, young adolescents should write at least 10 words per minute. Teachers also carefully observe students as they write because their behavior may indicate handwriting problems.

Voice. Teachers reread several compositions students have written to evaluate their unique style. There aren't standards to use in assessing voice, so teachers often compare one student's writing to peers' to rate its voice as comparable or above or below average.

Commercial tests aren't available to assess students' writing fluency, but these informal assessments are useful in diagnosing students who have writing fluency problems.

Obstacles to Fluency

Students who struggle with fluency may have a single problem, such as slow reading speed or delayed spelling development, or they may face numerous obstacles in both reading and writing. In the upcoming sections of this chapter, you'll read more about each obstacle and how to intervene to help students become more-fluent readers, so they can comprehend what they're reading, and more-fluent writers, so they can focus on creating meaning as they write. Providing targeted instruction is often necessary to help students overcome those obstacles; however, effective interventions require more than "fix-it" instruction. Curtis (2004) and other researchers recommend these components for the most effective interventions:

- Providing explicit instruction on diagnosed fluency problems
- Increasing the time for students to read books at their independent level
- Modeling fluent reading and writing
- Clarifying the connections between reading fluency and comprehension and between writing fluency and effective compositions so that students understand the importance of what they're learning
- Expanding opportunities for writing

"Fix-it" intervention programs for older students usually aren't successful because they target one area and ignore the larger problem. Ivey (2008) explains that not being able to identify multisyllabic words, for example, may only be a symptom of a student's limited reading experience, and being a slow writer may similarly be a symptom of a student's limited writing experience.

The amount of reading and writing that students do makes a critical difference. Guthrie (2004) found that capable readers spend 500% more time reading than struggling readers do, and Allington (2009a) warns that "older struggling readers probably will never become fluent and proficient readers unless teachers design interventions that

Check the Compendium of Instructional Procedures, which follows Chapter 12, for more information on the highlighted terms.

dramatically increase the volume of reading that they do" (p. 99). Teachers can increase students' independent reading time in several ways, including reading workshop, **Sustained Silent Reading**, or a 15- or 20-minute reading period during interventions, as Ms. Simmons did in the vignette. Two ways that teachers can increase students' writing is through writing workshop and a 15- or 20-minute writing period during interventions, as Ms. Simmons did.

Reading fluency typically precedes writing fluency, but the two are clearly linked. The more reading students do, the sooner they'll reach writing fluency, and the more writing students do, the sooner they'll achieve reading fluency.

OBSTACLE 1: Accurate Reading and Writing

Fluent readers recognize and spell most high-frequency words, such as *what* and *thought*, automatically, and they've learned word-identification and spelling strategies for reading and writing longer, multisyllabic words. In contrast, many dysfluent students struggle to read and write common words. This obstacle to fluent reading and writing is the most serious one because students can't develop the other components until they're able to read and write words accurately. In addition, all middle-grade students are refining their knowledge about syllabication and root words, so teachers include lessons on these topics as part of vocabulary instruction.

High-Frequency Words

The most common words that students read and write are called *high-frequency words*. There have been numerous attempts to identify these words and to calculate their frequency in reading materials. The 100 most common words account for half of the words people read and write, and the 300 high-frequency words account for nearly three quarters of the words we use (Eldredge, 2005). Figure 5–2 presents a list of 300 high-frequency words; the 100 most common ones are marked with an asterisk. Most students learn the 100 highest-frequency words in first grade and the rest of the words during second and third grades, but if dysfluent readers and writers don't know these words, it's essential that they learn them now.

Many high-frequency words are tough to learn because they can't be easily decoded (Cunningham, 2008): Try sounding out the words *to*, *what*, and *could* and you'll see how difficult they are. A further complication is that many of these words are function words, so they don't carry much meaning. It's easier to learn to recognize *whale* than *what*, because *whale* conjures up the image of the huge aquatic mammal, but *what* is abstract; however, *what* is used much more frequently, and students must learn to read and write it.

How to Intervene

Teachers use explicit instruction to teach students to read and write the unfamiliar words on the list of 300 high-frequency words. Even though they're listed alphabetically in Figure 5–2, they shouldn't be taught in that order; instead, teachers choose words that students are using but are confusing or words they can connect with books students are reading. The goal is for students to recognize the words automatically when they're reading and to write without having to stop and think about how to spell them.

FIGURE 5–2 ◆ The 300 High-Frequency Words

*a	children	great	looking	ran	through
*about	city	green	made	read	*time
*after	come	grow	make	red	*to
again	*could	*had	*man	ride	toad
*all	couldn't	hand	many	right	together
along	cried	happy	may	road	told
always	dad	has	maybe	room	*too
*am	dark	hat	*me	run	took
*an	*day	*have	mom	*said	top
*and	*did	*he	more	sat	tree
animals	*didn't	head	morning	*saw	truck
another	*do	hear	*mother	say	try
any	does	heard	mouse	*school	*two
*are	dog	help	Mr.	sea	under
*around	*don't	hen	Mrs.	*see	until
*as	door	*her	much	*she	*up
asked	*down	here	must	show	*us
*at	each	hill	*my	sister	*very
ate	eat	*him	name	sky	wait
away	end	*his	need	sleep	walk
baby	even	*home	never	small	walked
*back	ever	*house	new	*so	want
bad	every	*how	next	*some	wanted
ball	everyone	*I	nice	something	*was
*be	eyes	I'll	night	soon	water
bear	far	I'm	*no	started	way
*because	fast	*if	*not	stay	*we
bed	father	*in	nothing	still	*well
been	find	inside	*now	stop	*went
before	fine	*into	*of	stories	*were
began	first	*is	off	story	*what
behind	fish	*it	oh	sun	*when
best	fly	it's	old	take	where
better	*for	its	*on	tell	while
big	found	jump	once	than	*who
bird	fox	jumped	*one	*that	why
birds	friend	*just	only	that's	*will
blue	friends	keep	*or	*the	wind
book	frog	king	other	their	witch
books	*from	*know	*our	*them	*with
box	fun	last	*out	*then	wizard
boy	garden	left	*over	*there	woman
brown	gave	let	*people	these	words
*but	*get	let's	picture	*they	work
*by	girl	*like	pig	thing	*would
called	give	*little	place	*things	write
*came	go	live	play	*think	yes
*can	going	long	pulled	*this	*you
can't	good	look	*put	thought	*your
cat	*got	looked	rabbit	three	you're

*The first 100 most frequently used words.

From *Teach Decoding: How and Why* (2nd ed., pp. 119–120), by J. L. Eldredge,
© 2005. Adapted by permission of Prentice Hall, Inc., Upper Saddle River, NJ.

Each week, teachers introduce approximately five words, and they involve students in these activities each day to practice reading and writing the words:

- Students locate examples of the words in books they're reading.
- Students practice reading flash cards with the words to partners.
- Students do choral reading of poems and other short texts containing the words.
- Students play games, such as Concentration, using the words.
- Students write the words and sentences they compose with the words on whiteboards.
- Students spell the words with letter cards or magnetic letters.
- Students write the words in interactive writing activities.

These activities provide the practice that's necessary for students to learn to recognize and spell high-frequency words automatically.

Teachers create word walls with the high-frequency words that they post in the classroom when most students are still learning them, or they make individual word lists for older dysfluent students. They type up a list of words in alphabetical order and make copies to cut into bookmarks, to glue on a file folder, or to create personal dictionaries. Students practice reading the words on the word wall or refer to it when they're writing so that they can spell the words accurately and quickly. Teachers also use word walls for practice activities. For example, teachers play word games where they ask students to identify the two-syllable word on the word wall that means the opposite of "in front" (*behind*) and write it on a whiteboard. Or, they have students take "mock" spelling tests where they spell as many of the high-frequency words as they can, but they're allowed to check the word wall, if needed (Allington, 2009a).

Students also create word banks of high-frequency words that they've learned to read. When teachers introduce new words, they distribute small word cards and students practice reading them, often adding a checkmark on the back of the card each time they read the word correctly. Once they can consistently identify the word, students add it to their word banks. Then they continue to practice reading the words and refer to them, if necessary, when they're writing. Students' confidence increases as their bank of word cards grows to 20, 50, or 100 word or more.

Targeted instruction on high-frequency words is only part of an effective intervention. It's equally important to increase the amount of time students are reading and writing. They need to spend at least 15 minutes reading books at their independent reading level and another 15 minutes quickwriting, writing in reading logs and other journals, and doing other writing activities every day. Authentic reading and writing activities are essential for building students' store of high-frequency words.

How to Monitor Progress. Teachers monitor students' learning to read and write high-frequency words by observing them as they participate in literacy activities and through these assessment procedures:

- Teachers listen as students read aloud texts containing the words.
- Teachers have students read aloud the words written on flash cards.
- Teachers examine students' writing to check that the words are spelled correctly.
- Teachers have students use magnetic letters to spell the words.
- Teachers have students write the words on whiteboards.

These informal procedures are easy for teachers to include in small-group lessons.

Word-Identification Strategies

Students use word-identification strategies to read unfamiliar words. Struggling readers often depend on phonics to sound out unfamiliar words, but they need to develop all four strategies to identify unfamiliar words:

◆ Phonic analysis
◆ Analogies
◆ Syllabic analysis
◆ Morphemic analysis

Be Strategic!

Word-Identification Strategies

Students use these strategies to pronounce unfamiliar words when they're reading:

▶ Use phonic analysis
▶ Decode by analogy
▶ Divide into syllables
▶ Apply morphemic analysis

Students' choice of strategy depends on their knowledge about words and the complexity of the unfamiliar word.

Writers use similar strategies to spell words. As with reading, struggling writers depend on phonics to spell parts of words, but they need to learn more-sophisticated strategies to spell academic vocabulary words.

Phonic Analysis. Students use what they've learned about phoneme–grapheme correspondences, phonics rules, and vowel patterns to decode words such as *peach, spring, blaze,* and *chin.* Even though English is an imperfect phonetic language, phonic analysis is a very useful strategy because almost every word has some phonetically regular parts. Researchers report that the biggest difference between students who identify words effectively and those who don't is whether they notice all or almost all the letters in a word and analyze the letter sequences (Stanovich, 1992). Struggling readers often try to decode a word by guessing at it based on the beginning sound. As you might imagine, their guesses are usually wrong; sometimes they don't even make sense in the sentence.

Figure 5–3 presents a review of phonics concepts that students need to know to use phonic analysis effectively. Most students who have difficulty identifying one-syllable words struggle with vowels, especially vowel digraphs, long-vowel patterns, and diphthongs.

Decoding by Analogy. Students identify some words by associating them with words they already know; this strategy is known as *decoding by analogy* (Cunningham, 2008). When readers come to *fright,* for example, they might notice *-ight,* think of the word *light,* and decode the word by analogy. Students use analogies to figure out the spelling of unfamiliar words, too; they might use the familiar word *game* to help them spell *frame,* for example. This strategy accounts for students' common misspelling of *they* as *thay,* because *they* rhymes with *day* and *say.*

Students learn to decode by analogy when they read and write "word families" using familiar phonograms, such as *-at, -ell, -ice, -own,* and *-unk.* They must be familiar with consonant blends and digraphs and be able to manipulate sounds to apply this strategy. Using *-ill,* for example, students can read and spell 15 words: *bill, chill, fill, gill, grill, hill, kill, mill, pill, quill, shrill, spill, still, thrill,* and *will.* They can add affixes to create even more words (*hills, miller, chilly, killers, refilled, illness, grilling*) and to read and write longer words (*hilltop, brilliant, pillow, killjoy, vanilla*).

Syllabic Analysis. Readers divide longer words, such as *biodegradable, admonition,* and *unforgettable,* into syllables to identify them. Once a word is divided into syllables, it's easier to decode. Identifying syllable boundaries is important, because these affect the vowel sound's pronunciation. For example, compare the vowel sound in the first syllable of *cabin* and *cable.* In *cabin,* the syllable boundary comes after *b,* but in *cable,* it's

FIGURE 5–3 ◆ *Phonics Concepts*

Phonics explains the relationships between phonemes (sounds) and graphemes (letters). The 44 phonemes in English are represented by the 26 letters. The alphabetic principle suggests a one-to-one correspondence between phonemes and graphemes, with each sound represented consistently by a letter, but English isn't a perfect phonetic language: There are more than 500 ways to spell the 44 phonemes using single letters or combinations of letters.

Consonants

The consonants are *b, c, d, f, g, h, j, k, l, m, n, p, q, r, s, t, v, w, x, y,* and *z*. Most represent one sound consistently, but there are exceptions:

- *C* doesn't represent a unique sound: When followed by *a, o,* or *u*, it's pronounced /k/ (*cat*), and when followed by *e, i,* or *y*, it's pronounced /s/ (*city*).
- *G* represents two sounds: It's usually pronounced /g/ (*goat*), but when followed by *e, i,* or *y*, it's pronounced /j/ (*giant*).
- *X* is pronounced according to its location in a word: At the beginning, it's often pronounced /z/ (*xylophone*) or as its letter name (*x-ray*), and at the end, it's pronounced /ks/ (*box*).
- *W* and *y* can be consonants or vowels: They're consonants at the beginning of a word or syllable (*wind, yard*), but in the middle or at the end, they're vowels (*saw, flown, day*).

Blends and digraphs are consonant combinations. Blends occur when two or three consonants appear next to each other and their individual sounds are blended together (*grass, belt*). Consonant digraphs are two-letter combinations standing for single sounds that aren't represented by either letter: *ch* (*chair*), *sh* (*wish*), *th* (*mother*), *wh* (*whale*), *gh* (*laugh*), and *ph* (*photo*).

Vowels

Five letters—*a, e, i, o,* and *u*—are always vowels, and *w* and *y* are vowels in the middle or at the end of syllables and words. Vowels represent different sounds; for example, consider the sounds *e* represents in these words: *egg, feet, she, her, pear, eagle, sew, toe, eight, fuel, towel*. These are the most important vowel concepts:

Short Vowels. Short vowels represent these sounds: /ă/ *cat*, /ĕ/ *bed*, /ĭ/ *in*, /ŏ/ *hot*, and /ŭ/ *cup*. They're marked with a curved line symbol called a *breve*. Common short-vowel patterns are CVC (*pet, black*) and VC (*up*); C stands for *consonant* and V for *vowel*.

Long Vowels. Long vowels are pronounced using their letter names: /ā/ *say*, /ē/ *feet*, /ī/ *ice*, /ō/ *snow*, and /ū/ *rule*. They're marked with a straight line symbol called a *macron*. Long vowel sounds are usually spelled with two vowels, except when the long vowel sound is at the end of a word or syllable (*go, hotel*). When *y* is by itself at the end of a word, it's pronounced as long *e* or *i*, depending on the word's length (*cry, happy*). Common long-vowel patterns are CVCe (*smile*), VCe (*ate*), CVVC (*soap*) CVV (*day*), and CV (*no*).

***r*-Controlled Vowels.** Vowels followed by *r* are known as *r-controlled vowels* because the *r* influences the vowel sound (*car, hair, very, wear, birth, work, fourth, cure*). They're neither short nor long, and words with the same vowel sequence are often pronounced differently (*bear, fear, heart, pearl*).

Vowel Digraphs. Combinations of vowels representing a single sound are *vowel digraphs*: *ai* (*snail*), *au* (*laugh, caught*), *aw* (*saw*), *ea* (*peach*), *oa* (*coat*), *oo* (*cook, moon*), *ou* (*through*), and *ow* (*snow*).

Diphthongs. Vowel combinations where the sounds glide from one to another are *diphthongs*. Vowel combinations *oi* and *oy* (*soil, toy*) are always diphthongs, but other combinations, such as *ou* (*house*) and *ow* (*now*), are diphthongs when they represent a glided sound.

Schwa Sound. The vowel sound in an unaccented syllable of a multisyllabic word is a *schwa*; the sound is pronounced "uh" (*about, circus*). It's indicated in dictionaries with ə.

Students apply these phonics concepts when they use phonic analysis to decode unfamiliar words.

before *b*. Readers can predict that the *a* in *cabin* is short because the syllable follows the CVC pattern, and that the *a* in *cable* is long because the syllable follows the CV pattern.

The most basic rule about syllabication is that there's one vowel sound in each syllable. Consider the words *bit* and *bite*. *Bit* is a one-syllable word because there's one vowel letter representing one vowel sound. *Bite* is a one-syllable word, too, because even though there are two vowels, they represent one vowel sound. *Magic* and *curfew* are two-syllable words; there's one vowel letter and sound in each syllable in *magic*, but in the second syllable of *curfew*, the vowel letters *ew* represent a single vowel sound. Let's try a longer word: How many syllables are in *inconvenience*? There are six vowel letters representing four sounds in four syllables.

Syllabication rules teach students how to divide words into syllables. Five useful rules are presented in Figure 5–4. The first rule is the easiest one; examples include *cof-fee* and *jour-ney*. The second rule deals with words where three consonants appear together in a word, such as *com-plain*: The word is divided between *m* and *p* to preserve the *pl* blend. The third and fourth rules involve the VCV pattern. Usually the syllable boundary comes after the first vowel, as in *bo-nus* and *ca-jole*; however, the division comes after the consonant in *cour-age* because dividing the word *cou-rage* doesn't produce a recognizable word. The syllable boundary comes after the consonant in *without*, too, but this compound word has easily recognizable word parts. According to the fifth rule, words such as *qui-et* and *po-et* are divided between the two vowels because the vowels don't represent a vowel digraph or diphthong.

FIGURE 5–4 ◆ *Syllabication Rules*	
Rules	**Examples**
When two consonants come between two vowels in a word, divide syllables between the consonants.	*cof-fee* *bor-der* *plas-tic* *jour-ney*
When there are more than two consonants together in a word, divide the syllables keeping the blends together.	*em-ploy* *mon-ster* *en-trance* *bank-rupt*
When there is one consonant between two vowels in a word, divide the syllables after the first vowel.	*ca-jole* *bo-nus* *plu-ral* *gla-cier*
If following the previous rule doesn't make a recognizable word, divide the syllables after the consonant that comes between the vowels.	*doz-en* *ech-o* *meth-od* *cour-age*
When there are two vowels together that don't represent a long vowel sound or a diphthong, divide the syllables between the vowels.	*cli-ent* *po-em* *cha-os* *li-on* *qui-et*

Morphemic Analysis. Students apply their knowledge of affixes and root words to read and spell multisyllabic words such as *hemisphere, lackluster, pseudonym, antiseptic,* and *vegetarian.* During the middle grades, teachers teach grade-level, struggling, and advanced students about morphemic analysis as part of vocabulary instruction because it expands their ability to pronounce and spell new words and understand their meaning. Students learn about prefixes and suffixes and how they change the meaning of words (*responsible–irresponsible, import–export, marine–submarine*). Once students learn that the word *immortal* means "cannot die" and that the prefix *im-* means "not" and the root *mort* means "death," students can access other words, including *immobilize, immature, mortality,* and *mortician.* They also learn to identify English, Latin, and Greek root words and their related forms; for example, consider these words from three languages that are related to the English word *see: sightseeing* (E), *television* (L), and *horoscope* (Gr). The minilesson on the next page shows how Mr. Morales teaches his sixth graders about morphemic analysis as part of a thematic unit on ancient civilizations. To read more about root words and affixes, turn to Chapter 6, Expanding Academic Vocabulary.

How to Intervene

Teachers include these components in their intervention programs to develop students' ability to read and spell words:

- Develop students' background knowledge and introduce new vocabulary words before reading
- Teach word-identification strategies
- Provide more time for reading and writing practice

These components help dysfluent readers and writers develop automaticity.

Some middle-grade students continue to struggle to decode words. Too often, struggling readers simply guess at words based on the first letter, but their guesses don't make sense when they lack adequate background knowledge. For example, if you were reading a passage about Abraham Lincoln and didn't know a five-letter word beginning with a capital *C* and followed by the capitalized word *War,* would you have any difficulty identifying the word *Civil?* A surprising number of young adolescents would. It's essential that teachers build students' background knowledge and introduce new vocabulary words before reading so that struggling readers will have additional sources of information to apply while they're reading.

Students need to learn strategies for identifying unfamiliar words. Teachers use minilessons to teach phonic analysis, decoding by analogy, syllabic analysis, and morphemic analysis using words that students are attempting to read and write. Curtis (2004) recommends focusing on spelling rather than on decoding because older students are often embarrassed that they can't identify words effectively. For example, when a student spells *lake* as *lack* or *jungle* as *jungul,* teachers have opportunities to review phonics and spelling concepts in a meaningful way.

Dysfluent students need more time for reading books at their independent reading level and for writing on topics that interest them. Even though teachers often think that additional instruction, and phonics instruction in particular, will solve students' reading problems, researchers have concluded that older struggling students rarely benefit from it (Ivey & Baker, 2004; National Reading Panel, 2000). Instead, lots of reading and writing practice is more important in developing students' ability to identify and spell words without conscious effort, but struggling students who don't do as much reading and writing lack the necessary experience.

TOPIC: *Using Morphemic Analysis to Identify Words*
GRADE: *Sixth Grade*
TIME: *Three 30-minute periods*

As part of a thematic unit on ancient civilizations, Mr. Morales introduces the concepts *democracy, monarchy, oligarchy,* and *theocracy* and adds the words to the word wall; however, he notices that many of his sixth graders have difficulty pronouncing the words and remembering what they mean even though they've read about them in the social studies textbook.

❶ Introduce the Topic

Mr. Morales looks over the ancient civilizations word wall and reads aloud these words: *democracy, monarchy, oligarchy,* and *theocracy.* Marcos volunteers that he thinks the words have something to do with kings or rulers, but he's not sure.

❷ Share Examples

The teacher writes the words on the chalkboard, dividing them into syllables so that the sixth graders can pronounce them more easily. The students practice saying the words several times, but they're still puzzled about their meanings.

❸ Provide Information

Mr. Morales explains that he can help them figure out the meaning of the words. "The words are Greek," he says, "and they have two word parts. If you know the meaning of the word parts, you'll be able to figure out the meaning of the words." He writes the four words and breaks them into word parts this way:

democracy = demo + cracy *monarchy = mono + archy*
oligarchy = olig + archy *theocracy = theo + cracy*

Then he explains that Marcos was right—the words have to do with kings and rulers: They describe different kinds of government. *Cracy* means *government* and *archy* means *leader.* The first word part tells more about the kind of government; one of them means *gods,* and the others mean *one, people,* and *few.* The students work in small groups to figure out that *democracy* means government by the people, *monarchy* means one leader, *oligarchy* means rule by a few leaders, and *theocracy* means government by the gods.

❹ Guide Practice

The next day, Mr. Morales divides the class into four groups, and each group makes a poster to describe one of the four types of government. On each poster, students write the word, the two Greek word parts, and a definition. They also create an illustration based on what they've learned about this type of government. Afterward, students share their posters with the class and display them in the classroom.

❺ Assess Learning

On the third day, Mr. Morales passes out a list of six sentences about the different types of government taken from the social studies textbook and asks students to identify the type. He encourages the sixth graders to refer to the posters the class made as they complete the assignment. Afterward, he reviews their papers to determine which students can use the words correctly to identify the four types of government.

How to Monitor Progress

Teachers monitor students' progress by listening to them read aloud. As they listen, teachers notice the word-identification strategies students use effectively to identify unfamiliar words and examine the words they can't decode. Are these words high-frequency words, one-syllable words that can be sounded out, or longer words that can be divided into syllables? Knowing which types of errors students are making provides information that teachers use as they plan for instruction. Teachers analyze students' spelling errors the same way, thinking about which strategies might help them spell words correctly. To learn more about diagnosing students' spelling errors, turn to Chapter 9, Teaching Writing.

OBSTACLE 2: Reading Speed

Many dysfluent students read too slowly. When students haven't developed an adequate reading speed by the middle grades, they don't have the cognitive resources available to focus on meaning, and when they can't attend to ideas, their comprehension suffers. Researchers have identified representative oral and silent reading speeds for each grade level (end of the school year), which are shown in Figure 5–5 (Allington, 2009a; Fountas & Pinnell, 2006c; Rasinski & Padak, 2008). You'll notice that students' reading speed gradually increases; silent reading is faster than oral reading because pronouncing each word takes time. Teachers should use these numbers cautiously because many factors affect reading speed, including the difficulty level of the text and students' background knowledge.

As students become more-fluent readers, they learn to vary their reading speed depending on their purpose and the text they're reading. Fountas and Pinnell (2006c) identified these factors that affect students' reading speed:

The Topic. When students have background knowledge about the topic, they're able to read more quickly and connect the ideas they're reading to what they already know. They can also identify new words more easily because even though they don't recognize the words in print, they may have heard them before.

Text Format. When students are knowledgeable about genre, text structure, and text layout and other book features, their familiarity with these factors makes it easier to anticipate what they're reading. Students who have read other books in the same genre with similar structural elements and book features have an easier time than those students for whom the text format features are new.

FIGURE 5–5 ◆ Reading Speed by Grade Levels		
Grade	**Oral Reading**	**Silent Reading**
4	100–150 wpm*	125–170 wpm
5	110–170 wpm	140–190 wpm
6	120–180 wpm	160–210 wpm
7	135–190 wpm	170–220 wpm
8	150–200 wpm	190–230 wpm
*wpm = words per minute		

FIGURE 5–6 ◆ Factors That Affect Reading Speed

Category	Factors	How the Factors Affect Reading Speed
Topic	Background knowledge	When students have adequate background knowledge about the topic, they read confidently and identify new words more quickly.
Text Format	Genre	When students know about the genre, they vary their expression to match their interpretation.
	Text structure	When students recognize the text structure, they anticipate the flow of the text and vary their speed appropriately.
	Text features	When students know how to use headings, margin notes, and other text features, they read more confidently.
English Language Knowledge	Vocabulary	When students know most words, they read more smoothly because they don't have to stop often to identify words.
	Sentence complexity	When students are familiar with the syntax, they chunk words into phrases and apply intonation appropriately as they read.
	Literary features	When students know about metaphors, personification, and other literary features, they vary their volume and expression to match their interpretation.

English Language Development. Students who speak English fluently have an advantage in developing reading speed because they know the meanings of more words, are familiar with English sentence structures, especially more complex ones, and recognize metaphors, alliteration, and other literary features.

Students become more-strategic readers as they learn to use speed appropriately and to vary their reading rate depending on the text. For example, students who are reading to locate information typically skim a text quickly, but they generally slow down to appreciate the author's use of descriptive language when they're reading a novel or a poem. These factors are reviewed in Figure 5–6; they emphasize the importance of background knowledge and lots of experience reading books and listening to books aloud.

How to Intervene

The most important way that teachers intervene is by providing daily practice opportunities to develop students' reading speed and stamina. Allington (2009a) reports that "by fourth grade, struggling readers have read millions fewer words than their achieving classmates" (p. 101). Struggling readers typically don't read outside of school; in contrast, most grade-level students in the middle grades read 15 to 30 minutes a day in addition to doing homework assignments. To increase reading volume, teachers provide a combination of teacher-guided and independent reading practice, including these activities:

Choral Reading. Students work in small groups or together as a class for choral reading. They experiment with different ways to read poems and other short texts aloud (Rasinski, 2003). More-fluent peers serve as models and set the reading speed for struggling readers.

Guided Reading. Teachers have students reread passages as part of **guided reading** lessons. Sometimes the teacher reads a passage aloud at an appropriate speed while students read along, and after several repetitions, students read it independently.

Readers Theatre. Students practice reading a story script to develop reading speed and prosody before performing for classmates. Researchers report that **readers theatre** results in significant improvement in students' reading fluency (Martinez, Roser, & Strecker, 1998/1999).

Listening Center. Students read along in a book at their independent reading level while listening to it being read aloud on a CD or audiocassette at a listening center (Kuhn & Stahl, 2004).

Partner Reading. Pairs of students who read at approximately the same level read or reread books together (Griffith & Rasinski, 2004). They choose a book that interests them and decide how they'll read it. They may read aloud in unison or take turns reading aloud while the partner follows along.

To develop fluency through these practice activities, books must be appropriate; that is, students must be interested in their topics and be able to read them with 98 or 99% accuracy.

Another way to improve reading speed is the repeated readings procedure, in which students practice reading a text aloud three to five times, striving to improve their reading speed and reduce their accuracy errors with each reading (Samuels, 1979). Students time their reading and plot their speed on a graph so they can track their improvement. For years, researchers have advocated repeated readings as an effective way to increase students' reading fluency, but now researchers suggest that reading a variety of books is at least as effective and perhaps even more beneficial (Allington, 2009a; Kuhn & Stahl, 2004). When teachers have students use the repeated readings procedure, it should be done one or two days a week or only for month or two so that students have plenty of time for independent reading.

Reading Stamina. Once students reach the fluency level, the focus shifts to helping them develop reading stamina, or the strength to read silently for increasingly longer periods. Students develop this stamina through daily opportunities to read independently for extended periods. When students' reading is limited to basal reader selections or magazine articles that can be completed in 15 or 20 minutes, they won't develop the endurance they need. Many teachers report that by sixth or seventh grade, their students can't read comfortably for more than 20 minutes. It's essential that they develop the stamina to read for longer periods so they can read novels and handle the lengthier texts they're expected to read. Teachers include extended opportunities each day for independent reading of self-selected texts through reading workshop or **Sustained Silent Reading**. In the middle grades, students' independent reading time begins at 40 or 45 minutes and increases to 60 minutes, if the schedule permits. Students also benefit from doing additional independent reading at home.

Another way of looking at how students develop stamina is by the number of words they're expected to read. Many school districts now call for students to read 500,000 words in fourth grade and gradually increase the number of words until they read one million words in eighth grade. You may wonder how the number of words translates to books: Students in fourth, fifth, and sixth grades often read novels that are approximately 200 pages long, and these books typically have about 35,000 words; for example, *Esperanza Rising* (Ryan, 2002), *Loser* (Spinelli, 2002), and *Homeless Bird* (Whelan,

2001). Therefore, students need to read approximately 14 books to reach 500,000 words. Those who read two novels each month will reach the 500,000-word mark.

Students in seventh and eighth grades usually read longer books with 250 pages or more. Books with 250 pages, such as *Bud, Not Buddy* (Curtis, 1999), *Holes* (Sachar, 2008), and *Crispin: The Cross of Lead* (Avi, 2005), contain at least 50,000 words. Books containing more than 300 pages, such as *Harry Potter and the Chamber of Secrets* (Rowling, 1999), range from 75,000 to 100,000 words. Students need to read 10 to 20 books, depending on length, to reach one million words. So, those who read two books with 250 to 350 pages each month will reach the one million–word mark.

How to Monitor Progress

Teachers monitor students' reading speed by listening to them read aloud. During reading workshop, Sustained Silent Reading, and other reading activities, teachers move around the classroom and spend a few minutes with each student. The teacher squats down beside or sits alongside a student and asks him or her to read aloud, but quietly. The student reads several paragraphs or a page of text while the teacher looks on, and then the teacher stops the student to check comprehension. They talk about the book and the reading strategies the student is using.

At the end of each quarter, teachers often have dysfluent students read a passage for one minute and count the number of words read correctly to track their reading speed. This score isn't very meaningful, however, if teachers don't also check students' comprehension because it doesn't matter whether students meet grade-level expectations if they don't understand what they're reading.

OBSTACLE 3: Prosody

When students read expressively, they use their voices to add meaning to the words. Rasinski and Padak (2008) identified these components of prosody:

Expression. Students read with enthusiasm and vary their expression to match their interpretation of the text.

Phrasing. Students chunk words into phrases as they read and apply stress and intonation appropriately.

Volume. Students vary the loudness of their voices to add meaning to the text.

Smoothness. Students read with a smooth rhythm and quickly self-correct any breakdowns.

Pacing. Students read at a conversational speed.

These components seem more related to oral reading, but prosody plays an important role during silent reading, too, because students' internal voice affects comprehension.

How to Intervene

Teachers emphasize prosody by modeling expressive reading every time they read aloud and using the **think-aloud** procedure to reflect on how they varied their expression, chunked words into phrases, modulated the loudness of their voice, or varied their pacing. They talk about the importance of prosody for both fluency and comprehension and show students how meaning is affected when they read in a monotone or slow down their reading speed.

Schreider (1991) recommends teaching students to phrase or chunk words together to read with expression. Fluent readers understand how to chunk words into meaningful units, perhaps because they've been read to or have had numerous reading experiences themselves, but many dysfluent readers can't. Consider this sentence from *Sarah, Plain and Tall* (MacLachlan, 2004): "A few raindrops came, gentle at first, then stronger and louder, so that Caleb and I covered our ears and stared at each other without speaking" (p. 47). This sentence comes from the chapter describing a terrible storm that the pioneer family endured, huddled with their animals in their sturdy barn. Three commas help students read the first part of this sentence, but then they must decide how to chunk the second part.

Teachers work with dysfluent readers to break sentences into phrases and read the sentences expressively. They make copies of a page from a book students are reading so they can mark pauses in longer sentences, then students practice rereading the sentence. After practicing with one sentence, they work with a partner to chunk and read another sentence.

Choral reading and readers theatre are two other ways to improve students' prosody. In **choral reading**, students work together in small groups to read poems and other texts. They practice reading the text until they can read it smoothly, and they experiment with ways to read more expressively, including varying the loudness of their voices, their intonation patterns, and their pacing. In **readers theatre**, students assume the roles of characters and practice reading aloud a script without performing it. The emphasis is on reading smoothly at a conversational pace and using expression so their voices add meaning to the words.

Sometimes teachers use round-robin reading to improve prosody, but this outmoded oral reading activity, in which the teacher calls on students to take turns reading aloud to the class, isn't recommended (Johns & Berglund, 2006). Many problems are associated with round-robin reading (Opitz & Rasinski, 1998): Students may develop inefficient reading habits because they adjust their silent reading speed to match classmates' oral reading speeds, and not surprisingly, listeners are often inattentive as they await their turn to read. Round-robin reading is stressful for struggling readers who are anxious or embarrassed when they read aloud. In addition, round-robin reading wastes valuable instructional time that could be spent on more-productive reading activities (Allington, 2009a).

How to Monitor Progress

Teachers monitor students' expressive reading by listening to them read aloud and assessing their expression, phrasing, volume, smoothness, and pacing. Sometimes teachers tape-record students as they read aloud a passage that they've practiced to track their improvement and so students can self-assess their own progress. Teachers can also use the rubric in the Assessment Tools feature on the next page to evaluate students' expressive reading according to the five components of prosody.

OBSTACLE 4: Writing Speed and Legibility

Speed is as important for fluent writing as it is for fluent reading. Students must be able to write quickly enough to get their ideas down on paper. To be considered fluent, writers must write at least 10 words per minute. When writers can't keep pace with their thinking, their writing won't make sense. For students to

Assessment Tools

A Rubric to Assess Prosody

	1	2	3	4
Expression	Monotone	Some expressiveness	Reasonable expressiveness	Expression matches interpretation
Phrasing	Word-by-word reading	Choppy reading	Reasonable chunking and intonation	Effective phrasing
Volume	Very quiet voice	Quiet voice	Appropriate volume	Volume matches interpretation
Smoothness	Frequent extended pauses and breakdowns	Some pauses and breakdowns	A few pauses or breakdowns	Smooth rhythm
Pacing	Laborious reading	Slow reading	Uneven combination of fast and slow reading	Appropriate conversational pace

Adapted from Rasinski & Padak, 2008.

become fluent writers, their transcription of ideas onto paper must be automatic; that means students spell most words automatically and handwrite without thinking about how to form letters or keyboard without hunting for letter keys.

Dysfluent writers' handwriting is often difficult to read, as if they don't want teachers to be able to read what they've written. Students need to know how to hold writing instruments comfortably, so their hands and arms don't hurt, and they need to learn how form both manuscript and cursive letters to improve their speed and legibility. Sometimes teachers require students to write only in cursive, but students should be allowed to use either form, as long as it's easy to read and can be written quickly.

Left-handed writers face unique handwriting problems. The basic difference between right- and left-handed writers is physical orientation: Right-handed students pull their hand and arm away from the body, but left-handed students move their left hand across what has just been written, often covering it. As a result, students too often adopt a "hook" position to avoid covering what they've just written. To address that problem, left-handed writers should hold pencils and pens an inch or more father back from the tip than right-handed writers so they can see what they've just written. The tilt of their papers is a second issue: Left-handed students should tilt their papers slightly to the right, in contrast to right-handed writers, who tilt their papers to the left to more comfortably form letters. Slant is a third concern: Left-handed students should slant their letters in a way that allows them to write comfortably. It's acceptable for them to write cursive letters vertically or even slightly backward, in contrast to right-handed students, who slant cursive letters to the right.

Keyboarding is an essential 21st-century literacy skill, and it's a necessary alternative for students with severe handwriting problems. Most schools use commercial tutorial programs to teach typing skills, beginning with the location of the home keys and correct fingering on the keyboard. Most programs have students practice using the keys to write words and sentences, and they receive feedback about their accuracy and speed. Students usually learn keyboarding before the middle grades, and this instruction is critical, because when students don't know how to keyboard, they use the inefficient hunt-and-peck technique and their writing speed is very slow.

In addition, students won't develop writing speed if they can't think of anything to write about. As they learn about the writing process, students learn how to generate ideas about a topic by brainstorming lists of words, drawing pictures, creating a cluster or other graphic organizer, or talking about a topic with a classmate, and through lots of practice, they internalize these strategies so that they can handle almost any writing task.

How to Intervene

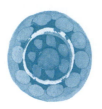

The best way to improve students' writing speed is through lots of writing. Dysfluent writers often have trouble sustaining a writing project through the five-stage writing process, but these informal writing activities are productive ways to increase writing speed:

Quickwriting. Students choose a topic for **quickwriting** and write without stopping for 5 or 10 minutes to explore the topic and deepen their understanding. The writing is informal, and students are encouraged to pour out ideas without stopping to organize them. Students can choose words from the word wall to write about, write in response to a prompt, write to answer a question, or write to summarize their learning.

Quickwriting

These sixth graders do daily timed quickwrites to develop writing fluency. They write for 5 minutes on topics related to thematic units, or current events. The boys are becoming faster writers; their writing speed has just reached 10 words per minute! They've become stronger spellers who can now spell more difficult common words including *about*, and *could*, automatically. The teacher has noticed that the students are writing more effective paragraphs with topic sentences. After writing, they share their quickwrites in small groups. Their writer's voices are rapidly improving, too, because the boys are experimenting with style to impress their classmates.

Reading Logs. Students write entries in **reading logs** as they read a story or listen to the teacher read a novel aloud. In their entries, students share their predictions, write summaries, ask questions, collect quotes, and reflect on the reading experience.

Simulated Journals. Students assume the role of a book character and write entries from that character's viewpoint in simulated journals. They delve into the character's thoughts and actions to deepen their understanding of the novel they're reading or that the teacher is reading aloud.

Learning Logs. Students write entries in **learning logs** as part of thematic units. They're using writing as a tool for learning as they take notes, brainstorm lists of words, draw graphic organizers, summarize big ideas, and write answers to questions.

It's important to have available a list of high-frequency words as well as a word wall with vocabulary related to the book or the thematic unit for struggling writers to refer to while they're writing.

For students with legibility problems, teachers check that they know how to hold writing instruments and form manuscript and cursive letters. It may be necessary to have students slow down their writing at first and concentrate on forming letters carefully and including all letters in each word before they focus on increasing their writing speed. **Interactive writing** is a useful procedure for examining students' handwriting skills and demonstrating how to write legibly. For students with serious handwriting problems, developing keyboarding skills may be a better alternative.

How to Monitor Progress

Teachers monitor students' progress toward writing fluency by having them quickwrite for 5 or 10 minutes about a familiar topic and then counting the number of words they've written. By dividing the number of words written by the number of minutes, teachers can track student's writing rates. For example, if a student writes 43 words in 5 minutes, her speed is nearly 9 words per minute; she's almost reached the threshold fluency rate of 10 words per minute. Another student writes 71 words in 10 minutes, and his speed is 7 words per minute; even though this student wrote more words, his writing speed is slower. Teachers often repeat this assessment monthly using a different, but equally familiar, topic. It's essential that the topic be accessible because the purpose of the assessment is to monitor students' writing speed, not their knowledge about the topic.

OBSTACLE 5: Writer's Voice

The writer's voice reflects the person doing the writing. It sounds natural, not stilted. Pulitzer prize–winning author and teacher Donald Murray (2003) says that a writer's voice is the person in the writing. As students gain experience as readers and writers, their writers' voices will emerge, especially when they're writing on topics they know well.

Once students develop their writers' voices, they'll learn to alter them according to purpose, genre, and audience. Their voices vary when they're writing to entertain, inform, or persuade, and some writing forms require a more informal or formal voice: Think about the difference when you're writing an e-mail message or a business letter. Similarly, students' voices are more casual and relaxed when they're writing for peers than when they're writing for adults.

How to Intervene

Doing lots of reading and writing helps dysfluent writers develop their voices. As they read books and listen to the teacher read others aloud, students develop an awareness of the writer's voice. While reading aloud the hilarious *My Dad's a Birdman* (Almond, 2007), a story about Lizzie and her dad who enter the Great Human Bird Competition, a fifth-grade teacher pointed out how the author emphasized his writer's voice through dialogue, onomatopoeia, lots of detail, alliteration, and British jargon. Even the character names—Jackie Crow, Mortimer "Missile" Mint, Doreen Doody, and Mr. Poop—are humorous. The fifth graders also collected alliterative phrases from the fanciful novel, including "the nits, the ninnies, the nincompoopy noodleheads" (n.p.), and made a list of words and phrases that emphasized David Almond's voice:

an ordinary day	*shenanigans*	*scruffy*
tweakling and twockling	*smacked his lips*	*rustled his wings*
little chubby man	*megaphone*	*little wormies*
method of propulsion	*wobbly*	*flinched*
with a flourish	*don't be daft*	*thundering and thumpling*
potty as a pancake	*blitheration*	*angry marbly beady eyes*

Through **minilessons** and word-study activities, students become aware of some of the techniques they can apply in their own writing so their voices will be heard.

At the same time they're examining authors' voices in books they're reading, students do lots of informal writing to develop their own writers' voices. To become fluent, students need to write every day for at least 15 or 20 minutes, and most intervention programs include writing components. If students haven't done much writing, keeping a personal journal is a good way to begin, or they can **quickwrite** or write in **reading logs** on topics they choose or on topics provided by the teacher. Students can try writing from varied viewpoints to experiment with voice. For example, for the topic "what I'm thankful for," it's not hard to imagine how the writer's voice would differ if the writing were done by a child or a parent, a police officer or a criminal, a farm worker or a film star. Another way to emphasize voice is by having students talk out their writing ideas with a partner before beginning to write; this prewriting conversation serves as a rehearsal and makes students' writing more effective. Through this daily writing practice, students gain experience in brainstorming ideas, organizing ideas into sentences and paragraphs, spelling high-frequency words correctly, and developing writing speed as well as nurturing their emerging writers' voices.

How to Monitor Progress

Teachers have students keep quickwriters and other informal pieces of writing as well as polished compositions in their portfolios. At the end of each grading period, both teachers and students can examine and compare the writing samples, looking for evidence of students' evolving writers' voices. Having students read aloud a piece from the beginning of the school year and one written recently is a good way to highlight the changes; afterward, students can write brief reflections, pointing out how their writers' voices are developing.

Scaffolding English Learners

To become fluent readers, English learners need to read words accurately, quickly, and expressively, like native English speakers do; however, it's unlikely that they'll become fluent readers until they speak English fluently because their lack of oral language proficiency limits their recognition of high-frequency words and use of word-identification strategies, and it interferes with their ability to understand word meanings, string words together into sentences, and read expressively (Peregoy & Boyle, 2008). It's also unlikely that ELs will become fluent writers before they develop oral language proficiency.

Young adolescents who are learning English are immersed in reading and writing instruction in English at the same time they're learning to speak the language. Teachers help them to make connections between the oral and written language modes to accelerate their achievement and overcome the obstacles that get in the way of their becoming fluent readers and writers.

Accuracy. Developing reading and writing accuracy is challenging for many English learners, and it takes longer than it does for native English speakers. High-frequency words are difficult to recognize because so many of them are abstract (*about*, *this*, *which*), and many are hard to spell because they violate spelling rules (*could*, *said*, *what*, *who*). ELs often speak with a native-language accent, which makes phonic analysis more arduous, but their pronunciation differences needn't hamper their reading fluency. For example, even though some Hispanic students, especially more-recent immigrants, pronounce *check* as /shĕk/ because the *ch* digraph doesn't exist in Spanish, they're reading the word accurately. Everyone has an accent, even native English speakers, so ELs shouldn't be expected to eliminate their accents to be considered fluent readers. Students' limited background knowledge also contributes to their dysfluency. Applying syllabic and morphemic analysis to identify words that aren't in their speaking vocabularies can be a formidable task, especially if they're not familiar with cognates or related words in their native language.

Reading Speed. English learners' difficulty in developing reading speed is generally the result of their limited background knowledge and lack of academic vocabulary. By building background knowledge and introducing new words before reading, teachers can help ELs improve their reading speed. In addition, Garcia and Godina (2004) recommend that students have opportunities to reread culturally relevant books and other materials at their reading levels that they've read and discussed previously.

Prosody. Students' knowledge of spoken English plays a critical role in developing expressive reading. When students chunk words into phrases, their intonation patterns reflect their native language. This common problem is due to ELs' limited knowledge of English syntax, and the fact that punctuation marks provide the only clues about how to chunk words in printed English (Allington, 2009a). Teachers teach students about punctuation marks and provide lots of oral reading practice. They also serve as models as they read a text with students in an activity called *unison reading* (Reutzel & Cooter, 2008). The teacher is the leader and reads loudly enough to be heard above the group. Another activity is echo reading, in which the teacher reads the first sentence expressively and the students reread it, trying to imitate the teacher's prosody. If the students are successful, the teacher moves to the next sentence; however, if students struggle to read the sentence, the teacher repeats it.

Writing Speed. English learners' limited background knowledge is more likely than a lack of writing stamina to hinder their writing speed. Students who are learning English are often more successful writing in **reading logs** about books they're reading and **quickwriting** about topics they're learning in thematic units and content-area classes because they're familiar with the topics and technical vocabulary. When students need more support, teachers can create graphic organizers and word banks or provide opportunities for students to talk with peers before they begin writing. In addition, Garcia and Godina (2004) warn that if teachers are overconcerned with grammatical correctness, students' writing will be inhibited because they'll stick with safe, grammatically correct sentences they already know how to write.

Voice. Developing a voice for writing is just as challenging for English learners as becoming an expressive reader. Students learn to use sentence structures, figurative language, idioms, and other features of voice when teachers talk about the author's voice in books they're reading aloud and through lots of reading and writing practice. It's also helpful to have students collect sentences from books they're reading and use them as models for their own writing (Garcia & Godina, 2004). For example, *Middle School Is Worse Than Meatloaf: A Year Told Through Stuff* (Holm, 2007) is a clever multigenre novel exhibiting multiple voices, including those of a seventh grader named Ginny, her parents, teachers, and friends. Students can compare Ginny's voice with the others and adapt sentences from the book for their own writing. For example, they can incorporate "There's nothing quite like the first day of school," a repeated line from one of Ginny's poems, into their own poems, or they can write memos using Ginny's memo to her mom about exchanging dishwashing duties for money to buy a new sweater as a model.

It's just as important that English learners overcome the obstacles to fluency because automaticity, speed, and expressiveness are necessary for young adolescents to handle the demands of reading and writing in the middle grades. The same combination of explicit instruction and authentic practice activities that is recommended for native speakers is effective with English learners; however, ELs often require more time because they're learning to speak English at the same time they're learning to read and write.

CHAPTER 5

How Effective Teachers Eliminate Obstacles to Fluency

▶ Teachers teach dysfluent students to read and spell high-frequency words.

▶ Teachers teach four word-identification strategies—phonic analysis, decoding by analogy, syllabic analysis, and morphemic analysis—to help students become more-accurate readers and writers.

▶ Teachers increase the amount of reading students do to develop their reading speed and prosody.

▶ Teachers increase the amount of writing students do to develop their writing speed.

▶ Teachers help dysfluent writers develop their voice or writing style through minilessons and lots of reading and writing.

CHAPTER 6

Expanding Academic Vocabulary

Mrs. Sanom's Word Wizards Club

Mrs. Sanom is the resource teacher, and she sponsors an after-school Word Wizards Club for fifth and sixth graders; the club meets for an hour on Wednesday afternoons. Nineteen students, many of them English learners, are club members this year. Mrs. Sanom teaches vocabulary lessons during the club meetings using costumes, books, and hands-on activities. She focuses on different word-study topics each week, including writing alliterations, choosing synonyms carefully, applying context clues to figure out unfamiliar words, understanding multiple meanings of words, choosing between homonyms, and studying root words.

She devised this club because students' limited vocabularies affect their reading achievement. In the letters that club members write to Mrs. Sanom at the end of the school year, they report paying more attention to words an author uses, and they're better at using context clues to figure out the meaning of unfamiliar words. Most importantly, the students say that participation in the Word Wizards Club gives them an appreciation for words that will last a lifetime. Rosie writes:

I love being a Word Wizard. I learned lots of new words and that makes me smart. I have a favorite word that is hypothesis. Did you know that I am always looking for more new words to learn? My Tio Mario gave me a dictionary because I wanted it real bad. I like looking for words in the dictionary and I like words with lots of syllables the best. I want to be in the club next year in 6th grade. Ok?

At the first club meeting, Mrs. Sanom read aloud *Miss Alaineus: A Vocabulary Disaster* (Frasier, 2007), about a girl named Sage who loves words. In the story, Sage misunderstands the meaning of *miscellaneous*, but what begins as embarrassment turns into victory when she wins an award for her costume in the school's annual vocabulary parade. The students talked about the story in a **grand conversation**, and they decided to dress in costumes and have a vocabulary parade themselves, just as Mrs. Sanom knew they would. "I like to dress in vocabulary costumes," Mrs. Sanom explained. "I plan to dress up in clothes or a hat that represents a vocabulary word at each club meeting." With that introduction, she reached into a shopping bag and pulled out an oversized, wrinkled shirt and put it on over her clothes. "Here is my costume," she announced. "Can you guess the word?" She modeled the shirt, trying to smooth the wrinkles, until a student guessed the word *wrinkled*.

The students talked about *wrinkle*, forms of the word (*wrinkled*, *unwrinkled*, and *wrinkling*), and the meanings. They checked the definitions of *wrinkle* in the dictionary. They understood the first meaning, "a crease or fold in clothes or skin," but the second meaning—"a clever idea or trick"—was more difficult. Mrs. Sanom called their idea to have a vocabulary parade "a new wrinkle" in her plans for the club, and then the students began to grasp the meaning.

The borders of each page in *Miss Alaineus* are decorated with words beginning with a specific letter; the first page has words beginning with A, the second page B, and so on. To immerse students in words, Mrs. Sanom asked them each to choose a letter from a box of plastic letters, turn to that page in the book, and choose a word beginning with that letter for an activity. The words they chose included *awesome*, *berserk*, *catastrophe*, and *dwindle*. Students wrote the word on the first page of their Word Wizard Notebooks (small, spiral-bound notebooks that Mrs. Sanom purchased for them), checked its meaning in a dictionary and wrote it beside the word, and then drew a picture to illustrate the meaning. While they worked, Mrs. Sanom wrote the words on the alphabetized **word wall** she posted in the classroom. Afterward, the students shared their words and illustrations in a **tea party** activity.

At today's meeting, Mrs. Sanom is wearing a broad-brimmed hat with two wrecked cars and a stop sign attached. The students check out Mrs. Sanom's costume because they know it represents a word. They quickly begin guessing: "Is it *crash*?" Oscar asks. "I think the word is *accident*. My dad had a car accident last week," says Danielle. Ramon suggests, "Those cars are *wrecked*. Is that the word?" Mrs. Sanom commends the club members for their good guesses and says they're on the right track. To provide a little help, she draws a row of nine letter boxes on the chalkboard and fills in the first letter and the last four letters. Then Martha guesses it—*collision*. Mrs. Sanom draws a cluster on the chalkboard with the word *collision* written in the middle circle and related words on each ray. Students compare the noun *collision* and the verb *collide*. They also check the dictionary and a thesaurus for more information and write *crash*, *accident*, *wreck*, *hit*, *smashup*, and *collide* on the rays to complete the cluster. They talk about how to use *collide* and *collision*. Ramon offers, "I know a sentence: On 9-11, the terrorists' airplanes collided with the World Trade Center."

Mrs. Sanom explains that ships can be involved in collisions, too: A ship can hit another ship, or it can collide with something else in the water—an iceberg, for example. Several students know about the *Titanic*, and they share what they know about that ship's fateful ocean crossing. Mrs. Sanom selects *Story of the Titanic* (Kentley, 2001) and shows photos of the ship to build background knowledge. They make a

K-W-L chart, listing what they know in the K column and what they wonder about in the W column.

Next, Mrs. Sanom presents a list of words—some about the *Titanic* article they'll read and some not—for an **exclusion brainstorming** activity; the words include *unsinkable, crew, liner, passengers, voyage, airplane, catastrophe, ship, mountain, lifeboat,* and *general*. The students predict which words relate to the article and which don't. The word *general* stumps them because they think of it as an adjective meaning "having to do with the whole, not specific." A student checks the dictionary to learn about the second meaning—a high-ranking military officer. The students are still confused, but after reading the article, they realize that the word *general* isn't related: The officer in charge of the *Titanic* (or any ship, for that matter) is a *captain*.

Mrs. Sanom passes out copies of the one-page article and reads it aloud while students follow along. They discuss the article, talking about the needless tragedy. Then they complete the L section of the K-W-L chart and the exclusion brainstorming activity. Because everyone wants to learn more about the disaster, Mrs. Sanom introduces her text set of books about the *Titanic*, including *Inside the Titanic* (Brewster, 1997), *Tonight on the Titanic* (Osborne & Osborne, 1995), *Titanic: A Nonfiction Companion to Tonight on the Titanic* (Osborne & Osborne, 2002), *On Board the Titanic: What It Was Like When the Great Liner Sank* (Tanaka, 1996), and *Voyage on the Great Titanic: The Diary of Margaret Ann Brady* (White, 1998). She invites the students to spend the last few minutes of the club meeting choosing a book to take home and read.

Mrs. Sanom wears a different costume or hat each week. Here are her favorites:

bejeweled	A silky shirt with "jewels" glued across the front
champion	Racing shorts, tee shirt, and a medal on a ribbon worn around her neck
hocus-pocus	A black top hat with a stuffed rabbit stuck inside, white gloves, and a magic wand
international	A dress decorated with the flags of many countries and a globe cut in half for a hat
slick	A black leather jacket, sunglasses, and hair slicked back with mousse
transparent	A clear plastic raincoat, clear plastic gloves, and a clear shower cap
vacant	A bird cage with a "for rent" sign worn as a hat with an artificial bird sitting on her shoulder

One week, however, Mrs. Sanom forgot to bring a costume, so after a bit of quick thinking, she featured the word *ordinary* by wearing her everyday clothes as her costume!

For their 17th weekly club meeting, Mrs. Sanom dressed as a queen with a flowing purple robe and a tiara on her head. The focus was words beginning with Q, the 17th letter of the alphabet. They began by talking about queens—Queen Isabella of Spain and Great Britain's Queen Elizabeth II. Next, Mrs. Sanom started a list of Q words with *queen*, and then the students added words to it. They checked the Q page in alphabet books and examined dictionary entries for additional Q words, including *quadruped, quadruplet, qualify, quest, quarantine, quintet, quiver, quench,* and *quotation*. After they had more than 20 words on their list, Mrs. Sanom asked each student to choose a Q word, study it, and make a square poster to share what he or she learned. Afterward, Mrs. Sanom, taped the posters together to make a quilt and hung it on

A Student's Square on Quadruped for the Q Quilt

Is a rabbit a quadruped? <u>Yes.</u>

Is a cat a quadruped? <u>Yes.</u>

quadruped

A lizard is a quadruped.

quadr = 4
ped = feet

an animal with 4 feet

Is a fish a quadruped? <u>No.</u>

Is a bird a quadruped? <u>No.</u>

the wall outside the classroom. One student's square about *quadruped* is shown here; it documents the student's understanding of root words.

The Word Wizards proudly wear word bracelets to highlight special words; in October, they made bracelets with the word they'd chosen to describe themselves, *genius, ornery,* or *sincere,* for instance. Mrs. Sanom's word was *sassy*; she demonstrated how to make a bracelet using small alphabet beads strung on an elastic string, and students made their own bracelets. In February, they studied patriotic words, such as *allegiance, citizen, equality,* and *independence,* and chose a word for a second bracelet. For their third word bracelet, they selected their favorite word from all they'd collected in their Word Wizard Notebooks; their choices included *valiant, awesome, phenomenon, plethora, incredulous, cryptic, guffaw, mischievous,* and *razzle-dazzle.*

The vocabulary parade is the highlight of the year. Every club member creates a costume and participates in the parade. Mrs. Sanom dresses as a wizard—a word wizard, that is—and she leads the parade from classroom to classroom in the school's intermediate wing. The students dress as *camouflage, victory, shimmer, monarch, liberty, uncomfortable, fortune, emerald,* and *twilight,* for example, and carry word cards so that everyone will know the words they represent. As they tour each classroom, the students talk about their words. Students' parents come to school to view the parade, and a local television station films it for the evening news.

Capable students' vocabularies grow at an astonishing rate—about 3,000 to 4,000 words a year, or roughly 7 to 10 new words every day. By the time they graduate from high school, their vocabularies reach 25,000 to 50,000 words or more.

These students learn the meanings of words by being immersed in a word-rich environment and through a combination of daily independent reading, **interactive read-alouds**, and explicit instruction. They learn most words incidentally through reading, hobbies, and family activities, but teachers expand students' vocabulary development by explicitly teaching some words and word-learning strategies and by fostering students' interest in words (Graves, 2006). In the vignette, Mrs. Sanom expanded her fifth and sixth graders' vocabularies as they participated in lively Word Wizard Club activities.

Vocabulary knowledge and reading achievement are closely related: Students with larger vocabularies are more-capable readers, and they know more strategies for figuring out the meanings of unfamiliar words than less capable readers do (Graves, 2006). One reason why capable readers have larger vocabularies is that they do more reading. This idea is an example of the Matthew effect, which suggests that "the rich get richer and the poor get poorer" (Stanovich, 1986): Capable readers get better because they read more, and the books they read are more challenging, with academic vocabulary words. The gulf between more-capable and less capable readers grows larger each year because less capable readers do less reading and the books they read have fewer grade-level academic words.

Vocabulary learning can't be left to chance, because students' word knowledge influences whether they comprehend what they're reading, write effectively, and learn content-area information (Stahl & Nagy, 2006). Students come to school with varying levels of word knowledge, both in the number of words they know and the depth of their understanding. Students from low-income homes have less than half of the vocabulary of more-affluent students, and some researchers estimate that they know less than one quarter of the words that their classmates do. To make matters worse, this gap widens each year (Cunningham, 2009). Therefore, it's essential that teachers recognize the impact of socioeconomic level on students' vocabulary knowledge and emphasize word learning for students who know fewer words.

> Check the Compendium of Instructional Procedures, which follows Chapter 12, for more information on the highlighted terms.

Academic Vocabulary

The words that are frequently used in language arts, social studies, science, and math are called *academic vocabulary* (Burke, 2008). These words are used in textbooks, **minilessons**, classroom assignments, and directions for high-stakes tests. Here's a sampling of academic vocabulary words that fourth through eighth graders learn:

adjacent	diameter	jargon	quotation
biome	diplomacy	key	random
brief	edible	lunar	ray
census	evaluate	nomadic	revolution
colonial	imagery	nucleus	strategy
concave	industrial	plagiarize	summarize
condensation	infer	proofread	variable
democracy	infinite	purpose	voice

You probably recognized *infer*, *plagiarize*, and *voice* as language arts words; *biome*, *condensation*, and *nucleus* as science words; *census*, *diplomacy*, and *nomadic* as social studies words; and *diameter*, *infinite*, and *ray* as math words. Knowing these words is especially useful because they often have multiple forms and are used in different ways. Consider these nine forms for the word *brief*:

Noun: *brief, briefs*

Verb: *brief, briefed, briefing*

Adjective: *brief, briefer, briefest*

Adverb: *briefly*

Some words are technical (e.g., *concave* and *proofread*), and their use is limited to specific content areas, but others (e.g., *adjacent* and *nucleus*) are used more broadly. In addition, a few words, such as *key* and *voice*, are common words being used in new ways. Young adolescents' knowledge of academic vocabulary is part of their background knowledge, and it affects their school success (Marzano & Pickering, 2005).

Three Tiers of Words

Beck, McKeown, and Kucan (2002) have devised a tool to assist teachers in identifying academic vocabulary—they suggest that teachers categorize words into three tiers:

Tier 1: Basic Words. These common words are used socially, in informal conversation at home and on the playground. Examples include *traffic, relaxed, breeze, anger, escape,* and *truthful*. Native English-speaking students rarely require instruction about these words.

Tier 2: Academic Vocabulary. These words have wide application in school contexts and are used more frequently in written than in oral language. Some are related to literacy concepts, including *mythical, apostrophe, thesis, feign, perplexed,* and *trait*. Others are more-sophisticated words related to familiar concepts. For example, students understand the concept of *smell* but not the words *scent, odor,* or *aroma*, or they know the word *sharp* but aren't familiar with its synonyms *keen* and *acute*. Teaching these words and their related word forms has a powerful impact on students' learning.

Tier 3: Specialized Terms. These technical words are content-specific and often abstract. Examples include *minuend, volume, osmosis, opaque, transcontinental,* and *suffrage*. They aren't used frequently enough to devote time to teaching them when they come up in texts students are reading in language arts, but they're the words that teachers explicitly teach during thematic units and in content-area classes.

As teachers choose words for instruction and word-study activities, they focus on Tier 2 words even though words representing all three levels are written on **word walls** and explained when necessary.

During a fifth-grade unit on America in the 20th century, students learned to sing Woody Guthrie's folk ballad "This Land Is Your Land" (Guthrie, 2002) and then read the biography *Woody Guthrie: Poet of the People* (Christensen, 2001). The fifth graders created a word wall that included these words:

ballads	Great Depression	nightmare	spirit
celebrate	guitar	ordinary	stock market
criss-cross	hardship	original	tragedy
depression	harmonica	rallies	unfair
desperate	hitchhiked	restless	unions
devastated	lonesome	scorn	unsanitary
drought	migrant	severe	wandering
Dust Bowl	migration	sorrow	worries

From this list, their teacher identified some Tier 1, 2, and 3 words:

Tier 1 words: *guitar, harmonica, worries, nightmare, unfair, celebrates*

Tier 2 words: *ordinary, spirit, desperate, original, sorrow, tragedy*

Tier 3 words: *drought, Dust Bowl, stock market, Great Depression, unsanitary*

Only one Tier 1 word—*harmonica*—needed to be taught, so the teacher invited a friend who played the instrument to visit the classroom. The teacher focused on teaching both Tier 2 and Tier 3 words because this was a social studies unit.

Scaffolding English Learners

English learners often need more-explicit vocabulary instruction than native English speakers do. Sometimes English learners only need to have a word translated, but at other times, they're confused about a new meaning of a familiar word, or they're unfamiliar with both the underlying concept and words that describe it, and instruction is necessary.

Tier 1 Words. These words are easiest for English learners to learn because they often know the words in their native language; what they don't know are the equivalent words in English. If teachers speak students' native language, they can translate the words and help students learn these English equivalents. English-speaking teachers can use pictures and pantomime to explain them. It's often helpful for teachers to put together collections of small objects and pictures to share with students during literature focus units and thematic units.

Tier 2 Words. Teachers preteach some unfamiliar words, including essential Tier 2 words, before students read a book or when they introduce a writing project, and later, through explicit instruction and a variety of word-study activities, they teach other Tier 2 words. In addition, Calderon (2007) points out that ELs need to understand transition words and phrases, words with multiple meanings, and English words with cognates. Transition words, such as *consequently, yet, likewise, against, meanwhile, afterward,* and *finally,* are used to bridge ideas in sentences, paragraphs, and longer texts. Teachers can help ELs recognize these words and phrases, understand their meaning, and use them in their own writing.

Learning new meanings for familiar words is another Tier 2 activity. Some everyday words, such as *key, soft,* and *ready,* have less frequently used meanings that confuse English learners even though they know the most common meanings. Students also learn to choose among related words. For example, *instrument* means a device for doing work; *tool* and *utensil* are also devices for doing work, but they don't mean exactly the same thing. *Instruments,* such as stethoscopes and scalpels, are used for doing complicated work; *tools,* such as hammers and screwdrivers, are used for skilled jobs; and *utensils* are simple devices, such as whisks and spoons, for working in the kitchen.

Teachers also point out cognates, English words that are related to words in students' native language. Many Tier 2 words are Latin-based, so it's important to teach English learners who speak Spanish, Portuguese, Italian, and French to ask themselves whether an unfamiliar word is similar to a word in their native language.

Tier 3 Words. It's less important to teach these technical words because of their limited usefulness, and only a few have cognates that English learners would know. Calderon (2007) recommends that teachers translate the words or briefly explain them. However, during thematic units, teachers do teach Tier 3 words that are important to understanding the big ideas through a combination of explicit instruction and word-study activities.

Levels of Word Knowledge

Students develop knowledge about a word gradually, through repeated oral and written exposures to it. They move from not knowing a word at all to recognizing that they've seen the word before, and then to partial knowledge where they have a general sense of the word or know one meaning. Finally, students know the word fully: They understand multiple meanings and can use the word in a variety of ways. Here are the four levels:

Level 1: Unknown Word. Students don't recognize the word.

Level 2: Initial Recognition. Students have seen or heard the word or can pronounce it, but they don't know the meaning.

Level 3: Partial Word Knowledge. Students know one meaning of the word and can use it in a sentence.

Level 4: Full Word Knowledge. Students know more than one meaning of the word and can use it in several ways. (Allen, 1999)

Once students reach the third level, they can generally understand the word in context and use it in writing. In fact, they don't reach the fourth level with every word they learn, but when they do develop full word knowledge, they're flexible word users because they understand the core meaning of a word and how it changes in different contexts (Stahl, 1999).

Word Consciousness

Students' interest in learning and using words is known as *word consciousness* (Graves & Watts-Taffe, 2002). According to Scott and Nagy (2004), word consciousness is "essential for vocabulary growth and comprehending the language of schooling" (p. 201). Students who have word consciousness exemplify these characteristics:

- Students use words skillfully, understanding the nuances of word meanings.
- Students gain a deep appreciation of words and value them.
- Students are aware of differences between social and academic language.
- Students understand the power of word choice.
- Students are motivated to learn the meaning of unfamiliar words.

Students' interest in learning words and appreciation of the power of language vary. The Spotlight feature on page 152 shows how Ales, Graciela, and Kolei differ in word consciousness.

As students develop word consciousness, they become more aware of words, manipulate them playfully, and appreciate their power. Teachers foster awareness in a variety of ways, as Mrs. Sanom did in the vignette at the beginning of the chapter. Most importantly, they model interest in words and precise use of vocabulary (Graves, 2006). To encourage students' awareness, teachers share books about words, including *Miss Alaineus: A Vocabulary Disaster* (Frasier, 2007), *Baloney (Henry P.)* (Scieszka, 2005), and *Mom and Dad Are Palindromes* (Shulman, 2006). They call students' attention to words by highlighting words of the day, posting words on **word walls**, and having students collect words from books they're reading. They promote wordplay by sharing riddles, jokes, puns, and poems and by encouraging students to experiment with words and use them in new ways. Through these activities, students become more-powerful word users.

Spotlight on . . .
Academic Vocabulary

Ales likes to learn new words, so her mom bought her a dictionary to learn more words. She knows the meaning of many eighth-grade words. Ales defines *economical* as "being smart about money" and identifies *expensive* as an antonym.

She can define the "nyms"—synonyms, antonyms, and homonyms—and give examples. She explains that homonyms are words that sound alike but are spelled differently. She offers these examples: *sun–son*, *write–right*, and *there–their–they're*.

When asked about the multiple meanings of the word *tie*, Ales responds that she can think of several meanings: "Men wear ties, I tie my shoelaces, games end in a tie when the score is same."

Ales volunteers information about her coach's favorite idiom, *you can't make an omelet without breaking eggs*. She explains, "It means there are always setbacks on the road to victory. There's another one that I know," she offers. "It's 'when pigs fly.' My nana says it a lot to mean that some things will never happen, like winning the lottery."

"When I was in sixth grade, my teacher read a book called *Miss Alaineus* (Frasier, 2007). That's when I started paying attention to words," Ales concludes.

Graciela isn't interested in words, and she blames her teachers for using hard words: "My teachers are mean; they're always saying hard words." When she's listening to her teachers or reading, her strategy is to ignore the "hard" words.

When she's asked to define the word *secret*, she responds that "a secret is something you can't tell other people," but she doesn't recognize *confidential* or *private* as synonyms. She can't define *grip*, *recent*, or *alert*.

Graciela can identify a few common antonyms, including *clean–dirty* and *easy–hard*, but she usually forms opposites using "not": *noisy–not noisy*, and *shiny–not shiny*.

This struggling student sees a one-to-one correspondence between words and meanings. When asked about meanings of the word *fall*, Graciela provides an example: "It's like when you fall down." When pressured about additional meanings, she says there aren't any even though most young adolescents recognize that *fall* means "to surrender," "to lower," or "to occur." It's also another name for *autumn*.

Graciela isn't familiar with idioms. When asked what "it's raining cats and dogs" means, she responds, "That there are too many animals."

Kolei is curious about words. His dad bought him a copy of *100 Words Every High School Freshman Should Know* (Editors of the American Heritage Dictionary, 2004), and they learn the words together. "I was surprised that *alliteration* was there because I already knew it," he explains, "and my favorite word is *bamboozle*. It means to trick someone."

This eighth grader knows a lot of words, including *prudent*, *absolute*, *motto*, and *remedy*. He can cite examples of synonyms (e.g., *rapid–speedy*), antonyms (e.g., *expensive–cheap*), and homonyms (e.g., *soul–sole*).

His favorite idiom is "slow and steady wins the race," which means that if you work hard, you'll be successful. Kolei has it posted on a sign over his desk at home.

When asked about multiple meanings, Kolei says he knows that lots of words have more than one meaning. He identifies these meanings for *tip*: "It's the point on the end of a finger. It's the money you give a waiter at a restaurant for good service. It's when you knock over a glass full of milk. And, one more thing: A tip is secret information that someone tells the police. There are probably even more meanings that I don't know yet."

Word-Study Concepts

I t's not enough to have students memorize one definition of a word; to develop full word knowledge, they need to learn more about a word (Stahl & Nagy, 2006). Consider the word *brave*: It can be used as an adjective, a noun, or a verb. It often means "showing no fear," but it can also mean an "American Indian warrior" or "to challenge or defy." These forms are related to the first meaning: *braver, bravest, bravely,* and *bravery.* Synonyms related to the first meaning include *courageous, bold, fearless, daring, intrepid, heroic,* and *valiant;* antonyms include *cowardly* and *frightened.* Our word *brave* comes from the Italian word *bravo.* Interestingly, the Italian word *bravo* and a related form—*bravissimo*—have entered English directly, and they're used to express great approval; these words mean "excellent," an obsolete meaning of *brave.* In addition, there's *bravado,* a Spanish word that means "a pretense of courage." As students learn some of this information, they're better able to understand the word *brave* and use it orally and in writing.

As students learn about a word, they acquire a wide range of information. They learn one or more meanings for a word and synonyms and antonyms to compare meanings. Sometimes they confuse a word they're learning with a homonym that sounds or is spelled the same. Students also learn about idioms and figurative sayings that make our language more colorful. A seventh grader's investigation of the word *vaporize* is shown in Figure 6–1.

FIGURE 6–1 ◆ *An Investigation of* Vaporize		
Morphemic Analysis vapor + ize	**Root Word** vapor	**Suffix** ize It is used to change a noun into a verb.
 **To change from a solid into a vapor (gas) (verb)**		
Word History It became a word in the 1600's. It came from the Latin word "steam".	**Related Words** evaporate vaporizer vaporous	**Figurative Use** The boy's thoughts vaporized and he couldn't remember the answer.

Multiple Meanings of Words

Many words have more than one meaning. For some words, multiple meanings develop for the noun and verb forms, but additional meanings can develop in other ways. The common word *bank*, for example, has these meanings:

a piled-up mass of snow or clouds

the slope of land beside a lake or river

the slope of a road on a turn

the lateral tilting of an airplane in a turn

to cover a fire with ashes for slow burning

a business establishment that receives and lends money

a container in which money is saved

a supply for use in emergencies (e.g., a blood bank)

a place for storage (e.g., a computer's memory bank)

to count on

similar things arranged in a row (e.g., a bank of elevators)

to arrange things in a row

You may be surprised that there are at least a dozen meanings for this word! Some are nouns and others are verbs, but grammatical form alone doesn't account for so many meanings.

The meanings of *bank* come from three sources. The first five meanings developed from a Viking word, and they all deal with something slanted or making a slanted motion. The next five come from the Italian word *banca*, a money changer's table; these meanings deal with financial banking except for the 10th meaning, "to count on," which requires a bit of thought. We use the saying "to bank on" figuratively to mean "to depend on," but it began more literally from the actual counting of money on a table. The last two meanings developed from the French word *banc*, meaning "bench." Words acquired multiple meanings as society became more complex and finer shades of meaning were necessary; for example, the meanings of *bank* as an emergency supply and a storage place are fairly new. As with many words with multiple meanings, it's just a linguistic accident that three original words from different languages with related meanings came to be spelled the same way. A list of other common words with more than five meanings is shown in Figure 6–2.

Students gradually acquire additional meanings for words, and they usually learn these new meanings through reading. When a familiar word is used in a new way, students often notice the new application and may be curious enough to check the meaning in a dictionary.

Synonyms: Words With Nearly the Same Meaning

Words that have nearly the same meaning are *synonyms*. English has so many synonyms because numerous words have been borrowed from other languages. Synonyms are useful because they're more precise. Think of all the synonyms for the word *cold: cool, chilly, frigid, icy, frosty,* and *freezing*. Each word expresses a different shade of meaning: *Cool*

FIGURE 6–2 ◆ Common Words With More Than Five Meanings

act	cross	high	now	range	sign	stuff
air	crown	hold	off	rear	sing	sweep
away	cut	hot	open	rest	sink	sweet
bad	draw	house	out	return	slip	swing
bar	drive	key	paper	rich	small	take
base	dry	knock	part	ride	sound	thick
black	dull	know	pass	right	spin	think
blow	eye	lay	pay	ring	spread	throw
boat	face	leave	pick	rise	spring	tie
break	fail	line	piece	roll	square	tight
carry	fair	low	pitch	run	stamp	time
case	fall	make	place	scale	stay	touch
catch	fast	man	plant	score	step	train
change	fire	mark	plate	serve	stick	trip
check	fly	mind	point	set	stiff	turn
clear	green	mine	post	sharp	stock	under
color	hand	natural	print	shine	stop	up
count	have	new	quiet	shoot	strike	watch
cover	head	nose	rain	short	stroke	way
crack	heel	note	raise	side	strong	wear

means moderately cold; *chilly* is uncomfortably cold; *frigid* is intensely cold; *icy* means very cold; *frosty* means covered with frost; and *freezing* is so cold that water changes into ice. English would be limited if we had only the word *cold*.

Teachers should carefully articulate the differences among synonyms. Nagy (1988) emphasizes that teachers should teach concepts and related words, not just provide single-word definitions using synonyms. For example, to tell a student that *frigid* means *cold* provides limited information; it doesn't help the student to understand the degrees of cold.

Antonyms: Words That Mean the Opposite

Words that express opposite meanings are *antonyms*. For the word *loud*, antonyms include *soft*, *subdued*, *quiet*, *silent*, *inaudible*, *sedate*, *somber*, *dull*, and *colorless*. These antonyms express shades of meaning just as synonyms do, and some opposites are more appropriate for one meaning of *loud* than for another. When *loud* means *gaudy*, for instance, antonyms are *somber*, *dull*, and *colorless*; when *loud* means *noisy*, the opposites are *quiet*, *silent*, and *inaudible*.

Students use a thesaurus to locate both synonyms and antonyms. *Scholastic Children's Thesaurus* (Bollard, 2006) and *The American Heritage Children's Thesaurus* (Hellweg, 2006) are excellent reference books. Students need to learn how to use these handy references to locate more-effective words when they're revising their writing and during word-study activities.

Homonyms: Words That Confuse

Homonyms are confusing because even though these words have different meanings, they're either pronounced the same or spelled the same as other words. Homophones are words that sound alike but are spelled differently, such as *right–write*, *air–heir*, and *there–their–they're*. A list of homophones is presented in Figure 6–3. Sometimes students confuse the meanings of these words, but more often they confuse their spellings. Most homophones are linguistic accidents, but *stationary* and *stationery* share an interesting history: *Stationery*, meaning paper and books, developed from *stationary*. In medieval England, merchants traveled from town to town selling their wares. The merchant who sold paper goods was the first to set up shop in one town. His shop was "stationary" because it didn't move, and he came to be the "stationer." The spelling difference between the two words signifies the semantic difference. In contrast, words with identical spellings but different meanings and pronunciations, such as the noun and verb forms of *wind* and the noun and adjective forms of *minute*, are homographs. Other examples include *live*, *read*, *bow*, *conduct*, *present*, and *record*.

There are many useful books of homonyms, including Gwynne's *The King Who Rained* (2006) and *A Chocolate Moose for Dinner* (2005), Barretta's *Dear Deer: A Book of Homophones*

FIGURE 6–3 ◆ Homophones

air–heir	colonel–kernel	hole–whole	patience–patients	sew–so–sow
allowed–aloud	complement–compliment	hour–our	peace–piece	side–sighed
ant–aunt	creak–creek	knead–need	peak–peek–pique	slay–sleigh
ate–eight	days–daze	knew–new	peal–peel	soar–sore
ball–bawl	dew–do–due	knight–night	pedal–peddle–petal	soared–sword
bare–bear	die–dye	knot–not	plain–plane	sole–soul
beat–beet	doe–dough	know–no	pleas–please	some–sum
berry–bury	ewe–you	lead–led	pole–poll	son–sun
billed–build	eye–I	leak–leek	poor–pore–pour	stairs–stares
blew–blue	fair–fare	lie–lye	praise–prays–preys	stake–steak
boar–bore	feat–feet	loan–lone	presence–presents	stationary–stationery
board–bored	fined–find	made–maid	pride–pried	steal–steel
bough–bow	fir–fur	main–mane	prince–prints	straight–strait
brake–break	flair–flare	manner–manor	principal–principle	suite–sweet
brews–bruise	flea–flee	marshal–martial	profit–prophet	taught–taut
bridal–bridle	flew–flu	meat–meet–mete	quarts–quartz	tear–tier
brows–browse	flour–flower	medal–meddle–metal	rain–reign–rein	their–there–they're
buy–by–bye	for–fore–four	might–mite	raise–rays–raze	threw–through
capital–capitol	forth–fourth	mind–mined	rap–wrap	throne–thrown
ceiling–sealing	foul–fowl	miner–minor	red–read	tide–tied
cell–sell	gorilla–guerrilla	missed–mist	reed–read	to–too–two
cellar–seller	grate–great	moan–mown	right–rite–write	toad–toed–towed
cent–scent–sent	groan–grown	morning–mourning	ring–wring	toe–tow
chews–choose	guessed–guest	muscle–mussel	road–rode–rowed	troop–troupe
chic–sheik	hair–hare	naval–navel	role–roll	vain–vane–vein
chili–chilly	hall–haul	none–nun	root–route	wade–weighed
choral–coral	hay–hey	oar–or–ore	rose–rows	waist–waste
chord–cord–cored	heal–heel	one–won	rung–wrung	wait–weight
chute–shoot	hear–here	pail–pale	sail–sale	wares–wears
cite–sight–site	heard–herd	pain–pane	scene–seen	way–weigh
close–clothes	hi–high	pair–pare–pear	seam–seem	weak–week
coarse–course	hoarse–horse	passed–past	serf–surf	wood–would

FIGURE 6–4 ◆ A Sixth Grader's Homonym Poster

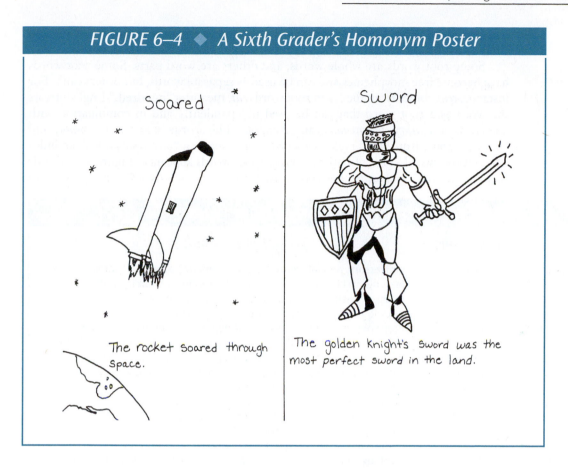

(2007), *The Dove Dove: Funny Homograph Riddles* (Terban, 1992), and *Eight Ate: A Feast of Homonym Riddles* (Terban, 2007a). Sharing these books with students helps to develop their understanding of homophones and homographs.

Primary-grade teachers introduce homonyms and teach the easier pairs, including *see–sea, I–eye, right–write,* and *dear–deer.* In fourth through eighth grades, teachers focus on homographs and the homophones that students confuse, such as *there–their–they're* and more-sophisticated pairs, including *morning–mourning, flair–flare, serf–surf,* and *complement–compliment.* Teachers teach **minilessons** to explain the concept of homonyms and have students make charts of the homophones and homographs; calling attention to differences in spelling, meaning, and pronunciation helps to clarify the words. This explicit instruction is especially important for English learners (Jacobson, Lapp, & Flood, 2007). Students can also make homonym posters with pictures and sentences to contrast homophones and homographs, as shown in Figure 6–4.

Root Words and Affixes

Students examine the root word and affixes of multisyllabic words to identify them. A root word is a *morpheme,* the basic part of a word to which affixes are added. Many words are developed from a single root word; for example, the Latin words *portare* (to carry), *portus* (harbor), and *porta* (gate) are the sources of at least 12 English words: *deport, export, exporter, import, port, portable, porter, report, reporter, support, transport,* and *transportation*. Latin is the most common source of English root words; Greek and English are two other sources.

Some root words are whole words, and others are word parts. Some root words have become free morphemes and can be used as separate words, but others can't. For instance, *cent* comes from the Latin root word *cent*, meaning "hundred." English treats the word as a root word that can be used independently and in combination with affixes, as in *century*, *bicentennial*, and *centipede*. The words *cosmopolitan*, *cosmic*, and *microcosm* come from the Greek root word *cosmo*, meaning "universe"; it isn't an independent root word. A list of Latin and Greek root words appears in Figure 6–5. Words such as *eye*, *tree*, and *water* are root words, too. New words are formed through

FIGURE 6–5 ◆ *Latin and Greek Root Words*

Root	Language	Meaning	Sample Words
ann/enn	Latin	year	anniversary, annual, centennial, millennium, perennial, semiannual
arch	Greek	ruler	anarchy, archbishop, architecture, hierarchy, monarchy, patriarch
astro	Greek	star	aster, asterisk, astrology, astronaut, astronomy, disaster
auto	Greek	self	autobiography, automatic, automobile, autopsy, semiautomatic
bio	Greek	life	biography, biohazard, biology, biodegradable, bionic, biosphere
capit/capt	Latin	head	capital, capitalize, Capitol, captain, caption, decapitate, per capita
cent	Latin	hundred	bicentennial, cent, centennial, centigrade, centipede, century, percent
circ	Latin	around	circle, circular, circus, circumspect, circuit, circumference, circumstance
cosmo	Greek	universe	cosmic, cosmopolitan, microcosm
cred	Latin	believe	credit, creed, creditable, discredit, incredulity
cycl	Greek	wheel	bicycle, cycle, cyclist, cyclone, recycle, tricycle
dict	Latin	speak	contradict, dictate, dictator, prediction, verdict
gram	Greek	letter	cardiogram, diagram, grammar, monogram, telegram
graph	Greek	write	autobiography, biographer, cryptograph, epigraph, graphic, paragraph
jus/jud/jur	Latin	law	injury, injustice, judge, juror, jury, justice, justify, prejudice
lum/lus/luc	Latin	light	illuminate, lucid, luminous, luster
man	Latin	hand	manacle, maneuver, manicure, manipulate, manual, manufacture
mar/mer	Latin	sea	aquamarine, marine, maritime, marshy, mermaid, submarine
meter	Greek	measure	centimeter, diameter, seismometer, speedometer, thermometer
mini	Latin	small	miniature, minibus, minimize, minor, minimum, minuscule, minute
mort	Latin	death	immortal, mortality, mortuary, postmortem
ped	Latin	foot	biped, pedal, pedestrian, pedicure
phono	Greek	sound	earphone, microphone, phonics, phonograph, saxophone, symphony
photo	Greek	light	photograph, photographer, photosensitive, photosynthesis
pod/pus	Greek	foot	octopus, podiatry, podium, tripod
port	Latin	carry	exporter, import, port, portable, porter, reporter, support, transportation
quer/ques/quis	Latin	seek	query, quest, question, inquisitive
scope	Greek	see	horoscope, kaleidoscope, microscope, periscope, telescope
scrib/scrip	Latin	write	describe, inscription, postscript, prescribe, scribble, scribe, script
sphere	Greek	ball	atmosphere, atmospheric, hemisphere, sphere, stratosphere
struct	Latin	build	construct, construction, destruction, indestructible, instruct, reconstruct
tele	Greek	far	telecast, telegram, telegraph, telephone, telescope, telethon, television
terr	Latin	land	subterranean, terrace, terrain, terrarium, terrier, territory
vers/vert	Latin	turn	advertise, anniversary, controversial, divert, reversible, versus
vict/vinc	Latin	conquer	convince, convict, evict, invincible, victim, victor, victory
vis/vid	Latin	see	improvise, invisible, revise, supervisor, television, video, vision, visitor
viv/vit	Latin	live	revive, survive, vital, vitamin, vivacious, vivid, viviparous
volv	Latin	roll	convolutions, evolve, evolution, involve, revolutionary, revolver, volume

compounding—for example, *eyelash*, *treetop*, and *waterfall*—and other root words, such as *read*, combine with affixes, as in *reader* and *unreadable*.

Affixes are bound morphemes that are added to words: *Prefixes* are placed at the beginning, as in *replay*, and *suffixes* are placed at the end, as in *playing*, *playful*, and *player*. Like root words, some affixes are English and others come from Latin and Greek. Affixes often change a word's meaning, such as adding *un-* to *happy* to form *unhappy*. Sometimes they change the part of speech, too; for example, when *-tion* is added to *attract* to form *attraction*, the verb *attract* becomes a noun.

There are two types of suffixes: inflectional and derivational. Inflectional suffixes are endings that indicate verb tense and person, plurals, possession, and comparison; these suffixes are English. Here are some examples:

the *-ed* in *walked*	the *-es* in *beaches*
the *-ing* in *singing*	the *-'s* in *girl's*
the *-s* in *asks*	the *-er* in *faster*
the *-s* in *dogs*	the *-est* in *sunniest*

In contrast, derivational suffixes show the relationship of the word to its root word. Consider these words containing the root word *friend*: *friendly*, *friendship*, and *friendless*.

When a word's affix is "peeled off," the remaining word is usually a real word. For example, when the prefix *pre-* is removed from *preview* or the suffix *-er* is removed from *viewer*, the word *view* can stand alone. Sometimes, however, Latin and Greek root words cannot stand alone. One example is *legible*: The *-ible* is a suffix, and *leg* is the root word even though it can't stand alone. Of course, *leg*—meaning part of the body—is a word, but the root word *leg-* from *legible* isn't: It's a Latin root word, meaning "to read."

A list of English, Greek, and Latin prefixes and suffixes is presented in Figure 6–6. White, Sowell, and Yanagihara (1989) researched affixes and identified the most common ones; these are marked with an asterisk in the figure. White and his colleagues recommend that the commonly used affixes be taught because of their usefulness. Some of the most commonly used prefixes can be confusing, however, because they have more than one meaning; the prefix *un-*, for example, can mean *not* (e.g., *unclear*) or it can reverse the meaning of a word (e.g., *tie–untie*).

Etymologies: The History of the English Language

Glimpses into the history of the English language provide interesting information about word meanings (Tompkins & Yaden, 1986). The English language began in A.D. 447 when Angles, Saxons, and other Germanic tribes invaded England. This Anglo-Saxon English was first written down by Latin missionaries in approximately A.D. 750. The English from 450 to 1100 is known as Old English. During this time, English was a very phonetic language and followed German syntactic patterns. Words, including *ugly*, *window*, *egg*, *they*, *sky*, and *husband*, were contributed by the marauding Vikings who plundered villages along the English coast.

Middle English (1100–1500) began with the Norman Conquest in 1066. William, Duke of Normandy, invaded England and became king. William and his lords spoke French, so it became the official language of England for nearly 200 years. Many French loan words were added, and French spellings were substituted for Old English spellings. For example, *night* was spelled *niht* and *queen* was spelled *cwen* in Old English to reflect how they were pronounced; their modern spellings reflect changes made by French scribes. Words from Dutch, Latin, and other languages were added during this period, too.

FIGURE 6–6 ◆ English, Greek, and Latin Affixes

Language	Prefixes	Suffixes
English	* **over-** (too much): overflow **self-** (by oneself): self-employed * **un-** (not): unhappy * **un-** (reversal): untie **under-** (beneath): underground	**-ed** (past tense): played **-ful** (full of): hopeful **-ing** (participle): eating, building **-ish** (like): reddish **-less** (without): hopeless **-ling** (young): duckling * **-ly** (in the manner of): slowly * **-ness** (state or quality): kindness **-s/-es** (plural): cats, boxes **-ship** (state of, art, or skill): friendship, seamanship **-ster** (one who): gangster **-ward** (direction): homeward * **-y** (full of): sleepy
Greek	**a-/an-** (not): atheist, anaerobic **amphi-** (both): amphibian **anti-** (against): antiseptic **di-** (two): dioxide **hemi-** (half): hemisphere **hyper-** (over): hyperactive **hypo-** (under): hypodermic **micro-** (small): microfilm **mono-** (one): monarch **omni-** (all): omnivorous **poly-** (many): polygon **sym-/syn-/sys-** (together): symbol, synonym, system	**-ism** (doctrine of): communism **-ist** (one who): artist **-logy** (the study of): zoology
Latin	**bi-** (two, twice): bifocal, biannual **contra-** (against): contradict **de-** (away): detract * **dis-** (not): disapprove * **dis-** (reversal): disinfect **ex-** (out): export * **il-/im-/in-/ir-** (not): illegible, impolite, inexpensive, irrational * **in-** (in, into): indoor **inter-** (between): intermission **mille-** (thousand): millennium * **mis-** (wrong): mistake **multi-** (many): multimillionaire **non-** (not): nonsense **post-** (after): postwar **pre-** (before): precede **quad-/quart-** (four): quadruple, quarter **re-** (again): repay * **re-/retro-** (back): replace, retroactive * **sub-** (under): submarine **super-** (above): supermarket **trans-** (across): transport **tri-** (three): triangle	**-able/-ible** (worthy of, can be): lovable, audible * **-al/-ial** (action, process): arrival, denial **-ance/-ence** (state or quality): annoyance, absence **-ant** (one who): servant **-ary/-ory** (person, place): secretary, laboratory **-cule** (very small): molecule **-ee** (one who is): trustee * **-er/-or/-ar** (one who): teacher, actor, liar **-ic** (characterized by): angelic **-ify** (to make): simplify **-ment** (state or quality): enjoyment **-ous** (full of): nervous * **-sion/-tion** (state or quality): tension, attraction **-ure** (state or quality): failure

The * indicates the most commonly used affixes (White, Sowell, & Yanagihara, 1989).

The invention of the printing press marks the transition from Middle English to Modern English (1500–present). William Caxton brought the first printing press to England in 1476, and soon books and pamphlets were being mass-produced. Spelling became standardized as Samuel Johnson and other lexicographers compiled dictionaries, even though English pronunciation of words was still evolving. New words continued to flow into English from almost every language in the world, including *zero* (Arabic), *tattoo* (Polynesian), *robot* (Czech), *yogurt* (Turkish), *restaurant* (French), *dollar* (German), *jungle* (Hindi), and *umbrella* (Italian). Some words, such as *electric*, *democracy*, and *astronaut*, were created using Greek word parts. New words continue to be added to English every year, and these words reflect new inventions and cultural practices. Many new words today, such as *e-mail*, relate to the Internet. The word *Internet* is a recent word, too; it's less than 25 years old!

Students use etymological information in dictionaries to learn how particular words evolved and what they mean. Etymological information is included in brackets at the beginning or end of dictionary entries. Here's the etymological information for three words:

democracy [1576, < MF < LL < Gr demokratia, demos (people) + kraia (cracy = strength, power)]

Explanation: The word *democracy* entered English in 1576 through French, and the French word came from Latin and before that Greek. The Greek word *demokratia* means "power to the people."

house [bef. 900, ME hous, OE hus]

Explanation: *House* is an Old English word that entered English before 900. It was spelled *hus* in Old English and *hous* in Middle English.

moose [1603, <Algonquin, "he who strips bark"]

Explanation: *Moose* is a Native American word—from an Algonquin tribe in the northeastern United States—and entered English in 1603. The Algonquin word meant "he who strips bark."

Even though words have entered English from around the world, the three main sources of words are English, Latin, and Greek. Students learn to identify the languages that these words came from because knowing the language backgrounds helps to predict the spellings and meanings (Venezky, 1999). English words are usually one- or two-syllable common words that may or may not be phonetically regular, such as *fox, arm, Monday, house, match, eleven, of, come, week, horse, brother,* and *dumb.* Words with *ch* (pronounced as /ch/), *sh, th,* and *wh* digraphs are usually English, as in *church, shell, bath,* and *what.* Many English words are compound words or use comparative and superlative forms, such as *starfish, toothache, fireplace, happier, fastest.*

Many words from Latin are similar to comparable words in French, Spanish, or Italian, such as *ancient, judicial, impossible,* and *officer.* They have related words or derivatives; for example, *courage* has these derivatives: *courageous, encourage, discourage,* and *encouragement.* Also, many Latin words have *-tion/-sion* suffixes: *imitation, extension,* and *possession.*

Greek words are unusual. Many are long words with unfamiliar spellings. The digraph *ph* is pronounced /f/, and *ch* is pronounced /k/, as in *autograph, chaos,* and *architect.* Longer words with *th,* such as *thermometer* and *arithmetic,* are Greek. The suffix *-ology* is Greek, as in the words *biology, psychology,* and *geology.* The letter *y* is used in place of *i* in the middle of some words, such as *bicycle* and *myth.* Many Greek words are composed of two parts: *bibliotherapy, microscope, biosphere, hypodermic,* and

FIGURE 6–7 ◆ *Words From English, Latin, and Greek*

English	Latin	Greek
apple	addiction	ache
between	administer	arithmetic
bumblebee	advantage	astronomy
child	capital	atomic
cry	confession	biology
cuff	continent	chaos
earth	discourage	chemical
fireplace	erupt	democracy
fourteen	explosion	disaster
freedom	fraction	geography
Friday	fragile	gymnastics
get	frequently	helicopter
have	heir	hemisphere
horse	honest	hieroglyphics
knight	identify	kaleidoscope
know	January	myth
lamb	junior	octopus
lip	nation	photosynthesis
lock	occupy	pseudonym
mouth	organize	rhythm
out	principal	sympathy
quickly	procession	telescope
silly	salute	theater
this	special	thermometer
twin	uniform	trophy
weather	vacation	zodiac
wild	vegetable	zoo

telephone. Figure 6–7 presents sample English, Latin, and Greek words that teachers can use for **word sorts** and other vocabulary activities.

Conceptually related words have developed from English, Latin, and Greek sources. Consider the words *tooth, dentist,* and *orthodontist. Tooth* is an English word, which explains its irregular plural form, *teeth. Dentist* is a Latin word; *dent* means "tooth," and the suffix *-ist* means "one who does." The word *orthodontist* is Greek. *Ortho* means "straighten" and *dont* means "tooth"; thus, *orthodontist* means "one who straightens teeth." Here are other conceptually related triplets:

book	bookstore (E), bibliography (Gr), library (L)
eye	eyelash (E), optical (Gr), binoculars (L)
foot	foot-dragging (E), tripod (Gr), pedestrian (L)
great	greatest (E), megaphone (Gr), magnificent (L)
see	foresee (E), microscope (Gr), invisible (L)
star	starry (E), astronaut (Gr), constellation (L)
time	time-tested (E), chronological (Gr), contemporary (L)
water	watermelon (E), hydrate (Gr), aquarium (L)

When students understand English, Latin, and Greek root words, they appreciate the relationships among words and their meanings.

Figurative Meanings

Many words have both literal and figurative meanings: Literal meanings are explicit, dictionary meanings, and figurative meanings are metaphorical. For example, to describe *winter* as the coldest season of the year is literal, but to say that "winter has icy breath" is figurative. Two types of figurative language are idioms and comparisons.

Idioms are phrases, such as "in hot water," that have a symbolic meaning. Idioms can be confusing because they must be interpreted figuratively. "In hot water" is an old expression meaning to be in trouble. In the Middle Ages, people had to protect themselves from robbers. When a robber tried to break into a house, the homeowner might pour boiling water from a second-floor window onto the head of the robber, who would then be "in hot water." There are hundreds of idioms in English that make language more colorful; examples include "out in left field," "a skeleton in the closet," "raining cats and dogs," and "a chip off the old block." Students can examine books that explain the stories behind the idioms, including *Scholastic Dictionary of Idioms* (Terban, 2006a), *Mad as a Wet Hen! And Other Funny Idioms* (Terban, 2007c), *In a Pickle and Other Funny Idioms* (Terban, 2007b), *My Teacher Likes to Say* (Brennan-Nelson, 2004), and *There's a Frog in My Throat! 440 Animal Sayings a Little Bird Told Me* (Leedy, 2003).

Because idioms are figurative sayings, many students—especially English learners—have difficulty understanding them (Palmer, Shackelford, Miller, & Leclere, 2006/2007). It's crucial that teachers provide explicit instruction so that students learn their figurative meanings. They can create idiom posters to compare their literal and figurative meanings, as illustrated in Figure 6–8.

FIGURE 6–8 ◆ *A Sixth Grader's Idiom Poster for "In Hot Water"*

Indiana Jones was stuck in the cave; he was in hot water.

Metaphors and similes are comparisons that liken something to something else. A simile is signaled by the use of *like* or *as*: "The crowd was as rowdy as a bunch of marauding monkeys" is an example. In contrast, a metaphor compares two things by implying that one is the other, without using *like* or *as*: "The children were frisky puppies playing in the yard" is an example. Metaphors are stronger comparisons.

Teaching Students to Unlock Word Meanings

Vocabulary instruction plays a crucial role in the middle grades because students' knowledge of academic vocabulary directly affects their literacy achievement. Baumann, Kame'enui, and Ash (2003) and Graves (2006) identified these components of effective vocabulary instruction:

- Immerse students in words through listening, talking, reading, and writing
- Teach specific words through active involvement
- Teach word-learning strategies
- Develop students' word consciousness

Teachers address these components when they teach vocabulary. Too often, vocabulary instruction has emphasized only the second component, teaching specific words, without developing students' ability to learn words independently and use them effectively. The feature below lists guidelines for teaching vocabulary.

Guidelines
for Teaching Vocabulary

- Highlight on word walls key words from books students are reading and from thematic units.
- Choose Tier 2 words—academic vocabulary—for explicit instruction.
- Scaffold students as they develop full word knowledge by teaching multiple meanings, synonyms, antonyms, word histories, root words and affixes, and figurative meanings.
- Teach minilessons about the meanings of individual words and vocabulary concepts.
- Teach students to use word-learning strategies to unlock the meanings of unfamiliar words.
- Engage students in word-study activities, such as word posters and word sorts, so they can deepen their understanding of specific words.
- Develop students' word consciousness by demonstrating curiosity about words, teaching about words, and involving students in wordplay activities.
- Encourage incidental word learning by having students read independently for 30–60 minutes each day.

Highlighting Words on Word Walls

Teachers post **word walls** in the classroom; usually they're made from large sheets of butcher paper divided into sections for each letter of the alphabet. Students and the teacher write interesting and important words representing all three tiers on the word wall. Usually students choose the words to write and do the writing themselves, but teachers add any important words that students haven't chosen. Words are added to the word wall as they come up in books students are reading or during a thematic unit, not in advance. Allen (2007) says that word walls should be "a living part of the classroom with new words being added each day" (p. 120). Word walls are useful resources: Students locate words that they want to use during **grand conversations** or check the spelling of a word they're writing, and teachers use the words for word-study activities.

Students also make individual word walls by dividing a sheet of paper into boxes and labeling the boxes with the letters of the alphabet. Then they write important words in the boxes as they read or when they're added to the classroom word wall. Individual word walls often work better in middle school settings where teachers are departmentalized because it's not practical to hang different word walls for each class.

Explicit Instruction

Teachers explicitly teach specific words, usually Tier 2 words. McKeown and Beck (2004) emphasize that instruction should be rich, deep, and extended. That means that teachers provide multiple encounters with words; present a variety of information, including definitions, contexts, examples, and related words; and involve students in activities using the word. The procedure is time-consuming, but researchers report that students are more successful in learning and remembering word meanings this way.

Teachers use **minilessons** to teach specific words. They provide information about words, including both definitions and contextual information, and they engage students in activities to get them to think about and use words orally and in reading and writing. Sometimes teachers present minilessons before reading; at other times, they teach them afterward. The minilesson on page 166 shows how Mrs. Cramer introduces vocabulary before reading a chapter in a content-area textbook.

Word-Study Activities

Students examine words, visualize word meanings, and think more deeply about them as they participate in word-study activities (Allen, 2007). In these activities, they create visual representations of words, categorize words, or investigate related words:

Word Posters. Students choose a word and write it on a small word poster; then they draw a picture to illustrate it. They also use the word in a sentence on the poster.

Word Maps. Students create diagrams known as *word maps* to examine words. They write a word, make a box around it, draw several lines from the box, and add information about the word in additional boxes they put at the end of each line. Students usually identify a category for the word, several examples, and characteristics or associations for the word. Figure 6–9 shows a word map for *glistened* made by a fifth grader while he was reading *Bunnicula: A Rabbit-Tale of Mystery* (Howe & Howe, 2006).

Minilesson

TOPIC: *Introducing Content-Area Vocabulary Words*
GRADE: *Fifth Grade*
TIME: *Three 30-minute periods*

Mrs. Cramer's fifth-grade class is involved in a social studies unit on immigration. They've already created a K-W-L chart on immigration to activate students' background knowledge, and students have written about how their families came to the United States. They've also marked their countries of origin on a world map hanging in the classroom. In this 3-day minilesson, Mrs. Cramer introduces five key vocabulary words before students read a chapter in their social studies textbook. Because many of her students are English learners, she takes more time to practice vocabulary before reading the chapter.

❶ Introduce the Topic

Mrs. Cramer explains that the fifth graders are now getting ready to read the chapter about immigration in the social studies text. She places these five words written on word cards in a pocket chart and reads each one aloud: *culture, descendant, immigrant, prejudice,* and *pluralism*. She tells students that these words are used in the chapter and that it's important to be familiar with them before reading.

❷ Share Examples

The teacher distributes anticipation guides for students to rate their knowledge of the new words. The new words are listed in the left column of the guide, and the other three columns have these headings: I know the word well, I've heard of it, I don't know this word. For each word, the students put a checkmark in the appropriate column. At the end of the unit, they'll again rate their knowledge of the words and compare the two ratings to assess their learning.

❸ Provide Information

Mrs. Cramer divides the students into small groups for a word sort. Each group receives a pack of 10 cards; the new vocabulary words are written on five of the cards and their definitions on the other cards. Students work together to match the words and definitions, and then Mrs. Cramer reviews the meaning of each word.

❹ Guide Practice

The next day, the students repeat the word sort activity to review the meanings of the words. Next, they work with partners to complete a cloze activity: Mrs. Cramer has prepared a list of sentences taken from the chapter with the new words omitted, and students write the correct word in each blank. Then she reviews the sentences, explaining any sentences completed incorrectly.

❺ Assess Learning

On the third day, Mrs. Cramer adds the new words to the word wall displayed in the classroom. Next, she models writing a quickwrite using the new words and other words from the word wall. Following the teacher's model, students write quickwrites using at least three of the new words and three additional words from the word wall. Afterward, students use highlighters to mark the immigration-related words they've incorporated in their quickwrites. Later, Mrs. Cramer reads the quickwrites to assess the students' vocabulary knowledge.

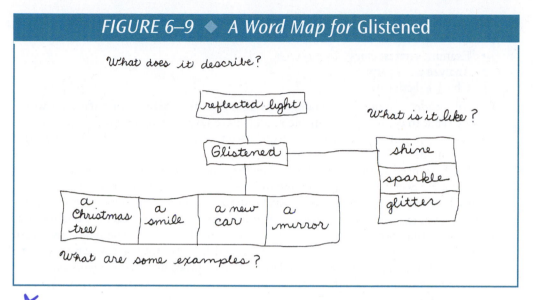

FIGURE 6–9 ◆ A Word Map for Glistened

Word Sorts. Students sort a group of words into two or more categories in a **word sort** (Bear, Invernizzi, Templeton, & Johnston, 2008). Usually students choose the categories, but sometimes the teacher does. For example, words from a novel might be sorted by character, or words from a thematic unit on machines might be sorted according to type of machine. The words can be written on cards, or students can cut apart a list of words and sort them into categories.

Word Chains. Students choose a word and then identify three or four synonyms or other related words to sequence before or after it to make a chain. For example, the word *aggravate* can be chained like this to indicate shades of meaning: *irritate, bother, aggravate, annoy*. Students can write their chains on a sheet of paper, or they can make a chain out of construction paper and write a word on each link.

Semantic Feature Analysis. Students analyze the meanings of a group of related words in a **semantic feature analysis** (Allen, 2007). Teachers select a group of words and make a grid to classify them according to distinguishing characteristics (Rickelman & Taylor, 2006). Students consider a word, characteristic by characteristic, and mark each cell to indicate whether the word represents that characteristic. The word *sloth* might be included in a semantic feature analysis about the rain forest, for example, and students would add marks in the grid to indicate that a sloth is a mammal and lives in the canopy, and a different mark to indicate that it's not dangerous to people or used for medicine.

These word-study activities provide opportunities for students to deepen their understanding of words. None of them require students to simply write words and their definitions or to use words in sentences or a contrived story.

Word-Learning Strategies

When students come across an unfamiliar word while reading, they can reread the sentence, examine root words and affixes in the word, check a dictionary, pronounce the word, look for context clues in the sentence, skip the word and keep reading, or ask a classmate for help (Allen, 1999). Some techniques, however, work better than others. After studying the research on ways to deal

Be Strategic!
Word-Learning Strategies

When students come across an unfamiliar word, they use these strategies to figure out the word's meaning:

▶ Examine context clues
▶ Analyze word parts
▶ Check a dictionary

These three strategies are effective when students know how to apply them and are interested in learning new words.

with unfamiliar words, Graves (2006) recommends these three effective word-learning strategies:

- Examine context clues
- Analyze word parts
- Check a dictionary

Capable students apply these strategies to figure out the meaning of unfamiliar words as they read. In contrast, less capable readers have fewer strategies available: They often depend on just one or two less effective strategies, such as pronouncing the word or skipping it.

Students need to know what to do when they encounter unfamiliar words, especially those that are essential to understanding the meaning of the text they're reading (Graves, 2006). Teachers teach **minilessons** about the strategies and how to apply them, and students practice examining context clues, analyzing word parts, and checking a dictionary as they read fiction, nonfiction, and content-area textbooks. Also, during **interactive read-alouds**, teachers demonstrate how to use the word-learning strategies when they come across words that might be new to students. Here's a procedure that students can use to figure out the meaning of unfamiliar words:

1. Reread the sentence containing the word.
2. Examine context clues to figure out the word's meaning, but if that doesn't work, continue to the next step.
3. Analyze word parts, looking for root words and affixes to aid in figuring out the meaning, but if that's not successful, continue to the next step.
4. Pronounce the word to see if it sounds familiar, but if that doesn't work, continue to the next step.
5. Check the word in a dictionary or ask the teacher for help.

This procedure has the greatest chance of success because it incorporates all three word-learning strategies.

Using Context Clues. Students learn many words from context as they read. The surrounding words and sentences offer context clues; some clues provide information about the meaning of the word, and others provide information about the part of speech and how the word is used in a sentence. This contextual information helps students infer the word's meaning. Illustrations also provide information that helps identify words. The types of context clues that readers use are presented in Figure 6–10. Interestingly, two or three types of contextual information are often found in the same sentence.

Nagy, Anderson, and Herman (1987) found that students who read books at their grade level have a 1 in 20 chance of learning a word's meaning from context. Although that might seem insignificant, if students read 20,000 words a year and learn 1 of every 20 words from context, they will learn 1,000 words, or one third of their annual vocabulary growth. That's significant! How much time does it take to read 20,000 words? Nagy (1988) estimated that if teachers provide 30 minutes of daily reading time, students will learn an additional 1,000 words a year! It's interesting to note that both more- and less capable readers learn from context at about the same rate (Stahl, 1999).

The best way to teach students about context clues is by modeling. When teachers read aloud, they can stop at a difficult word and talk about how to use context clues to figure out its meaning. If the context provides adequate information, teachers deduce the word's meaning and continue reading, but when it doesn't, teachers demonstrate another strategy to figure out the word's meaning.

Analyzing Word Parts. Students can use their knowledge of affixes and root words to unlock many multisyllabic words when they understand how word parts function. For example, *omnivorous*, *carnivorous*, and *herbivorous* relate to the foods that animals eat: *Omni*

FIGURE 6–10 ◆ Types of Context Clues

Clue	Description	Sample Sentence
Definition	Readers use the definition in the sentence to understand the unknown word.	Some spiders spin silk with tiny organs called *spinnerets*.
Example-Illustration	Readers use an example or illustration to understand the unknown word.	Toads, frogs, and some birds are *predators* that hunt and eat spiders.
Contrast	Readers understand the unknown word because it's compared or contrasted with another word in the sentence.	Most spiders live for about one year, but *tarantulas* sometimes live for 20 years or more!
Logic	Readers think about the rest of the sentence to understand the unknown word.	An *exoskeleton* acts like a suit of armor to protect the spider.
Root Words and Affixes	Readers use their knowledge of root words and affixes to figure out the unknown word.	People who are terrified of spiders have *arachnophobia*.
Grammar	Readers use the word's function in the sentence or its part of speech to figure out the unknown word.	Most spiders *molt* five to ten times.

means "all," *carno* means "flesh," and *herb* means "vegetation." The common word part *vorous* comes from the Latin word *vorare*, meaning "to swallow up." When students know *carnivorous* or *carnivore*, they use morphemic analysis to figure out the other words.

Teaching prefixes, derivational suffixes, and non-English root words in the middle grades improves students' ability to unlock the meaning of unfamiliar words (Baumann, Edwards, Font, Tereshinski, Kame'enui, & Olejnik, 2002; Baumann, Font, Edwards, & Boland, 2005). For example, when students recognize that the Latin roots *-ann* and *-enn* mean "year," they can figure out the meanings of *annual, biennial, perennial, centennial, bicentennial, millennium,* and *sesquicentennial*. Graves (2006) recommends that teachers teach morphemic analysis when non-English root words appear in books students are reading and during thematic units. Teachers break apart the words and discuss the word parts when they're posted on the word wall and through minilessons.

Checking the Dictionary. Looking up unfamiliar words in the dictionary is often frustrating because the definitions don't provide enough useful information or because words used in the definition are forms of the word being defined (Allen, 1999). Sometimes the definition that students choose—usually the first one—is the wrong one, or the definition doesn't make sense. For example, the word *pollution* is usually defined as "the act of polluting"—not very useful! Students could look for an entry for *polluting*, but they won't find it. They might notice an entry for *pollute*, where the first definition is "to make impure." The second definition is "to make unclean, especially with man-made waste," but even this definition may be difficult to understand.

Teachers play an important role in teaching students how to read a dictionary entry. During interactive read-alouds, for example, teachers pause when they come across an unfamiliar word. A student locates the word in a dictionary and reads the entry aloud; then the class decides which definition is most appropriate.

Incidental Word Learning

Students learn words incidentally all the time, and because they learn so many words this way, teachers know that it isn't necessary to teach the meaning of every unfamiliar word. Students learn words from many sources, but researchers report that reading is

STRUGGLING READERS AND WRITERS

Lots of Words

Struggling readers need to know more words.

One of the biggest challenges facing struggling readers is their limited word knowledge. Even though independent reading is an important way to acquire a large vocabulary, it isn't enough for struggling students (Allington, 2006). Students who exhibit reading difficulties don't do as much reading as their peers, and the books they read don't introduce them to grade-level vocabulary words. To expand students' vocabularies, it's essential that teachers provide daily activities to draw students' attention to words and instruction on Tier 2 words and word-learning strategies. Cooper, Chard, and Kiger (2006) offer these instructional recommendations:

- ▶ *Nurture students' awareness of words using word walls, independent reading, and interactive read-alouds.*
- ▶ *Explicitly teach the meanings of 8–10 words each week by introducing key words before reading and providing engaging practice activities afterward.*
- ▶ *Develop students' ability to figure out the meaning of unfamiliar words.*

Teachers can accelerate students' vocabulary development by implementing a more-structured program with daily lessons based on these recommendations.

Sometimes teachers thwart students' vocabulary development. Allington (2006) identified these activities that waste instructional time: First, students shouldn't read books that are too difficult because they won't understand them. Next, teachers can't expect students to figure out the meaning of unfamiliar words if they haven't been taught to use context clues or other word-learning strategies. Third, students shouldn't be given a list of words and asked to copy the definition for each word or write a sentence using it. These activities don't develop in-depth word knowledge.

the best source of vocabulary growth (Swanborn & de Glopper, 1999).

Independent Reading. Students need daily opportunities for independent reading to learn lots of words, and they need books that they can read easily. Reading workshop is the best way to provide time for independent reading. Students choose books from age-appropriate and reading-level-suitable collections in classroom libraries, and because they've chosen the books themselves, they're more likely to keep reading. **Sustained Silent Reading** (SSR) is another way to encourage independent reading: Students spend 30 minutes or more reading books they they've chosen themselves, and even the teacher takes time to read. Simply providing time for independent reading, however, doesn't guarantee that students will learn lots of words because they need to know how to use context clues and other word-learning strategies to increase their vocabulary (Stahl & Nagy, 2006).

Reading Aloud to Students. Teachers also provide for incidental word learning when they read aloud fiction, nonfiction, and poetry. Daily read-aloud activities are important for students at all grade levels, even in seventh and eighth grades. Teachers use the **interactive read-aloud** procedure and focus on a few key words in the book, model how to use context clues to understand new words, and talk about the words after reading. Two recent studies found that teachers enhance students' vocabulary knowledge and their comprehension when they add a focus on vocabulary to their read-alouds (Fisher, Frey, & Lapp, 2008; Santoro, Chard, Howard, & Baker, 2008).

Assessing Students' Vocabulary Knowledge

It's difficult to assess students' vocabulary knowledge because there aren't any grade-level standards to indicate which words students should know or even how many words they should learn. Moreover, assessing vocabulary is complicated because students learn words gradually, moving to deeper levels of "knowing" a word. Teachers typically monitor students' independent reading and use these informal assessment tools to evaluate whether students have learned the words that were taught and the depth of their knowledge:

Observations. Teachers watch how students use new words during word-study activities, **minilessons**, and discussions. They also notice how students apply word-learning strategies during **guided reading** lessons and **interactive read-alouds**.

Rubrics. Teachers include vocabulary items on **rubrics**. For oral-presentation rubrics, teachers can emphasize technical terms, and for writing, they stress precise vocabulary.

Tests. Teachers also create a variety of paper-and-pencil tests to monitor students' vocabulary knowledge. For example, students use the **cloze procedure** to complete a passage, **quickwrite** about a word, or create a word map for a word.

These informal assessments are more useful than formal tests because they go beyond simply asking students to provide a definition or use a word in a sentence (Bean & Swan, 2006).

Students also self-assess their knowledge of specific words, using levels of word knowledge (Cunningham & Allington, 2007). Teachers develop a list of word knowledge levels using language that's appropriate for their students. This list was developed by a sixth-grade teacher:

1 = I don't know this word at all.

2 = I've heard this word before, but I don't know the meaning.

3 = I think I know what this word means.

4 = I know one meaning for this word, and I can use it in a sentence.

5 = I know several meanings or other things about this word.

Teachers prepare a list of words related to a novel or at the beginning of a thematic unit and give it to students. Students assess their word knowledge by writing a number beside each word to indicate their knowledge level, and then they repeat the procedure after reading the novel or at the end of the unit to see how their knowledge has expanded. Or, before introducing a new word, teachers informally ask students to raise their hands and hold up the number of fingers corresponding to their level of word knowledge.

CHAPTER 6

Review

How Effective Teachers Expand Academic Vocabulary

▶ Teachers categorize unfamiliar words into three tiers—basic words, academic vocabulary, and specialized terms.

▶ Teachers nurture students' word consciousness.

▶ Teachers teach Tier 2 words using explicit instruction and a variety of word-study activities.

▶ Teachers support students' development of word-learning strategies.

▶ Teachers provide daily opportunities for students to read books and listen to them read aloud.

Promoting Comprehension: Reader Factors

Mrs. Donnelly Teaches Comprehension Strategies

Posters about comprehension strategies, including connecting, repairing, and summarizing, hang on the wall in Mrs. Donnelly's classroom. She introduced comprehension by explaining that sixth graders think while they read, and that they do different kinds of thinking; these kinds of thinking are called *strategies*. Her students made the posters as they studied each strategy. Tanner, Vincente, and Ashante's poster for monitoring is shown in the box on the next page.

One of the first strategies that Mrs. Donnelly taught was predicting, and even though her students were familiar with it, they didn't know why they were using it. She explained that predictions guide thinking. Together they made a chart about the strategy and practiced making predictions as Mrs. Donnelly read *The Garden of Abdul Gasazi* (Van Allsburg, 1993a), about an evil magician who hates dogs. The students made predictions about the surrealistic story based on the title and the cover illustration, but making predictions got tougher in the middle because they didn't know whether the dog would escape the magician's garden. Mrs. Donnelly emphasized the importance of continuing to think and make predictions when the story gets confusing. She stopped reading and talked first about why the dog was likely to be successful and then why he wouldn't be. Only about two thirds of the students predicted he would make it home safely, but he did.

The next day, they read *La Mariposa* (Jiménez, 1998), an autobiographical story about a migrant child with exceptional artistic ability. The title, which means "the butterfly," and the illustration on the cover of a boy flying toward the sun didn't provide enough information on which to base a prediction, so the students learned that sometimes they have to read a few pages before they can make useful predictions.

	Monitoring
What is it?	*It is checking that you are understanding what you are reading.*
Why use it?	*Monitoring helps you solve problems so you can be successful.*
When?	*You should use this strategy while you are reading.*
What do you do?	*1 Keep asking: Does this make sense?*
	If you understand, keep reading, but if it doesn't make sense, take action to solve the problem.
	2 Try these solutions:
	• Go back several pages or to the beginning of the chapter and reread.
	• Keep reading for one or two more pages.
	• Reread the last prediction, connection, or summary you wrote.
	• Talk to a friend about the problem.
	• Write a quickwrite about the problem.
	• Talk to Mrs. Donnelly.

After reading about Francisco's difficult first day of school in an English-only classroom, Norma figured out that the caterpillar the boy is watching in the classroom will become a butterfly, and that the boy on the front cover is flying like a butterfly, but she didn't know why that connection was important. Several students pointed out that the butterfly might symbolize freedom. Moises predicted that Francisco will be rescued from the migrant tent city where he and his family live, and Lizette suggested that he'll move to a bilingual classroom where his teacher will understand him and he'll make friends. Even though those predictions were wrong, the students became more engaged in the story. Mrs. Donnelly wrote their predictions on small self-stick notes and attached them to the edge of the pages. She modeled how to use these notes because she wanted to make their thinking more visible, and she explained that she wants them to use self-stick notes, too: "I want you to show me your thinking."

Next, she taught the connecting strategy using *So Far From the Sea* (Bunting, 1998), about life at a Japanese relocation camp during World War II. She explained that readers make three kinds of connections—text-to-self, text-to-world, and text-to-text. As she read the book aloud, she modeled making connections and encouraged the sixth graders to share their connections. Each time they made a connection, Mrs. Donnelly wrote it on a self-stick note; after she finished reading the book, she collected the notes, sorted them according to the type of connection, and posted them in text-to-self, text-to-world, and text-to-text columns on a chart. The chart is shown on page 174.

After reviewing the comprehension strategies, Mrs. Donnelly explained that readers rarely use just one strategy in a book; instead, they integrate their use as they read. The students read *Joey Pigza Loses Control*, a Newbery Honor book by Jack Gantos (2005), to practice using the strategies. She introduced the book this way:

The Connections Chart About So Far From the Sea

Text-to-Self	Text-to-World	Text-to-Text
My grandmother takes flowers when she goes to the cemetery because one of her husbands died.	I know that in World War II, Americans were fighting the Japanese because of Pearl Harbor, and they were fighting Hitler, too.	This story is like _The Bracelet_. That girl's family was taken to a camp in the desert. It was miserable there and they didn't deserve to go.
My great-granddad had to go too, and it wasn't fair because he was a loyal American, but his parents were from Japan.	In the book it's World War II, but I'm thinking about our war in Iraq.	Another book I know is _Journey to Topaz_. Topaz was another war relocation center and it was a terrible prison, too.
I know how to make origami birds. My cousin and I learned last summer.		I've heard about a book called _Anne Frank_. She was Jewish and this sorta happened to her in Germany and she died, too.
We have an American flag on our car so everyone knows we love America.		

This is a story about a boy named Joey who is about your age. His parents are divorced, and he's going to spend the summer with his dad. Joey is ADHD. His mother says he's "wired," and he uses medicine patches to control his behavior. He doesn't know his dad very well, so he doesn't know what to expect. His mom tells him not to expect too much.

She asks the sixth graders to think about what they know about divorced parents, summer vacations, and ADHD kids. They talk about those topics to stimulate their thinking about the story and brainstorm these questions:

What is Joey's dad like?

Will they have fun together?

Will Joey be in the way?

Does he hope his parents will get back together?

Does Joey's dad love him?

Will Joey's dad disappoint him?

Will Joey disappoint his dad?

Will Joey's medicine work, or will he be "wired"?

Will Joey's mom be lonely without him?

Will Joey stay with his dad all summer or come back home sooner?

Mrs. Donnelly passes out copies of the book and stacks of small self-stick notes so students can record their thinking as they read. They read the first chapter together, and then students continue reading on their own or with a partner. The sixth graders quickly get interested in the story, and it's easy reading for most of them. Mrs. Donnelly chose it so they'd have the cognitive resources available while reading to concentrate on their strategy use.

After reading the first chapter, the students talk about it in a **grand conversation**. They begin by talking about what they remember, and then Mrs. Donnelly reads the sentence from page 10 where Joey talks about the dad he doesn't know very well: "I just want him to love me as much as I already love him." She asks, "How do parents show that they love their children?" She hangs up a sheet of chart paper, divides it into two columns, and writes the question at the top of the first column. The students suggest a number of ways: giving them presents, taking care of them, spending time with them, taking them to church, keeping them safe, and having dinner with them. Mrs. Donnelly writes their ideas in the first column. Then she narrows the question and asks, "What do you think Joey is looking for from his dad?" Ashante says, "He wants his dad to pay attention to him." Leticia suggests, "He wants him to say 'I love you, son,' tell him he's missed him, and play basketball with him." Students continue to offer ideas, which Mrs. Donnelly adds to the chart. Then she asks, "How do kids show love to their parents?" and she writes the question at the top of the second column. The students suggest that kids show their love by behaving, making their parents proud, being responsible, and doing their chores; she writes these answers in the second column. Finally, Mrs. Donnelly asks, "What is Joey's dad expecting from his son?" It's much harder for the students to put themselves in this role. Henry offers, "I think he just wants to have him live with him every day." The sixth graders also reflect about their strategy use. Several students share the predictions they made, and others talk about how they monitored their reading and made connections while they were reading.

After reading and discussing each chapter, the students collect the self-stick notes they've used to keep track of their thinking, and they write about the strategies they've used in a **double-entry journal**. Normally, double-entry journals have two columns, but Mrs. Donnelly asks the students to include three columns—she's calling it a triple-entry journal: They write what was happening in the text or copy a quote from the text in the first column, explain their thinking in the second column, and identify the strategy they used in the third column. Excerpts from Tanner's triple-entry thinking journal are shown on page 176.

The students continue to read, discuss, and write about their strategy use. After they've read half the book, Mrs. Donnelly brings the class together for a **minilesson**. She explains that she's reviewed their thinking journals and has noticed that students aren't

Excerpts From Tanner's Triple-Entry Thinking Journal

Chapter	The Text	Your Thinking	The Strategy
1	Joey's mom warns him that his dad is wired like he is.	I'm thinking that this book is about a kid who doesn't know his dad and he's going to be disappointed by him. His Mom doesn't think it's going to be a good vacation.	Identifying big ideas
4	Joey's dad doesn't act like a dad and his Grandma doesn't act like a grandma.	My stomach feels queasy. Joey doesn't belong with these people. His dad doesn't stop talking to listen to him and his grandma doesn't even like him. I predict bad things are going to happen.	Predicting
7	After the game they go to the mall to see Leezy.	My mind is asking questions. Why would Carter let Joey drive the car to the mall? Why would his dad tell him it's OK to steal money out of the wishing pond? Is the author trying to show us what a terrible dad he is? We already know that.	Questioning
8	His dad thinks Joey doesn't need the patches and he won't let him have them.	What is wrong with his dad? The patch is medicine that he needs. I am so mad at his dad. That's all I can think. I'm glad my parents take good care of me.	Connecting
14	Joey calls his mom to come get him at the mall.	I think Joey is really a smart kid. He knows how to save himself. He calls his mom and she comes to get him. Joey is right to call his dad a J-E-R-K because that's what he is. The visit was a fiasco just like I predicted. This is a really great book and I want to read it all over again.	Evaluating

using summarizing very much. They review the summarizing strategy, how and when to use the strategy, and why they should use it. Mrs. Donnelly demonstrates how to summarize as she reads the beginning of the next chapter aloud, and then she encourages students to use the strategy as they read the next chapter.

After they finish reading *Joey Pigza Loses Control*, the students have another grand conversation. They talk about how Joey's mom rescues him and how disillusioned Joey is about his dad. Next, they return to the questions they brainstormed before they began reading and answer them. Jake answers the question "Does Joey's dad love him?" this way: "I think his dad does love him but it's a strange kind of love because his dad is selfish. He loves him as much as he can, but it's not very good love." Lizette answers these two questions: "Will Joey's dad disappoint him?" and "Will Joey disappoint his dad?" She says, "I'm positive that Joey's dad disappointed him. His dad wasn't a good dad. The second question is harder to answer. I know Joey tried to be a good son, but it's impossible to satisfy his dad. His dad made him wired and then got mad at him for being wired."

Then they reread the chart they began after reading the first chapter about parents showing their love for their children and children showing their love for their parents. They talk about the things they learned that Joey wanted from his dad: for his dad to listen to him, to take care of him, to be responsible for him. They also talk about what Joey's dad wanted from him. Dillan explains, "I think Joey's dad wanted Joey to be his friend and to take care of him. I think Joey will be a better dad than his dad was." Then Mrs. Donnelly asks about Joey's mom: "Does Joey's mom love him?" Everyone agrees that she does, and they name the ways that she shows her love, including giving him money so he can call her, listening to him, worrying about him, hugging him, and telling him she loves him. They complete the chart by adding the new suggestions and then circling the behaviors that his dad exemplified in blue, his mom's in green, and Joey's in red. Later, students will use the information on this chart as they write an essay about how parents and children show their love for one another.

As they reflect on their strategy use, the students are amazed that they remember so much from the story and how well they understand it. Jake says, "I was thinking all the time in this story. I guess that's why I know so much about it. This thinking is a good idea." Richard agrees, saying, "I don't even have to remember to use strategies now. I just naturally think that way." Mrs. Donnelly smiles at Richard's comment. Her goal is for her students to use comprehension strategies independently. She'll continue to have the sixth graders to use self-stick notes to track their thinking for several more months, but she'll gradually remove this scaffold once she sees that they've become strategic readers.

Comprehension is the goal of reading; it's the reason why people read. Young adolescents must understand what they're reading to learn from the experience, to make sense of the words in the text to maintain interest, and to become lifelong readers. Mrs. Donnelly was teaching her students to use comprehension strategies because strategic readers are more likely to comprehend what they're reading. Struggling readers, in contrast, are frustrated; they don't understand what they're reading, don't like to read, and aren't likely to read in the future.

Comprehension involves four levels of thinking:

◆ Literal comprehension
◆ Inferential comprehension
◆ Critical comprehension
◆ Evaluative comprehension

The most basic level is literal comprehension: Readers pick out main ideas, sequence details, notice similarities and differences, and identify explicitly stated reasons. The higher levels differ from literal comprehension because readers use their own knowledge along with the information presented in the text. In inferential comprehension, readers use clues in the text, implied information, and their background knowledge to draw inferences. They make predictions, recognize cause and effect, and determine the author's purpose. Critical comprehension is the third level: Readers analyze symbolic meanings, distinguish fact from opinion, and draw conclusions. The most sophisticated level is evaluative comprehension: Readers assess the value of a text using generally accepted criteria and personal standards. They detect bias, identify faulty reasoning, determine the effectiveness of persuasive techniques, and judge the quality of texts. These levels point out the range of thinking readers do. Because it's important to involve students in higher-level thinking, teachers ask questions and plan activities that require inferential, critical, and evaluative comprehension.

What Is Comprehension?

Comprehension is a creative, multifaceted thinking process in which students engage with the text (Tierney, 1990). You've read about the word *process* before—both reading and writing have been described as processes. A process is more complicated than a single action: It involves a series of behaviors that occur over time. The comprehension process begins during prereading as students activate their background knowledge and preview the text, and it continues to develop as students read, respond, explore, and apply their reading. Readers construct a mental "picture" or representation of the text and its interpretation through the comprehension process (Van Den Broek & Kremer, 2000).

Irwin (1991) defines comprehension as a reader's process of using prior experiences and the author's text to construct meaning that's useful to that reader for a specific purpose. This definition emphasizes that comprehension depends on two factors: the reader and the text. Whether comprehension is successful, according to Sweet and Snow (2003), depends on the interaction of reader factors and text factors.

Reader and Text Factors

Readers are actively engaged with the text; they think about many things as they read to comprehend the text. For example, they do the following:

Activate prior knowledge

Examine the text to uncover its organization

Make predictions

Connect to their own experiences

Create mental images

Draw inferences

Notice symbols and other literary devices

Monitor their understanding

These activities can be categorized as reader and text factors (National Reading Panel, 2000). Reader factors include the background knowledge that readers bring to the reading experience as well as the strategies they use while reading and their engagement during reading. Text factors include the author's ideas, the organization of ideas, and the words used to express the ideas. Both reader and text factors affect comprehension. Figure 7–1 presents an overview of these two factors. This chapter focuses on reader factors, and Chapter 8 addresses text factors.

In the Spotlight feature on page 180, Ales, Graciela, and Kolei share their insights about comprehension, both reader and text factors. They reflect on the kinds of reading they do, explain what they do to understand what they're reading, and talk about books they've read and their favorite authors.

FIGURE 7–1 ◆ The Comprehension Factors

Type	Factors	Role in Comprehension
Reader	Background Knowledge	Students activate their world and literary knowledge to link what they know to what they're reading.
	Vocabulary	Students recognize the meaning of familiar words and apply word-learning strategies to understand what they're reading.
	Fluency	Students have adequate cognitive resources available to understand what they're reading when they read fluently.
	Comprehension Strategies	Students actively direct their reading, monitor their understanding, and troubleshoot comprehension problems when they occur.
	Comprehension Skills	Students automatically note details that support main ideas, sequence ideas, and use other skills.
	Motivation	Motivated students are more engaged in reading, more confident, and more likely to comprehend successfully.
Text	Genres	Students' knowledge of the characteristics of genres provides a scaffold for comprehension.
	Text Structures	Students recognize the important ideas more easily when they understand how authors organize text.
	Text Features	Students apply their knowledge of literary devices to deepen their understanding.

Prerequisites for Comprehension

Comprehension is dependent on students having adequate background knowledge about the topic and the genre, being familiar with most words in the text, and being able to read it fluently (Allington, 2006). When one of these requirements is lacking, students are unlikely to comprehend what they're reading (Cooper, Chard, & Kiger, 2006). When students lack any of these prerequisites, teachers differentiate instruction to increase the likelihood that they'll be successful.

Background Knowledge. Having adequate background knowledge is a prerequisite because when students have both world knowledge and literary knowledge, it provides a bridge to a new text (Braunger & Lewis, 2006). Teachers use prereading activities to build students' background knowledge; first they determine whether students need world or literary knowledge and then provide experiences and information to develop their schema. They use a combination of experiences, visual representations, and talk to build knowledge. Involving students in authentic experiences such as taking field trips, participating in dramatizations, and examining artifacts is the best way to build background knowledge, but photos, picture books, websites, videos, and other visual representations can also be used. Talk is the least effective way, especially for English learners, but sometimes explaining a concept or listing the characteristics of a genre provides enough information.

Spotlight on . . . Comprehension

GRADE-LEVEL STUDENT

Ales is a grade-level reader who likes to read and who knows about comprehension. "I think about what I'm reading," she explains. "I visualize, make connections, summarize, and monitor so I'll understand." She applies fix-up strategies—especially slowing down and rereading—when she gets confused.

"I want to become a better reader so I can go to college," Ales says. "I think the most important thing my teachers can do to help me is to give me more time for reading. My mom makes me read 30 minutes every night and that's why I get good grades."

Ales likes to read realistic fiction, especially inspirational stories about girls. Now she's reading *Reach for Tomorrow* (McDaniel, 1999), a book in the One Last Wish series about the residents and counselors of Jenny House, a group home for critically ill girls. Ales explains that she likes reading about miracles, and the stories teach her how to cope in a crisis. She also reads *Essence* magazine.

Her favorite author is Sharon Flake, author of *The Skin I'm In* (2007) and other novels about hope and perseverance set in inner-city neighborhoods. Ales is a member of Sharon Flake's fan club, and she likes to visit the author's website.

STRUGGLING STUDENT

Graciela's instructional reading level is fourth grade; even so, she describes herself as "a pretty good reader." She can read texts in both English and Spanish, but she's stronger in English.

The most important thing when you're reading is "to say all the words right," according to Graciela. She thinks she's better at comprehension than at getting the words right and would like to get better at word identification.

Sometimes her teacher talks about the comprehension strategies, but Graciela doesn't listen because she doesn't plan to use them. "They're for thinking," she says, "not for reading."

Graciela says she's read all the Harry Potter books, but she doesn't remember anything about them. She does know about the 6-year-old main character of the Junie B. Jones early chapter-book series, and she has *Junie B. Jones Is a Party Animal* (Park, 1997) tucked into her book bag; the book's reading level is second grade. In addition, Graciela says that she likes to read the Spanish magazines her mom buys at the grocery store.

"I don't really like to read very much," Graciela admits. "I'd rather go outside and play touch football with my girlfriends."

ADVANCED STUDENT

Kolei reads two grade levels above his grade placement. He says, "I love to read because that's how I learn." His teachers often call on him to read aloud in class because he's such an expressive reader.

"I always use strategies to understand what I'm reading." Kolei explains. "I think about the topic and the purpose before I start reading, and I'm good at drawing inferences and summarizing. I monitor my reading so I'll know when I don't understand."

Kolei reads for an hour or more most days. He's read the popular Harry Potter series and the Lemony Snicket series, but he doesn't really like fantasy. He prefers historical fiction because "history is interesting." He really enjoyed Avi's *The Fighting Ground* (1994), set during the American Revolution, and *Crispin: The Cross of Lead* (2004), set in 14th-century England.

The book he prizes most is a biography, *Queen Salote of Tonga* (Wood-Ellem, 2001), and he also reads his grandmother's books, which are written in Tongan or Tahitian.

His parents often buy books for him, and on weekends he can often be found browsing in the psychology section at the local Barnes and Noble bookstore.

Vocabulary. Students' knowledge of words plays a tremendous role in comprehension because it's difficult to understand a text that's loaded with unfamiliar words. It's also possible that when students don't know many words related to a topic, they don't have adequate background knowledge. Blachowicz and Fisher (2007) recommend creating a word-rich classroom environment to immerse students in words and teaching word-learning strategies so they can figure out the meaning of new words. In addition, teachers preteach key words when they're building background knowledge using **K-W-L charts, anticipation guides,** and other prereading activities.

Check the Compendium of Instructional Procedures, which follows Chapter 12, for more information on the highlighted terms.

Fluency. Fluent readers read efficiently. Because they recognize most words automatically, their cognitive resources aren't depleted by decoding unfamiliar words, and they can devote their attention to comprehension (Pressley, 2002a). For many struggling readers, their lack of fluency severely affects their ability to understand what they read. Teachers help dysfluent readers by teaching word-identification strategies, having students do repeated readings, and providing students with books at their instructional levels so that they can be successful. When teachers use grade-level texts that are too difficult for struggling students, they read them aloud so that everyone can comprehend and participate in related activities.

Comprehension Strategies

Comprehension strategies are thoughtful behaviors that students use to facilitate their understanding as they read (Afflerbach, Pearson, & Paris, 2008). Some strategies are *cognitive*—they involve thinking; others are *metacognitive*—students reflect on their thinking. For example, readers make connections while they're reading: They relate what they're reading to something that's happened to them or to another book they've read. Connecting is a cognitive strategy because it involves thinking. Readers also monitor their reading, and monitoring is a metacognitive strategy. They notice whether they're understanding; and if they're confused, they take action to solve the problem. For example, they may go back and reread or talk to a classmate to clarify their confusion. Students are being metacognitive when they're alert to the possibility that they might get confused, and they know several ways to solve the problem (Pressley, 2002b).

Be Strategic!

Comprehension Strategies

Students use these strategies to understand texts they're reading:

- ► Activate background knowledge
- ► Connect
- ► Determine importance
- ► Draw inferences
- ► Evaluate

- ► Monitor
- ► Predict
- ► Question
- ► Repair
- ► Set a purpose
- ► Summarize
- ► Visualize

These strategies emphasize what students think about as they read; they're reader factors.

Students learn to use a variety of cognitive and metacognitive strategies to ensure that they understand what they're reading. Here's a list of the most important comprehension strategies:

- ◆ Activating background knowledge
- ◆ Connecting
- ◆ Determining importance
- ◆ Drawing inferences
- ◆ Evaluating
- ◆ Monitoring

- ◆ Predicting
- ◆ Questioning
- ◆ Repairing
- ◆ Setting a purpose
- ◆ Summarizing
- ◆ Visualizing

Students use these comprehension strategies not only to understand what they're reading, but also for comprehending while they're listening to books read aloud and when they're writing. Students use the determining importance strategy, for example, when they're listening or reading to identify the big ideas, and when they're writing, they or-

FIGURE 7–2 ◆ *Comprehension Strategies*

Strategy	What Readers Do	How It Aids Comprehension
Activating Background Knowledge	Readers make connections between what they already know and the information in the text.	Readers use their background knowledge to fill in gaps in the text and enhance their comprehension.
Connecting	Readers make text-to-self, text-to-world, and text-to-text links.	Readers personalize their reading by relating what they're reading to their background knowledge.
Determining Importance	Readers notice the big ideas in the text and the relationships among them.	Readers focus on the big ideas so they don't become overwhelmed with details.
Drawing Inferences	Readers use background knowledge and clues in the text to "read between the lines."	Readers move beyond literal thinking to grasp meaning that isn't explicitly stated in the text.
Evaluating	Readers evaluate both the text itself and their reading experience.	Readers assume responsibility for their own strategy use.
Monitoring	Readers supervise their reading experience, checking that they're understanding the text.	Readers expect the text to make sense, and they recognize when it doesn't so they can take action.
Predicting	Readers make thoughtful "guesses" about what will happen and then read to confirm their predictions.	Readers become more engaged in the reading experience and want to continue reading.
Questioning	Readers ask themselves literal and higher-level questions about the text.	Readers use questions to direct their reading, clarify confusions, and make inferences.
Repairing	Readers identify a problem interfering with comprehension and then solve it.	Readers solve problems to regain comprehension and continue reading.
Setting a Purpose	Readers identify a broad focus to direct their reading through the text.	Readers focus their attention as they read according to the purpose they've set.
Summarizing	Readers paraphrase the big ideas to create a concise statement.	Readers have better recall of the big ideas when they summarize.
Visualizing	Readers create mental images of what they're reading.	Readers use the mental images to make the text more memorable.

ganize their writing around the big ideas so that readers also will comprehend what they're reading. Figure 7–2 presents an overview of the comprehension strategies and explains how readers use them.

Activating Background Knowledge. Readers bring their background knowledge to every reading experience; in fact, they read a text differently depending on their prior experiences. Zimmermann and Hutchins (2003) explain that "the meaning you get from a piece is intertwined with the meaning you bring to it" (p. 45). Readers think about the topic before they begin reading and call up relevant information and related vocabulary to use while reading. The more background knowledge and prior experiences readers have, the more likely they are to comprehend what they're reading (Harvey & Goudvis, 2007).

Teachers use a variety of prereading activities to scaffold students as they learn to activate their background knowledge, including **anticipation guides**, **exclusion brainstorming**, **K-W-L charts**, and **prereading plans**. Through these activities, students think about the topic, use related vocabulary, and get engaged or interested in reading.

Connecting. Readers make three types of connections between the text and their background knowledge: text-to-self, text-to-world, and text-to-text connections (Harvey & Goudvis, 2007). In text-to-self connections, students link the ideas they're reading about to events in their own lives; these are personal connections. A story event or character may remind them of something or someone in their own lives, and information in a nonfiction book may remind them of a past experience. In text-to-world connections, students relate what they're reading to their "world" knowledge, learned both in and out of school. When students make text-to-text connections, they link the text itself or an element of it to another text they've read or to a familiar film or television program. Students often compare different versions of folktales, novels and their sequels, and sets of books by the same author. Text-to-text connections require higher-level thinking, and they're often the most difficult, especially for students with less reading experience.

Teachers use connection charts to teach students about this strategy. They make charts with three columns labeled *text-to-self*, *text-to-world*, and *text-to-text*, then students write connections on small self-stick notes and post them on the chart, as Mrs. Donnelly's students did in the vignette at the beginning of the chapter. Students can also make connection charts in their **reading logs** and write connections in each column. Later in the reading process, students make connections as they assume the role of a character and are interviewed by classmates during **hot seat**, create **open-mind portraits** to share the character's thinking, or write simulated journals from the viewpoint of a character, for example.

Determining Importance. Readers sift through the text to identify the important ideas as they read because it isn't possible to remember everything (Harvey & Goudvis, 2007; Keene & Zimmermann, 2007). Students learn to distinguish the big ideas and the details and to recognize what's important as they read and talk about the books they've read. This strategy is important because students need to be able to identify significant ideas in order to summarize.

Teachers often direct students toward the big ideas through the questions they ask. In the vignette, for example, Mrs. Donnelly directed her sixth graders' thinking as she introduced *Joey Pigza Loses Control* (Gantos, 2005) and asked questions about how parents and children show their love. Teachers also have students create graphic organizers to highlight the big ideas. They make story diagrams about the plot, characters, and setting. Similarly, students make diagrams that reflect the structure of the text when they read nonfiction articles and chapters in content-area textbooks. Sometimes teachers provide the diagrams with the big ideas already identified, and sometimes students analyze the text to determine its structure and then develop their own graphic organizers.

Drawing Inferences. Readers seem to "read between the lines" to draw inferences, but what they actually do is synthesize their background knowledge with the author's clues to ask questions that point toward inferences. Keene and Zimmermann (2007) explain that when readers draw inferences, they have "an opportunity to sense a meaning not explicit in the text, but which derives or flows from it" (p. 145). Readers make both unconscious and conscious inferences about characters in a story and its theme, the big ideas in an article or nonfiction book, and the author's purpose in a poem (Pressley, 2002a). In fact, readers may not even be aware that they're drawing inferences, but when they wonder why the author included this or omitted that information, they probably are.

Students often have to read a picture-book story or an excerpt from a novel several times to draw inferences because at first they focus on literal comprehension, which precedes higher-level thinking. Capable students draw inferences on their own as they read, but other students don't notice opportunities to make them. Sometimes students do draw inferences when prompted by the teacher, but it's important to teach students how to draw inferences so that they can think more deeply when they read independently.

Teachers begin by explaining what inferences are, how inferential thinking differs from literal thinking, and why inferences are important. Then they teach these steps in drawing inferences:

1. Activate background knowledge about topics related to the text.
2. Look for the author's clues as you read.
3. Ask questions, tying together background knowledge and the author's clues.
4. Draw inferences by answering the questions.

Teachers can create charts to make the steps more visible as students practice making inferences. Figure 7–3 shows an inference chart developed by a seventh-grade class as they analyzed *The Wretched Stone* (Van Allsburg, 1991). The story, told in diary format, is about a ship's crew that picks up a strange, glowing stone on a sea voyage. The stone captivates the sailors and has a terrible transforming effect on them. After reading the story and talking about what they understood and what confused them, students began making the chart. First, they completed the "background knowledge" column. The students thought about what they needed to know to understand the story: the meaning of the word *wretched*, sailors, the author/illustrator, Chris Van Allsburg, and the fantasy genre. Then they reread the story, searching for clues that might affect the meaning. They noticed that the ship captain's name was Hope, the island was uncharted, and the sailors who could read recovered faster, and they wrote these clues in the second column. Next, they thought about their lingering questions about the story and wrote them in the third column. Finally, the teacher reread the book one more time, and students listened more confidently, recognizing clues and drawing inferences they had missed earlier. Finally, they completed the last column of the chart with their inferences.

FIGURE 7–3 ◆ *Seventh Graders' Inference Chart About* The Wretched Stone

Background Knowledge	Clues in the Story	Questions	Inferences
• The word <u>wretched</u> means "causing misery." • Usually the sailors are hard workers but not readers and musicians. • Chris Van Allsburg has brown hair and a beard, and he wears glasses. • Impossible things can happen in fantasies.	• The captain's last name is Hope. • The crew can read, play music, and tell stories. • It's odd that the island isn't on any maps. • The crew stare at the glowing stone and stop working. • Capt. Hope looks just like Chris Van Allsburg.	• Why did Chris Van Allsburg make himself the captain? • Was the island real? • What's the wretched stone? Is it a symbol? • Why did the sailors turn into monkeys? • Why did the sailors who could read get well faster?	• Chris Van Allsburg wrote this book with hope for kids. • The wretched stone is a television. • This book is a warning that watching too much TV is bad for you. • He wants kids to read more books and spend less time watching television.

Evaluating. Readers reflect on their reading experience and evaluate the text and what they're learning. They use this strategy throughout the reading process, monitoring their interest from the moment they pick up the book and judging their success in solving reading problems when they arise. They evaluate their reading experience, including these aspects:

> Their ease in reading the text
> The adequacy of their background knowledge
> Their use of comprehension strategies
> How they solved reading problems
> Their interest and engagement during reading

They also consider the text:

> Whether they like the text
> Their opinions about the author
> The world knowledge they gain
> How they'll use what they're learning

Students usually write about their reflections in **reading log** entries and talk about their evaluations in conferences with the teacher. Evaluating is important because it helps students assume more responsibility for their own learning.

Monitoring. Readers monitor their understanding as they read, although they may be aware that they're using this strategy only when their comprehension breaks down and they have to take action to solve a problem. Harvey and Goudvis (2007) describe monitoring as the inner conversation that students carry on in their heads as they read—expressing wonder, making connections, asking questions, reacting to information, drawing conclusions, noticing confusions, for example.

Monitoring involves regulating reader and text factors at the same time. Readers often ask themselves these questions:

> What's my purpose for reading?
> Is this book too difficult for me to read on my own?
> Do I need to read the entire book or only part of it?
> What's special about the genre?
> How is text structure used?
> What's the author's viewpoint?
> Do I understand the words I'm reading? (Pressley, 2002b)

Once students detect a problem, they shift into problem-solving mode to repair their comprehension.

Teachers use **think-alouds** to demonstrate the monitoring strategy during **minilessons** and when they're reading aloud. Students also write about their thinking on small self-stick notes and place them in the book, next to text that stimulated their thinking. Later, students share their notes during a discussion about how students monitor their reading.

Predicting. Readers make thoughtful "guesses" or predictions about what will happen or what they'll learn in the book they're reading. These guesses are based on what students already know about the topic and genre or on what they've read thus far. Students often make a prediction before beginning to read and several others at pivotal points in a text—no matter whether they're reading fiction, nonfiction, or poetry—and then as they read, they confirm or revise their predictions. Predictions about nonfiction are different than for stories and poems; here students are generating questions about the topic that they would like to find answers to as they read.

Questioning. Readers ask themselves questions about the text as they read (Duke & Pearson, 2002). They ask self-questions out of curiosity, and as they use this strategy, they become more engaged and want to keep reading to find answers to their questions (Harvey & Goudvis, 2007). These questions often lead to making predictions and drawing inferences. Students also ask themselves questions to clarify misunderstandings. This strategy is used throughout the reading process—to activate background knowledge and make predictions before reading, to engage with the text and clarify confusions during reading, and to evaluate and reflect on the text after reading.

Traditionally, teachers have been the question-askers and students have been the question-answerers, but when students learn to generate questions about the text, their comprehension improves. In fact, students comprehend better when they generate their own questions than when teachers ask questions (Duke & Pearson, 2002). Many students don't know how to ask questions to guide their reading, so it's important that teachers teach students how to do so. They model generating questions and then encourage students to do the same. Tovani (2000) suggests having students brainstorm a list of "I

New Literacies

Online Comprehension Strategies

Websites are dynamic learning contexts that create new challenges for readers, because online texts differ from print texts in significant ways (Castek, Bevans-Mangelson, & Goldstone, 2006). Print texts are linear and unchanging; they contain a finite number of pages with information arranged in predictable fiction, nonfiction, and poetic genres. Online texts, in contrast, are multilayered, with unlimited multimodal information available through hypertext links.

Students use traditional comprehension strategies to read Web-based texts, but they use them in new ways:

Activating Background Knowledge. Readers need to know about websites and how to navigate search engines to locate useful ones.

Predicting. Readers predict which links will be useful; otherwise, students get distracted or waste time finding their way back from unproductive links.

Evaluating. Students determine the accuracy, objectivity, relevance, and quality of information at websites, because the information on some websites is erroneous and biased.

Monitoring. Students monitor their navigational choices and decide whether the links they've reached are useful.

Repairing. Readers use the repairing strategy to correct poor navigational choices.

As researchers learn more about online reading, it's likely that they'll identify additional ways students adapt traditional comprehension strategies.

Readers also learn comprehension strategies that address the unique characteristics and complex applications of online texts (Coiro, 2003). Coauthoring is a comprehension strategy that readers use to impose an organization on information they read online (Leu, Kinzer, Coiro, & Cammack, 2004). More recently, Coiro and Dobler (2007) examined the strategies that sixth graders used for Internet reading and found that these students use a self-directed process of text construction. Readers make a series of decisions as they move from one link to another: They plan, predict, monitor, and evaluate each time they make a navigational choice. More than 25 years ago, Tierney and Pearson (1983) asserted that reading is a composing process, and these comprehension strategies emphasize the interrelatedness of reading and writing.

It's essential that teachers prepare students to use 21st-century technology. Students need to understand how print and Web-based texts differ so they can adjust how they apply traditional comprehension strategies and learn ones to use when they're reading Internet texts.

wonder" questions on a topic because they need to learn how to generate questions; in the vignette at the beginning of the chapter, for example, Mrs. Donnelly's sixth graders brainstormed questions before they began reading *Joey Pigza Loses Control* (Gantos, 2005).

The questions students ask shape their comprehension: If they ask literal questions, their comprehension will be literal, but if students generate inferential, critical, and evaluative questions, their comprehension will be more sophisticated. **Question-Answer-Relationships** (QARs) (Raphael, Highfield, & Au, 2006) is an effective way to teach students about the types of questions they can ask about a text. QARs was developed for analyzing the end-of-chapter questions in content-area textbooks, but it's also useful for teaching students to categorize questions and ultimately to ask higher-level questions.

Repairing. Readers use repairing to fix comprehension problems that arise while reading (Zimmermann & Hutchins, 2003). When students notice that they're confused or bored, that they can't remember what they just read, or that they're not asking questions, they need to use this strategy (Tovani, 2000). Repairing involves detecting the problem and then taking action to solve it: Sometimes students go back and reread or skip ahead and read; sometimes they try visualizing, questioning, or another strategy that might help; and at other times, they check the meaning of an unfamiliar word, examine the structure of a confusing sentence, learn more about an unfamiliar topic related to the text, or ask a classmate or the teacher for assistance. These solutions are often referred to as *fix-up strategies*.

Setting a Purpose. Readers read for different reasons—for entertainment, to learn about a topic, for directions to accomplish a task, or to find the answer to a question, for instance—and the purposes they set direct their attention during reading (Tovani, 2000). Setting a

STRUGGLING READERS AND WRITERS

Strategic Readers

Struggling students need to become strategic readers.

Struggling readers often complain that they don't understand what they're reading. Comprehension difficulties are due to a variety of problems, but one of the most common is that students don't read strategically (Cooper, Chard, & Kiger, 2006). They read passively without using comprehension strategies to think about what they're reading. Without learning to thoughtfully engage in the reading process, it's unlikely that students who struggle with comprehension will improve very much.

The good news is that teachers can help struggling students become better readers by teaching them to use comprehension strategies to be more thoughtful readers (Allington, 2006). The most important strategies for struggling readers are activating background knowledge, determining importance, summarizing, questioning, visualizing, and monitoring.

As teachers teach comprehension strategies, they explain each one, including how, when, and why to use it, and they make the strategy visible by demonstrating it during minilessons, interactive read-alouds, and guided reading lessons. They use think-alouds to show that capable readers are active thinkers. Students participate in small-group and partner activities as they practice using the strategy and verbalize their thinking. At first, teachers provide lots of support, and they withdraw it slowly as students become responsible for using the strategy independently. Once students have learned to apply two or three strategies, they begin to use them together. Integrating strategy use is important because capable readers don't depend on a single comprehension strategy; instead, they have a repertoire of strategies available that they use as needed while they're reading (Allington, 2006).

purpose activates a mental blueprint, which determines how readers focus their attention and how they sort relevant from irrelevant information (Blanton, Wood, & Moorman, 1990). Before they begin to read, students identify a single, fairly broad purpose that they sustain while reading the entire text; it must fit both students' reason for reading and the text. Students can ask themselves "Why am I going to read this text?" or "What do I need to learn from this book?" to help identify their purpose. It's important that students have a purpose, because readers vary how they read and what they remember according to their purpose. When students don't have a purpose, they're likely to misdirect their attention and often focus on unimportant ideas.

Summarizing. When readers summarize, they pick out the important ideas and relationships among them and briefly restate the ideas so they can be remembered (Harvey & Goudvis, 2007). Identifying the most important ideas is crucial because if students focus on tangential ideas or details, their comprehension is compromised. To create effective summaries, students need to learn to paraphrase, or restate ideas in their own words. Summarizing is a difficult task, but instruction and practice improve not only students' ability to summarize but their overall comprehension as well (Duke & Pearson, 2002).

Visualizing. Readers create mental images of what they're reading (Harvey & Goudvis, 2007; Keene & Zimmermann, 2007). They often place themselves in the images they create, becoming a character in the novel they're reading, traveling to that setting, or facing the conflict situations the characters face. Teachers sometimes ask students to close their eyes to help visualize the story or to draw pictures of the scenes and characters they visualize. How well students use visualization often becomes clear when they view film versions of books they've read: Students who are good visualizers are often disappointed with the film and the actors who perform as the characters; in contrast, those who don't visualize often prefer the film to the book.

Students use comprehension strategies at every stage in the reading process, but their activities vary from stage to stage. Figure 7–4 explains what readers do to comprehend at each stage and the strategies they use. Sometimes strategies are grouped into *before reading*, *during reading*, and *after reading* clusters, but that categorization doesn't work: Although setting a purpose is almost always a prereading strategy and monitoring and

FIGURE 7–4 ◆ How Comprehension Strategies Fit Into the Reading Process

Stage	What Readers Do	Strategies Readers Use
Prereading	Students prepare to read by setting purposes, thinking about the topic and genre, and planning for the reading experience.	Activating background knowledge Predicting Questioning Setting a purpose
Reading	Students read the text, thinking about it as they read, monitoring their understanding, and solving problems as they arise.	Monitoring Repairing All other strategies
Responding	Students share their reactions, making comments, asking questions, and clarifying confusions, by talking with classmates and the teacher and writing in reading logs.	Connecting Determining importance Drawing inferences Evaluating Questioning Visualizing
Exploring	Students reread parts of the text, examine it more analytically, and study the genre.	Determining importance Drawing inferences Evaluating Summarizing
Applying	Students create projects to deepen their understanding and reflect on their reading experience.	Connecting Evaluating Questioning

repairing are usually reading-stage strategies, students use connecting, drawing inferences, questioning, and other strategies in more than one stage.

Comprehension Skills

Even though there's controversy regarding the differences between strategies and skills, it's possible to identify some comprehension skills that students need to learn to become successful readers. These skills are related to strategies, but the big difference is that skills involve literal thinking; they're like questions to which there's one correct answer. One group of skills focus on main ideas and details. Students use the determining importance strategy to identify main ideas, and they use these related skills:

> Recognizing details
> Noticing similarities and differences
> Identifying topic sentences
> Comparing and contrasting main ideas and details
> Matching causes with effects
> Sequencing details
> Paraphrasing ideas
> Choosing a good title for a text

In contrast, when main ideas and relationships among them aren't explicitly stated in the text, students use the drawing inferences strategy to comprehend them because higher-level thinking is required. Another group of comprehension skills are related to the evaluating strategy:

> Recognizing the author's purpose
> Detecting propaganda
> Distinguishing between fact and opinion

Teachers teach these skills and students practice them until they become automatic procedures that don't require conscious thought or interpretation.

Teaching About Reader Factors

Comprehension instruction involves teaching students about comprehension and the strategies they use to understand what they're reading. Three components are explicit instruction, reading, and writing (Duke & Pearson, 2002). Researchers emphasize the need to establish the expectation that the books students read and the compositions they write will make sense. Teachers create an expectation of comprehension in these ways:

- Involving students in authentic reading and writing activities every day
- Providing access to well-stocked classroom libraries
- Teaching students to use comprehension strategies
- Ensuring that students are fluent readers
- Providing opportunities for students to talk about the books they're reading
- Linking vocabulary instruction to underlying concepts

Teachers can't assume that students will learn to comprehend simply by doing lots of reading; instead, students develop an understanding of comprehension and what readers do to be successful through a combination of instruction and authentic reading activities (Block & Pressley, 2007). Guidelines for teaching comprehension are presented on page 190.

Guidelines
for Teaching Comprehension

▶ Teach students about both reader and text factors.

▶ Teach comprehension strategies using a combination of explanations, demonstrations, think-alouds, and practice activities.

▶ Read aloud picture books and novels to teach strategies.

▶ Have students apply strategies in literacy activities as well as in thematic units.

▶ Teach groups of strategies in routines so that students learn to orchestrate their use of multiple strategies.

▶ Ask students to reflect on their use of individual strategies and strategy routines.

▶ Hang charts in the classroom of the strategies and strategy routines students are learning.

▶ Differentiate between strategies and skills so that students understand that strategies are problem-solving tactics and skills are automatic behaviors.

Explicit Comprehension Instruction

The fact that comprehension is an invisible mental process makes it difficult to teach; however, through explicit instruction, teachers can make comprehension more visible. They explain what comprehension is and why it's important, and they model how they do it, by thinking aloud. Next, teachers encourage students to direct their thinking as they read, gradually releasing responsibility to students through guided and independent practice. Finally, they move students from focusing on a single comprehension strategy to integrating several strategies in routines, such as reciprocal teaching. Mrs. Donnelly demonstrated the concept of gradual release in the vignette at the beginning of the chapter as she reviewed each comprehension strategy and had the students practice it as they read picture books; then she had them apply all the strategies as they read *Joey Pigza Loses Control* (Gantos, 2005).

Teaching Comprehension Strategies. Teachers teach individual comprehension strategies and then show students how to integrate several strategies simultaneously (Block & Pressley, 2007). They introduce each comprehension strategy in a series of **minilessons**. Teachers describe the strategy, model it for students as they read a text aloud, use it collaboratively with students, and provide opportunities for guided and then independent practice; the independent practice is important because it's motivational.

Teachers also support students' learning about comprehension strategies in other ways: Figure 7–5 suggests several activities to teach each strategy. Sixth graders, for example, practice the connecting strategy when they write favorite quotes in one column of a **double-entry journal** and then explain in the second column why each quote is meaningful. When teachers involve students in an activity, it's important that they explain that students will be practicing a particular strategy so that they think about what they're doing and how it helps them to comprehend better.

Teaching Comprehension Routines. Once students know how to use individual strategies, they learn to use routines, or combinations of strategies, because capable readers rarely use comprehension strategies one at a time (Duke & Pearson, 2002). In the vignette, for example, Mrs. Donnelly was teaching her sixth graders to use multiple strategies as

FIGURE 7–5 ◆ Ways to Teach the Comprehension Strategies

Strategy	Instructional Procedures
Activating Background Knowledge	• Students complete an anticipation guide. • Students do an exclusion brainstorming activity. • Students develop a K-W-L chart.
Connecting	• Students add text-to-self, text-to-world, and text-to-text connections to a class chart. • Students write a double-entry journal with quotes and reflections about each one. • Students become a character and participate in a hot seat activity.
Determining Importance	• Students create graphic organizers. • Students make posters highlighting the big ideas.
Drawing Inferences	• Students use small self-stick notes to mark clues in the text. • Students create charts with author's clues, questions, and inferences. • Students quickwrite about an inference they've made.
Evaluating	• Students write reflections and evaluations in reading logs. • Students conference with the teacher about a book they've read.
Monitoring	• Students think aloud to demonstrate how they monitor their reading. • Students write about their strategy use on small self-stick notes and in reading logs.
Predicting	• Students make and share predictions during read-alouds. • Students write a double-entry journal with predictions in one column and summaries in the other. • Students make predictions during guided reading lessons.
Questioning	• Students brainstorm a list of questions before reading. • Students ask questions during grand conversations and other discussions. • Students analyze the questions they pose using QARs.
Repairing	• Students make personal charts of the ways they solve comprehension problems. • Students think aloud to demonstrate how they use the repairing strategy. • Students write about their repairs on small self-stick notes and place them in a book they're reading.
Setting a Purpose	• Students identify their purpose in a discussion before beginning to read. • Students write about their purpose in a reading log entry before beginning to read.
Summarizing	• Students write a summary using interactive writing. • Students create visual summaries on charts using words, diagrams, and pictures.
Visualizing	• Students create open-mind portraits of characters. • Students draw pictures of episodes from a book they're reading. • Students role-play episodes from a book they're reading.

they read *Joey Pigza Loses Control* (Gantos, 2005) and reflected on their strategy use in their thinking logs.

One of the most effective comprehension routines is reciprocal teaching (Palincsar & Brown, 1986), in which students use predicting, questioning, clarifying, and summarizing strategies to figure out the meaning of a text, paragraph by paragraph. Teachers can use this procedure with the whole class when students are reading chapters in content-area textbooks or novels in literature circles.

Developing Comprehension Through Reading

Students need to spend lots of time reading authentic texts independently and talking about their reading with classmates and teachers. Having students read interesting books written at their reading level is the best way for them to apply comprehension strategies. As they read and discuss their reading, students are practicing what they're learning about comprehension. Reading a selection in a basal reader each week isn't enough; instead, students need to read many books representing a range of genres.

In addition to providing opportunities for students to read independently, teachers read some books aloud, especially when struggling readers can't read age-appropriate books themselves; when teachers do the reading, students have more cognitive resources available to focus on comprehension. Teachers often read books aloud when they introduce comprehension strategies so that they can model procedures and scaffold students' thinking.

Scaffolding English Learners

Comprehension is often difficult for English learners, and there are a number of reasons why (Bouchard, 2005). Many ELs lack the necessary background knowledge for understanding the book they're attempting to read. Sometimes they lack culturally based knowledge, and at other times, they're unfamiliar with a genre or can't understand the meaning of figurative vocabulary. There can be a mismatch between the level of students' English proficiency and the reading level of the book, too: Like all students, ELs won't understand what they're reading if the book is too difficult.

Teachers can address these issues by carefully choosing books that are appropriate for English learners, building their world and literary knowledge, and introducing key vocabulary words in advance. Peregoy and Boyle (2008) also point out that many ELs read texts passively, as if they were waiting for the information they're reading to organize itself and highlight the big ideas. To help these students become more active readers, teachers explicitly teach the comprehension strategies. During the lessons, teachers explain each strategy, including why it will help students become better readers and how and when to use it. They spend more time modeling how to apply each strategy and thinking aloud to share their thoughts. Next, teachers provide guided practice with the students working together in small groups and with partners, and they assist students as they use the strategy. Finally, students use the strategy independently and apply it in new ways.

Assessing Comprehension

Teachers assess students' comprehension in a variety of ways. Each day they informally monitor students' comprehension as they listen to the comments students make during **grand conversations**, conference with students about books they're reading, and examine their entries in **reading logs**, for example. They also use these procedures to assess students' use of comprehension strategies and their understanding of books they're reading:

Cloze Procedure. Teachers examine students' understanding of a text using the **cloze procedure**, in which students supply the deleted words in a passage taken from a text they've read. Although filling in the blanks may seem like a simple activity, it isn't because students must consider the content, vocabulary words, and sentence structure to choose the exact word that was deleted.

Running Records. Teachers use **running records** to examine students' oral reading and analyze their comprehension (Clay, 2007). Although they're more commonly used with young children, running records can also be used with older struggling readers. Students orally read a text and then retell it. Teachers ask questions to prompt their recall, when necessary, and sometimes pose other questions to probe the depth of their understanding. Finally, they evaluate the completeness of the retelling.

Think-Alouds. Teachers assess students' ability to apply comprehension strategies by having them **think aloud** and share their thinking as they read a passage (Wilhelm, 2001). Students usually think aloud orally, but they can also record their thoughts on small self-stick notes that they place beside sections of text or write entries in **reading logs**.

Teachers also use other assessment tools, including tests, to evaluate students' comprehension; the Assessment Tools feature on page 194 presents more information about comprehension tests. No matter whether teachers are using informal assessments or tests, they need to consider whether they're assessing literal, inferential, critical, or evaluative thinking. The emphasis in both assessment and instruction should be on higher-level comprehension.

Motivation

Motivation is intrinsic, the innate curiosity that makes us want to figure things out. It involves feeling self-confident, believing you'll succeed, and viewing the activity as pleasurable (Guthrie & Wigfield, 2000). It's based on the engagement theory that you read about in the first chapter. Motivation is social, too: People want to socialize, share ideas, and participate in group activities. Motivation is more than one characteristic, however; it's a network of interacting factors (Alderman, 1999). Often students' motivation to become better readers and writers diminishes as they reach the middle grades, and struggling students demonstrate significantly less enthusiasm for reading and writing than other students do.

Many factors contribute to students' engagement or involvement in reading and writing. Some focus on teachers' role—what they believe and do—and others focus on students (Pressley, Dolezal, Raphael, Mohan, Roehrig, & Bogner, 2003; Unrau, 2004). Figure 7–6 summarizes the factors affecting students' engagement in literacy activities and what teachers can do to nurture students' interest.

The Teacher's Role

Everything teachers do affects their students' interest and engagement with literacy, but four of the most important components are teachers' attitude, the learning community teachers create, the instructional approaches they use, and their reward systems.

Attitude. It seems obvious that when teachers show that they care about their students and exhibit excitement and enthusiasm for learning, students are more likely to become engaged. Effective teachers also stimulate students' curiosity and encourage them to explore ideas. They emphasize intrinsic over extrinsic motivation because they understand that students' intrinsic desire to learn is more powerful than grades, rewards, and other extrinsic motivators.

Community. Students are more likely to engage in literacy activities when their classroom is a learning community that respects and nurtures everyone. Students and the teacher show respect for each other, and students learn to work well in small groups. In a community of learners, students enjoy social interaction and feel connected to classmates and their teacher.

Instruction. The types of literacy activities in which students are involved affect their motivation. Turner and Paris (1995) compared authentic literacy activities such as reading and writing workshop with skills-based reading programs and found that

Assessment Tools

Comprehension

Teachers use a combination of informal assessment procedures, including think-alouds and commercially available tests, to measure students' comprehension. These tests are often used in middle-grade classrooms:

◆ **Comprehension Thinking Strategies Assessment** (Keene, 2006)

The Comprehension Thinking Strategies Assessment examines students' ability to think about the fiction and nonfiction texts they're reading. Activating background knowledge, determining importance, drawing inferences, monitoring, noticing text structure, questioning, setting a purpose, and visualizing are assessed. As students read a passage, they pause and reflect on their use of strategies. Teachers score students' responses using a rubric. This test can be administered to individuals or to the class, depending on whether students' responses are oral or written. This flexible assessment tool, published by Shell Education, can be used to evaluate students' learning after teaching a strategy or to survey progress at the beginning or monitor progress during the school year.

◆ **Developmental Reading Assessment (2nd ed.)(DRA2)** (Beaver & Carter, 2005)

The DRA2 measures reading comprehension, determines reading levels, and assesses readers' strengths and weaknesses. The kit contains a collection of leveled books, and teachers choose a book at the student's instructional level. The student reads the book and then retells everything he or she remembers. Retellings are scored using a 4-point rubric; the highest score indicates a well-organized retelling that includes the main idea with supporting details.

◆ **Informal Reading Inventories (IRIs)**

Teachers use individually administered IRIs to assess students' comprehension of fiction and nonfiction texts. Comprehension is measured by students' ability to retell what they've read and to answer questions about the passage. The questions examine how well students use literal and higher-level thinking and their knowledge about word meanings. A number of commercially published IRIs are available:

  Analytical Reading Inventory (Woods & Moe, 2007)
  Comprehensive Reading Inventory (Cooter, Flynt, & Cooter, 2007)
  Critical Reading Inventory (Applegate, Quinn, & Applegate, 2008)
  Qualitative Reading Inventory (Leslie & Caldwell, 2006)

Other IRIs accompany basal reading series.

These tests provide valuable information about whether students meet grade-level comprehension standards.

FIGURE 7–6 ◆ *Factors Affecting Students' Motivation*

Role	Factors	What Teachers Do
Teachers	Attitude	• Show students that you care about them. • Display excitement and enthusiasm about what you're teaching. • Stimulate students' curiosity and desire to learn.
	Community	• Create a nurturing and inclusive classroom community. • Insist that students treat classmates with respect.
	Instruction	• Focus on students' long-term learning. • Teach students to be strategic readers and writers. • Engage students in authentic activities. • Offer students choices of activities and reading materials.
	Rewards	• Employ specific praise and positive feedback. • Use external rewards only when students' interest is very low.
Students	Expectations	• Expect students to be successful. • Teach students to set realistic goals.
	Collaboration	• Encourage students to work collaboratively. • Minimize competition. • Allow students to participate in making plans and choices.
	Reading and Writing Competence	• Teach students to use reading and writing strategies. • Provide guided reading lessons for struggling readers. • Use interactive writing to teach writing skills to struggling writers. • Provide daily reading and writing opportunities.
	Choices	• Have students complete interest inventories. • Teach students to choose books at their reading levels. • Encourage students to write about topics that interest them.

the most successful were open-ended activities and projects in which students were in control of the processes they used and the products they created.

Rewards. Many teachers consider using rewards to encourage students to do more reading and writing, but Kohn (2001) and others believe that extrinsic incentives are harmful because they undermine students' intrinsic motivation. Incentives such as pizzas, free time, or "money" to spend in a classroom "store" are most effective when students are very reluctant to participate in literacy activities. Once students become more engaged, teachers withdraw these incentives and use less tangible ones, including positive feedback and praise (Stipek, 2002).

Students' Role

Motivation isn't something that teachers or parents can force on students; rather, it's an innate, intrinsic desire that students develop themselves. These factors influence students' motivation:

Expectations. Students who feel they have little hope of success are unlikely to get engaged in literacy activities. Teachers play a big role in shaping students' expectations, and teacher expectations are often self-fulfilling (Brophy, 2004): If teachers believe that their students can be successful, it's more likely that they will be. Stipek (2002) found that in classrooms where teachers take a personal interest in students, they're more successful.

Collaboration. When students work with peers, they're often more engaged in activities than when they read and write alone. Collaborative groups support students because they have opportunities to share ideas, learn from each other, and enjoy their classmates' collegiality. Competition, in contrast, doesn't develop intrinsic motivation; it decreases many students' interest in learning.

Reading and Writing Competence. Not surprisingly, students' competence in reading and writing affects their motivation: Students who read well are more likely to be motivated to read than those who read less well, and the same is true for writers. Effective instruction is an essential factor; teachers find that once struggling readers and writers improve, they become more motivated.

Choice. Students want to have a say in which books they read and which topics they write about. By making choices, they develop more responsibility and ownership of their accomplishments. Reading and writing workshop are instructional approaches that honor students' choices: In reading workshop, students choose books they want to read, and in writing workshop, students write about topics that interest them.

How to Engage Students in Reading and Writing

Oldfather (1995) conducted a 4-year study to examine the factors influencing students' motivation, and she found that students were more highly motivated when they had opportunities for authentic self-expression and when they had ownership of the learning activities. Ivey and Broaddus (2001) reported similar conclusions from their study of the factors that influence sixth graders' desire to read. Three of their conclusions are noteworthy: First, students are more motivated when their teachers make them feel confident and successful; a nurturing classroom community is an important factor. Second, students are more motivated when they have ownership of their literacy learning. Students place great value on being allowed to choose interesting books and other reading materials. Third, students are more engaged with books when they have time for independent reading and opportunities to listen to the teacher read aloud. Students reported that they enjoy listening to teachers read aloud because teachers make books more comprehensible and more interesting through the background knowledge they provide.

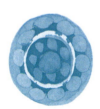

Some students aren't strongly motivated to learn to read and write, however, and they adopt defensive tactics for avoiding failure. Unmotivated readers give up or remain passive, uninvolved in reading. Some students feign interest or pretend to be involved even though they aren't. Others don't think reading is important, and they choose to focus on other curricular areas—math or sports, for instance. Some students complain about feeling ill or that classmates are bothering them. They place blame anywhere but on themselves.

Some students avoid reading and writing entirely, and others read books that are too easy for them or write short pieces so they don't have to exert much effort. Even though these strategies are self-serving, students use them because they lead to short-term success. The long-term result, however, is devastating because these students fail to learn to read and write well. Because it takes effort to read and write strategically, it's especially important that students experience personal ownership of literacy activities and know how to manage their own reading and writing behaviors.

Assessing Motivation

Because students' motivation and engagement affect their success in reading as well as writing, it's important that teachers learn about their students and work to ensure that they're motivated and have positive attitudes about literacy. Teachers observe students and conference with them and their parents to understand students' reading and writing habits at home, their interests and hobbies, and their view of themselves as readers and writers.

Teachers also administer surveys to quickly estimate students' motivation toward reading and writing; these surveys are described in the Assessment Tools feature on page 198.

Comparing Capable and Less Capable Readers and Writers

Researchers have compared capable readers and writers with students who are less successful and have found some striking differences (Baker & Brown, 1984; Faigley, Cherry, Jolliffe, & Skinner, 1985). Capable readers demonstrate these characteristics:

- Read fluently
- View reading as a process of creating meaning
- Have large vocabularies
- Understand the organization of fiction, nonfiction, and other genres
- Use comprehension strategies
- Monitor their understanding as they read

Similarly, capable writers demonstrate these characteristics:

- Vary how they write depending on their purpose and the audience that will read the composition
- Use the writing process flexibly
- Focus on developing ideas and communicating effectively
- Turn to classmates for feedback on how they're communicating
- Monitor how well they're communicating
- Use appropriate formats and structures for each genre
- Postpone attention to mechanical correctness until the end of the writing process

A comparison of the characteristics of capable and less capable readers and writers is presented in Figure 7–7.

Perhaps the most remarkable difference between more- and less capable students is that more-capable readers view reading as a process of comprehending or creating meaning, but less capable readers focus on decoding. In writing, less capable writers make cosmetic changes when they revise, rather than changes to communicate meaning more effectively. These important differences suggest that capable students focus on comprehension.

Another important difference is that those students who are less successful aren't strategic; they're reluctant to use unfamiliar strategies or those that require much effort. They aren't motivated and don't expect to be successful. Less capable readers and writers don't monitor their reading and writing, or, if they do use strategies, they remain dependent on primitive ones (Keene & Zimmermann, 2007). For example, less successful readers seldom look ahead or back into the text to clarify misunderstandings or make plans. Or, when they come to an unfamiliar word, they stop reading, unsure of what to do. They may try to sound out an unfamiliar word, but if that's unsuccessful, they give up. In contrast, capable readers know a variety of strategies, and if one isn't successful, they try another.

Less capable writers move through the writing process in a lockstep, linear approach. They use a limited number of strategies, most often a "knowledge-telling" strategy in which they list everything they know about a topic with little thought to choosing information to meet their readers' needs or to organizing the information to put related ideas together (Faigley et al., 1985). In contrast, capable writers understand the recursive nature of the writing process and turn to peers for feedback about how well they're communicating. They're more responsive to their audience's needs, and they work to organize their writing in a cohesive manner.

This research on capable and less capable readers and writers has focused on comprehension and students' use of strategies. It's noteworthy that all research comparing readers and writers focuses on how students use strategies, not on their use of skills.

Assessment Tools

Motivation

Teachers assess students' motivation as they observe students reading and writing and conference with them about their interests and attitudes. At the beginning of the school year, teachers often have students complete interest inventories with lists of things they're interested in, books they like to read, and favorite authors. Teachers also administer attitude surveys to assess students' motivation:

◆ **Elementary Reading Attitude Survey** (McKenna & Kear, 1990)

The Elementary Reading Attitude Survey assesses students' attitudes toward reading. All items begin with the stem "How do you feel . . ." and students mark one of four pictures of Garfield, the cartoon cat; each picture depicts a different emotional state, ranging from positive to negative. Teachers use this test to quickly estimate their students' attitudes.

◆ **Motivation to Read Profile** (Gambrell, Palmer, Codling, & Mazzoni, 1996)

The Motivation to Read Profile has two parts, a group test and an individual interview. The test consists of 20 items about students' view of themselves as readers and the value of reading. Students respond using a 4-point Likert scale. The interview consists of open-ended questions about the types of books students like best and where they get reading materials.

◆ **Reader Self-Perception Scale** (Henk & Melnick, 1995)

The Reader Self-Perception Scale measures how students feel about reading and about themselves as readers. Students respond to "I think I am a good reader" and other statements using a 5-point Likert scale where responses range from "strongly agree" to "strongly disagree." Teachers score students' responses and interpret the results to determine both overall and specific attitude levels.

◆ **Writing Attitude Survey** (Kear, Coffman, McKenna, & Ambrosio, 2000)

The Writing Attitude Survey examines students' feelings about writing and types of writing. It has 28 items, including "How would you feel if your classmates talked to you about making your writing better?" It features Garfield, the cartoon cat, as in the Elementary Reading Attitude Survey.

◆ **Writer Self-Perception Scale** (Bottomley, Henk, & Melnick, 1997/1998)

The Writer Self-Perception Scale assesses students' attitudes about writing and how they perceive themselves as writers. They respond to statements such as "I write better than my classmates do," using the same 5-point Likert scale that the Reader Self-Perception Scale uses.

These attitude surveys were originally published in *The Reading Teacher* and are readily available at libraries, online, and in collections of assessment instruments, such as *Assessment for Reading Instruction* (McKenna & Stahl, 2003).

FIGURE 7–7 ◆ *Capable and Less Capable Readers and Writers*

Component	Reader Characteristics	Writer Characteristics
Belief Systems	Capable readers view reading as a comprehending process, but less capable readers see reading as a decoding process.	Capable writers view writing as communicating ideas, but less capable writers see writing as putting words on paper.
Purpose	Capable readers adjust their reading according to purpose, but less capable readers approach all reading tasks the same way.	Capable writers adapt their writing to meet demands of audience, purpose, and form, but less capable writers don't.
Fluency	Capable readers read fluently, but less capable readers read word by word, don't chunk words into phrases, and read without much expression.	Capable writers sustain their writing longer and pause to think and reread what they've written, but less capable writers write less and don't pause to reread their writing.
Background Knowledge	Capable readers relate what they're reading to their background knowledge, but less capable readers don't make this connection.	Capable writers gather and organize ideas before writing, but less capable writers don't plan before beginning to write.
Decoding/ Spelling	Capable readers identify unfamiliar words efficiently, but less capable readers make nonsensical guesses or skip over unfamiliar words when they're reading.	Capable writers spell many words conventionally and use the dictionary, but less capable writers can't spell many high-frequency words, and they use phonics to spell unfamiliar words.
Vocabulary	Capable readers have larger vocabularies than less capable readers do.	Capable writers use more-sophisticated words and figurative language than less capable writers do.
Strategies	Capable readers use a variety of strategies as they read, but less capable readers use fewer strategies or less effective ones.	Capable writers use many strategies effectively, but less capable writers use fewer strategies or less effective ones.
Monitoring	Capable readers monitor their comprehension, but less capable readers don't realize or take action when they don't understand.	Capable writers monitor that their writing makes sense, and they turn to classmates for revising suggestions, but less capable writers don't.

Adapted from Faigley, Cherry, Jolliffe, & Skinner, 1985.

CHAPTER 7
Review

How Effective Teachers Promote Comprehension

▶ Teachers understand that comprehension involves both reader factors and text factors.

▶ Teachers ensure that students have adequate background knowledge, vocabulary, and fluency, the prerequisites for comprehension.

▶ Teachers understand how comprehension strategies support students' understanding of texts they're reading.

▶ Teachers teach students how to use comprehension strategies and skills.

▶ Teachers nurture students' motivation and engagement in literacy activities.

CHAPTER 8

Promoting Comprehension:
Text Factors

Mr. Abrams's Fourth Graders Learn About Frogs

Mr. Abrams's class is studying frogs. The fourth graders began the unit by making a **K-W-L chart**, listing what they already know about frogs in the "K: What We Know" column and things they want to learn in the "W: What We Wonder" column. At the end of the unit, students will finish the chart by listing what they've learned in the "L: What We Have Learned" column. The students want to know how frogs and toads are different and if it's true that you get warts from frogs. Mr. Abrams assures them that they will learn the answers to many of their questions and makes a mental note to find the answer to their question about warts.

Aquariums with frogs and frog spawn sit on one side of the classroom. Mr. Abrams has brought in five aquariums and filled them with frogs he collected in his backyard and others he "rented" from a local pet store, and he's also brought in frog spawn from a nearby pond. The fourth graders are observing the frogs and the frog spawn daily and drawing diagrams and making notes in their **learning logs**.

Mr. Abrams sets out a text set with fiction, nonfiction, and poetry books about frogs on a special shelf in the classroom library. He reads many of the books aloud using the **interactive read-aloud** procedure. To begin, he reads the title, shows students several pages, and asks them to classify the book as fiction, nonfiction, or poetry. After determining the genre, they talk about their purpose for listening. For nonfiction, Mr. Abrams writes a question or two on the chalkboard to guide their listening. After reading, the students answer the questions as part of their discussion. Students also reread many of these books independently.

Mr. Abrams also has a class set of *Amazing Frogs and Toads* (Clarke, 1990), a nonfiction book with striking photograph illustrations and well-organized presentations of information. He reads it once with the whole class using shared reading, and they talk about the important information in the book. He divides the class into small groups, and each group chooses a question about frogs to research. Students reread the book, hunting for the answer to their question. Mr. Abrams has already taught the students to use the table of contents and the index to locate facts. After they locate the information, they create a poster to answer the question and share what they've learned. He meets with each group to help them organize their posters and revise and edit their writing.

From the vast amount of information in *Amazing Frogs and Toads*, Mr. Abrams chooses nine questions, which he designs to address some of the questions on the "W: What We Wonder" section of the K-W-L chart, highlight important information in the text, and focus on the expository text structures, the organizational patterns used in nonfiction texts. Mr. Abrams is teaching the fourth graders that nonfiction texts have special organizational elements. Here are his questions organized according to the expository structures:

What are amphibians? (description)

What do frogs look like? (description)

What is the life cycle of a frog? (sequence)

How do frogs eat? (sequence)

How are frogs and toads alike and different? (comparison)

Why do frogs hibernate? (cause and effect)

How do frogs croak? (cause and effect)

How do frogs use their eyes and eyelids? (problem and solution)

How do frogs escape from their enemies? (problem and solution)

After completing their posters, the fourth graders share them through brief presentations, and the posters are displayed in the classroom. Two posters are shown on page 202; the life cycle poster emphasizes the sequence structure, and the "Frogs Have Big Eyes" poster explains that the frog's eyes help it solve problems—finding food, hiding from enemies, and seeing underwater.

Mr. Abrams's students use the information in the posters to write books about frogs. Students each choose three posters and write chapters to report the information from them. Students meet in writing groups to revise their rough drafts and then edit with a classmate and with Mr. Abrams. Finally, students word process their final copies and add illustrations, a title page, and a table of contents. Then they compile their books and "publish" them by sharing them with classmates from the author's chair.

Armin wrote this brief chapter on "Hibernation":

> *Hibernation means that an animal sleeps all winter long. Frogs hibernate because they are cold blooded and they might freeze to death if they didn't. They find a good place to sleep like a hole in the ground, or in a log, or under some leaves. They go to sleep and they do not eat, or drink, or go to the bathroom. They sleep all*

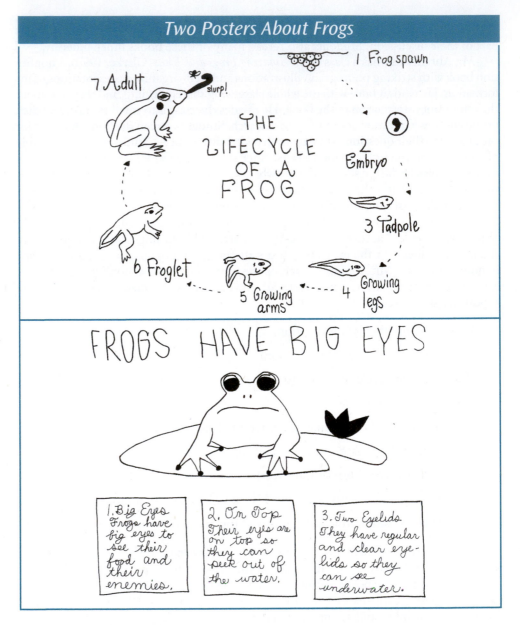

Two Posters About Frogs

THE LIFECYCLE OF A FROG

7 Adult slurp!

1 Frog spawn

2 Embryo

3 Tadpole

4 Growing legs

5 Growing arms

6 Froglet

FROGS HAVE BIG EYES

1. Big Eyes
Frogs have big eyes to see their food and their enemies.

2. On Top
Their eyes are on top so they can peek out of the water.

3. Two Eyelids
They have regular and clear eyelids so they can see underwater.

winter and when they wake up it is spring. They are very, very hungry and they want to eat a lot of food. Their blood warms up when it is spring because the temperature warms up and when they are warm they want to be awake and eat. They are awake in the spring and in the summer, and then in the fall they start to think about hibernating again.

Jessica wrote this longer chapter on "The Differences Between Frogs and Toads":

You might think that frogs and toads are the same, but you would be wrong. They are really different, but they are both amphibians. I am going to tell you three ways they are different.

First of all, frogs really love water so they stay in the water or pretty close to it. Toads don't love water. They usually live where it is dry. This is a big difference between frogs and toads.

Second, you should look at frogs and toads. They look different. Frogs are slender and thin but toads are fat. Their skin is different, too. Frogs have smooth skin and toads have bumpy skin. I would say that toads are not pretty to look at.

Third, frogs have long legs but toads have short legs. That probably is the reason why frogs are wonderful jumpers and toads can't. They move slowly. They just hop. When you watch them move, you can tell that they are very different.

Frogs and toads are different kinds of amphibians. They live in different places, they look different, and they move in different ways. You can see these differences when you look at them, and it is very interesting to study them.

Mr. Abrams helps his students develop a rubric to assess their books. Some points on the rubric address the chapters:

- The chapter title describes the chapter.
- The information in each chapter is presented clearly.
- Vocabulary from the word wall is used in each chapter.
- The information in each chapter is written in one or more indented paragraphs.
- The information in each chapter has very few spelling, capitalization, and punctuation errors.
- There is a useful illustration in each chapter.

Other points consider the book as a whole:

- The title page lists the title and the author's name.
- All pages in the book are numbered.
- The table of contents lists the chapters and the pages for each chapter.
- The title is written on the cover of the book.
- The illustrations on the cover of the book relate to frogs.

The students self-assess their books using a 4-point scale, and Mr. Abrams also uses the rubric to assess their writing. He conferences with students and shares his scoring with them. Also, he helps the students set goals for their next writing project.

At the end of the unit, the fourth graders finish the K-W-L chart. In the third column, "L: What We Have Learned," they list interesting information they've learned:

Tadpoles breathe through gills but frogs breathe through lungs.

Tadpoles are vegetarians but frogs eat worms and insects.

Snakes, rats, birds, and foxes are the frogs' enemies.

Some frogs in the rainforest are brightly colored and poisonous, too.

Some frogs are hard to see because they have camouflage coloring.

Male frogs puff up their air sacs to croak and make sounds.

Frogs have teeth but they swallow their food whole.

Frogs have two sets of eyelids and one set is clear so frogs can see when they are underwater.

Frogs can jump ten times their body length but toads can't—they're hoppers.

Mr. Abrams stands back to reread the fourth graders' comments. "I can tell how much you've learned when I read the detailed information you've added in the L column," he remarks with a smile. He knows that one reason why his students are successful is because he taught them to use text structure as a tool for learning.

What readers know and do during reading has a tremendous impact on how well they comprehend, but comprehension involves more than just reader factors: It also involves text factors. Stories, nonfiction, and poems can be easier or more difficult to read depending on factors that are inherent in them (Harvey & Goudvis, 2007). Authors use these text factors:

Genres. The three broad categories of literature are fiction, nonfiction, and poetry, and there are subgenres within each category. For example, science fiction and historical fiction are subgenres of fiction, and alphabet books and biographies are subgenres of nonfiction.

Structures. Authors use patterns to organize texts and emphasize the most important ideas. For example, sequence, comparison, and cause and effect are structures that authors use to organize nonfiction texts.

Features. Authors use conventions and literary devices to achieve particular effects in their writing, including symbolism and tone in fiction, headings and indexes in nonfiction, and page layout for poems.

When students understand how authors organize and present their ideas in books, this knowledge about text factors serves as a scaffold, making comprehension easier (Meyer & Poon, 2004; Sweet & Snow, 2003). Text factors make a similar contribution to students' writing; students apply what they've learned about genres, text structures, and text features when they're writing.

Text Factors of Fiction

Stories are narratives about characters trying to overcome problems or deal with difficulties. They've been described as "waking dreams" that people use to find meaning in their lives. Young children develop an understanding of what constitutes a story beginning in the preschool years when their parents read aloud to them, and they refine and expand their understanding of stories through literacy instruction at school. Students learn about the subgenres of fiction and read picture-book stories and novels representing each one, examine the structural patterns that authors use to organize fiction, and point out the narrative devices that authors use to breathe life into their writing.

Narrative Genres

Stories can be categorized in different ways, one of which is according to genre (Buss & Karnowski, 2000). Three general subcategories are folklore, fantasies, and realistic fiction. Figure 8–1 presents an overview of these narrative genres.

Folklore. Stories that began hundreds of years ago and were passed from generation to generation by storytellers before being written down are folklore. These stories, including fables, folktales, and myths, are an important part of our cultural heritage. Fables are brief narratives designed to teach a moral. The narrative format makes the lesson easier to understand, and the moral is usually stated at the end. Fables exemplify these characteristics:

- They are short, often less than a page long.
- The characters are usually animals.
- The characters are one-dimensional: strong or weak, wise or foolish.
- The setting is barely sketched; the stories could take place anywhere.
- The theme is usually stated as a moral at the end of the story.

FIGURE 8–1 ◆ Narrative Genres

Category	Genres	Description
Folklore	Fables	Brief tales told to point out a moral. For example: *Town Mouse, Country Mouse* (Brett, 2003) and *The Boy Who Cried Wolf* (Hennessy, 2006).
	Folktales	Stories in which heroes demonstrate virtues to triumph over adversity. For example: *Rumpelstiltskin* (Zelinsky, 1996) and *The Girl Who Spun Gold* (Hamilton, 2000), a West Indian version of "Rumpelstiltskin."
	Myths	Stories created by ancient peoples to explain natural phenomena. For example: *Why Mosquitoes Buzz in People's Ears* (Aardema, 2004) and *Raven* (McDermott, 2001).
	Legends	Stories that recount the courageous deeds of people who struggled against each other or against gods and monsters. For example: *John Henry* (Lester, 1999) and *The Adventures of Robin Hood* (Williams, 2007).
Fantasy	Modern Literary Tales	Stories written by modern authors that are similar to folktales. For example: *The Ugly Duckling* (Mitchell, 2007).
	Fantastic Stories	Imaginative stories that explore alternate realities and contain elements not found in the natural world. For example: *Inkheart* (Funke, 2003) and *Poppy* (Avi, 2005).
	Science Fiction	Stories that explore scientific possibilities. For example: *The House of the Scorpions* (Farmer, 2002) and *The Giver* (Lowry, 2006b).
	High Fantasy	Stories that focus on the conflict between good and evil and often involve quests. For example: the Harry Potter series and *The Lion, the Witch and the Wardrobe* (Lewis, 2005).
Realistic Fiction	Contemporary Stories	Stories that portray today's society. For example: *After Tupac & D Foster* (Woodson, 2008) and *Seedfolks* (Fleischman, 2004b).
	Historical Stories	Realistic stories set in the past. For example: *Sarah, Plain and Tall* (MacLachlan, 2004) and *Roll of Thunder, Hear My Cry* (Taylor, 2001).

The best-known fables, including "The Hare and the Tortoise" and "The Ant and the Grasshopper," are believed to have been written by a Greek slave named Aesop in the 6th century B.C.

Folktales began as oral stories, told and retold by medieval storytellers as they traveled from town to town. The problem in a folktale usually revolves around one of four situations: a journey from home to perform a task, a journey to confront a monster, the miraculous change from a harsh home to a secure home, or a confrontation between a wise beast and a foolish beast. Folktales exemplify these characteristics:

- The story often begins with the phrase "Once upon a time . . ."
- The setting is generalized and could be located anywhere.
- The plot structure is simple and straightforward.
- Characters are one-dimensional: good or bad, stupid or clever, industrious or lazy.
- The end is happy, and everyone lives "happily ever after."

The best-known folktales are fairy tales. They have motifs or small, recurring elements, including magical powers, transformations, enchantments, magical objects, trickery, and wishes that are granted, and they feature witches, giants, fairy godmothers, and other fantastic characters. Well-known examples are *Cinderella* (Ehrlich, 2004) and *Sleeping Beauty* (Craft, 2002).

People around the world have created myths to explain natural phenomena. Some explain the seasons, the sun, the moon, and the constellations, and others tell how the mountains and other physical features of the earth were created. Ancient peoples used myths to explain many things that have since been explained by science. Myths exemplify these characteristics:

- Myths explain creations.
- Characters are often heroes with supernatural powers.
- The setting is barely sketched.
- Magical powers are required.

For example, the Greek myth *King Midas: The Golden Touch* (Demi, 2002) tells about the king's greed. Other myths tell how animals came to be or why they look the way they do. Legends are myths about heroes who have done something important enough to be remembered in a story; they may have some basis in history but aren't verifiable. Stories about Robin Hood and King Arthur, for example, are legends. Legends about American heroes, including Johnny Appleseed, Paul Bunyan, Pecos Bill, and John Henry, are known as *tall tales*.

Fantasies. Fantasies are imaginative stories. Authors create new worlds for their characters, but these worlds must be based in reality so that readers will believe they exist. One of the most beloved fantasies is *Charlotte's Web* (White, 2006). Fantasies are classified as modern literary tales, fantastic stories, science fiction, and high fantasy.

Modern literary tales are related to fairy tales because they often incorporate many characteristics and conventions of traditional literature, but they've been written more recently and have identifiable authors. The best-known author of modern literary tales is Hans Christian Andersen, who wrote *The Snow Queen* (Ehrlich, 2006) and *The Ugly Duckling* (Mitchell, 2007).

Fantastic stories are realistic in most details, but some events require readers to suspend disbelief. They exemplify these characteristics:

- The events in the story are extraordinary; things that could not happen in today's world.
- The setting is realistic.
- Main characters are people or personified animals.
- Themes often deal with the conflict between good and evil.

Some are animal fantasies, such as *Babe: The Gallant Pig* (King-Smith, 2005). The main characters in these stories are animals endowed with human traits. Students often realize that the animals symbolize human beings and that these stories explore human relationships. Some are toy fantasies, such as *The Miraculous Journey of Edward*

Tulane (DiCamillo, 2008). Toy fantasies are similar to animal fantasies except that the main characters are talking toys, usually stuffed animals or dolls. Other fantasies involve enchanted journeys during which wondrous things happen. The journey has a purpose, but it's usually overshadowed by the fantastic world, as in Roald Dahl's *Charlie and the Chocolate Factory* (2007).

In science fiction, authors create a world in which science interacts with society. Many stories involve traveling through space to distant galaxies or meeting alien societies. Authors hypothesize scientific advancements and imagine technology of the future to create the plot. Science fiction exemplifies these characteristics:

- The story is set in the future.
- Conflict is usually between the characters and natural or mechanical forces, such as robots.
- The characters believe in the advanced technology.
- A detailed description of scientific facts is provided.

Time-warp stories, including Jon Scieszka's Time Warp Trio stories, in which the characters move forward and back in time, are also classified as science fiction.

Heroes confront evil for the good of humanity in high fantasy. The primary characteristic is the focus on the conflict between good and evil, as in C. S. Lewis's *The Lion, the Witch and the Wardrobe* (2005) and J. K. Rowling's Harry Potter stories. High fantasy is related to folklore in that it's characterized by motifs and themes. Most stories include magical kingdoms, quests, tests of courage, magical powers, and fantastic characters.

Realistic Fiction. These stories are lifelike and believable. The outcome is reasonable, and the story seems truthful. Realistic fiction helps readers discover that their problems aren't unique and that they aren't alone in experiencing certain feelings and situations. This genre also broadens students' horizons and allows them to experience new adventures. Contemporary stories and historical stories are two types.

In contemporary fiction, readers identify with characters who are their own age and have similar interests and problems. Here are the characteristics of these modern-day stories:

- Characters act like real people or like real animals.
- The setting is in the world as we know it today.
- Stories deal with everyday occurrences or "relevant subjects."

In *The Higher Power of Lucky* (Patron, 2006), for example, students read about an eccentric 10-year-old girl named Lucky, who finally comes to terms with her mother's death. Other examples are *I Am Not Joey Pigza* (Gantos, 2007) and *No More Dead Dogs* (Korman, 2000).

In contrast, historical fiction is set in the past. Details about food, clothing, and culture must be typical of the era in which the story is set because the setting influences the plot. These are the characteristics of this genre:

- The setting is historically accurate.
- Conflict is often between characters or between a character and society.
- The language is appropriate to the setting.
- Themes are universal, both for the historical period of the book and for today.

Examples of historical fiction include *Number the Stars* (Lowry, 1998) and *Crispin: The Cross of Lead* (Avi, 2004). In these stories, students are immersed in historical events, they appreciate the contributions of people who have lived before them, and they learn about human relationships.

New Literacies

A New Generation of Books

Many of the best new books for young adolescents blur the lines between genres and incorporate innovative forms. Students read these texts differently, much like they approach online texts (Kiefer, Price-Dennis, & Ryan, 2006). In *The Invention of Hugo Cabret* (Selznick, 2007), the first novel to win the Caldecott Medal, the author combined storytelling, meticulous drawings, and cinematic techniques to create a touching story about a Parisian orphan. Half of the 500-page novel is told through illustrations that readers must read as carefully as they do the text.

Sometimes authors combine genres. *Love That Dog* (Creech, 2001), about a boy who learns the power of poetry, and *Becoming Joe Di Maggio* (Testa, 2005), about a kid who escapes his difficult life by listening to baseball games with his grandfather, are poetic narratives—stories told in verse. Students focus on the characters and the plot, but they're aware of the unique page layout and appreciate the figurative qualities of poetic language as they read.

Other authors invent multiple voices to develop their stories. *Day of Tears: A Novel in Dialogue* (Lester, 2005a) tells about an 1859 slave auction using different voices to emphasize the anguish of slave families and the greed of owners, and *Good Masters! Sweet Ladies! Voices From a Medieval Village* (Schlitz, 2007) is an award-winning collection of 23 monologues, featuring people living at an English manor. Students read flexibly, adjusting to new viewpoints in each chapter.

Book-length comics called *graphic novels* are a new genre. Babymouse is a sassy mouse featured in *Babymouse: Queen of the World* (Holm, 2005) and numerous sequels. Fone Bone engages in battles of good versus evil in *Bone: Out of Boneville* (Smith, 2005) and other books in this series. *Diary of a Wimpy Kid* (Kinney, 2007) and its sequels combine text and graphics to recount Greg Heffley's middle school experiences. Students examine every illustration and use their imagination to understand what's happening between frames.

Some wordless picture books incorporate the characteristics of graphic novels. *The Arrival* (Tan, 2007), for example, is a compelling story about an immigrant's journey to build a better future. Readers develop a sense of the immigrant's isolation as they study the illustrations and recognize the visual metaphors.

Students are learning new strategies for reading books that they also use online. They combine visual and textual information to comprehend across genres, text structures, and conventions.

Elements of Story Structure

Fiction has unique structural elements that distinguishes it from other genres. The most important elements are plot, characters, setting, point of view, and theme. They work together to structure a story, and authors manipulate them to make their stories interesting.

Plot. The sequence of events involving characters in conflict situations is plot. It's based on the goals of one or more characters and the processes they go through to attain them (Lukens, 2006). The main characters want to achieve the goal, and other characters are introduced to prevent them from being successful. The story events are set in motion by characters as they attempt to overcome conflict and solve their problems. Figure 8–2 presents a list of stories with well-developed plots and other elements of story structure.

The most basic aspect of plot is the division of the main events into the beginning, middle, and end. Specific information is included in each part. Authors introduce the characters, describe the setting, and present a problem in the beginning. Together, the characters, setting, and events develop the plot and sustain the theme through the story. In the middle, the plot unfolds, with each event preparing readers for what follows. Conflict heightens as the characters face roadblocks that keep them from solving their problems; how the characters tackle these problems adds suspense to keep readers interested. In the end, all is reconciled, and readers learn whether the characters' struggles are successful.

Conflict is the tension or opposition between forces in the plot, and it's what interests readers enough to continue reading the story (Lukens, 2006). Conflict occurs in these four ways:

Between a Character and Nature. Conflict between a character and nature occurs in stories in which severe weather plays an important role and in stories set in isolated geographic locations, such as *Holes* (Sachar, 2008), in which Stanley struggles to survive at a boys' juvenile detention center.

Between a Character and Society. Sometimes the main character's activities and beliefs differ from those of others, and conflict arises between that character and society. In *The Witch of Blackbird Pond* (Speare, 2001), for example, Kit Tyler is accused of being a witch because she continues activities that were acceptable in the Caribbean community where she grew up but aren't in the New England Puritan community where she lives now.

Between Characters. Conflict between characters is very common. In *Tales of a Fourth Grade Nothing* (Blume, 2007), for instance, the never-ending conflict between Peter and his little brother, Fudge, is what makes the story entertaining.

Within a Character. The main character struggles to overcome challenges in his or her own life. In *Esperanza Rising* (Ryan, 2002), the title character must come to terms with her new life as a migrant worker after she leaves her family's ranch in Mexico.

Plot is developed through conflict that's introduced at the beginning, expanded in the middle, and finally resolved at the end. It involves these components:

- A problem that introduces conflict is presented at the beginning of the story.
- Characters face roadblocks in attempting to solve the problem in the middle.

FIGURE 8–2 ◆ *Stories Illustrating the Elements of Story Structure*

Plot

Paulsen, G. (2007). *Hatchet*. New York: Simon & Schuster. (grades 6–7)

Sachar, L. (2008). *Holes*. New York: Farrar, Straus & Giroux. (7–8)

Steig, W. (2006). *Sylvester and the magic pebble*. New York: Aladdin Books. (4–5)

Characters

Cushman, K. (1994). *Catherine, called Birdy*. New York: HarperCollins. (6–8)

Dahl, R. (2007). *James and the giant peach*. New York: Puffin Books. (4–6)

Lowry, L. (2006). *The giver*. New York: Delacorte. (6–8)

Setting

Curtis, C. P. (2000). *The Watsons go to Birmingham—1963*. New York: Laurel Leaf. (5–7)

Hale, S. (2005). *Princess Academy*. New York: Bloomsbury. (4–6)

Lowry, L. (1998). *Number the stars*. New York: Laurel Leaf. (5–6)

Patron, S. (2006). *The higher power of Lucky*. New York: Atheneum. (6–7)

Point of View

Hesse, K. (2001). *Witness*. New York: Scholastic. (6–8)

Lewis, C. S. (2005). *The lion, the witch and the wardrobe*. New York: HarperCollins. (6–8)

MacLachlan, P. (2004). *Sarah, plain and tall*. New York: HarperTrophy. (4–5)

Theme

Appelt, K. (2008). *The underneath*. New York: Atheneum. (6–8)

Babbitt, N. (2007). *Tuck everlasting*. New York: Square Fish Books. (6–8)

Bunting, E. (1999). *Smoky night*. San Diego: Harcourt Brace. (4–5)

DiCamillo, K. (2008). *The miraculous journey of Edward Tulane*. New York: Walker. (4–6)

Naylor, P. R. (2000). *Shiloh*. New York: Aladdin Books. (4–6)

- The high point in the action occurs when the problem is about to be solved. This high point separates the middle and the end.
- The problem is solved and the roadblocks are overcome at the end of the story.

Figure 8–3 presents a plot diagram that fifth graders completed after reading *Esperanza Rising* (Ryan, 2002). It incorporates all four components. The problem is that Esperanza and her mother must create a new life for themselves in California because they can't remain at their Mexican ranch home any longer. Certainly, there's conflict between characters here and conflict with society, too, but the most important conflict is within Esperanza as she leaves her comfortable life in Mexico to become a migrant laborer. Esperanza and her mother face many roadblocks in California. The work is very difficult. Esperanza wants to bring her grandmother to join them, but they don't have enough money for her travel expenses. Then Esperanza's mother becomes ill, and Esperanza takes over her mother's work. Finally, Esperanza saves enough money to bring her grandmother to California, but her money disappears. The high point occurs when Esperanza's mother recovers, and it turns out that her money wasn't stolen after all: Esperanza's friend Miguel used it to bring her grandmother to them. As the story ends, the problem is solved: Esperanza adjusts to her new life with her

FIGURE 8–3 ◆ *A Plot Diagram for* Esperanza Rising

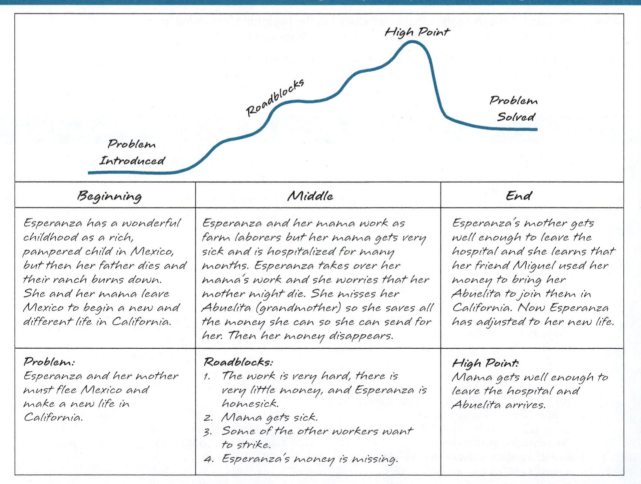

Beginning	Middle	End
Esperanza has a wonderful childhood as a rich, pampered child in Mexico, but then her father dies and their ranch burns down. She and her mama leave Mexico to begin a new and different life in California.	Esperanza and her mama work as farm laborers but her mama gets very sick and is hospitalized for many months. Esperanza takes over her mama's work and she worries that her mother might die. She misses her Abuelita (grandmother) so she saves all the money she can so she can send for her. Then her money disappears.	Esperanza's mother gets well enough to leave the hospital and she learns that her friend Miguel used her money to bring her Abuelita to join them in California. Now Esperanza has adjusted to her new life.
Problem: Esperanza and her mother must flee Mexico and make a new life in California.	**Roadblocks:** 1. The work is very hard, there is very little money, and Esperanza is homesick. 2. Mama gets sick. 3. Some of the other workers want to strike. 4. Esperanza's money is missing.	**High Point:** Mama gets well enough to leave the hospital and Abuelita arrives.

mother and grandmother. *Esperanza* means "hope" in Spanish, and readers have reason to be optimistic that the girl and her family will create a good life for themselves.

Characters. Characters are the people or personified animals in the story. This is often the most important structural element because the story is centered on a character or group of characters. Main characters have many traits, both good and bad; that is to say, they have all the characteristics of real people. Inferring a character's traits is an important part of comprehension: Through character traits, readers get to know a character well, and the character seems to come to life. A list of stories with fully developed main characters is included in Figure 8–2. Characters are developed in four ways:

Appearance. Readers learn about characters by the description of their facial features, body shapes, habits of dress, mannerisms, and gestures. The title character in *Skellig* (Almond, 2001) is a man-owl-angel who's as pale as dry plaster and is covered with dead flies. His legs are long, his fingers are gnarled, and wings protrude out of his back. He has a squeaky voice and coughs up furry balls. He smells of old clothes and sweat, and his breath in stinky. He's been known to eat mice and spiders, but he loves Chinese food and brown ale. It's Almond's description of Skellig that makes readers keep reading to learn more about this mysterious character.

Action. The best way to learn about characters is through their actions. In Van Allsburg's *The Stranger* (1986), readers deduce that the stranger is Jack Frost because of what he does: He watches geese flying south for the winter, blows a cold wind, labors long hours without becoming tired, has an unusual rapport with wild animals, and is unfamiliar with modern conveniences.

Dialogue. What characters say is important, but so is how they speak. The geographic location of the story and the characters' socioeconomic status also determine how they speak. Authors use dialogue to move the story along and to provide valuable insight into their characters. In Kinney's *Diary of Wimpy Kid* (2007) and other books in this hilarious series, Greg Heffley describes his efforts to get through life, including his father's efforts to turn him into a jock.

Monologue. Authors provide insight into characters by revealing their thoughts. In *Sylvester and the Magic Pebble* (Steig, 2006), thoughts and wishes are central to the story. Sylvester, a foolish donkey, wishes to become a rock, and he spends a miserable winter that way. Steig shares the donkey's thinking with readers: He thinks about his parents, who are frantic with worry, and readers learn how Sylvester feels in the spring when his parents picnic on the rock he has become.

Setting. The setting is generally thought of as the location where the story takes place, but that's only one aspect. There are four dimensions:

Location. Many stories take place in predictable settings that don't contribute to a story's effectiveness, but sometimes the location is integral. For instance, the Alaskan North Slope in *Julie of the Wolves* (George, 2005) is artfully described and makes the story unique.

Weather. Severe weather, such as a blizzard, a rainstorm, or a tornado, is crucial in some stories. A rainstorm is essential to the plot development in *Bridge to Terabithia* (Paterson, 2005), but in other books, the weather isn't mentioned because it doesn't affect the outcome of the story.

Time Period. For stories set in the past or in the future, the time period is important. If *Number the Stars* (Lowry, 1998) were set in a different era, for example, it would lose much of its impact; today, few people would believe that Jewish people are the focus of government persecution.

Time. Many stories span a brief period of time; *Hatchet* (Paulsen, 2007) takes place in less than 2 months. Other stories, however, span a year—long enough for the main character to grow to maturity.

In some stories, the setting is barely sketched; these are called *backdrop settings*. The setting in many fairy tales, for instance, is relatively unimportant, and the convention "Once upon a time . . ." is enough to set the stage. In other stories, the setting is elaborated and is essential to the story's effectiveness; these settings are called *integral settings* (Lukens, 2006). Stories with integral settings also are listed in Figure 8–2.

Point of View. Stories are written from a particular viewpoint, and this perspective determines to a great extent readers' understanding of the characters and events of the story (Lukens, 2006). Stories written from different viewpoints are presented in Figure 8–2. Here are the points of view:

First-Person Viewpoint. This point of view is used to tell a story through the eyes of one character using the first-person pronoun "I." The narrator, usually the main character, speaks as an eyewitness and a participant in the events. For example, in *The True Story of the 3 Little Pigs!* (Scieszka, 1996), the wolf tries to explain away his bad image in this version of the familiar folktale.

Omniscient Viewpoint. The author is godlike, seeing and knowing all. The author tells readers about the thought processes of each character without worrying about how the information is obtained. *Doctor De Soto* (Steig, 1990), a story about a mouse dentist who outwits a fox with a toothache, is told from the omniscient viewpoint. Steig lets readers know that the fox wants to eat the dentist as soon as his toothache is cured and that the mouse dentist is aware of the fox's thoughts and plans a clever trick.

Limited Omniscient Viewpoint. This viewpoint is used so that readers know the thoughts of one character. The story is told in third person, and the author concentrates on the thoughts, feelings, and experiences of the main character or another important character. Gary Paulsen used this viewpoint for *Hatchet* (2007) to explore Brian's thoughts as he struggles to survive in the wilderness and to accept his parents' divorce.

Objective Viewpoint. Readers assume the role of eyewitness and are confined to the immediate scene. They learn only what's visible and audible and aren't aware of what any characters think. Fairy tales are told from the objective viewpoint. The focus is on recounting events, not on developing the characters' personalities.

Some stories are told from multiple viewpoints, such as *Seedfolks* (Fleischman, 2004b), about a community garden that brings hope to a blighted neighborhood, and *Witness* (Hesse, 2001), about an event in 1924 when the Ku Klux Klan moved into a Vermont town. Each chapter in these stories is told by a different character.

Theme. Theme is the underlying meaning of a story; it embodies general truths about human nature (Lukens, 2006). Themes usually deal with the characters' emotions and values and can be stated either explicitly or implicitly: Explicit themes are stated clearly in the story, but implicit themes must be inferred. In a fable, the theme is often stated explicitly at the end, but in most stories, the theme emerges through the thoughts, speech, and actions of the characters as they try to overcome the obstacles that prevent them from reaching their goals.

Stories usually have more than one theme, and their themes generally can't be articulated with a single word. *Charlotte's Web* (White, 2006), for example, has several "friendship" themes, one explicitly stated and others that must be inferred. Friendship is a

TOPIC: *Analyzing the Theme*
GRADE: *Seventh Grade*
TIME: *20 minutes*

Mrs. Miller's seventh graders are studying the Middle Ages and are reading novels set in that period, such as *Catherine, Called Birdy* (Cushman, 1994), in literature circles. Mrs. Miller brings the class together to teach a minilesson on theme before asking the students in each literature circle to analyze the theme of the book they're reading.

❶ Introduce the Topic

"It's time to talk about theme because most of you are reaching the end of the book you're reading," Mrs. Miller begins. "Before, I asked you to focus on the setting to learn more about medieval life as you were reading and discussing the book. Now, I want you to think about your book in a different way: I want you to think about the theme. Let's review: Theme is the universal message in the book. It might be about friendship, courage, acceptance, determination, or some other important quality."

❷ Share Examples

Mrs. Miller uses *Hatchet* (Paulsen, 2007), a survival story that students read in September, as an example. "Did Brian save himself?" the teacher asks. Everyone agrees that he did. "So what is the theme of the story?" Mrs. Miller asks. Students identify survival as the theme, and Mrs. Miller asks them to explain it in a sentence. Jared suggests, "Sometimes you have to do a lot of disgusting things if you want to survive." Mrs. Miller agrees. Carole offers, "I think the theme is that you may not think that you have the guts and the brains to survive, but if you get trapped in the wilderness, you will find that you do." Again she agrees. Jo-Jo expresses the theme another way: "It's like in the movie *Castaway*. Brian has to get mad—really mad and a little crazy, too, but he gets mad enough to survive. You have to stand up and prove to yourself that you can survive." Again she agrees. Mrs. Miller draws a cluster on the chalkboard and writes *survival* in the center circle. Then she draws out rays and writes on them the sentences that the students offered.

❸ Provide Information

"Theme isn't obvious the way plot, characters, and setting are," Mrs. Miller explains. She tells the class that in order to uncover the theme, they need to think about the conflicts facing the character and how the character goes about solving the problem. "Then you have to answer the question: 'What is the author trying to tell me about life?'"

❹ Guide Practice

The minilesson ends as the students return to their literature circles to talk about the theme of their book. Mrs. Miller asks them to think of one or more one-word qualities and then to draw out at least three possible sentence-long themes. As they analyze the theme, they draw clusters on chart paper.

❺ Assess Learning

Mrs. Miller moves from group to group, talking with students about theme. She checks their clusters and helps them draw out additional themes to add to them.

Check the Compendium of Instructional Procedures, which follows Chapter 12, for more information on the highlighted terms.

multidimensional theme—qualities of a good friend, unlikely friends, and sacrificing for a friend, for instance. Teachers probe students' thinking as they work to construct a theme and move beyond simplistic one-word labels. The **minilesson** on page 213 demonstrates how Mrs. Miller, a seventh-grade teacher, reviewed the concept of theme. Afterward, her students analyzed the theme of books they were reading in literature circles.

Narrative Devices

Authors use literary devices to make their writing more vivid and memorable (Lukens, 2006).

- **Dialogue.** Written conversation where characters speak to each other.
- **Flashbacks.** An interruption, often taking readers back to the beginning of the story.

EXAMINING TEXT FACTORS

◀ *Fiction*

Project Mulberry
READING LEVEL: Fifth Grade
INTEREST LEVEL: Fourth to Sixth Grade

Genre	Fiction/contemporary realism
Elements of Story Structure	Character—Julie's thoughts and actions as she tries to deal with her conflict about being Korean and American.
	Point of view—Julie's first-person account of her science fair project with Patrick.
	Theme—Julie's acceptance of herself and the importance of building tolerance and eliminating racism.
Narrative Devices	Between-chapter conversations between the author and the main character

Project Mulberry (Park, 2007) is a contemporary realistic novel about Julie Song, a seventh-grade Korean American girl, and her friend, Patrick, who team up to create a project to win a blue ribbon at the state fair. The reading level of this multicultural novel is fifth grade, and the interest level is fourth through sixth grade. Newbery Medal–winning author Linda Sue Park has written a lively, engaging first-person narrative. Julie is a compelling character, and her thoughts and actions drive the story forward. Her mother suggests that she and Patrick raise silkworms for their state fair project, but at first Julie isn't interested because she thinks it's too Korean; instead, she wants to do something "American."

Self-acceptance is the most important theme in this story. Julie deals with conflict within herself as she struggles to fit in while honoring her Korean heritage. Another theme is prejudice: Julie fears that her mother may be racist because she doesn't want her to spend time with Mr. Dixon, the African American man who gives her mulberry leaves to feed to the silkworms. The story emphasizes the importance of doing small things to increase tolerance.

The most interesting feature in the book is a series of conversations between Julie and the book's author that are inserted between chapters. In these conversations, Julie complains about her character and asks the author questions about how she thinks of ideas and writes books. These witty conservations provide useful insights about the writing process. Most students will enjoy reading them, but those who don't can easily skip over them because they're set off from the rest of the story.

- **Foreshadowing.** Hinting at events to come later in the story to build readers' expectations.
- **Imagery.** Descriptive words and phrases used to create a picture in readers' minds.
- **Suspense.** An excited uncertainty about the outcome of conflict in a story.
- **Symbolism.** A person, place, or thing used to represent something else. For example, a lion often symbolizes courage and a dove symbolizes peace.
- **Tone.** The overall feeling or mood in a story, ranging from humorous to serious and sad.

Symbolism is an essential narrative device in Chris Van Allsburg's *The Wretched Stone* (1991), for example. The story, written as a ship captain's journal, tells about a voyage when the crew picks up a strange, glowing stone that distracts them from reading, spending time with friends, and doing their jobs. The stone symbolizes television or computers, and to understand the theme, students must recognize this symbol and what it represents.

Text Factors of Nonfiction

Nonfiction is different than fiction. Because young adolescents tend to be more familiar with fiction, teachers explicitly teach students about nonfiction books and how to read them. Consider these nonfiction books:

Off to War: Voices of Soldiers' Children (Ellis, 2008), a collection of interviews with kids whose lives have been upended by their military parents' deployment to Iraq or Afghanistan

The Way We Work: Getting to Know the Amazing Human Body (Macaulay, 2008), a presentation of complex and technical information about the body systems

We Are the Ship: The Story of Negro League Baseball (Nelson, 2008), a tribute to Satchel Paige, Josh Gibson, and other gifted athletes who overcame racial bias in segregated America

Lincoln Shot: A President's Life Remembered (Denenberg, 2008), an invented newspaper memorial of Lincoln's death, illustrated with period portraits, photos, and maps

Dogs and Cats (Jenkins, 2007), a unique flip-book presentation of scientific information that compares dogs and cats

They provide information on varied topics, use different text-structure patterns, and incorporate reader-friendly nonfiction features, such as headings and margin notes. For students to comprehend these books, they need to appreciate the differences between fiction and nonfiction, understand how nonfiction texts are organized, and recognize the text features authors include.

Nonfiction Genres

Nonfiction books provide facts about just about any topic you can think of. Consider, for example: *Flick a Switch: How Electricity Gets to Your Home* (Seuling, 2003), *Taj Mahal* (Arnold & Comora, 2007), *Saguaro Moon: A Desert Journal* (Pratt-Serafini, 2002), *The Brain* (Simon, 2006), *Ancient Inca* (Gruber, 2006), and *Right Dog for the Job: Ira's Path From Service Dog to Guide Dog* (Patent, 2004). Some of these books are picture books that use a combination of text and illustrations to present information, and others are chapter books that depend primarily on the text to provide information.

Other books present information within a story context; the Magic School Bus series is perhaps the best known. In *The Magic School Bus and the Science Fair Expedition* (Cole, 2006), for example, Ms. Frizzle and her class travel through time to learn how scientific thinking developed. The page layout is innovative, with charts and reports containing factual information presented at the outside edges of most pages.

Alphabet Books. Many alphabet books are designed for young children, but others are intended for older students. *The Alphabet From A to Y With Bonus Letter Z!* (Martin & Chast, 2007) is a clever wordplay book, and others, such as *SuperHero ABC* (McLeod, 2006) and *Q Is for Quark: A Science Alphabet Book* (Schwartz, 2001), provide a wealth of information. In these books, words representing each letter are explained in paragraph-long entries.

Biographies. Students read biographies to learn about a person's life. A wide range of biographies are available today, from those featuring well-known personalities, such as *Eleanor Roosevelt: A Life of Discovery* (Freedman, 1997), *Muhammad* (Demi, 2003), *Escape! The Story of the Great Houdini* (Fleischman, 2006), and *Isaac Newton* (Krull, 2006), to those about unsung heroes, such as *Delivering Justice: W. W. Law and the Fight for Civil Rights* (Haskins, 2006). These books are individual biographies that focus on a single person; others are collective biographies with short vignettes about a group of related people, such as *American Heroes* (Delano, 2005) and *Honky-Tonk Heroes and Hillbilly Angels: The Pioneers of Country and Western Music* (George-Warren, 2006). Only a few autobiographies are available for students, but the Meet the Author series of autobiographies for kindergarten through fifth-grade students and the Author at Work series for older students, from Richard C. Owen Publisher, are interesting to students who have read their books. These autobiographies of contemporary authors, including Janet S. Wong's *Before It Wriggles Away* (2006) and Ralph Fletcher's *Reflections* (2007), include information about their lives and insights into their writing.

Expository Text Structures

Nonfiction books are organized in particular ways called *expository text structures* (McGee & Richgels, 1985). Figure 8–4 summarizes these patterns, presents sample passages and cue words that signal use of each pattern, and suggests an appropriate graphic organizer. When readers are aware of these patterns, it's easier to understand what they're reading, and when writers use these structures to organize their writing, it's easier for readers to understand. Sometimes the pattern is signaled through the title, a topic sentence, or cue words, but sometimes it isn't. Here are the most common expository text structures:

Description. The author describes a topic by listing characteristics, features, and examples. Phrases such as *for example* and *characteristics are* cue this structure. When students delineate any topic, such as the Nile River, castles, or Australia, they use description.

Sequence. The author lists or explains items or events in numerical, chronological, or alphabetical order. Cue words for sequence include *first, second, third, next, then,* and *finally.* Students use this pattern to write directions for completing a math problem or the stages in an animal's life cycle. Biographies are often written using the sequence pattern, too.

Comparison. The author compares two or more things. *Different, in contrast, alike,* and *on the other hand* are cue words and phrases that signal this structure. When students compare and contrast book and movie versions of a story or life in ancient Greece with life in ancient Egypt, they use this organizational pattern.

FIGURE 8–4 ◆ *The Expository Text Structures*

Pattern	*Graphic Organizer*	*Sample Passage*
Description The author describes a topic. Cue words include *for example* and *characteristics are.*		The Olympic symbol consists of five interlocking rings that represent the continents athletes come from to compete in the games. The rings are black, blue, green, red, and yellow. At least one of these colors is found in the flag of every country sending athletes to the Olympic games.
Sequence The author lists items or events in numerical or chronological order. Cue words include *first, second, third, next, then,* and *finally.*	1. _____ 2. _____ 3. _____ 4. _____ 5. _____	The Olympics began as athletic festivals to honor Greek gods. The most important festival honored Zeus, and it became the Olympics in 776 B.C. The games ended in A.D. 394 and weren't held for 1,500 years. The modern Olympics began in 1896. Nearly 300 male athletes competed in these games. In 1900, female athletes also competed. The games have continued every four years since then except during World War II.
Comparison The author explains how two or more things are alike or how they're different. Cue words include *same, different, in contrast, alike,* and *on the other hand.*	Alike Different _____ _____ _____ _____ _____ _____ _____ _____	The modern Olympics is different than the ancient games. There weren't swimming races, for example, but there were chariot races. No female contestants participated, and all athletes competed in the nude. Of course, the ancient and modern Olympics are alike in many ways. Some events, such as the javelin and discus throws, are the same. Some people say that cheating, professionalism, and nationalism in the modern games are a disgrace to the Olympic tradition, but according to ancient Greek writers, these existed in their Olympics, too.
Cause and Effect The author lists one or more causes and the resulting effect or effects. Cue words include *reasons why, if . . . then, result, therefore,* and *because.*	Cause → Effect #1 Cause → Effect #2 Cause → Effect #3	There are several reasons why so many people attend the Olympics or watch the games on television. One reason is tradition. The word *Olympics* reminds people of the ancient games. People escape the ordinariness of daily life by attending or watching the Olympics. They like to identify with someone else's accomplishment. National pride is another reason, and an athlete's hard-earned victory becomes a nation's victory.
Problem and Solution The author states a problem and lists one or more solutions. A variation is the question-and-answer format, in which the author poses a question and then answers it. Cue words include *problem, dilemma, puzzle, solved,* and *question . . . answer.*	Problem → Solution	One problem with the modern games is that they're very expensive. A stadium, pools, and playing fields must be built for the athletic events, and housing is needed for the athletes. And these facilities are used for only 2 weeks! In 1984, Los Angeles solved these problems by charging a fee for official sponsors, and using many existing buildings in the area. The Coliseum where the 1932 games were held was used again, and local colleges became playing and living sites.

Cause and Effect. The author explains one or more causes and the resulting effect or effects. *Reasons why, if . . . then, as a result, therefore,* and *because* are words and phrases that cue this structure. Explanations of why dinosaurs became extinct, the effects of pollution, or the causes of the Civil War use this pattern.

Problem and Solution. The author states a problem and offers one or more solutions. A variation is the question-and-answer format, in which the writer poses a question and then answers it. Cue words and phrases include *problem, dilemma, puzzle, solved,* and *question . . . answer.* Students use this structure when they write about why money was invented or why dams are needed to ensure a permanent water supply.

Figure 8–5 lists books exemplifying each of the expository text structures.

Nonfiction Features

Nonfiction books have unique text features that fiction and poetry normally don't have, such as margin notes and glossaries; their purpose is to make text easier to read and understand. Here's a list of nonfiction text features:

- Headings and subheadings to direct readers' attention
- Photographs and drawings to illustrate the big ideas
- Figures, maps, and tables to present detailed information visually
- Margin notes to provide supplemental information or direct readers to additional information on a topic
- Highlighted vocabulary words to identify key terms
- A glossary to assist readers in pronouncing and defining key terms
- Review sections at the end of chapters or the entire book
- An index to assist readers in locating specific information

It's important that students understand these nonfiction text features so they can make their reading more effective and improve their comprehension (Harvey & Goudvis, 2007).

FIGURE 8–5 ◆ Nonfiction Books Illustrating the Expository Text Structures

Description
Cooper, M. L. (2007). *Jamestown, 1607.* New York: Holiday House. (5–8)
Simon, S. (2007). *Snakes.* New York: HarperCollins. (4–6)

Sequence
Cole, J. (2006). *The magic school bus and the science fair expedition.* New York: Scholastic. (4–5)
Minor, W. (2006). *Yankee Doodle America: The spirit of 1776 from A to Z.* New York: Putnam. (4–6)
Royston, A. (2006). *The life and times of a drop of water: The water cycle.* Chicago: Raintree. (4–5)

Comparison
Bidner, J. (2007). *Is my cat a tiger? How your cat compares to its wild cousins.* New York: Lark Books. (4–5)
Jenkins, S. (2007). *Dogs and cats.* Boston: Houghton Mifflin. (4–6)

Munro, R. (2001). *The inside-outside book of Washington, DC.* San Francisco: Chronicle Books. (4–6)

Cause-Effect
Burns, L. G. (2007). *Tracking trash: Flotsam, jetsam, and the science of ocean movement.* Boston: Houghton Mifflin. (4–8)
Collins, A. (2006). *Violent weather: Thunderstorms, tornadoes, and hurricanes.* Washington, DC: National Geographic. (4–6)

Problem-Solution
Bledsoe, L. J. (2006). *How to survive in Antarctica.* New York: Holiday House. (5–8)
Morrison, M. (2006). *Mysteries of the sea: How divers explore the ocean depths.* Washington, DC: National Geographic. (4–6)
Thimmesh, C. (2006). *Team moon: How 400,000 people landed Apollo 11 on the moon.* Boston: Houghton Mifflin. (4–8)

◀ **Nonfiction**

Team Moon: How 400,000 People Landed Apollo 11 on the Moon
READING LEVEL: Seventh Grade
INTEREST LEVEL: Fourth to Eighth Grade

Genre	Nonfiction picture book
Expository Text Structures	Sequence—The author uses sequence to describe the steps in the Apollo 11 mission, from dream to splashdown.
	Problem and Solution—The text describes eight challenges and explains how Team Moon solved them to land the first human beings safely on the moon.
Nonfiction Conventions	Photos of some the Team Moon workers
	Notes about each chapter
	Glossary
	Bibliography
	Additional sources of information, including recommended websites
	Index

Team Moon: How 400,000 People Landed Apollo 11 on the Moon (Thimmesh, 2006) is a nonfiction picture book that's a tribute to the men and women who put the first human being on the moon. The author tells the behind-the-scenes stories of some of the workers at the Kennedy Space Center, including the Grumman employees who built the lunar module, the seamstresses who constructed the 22-layer space suits, the engineers who created a special heat shield to protect the capsule during reentry, and the flight directors, computer programmers, and aerospace technicians at Mission Control.

The author leads readers in sequential order through the amazing story of the Apollo 11 mission. Each well-documented chapter focuses on one step, from President Kennedy's dream to the historic moon landing and, finally, to the astronauts' splashdown in the Pacific Ocean. Chapter titles guide readers through the events and highlight eight challenges facing Team Moon, including the moon's alien environment, frozen fuel slugs, and space suits. Thimmesh explains each problem, its threat to the mission's success, and how it was solved.

This large-format book was printed on black matte-finish paper that suggests the emptiness of space, and stunning NASA photos, some in black and white and others in color, jump from each page. Brief narratives accompanying each photo provide detailed information about the events, but more importantly, they share the suspense of Apollo 11's moon landing.

The miracle of Apollo 11 was the result of the dedication and perseverance of more than 400,000 people, not just the heroics of three astronauts. Quotes from some of the unsung NASA workers are included, together with their photos. *Team Moon* emphasizes that ordinary people who work behind the scenes, not just the superheroes, make valuable contributions to the success of a project.

Text Factors of Poetry

I t's easy to recognize a poem because the text looks different than a page from a story or a nonfiction book. Layout, or the arrangement of words on a page, is an important text factor. Poets use a variety of forms, ranging from free verse to haiku, and devices to make their writing more effective. Janeczko (2003) explains that it's important to point out poetic forms and devices to establish a common vocabulary for talking about poetry, and because poems are shorter than other types of text, it's often easier for students to examine poems, notice differences in forms, and find examples of devices that poets have used.

Formats of Poetry Books

Young adolescents read three types of poetry books. First, a number of picture-book versions of single poems in which each line or stanza is illustrated on a page are available, such as *The Midnight Ride of Paul Revere* (Longfellow, 2001). Others are specialized collections of poems, either written by a single poet or related to a single theme, such as *Tour America: A Journey Through Poems and Art* (Siebert, 2006). Comprehensive anthologies are the third type, and these books feature 50 to 500 or more poems arranged by category. One of the best is Jack Prelutsky's *The Random House Book of Poetry for Children* (2000). A list of poetry books that includes examples of each type is presented in Figure 8–6.

Sometimes authors use poetry, usually free verse, to tell their stories. Karen Hesse's Newbery Medal–winning story, *Out of the Dust* (1999), focuses on the grim realities of living in the Oklahoma dust bowl, and *Witness* (2001) recounts the Ku Klux Klan infiltration into a Vermont town, told through 12 people's voices. In *Locomotion* (2004), Jacqueline Woodson uses a collection of 60 poems to tell the hopeful story of a New York City fifth grader who grieves and then slowly recovers after his parents are killed

---

FIGURE 8–6 ◆ Collections of Poetry

Picture-Book Versions of Single Poems

Carroll, L. (2007). *Jabberwocky* (C. Myers, illus.). New York: Jump at the Sun. (7–8)

Frost, R. (2001). *Stopping by woods on a snowy evening* (S. Jeffers, illus.). New York: Dutton. (6–8)

Thayer, E. L. (2006). *Casey at the bat*. Tonawanda, NY: Kids Can Press. (5–8)

Specialized Collections

Florian, D. (2007). *Comets, stars, the moon, and Mars: Space poems and paintings*. Orlando, FL: Harcourt. (4–7)

Issa, K. (2007). *Today and today*. New York: Scholastic. (4–8)

Kuskin, K. (2003). *Moon, have you met my mother? The collected poems of Karla Kuskin*. New York: HarperCollins. (4–7)

Prelutsky, J. (2006). *Behold the bold umbrellaphant and other poems*. New York: Greenwillow. (4–6)

Sidman, J. (2006). *Butterfly eyes and other secrets of the meadow*. Boston: Houghton Mifflin. (5–7)

Soto, G. (2006). *A fire in my hands*. Orlando, FL: Harcourt. (7–8)

Comprehensive Anthologies

Paschem, E., & Raccah, D. (Sels.). (2005). *Poetry speaks to children*. Naperville, IL: Sourcebooks MediaFusion. (4–6)

Prelutsky, J. (Sel.). (2000). *The Random House book of poetry for children*. New York: Random House. (4–6)

in a house fire. Sharon Creech's *Love That Dog* (2001) is a sweet novel written in the form of a boy's journal as he discovers the power and pleasures of poetry.

Poetic Forms

Poems assume a variety of forms; some are traditional, such as narrative and rhyming poems, but others, such as concrete poems, are playful and innovative. Here are some commonly used poetic forms:

Concrete Poems. Concrete poems are collages of words, letters, and symbols; their arrangement on the page, sometimes as a picture or in the shape of an object, helps to convey the meaning. Three excellent collections are *A Poke in the I: A Collection of Concrete Poems* (Janeczko, 2005), *Blue Lipstick: Concrete Poems* (Grandits, 2007), and *Doodle Dandies: Poems That Take Shape* (Lewis, 2002).

Free Verse. Unrhymed poetry is *free verse*. Word choice and visual images take on greater importance in free verse, and rhythm is less important than in other types of poetry. Gary Soto's *Canto Familiar* (2007) is a collection of free verse. Poems for two voices are a unique form of free verse, written in two columns, side by side, and two readers read the columns simultaneously. The best-known collection is Paul Fleischman's Newbery Award–winning *Joyful Noise: Poems for Two Voices* (2004a).

Haiku. Haiku is a Japanese poetic form that contains 17 syllables arranged in three lines of 5, 7, and 5 syllables. It's a concise form, much like a telegram, and the poems normally deal with nature, presenting a single clear image. Books of haiku to share with students include *Dogku* (Clements, 2007) and *Cool Melons— Turn to Frogs! The Life and Poems of Issa* (Gollub, 2004).

Narrative Poems. Poems that tell a story are *narrative poems*. Perhaps our best-known narrative poem is Clement Moore's classic, "The Night Before Christmas." Other narrative poems include Longfellow's *The Midnight Ride of Paul Revere* (2001), illustrated by Christopher Bing, and *Casey at the Bat* (Thayer, 2006).

Odes. These poems celebrate everyday objects, especially those that aren't usually appreciated. The unrhymed poem, written directly to that object, tells what's good about it and why it's valued. The ode is a venerable poetic form, tracing its heritage back to ancient Greece. Traditionally, odes were sophisticated lyrical verses, such as Keats's "Ode to a Nightingale," but Chilean poet Pablo Neruda (2000) introduced this contemporary variation that's more informal. A great collection is Gary Soto's *Neighborhood Odes* (2005), which celebrates everyday things, such as water sprinklers and tennis shoes, in the Mexican American community in Fresno, California, where he grew up.

Rhymed Verse. Poets use various rhyme schemes, such as limericks, and the effect of the rhyming words is a poem that's fun to read. Examples include *My Parents Think I'm Sleeping* (Prelutsky, 2007) and *Today at the Bluebird Café: A Branchful of Birds* (Ruddell, 2007).

There are many other poetic forms, of course, but these forms are commonly used in poems written for young adolescents. To learn about other forms, check *A Kick in the Head: An Everyday Guide to Poetic Forms* (Janeczko, 2009) or *Handbook of Poetic Forms* (Padgett, 2007).

Poetry Unit
These fifth graders are studying Jack Prelutsky and reading his poems. They especially enjoy his CD of *The New Kid on the Block*. The students pick favorite poems and copy them on chart paper. Next, they choose a familiar tune, such as "Twinkle, Twinkle, Little Star" or "I've Been Working on the Railroad," that fits the cadence of the poem and sing the poem to that tune. Singing poems is a favorite daily activity. They're also writing their own verses collaboratively using Prelutsky's poetic forms, such as "My Fish Can Ride a Bicycle," that they will make into class books.

Poetic Devices

Poetic devices are especially important tools because poets express their ideas very concisely. Every word counts! Poets often use these devices:

- **Assonance:** The type of alliteration where vowel sounds are repeated in nearby words.
- **Consonance:** The type of alliteration where consonant sounds are repeated in nearby words.
- **Imagery:** Words and phrases that appeal to the senses and evoke mental pictures.
- **Metaphor:** Two unlikely things are compared, without using *like* or *as*.
- **Onomatopoeia:** Words that imitate sounds, such as *sizzle*, *cackle*, and *kerplunk*.
- **Repetition:** Words, phrases, or lines that are repeated for special effect.
- **Rhyme:** Words that end with similar sounds used at the end of the lines.
- **Rhythm:** The internal beat in a poem that's felt when poetry is read aloud.
- **Simile:** A comparison incorporating the word *like* or *as*.

Narrative and poetic devices are similar, and many of them, such as imagery and metaphor, are important in both genres.

Poets use conventions in unique ways, too. Capitalization and punctuation are used differently; poets choose where to use capital letters and decide whether or where to add punctuation marks in their poems. They think about the meaning they're conveying and the rhythm of their writing as they decide how to break poems into lines and whether to divide the lines into stanzas. Layout is another consideration: The arrangement of lines on the page is especially important in concrete poems, but it matters for all poems.

Teaching About Text Factors

Researchers have documented that when teachers teach students about text factors, their comprehension increases (Fisher, Frey, & Lapp, 2008; Sweet & Snow, 2003). In addition, when students are familiar with the genres,

Joyce Sidman   Illustrated by Pamela Zagarenski

◀ Poetry

This Is Just to Say: Poems of Apology and Forgiveness
READING LEVEL: Fifth Grade
INTEREST LEVEL: Fourth to Seventh Grade

Genre	Poetry
Poetic Forms	Main form—apology poems using William Carlos Williams's poem "This Is Just to Say" as a model Others—haiku, poems for two voices, odes, found poems, and free verse
Poetic Devices	Imagery, metaphors/similes, repetition, and rhythm

This Is Just to Say: Poems of Apology and Forgiveness (Sidman, 2007) is presented as a collection of poems written by Mrs. Merz's sixth graders. Student-editor Anthony K. explains that he and his classmates wrote apology poems using William Carlos Williams's poem "This Is Just to Say" as a model, and then the recipients wrote poems of forgiveness back to the students.

The book is arranged in two parts. The first part, Apologies, contains the sixth graders' apology poems, with each student's poem featured on a separate page with a drawing of the student-author and other illustrations related to the content of the poem. Readers are told that the illustrations were created by Bao Vang, an artistic class member. The second part, Responses, contains the poems that the sixth graders received.

Short poems written on a wide variety of topics are included in this captivating anthology; some are humorous, and others heartfelt. José, for example, wrote an apology to his dad for throwing a rock through the garage window. José's dad responds, telling him to forget about the broken window and expressing his pride in his son's accomplishments. Most of the poems follow the model, but a handful use different forms, including haiku, poems for two voices, odes, found poems, and free verse. The most striking feature is the range of voices: Some sound as if they were written by girls, some by boys, and others by siblings, parents, and grandparents.

In the author information, Joyce Sidman admits that she wrote the poems herself. Years before, she'd written an apology poem with a class of fourth graders and sent it to her mother, who responded with a letter of forgiveness, and the idea for this book was born!

organizational patterns, and literary devices in books they're reading, they're better able to create those text factors in their own writing (Buss & Karnowski, 2000). It's not enough to focus on fiction, however; students need to learn about nonfiction and poetry. In the vignette at the beginning of the chapter, Mr. Abrams used text factors to scaffold his students' learning about frogs. He taught them about the unique characteristics of nonfiction books, emphasized text structures through the questions he asked, and used graphic organizers to help students visualize big ideas.

Minilessons

Teachers teach students about text factors directly—often through **minilessons** (Simon, 2005). They highlight a genre, explain its characteristics, and then read aloud books representing that genre, modeling their thinking about text factors. Later, students make charts of the information they're learning and hang them in the classroom. Similarly, teachers introduce structural patterns and have students examine how authors use them to organize a book or an excerpt from a book they're reading. Students often create graphic organizers to visualize the structure of books they're reading and appreciate how the organization emphasizes the big ideas (Opitz, Ford, & Zbaracki, 2006). Teachers also focus on the literary devices that authors use to make their writing more vivid and the conventions that make a text more reader-friendly. Students often collect sentences with narrative devices from stories they're reading and lines of poetry with poetic devices to share with classmates, and they create charts of nonfiction features they've found in books to incorporate in reports they're writing.

Close Reading

Close reading is a procedure for interpreting literature that requires a careful, sustained analysis of brief passages of text. Students apply what they've learned about genres, structural patterns, and literary devices to think more deeply about the book they're reading. This activity grows out of responding to literature: During the middle grades, students transition from making personal responses to interpreting books.

Teachers guide students to interpret the books they're reading. As they read and discuss each chapter, students examine individual words and their meanings, attend to the flow of sentences, think about the structure of the text, and notice literary devices. Teachers reread key passages once or twice while students follow along; they often distribute copies of the passage so students can make notes as they listen. Then students discuss the passage, drawing inferences and talking about what they noticed to uncover the themes and big ideas evoked by the text. Students move from noticing small details to delving into larger issues as they follow these steps:

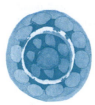

1. **Examine specific words.** Students investigate names and other proper nouns to see how their meanings deepen their understanding of the book. They also notice the author's choice of words and which words are repeated again and again. Teachers often include a discussion about words as part of **grand conversations**.

2. **Draw inferences.** Students draw inferences from information presented in the book to direct their attention toward themes and larger issues. Teachers encourage students to draw inferences during **interactive read-alouds** and grand conversations.

3. **Analyze single sentences.** Students talk and write about key sentences selected from the text to appreciate their meaning and importance to the story. Teachers use grand conversations and **reading logs** for this activity.

4. **Collect literary opposites**. Students identify pairs of opposites related to the book; the words can be either explicitly stated in the text or generalized from the context. Teachers make charts of literary opposites that students identify and have them **quickwrite** about a pair of opposites to think about the author's message.

5. **Reread passages.** Teachers read aloud a key passage, from a page to a chapter in length, that students have already read, and the class works together to analyze the words and sentences to deepen their understanding. Teachers ask questions to probe students' thinking, and students share their ideas and learn from their classmates.

6. **Learn about the author**. Students research the author to see what his or her experiences, knowledge, and beliefs reveal about this text. Sometimes author information is included in the book, but at other times, students check author websites or read articles and biographies about the author.

7. **Identify themes.** Students develop interpretations as they review what they've uncovered during the previous steps and identify the themes and larger issues addressed in the book. Students often talk about the themes during grand conversations.

Sometimes students apply what they've learned through close reading as they develop a project related to the theme or write an essay in which they explain their interpretation.

A sixth-grade class did a close reading of *Skellig* (Almond, 1998), the story of boy who discovers a strange owl-man-angel creature, named Skellig, dying in his garage and nourishes him back to health, to deepen their understanding of this complex book. Figure 8–7 shows what the sixth graders learned through their close reading of *Skellig* and the themes they identified.

FIGURE 8–7 ◆ *A Close Reading of* Skellig

Examine Specific Words
- *Skellig* is the name of two Irish islands; one is Skellig Michael, and in the Middle Ages, a hermit lived there.
- *Skell* is a slang term for a derelict or homeless person.
- Michael means "like an angel."
- Michael's friend Mina loves birds, and her name is like *myna* bird.
- The words *dead* and *death* are repeated often (e.g., "dead of night," "Dr. Death").

Draw Inferences
- Michael now lives on Falconer Road, and *falconers* train birds (inference: and other winged creatures).
- Michael's baby sister's name is *Joy* (inference: baby won't die).
- Michael moves to the new house at the end of winter (inference: spring and good times are coming).

Analyze Single Sentences
- "What do you want?" he whispered. "I said, "What do you want?" (p. 10)
- "They say that shoulder blades are where your wings were, when you were an angel," she said. (p. 37)
- "How can a bird that is born for joy/Sit in a cage and sing?' William Blake." (p. 50)
- "We have to allow ourselves to see what there is to see, and we have to imagine." (p. 140)

Collect Literary Opposites
healthy–sick	childhood–adulthood
people–angels	death–life
hope–hopeless	weak–strong
dreams–truth	positive–negative

Reread Passages
- Chapter 10: Michael visits Skellig.
- Chapter 20: Mina meets Skellig and decides how to help him.
- Chapter 41: Michael's baby sister survives heart surgery.
- Chapter 42: Skellig says good-bye to Michael and Mina.

Learn About the Author
- David Almond's baby sister died.
- He mentions birds and flying often in this book and in *My Dad's a Birdman* (Almond, 2007).

Identify Themes
- Flying: People who "have wings and fly" are courageous, determined risk-takers who follow their dreams and create their own success.
- Change: We may not like change, but it helps us grow and learn new things.
- Angels: There may be angels among us, and we can be angels to other people.

Comprehension Strategies

It's not enough that students can name the characteristics of a myth, identify cue words that signal expository text structures, or define *metaphor* or *assonance*; the goal is for students to actually use what they've learned about text factors when they're reading and writing. The comprehension strategy they use when they're applying what they've learned is *noticing text factors*; it involves considering genre, recognizing text structure, and attending to literary devices. Lattimer (2003) explains the strategy this way: Students need to think about "what to expect from a text, how to approach it, and what to take away from it" (p. 12). Teachers teach students about text factors through minilessons and other activities, but the last step is to help students internalize the information and apply it when they're reading and writing. One way teachers do this is by demonstrating how they use the strategy as they read books aloud with **think-alouds** (Harvey & Goudvis, 2007). Teachers also use think-alouds to demonstrate this strategy as they do modeled and shared writing.

Be Strategic!

Comprehension Strategies

Students apply what they've learned about text factors when they use these comprehension strategies:

- ▶ Consider genre
- ▶ Recognize text structure
- ▶ Attend to literary devices

When students notice text factors, they're better able to understand what they're reading.

Reading and Writing Activities

Students need opportunities to read books and listen to teachers read books aloud while they're learning about text factors. Lattimer (2003) recommends teaching genre studies where students learn about a genre while they're reading and exploring books representing that genre and then apply what they're learning through writing. For example, a small group of fifth graders wrote this poem for two voices as a project after reading *Number the Stars* (Lowry, 1998), the story of the friendship between two Danish girls, a Christian and a Jew, during World War II:

I am Annemarie, a Christian.

I hate this war.

The Nazis want to kill my friend.
Why?
I want to help my friend.

My mother will take you to my uncle.
He's a fisherman.

He will hide you on his ship.

He will take you to Sweden.
To freedom.
I am Annemarie, a Christian.

I want to help my friend.

I hate this war.

I am Ellen, a Jew.
I hate this war.
The Nazis want to kill me.

Why?

Can you help me?

Your uncle is a fisherman?

He will hide me on his ship?

To freedom.

I am Ellen, a Jew.

I need the help of my friends
or I will die.
I hate this war.

The fifth graders' choice of this poetic form is especially appropriate because it highlights one of the story's themes: These characters are very much alike even though one is Christian and one is Jewish. The students knew how to write poems for two voices because they participated in a genre study about poetry several months earlier.

Assessing Students' Knowledge of Text Factors

Although there aren't formal tests to assess students' knowledge of text factors, students demonstrate their knowledge in a variety of ways:

- Talking about the characteristics of the genre in book talks and grand conversations
- Using their knowledge of story elements to explain themes in reading log entries
- Applying their understanding of genre when writing in response to prompts for district and state writing assessments
- Documenting their ability to recognize text structures by making graphic organizers
- Writing poems that are modeled after poems they've read
- Choosing sentences with literary devices when asked to locate examples of narrative or poetic devices in books they're reading
- Incorporating literary devices in their own writing

It's up to teachers to notice how students are applying their knowledge about text factors, and to find new ways for students to share their understanding.

CHAPTER 8
Review

How Effective Teachers Focus on Text Factors

▶ Teachers teach students that fiction has unique text factors: narrative genres, story elements, and narrative devices.

▶ Teachers teach students that nonfiction has unique text factors: nonfiction genres, expository text structures, and nonfiction features.

▶ Teachers teach students that poems have unique text factors: poetic forms and poetic devices.

▶ Teachers encourage students to apply their knowledge of text factors when they're reading and writing.

CHAPTER 9

Teaching Writing

Fifth Graders' Revision Stations

Ms. Garza's fifth graders have become a supportive community of writers who use the writing process to draft and refine their compositions. The 28 students in the classroom spend 60 minutes each morning participating in writers' workshop. During the first 15 minutes, Ms. Garza teaches a **minilesson** on a writing topic, such as making conclusions more effective, writing odes, and eliminating homonym errors. Next, students work independently and with peers on writing projects for 40 minutes. For the last 5 minutes, they take turns sharing their published writings; when there's time, Ms. Garza asks, "Who's applied what we talked about during the minilesson in your writing today?" and students talk about their experiences.

The fifth graders learned about the six traits of effective writing—ideas, organization, word choice, sentence fluency, mechanics, and voice—in third and fourth grades, and they reviewed each trait several months ago. Ms. Garza used the fifth-grade Write Traits® Classroom Kit, published by Great Source, and supplemented it by reading picture books and examining how authors used the traits in their writing. Some of the students quickly demonstrated expertise in specific traits, and Ms. Garza began calling them "experts." Six of these student-experts talk about their talents:

Jax, on ideas:

"You got to have lots and lots of ideas to be a good writer, and that's what I do best. I don't know why, but I like thinking about ideas. At first I used to tell people all my ideas, but Ms. Garza taught me to ask questions to help people think of their own ideas."

Jade, on mechanics:

"I'm an expert on mechanics because I'm a very good speller. I know about when to capitalize letters and I know about putting in punctuation marks, except I'm still learning about colons and semicolons. When I'm being an expert, I mark their mistakes and help them fix them. It's like I'm a teacher."

Necie, on organization:

"It's fun making maps. I always make a map before I start to write so my writing will be organized. It's really not hard to do, and it helps me think. Some of the other kids ask me to help them make their maps, and I like to help them."

Owen, on sentence fluency:

"Did you ever notice that words have a beat like music? I can hear the beat in my mind. Poems are the best, but every kind of writing has it. My friends always ask me to read their papers and check their beat, and I can help them make their writing better."

Trevor, on voice:

"In third grade, my teacher, Mrs. Kim, taught us about the six traits, and I wanted to make my writer's voice strong. She helped me learn how. My dad's a chef and he adds spices to the food he cooks; well, I add spices to my writing."

Bree, on word choice:

"I'm a word collector, and I've always been one. When I was in first grade, my Grandpa Johnny gave me a pink-and-purple chest to hold my word cards. Yesterday I added the word 'glee.' When I'm being an expert, I help kids delete boring words and replace them with words that sparkle to make their writing better."

These middle graders' comments highlight their awareness about what writers think and do. So far, 17 students have been named as student-experts, and Ms. Garza believes every student will demonstrate the competence to be named an expert on one trait before the end of the school year. She also expects that some students will become experts on additional traits.

Ms. Garza set up six revision stations, one for each trait, and colorful student-made signs with icons representing the traits hang from the ceiling above them: The icon for organizing is a skeleton, the one for sentence fluency is a drum, and the one for mechanics is a car repair shop. Some of the stations are arranged on tables; others are placed on counters around the classroom. The supplies are stored in plastic tubs at each station. For example, materials at the word choice station include several student dictionaries and thesauri; the *Scholastic Dictionary of Idioms* (Terban, 2006a); charts Ms. Garza and the students have made about powerful nouns, vivid verbs, and tired words to avoid, such as *said*; and a plastic bag of highlighter pens that students use to mark words in their drafts. The student-experts for each trait take turns assisting classmates at the stations. They use brightly colored pens to sign their names and write their trait in the margin of their classmates' papers so Ms. Garza knows who's provided assistance to each writer.

Mrs. Garza's Revising Stations

Station	Icon	Expert Student's Role	Supplies
Ideas	Head with idea bubbles above it	The expert assists classmates to brainstorm and narrow ideas, search for more information, and add details.	Lined paper Pens and pencils Computer with online access Encyclopedias Self-stick notes
Mechanics	Car repair shop	The expert helps classmates proofread and correct spelling, punctuation, capitalization, and grammar errors.	Student dictionaries *Scholastic Dictionary of Spelling* (Terban, 2006b) Red pens Charts about capitalization and punctuation
Organization	Skeleton	The expert helps classmates draw diagrams to check the organization of their writing and offers suggestions for rearrangement, if necessary.	Whiteboards and pens Unlined paper Pens and pencils Correction fluid Self-stick notes
Sentence Fluency	Drum	The expert listens to classmates read their drafts aloud and marks spots where their rhythm falters, and assists in analyzing sentence types and eliminating run-ons and sentence fragments.	Checklist for analyzing sentence types Self-stick notes Pens and pencils Charts about sentence types
Voice	Mouth with a talking balloon extending from it	The expert listens to classmates read their drafts aloud and suggests ways to strengthen their voice, such as adding examples and questions, using repetitions and figurative language, and changing the viewpoint.	Self-stick notes Pens and pencils Highlighters A display of sentences with strong voice
Word Choice	Dart board with one dart in the center	The expert advises classmates about substituting livelier and more-precise words for less effective ones.	Highlighters Dictionaries and thesauri *Scholastic Dictionary of Idioms* (Terban, 2006a) Class word charts

This box lists the six stations, the student-experts' roles, and the supplies available at each station.

Several weeks ago, Ms. Garza's students chose topics they'd like to learn more about to research. Divina chose to investigate how dolphins communicate, Jamel to learn more about Barack Obama, Trevor to research tsunamis, Riley to study sword fighting, Larah to learn about the Grand Canyon, Jax to extend his already sizable knowledge about the Yankees, and Amber to read about the gemstone made from fossil tree resin—amber—because that's the source of her name. Now they're writing reports about the topics they've researched that they plan to share with parents at the upcoming back-to-school night.

The students move at their own pace through the stages of the writing process. Today most of the students are revising, but a few are still writing rough drafts, and a couple have moved on to proofreading. During revising, they meet in **writing groups** to share their rough drafts and get feedback on how well they're communicating and how they can refine their papers. The students go to two stations, based on the revision priorities they recognized or those identified in their writing groups. They share their rough drafts with the student-experts and classmates at the station, who analyze their papers and offer suggestions for revision. Sometimes the students make changes right there; at other times, they return to their desks to work.

Diego goes to the Organization station, and Necie's the student-expert there. He researched scuba diving, and his rough draft is nine handwritten pages long. He's worried that it's too long, and he asks Necie to think about whether he should divide it into chapters or cut out some parts. Evie and Jade also arrive at the center and decide to work together to check the organization of their papers while Diego reads his draft aloud to Necie. As he's reading, Ms. Garza joins the group. Necie draws a map with his ideas and offers this opinion: "Your organization is clear and easy to follow. I drew this map of your ideas. I think everything is important so you shouldn't delete any part. Maybe you could divide your paper into chapters with one big idea in each chapter." Ms. Garza agrees that his organization is clear, but she suggests that he add headings instead of dividing the paper into chapters. She goes over to the classroom library and grabs several nonfiction books to show Diego what headings look like. Both Diego and Necie agree that headings are a good way to organize his report.

Bree's the student-expert at the Word Choice station, and it's filled with five students needing her assistance. This future teacher passes out three highlighter pens to each student. First, she asks the students to read through their drafts and to highlight any of the words on the Tired Words list with the green pens; afterward, they use thesauri to locate more-effective words. Next they reread and highlight the remaining verbs in yellow; afterward, they decide whether the words are vivid or should be replaced. She asks them to improve five verbs, and again they consult the thesauri to choose replacements. Finally, they reread their drafts and highlight in pink three other words that they want to replace with more-precise words. Jamel tells Bree that he doesn't see any other words that need to be replaced in his paper about Barack Obama, so she reads his draft and points out that he uses some words, such as *boy*, *learned*, and *wanted*, too often. She suggests that he check a thesaurus to locate some alternatives.

Both Trevor and Riley are manning the Voice station. Trevor works with Jax, who's written about the New York Yankees, and Riley assists Divina, who's written about dolphin communication. They each listen intently as the writer reads his or her draft aloud. They respond to the author's language, expressing interest in the facts being presented, laughing at humorous remarks, and commenting "good" when the writer's voice is strong. After the writers finish reading, the student-experts point out examples of strong voice and make suggestions. For example, Riley wonders how Divina's paper would sound if the information were presented from a dolphin's viewpoint or from a scientist's. Divina is frustrated because she thinks her report lacks voice, so she's excited to try to recast it from a different viewpoint.

Ms. Garza keeps track of the students' progress. As students move from the minilesson to the writing period, they indicate what they're doing on the Status of the Class chart. Sign-in sheets are placed at each station, and both student-experts and other students sign in when they arrive. In addition, students write brief notes about their activities on the writing process chart they keep in their writing folders.

After revising, students complete the writing process by editing and then publishing their reports. With only a few days to spare before the back-to-school night, the reports are done, and students share them with classmates. Divina has turned her lackluster report into an entertaining interview between Professor Dolphin and Silver, a 15-year-old female bottle-nosed dolphin who has a calf named Splash. Here's an excerpt from the interview:

Professor Dolphin:

What is a signature whistle?

Silver:

My signature whistle sound is my name. Everybody in my pod knows mine and I know theirs. When Splash was born, I repeated my whistle for three whole days and nights because I wanted to make sure Splash would know me in case she got lost, but she's a good girl and she sticks nice and close. Splash has developed her own signature whistle now and I always know it.

Professor Dolphin:

Can you make other sounds?

Silver:

I can be very, very noisy. I make whistles, squeaks, chirps, groans, and grunts. They sound like air coming out of a balloon—that's what people tell me. I also imitate sounds and make other dolphins' signature whistles. You know, dolphins are very intelligent marine mammals!

Professor Dolphin:

Is there really a dolphin language?

Silver:

I knew you were going to ask me that question. That's what all the scientists want to know. It's a secret so I'm not going to tell you, but I hope you will keep up your researching and find out the answer. You will become very famous!

Professor Dolphin:

Do you have other ways to communicate?

Silver:

Yes, I do. I use body language. I roll my eyes, shake my head, and I even roll over and play dead. Splash always understands what I mean and now she has learned to shake her head. I also communicate with different moves. I hit with my snout, I kick with my tail, and I do a touch bite. Of course, I nuzzle Splash a lot. When she was little, I used to hold her hand. Don't you believe me? I would swim next to her and touch her fin with my fin. All the dolphin moms do that. Splash communicates by rubbing me and once when she was mad, she rammed me. She was so cute!

As soon as Divina completes the final copy of "My Dolphin Interview," she shows it to Riley. It's dedicated to him for suggesting that she write from a dolphin's perspective.

riting is a powerful tool for young adolescents (Graham, MacArthur, & Fitzgerald, 2007). They use writing to communicate, share knowledge, learn, persuade, and explore feelings. It's also the way most teachers evaluate academic achievement. Becoming an effective writer is essential to school success, and it's increasingly important in daily life because of e-mail, text messaging, and other forms of electronic communication. In *Writing Next*, Graham and Perin (2007) make these recommendations for improving the quality of writing instruction:

- Teach students to use the writing process.
- Coach students to use writing strategies to plan, draft, and refine their writing.
- Have students read, analyze, and model examples of good writing.
- Provide a supportive workshop environment for writing.
- Encourage students to work together on collaborative writing projects.
- Have students use word processors for writing assignments.

These recommendations are based on the authors' review of research examining the most effective approaches to writing instruction.

Every 4 years, the National Assessment of Educational Progress (NAEP) measures the reading and writing proficiency of fourth and eighth graders, and the NAEP results have repeatedly documented that students aren't capable writers: Only a quarter of students met NAEP's writing proficiency standard (Persky, Daane, & Jinn, 2003). Difficulty in writing has serious consequences (Shanahan, 2004). Reading and writing are related, so less capable writers are usually less capable readers as well. In addition, they're not as effective in using writing as a tool for learning in language arts and across the curriculum, and they're less likely to be successful in college or in the workplace because of the writing demands they'll face.

Components of Writing Instruction

Writing instruction in the middle grades has three components. First, the writing process: Students become more-strategic writers as they learn to employ the writing process to draft and refine their compositions. Second, the six traits: Students learn about traits of effective writing and use their knowledge to improve the quality of their writing. Third, writing genres: Students participate in genre studies to examine essays and other genres and then apply what they've learned in their own writing.

The Six Traits

What makes a piece of writing good? Spandel (2009) has identified six qualities, which she calls *traits*:

Ideas. The ideas are the essence of a composition. Students choose an interesting idea during prewriting, and as they draft and revise, they narrow and develop it using main ideas and details.

Organization. The organization is the skeleton of the composition: Students hook the reader in the beginning, identify the purpose, present ideas logically, provide transitions between ideas, and end with a satisfying conclusion so that the important questions are answered. Students organize their writing during prewriting and follow their plans as they draft.

Voice. The writer's distinctive style is voice; it's what breathes life into a piece of writing. Culham (2003) calls voice "the writer's music coming out through the words" (p. 102). During the drafting and revising stages, students create voice in their writing through the words they use, the sentences they craft, and the tone they adopt.

Word Choice. Careful word choice makes the meaning clear and the composition more interesting to read. As students craft their pieces, they learn to choose lively

New Literacies

Laptops for Writing

Technology has the potential to support writing instruction through word processing, spell-check programs, multimedia software, and the Internet (Karchmer-Klein, 2007). One of the most exciting programs is Maine's middle school laptop program. All of Maine's seventh and eighth graders were given laptops in 2002 as part of a 5-year program to get kids ready for 21st-century literacy demands, and teachers learned to use laptops to teach writing. Students used Apple iBook computers with AirPort wireless networking and Internet access. Software on the laptops included AppleWorks for word processing, web browsers, e-mail software, iMovie, iPhoto, and NoteShare. Students could take their laptops home in the evenings, on weekends, and on school vacations.

Teachers participated in professional development programs led by the Maine Writing Project's Literacy Through Technology Team to learn about composing, publishing, and teaching with digital tools. The team provided technical assistance and trained Teacher Leaders at each school site so they could help colleagues integrate the laptops into their instructional programs.

Researchers reported a positive link between laptop use and improving the quality of students' writing; they concluded that the Maine Learning Technology Initiative had a significant impact on students' writing achievement (Silvernail & Gritter, 2007). Eighth-grade student writing, as measured by the Maine Educational Assessment (MEA), the state's standardized assessment, improved significantly after the laptop program was implemented. MEA writing scores from 2000 were compared with 2005 scores: In 2000, 29% of eighth graders met the state's writing proficiency standard, but in 2005, 41% did! The researchers found that the way laptops were used in the writing process influenced students' writing achievement. Students who reported using their laptops at each stage in the writing process received the highest test scores; in contrast, students who said they didn't use laptops for writing had the lowest scores.

Silvernail and Gritter (2007) interviewed students and teachers about the program. They found that more than 70% of participating students believed that writing on laptops facilitated their learning. They reported doing more writing, working more quickly, and self-correcting a higher number of writing errors. In addition, they believed that the quality of their writing had improved. The teachers' perceptions were similar: Students did more revising and editing and were more actively involved in learning when they used laptops.

verbs and specific nouns, adjectives, and adverbs; create word pictures; and use idiomatic expressions. They focus on word choice as they draft and revise their writing.

Sentence Fluency. Sentence fluency is the rhythm and flow of language. Students vary the length and structure of their writing so that it has a natural cadence and is easy to read aloud. They develop sentence fluency as they draft, revise, and edit their writing.

Mechanics. The mechanics are spelling, capitalization, punctuation, and grammar. In the editing stage, students proofread their compositions and correct spelling and grammar errors to make them easier to read.

Teachers teach series of **minilessons** about each trait. They explain the trait, show examples from literature and students' own writing, involve students in activities to investigate and experiment with the trait, and have students apply what they've learned in their own writing. Figure 9–1 presents a list of books and activities that teachers can use in teaching the six traits.

As students study the six traits, they internalize what good writers do. They learn to recognize good writing, develop a vocabulary for talking about writing, become better able to evaluate their own writing, and acquire strategies for improving the quality of their writing.

> Check the Compendium of Instructional Procedures, which follows Chapter 12, for more information on the highlighted terms.

FIGURE 9–1 ◆ *Teaching the Six Traits*

Trait	Books	Ways to Examine the Traits
Ideas	Law, I. (2008). *Savvy*. New York: Dial Books. Van Allsburg, C. (1996). *The mysteries of Harris Burdick*. Boston: Houghton Mifflin. Tan, S. (2008). *Tales from outer suburbia*. New York: Scholastic. Wyeth, S. D. (2002). *Something beautiful*. New York: Dragonfly.	• Read or listen to books with well-developed ideas. • Choose photos, pictures, or objects to write about. • Quickwrite to narrow or develop an idea. • Make clusters to develop an idea.
Organization	Fleischman, P. (2004). *Seedfolks*. New York: Harper-Trophy. Sachar, L. (2008). *Holes*. New York: Farrar, Straus & Giroux. Wiesner, D. (2006). *Flotsam*. New York: Clarion Books. Woodson, J. (2005). *Show way*. New York: Putnam.	• Analyze the structure of a book using a graphic organizer. • Collect effective leads from books. • Find examples of effective transitions in books. • Collect effective endings from books.
Voice	Hesse, K. (2001). *Witness*. New York: Scholastic. Ives, D. (2005). *Scrib*. New York: HarperCollins. Mass, W. (2008). *Every soul a star*. Boston: Little, Brown. Scieszka, J. (1996). *The true story of the 3 little pigs!* New York: Puffin Books.	• Read or listen to books with strong voices. • Talk about the voice in a text. • Personalize a story by telling it from one character's viewpoint. • Add emotion to a voiceless piece of writing.
Word Choice	Cushman, K. (1994). *Catherine, called Birdy*. New York: HarperCollins. Leedy, L., & Street, P. (2003). *There's a frog in my throat! 440 animal sayings a little bird told me*. New York: Holiday House. McKissack, P. C. (2008). *Stitchin' and pullin': A Gee's Bend quilt*. New York: Random House. Scieszka, J. (2001). *Baloney (Henry P.)* New York: Viking.	• Read or listen to books with good word choice. • Collect lively and precise words. • Learn to use a thesaurus. • Craft metaphors and similes.
Sentence Fluency	Creech, S. (2008). *Hate that cat*. New York: HarperCollins. Grimes, N. (2002). *My man blue*. New York: Puffin Books. Locker, T. (2003). *Cloud dance*. San Diego: Voyager. White, E. B. (2006). *Charlotte's web*. New York: HarperTrophy.	• Do choral readings of books with sentence fluency. • Collect favorite sentences on sentence strips. • Practice writing alliterative sentences. • Reread favorite books.
Mechanics	Holm, J. L. (2007). *Middle school is worse than meatloaf: A year told through stuff*. New York: Atheneum. Pulver, R. (2003). *Punctuation takes a vacation*. New York: Holiday House. Truss, L. (2006). *Eats, shoots & leaves: Why commas really do make a difference!* New York: Putnam. Truss, L. (2008). *Twenty-odd ducks: Why, every punctuation mark counts!* New York: Putnam.	• Proofread excerpts from books to find mechanical errors that have been added. • Add capital letters to excerpts that have had them removed. • Add punctuation marks to excerpts that have had them removed. • Correct grammar errors that have been added to excerpts from books.

Adapted from Spandel, 2001, 2009; Culham, 2003.

Writing Genres

The forms of writing are called *genres*. That's the same term used for the types of litera-ture, and some literature and writing genres are the same, such as stories and poetry, but others are different. Students learn to use a variety of writing genres, and they're often ex-pected to apply their knowledge of writing genres on state- and district-mandated writing assessments. Through reading and examining writing samples, students become knowl-edgeable about these genres and how they're structured (Donovan & Smolkin, 2002).

Descriptive Writing. Descriptive writing paints vivid pictures of people, places, events, and things. Writers use sensory details to breathe life into their compositions. Young adolescents write descriptive paragraphs and essays that exemplify these characteristics:

- Students describe something from several viewpoints.
- Students use sensory words.
- Students write so that readers can imagine the thing being described.

In descriptive writing, students describe something by painting a word picture; they don't explain or tell a story about it.

Expository Writing. Expository writing is used to explain something or present infor-mation. Students write reports to share information they've learned, and essays to describe something, compare two things, explain a change using causes and effects, or specify how to make or do something. Expository writing exemplifies these characteristics:

- Writers introduce their topic, state their focus, and get readers' attention in the first paragraph.
- Writers present information with topic sentences and specific details that support the focus in the middle paragraphs.
- Writers sum up their ideas and make a final comment about the topic in the conclusion.
- Writers use expository text structures to organize their writing and cue words to guide readers.
- Writers define technical terms.

When writers are knowledgeable and enthusiastic about their topics, their writing is more effective.

Multimedia Writing. Multimedia writing is a 21st-century genre that integrates dig-ital technology with writing. Writers use word processors, digital cameras, video clips, websites, and other computer applications to create compositions with website links, multigenre projects, and PowerPoint presentations. Here are the characteristics of this new genre:

- Writers use appropriate technology to communicate information.
- Writers design the documents according to purpose and audience.
- Writers create multimedia documents that integrate software.
- Writers provide interactive components, including links to websites.

Through multimedia writing, students become familiar with emerging technologies and their applications.

Narrative Writing. Narratives are accounts of events or experiences, either true or imaginary. Writers create a context for readers to imagine the world of the account and provide insight into why it's memorable. Young adolescents write narratives that exemplify these characteristics:

- Students focus on a single event or story.
- Students organize their writing with a beginning, middle, and end.
- Students include specific details to make the narrative interesting.
- Students often use dialogue.
- Students use either first- or third-person viewpoint.

Three types of narrative writing are personal narratives, autobiographical incidents, and stories.

Persuasive Writing. Persuasion is a part of everyday life, and students write persuasive essays and letters to share their opinions and influence others. Persuasive writing exemplifies these characteristics:

- Writers use a "hook" to get their readers' attention.
- Writers state a clear position or opinion.
- Writers support their viewpoint with evidence.
- Writers address alternative positions and refute counterarguments.
- Writers persuade readers to accept their viewpoint.

Students organize persuasive writing into three parts. In the first part, they present their position or argument. In the second part, they explain the evidence supporting their argument, identify counterarguments, and refute them. This part usually includes three or more paragraphs. In the third part, students conclude the composition by summarizing the main points or asserting an appeal to readers. Figure 9–2 presents an organizer for developing a persuasive composition.

FIGURE 9–2 ◆ *Persuasive Writing Organizer*

Component	Information to Include	Student's Notes
Introduction	• Present the issue. • State your position. • Briefly mention reasons for your position.	
Reason #1	• Explain the evidence. • Address pros and cons (or counterarguments).	
Reason #2	• Explain the evidence. • Address pros and cons (or counterarguments).	
Reason #3	• Explain the evidence. • Address pros and cons (or counterarguments).	
Other Reasons	• Explain the evidence. • Address pros and cons (or counterarguments).	
Conclusion	• Restate the issue. • Summarize. • Add an emotional or thoughtful appeal.	

238 ◆ **PART 2** Powerful Teaching

Poetry. Poetry is unique among writing genres: It's a concise form that explores the meaning of life and evokes readers' emotional responses. Poets see the world in unexpected ways, and their insights often surprise us. Modern poetry has few rules; poems can address any topic, and rhyming isn't required. Poetry is meant to be read aloud so that readers and listeners can appreciate the sounds of language as well as its meaning. Young adolescents write poems that exemplify these characteristics:

- Students use poetic forms to structure their poems.
- Students choose their words carefully, often using figurative language and wordplay.
- Students organize the words they write into lines, not sentences.
- Students may use capitalization and punctuation to enhance the meaning, or they may ignore these conventions.
- Students arrange words and lines to heighten the meaning of their poems.

Students write free verse, imitate poems written by adult poets, and use many other poetic forms.

Free Verse. Students arrange words and phrases together to express a thought or tell a story without concern for rhyme, repetition, or other poetic devices; the image that's evoked by the words and the placement of words on the page matter most. An eighth grader eloquently describes loneliness in this free-verse poem:

A lifetime
of broken dreams
and promises.
Lost love hurts.
My heart
cries
in silence.

The student uses capitalization and punctuation to guide the reader. Concrete poems and found poems are other examples of free-form poems. Four types of free verse are concrete poems, "I Am. . . " poems, odes, and found poems:

- Students write concrete poems by arranging words to create an image or picture on the page.
- Students write "I Am . . ." poems by assuming the viewpoint of a person or thing, and the first and last lines of each stanza begin "I am . . ."
- Students write odes to celebrate people and things. In contrast to traditional odes, which are quite formal, the odes that students write don't have rhyme schemes or stanza patterns.
- Students write found poems by choosing words from a story, song, nonfiction book, or newspaper article and arranging the words to form a poem.

Model Poems. Writers imitate poems composed by adults using an approach Kenneth Koch suggested in *Rose, Where Did You Get That Red?* (1990); the adult poem serves as the model for their writing. Students write apology poems using William Carlos Williams's poem "This Is Just to Say" as a model, and in their poems, they apologize for something they're secretly glad they did, and they write poems for two voices when they explore a topic from two perspectives. The poem is written in two side-by-side columns and read simultaneously by two readers.

Rhymed Verse. Writers often use rhyme schemes to structure their poems. Jack Prelutsky, perhaps the best known contemporary poet writing for young adolescents, often incorporates rhyme in his poems. Limericks are one type of rhymed verse; this humorous verse form was popularized in the 19th century by Edward Lear. Students combine rhyme and rhythm to create five-line poems using an a-a-b-b-a rhyme scheme; the third and fourth lines rhyme and are shorter than others, and the last line usually contains a surprise ending.

Syllable-Count Poems. Students use numerical formulas to structure some poems, but these restrictions often inhibit students' natural expression. Haiku is probably the best known example of syllable-count poetry: Students arrange words containing 17 syllables in three lines of 5, 7, and 5 syllables each to craft brief but powerful unrhymed Japanese poems. Haiku usually describe a natural scene; when poems follow the same pattern but describe human nature, they're called *senryu*.

Janeczko's *A Kick in the Head: An Everyday Guide to Poetic Forms* (2009) provides samples of more than two dozen poetic forms, and Figure 9–3 lists books with examples of these types of poems.

Response to Literature. Students write responses to literature to share their interpretation of a story or other text; they apply what they've learned about the elements of story structure, narrative devices, and genre when they respond to a text they've read. Here are the characteristics of this genre:

- Writers demonstrate a clear understanding of the text.
- Writers include specific references to the text.
- Writers apply knowledge of story elements in their responses.
- Writers comment on the author's use of literary devices.
- Writers identify and compare literary genres.
- Writers make connections to their own lives, the world, and other literature.

Students develop their ideas, present evidence and examples from the text, and organize their writing into book reviews and literary response essays. Their responses reflect their knowledge of text factors and the depth of their comprehension.

A fifth-grade class collaborated on this literary response essay about *The Wretched Stone* (Van Allsburg, 1991):

> The Wretched Stone *by Chris Van Allsburg is a story about a sea captain who has terrible things happen on his ship after be brings on board an unusual glowing rock. The crew stares at it for days and hours and forgets to do their jobs. Finally, the captain throws the rock overboard in order to save his ship.*
>
> *The author calls the rock "a wretched stone."* Wretched *means bad. The rock is bad because it distracts people from their jobs and from reading, singing, and talking to other people. It changed the crew so much that they seemed to become apes.*
>
> *We think the wretched stone is a symbol for new technology including computers, video games, and ipods. It also might symbolize television. Chris Van Allsburg is warning us not to be couch potatoes. We should use our brains to read, do our homework, and stay smart, or we will turn into apes, too!*

FIGURE 9–3 ◆ *Books Illustrating the Poetic Forms*

Concrete Poems

Grandits, J. (2004). *Technically, it's not my fault: Concrete poems.* New York: Sandpiper.

Grandits, J. (2007). *Blue lipstick: Concrete poems.* New York: Sandpiper.

Janeczko, P. B. (2009). *A poke in the I: A collection of concrete poems.* Cambridge: Candlewick Press.

Lewis, J. P. (2002). *Doodle dandies: Poems that take shape.* New York: Atheneum.

Free Verse

Fleischman, P. (2004). *Joyful noise: Poems for two voices.* New York: HarperCollins.

Fletcher, R. (2005). *A writing kind of day: Poems for young poets.* Honesdale, PA: Boyds Mills Press.

Heard, G. (Ed). (2009). *Falling down the pages: A book of list poems.* New York: Roaring Brook Press.

Janeczko, P. B. (2001). *Dirty laundry pile: Poems in different voices.* New York: HarperCollins.

Soto, G. (2007). *Canto familiar.* Orlando: Harcourt.

Model Poems

Shapiro, K. J. (2003). *Because I could not stop my bike and other poems.* Watertown, MA: Charlesbridge.

Shapiro, K. J. (2007). *I must go down to the beach again and other poems.* Watertown, MA: Charlesbridge.

Sidman, J. (2007). *This is just to say: Poems of apology and forgiveness.* Boston: Houghton Mifflin.

Soto, G. (2005). *Neighborhood odes.* Orlando: Harcourt.

Rhymed Verse

Ciardi, J. (1992). *The hopeful trout and other limericks.* New York: Sandpiper.

Dakos, K. (1995). *If you're not here, please raise your hand: Poems about school.* New York: Aladdin Books.

Krensky, S. (2004). *There once was a very odd school.* New York: Dutton.

Prelutsky, J. (2008). *Be glad your nose is on your face and other poems.* New York: HarperCollins.

Whitehead, J. (2001). *Lunch box mail and other poems.* New York: Henry Holt.

Syllable-Count Poems

Chaikin, M. (2002). *Don't step on the sky: A handful of haiku.* New York: Henry Holt.

Gollub, M. (2004). *Cool melons—Turn to frogs! The life and poems of Issa.* New York: Lee & Low.

Janeczko, P. B., & Lewis, J. P. (2006). *Wing nuts: Screwy haiku.* Boston: Little, Brown.

Spivak, D. (1997). *Grass sandals: The travels of Basho.* New York: Atheneum.

This composition shows that the students have inferred the author's message. Their focus on the wretched stone continues through all three paragraphs: In the first paragraph, they summarize the story and explain the stone's role; in the second, they discuss the stone's impact using evidence from the text; and in the third, they recognize that the stone is a symbol and infer the author's message.

Workplace Writing. Workplace or technical writing is another new genre. Students are familiar with this genre because they read instruction manuals to operate cell phones and bus schedules to go to the mall with their friends, for example. This on-the-job writing is practical and purposeful, and it exhibits these characteristics:

- Writers sequence step-by-step directions and instructions.
- Writers choose precise vocabulary, including sequencing and spatial words.
- Writers use formatting, color, and font sizes and styles to emphasize their message.
- Writers demonstrate an awareness of the intended audience.

Spotlight on . . . Writing

"Of course I like to write!" Ales declares. "It's fun, and it helps me become a better reader." Her favorite genre is essays because that's what she's learning now. Her mom reads everything she writes and saves her papers in a special box.

Ales has a computer at home, and she uses it to word process some of her writing assignments. "I'm just learning to type, so you could say I just hunt and peck when I'm word processing on the computer," she explains. "I'm getting better but I need to take a word processing course next summer."

Ales has learned to use the writing process. She explains, "I make notes with all my ideas before I start writing. Then I keep thinking about what I'm writing. I ask myself if my writing is good, and I know I can revise to make it better. I think a lot faster than I write, so I skip words. When I'm revising, I go back and add them. I like sharing and getting feedback. Proofreading is the easiest part because I'm a good speller."

Ales writes at home, too: "I have a diary that I write in almost every day. I keep it hidden so no one can read it. And, I write letters to my dad, and he always writes back to me."

Graciela says she doesn't do much writing at school, and she can't remember any compositions she's written. When asked specifically about the writing project that's going on in her classroom that week, she admits that she's writing a response to *Freak the Mighty* (Philbrick, 2001), the compelling story of an extraordinary friendship between two eighth-grade misfits, which her teacher has read aloud.

In response to questions about the writing process, this struggling writer explains, "I just pick up my pen and start writing. It's hard to think of things to write about, so I just try to get done." She doesn't like to share her writing with classmates and tries to get everything right the first time so she doesn't have to revise. Her friend Angela is a good proofreader, so she checks Graciela's writing.

"Writing is good when it's neat and there aren't any mistakes," according to Graciela. "I erase my mistakes."

Graciela claims to like to write at home but later she says she never writes at home. With prompting, she recalls adding items to grocery lists, sending birthday cards, and jotting notes to friends. She has pencils and pens available at home, but no computer.

Kolei prefers writing to reading, and he's interested in a variety of genres. He recently completed a lengthy science report on the accuracy of eyewitness testimony. In that report, he concluded that girls and boys provide similar eyewitness testimony. He also likes to write poetry: "Have you noticed that words have color? I use words to create pictures in the poems I write. Rhyme isn't important; word choice is what matters. That's why I like poetry."

Like most writers, Kolei says that revising is the toughest part of the writing process for him. He rereads his drafts, thinking about the audience's needs more than his own, checks to make sure his writing is well organized, and deletes or "tosses" lots of sentences because that's what authors do when they revise. He also gets feedback from peers and uses their suggestions when he revises.

When asked about what makes writing effective, Kolei identified these traits: introductions that grab readers' attention, well-developed ideas, clear organization, precise words, interesting sentences, and a powerful voice.

This dedicated writer keeps three notebooks at home. In one journal, Kolei writes song lyrics; in the second, he creates stories; and in the third, he sketches fashion designs.

FIGURE 9–4 ◆ Writing Genres

Genre	Description	Examples
Descriptive Writing	Descriptive writing paints vivid pictures of people, places, events, and things. Writers use sensory details to breathe life into their compositions.	Descriptive paragraphs Descriptive essays
Expository Writing	Expository writing presents information. Writers use the expository text structures to organize their presentation of information and cue words to guide readers.	Cause-and-effect essays Comparison essays How-to essays Reports
Multimedia Writing	Multimedia writing integrates digital technology with writing. Writers use word processors, digital cameras, video clips, websites, and other computer applications to create compositions.	Compositions with website links Multigenre projects PowerPoint presentations
Narrative Writing	Narratives are accounts of events or experiences that may be true or imaginary. Writers create a context for readers to imagine where the story takes place and provide insight into why it's memorable.	Personal narratives Autobiographical incidents Stories
Persuasive Writing	Persuasion is winning someone to your viewpoint or cause using appeals to logic, moral character, and emotion. Writers state a position clearly, support it with relevant evidence, and address reader concerns.	Persuasive letters Persuasive essays
Poetry	Poems are concise word images. Writers use figurative language, rhyme, and other poetic devices to evoke an emotional response.	Concrete poems Haiku "I Am. . ." poems Odes
Response to Literature	Response to literature is an interpretation of a story or other text. Writers support their opinions with evidence from the text.	Book reviews Literary response essays
Workplace Writing	Workplace writing is a new genre that includes the real-life compositions and technical documents that people write on the job. Writers use bulleted lists, boldface type, and other stylistic devices.	E-mail messages Business letters Directions Instructions

Ward (2006) emphasizes that workplace writing must be clear, concise, and compelling. Students learn to write and format "how to" instructions for making a sandwich or tying a shoe, e-mail messages, business letters, directions, and memos.

The eight writing genres are summarized in Figure 9–4.

The Teacher's Role

Teachers use an apprenticeship model of writing where they cultivate a community of writers, and students employ the writing process to draft and refine their compositions. In many classrooms, including Ms. Garza's in the vignette, teachers choose the writing workshop approach. They combine explicit instruction with authentic practice as students examine the traits of effective writing, participate in genre studies, learn about authors, and use literature as a model for their writing. Students apply what they're

Guidelines
for Writing Instruction

▶ Cultivate a community of writers.

▶ Provide daily opportunities for extended writing activities.

▶ Guide students to apply the writing process, with particular emphasis on revising.

▶ Model and teach writing strategies, including organizing, revising, and proof-reading.

▶ Teach the six traits so students can incorporate these qualities into their writing.

▶ Involve students in genre studies to learn about writing forms and use them in their own writing.

▶ Train students to self-assess their writing using rubrics.

▶ Collect students' writing in portfolios.

learning to their own writing, and the quality of their writing reflects their learning. The guidelines feature above lists the components of effective writing instruction.

Writing Strategies. Writing is a constructive process, and writers make deliberate choices as they construct meaning (Flower, 1989). They apply strategies purposefully as they plan, revise, and edit their compositions. Researchers have found that strategic students' compositions are dramatically better than those of other students, and that instruction in writing strategies is particularly important for struggling students (Graham & Perin, 2007; Olson & Land, 2007). Writers apply some of the same strategies that readers use, but they also draw on other, more-specific strategies at each stage of the writing process and for varied types of writing activities (Dean, 2006). Middle graders learn to apply these writing strategies:

Generating. Writers brainstorm ideas and the words to express them. Sometimes they activate their background knowledge and brainstorm lists, but at other times, they read books, conduct interviews, or research a topic.

Organizing. Writers impose an order on their presentation of ideas using their knowledge of narrative elements, expository structures, or poetic forms. Outlining is the traditional form of organizing, but clusters and other graphic organizers are usually more effective.

Narrowing. Writers limit the scope of their topic to make it more manageable. When students attempt to write about a broad topic, they're often so overwhelmed with information that they can't complete the assignment.

Elaborating. Writers expand their ideas by adding details, examples, and quotes; it's the opposite of narrowing. Sometimes students brainstorm additional words and ideas; at other times, however, they have to do more research to elaborate their ideas.

 Be Strategic!
Writing Strategies

Students use writing strategies to draft and refine their compositions:

▶ Generate   ▶ Reread
▶ Organize   ▶ Revise
▶ Narrow   ▶ Proofread
▶ Elaborate   ▶ Format

Students learn to apply these strategies through a combination of explicit instruction and authentic writing activities.

STRUGGLING READERS AND WRITERS

Apprehensive Writers

Most struggling writers are apprehensive.

Struggling writers don't have much confidence in themselves because year after year teachers have responded negatively to their writing attempts (Blasingame & Bushman, 2005). Their writing is noticeably shorter than their classmates' and not as well developed, and they have more difficulty with spelling, capitalization, punctuation, and Standard English usage. It's critical that teachers diagnose students' writing problems and that teachers and students work together to solve them.

An effective writing program for struggling writers combines explicit instruction with authentic writing activities. Writing instruction is more structured for struggling students and involves these components:

The Writing Process. Teachers teach students how to use the writing process and apply writing strategies.

The Six Traits. Teachers explain the traits of effective writing so students can apply them in their own writing.

Genre Study. Teachers present information about the writing genres and provide scaffolding as students write collaborative compositions using the genres.

The Reading–Writing Connection. Teachers link reading with writing by reading literature aloud, teaching about authors, and using literature passages as models for students' writing.

Models. Teachers select passages from trade books and students' writing to use as models for struggling writers.

Rubrics. Teachers create rubrics with students so they understand how they'll be assessed and so they can learn to self-assess their writing.

On-Demand Writing Assessments. Teachers prepare students for on-demand writing assessments so that they can be more successful.

Teachers also provide daily opportunities for struggling writers to participate in authentic writing activities. They scaffold the opportunities in these ways to ensure that students will be successful:

► Creating a nurturing classroom environment where students are encouraged to take risks
► Providing time each day for students to write
► Allowing students to choose topics for writing
► Encouraging students to collaborate on writing projects

Teachers also assess struggling writers to diagnose their writing problems and provide interventions to accelerate their achievement. Once students are more successful, they'll be less apprehensive and will gain confidence in themselves as writers.

Rereading. Writers often stop writing to read what they've written. They use this strategy for many purposes: to check that they're achieving their purpose, to monitor their flow of ideas, or to appreciate the voice they're creating. After a break, students reread to remember where they left off so they can begin to write again.

Revising. Revising isn't just a stage in the writing process; it's also a strategy writers to use improve the quality of their compositions. The four most important aspects are adding, deleting, substituting, and moving words, sentences, and longer pieces of text. For example, students add dialogue, delete redundant sentences, substitute more-vivid verbs, and move a paragraph to improve the organization.

Proofreading. Writers proofread to identify mechanical errors in their compositions, including spelling, capitalization, punctuation, and grammar mistakes. It's a special type of reading where students focus on the physical details of words rather than on their meaning.

Formatting. Writers design the layout of the final copies of their compositions. Formatting plays a more important role in some genres; for example, students spend a great deal of time formatting the poems they write and digital compositions of information, including PowerPoint presentations and websites.

Figure 9–5 shows how these writing strategies plus some reading and writing strategies fit into the writing process.

Teachers teach writing strategies using **minilessons**. They explain the strategy, model its use during **interactive writing** activities, and reflect on how they've used it using **think-alouds**. They also encourage students to use think-alouds to reflect on how they've employed the strategy during their own writing activities. When teachers use writing workshop, minilessons on writing strategies fit naturally into the instructional approach.

FIGURE 9–5 ◆ How the Writing Strategies Fit Into the Writing Process

Stage	What Writers Do	Strategies Writers Use
Prewriting	Students plan their compositions by activating their background knowledge about the topic, gathering ideas, and organizing them.	Activate background knowledge* Set a purpose* Generate Organize
Drafting	As students get their ideas down on paper, they focus on organizing the ideas and developing them using narrowing and elaborating. They monitor their progress and, from time to time, stop writing to reread their drafts.`	Organize Narrow Elaborate Monitor* Reread
Revising	Students reread and examine their drafts to discover ways to refine them. They add, delete, substitute, and move text and monitor the changes they're making to ensure that they're communicating more effectively.	Reread Revise Narrow Elaborate Monitor*
Editing	Students proofread their writing to identify mechanical errors and then correct the errors so they won't interfere with reader's understanding their compositions.	Proofread Monitor*
Publishing	Students design the layout and create the final copy of their compositions. They also evaluate the quality of the composition and their use of writing strategies.	Format Evaluate*

* = reading and writing strategy

Writing Workshop. Writing workshop is the foundation of good writing instruction (Angelillo, 2005). Students become a community of learners where they learn about writing. Teaching is organized into genre studies, author studies, the six traits, and writing strategies. In the workshop approach, teachers present minilessons where they provide information, demonstrate strategies, and have students read and examine mentor texts, but most of the time is devoted to writing. Students usually choose topics for writing, but they're responsible for using the writing process, practicing writing strategies, conferencing with classmates and the teacher, and publishing regularly.

Assessing Students' Writing

Teachers assess both the process students use as they write and the quality of their compositions. They observe as students use the writing process to develop their compositions and conference with students as they revise and edit their writing. Teachers notice, for example, whether students use strategies to organize ideas for writing and whether they take into account feedback from classmates when they revise. So that students can document their writing process activities, teachers also have them keep all drafts of their compositions in writing folders.

Teachers develop rubrics, or scoring guides, to assess the quality of students' writing (Farr & Tone, 1994). Rubrics make the analysis of writing simpler and the assessment process more reliable and consistent. They may have 4, 5, or 6 levels, with descriptors at each level related to ideas, organization, language, and mechanics. Some rubrics are general and are appropriate for almost any writing assignment, but others are designed for a specific writing assignment. The Assessment Tools feature on the next page presents a fifth-grade rubric.

Teachers use rubrics to assess writing. As they read the composition, they highlight words and phrases in the rubric that best describe it. Usually words and phrases in more than one level are marked, so the score is determined by noting which level has the most highlighted words.

Students, too, can learn to create rubrics to assess the quality of their writing. To be successful, they first need to examine examples of other students' writing and determine the qualities that demonstrate strong, average, and weak papers; teachers model how to address the qualities at each level in the rubric. Perhaps the most important outcome of teaching students to create rubrics, according to Skillings and Ferrell (2000), is that students develop metacognitive strategies and the ability to think about themselves as writers.

On-Demand Writing Tests. In most school districts, students take on-demand writing tests every year, and most states have implemented similar assessments in fourth and seventh or eighth grades. There's also a new writing on-demand component on the SAT, and California and other states are instituting tests with an on-demand writing component that students must pass to graduate from high school. These writing tests present a prompt for students to respond to within a set time period, and they're scored holistically using a 4-, 5-, or 6-point scale.

Good writing instruction is the most important way to prepare students for on-demand writing assessments (Angelillo, 2005). Students who apply the six traits, vary their writing according to genre, use writing strategies, and assess their own writing will do well on almost any type of writing. Nevertheless, writing tests place additional demands on students:

The Prompt. Students need to know how to read and interpret the prompt (Kiester, 2006a). They must identify the genre and audience and look for clue words, such as *describe* and *convince*, to figure out what they're expected to do. Prompts usually have several parts, so students must read the entire prompt carefully without jumping to conclusions.

The Topic. Students often choose their own topics for writing, so they need to get used to writing on test topics that may not interest them.

Time Restrictions. Students aren't usually limited in the time they have available for writing, so they need to practice writing compositions under test conditions so that they'll know how to allocate their time for planning, writing, and proofreading.

Teachers teach students about prompts, model how to write in response to a prompt, and have students practice taking writing tests so that they'll be familiar with the procedures before they're tested.

To prepare his students, Gallagher (2006) teaches the ABCs (and D) of on-demand writing:

A = Attack the prompt

B = Brainstorm possible answers

C = Choose the order of your response

D = Detect errors before turning the draft in (p. 41)

Students begin by reading and analyzing the prompt to determine what it's really asking them to do. Once they understand the prompt, they prewrite by brainstorming and

Assessment Tools

Writing

Teachers use rubrics to assess students' writing. Some rubrics, such as the one below, are general and can be used for almost any writing assignment, but others are designed for a specific writing assignment. Rubrics should have 4 to 6 achievement levels and address ideas, organization, language, and mechanics at each level. Sometimes teachers develop their own rubrics to assess the specific traits, genres, or skills they've taught; at other times, they use rubrics that have been developed by other teachers, school districts, state departments of education, and publishers of educational materials. In addition, many rubrics are available on the Internet that teachers can adapt and use.

Fifth-Grade Writing Rubric

4 EXCELLENT

___ Creative and original
___ Clear organization
___ Precise word choice and figurative language
___ Sophisticated sentences
___ Essentially free of mechanical errors

3 GOOD

___ Some creativity, somewhat predictable
___ Definite organization
___ Good word choice, but no figurative language
___ Varied sentences
___ Only a few mechanical errors

2 BASIC

___ Predictable paper
___ Some organization
___ Adequate word choice
___ Little sentence variety and some run-on sentences
___ Some mechanical errors

1 MINIMAL

___ Brief and superficial
___ Little organization
___ Imprecise language
___ Many incomplete and run-on sentences
___ Many spelling, grammar, and other mechanical errors

developing ideas. Gallagher recommends that students create a graphic organizer with their ideas and number them to organize their responses; he's found that when students spend 5 or 6 minutes prewriting, their writing is better. Finally, students take a minute or two at the end of the writing time to proofread their compositions and correct spelling, capitalization, punctuation, and grammar errors.

Shelton and Fu (2004) describe how a fourth-grade teacher interrupted her students' writing workshop to provide an intensive 6-week test preparation before the state on-demand writing assessment. During the test preparation, the students learned to read prompts, studied the two genres that might be tested, and practiced writing under test conditions. These fourth graders scored higher than the state average, but even though they did well, they disliked writing for the test and eagerly returned to writing workshop where they chose their own topics, collaborated with classmates, and didn't have to adhere to time restrictions.

Spelling

Students need to learn to spell words conventionally so that they can communicate effectively through writing. Learning phonics during the primary grades is part of spelling instruction, but middle graders learn other strategies and information about English orthography. In the past, weekly spelling tests were the main instructional strategy; now, they're only one part of a comprehensive spelling program. Guidelines for spelling instruction are presented below.

Stages of Spelling Development

Based on examinations of students' spellings, researchers have identified five stages that students move through on their way to becoming conventional spellers (Bear, Invernizzi, Templeton, & Johnston, 2008). Most young adolescents are at the fourth and fifth stages, but struggling readers and writers still depend on phonics skills and are often stuck at the third stage. At each stage, students use different strategies and focus on particular aspects of spelling.

Stage 1: Emergent Spelling. Young children string scribbles, letters, and letter-like forms together, but they don't associate the marks with specific phonemes. They may write from left to right, right to left, top to bottom, or randomly across the

Guidelines
for Teaching Spelling

► Analyze the errors in students' writing to provide appropriate spelling instruction based on their stage of development.

► Teach students to use spelling strategies to spell unfamiliar words.

► Involve students in daily authentic reading and writing activities.

► Involve students in making words, word sorts, and other hands-on spelling activities.

► Teach students to proofread their writing.

► Consider spelling tests as only one part of a spelling program.

page, but by the end of the stage, they have an understanding of directionality. Some children have a large repertoire of letterforms to use, but others repeat a small number of letters over and over. They use both upper- and lowercase letters but show a distinct preference for uppercase letters. This stage is typical of 3- to 5-year-olds who learn these concepts:

- The distinction between drawing and writing
- How to make letters
- The direction of writing on a page
- Some letter–sound matches

Stage 2: Letter Name-Alphabetic Spelling. Students develop an understanding of the alphabetic principle, that a link exists between letters and sounds, and represent phonemes in words with letters. At first, students' spellings are quite abbreviated and represent only the most prominent features in words. They use only one or two letters to represent an entire word, such as D (*dog*) and KE (*cookie*). Students learn to use most beginning and ending consonants and include a vowel in most syllables; for example, they spell *like* as *lik* and *bed* as *bad*. By the end of the stage, they use consonant blends (e.g., *bl-*, *gr-*, *-nt*) and digraphs (e.g., *ch*, *sh*, *th*, *wh*) and short-vowel patterns to spell words. They can also spell some CVCe words correctly. Spellers at this stage are usually 5- to 7-year-olds who learn these concepts:

- The alphabetic principle
- Consonant sounds
- Short vowel sounds
- Consonant blends and digraphs

Stage 3: Within-Word Pattern Spelling. Students learn to spell long-vowel patterns and *r*-controlled vowels. They may confuse spelling patterns and spell *meet* as *mete*, and reverse the order of letters, such as *gril* for *girl*. They also learn about complex consonant sounds, including *-tch* (*match*) and *-dge* (*judge*), and less frequent vowel patterns, such as *oi/oy* (*boy*), *au* (*caught*), *aw* (*saw*), *ew* (*sew*, *few*), *ou* (*house*), and *ow* (*cow*). Students compare long- and short-vowel combinations (*hope–hop*). Spellers at this stage are typically 7- to 9-year-olds who learn these concepts:

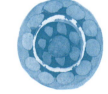

- Long-vowel spelling patterns
- *r*-controlled vowels
- More-complex consonant patterns
- Diphthongs and other less common vowel patterns

Stage 4: Syllables and Affixes Spelling. Students focus on syllables and apply what they've learned about one-syllable words to two-syllable and longer words. They learn about inflectional endings (*-s*, *-es*, *-ed*, and *-ing*) and rules about consonant doubling, changing the final *y* to *i*, or dropping the final *e* before adding an inflectional suffix. They also learn about homophones and compound words and are introduced to the more-common prefixes and suffixes. Spellers in this stage are generally 9- to 11-year-olds who learn these concepts:

- Inflectional endings
- Rules for adding inflectional endings
- Syllabication
- Homophones

FIGURE 9–6 ◆ *Stages of Spelling Development*

Stage 1: Emergent Spelling

Young children string scribbles, letters, and letterlike forms together, but they don't associate the marks they make with any specific phonemes. Preschoolers and kindergartners learn these concepts:

- The distinction between drawing and writing
- How to make letters
- The direction of writing on a page
- Some letter–sound matches

Stage 2: Letter Name-Alphabetic Spelling

Students represent phonemes in words with letters. At first, their spellings are quite abbreviated, but they learn to use consonant blends and digraphs and short-vowel patterns to spell many short-vowel words. Spellers are typically 5- to 7-year-olds who learn these concepts:

- The alphabetic principle
- Consonant sounds
- Short vowel sounds
- Consonant blends and digraphs

Stage 3: Within-Word Pattern Spelling

Students learn long-vowel patterns and *r*-controlled vowels, but they may confuse spelling patterns and spell *meet* as *mete*. They also reverse the order of letters, such as *gril* for *girl*. Spellers are generally 7- to 9-year-olds who learn these concepts:

- Long-vowel spelling patterns
- *r*-controlled vowels
- More-complex consonant patterns
- Diphthongs and other less common vowel patterns

Stage 4: Syllables and Affixes Spelling

Students break words into syllables and apply their knowledge about one-syllable words to spell longer words. They also add inflectional endings (e.g., *-es*, *-ed*, *-ing*) and differentiate between homophones, such as *your–you're*. Spellers are often 9- to 11-year-olds who learn these concepts:

- Inflectional endings
- Rules for adding inflectional endings
- Syllabication
- Homophones

Stage 5: Derivational Relations Spelling

Students discover that words with related meanings have similar spellings despite changes in sound (e.g., *wise–wisdom, sign–signal, nation–national*). They also learn Latin and Greek root words and derivational affixes (e.g., *amphi-, pre-, -able, -tion*). Spellers are 11- to 14-year-olds who learn these concepts:

- Consonant alternations
- Vowel alternations
- Latin and Greek affixes and root words
- Etymologies

Adapted from Bear, Invernizzi, Templeton, & Johnston, 2008.

Stage 5: Derivational Relations Spelling. Students explore the relationship between spelling and meaning, and they learn that words with related meanings are often related in spelling, even though vowel and consonant sounds change. Note how the sounds in these pairs of related words change: *wise–wisdom, sign–signal, nation–national,* and *magic–magician.* The first three pairs have vowel changes, and the last pair has a consonant change; these changes are called *alternations.* The focus in this stage is on morphemes, and students learn Greek and Latin root words and affixes. They also begin to examine etymologies and the role of history in shaping how words are spelled. They learn about eponyms (words from people's names), such as *maverick* and *sandwich.* Spellers at this stage are 11- to 14-year-olds who learn these concepts:

- Consonant alternations
- Vowel alternations
- Greek and Latin affixes and root words
- Etymologies

Students' spelling provides evidence of their growing understanding of English orthography. The words they spell correctly show which spelling patterns and language features they've learned to apply, and the words they misspell show what they're still learning to use and those features they haven't noticed or learned. The characteristics of the five stages are summarized in Figure 9–6.

Scaffolding English Learners

English learners move through the same five developmental stages that native English speakers do, but they move more slowly because they're less familiar with the letter–sound correspondences, spelling patterns, and grammar of English (Bear, Helman, Invernizzi, Templeton, & Johnston, 2007). Students' spelling development reflects their reading achievement, but it lags behind it: When ELs learn a word, they begin by learning its meaning and how to pronounce it. Almost immediately, they're introduced to the word's written form, and with practice, they learn to recognize and read it. Soon they're writing the word, too. At first their spellings reflect what they know about the English spelling system, but with spelling instruction and reading and writing practice, they learn to spell words correctly. Because spelling is more demanding than reading, it's not surprising that students' knowledge about spelling grows this way.

It's essential that teachers learn about English learners' home language, especially about the ways it differs from English, and then they need to explicitly teach students about the contrasts because they're harder to learn than the similarities (Bear et al., 2007). Consider these written language differences, for example: Chinese uses syllable-length characters instead of letters; Arabic is written from right to left, and the way letters are formed varies according to their location within a word; and vowels aren't used in Croatian and Czech. Some languages, including Arabic, Spanish, Kiswahili (Swahili), and Russian, are more phonetically consistent than English; students who speak these languages are often confused by the number of ways a sound can be spelled in English.

There are phonological differences, too: Many languages, including Korean, don't have the /th/ sound; there's no /p/ in Arabic, so Arabic speakers often substitute /b/ in

English; and /l/ and /r/ sound alike to speakers of Asian languages. Vowels are particularly difficult for English learners because they're often pronounced differently in their home language. For example, Russian speakers don't differentiate between short and long vowels, and Spanish speakers often substitute /ĕ/ for /ā/ and /ō/ for /ŏ/. Many African and Asian languages, including Kiswahili, Punjabi, Chinese, and Thai, as well as Navajo, a Native American language, are tonal; in these languages, pitch, not spelling differences, is used to distinguish between words.

In addition, there are syntactic differences that affect spelling: Hmong speakers don't add plural markers to nouns; Korean speakers add grammatical information to the end of verbs instead of using auxiliary verbs; and Chinese speakers aren't familiar with prefixes or suffixes because they're not used in their language.

Teachers base their instruction on English learners' stage of spelling development, and they emphasize the contrasts between students' home languages and English. At each developmental stage, teachers focus their instruction on concepts that confuse English learners, according to Bear and his colleagues (2007):

Emergent Stage. Students learn English letters, sounds, and words, and they learn that English is written from left to right and top to bottom, with spaces between words. Developing this awareness is more difficult for students whose home languages are not alphabetic.

Letter Name–Alphabetic Stage. Students learn that letters represent sounds, and the sounds that are the same in ELs' home languages and English are the easiest to learn. They learn both consonant and vowel sounds. Those consonant sounds that are more difficult include /d/, /j/, /r/, /sh/, and /th/. English learners often have difficulty pronouncing and spelling final consonant blends (e.g., *-st* as in *fast*, *-ng* as in *king*, *-mp* as in *stomp*, and *-rd* as in *board*). Long and short vowel sounds are especially hard because they're often pronounced differently than in students' home languages.

Within-Word Pattern Stage. Students move from representing individual sounds in words to using spelling patterns. They practice CVCe and CVVC spelling patterns and words that are exceptions to these rules; *r*-controlled vowels are especially tricky because they're found in common words, and sound often doesn't predict spelling (e.g., *bear/care/hair, bird/heard/fern/burst*). English learners also learn to spell contractions during this stage.

Syllables and Affixes Stage. Students learn spelling and grammar concepts together as they investigate verb forms (e.g., *talk–talked, take–took–taken, think–thought*), change adjectives to adverbs (e.g., *quick–quickly*), and add inflectional endings (e.g., *walks–walked–walking*) and comparatives and superlatives (e.g., *sunny–sunnier–sunniest*). They also learn to pronounce accented and unaccented syllables differently and to use the schwa sound in unaccented syllables.

Derivational Relations Stage. Students learn about Latin and Greek root words and vowel alternations in related words (e.g., *define–definition*). Some ELs use tonal changes to signal these relationships in their home languages, but they must learn that related words in English are signaled by similar spelling and changes in how the vowels are pronounced.

Spelling instruction for English learners is similar to that for native speakers: Teachers use a combination of explicit instruction, **word sorts** and other practice activities, and authentic reading and writing activities. The biggest difference is that ELs need more instruction on the English spelling concepts that confuse them, often because these features aren't used in their home languages.

Teaching Spelling

The best-known way to teach spelling is through weekly spelling tests, but tests should never be considered a complete spelling program. To become good spellers, students need to learn about the English orthographic system and move through the stages of spelling development. They develop strategies for spelling unknown words and gain experience in using dictionaries and other resources. A complete spelling program includes the following components:

- Providing daily reading and writing opportunities
- Matching instruction to students' stage of spelling development
- Teaching spelling strategies

Two of the most important ways that students learn to spell are through daily reading and writing activities. Students who are good readers tend to be good spellers, too: As they read, students visualize words—the shape of the word and the configuration of letters within it—and they use this knowledge to spell many words correctly and to recognize when a word they've written doesn't look right. Through writing, of course, students gain valuable practice using the strategies they have learned to spell words. And, as teachers work with students to proofread and edit their writing, they learn more about spelling and other writing conventions.

Spelling Strategies. Students learn strategies for figuring out the spelling of unfamiliar words. As students move through the stages of spelling development, they become increasingly more sophisticated in their use of phonological, semantic, and historical knowledge to spell words; that is, they become more strategic. Important spelling strategies include the following:

- Sound it out
- Apply affixes
- Proofread
- Check a dictionary

Be Strategic!
Spelling Strategies

Students use these strategies to spell words and to verify that words they've written are spelled correctly:

► Sound it out
► Apply affixes
► Proofread
► Check a dictionary

The "sound it out" strategy works best for spelling phonetically regular words during the primary grades; older students learn more-effective strategies to think out the spellings for longer words.

Teachers often give the traditional "sound it out" advice when students ask how to spell an unfamiliar word, but that's rarely productive; they provide more-useful information when they suggest that students use a strategic "think it out" approach. This advice reminds students that spelling involves more than phonological information and encourages them to think abut spelling patterns, root words and affixes, and what the word looks like.

Spelling Activities. Teachers use a variety of spelling activities to expand students' spelling knowledge and help them move through the stages of spelling development.

Word Walls. Teachers post commonly misspelled words on a **word wall** to draw students' attention to them and to use them in spelling activities. A list of words that fourth through eighth graders commonly misspell is presented in Figure 9–7.

FIGURE 9–7 ◆ Commonly Misspelled Words

A	B	C	D
again	beautiful	calendar	decide
although	because	caught	definitely
anonymous	believe	characteristic	desperate
apologize	breathe	clothes	dessert
	brought	committee	different
	business	courageous	disappoint
		curiosity	discussed
			doesn't

E	F	G	H
eighth	familiar	government	height
either	favorite		humorous
embarrass	February		hungry
enough	foreign		
especially	fourth		
etc.	friend		
everywhere			
experience			

I J K	L M	N O	P
immediately	library	necessary	parallel
independent	license	neighbor	particular
judgment	lightning	ninety	people
knowledge	literature	nuisance	permanent
	loneliness	occasionally	persuade
	lying	once	pleasant
	minimum	opinion	please
	mischievous	opportunity	possibility
			principal
			probably

Q R	S	T	U V W X Y Z
realize	safety	temperature	unnecessary
receipt	schedule	thorough	until
receive	scissors	throughout	usable
recognize	serious	together	usually
recommend	similar	tomorrow	weight
restaurant	sincerely	traffic	weird
rhythm	special	truly	whether
ridiculous	success	Tuesday	
	surprise	twelfth	

Teachers should choose words from the list that are appropriate for their students; words such as *remember* and *believe* are intended for fourth and fifth graders, and others, such as *characteristic* and *occasionally*, are more appropriate for older students.

Making Words. Teachers choose a word and prepare sets of letter cards for a **making words** activity (Cunningham & Cunningham, 1992). Then students use the cards to spell words; they arrange and rearrange the cards to spell two-letter words, three-letter words, and so forth, until they use all the letters to spell the original word. Fourth graders, for example, can create these words using the letters in *weather*: *at, we, he, the, are, art, ear, eat, hat, her, hear, here, hate, heart, wheat, there*, and *where*.

Word Sorts. Students use **word sorts** to compare and contrast word features as they examine a pack of word cards. Teachers prepare word cards for students to sort into two or more categories according to their spelling patterns or other criteria (Bear et al., 2008). Sometimes teachers tell students what categories to use, which makes it a closed sort; when students determine the categories themselves, it's an open sort. Students sort word cards and then return them to an envelope for future use, or they can glue the cards onto a sheet of paper.

Proofreading. Proofreading is a special kind of reading that students use to locate misspelled words and other mechanical errors in rough drafts. As students learn about the writing process, they're introduced to proofreading in the editing stage. More in-depth instruction about how to use proofreading to locate spelling errors and then correct these misspelled words is part of spelling instruction. Through a series of minilessons, students can learn to proofread sample student papers and mark misspelled words. Then, working in pairs, students can correct the misspellings.

Dictionary Use. Students need to know how to locate the spelling of unfamiliar words in the dictionary. Although it is relatively easy to find a "known" word, it's hard to locate unfamiliar words, and students need to learn what to do when they don't know how to spell a word. One approach is to predict possible spellings for unknown words, then check the most probable ones in a dictionary. Students should be encouraged to check the spellings of words in a dictionary and to check multiple meanings of a word or its etymology. Too often, students view consulting a dictionary as punishment, so teachers must work to change this view of dictionary use. One way is to appoint some students in the classroom as dictionary checkers: These students keep dictionaries on their desks, and they're consulted whenever questions about spelling and the meanings of words arise.

Spelling Options. In English, alternate spellings occur for many sounds because so many words borrowed from other languages retain their native spellings. Students can focus on /ûr/, /ə/, or /shun/, for example, and develop a list of the various ways the sound is spelled, giving examples of each spelling.

In these activities, students increase their spelling knowledge because they're actively involved in investigating words and how they're spelled.

Weekly Spelling Tests

Many teachers question the usefulness of spelling tests, because research on invented spelling suggests that spelling is best learned through reading and writing (Gentry & Gillet, 1993). In addition, teachers complain that lists of spelling words are unrelated to the words students are reading and writing and that the 30 minutes of valuable instructional time spent each day in completing spelling activities is excessive. Even so, parents and school board members value spelling tests as evidence that spelling is being taught. Weekly spelling tests, when they're used, should be individualized so that students learn to spell the words they need for writing.

In the individualized approach to spelling instruction, students choose the words they'll study, many of which are words they use in their writing projects. Students study 5 to 10 specific words during the week using a study strategy; this approach places more responsibility on students for their own learning. Teachers develop a weekly word list of 20 or more words of varying difficulty from which students select words to study. Words for the master list include high-frequency words, words from the word wall related to literature focus units and thematic units, and words students needed for their writing projects during the previous week. Words from textbook spelling programs can also be added to the list.

On Monday, the teacher administers a pretest using the master list of words, and students spell as many of the words as they can. Students correct their own pretests, and from the words they misspell they create individual spelling lists. They make two copies of their study list, using the numbers on the master list to make it easier to take the final test on Friday. Students use one copy of the list for study activities, and the teacher keeps the second copy.

Students spend approximately 5 to 10 minutes studying the words on their study lists each day during the week. Instead of "busy-work" activities such as using spelling words in sentences, it's more effective to use this study strategy:

1. Look at the word and say it to yourself.
2. Say each letter in the word to yourself.
3. Close your eyes and spell the word to yourself.
4. Write the word, and check that you spelled it correctly.
5. Write the word again, and check that you spelled it correctly.

This strategy focuses on the whole word rather than on breaking the word apart into sounds or syllables. Teachers explain how to use the strategy during a minilesson at the beginning of the school year and then post the steps in the classroom. In addition to using this study strategy, students often trade word lists on Wednesday and give each other a practice test.

A final test is administered on Friday. The teacher reads the master list, and students write only those words they've practiced during the week. To make the test easier to administer, students first write on their test papers the numbers of the words they've practiced from their study lists. Any words that students misspell should be included on their lists the following week.

Assessing Students' Spelling

The choices students make as they spell words are important indicators of their knowledge of spelling. Teachers classify and analyze the words students misspell in their writing to gauge their level of spelling development and to plan for instruction. They analyze the errors in students' compositions, analyze their errors on weekly spelling tests, and administer diagnostic tests. The Assessment Tools feature on the next page lists tests that teachers use to assess their students' stage of spelling development.

Assessment Tools

Spelling

Teachers assess students' spelling development by examining misspelled words in the compositions they write; they classify students' spelling errors according to the five stages of spelling development and plan instruction based on their analysis. Teachers also examine students' misspellings in weekly spelling tests and in diagnostic tests. These tests are designed for classroom teachers to screen, monitor, diagnose, and document students' spelling development:

◆ **Developmental Spelling Analysis (DSA)** (Ganske, 2000)

The DSA is a dictated spelling inventory with two components: a Screening Inventory for determining students' stage of spelling development, and Feature Inventories to highlight students' knowledge of specific spelling concepts. The DSA with detailed guidelines is available in Ganske's book, *Word Journeys: Assessment-Guided Phonics, Spelling, and Vocabulary Instruction* (2000).

◆ **Qualitative Spelling Inventory (QSI)** (Bear et al., 2008)

The QSI has two forms, one for grades K–6 and another for grades 6–8. These tests each include 20 or 25 spelling words listed according to difficulty and can easily be administered to small groups or whole classes. It's available in *Words Their Way: Word Study for Phonics, Vocabulary, and Spelling Instruction* (Bear et al., 2008).

Through these tests, teachers identify students' stage of spelling development and use this information to monitor their progress and plan for instruction.

CHAPTER 9

How Effective Teachers Teach Writing

▶ Teachers improve the quality of students' writing using the six traits.

▶ Teachers teach students about writing genres.

▶ Teachers teach writing strategies and how to incorporate them during the writing process.

▶ Teachers use rubrics to assess writing.

▶ Teachers include spelling as part of writing instruction.

PART 3

Effective Instructional Programs

 eachers organize their instructional programs using student-centered and teacher-led approaches that they usually combine or alternate to ensure that students participate in both explicit instruction and genuine application activities.

Literature Focus Units

Teachers guide students as they read and respond to award-winning or other high-quality books together as a class. In this teacher-centered approach, the book is used to teach academic vocabulary, comprehension strategies, and text analysis. Students also develop projects to culminate their learning.

Literature Circles

Students participate in four- to six-member collaborative groups or literature circles to read and respond to books. They take on roles to explore the piece of literature and engage in critical thinking and reflection to deepen their comprehension. Through their participation in this student-centered approach, students become more responsible and motivated.

Reading and Writing Workshop

Reading and writing workshop are authentic, student-centered approaches to literacy instruction. Students form a learning community to read real books at their reading level that they've chosen themselves and use the writing process to draft and refine compositions, often on topics they've chosen themselves. Teachers provide explicit instruction through minilessons.

Textbooks

Elementary and middle school literacy textbooks are commercial programs with literature selections, research-based instruction on reading and writing strategies and skills, numerous practice activities, and a strong emphasis on ongoing assessment and monitoring student progress. The teacher's guide provides directions for using the textbooks including scripts that teachers follow as they present instruction.

WHAT'S AHEAD

In Part 3, you'll read about a variety of approaches to literacy instruction:

Chapter 10: Teaching With Trade Books

Chapter 11: Teaching With Textbooks

Chapter 12: Using Literacy in the Content Areas

These chapters describe the ways teachers organize literacy instruction in response to state- and federally mandated initiatives. Some programs incorporate trade books, and others are textbook based. Teachers also integrate literacy with content-area instruction because students use reading and writing as learning tools and to demonstrate learning.

CHAPTER 10

Teaching With Trade Books

Fourth Graders Participate in a Yearlong Author Study

There's a busy hum in Miss Paniccia's fourth-grade classroom. The students are involved in a 40-minute writing workshop; it's the time when students develop and refine pieces of writing on topics they've chosen themselves. They work with peers to revise and edit their rough drafts and then use AlphaSmart® keyboards for word processing. Next, they transfer their compositions to a classroom computer and print out clean copies of their writing for a final editing conference with Miss Paniccia.

Today, the fourth graders are putting the finishing touches on the collections of stories they've worked on for months. Each student has written at least seven stories, and now they're publishing them by pasting them into bound books with blank pages. The spring back-to-school night is 2 days away, and everyone is eager for parents to read their books.

The class has been involved in an ambitious yearlong project on Chris Van Allsburg, the popular author and illustrator of award-winning fantasy picture books, including *Probuditi* (2006) and *The Polar Express* (2005). The students read some of his stories in their basal readers and during literature circles, and Miss Paniccia has read others aloud. The stories they've been writing accompany the illustrations in *The Mysteries of Harris Burdick* (Van Allsburg, 1996).

The Chris Van Allsburg unit began in September when Miss Paniccia read aloud *Jumanji* (Van Allsburg, 1982), the story of two kids who play a jungle adventure board game that comes to life. She also read aloud the sequel, *Zathura* (2002), about a space adventure board game, and students watched the movie version. They also made board games and wrote directions for playing them. She used the story to emphasize the importance of listening to directions in the classroom, following parents' directions at home, and reading directions on state achievement tests.

Miss Paniccia regularly teaches **minilessons** on writing strategies that students then apply in their own writing. She began with a series of lessons on revising and proofreading; next, she taught about story structure. Posters about each story element hang in the classroom, testimony to the instruction taking place there. Students apply what they've learned as they craft their own stories. They use the writing process, as shown in the box below, to draft and refine their stories. These students took an afterschool touch-typing course last year, so they know the fundamentals of finger placement on the keyboard and are becoming more-fluent typists as they use AlphaSmart® word processing machines.

Month after month, the students have been writing stories. Seth's story for the illustration entitled "Mr. Linden's Library" is shown on page 262. The illustration depicts a sleeping girl with an open book beside her; vines are growing out of the book and spreading across her bed. As you read Seth's story, you'll see how his story developed from the illustration and how he applied what he's learned about story structure.

Today Miss Paniccia is meeting with Alfonso, Martha, and Yimleej to proofread their stories and correct errors. Other students are word processing their last stories or printing out final copies and gluing them into their books. Miguel and Lindsey have

Students' Writing Process Activities

Stage	Activities	Description
Prewriting	Story Cards	Students create cards to develop their ideas.
	One-on-One	Students meet with peers to talk out their ideas.
Drafting	Rough Drafts	Students write rough drafts in pencil, working from their story cards.
Revising	Writing Groups	Students meet with peers to share their drafts, get feedback, and make revisions.
	Conference with Miss P.	Miss Paniccia reads and responds to their drafts; then students make additional revisions based on their teacher's feedback.
Editing	Proofreading	Students proofread and correct errors. Then two peers help them identify and correct the remaining errors.
	Word Processing	Students type their stories using word processing machines, transfer files to the classroom computer, and print out copies.
	Conference with Miss P.	Students meet with Miss Paniccia to proofread and correct the remaining errors.
Publishing	Final Copy	Students print out a final copy, glue the pages into a book, and add illustrations.

Seth's Story About "Mr. Linden's Library"

"I would like to check out this book," Sally Olger said. The book that she wanted to check out was called <u>Adventures in the Wild</u>. She had skipped as she had gone up to the counter. Sally loved to go to this library. It was owned by Mr. Linden, so everybody just called it Mr. Linden's library.

The expression on the man at the counter's face changed when he saw the book that Sally was holding. The man warned Sally that if she left the book out on one page for over an hour, something dangerous would come out of the book.

Sally didn't really hear or care about what the man said. She checked out the book and started reading it in bed that night. The book was really interesting. It had tons of short stories in it. At 12:00 midnight, Sally turned the page to a story called "Lost in the Jungle," yawned, and fell asleep. At 1:00 A.M. vines started to grow out of the book. He had warned her about the book. Now it was too late. Soon Sally's whole room was covered in vines. By 2:00, they were making their way up the stairs.

BBBRRRRIIIIINNNNNNGGGGGG! went Sally's alarm clock.

"AAAAAAAHHHHHHHH!" screamed Sally. Now the whole house was covered in vines. Sally slowly made her way to her parents' bedroom through the vines and woke them up. They screamed too. As quickly as possible (which wasn't very fast) the Olgers got out of their house, got in their car and drove to the library. They told the man at the desk what had happened. He said that the only way to get rid of the vines was to cut their roots (they would be sticking right out of the book) and then haul all of the vines off to the dump. Luckily, the town dump wasn't very far away from the Olgers' house.

By the time Mr. Olger had found and cut the roots away from the book, Sally and Mrs. Olger had rounded up the whole neighborhood to help take the vines to the dump. By 5:00 P.M. in the afternoon they had cleared away all of the vines. Sally had learned her lesson to listen when someone warns you about something.

finished their books, so they're helping classmates word process, transfer to the computer, and print out their stories. Miss Paniccia's optimistic that everyone will be finished by lunchtime tomorrow. She plans to start author's chair tomorrow: Students will take turns reading their favorite stories to classmates.

Last week, the class created this introductory page for their story collections:

Thirty years ago a man named Harris Burdick came by Peter Wenders's publishing office. Mr. Burdick claimed that he had written 15 stories and illustrated them. All he brought with him on that day were the illustrations with titles. The next day Harris Burdick was going to bring the stories to Mr. Wenders, but he never returned. In fact, Harris Burdick was never seen again.

Chris Van Allsburg met with Mr. Wenders and that is where he came across the illustrations. Mr. Wenders handed Mr. Van Allsburg a dust-covered box full of drawings, and Chris Van Allsburg was inspired to reproduce them for children across the nation.

Right here in Room 30, we have worked hard all year creating stories for the illustrations. Even though we have completed our stories, the mystery of Harris Burdick still remains.

It's a class collaboration: Miss Paniccia and the students developed the introduction together, and copies were made for each student. By collaborating, the teacher ensured that they had a useful introduction for their books.

After beginning the author study in September, Miss Paniccia continued to read stories each month. In October, she and her students read *The Stranger* (Van Allsburg, 1986), a story included in their basal readers. In the story, the Baileys take in an injured stranger, a man who doesn't speak or seem to know who he is, but he appears to be attuned with the seasons and has an amazing connection with wild animals. The stranger is Jack Frost, although it's never explicitly stated in the story. They take several days to read the story. On the first day, the teacher introduced the key vocabulary words, including *autumn*, *etched*, and *peculiar*, and the class previewed the story, examining the illustrations and making predictions. Miss Paniccia used a shared reading procedure: The students listened to the story read aloud on the professional CD that accompanies the textbook and followed along in their textbooks. Some inferred that the stranger is Jack Frost, but others didn't. That's when the teacher introduced the drawing inferences strategy, which she called "reading between the lines."

They read the story a second time, searching for clues that led their classmates to guess that the stranger is Jack Frost, and afterward made a cluster, a spider web–like diagram, with the clues. They wrote the words *The Stranger* in the center circle, drew out rays from this circle, and wrote these clues at the end of each one: He wears odd clothing, is confused by buttons, and works hard but doesn't get tired. Afterward, they completed page 156 in the Practice Book that accompanies the textbook as well as other pages that emphasize comprehension. Then Miss Paniccia asked students to closely examine the illustrations in the story. They noticed how the perspective in the illustrations varies to draw readers into the scenes and create the mood. The students read the story a third time with partners, talking about how Chris Van Allsburg used viewpoint in the illustrations.

In November, students read other books by Chris Van Allsburg in literature circles. Miss Paniccia presented **book talks** about these four books: *Two Bad Ants* (Van Allsburg, 1988), *Just a Dream* (Van Allsburg, 1990), *The Sweetest Fig* (Van Allsburg, 1993b), and *The Wreck of the Zephyr* (Van Allsburg, 1983). Then students formed small groups to read one of the books. They assumed roles and took on responsibilities in the small groups as they read and discussed the book. Then students read another of the books during a second literature circle in January.

Miss Paniccia read aloud the award-winning holiday story *The Polar Express* (Van Allsburg, 2005) in December. In the story, being able to hear Santa's bells jiggle represents belief in the magic of Christmas, so Miss Paniccia gave each student a small bell to jiggle each time it was mentioned in the story. The students discussed the story in a **grand conversation**; much of their discussion focused on the theme and how the author states it explicitly at the end of the story. "What an awesome story!" Hunter concluded, and his classmates agreed. They also talked about their own holiday traditions and wrote about them during writing workshop.

They continued to read additional books by Chris Van Allsburg: In February, Miss Paniccia read *The Garden of Abdul Gasazi* (Van Allsburg, 1993a), and in March, she read *The Wretched Stone* (Van Allsburg, 1991). These books are difficult to comprehend because students have to make inferences: In *The Garden of Abdul Gasazi*, readers have to decide whether the magician really changes the dog into a duck, and in *The Wretched Stone*, they need to understand that the stone is a symbol, representing television, computers, or video games. Miss Paniccia taught a series of minilessons on drawing inferences, and she modeled the strategy as she reread the stories, showing the fourth graders how to use background knowledge, the clues in the story, and self-questions to read between the lines. Then students reread the stories with partners, talked about clues in the stories, and drew inferences as their teacher had.

In March, Miss Paniccia also taught minilessons about the fantasy genre. Then students divided into small groups to reread the Chris Van Allsburg books and examine them for fantasy characteristics. They developed a chart with the titles of the books written across the top and the characteristics of fantasies written down the left side. Then they completed the chart by indicating how the characteristics are represented in each book.

This month, students are reading Chris Van Allsburg's books independently; some students are reading those they haven't yet read, and others are rereading favorite ones. As they read, they search for the white dog that Van Allsburg includes in each book. In some books, such as *The Garden of Abdul Gasazi*, the dog is alive, but in others, he's a puppet, a hood ornament, or a picture. In several books, only a small part of him shows; in *The Wretched Stone*, for example, you see only his tail on one page. In addition, they continue to notice the fantasy elements of the stories, they draw inferences when needed, and they reflect on Van Allsburg's use of perspective in his illustrations.

There's no one best way to teach reading and writing. Instead, teachers create a balanced literacy program using two or more instructional approaches. Some approaches use trade books, and others use textbooks. Miss Paniccia's author study in the vignette was successful because her literacy program was balanced with a combination of explicit instruction, small-group and whole-class literacy activities, and independent reading and writing opportunities. By combining several instructional approaches, Miss Paniccia juggled the district's adopted basal reading program with other instructional approaches that enriched and extended her students' literacy learning.

This chapter looks at literature focus units, literature circles, and reading and writing workshop. These programs are literature based because trade books, rather than textbooks, are used for instruction. Students read and respond to authentic literature. They often choose which books they read and how they'll respond to them. These programs do include teaching components, and teachers use the trade books as instructional resources as they teach minilessons.

Teaching With Literature Focus Units

Teachers plan literature focus units featuring popular and award-winning novels, nonfiction books, and books of poetry. Some literature focus units feature a single book but others feature several books for a genre unit or an author study. Teachers guide and direct students as they read, respond to, and analyze a book. The emphasis in this instructional approach is on teaching students about literature. An overview of this instructional approach is shown on the next page.

Literature focus units include activities incorporating the five stages of the reading process:

Prereading. Teachers involve students in activities to build background knowledge and interest them in reading the book, including sharing book boxes, reading related books, showing DVDs, and talking about related topics.

OVERVIEW OF THE INSTRUCTIONAL APPROACH

Literature Focus Units

TOPIC	DESCRIPTION
Purpose	To teach reading through literature, using high-quality, grade-appropriate trade books, especially novels.
Components	Teachers involve students in three activities: Students read, respond to, and analyze a trade book together as a class, the teacher teaches minilessons on strategies and skills using the book, and students create projects to extend their understanding.
Theory Base	Literature focus units are more teacher centered because the teacher guides students as they read a book. This approach also reflects information-processing theory because teachers develop students' background knowledge, read aloud when students can't read fluently, and teach vocabulary words and comprehension strategies, and critical literacy theory because issues of social justice often arise in the trade books.
Applications	Teachers teach units featuring a novel or other book, generally using books on a district-approved list, or units featuring a genre or author. Literature focus units are often alternated with another approach where students read books at their own reading levels.
Strengths	• Teachers select award-winning literature for these units. • Teachers scaffold students' comprehension. • Teachers teach minilessons on reading strategies and skills. • Students learn academic vocabulary related to the book. • Students learn about genres, structural forms, and literary devices.
Limitations	• All students read the same book whether or not it's at their reading level. • Many activities are teacher directed.

Reading. Students read the featured selection independently, or the teacher reads it aloud or uses shared reading if it's too difficult for students to read themselves.

Responding. Students participate in **grand conversations** to talk about the book and write entries in **reading logs** to deepen their understanding.

Exploring. Students post vocabulary on **word walls**, participate in word-study activities, learn comprehension strategies, do close reading to examine text factors, and research the book's author or related topics.

Applying. Students apply their learning as they create visual, oral, and written projects.

Through these activities, teachers guide students as they read and respond to high-quality literature.

Check the Compendium of Instructional Procedures, which follows Chapter 12, for more information on the highlighted terms.

Steps in Developing a Unit

Teachers develop a literature focus unit through a series of steps, beginning with choosing the literature and setting goals, then identifying and scheduling activities, and finally deciding how to assess students' learning. Effective teachers don't simply follow directions in literature focus unit planning guides that are available for purchase in school supply stores; rather, they do the planning themselves because they're the ones who are most knowledgeable about their students, the time available for the unit, the strategies and skills they need to teach, and the activities they want to develop.

Step 1: Select the Literature. Teachers select the book for the literature focus unit—a novel, a nonfiction book, or a book of poetry—and collect multiple copies so students will each have a copy to read. Many school districts have class sets of selected books available; however, sometimes teachers have to ask administrators to purchase multiple copies or buy books themselves through book clubs.

Teachers collect related books for the text set, too, including sequels, other books written by the same author, or more books in the same genre. Teachers collect one or two copies of 10 or more books at varying reading levels for the text set and add them to the classroom library for the unit. Books for the text set are placed on a special shelf or in a crate in the library. At the beginning of the unit, teachers introduce the books using **book talks** and provide opportunities for students to read them independently.

Teachers also identify and collect supplemental materials related to the featured selection, including book boxes of materials to use in introducing the book, charts and diagrams, and information about the author and the illustrator. Teachers also locate multimedia resources, such as film versions of the book, DVDs to provide background knowledge on the topic, and websites about the author and the illustrator.

Step 2: Set Goals. Teachers decide what they want their students to learn during the unit, and they connect the goals they set with grade-level standards.

Step 3: Develop a Unit Plan. Teachers read or reread the selected book and then think about their focus for the unit; sometimes they concentrate on an element of story structure, the historical setting, wordplay, the author or genre, or a topic related to the book, such as homelessness. After determining the focus, they choose activities to use at each of the five stages of the reading process. Teachers often jot notes on a chart divided into sections for each stage; then they use the ideas they've brainstormed as they plan the unit. Generally, not all of the activities will be used, but teachers select the most important ones according to their focus and the time available.

Step 4: Differentiate Instruction. Teachers think about the activities they'll use to teach the unit and how to adapt them to ensure that every student will be successful. They decide how to use grouping, tiered activities, centers, and projects to accommodate their students' learning differences.

Step 5: Create a Time Schedule. Teachers create a schedule that provides sufficient time for students to move through the reading process and complete the activities they've planned. They also develop minilessons to teach reading and writing strategies and skills identified in their goals and those needed for students to complete the unit activities. Teachers usually have a set time for minilessons in their weekly schedule, but sometimes they arrange their schedules to provide instruction just before they introduce specific activities or assignments.

Step 6: Assessing Students. Teachers often distribute unit folders in which students keep all their work. Keeping all the materials together makes the unit easier for both students and teachers to manage. Teachers also plan ways to document students' learning and assign grades. One type of record keeping is an assignment checklist, which is developed with students and distributed at the beginning of the literature focus unit. Students keep track of their work during the unit and sometimes negotiate to change the checklist as the unit evolves. They file the lists in their unit folders and mark off each item as it's completed. At the end of the unit, students turn in their assignment checklist and other completed work. Although this list doesn't include every activity students were involved in, it identifies those that will be graded.

Units Featuring a Novel

Teachers develop literature focus units using novels, such as *Bunnicula: A Rabbit-Tale of Mystery* (Howe & Howe, 2006), a hilarious fantasy about a vampire bunny; *The Wednesday Wars* (Schmidt, 2007), a realistic coming-of-age novel; and *Number the Stars* (Lowry, 1998), a story of courage set during World War II. Teachers choose popular and award-winning novels and consider the book's reading level, its instructional value, and the appropriateness of the topic for their students. Figure 10–1 presents a list of recommended novels by grade level, but teachers regularly choose novels at adjacent levels if they're a better fit for their students. Teachers also check that the books they select are included on district- and state-approved lists, especially if they're controversial.

Figure 10–2 presents a 4-week lesson plan for Lowry's *Number the Stars*, a story of friendship and courage set in Nazi-occupied Denmark during World War II. The daily routine during the first 2 weeks is as follows:

Reading. Students and the teacher read two chapters using shared reading.

Responding After Reading. Students participate in a **grand conversation** about the chapters they've read, write in **reading logs**, and add important words to the class **word wall**.

Minilesson. The teacher teaches a **minilesson** on a reading strategy or presents information about World War II or about the author.

More Reading. Students read related books from the text set independently.

The schedule for the last 2 weeks is different. During the third week, students choose a class project (interviewing people who were alive during World War II) and individual projects. They work in teams on activities related to the book and continue to read other books about the war. During the final week, students finish the class interview project and share their completed individual projects.

Units Featuring a Genre

Students learn about a particular genre, such as myths, science fiction, or biographies. They read several books illustrating the genre, participate in a variety of activities to deepen their knowledge about the text factors, and sometimes apply what they've learned through a project. For example, during a genre unit on biographies, fourth graders choose a person to research, read a biography, do more research online, and then write a biography to share what they've learned; or during a poetry unit, sixth graders write poems applying the forms of the poetry they've read.

Units Featuring an Author

During an author study, students learn about an author's life and read one or more books he or she has written. Most authors post websites where they share information about themselves, their books, and how they write, and each year, more authors are writing autobiographies. As students learn about authors, they develop a concept of author; this awareness is important so that students will think of them as real people who eat breakfast, ride bikes, and take out the garbage, just as they do. When students think of authors as real people, they view reading in a more personal way. This awareness also carries over to their own

FIGURE 10–1 ◆ *Novels for Literature Focus Units*

Grade 4

Almond, D. (2001). *Skellig*. New York: Laurel Leaf.

Blume, J. (2007). *Tales of a fourth grade nothing*. New York: Puffin Books.

DiCamillo, K. (2008). *Miraculous journey of Edward Tulane*. New York: Walker.

Gardiner, J. R. (1980). *Stone fox*. New York: HarperTrophy.

King-Smith, D. (2005). *Babe: The gallant pig*. New York: Knopf.

MacLachlan, P. (2004). *Sarah, plain and tall*. New York: HarperTrophy.

Naylor, P. R. (2000). *Shiloh*. New York: Aladdin Books.

O'Connor, B. (2007). *How to steal a dog*. New York: Farrar, Straus & Giroux.

White, E. B. (2006). *Charlotte's web*. New York: HarperCollins.

Grade 5

Coville, B. (2007). *Jeremy Thatcher, dragon hatcher*. San Diego: Harcourt.

Dahl, R. (2007). *Charlie and the chocolate factory*. New York: Puffin Books.

Gantos, J. (2007). *I am not Joey Pigza*. New York: Farrar, Straus & Giroux.

Hale, S. (2009). *Princess academy*. New York: Bloomsbury.

Hiaasen, C. (2002). *Hoot*. New York: Knopf.

Ryan, P. M. (2002). *Esperanza rising*. New York: Scholastic.

Speare, E. G. (1984). *Sign of the beaver*. New York: Yearling.

Spinelli, J. (1999). *Maniac Magee*. Boston: Little, Brown.

Woodson, J. (2002). *Hush*. New York: Putnam.

Grade 6

Babbitt, N. (2007). *Tuck everlasting*. New York: Square Fish.

Creech, S. (2003). *Walk two moons*. New York: HarperTrophy.

George, J. C. (2005). *Julie of the wolves*. New York: HarperTrophy.

L'Engle, M. (2007). *A wrinkle in time*. New York: Square Fish.

Mikaelsen, B. (2001). *Touching Spirit Bear*. New York: HarperCollins.

Patron, S. (2006). *The higher power of Lucky*. New York: Atheneum.

Paulsen, G. (2007). *Hatchet*. New York: Simon & Schuster.

Taylor, M. D. (2001). *Roll of thunder, hear my cry*. New York: Dial Books.

White, R. (2003). *Tadpole*. New York: Farrar, Straus & Giroux.

Grade 7

Avi. (2002). *Crispin: The cross of lead*. New York: Hyperion Books.

Farmer, N. (2002). *The house of the scorpion*. New York: Atheneum.

Levine, G. C. (2006). *Fairest*. New York: HarperCollins.

Lowry, L. (2006). *The giver*. New York: Delacorte.

O'Dell, S. (1987). *Island of the blue dolphins*. New York: HarperTrophy.

Rowling, J. K. (1999). *Harry Potter and the sorcerer's stone*. New York: Scholastic.

Sachar, L. (2008). *Holes*. New York: Farrar, Straus & Giroux.

Schmidt, G. D. (2007). *The Wednesday wars*. New York: Clarion Books.

Taylor, T. (2003). *The cay*. New York: Laurel Leaf.

Grade 8

Avi. (2004). *Nothing but the truth: A documentary novel*. New York: HarperTrophy.

Cooper, S. (2007). *The dark is rising*. New York: Simon & Schuster.

Fleischman, P. (1995). *Bull Run*. New York: HarperCollins.

Kidd, S. M. (2002). *The secret life of bees*. New York: Viking.

Lee, H. (2006). *To kill a mockingbird*. New York: HarperCollins.

Peck, R. N. (1999). *A day no pigs would die*. New York: Knopf.

Pfeffer, S. B. (2006). *Life as we knew it*. Orlando, FL: Harcourt.

Sleator, W. (1995). *Interstellar pig*. New York: Puffin Books.

Wiesel, E. (2006). *Night*. New York: Farrar, Straus & Giroux.

FIGURE 10–2 ◆ A Lesson Plan for Number the Stars

	Monday	Tuesday	Wednesday	Thursday	Friday
Week 1	Build background on World War II The Resistance movement ML: Reading maps of Nazi-occupied Europe Read aloud *The Lily Cupboard*	Introduce NTS Begin word wall Read Ch. 1 & 2 Grand conversation Reading log Add to word wall Book talk on text set	Read Ch. 3 & 4 Grand conversation Reading log Word wall ML: Connecting with a character Read text set books	Read Ch. 5 Grand conversation Reading log Word wall ML: Visualizing Nazis in apartment (use drama)	Read Ch. 6 & 7 Grand conversation Reading log Word wall ML: Information about the author and why she wrote the book
Week 2	Read Ch. 8 & 9 Grand conversation Reading log Word wall ML: Compare home front and war front Read text set books	Read Ch. 10 & 11 Grand conversation Reading log Word wall ML: Visualizing the wake (use drama) ↑	Read Ch. 12 & 13 Grand conversation Reading log Word wall ML: Compare characters – make Venn diagram ↑	Read Ch. 14 & 15 Grand conversation Reading log Word wall ML: Make word maps of key words ↑	Finish book Grand conversation Reading log Word wall ML: Theme of book ↑
Week 3	Plan class interview project Choose individual projects Independent reading/projects ↑	Centers: 1. Story map 2. Word sort 3. Plot profile 4. Quilt ↑	↑	↑	↑
Week 4	Revise interviews Independent reading/projects ↑	↑	Edit interviews Share projects	Make final copies ↑	Compile interview book ↑

Author Study

These sixth graders participate in an author study featuring books by Gary Paulsen. They begin by reading *Hatchet*, a coming-of-age story about a boy who survives alone in the wilderness after a plane crash. Then they read other adventure stories by Gary Paulsen, including two sequels to *Hatchet*. For each book, they participate in grand conversations to discuss the book and write in reading logs. Their teacher also taught them about the contemporary realism genre and helped them analyze the author's writing style. During writing workshop, the students write adventure stories using some of Gary Paulsen's techniques.

writing: Students gain a new perspective as they realize that they, too, can write books. They learn about the writing process that authors use, too.

In the vignette at the beginning of the chapter, Miss Pannicia's students participated in a yearlong author study on Chris Van Allsburg: They read his fantasy picture books, hunted for the picture of the white dog that he includes in every book, and wrote their own fantasy stories based on *The Mysteries of Harris Burdick* (Van Allsburg, 1996). Figure 10–3 presents a list of recommended authors for author studies. Some authors appear in more than one list because they write books that are often used at different grade levels; Jerry Spinelli and Sharon Creech, for instance, are prolific authors who write books that appeal to 10- to 14-year-olds.

FIGURE 10–3 ◆ *Popular Authors for Author Studies*

Fourth–Fifth Grade	*Sixth Grade*	*Seventh–Eighth Grade*
Bruce Coville	Joseph Bruchac	Avi
Sharon Creech	Christopher Paul Curtis	Karen Cushman
Kate DiCamillo	Jack Gantos	Cornelia Funke
Paul Fleischman	Kate Klise	Karen Hesse
Dick King-Smith	Linda Sue Park	S. E. Hinton
Gordon Korman	Gary Paulsen	Jeff Kinney
Patricia MacLachlan	J. K. Rowling	Lois Lowry
Robert Newton Peck	Lemony Snicket	Walter Dean Myers
Pam Muñoz Ryan	Gary Soto	Scott O'Dell
William Steig	Jerry Spinelli	Richard Peck
Jon Scieszka	Mildred Taylor	Louis Sachar
Chris Van Allsburg	Jacqueline Woodson	David Wiesner

Reality Check! Managing Literature Focus Units

Although many teachers love teaching their favorite books in literature focus units, this instructional approach requires them to invest time and energy to plan the unit. Teachers read and analyze the books they've chosen and plan for instruction, including vocabulary activities, minilessons about text factors, and writing assignments. They need to connect what they're teaching to grade-level standards and differentiate instruction so all students can be successful.

Timing is another issue. Teachers usually complete literature focus units in 2 to 4 weeks; rarely, if ever, do the units continue for more than a month. When teachers drag out a unit, they risk killing students' interest in that particular book or, worse yet, their interest in reading. In addition, teachers have to decide how to balance teaching literature with teaching reading, especially if some of their students can't read the books selected for literature focus units. It's essential that struggling students have opportunities to read books at their reading levels every day.

Orchestrating Literature Circles

One of the best ways to nurture students' love of reading and ensure that they become lifelong readers is through literature circles—small, student-led book discussion groups that meet regularly in the classroom (Daniels, 2001). Sometimes literature circles are called *book clubs*. The reading materials are quality trade books, including stories, poems, biographies, and other nonfiction books, and what matters most is that students are reading something that interests them and is manageable. Students choose the books to read and form temporary groups. Next, they set a reading and discussion schedule. Then they read independently or with partners and come together to talk about their reading in discussions that are like grand conversations. Sometimes the teacher meets with the group, and at other times, the group meets independently. A literature circle lasts a week or two, depending on the length of the book.

Key Features of Literature Circles

The three key features of literature circles are choice, literature, and response. As teachers organize for literature circles, they make decisions about these features: They structure the program so that students can make choices about what to read, and they develop a plan for response so that students can think deeply about books they're reading and respond to them.

Choice. Students make many choices in literature circles. They choose the books they'll read and the groups in which they participate. They share in setting the schedule for reading and discussing the book, and they choose the roles they assume in the discussions. They also choose how they'll share the book with classmates. Teachers structure literature circles so that students have these opportunities, but even more important, they prepare students for making choices by creating a community of learners in their classrooms in which students assume responsibility for their learning and can work collaboratively with classmates.

Literature. The books chosen for literature circles should be interesting and at students' reading level. The books must seem manageable to students, especially during their first literature circle experiences. Samway and Whang (1996) recommend choosing shorter books or picture books at first so that students don't become bogged down. It's also important that teachers have read and liked the books because otherwise they won't do convincing book talks to introduce them or contribute meaningfully to the book discussions.

Students typically read fiction during literature circles, but they can also read nonfiction books or nonfiction books paired with stories (Heller, 2006; Stien & Beed, 2004). Students often read nonfiction related to thematic units or biographies during a genre unit. Many fourth graders choose books from the Magic Tree House series of easy-to-read chapter books that features pairs of fiction and nonfiction books, including *Hour of the Olympics* (Osborne, 1998) and *Olympics of Ancient Greece* (Osborne & Boyce, 2004).

Response. Students meet several times during a literature circle to discuss the book because comprehension develops in layers. From an initial comprehension gained through reading, students deepen their understanding through the discussions. They return to the text to reread sentences and paragraphs in order to clarify a point or state an opinion, learn vocabulary, or examine text structure. Gilles (1998) examined students' talk during literature circle discussions and identified four types of talk, which are presented in Figure 10–4.

Karen Smith (1998) describes the discussions her students have as "intensive study," often involving several group meetings. At the first session, students share personal responses. They talk about the characters and events of the story, share favorite parts, and ask questions to clarify confusions. At the end of the first session, students and the teacher decide what they want to study at the next session, such as characters or another element of story structure. Students prepare for the second discussion by rereading excerpts related to the chosen focus. Then, during the second session, students talk about how the author used that element, often making charts and diagrams, such as an **open-mind portrait**, to organize their thoughts.

Students need many opportunities to respond to literature before they'll be successful in literature circles. One of the best ways to prepare students is by reading

---

FIGURE 10–4 ◆ *Types of Talk During Literature Circle Discussions*

Talk About the Book

Students summarize their reading and talk about the book by applying what they've learned about text factors as they do the following:

- Retell events or big ideas
- Examine the theme or genre
- Explore the organizational elements or patterns the author used
- Find examples of literary devices

Talk About Connections

Students make connections between the book and their own lives, the world, and other literature they've read in these ways:

- Explain connections to their lives
- Compare this book to another book
- Make connections to a film or television show they've viewed

Talk About the Reading Process

Students think metacognitively and reflect on the strategies they used to read the book as they do the following:

- Reflect on how they used strategies
- Explain their reading problems and how they solved them
- Identify sections that they reread and why they reread them
- Talk about their thinking as they were reading
- Identify parts they understood or misunderstood

Talk About Group Process and Social Issues

Students use talk to organize the literature circle and maintain the discussion. They also examine social issues and current events related to the book, such as homelessness and divorce, as they do the following:

- Decide who will be group leader
- Determine the schedule, roles, and responsibilities
- Draw in nonparticipating students
- Bring the conversation back to the topic
- Extend the discussion to social issues and current events

FIGURE 10–5 ◆ *Roles Students Play in Literature Circles*

Role	Responsibilities
Discussion Director	The discussion director guides the group's conversation and keeps the group on task. To get the discussion started or to redirect it, the student may ask: • What did the reading make you think of? • What questions do you have about the reading? • What do you predict will happen next?
Passage Master	The passage master focuses on the literary merits of the book. This student chooses several memorable passages to share with the group and tells why each one was chosen.
Word Wizard	The word wizard is responsible for vocabulary. This student identifies four to six important, unfamiliar words from the reading and looks them up in the dictionary. He or she selects the most appropriate meaning and other interesting information about the word to share with the group.
Connector	The connector points out links between the book and the students' lives. These connections might include happenings at school or in the community, current events or historical events from around the world, or something from the connector's own life. Or the connector can make comparisons with other books by the same author or on the same topic.
Summarizer	The summarizer prepares a brief summary of the reading to convey the big ideas to share with the group. This student often begins the discussion by reading the summary aloud.
Illustrator	The illustrator draws a picture or diagram related to the reading. The illustration might relate to a character, an exciting event, or a prediction. The student shares the illustration with the group, and the group talks about it before the illustrator explains it.
Investigator	The investigator locates some information about the book, the author, or a related topic to share with the group. This student may search the Internet, check an encyclopedia or library book, or interview a person with special expertise on the topic.

Adapted from Daniels, 2001; Daniels & Bizar, 1998.

aloud and involving them in **grand conversations** (Peterson & Eeds, 2007). Teachers demonstrate reflective ways to respond and reinforce students' comments when they share their thoughts and talk about their use of comprehension strategies.

Some teachers have students assume roles and complete assignments in preparation for group meetings (Daniels, 2001). One student is the discussion director, and he or she assumes the leadership role and directs the conversation. This student chooses topics and formulates questions to guide the discussion. Other students prepare by selecting a passage to read aloud, drawing a picture or making a diagram related to the book, or investigating a topic connected to the book. The roles are detailed in Figure 10–5. Although having students assume roles may seem artificial, it's an effective way to teach them how to respond in literature circles.

Teachers often prepare assignment sheets for each of the roles their students assume during a literature circle and then pass out copies before students begin reading. Students complete one of the assignment sheets before each discussion. Figure 10–6 shows a "word wizard" assignment sheet that an eighth grader completed as he read *Holes* (Sachar, 2008), the story of a boy named Stanley Yelnats who is falsely sent to a correctional camp where he finds a real friend, a treasure, and a new sense of himself. As word wizard, this student chose important words from the story to study. In the first column on the assignment sheet, he wrote the words and the pages on which they were found. Next, he checked each word's meaning in the dictionary, and in the second column listed several meanings when possible and placed checkmarks next to the appropriate ones. The student also checked the etymology of each word, and in the third column, he listed the language the word came from and when it entered English.

During the discussion about the second section of *Holes*, the word *callused* became important. The word wizard explained that *callused* means "toughened" and "hardened," and that in the story, Stanley and the other boys' hands became callused from digging holes. He continued to say that the third meaning, "unsympathetic," didn't make sense. This comment provided an opportunity for the teacher to explain how *callused* could mean "unsympathetic," and students decided to make a chart to categorize characters in the story who had callused hands and those who were unsympathetic. The group concluded that the boys with callused hands were sympathetic to each other, but the adults at the camp who didn't have callused hands were often unsympathetic—they had callused

---

FIGURE 10–6 ◆ An Eighth Grader's Literature Circle Role Sheet

𝕎𝕠𝕣𝕕 𝕎𝕚𝕫𝕒𝕣𝕕

Name _Ray_   Date _Dec. 7_   Book _Holes_

You are the Word Wizard in this literature circle. Your job is to look for important words in the book and learn about them. Complete this chart before your literature circle meets.

Word and Page Number	Meanings	Etymology
callused p. 80 "his callused hands"	✓ to toughen ✓ to make hard ? unsympathetic	Latin 1565
penetrating p. 82 "a penetrating stare"	? to enter ✓ sharp or piercing	Latin 1520
condemned p. 88 "a condemned man"	✓ found guilty	Latin 1300
writhed p. 91 "his body writhed with pain"	✓ to twist the body in pain	English 900

OVERVIEW OF THE INSTRUCTIONAL APPROACH

Literature Circles

TOPIC	DESCRIPTION
Purpose	To provide students with opportunities for authentic reading and literary analysis.
Components	Students form literature circles to read and discuss books that they choose themselves. They often assume roles to prepare for the book discussion.
Theory Base	Literature circles reflect sociolinguistic, transactive, and critical literacy theories because students work in small, supportive groups to read and discuss books, and the books they read often involve cultural and social issues that require them to think critically.
Applications	Teachers often use literature circles in conjunction with a basal reading program or with literature focus units so students have opportunities to do independent reading and literary analysis.
Strengths	• Books are available at a variety of reading levels. • Students are more strongly motivated because they choose the books they read. • Students have opportunities to work with peers. • Students participate in authentic literacy experiences. • Students learn to respond to literature. • Teachers may participate in discussions to help students clarify misunderstandings and think more critically about the book.
Limitations	• Teachers often feel a loss of control because students are reading different books. • Students must learn to be task oriented and to use time wisely to be successful. • Sometimes students choose books that are either too difficult or too easy.

hearts. Talking about the meaning of a single word—*callused*—led to a new way of looking at the characters.

This instructional approach is effective because it's authentic. As students read and discuss books they've chosen themselves with small groups of peers, they often become more engaged than in teacher-directed approaches. The box above presents an overview of literature circles.

Implementing Literature Circles

The success of literature circles depends on how teachers organize their classrooms and what they've taught students about working collaboratively and about reading and responding to literature. Teachers organize literature circles through a series of steps, beginning with choosing the novels or other books students will read, setting deadlines, and deciding which strategies and skills to teach in minilessons.

Step 1: Choose Books. Teachers prepare text sets with five to seven related titles at students' reading levels and collect six or seven copies of each one. They often consult online book-search systems when they're choosing books; check the New Literacies feature on page 276 to read about Scholastic's Teacher Book Wizard. The teachers give a brief book talk to introduce the books, and students sign up for the one they want to read. Students need time to preview the books and decide which one they want to read. Once in a while, students don't get to read their first choice, but they can always read it another time, either during another literature circle or during reading workshop.

Step 2: Form Literature Circles. Students get together to read each book; usually no more than six students participate in a group. They begin by setting a schedule for reading and discussing the book within the time limits the teacher gives and by choosing discussion roles so that they can prepare for the discussion after reading.

Step 3: Read the Book. Students read part of the book independently or with a partner, depending on the book's difficulty level. Afterward, they prepare for the discussion by completing the assignment for the role they assumed.

Step 4: Participate in a Discussion. Students meet in a literature circle to talk about the book; these **grand conversations** usually last about 30 minutes. The discussion director or another student who has been chosen as the leader begins the discussion, and then peers continue as in any other grand conversation. They take turns sharing responses according to the roles they assumed. The discussion is meaningful because students know how to respond to literature, and they talk about what interests them in the book.

New Literacies

Online Book-Search Systems

The Teacher Book Wizard™ (http://bookwizard. scholastic.com/tbw/homepage.do) is a free book-search system at Scholastic's website. Teachers can search the 50,000 books in its database to locate selections at a student's reading level or determine the reading level of a particular book. There are three ways to access this quick and easy search system:

- **Quick Search.** Teachers search for particular books, themed book lists, or books by an author.
- **Leveled Search.** Teachers customize the search by students' interests, reading level, language (English or Spanish), topic, or genre.
- **BookAlike Search.** Teachers enter a book title to locate similar books at the same reading level or other reading levels.

Teachers can also download the Widget, a free version of the Teacher Book Wizard search system, to their website or their school's homepage and use it to search for books instead of going to the Scholastic website.

The search results present useful information about each book, including its title and author, a photo of the book cover, the book's interest and reading levels, the genre, a summary, and a list of topics related to the book. The reading level is expressed as a grade-level equivalent (e.g., RL 7.2 or seventh grade, second month) and according to both Fountas and Pinnell's levels and Lexile Framework scores. Links are also provided to author information and teaching resources.

The Scholastic website offers a variety of related literature resources for teachers:

- **My Book List.** Teachers make and customize book lists using the results of their Teacher Book Wizard searches.

- **List Exchange.** Teachers join an online community to share their book lists and collect book lists from other teachers.

- **All About Authors.** Teachers locate information about authors, including video clips of author interviews, lists of their books, and ideas and lesson plans for author studies.

- **Teaching With Books.** Teachers search for information about particular books, including lists of vocabulary words, discussion guides, extension activities, and lesson plans.

In addition, a variety of resources for young adolescents are also available at the Scholastic website, including the Flashlight Readers Club, for kids who love books, and Stacks for Kids, with information about books and authors, games, videos, blogs, and message boards.

Step 5: Teach Minilessons. Teachers teach **minilessons** before or after group meetings on a variety of topics related to responding to literature, including asking insightful questions, completing role sheets, using comprehension strategies, and examining text factors (Daniels & Steineke, 2004).

Step 6: Share With the Class. Students in each literature circle share the book they've read with their classmates through a **book talk** or another presentation.

As students participate in literature circles, they're involved in activities representing all five stages of the reading process:

Prereading. Teachers give book talks, and then students choose books to read, form groups, and get ready to read by making schedules and choosing roles.

Reading. Students read the book independently or with a partner, and they prepare for the group meeting.

Responding. Students respond to the book and take responsibility to come to the discussion prepared to participate actively.

Exploring. Students learn vocabulary words, analyze text factors, and participate in other exploring-stage activities as part of their discussions. In addition, teachers teach minilessons to rehearse literature circle procedures, learn comprehension strategies, and examine text factors.

Applying. Students give brief presentations to the class about the books they've read.

As students make choices and move through the reading process, they assume increasingly more responsibility for their own learning.

Reality Check! Managing Literature Circles

When teachers introduce literature circles, they teach students how to participate in small-group discussions and respond to literature. At first, many teachers participate in discussions, but they quickly step back as students become comfortable with the procedures and get engaged in the discussions.

Unfortunately, groups don't always work well. Sometimes conversations get off track because of disruptive behavior, or students monopolize the discussion, hurl insults at peers, or exclude certain students. Clarke and Holwadel (2007) describe an inner-city sixth-grade classroom where literature circles deteriorated because of race, gender, and class tensions. They identified students' negative feelings toward classmates and their limited conversational skills as two problems they could address, and they improved the quality of literature circles in this classroom through these activities:

- **Minilessons.** The teachers taught minilessons to develop more-positive relationships among group members and build more-effective discussion skills, including learning how to listen to each other and take turns when talking (Daniels & Steineke, 2004).
- **Videotapes.** The teachers videotaped students participating in a literature circle and viewed it with group members to make them more aware of how their behavior affected their discussions. They talked about how the discussions went, identified problems, and brainstormed ways to solve them.
- **Books.** The teachers reconsidered the ones they'd chosen and looked for ones that might relate better to students' lives and inspire more-powerful discussions.

These books were especially effective in this classroom: *Sang Spell* (Naylor, 1998), *Hush* (Woodson, 2002), *Slave Dancer* (Fox, 2001), and *Stargirl* (Spinelli, 2004).

- **Coaching.** The teachers became coaches to guide students in becoming more-effective participants. They modeled positive group behavior and appropriate discussion skills and demonstrated how to use their responses to deepen their understanding of a book. At times, they assumed the teacher role to ensure that everyone participated and to keep the discussion on track.

Even though some problems persisted, Clarke and Holwadel improved the quality of their students' literature circles. The classroom environment became more respectful, and students' improved conversation skills transferred to other discussions. And, once students became more successful, their interest in reading increased, too.

Implementing Reading and Writing Workshop

tudents are involved in authentic reading and writing projects during reading and writing workshop. This approach involves three key characteristics: time, choice, and response. First, students have large chunks of time and the opportunity to read and write. Instead of being add-ons for after students finish assignments, reading and writing become the core of the literacy curriculum.

Second, students assume ownership of their learning through self-selection of books they read and their topics for writing. Instead of reading books that the teacher has selected or reading the same book together as a group, students choose the books they want to read, books that are suitable to their interests and reading levels. Usually students choose whatever book they want to read, but sometimes teachers set parameters. For example, during a genre unit on science fiction, teachers ask students to choose a science fiction novel. During writing workshop, students plan their writing projects: They choose topics related to hobbies, thematic units, and other interests, and they also select the genre.

The third characteristic is response. Students respond to books in **reading logs** that they share during conferences with the teacher. They also do book talks to share books they've finished reading with classmates. Similarly, in writing workshop, students share rough drafts they're writing with peers, and they share their published compositions with genuine audiences.

Reading workshop and writing workshop are distinct programs. Reading workshop fosters real reading. Students choose and read many books; it's not unusual for students read 30 to 60 books in a school year. Similarly, writing workshop fosters real writing: Students write 20 to 30 compositions during the year. As they write, students come to see themselves as authors and become interested in learning about the authors of the books they read.

Teachers often use both workshops, or if their schedule doesn't allow, they may alternate the two. Schedules for reading and writing workshop at the fourth-, sixth-, and eighth-grade levels are presented in Figure 10–7.

Reading and writing workshop can be used as the primary instructional approach, or it can be used along with other instructional approaches to provide authentic literacy experiences. This approach is student centered because students make many choices and work independently as they read and write. Providing authentic activities and independent work opportunities reflects the constructivist theory, which emphasizes that learners create their own knowledge through exploration and experimentation.

FIGURE 10–7 ◆ Workshop Schedules

Fourth Grade	
10:30–11:00	Students read self-selected books and respond to them in reading logs.
11:00–11:15	Students share with classmates books they've finished reading and do informal book talks about them. They pass the "good" books to those who want to read them next.
11:15–11:30	The teacher teaches a reading/writing minilesson.
11:30–11:55	The teacher reads aloud and afterward, students participate in a grand conversation.
	—Continued after lunch—
12:45–1:15	Students write independently.
1:15–1:30	Students share their published writings with classmates.
Sixth Grade	
8:20–8:45	The teacher reads aloud a chapter book, and students talk about it in a grand conversation.
8:45–9:30	Students write independently and conference with the teacher.
9:30–9:40	The teacher teaches a reading/writing minilesson.
9:40–10:25	Students read self-selected books independently.
10:25–10:40	Students share published writings and give book talks about books they've read.
Eighth Grade	
	During alternating months, students participate in reading and writing workshop.
1:00–1:45	Students read or write independently.
1:45–2:05	The teacher presents a minilesson on a reading or writing procedure, concept, strategy, or skill.
2:05–2:15	Students share the books they've read or compositions they've published.

Reading Workshop

Nancie Atwell introduced reading workshop in 1987 as an alternative to traditional reading instruction using basal readers and other textbooks. In reading workshop, students read books that they choose themselves and respond to books in **reading logs** and conferences with teachers (Atwell, 1998, 2007). This approach represented a change in what teachers believe about how students learn and how literature should be used in the classroom. Textbook programs emphasize dependence on a teacher's guide to determine how and when strategies and skills are taught, but reading workshop is an individualized program. Atwell developed reading workshop with her seventh and eighth graders, but it's been used successfully at all grade levels. Teachers implement reading workshop in different ways, but it normally involves five components: reading, responding, sharing, teaching minilessons, and reading aloud to students.

Reading. Students spend 30 to 60 minutes independently reading. They choose the books they read, often using recommendations from classmates. They also choose books on favorite topics—horses, science fiction, or World War II, for example—or written by favorite authors, such as Jacqueline Woodson or Louis Sachar. It's crucial

FIGURE 10–8 ◆ *The Goldilocks Strategy*

How to Choose the Best Books for YOU

"Too Easy" Books
1. The book is short.
2. The print is big.
3. You have read the book before.
4. You know all the words in the book.
5. The book has a lot of pictures.
6. You are an expert on this topic.

"Just Right" Books
1. The book looks interesting.
2. You know most of the words.
3. A teacher has read this book aloud to you.
4. You have read other books by this author.
5. There's someone to give you help if you need it.
6. You know something about this topic.

"Too Hard" Books
1. The book is long.
2. The print is small.
3. There aren't many pictures in the book.
4. There are a lot of words that you don't know.
5. There's no one to help you read this book.
6. You don't know much about this topic.

that students be able to read the books they choose. Ohlhausen and Jepsen (1992) developed a strategy for choosing books called the *Goldilocks Strategy*. These teachers created three categories of books—"Too Easy" books, "Too Hard" books, and "Just Right" books—using "The Three Bears" folktale as their model. The books in the "Too Easy" category were those students could read fluently; "Too Hard" books were confusing; and books in the "Just Right" category were interesting, with just a few unfamiliar words. The books in each category vary according to the student's reading level. Figure 10–8 presents a chart about choosing books using the Goldilocks Strategy.

Classroom libraries need to contain literally hundreds of books, including books at a range of reading levels, so that every student can find appropriate books to read. Teachers introduce students—especially reluctant readers—to books so that they can find interesting books to read. The best way to preview books is using a very brief **book talk** where teachers tell a little about the book, show the cover, and perhaps read the first paragraph or two.

Responding. Students usually keep **reading logs** in which they write their initial responses to the books they're reading. Sometimes students dialogue with the teacher about the book they're reading; a journal allows for ongoing written conversation between the teacher and individual students (Atwell, 1998). Responses often demonstrate students' reading strategies and offer insights into their thinking about literature. Seeing how students think about their reading helps teachers guide their learning.

Teachers play an important role in helping students expand and enrich their responses to literature. They collect students' reading logs periodically to monitor their responses. They write back and forth to students; however, because responding is very time-consuming, teachers should write brief responses and not respond to every entry.

Hancock (2007) identified three types of response that students use as they write about novels they're reading: immersion responses, involvement responses, and literary evaluation. The categories and the various patterns that exemplify each one are summarized in Figure 10–9. In most reading log entries, students address several patterns as they reflect on the story and explore their understanding.

In the first category, immersion responses, students indicate whether the book makes sense to them. They draw inferences about characters, offer predictions, ask

FIGURE 10–9 ◆ Response Patterns

Category	Patterns	Description
Immersion Responses	Understanding	Students write about their understanding of characters and plot. Their responses include personal interpretation as well as summarizing.
	Character Introspection	Students share their insights into the feelings and motives of a character. They often begin their comments with "I think . . .".
	Predicting	Students speculate about what will happen and confirm predictions they made previously.
	Questioning	Students ask "I wonder why" questions and write about confusions.
Involvement Responses	Character Identification	Students identify with a character, sometimes writing "If I were _____, I would . . ." They express empathy, share related experiences from their own lives, and give advice to the character.
	Character Assessment	Students judge a character's actions, often using evaluative terms such as "nice" or "dumb."
	Story Involvement	Students reveal their involvement as they express satisfaction with how the story's developing. They comment about wanting to continue reading or use terms such as "disgusting," "weird," or "awesome" to react to sensory aspects of the novel.
Literary Connections	Connections	Students make text-to-self, text-to-world, text-to-text, and text-to-media (TV shows and movies) connections.
	Literary Evaluation	Students evaluate part or all of the book. They offer "I liked/I didn't like" opinions and praise or condemn an author's style.

Adapted from Hancock, 2007.

questions, or discuss confusions. These responses were excerpted from sixth graders' reading logs about *Bunnicula: A Rabbit-Tale of Mystery* (Howe & Howe, 2006):

I think the Monroes will find out what Chester and Harold are doing.

Can a bunny be a vampire? I don't think so. A bunny couldn't suck the blood out of a vegetable. They don't even have blood.

I guess Bunnicula really is a vampire.

I was right! I knew Harold and Chester would try to take care of Bunnicula. What I didn't know was that the Monroes would come home early.

I wonder why the vegetables are turning white. I know it's not Bunnicula but I don't know why.

In the second category, involvement responses, students show that they're personally involved with a character, often giving advice or judging a character's actions. They reveal their own involvement in the story as they express satisfaction with how it's developing. Here are some examples:

I know how Chester and Harold feel. It's like when I got a new baby sister and everyone paid attention to her. I got ignored a lot.

If I were Bunnicula, I'd run away. He's just not safe in that house!

Gross!!! The vegetables are all white and there are two little fang holes in each one.

I just can't stop reading. This book is so cool. And it's funny, too.

In the third category, literary connections, students make connections and evaluate the book. They offer opinions, sometimes saying "I liked . . ." or "I didn't like . . ." and compare the book to others they've read. Here are some examples:

My dog is a lot like Harold. He gets on my bed with me and he loves snacks, but you should never feed a dog chocolate.

This is a great book! I know stuff like this couldn't happen but it would be awesome if it could. It's just fantasy but it's like I believe it.

This book is like <u>Charlotte's Web</u> because the animals can talk and have a whole life that the people don't know about. But the books are different because <u>Bunnicula</u> is much funnier than <u>Charlotte's Web</u>. It made me laugh and <u>Charlotte's Web</u> made me cry.

When students use only a few types of responses, teachers teach minilessons to model the types that students aren't using and ask questions to prompt them to think in new ways about the story they're reading.

Some students write minimal responses. It's important that students choose books that they find personally interesting and that they feel free to share their thoughts, feelings, and questions with a trusted audience—usually the teacher. Sometimes writing entries on a computer and using e-mail to share them with students in another class or with other interested readers will increase students' interest in writing more-elaborated responses.

There's little or no talking as students read and respond because they're engrossed in reading and writing independently. Rarely do students interrupt classmates, go to the rest room, or get drinks of water, except in case of emergency, nor do they use reading workshop time to do homework or catch up on other schoolwork.

Sharing. For the last 15 minutes of reading workshop, the class gathers together to discuss books they've finished reading. Students talk about a book and why they liked it. Sometimes they read a brief excerpt aloud or formally pass the book to a classmate who wants to read it. Sharing is important because it helps students become a community to value and celebrate each other's accomplishments.

Minilessons. Teachers also teach **minilessons** on reading workshop procedures, comprehension strategies, and text factors. Sometimes minilessons are taught to the whole class, but at other times, they're taught to small groups. At the beginning of the school year, teachers teach minilessons to the whole class on choosing books and other reading workshop procedures; later in the year, they teach minilessons on drawing inferences and other comprehension strategies and text factors. Teachers teach minilessons on particular authors when they introduce their books to the class and on literary genres when they set out collections of books representing a genre in the classroom library.

Reading Aloud to Students. Teachers use the **interactive read-aloud** procedure to read books to the class. They choose high-quality literature that students might not be able to read themselves, award-winning books that they believe every student should be exposed to, or books that relate to a thematic unit. After reading, students talk about the book and share the reading experience. This activity is important because students listen to a book read aloud and respond to it together as a community of learners, not as individuals.

Even though reading workshop is different from other instructional approaches, students work through the same five stages of the reading process:

Prereading. Students choose books at their reading level to read, and they activate background knowledge as they look at the cover and think about the title.

Reading. Students read books independently, at their own pace.

Responding. Students talk about the books they're reading during conferences with the teacher, and they often write responses in reading logs.

Exploring. Teachers teach minilessons about text factors, authors, and comprehension strategies.

Applying. Students often give book talks to share the books they've finished reading with classmates.

Sustained Silent Reading Isn't the Same as Reading Workshop. **Sustained Silent Reading** (SSR) is an independent reading time set aside during the school day for students in one class or the entire school to read self-selected books. It's used to increase reading volume and to encourage students to develop the habit of daily reading (Pilgreen, 2000). The goal of both programs is to provide opportunities for students to read self-selected books independently. Both programs work best in classrooms that are communities of learners. It seems obvious that students need to feel relaxed and comfortable in order to read for pleasure, and a community of learners is a place where students do feel comfortable because they're respected and valued.

There are important differences, however. Reading workshop has five components—reading, responding, sharing, teaching minilessons, and reading aloud to students—but SSR has only one—reading. Reading workshop is recognized as an instructional approach because it includes instruction; in contrast, SSR is a supplemental program without an instructional component.

Writing Workshop

Writing workshop is the best way to implement the writing process (Fletcher & Portalupi, 2001). Students write on topics that they choose themselves and assume ownership of their writing and learning. At the same time, the teacher's role changes from provider of knowledge to guide. The classroom becomes a community of writers who write and share their writing.

Students have writing folders where they keep all papers related to the writing project they're working on. They also keep writing notebooks in which they jot down images, impressions, dialogue, and experiences that they can build on for writing projects (Calkins, 1994). Students have access to different kinds of paper, some lined and some unlined, as well as writing instruments, including pencils and red and blue pens. They also have access to the classroom library because students' writing often grows out of books they've read; they may write a sequel to a book or retell a story from a different viewpoint, for example.

As they write, students sit at desks or tables arranged in small groups. The teacher circulates, conferencing briefly with students, and the classroom atmosphere is free enough that students converse quietly with peers and move around to assist each other or share ideas. There's space for students to meet for writing groups, and often a sign-up sheet for writing groups is posted in the classroom. A table is available for the teacher to meet with individual students or small groups for conferences, writing groups, proof-reading, and minilessons.

Writing workshop is a 60- to 90-minute period scheduled each day. During this time, students are involved in three components: writing, sharing, and minilessons. Sometimes a fourth activity, reading aloud to students, is added when it's not used in conjunction with reading workshop. The feature on the next page presents an overview of the workshop approach.

Writing. Students spend 30 to 45 minutes or longer working independently on writing projects. Just as students in reading workshop read at their own pace, in writing workshop, they work independently on writing projects they've chosen themselves. Students move through all five stages of the writing process as they plan, draft, and refine their writing.

Teachers conference with students as they write. Many teachers prefer moving around the classroom to meet with students rather than having students come to a table to meet with them: Too often, a line forms, and students lose precious writing time. Some teachers move around the classroom in a regular pattern, meeting with one fifth of the class each day so that they're sure to conference with everyone during the week.

Other teachers spend the first 15 to 20 minutes of writing workshop stopping briefly to check on 10 or more students. Many use a zigzag pattern to reach all areas of the classroom each day. These teachers often kneel down beside each student, sit on the edge of the student's seat, or carry their own stool around to each student's desk. During the 1- or 2-minute conferences, teachers ask what students are writing, listen to them read a paragraph or two, and ask what they plan to do next. Then these teachers use the remaining time to conference more formally with students who are revising and editing their compositions; they identify strengths in students' writing, ask questions, and discover possibilities during revising conferences. Some teachers like to read the

OVERVIEW OF THE INSTRUCTIONAL APPROACH

Reading and Writing Workshop

TOPIC	DESCRIPTION
Purpose	To provide students with opportunities for authentic reading and writing activities.
Components	Reading workshop involves reading, responding, sharing, teaching minilessons, and reading aloud to students. Writing workshop consists of writing, sharing, and teaching minilessons.
Theory Base	The workshop approach reflects sociolinguistic and information-processing theories because students participate in authentic activities that encourage them to become life-long readers and writers.
Applications	Teachers often use reading workshop in conjunction with a textbook program or with literature focus units so students have opportunities to do independent reading. They often add writing workshop to other instructional approaches so students have more sustained opportunities to use the writing process to develop and refine compositions.
Strengths	• Students read books that are appropriate for their reading levels. • Students are more motivated because they choose the books to read that interest them. • Students work through the stages of the writing process. • Activities are student directed, and students work at their own pace. • Teachers have opportunities to work individually with students during conferences.
Limitations	• Teachers often feel a loss of control because students are reading different books and working at different stages of the writing process. • Teachers have responsibility to teach minilessons on strategies and skills, both in whole-class groups and small groups. • Students must learn to be task oriented and to use time wisely to be successful.

pieces themselves, and others like to listen to students read their papers aloud. As they interact with students, teachers model the kinds of responses that students are learning to give to each other.

Students work with classmates to revise and edit their writing. They share their rough drafts in **writing groups** composed of four or five students. Sometimes teachers join in, but students normally run the groups themselves. They take turns reading their rough drafts to each other and listen as peers offer compliments and suggestions for revision. Students also participate in revising and editing centers. They know how to work at each center and understand the importance of working with classmates to make their writing better.

After proofreading their drafts with a classmate and then meeting with the teacher for final editing, students make the final copy of their writings. They often want to word process their writing so that it looks professional. Many times, students compile their final copies to make books, but sometimes they attach their writing to artwork, make posters, write letters that will be mailed, or perform scripts. Not every piece is necessarily published; sometimes students decide not to continue with a piece of writing, and they file that piece in their writing folders and start something new.

Sharing. For the last 10 to 15 minutes of writing workshop, students share their new publications (Mermelstein, 2007). If an author's chair is available, each student sits in the special chair to read his or her composition aloud. After each sharing, classmates clap and offer compliments. They may also make other comments and suggestions, but the focus is on celebrating completed writing projects, not on revising the composition.

Minilessons. Teachers teach minilessons on writing workshop procedures, the six traits of good writing, and writing strategies and skills, such as organizing ideas, proofreading, and using quotation marks (Fletcher & Portalupi, 2007). Teachers often display an anonymous piece of writing (from a student in another class or from a previous year) for students to read and use it to teach the lesson. Teachers also select excerpts from books students are reading for minilessons to show how published authors use writing strategies and skills. A minilesson on developing paragraphs is presented on the next page.

Writing workshop is the best way for students to apply the writing process. Students move through the five stages as they plan, draft, revise, edit, and, finally, publish their writing:

Prewriting. Students choose topics and set their own purposes for writing. Then they gather and organize ideas, often making graphic organizers or talking out their ideas with classmates.

Drafting. Students work independently to write rough drafts using the ideas they developed during prewriting.

Revising. Students participate in writing groups to share their rough drafts and get feedback to help them revise their writing.

Editing. Students work with peers to proofread and correct mechanical errors in their writing, and they also meet with the teacher for a final editing.

Publishing. Students prepare a final copy of their writing, and they sit in the author's chair to share it with classmates.

As students participate in writing workshop, they gain valuable experience using the writing process.

Reality Check! Managing a Workshop Classroom

It takes time to implement the workshop approach because students have to develop new ways of working and learning, and they have to form a learning community (Gillet & Beverly, 2001). For reading workshop, students need to know how to select books and other reading workshop procedures, and for writing workshop, they need to know how to use the writing process to develop and refine a piece of writing and other writing workshop procedures. Sometimes students complain that they don't know what to write about, but in time, they learn how to brainstorm possible topics.

Teachers develop a schedule for reading and writing workshop with time allocated for each component, as was shown in Figure 10–7. In their schedules, teachers allot as much time as possible for students to read and write. After developing the schedule, teachers post it in the classroom and talk with students about the activities and their expectations. They teach the workshop procedures and continue to model them until students become comfortable with the routines. As students gain experience with the workshop approach, their enthusiasm grows, and the workshop approach is successful.

Minilesson

TOPIC: *Writing Well-Developed Paragraphs*
GRADE: *Sixth Grade*
TIME: *20 minutes*

Ms. Hodas's sixth graders have been researching inventions, and now they're writing reports about the ones they've studied—superglue, air bags, and crossword puzzles, for example. The students are using the writing process to craft their reports. They've organized ideas and written rough drafts; now they're meeting in writing groups. Ms. Hodas notices that many students aren't crafting strong middle paragraphs, so she gets the class together for a minilesson on developing paragraphs. The students bring their rough drafts with them.

❶ Introduce the Topic

Ms. Hodas asks, "What do you remember about paragraphs?" Students talk about organizing ideas into paragraphs, keeping to one topic, using a topic sentence, and adding details to develop the topic. The teacher is pleased that students remember what she's taught them about paragraphing, and she refers them to the chart on paragraphs posted in the classroom that they created months ago.

❷ Share Examples

The teacher asks students to reread their rough drafts to themselves. Afterward, she has them mark their middle paragraphs. "Today we're going to focus on your middle paragraphs," she explains. "What's special about these paragraphs?" Tori explains, "I have four middle paragraphs, and each one tells one idea about superglue." Grant continues, "I add details so my ideas are complete." "I did that too," Amber agrees. "For my details, I have some examples and some facts." Keifer read one of the middle paragraphs in his report on the computer mouse, and the students pick out the topic sentence and the detail sentences.

❸ Provide Information

Next, Ms. Hodas asks students to read their paragraphs aloud. Simona reads aloud her well-developed middle paragraphs about velcro, and students pick out the topic sentences and the detail sentences. Next, William reads aloud his middle paragraphs about the invention of the helicopter, and students pick out the components. His third and fourth paragraphs aren't complete, so students offer suggestions on how he might develop them.

❹ Guide Practice

The students divide into pairs to share their rough drafts. They read to their paragraphs to each other, and when they find they aren't well developed, they jot revision ideas on self-stick notes. The teacher moves among the groups, listening and offering suggestions. After everyone has shared, Ms. Hodas asks students to raise their hands to indicate who needs more time to revise and who needs more assistance.

❺ Assess Learning

Ms. Hodas invites students who want more assistance revising their paragraphs to meet with her at the conferencing table while other students return to their desks.

Assessment Tools

"Status of the Class" Chart

Names	Dates 3/15	3/16	3/17	3/18	3/19	3/22	3/23	3/24
Antonio	4	5	5	5	5	1	1	1 2
Bella	2	2	2 3	2	2	4	5	5
Charles	3	3 1	1	2	2 3	4	5	5
Dina	4 5	5	5	1	1	1	1	2 3
Dustin	3	3	4	4	4	5	5 1	1
Eddie	2 3	2	2 4	5	5	1	1 2	2 3
Elizabeth	2	3	3	4	4	4 5	5	1 2
Elsa	1 2	3 4	4 5	5	5	1	2	2

Code: 1 = Prewriting   2 = Drafting   3 = Revising   4 = Editing   5 = Publishing

Many teachers use a classroom chart, which Nancie Atwell (1998) calls "status of the class," to monitor students' work. At the beginning of reading workshop, students (or the teacher) record what book they're reading or if they're writing in a reading log, waiting to conference with the teacher, or browsing in the classroom library. For writing workshop, students identify the stage of the writing process they're involved in. An excerpt from a writing workshop chart is shown above. Teachers can also use the chart to award weekly "effort" grades or to have students request a conference.

Teachers take time during reading and writing workshop to observe students as they work together in small groups. Some students exclude others from group activities because of gender, ethnicity, or socioeconomic status; the socialization patterns in classrooms seem to reflect society's. If teachers see instances of discrimination, they should confront the situation directly and continue to work to foster a nurturing classroom environment.

Many teachers fear that when they implement the workshop approach, students' scores on high-stakes achievement tests will decline, even though teachers have reported either an increase in test scores or no change at all. Swift (1993) reported the results of a yearlong study comparing two groups of her students; one group read basal reader selections, and the other participated in reading workshop. The reading workshop group showed significantly greater improvement, and Swift also reported that students participating in reading workshop showed more-positive attitudes toward reading.

CHAPTER 10

How Effective Teachers Teach With Trade Books

▶ Teachers use a combination of instructional approaches to provide effective literacy instruction because they understand that no one approach is a complete program.

▶ Teachers present literature focus units to share award-winning books and teach literary analysis.

▶ Teachers incorporate choice, literature, and response into literature circles.

▶ Teachers provide opportunities for students to read self-selected books during reading workshop and write on self-selected topics during writing workshop.

CHAPTER 11

Teaching With Textbooks

Seventh Graders Read About the Vietnam War

The seventh graders in Ms. Williams's first-period class are reading literature about "The Legacy of the Vietnam War" in Holt McDougal's *Language of Literature* (2009) textbook. To introduce the unit, Ms. Williams reads aloud *Patrol* (Myers, 2005), a book-length poem that evokes the experiences of a young soldier. Her students, who were born nearly 25 years after Saigon fell, are unfamiliar with that war, except for Diamond, Paloma, and Bryan, whose grandfathers fought in Vietnam. In contrast, everyone knows about the military operations in Iraq and Afghanistan and talk about combat troops, insurgents, casualties, public opinion, and media coverage. Aden explains how the War on Terror led to our involvement there. Then Chase asks, "Is that how America got sucked into the Vietnam War, too?" Ms. Williams explains that Americans' worry about the spread of Communism in Asia led to the "domino theory."

Next, Ms. Williams distributes copies of *Vietnam War* (DK Publishing, 2005), a nonfiction book with detailed color photos accompanied by brief explanations, for students to examine with partners or in small groups. The students read and talk while Ms. Williams circulates around the classroom, listening to Blake and Shawn examine a photo of a Chinook helicopter, Diamond's group discuss Agent Orange, and Kelsey and Paloma read about the Viet Cong. Bryan stops her to ask if the DMZ is the same as the Green Zone in Baghdad.

The students read four selections in their language arts textbook during the 2-week unit:

- "Zebra," a short story about boy who learns a powerful lesson from a Vietnam vet
- "The Collected Grief of a Nation," a feature article about an exhibition of mementos left at the Vietnam Veterans Memorial
- "A Mother's Words," the letter that Eleanor Wimbish wrote to her son on the 15th anniversary of his death and left at the Wall
- "Timeline: U.S. Involvement in Vietnam," a chronology comparing war-related events in the United States and Vietnam from 1950 to 1995

The textbook directs teachers to focus on standards addressing characterization, nonfiction genres, summarization, and verb tenses as students read these selections.

Ms. Williams introduces "Zebra" and previews the new vocabulary, including *grimace, intricate, disciplinarian, gaunt, jauntily, chafe,* and *contour*. They read the first two pages about a runner nicknamed Zebra, who's hurt in an accident. The story doesn't tell how he's injured, but the students infer that he was hit by a car. After the accident, Zebra is shy and insecure. The students talk about Zebra's changes and wonder how this story relates to the Vietnam War. They continue reading, and learn that Zebra meets Mr. Wilson, who's picking junk out of trashcans. Mr. Wilson tells Zebra that he's interested in teaching a summer-school art class. The students speculate that he's a Vietnam vet when they read that he has only one arm and wears an old army jacket. Zebra attends Mr. Wilson's summer art class, and Mr. Wilson teaches him to draw and to imagine a different life for himself.

After they finish reading, Ms. Williams focuses on character analysis. The students identify the two main characters—Zebra and Mr. Wilson—and examine their thoughts, words, and actions to determine whether they're static or dynamic characters. They do a close reading of two brief passages to analyze the characters. Then Paloma blurts out, "Now I get it! It was Zebra—not Mr. Wilson—who changed. He's the dynamic character." "Zebra used to run all the time, but he stopped when he got hit," Blake continues, "but that's not his biggest change." Aden completes the idea: "He was feeling sorry for himself, and I don't blame him for that, but Mr. Wilson showed him how to imagine a happier life." "And now he's a 'pleasant life form'—that's what Andrea says at the end of the story," Cristal adds. As their lesson ends, Diamond draws everyone's attention back to the first page of the unit, and exclaims, "Look at what it says here about injuries to the body and the spirit. That's Zebra! This story is about how Mr. Wilson helped Zebra heal his body and his spirit."

The next day, Ms. Williams reviews vocabulary from the story, and the students complete a vocabulary practice activity in the textbook before they reread the story independently. Afterward, the students participate in a **word sort** using words from the story. Working in small groups, the students sort a pack of word cards into categories and write the category labels on additional cards. Ms. Williams also reviews the information on verb tenses on page 207, and then students complete the grammar exercises at the bottom of the page.

One morning, Joe, one of the school's custodians, stops by to thank Ms. Williams for increasing the students' awareness about the Vietnam War. He's noticed the bulletin board display in the classroom and overheard the seventh graders talking in the lunch room. As soon as he explains that he's a Vietnam vet, Ms. Williams invites him to share his experiences with the students. The following day, Joe arrives slightly nervous but dignified in his old uniform. He talks quietly about his memories and answers most of their questions, but when he's asked whether he ever killed anyone, he responds, "I'm not comfortable answering that." Joe's visit heightens everyone's interest in the unit, but more importantly, Ms. Williams notices that the students are treating Joe with greater respect now.

Ms. Williams uses these three websites to introduce the Vietnam Veterans Memorial before students read the second and third selections in the unit:

The Vietnam Veterans Memorial Wall, at http://thewall-usa.com

Vietnam Women's Memorial, at www.vietnamwomensmemorial.org

The Virtual Wall, at www.thevirtualwall.org

She accesses these websites on her computer and displays them on a large wall screen using a digital projector. The students pay close attention as she navigates the websites; they examine video footage and photos of the Vietnam Veterans Memorial—the Wall, the statue The Three Servicemen, and the Vietnam Women's Memorial. Next, Ms. Williams sets out an Army helmet filled with objects like those that people leave at the Vietnam Veterans Memorial, including her dad's dog tags, insignia from his uniform, the rabbit's foot he carried, a dog-eared black-and-white photo of her dad and another soldier who was his friend, and a small American flag with a poem attached, like the one she and her dad left near his friend's name at the Wall.

Ms. Williams explains that "The Collected Grief of a Nation" is a feature article about an exhibit of mementos from the Vietnam Wall. The class previews the three-page article and examines photos of items left at the Wall. While students follow along in their textbooks, Ms. Williams reads aloud the first 25 lines of the article; then she asks which sentence states the most important idea in this section. Students conclude that "a collection of war memorabilia unlike any other" (p. 209) is the most important idea. They continue reading the article independently or with partners, stopping three more times to choose the sentence that sums up the most important idea in that section. In the article, the Wall is described as "a black gash," "a mirror of America," "a bulletin board," and "a protest site." Ms. Williams makes a chart with four columns, as shown on the next page, as they talk about these descriptors and infer their meaning.

The next day, students read the two-page letter, "A Mother's Words." They read silently while Ms. Williams passes out tissues; almost everyone in the classroom is choked up by the mother's heart-wrenching words. After sharing their reactions, Ms. Williams reviews summarizing, and following the directions in the textbook, students reread the letter to identify the main ideas and write summaries of the mother's message.

The last selection in the unit is a timeline of American involvement in Vietnam. Ms. Williams has the students work in small groups to preview the one-page chart and decide how to read it. They notice that it's formatted in two columns and that the decades from the 1950s to the 1990s are marked on the left edge of the chart. They read the timeline and then talk about how it helps them deepen their understanding of the feature article they read several days earlier.

Ms. Williams supplements the textbook with a text set of books about the Vietnam War, including *Fallen Angels* (Myers, 2008), *The Wednesday Wars* (Schmidt,

An Inference Chart About the Vietnam Veterans Memorial Wall

A Black Gash	A Mirror of America	A Bulletin Board	A Protest Site
The Vietnam War was extremely controversial. Some people believed in it, but others marched in protest and refused to go there and fight. It was like America had a serious wound in its heart.	The black granite wall is shiny like a mirror, and it reflects the diversity of people in our country. It also reflects our different beliefs, hopes, and dreams. We're different but we're all Americans.	Families and friends leave letters, photos, and other mementos to express their grief. The wall is like a bulletin board because people leave messages there for the soldiers who have died.	The wall lists the names of all the soldiers who died. It's a tribute to the heroes, but it's warning about the terrible price of war: sacrifice and suffering. People should stop and think before they go to war again.

2007), *10,000 Days of Thunder: A History of the Vietnam War* (Caputo, 2005), *Cracker! The Best Dog in Vietnam* (Kadohata, 2008), *The Things They Carried* (O'Brien, 1998), and *Escape From Saigon: How a Vietnam War Orphan Became an American Boy* (Warren, 2008). She has several copies of each book, and students choose one to read outside of class.

To bring closure to the unit, Ms. Williams reminds students that this unit was about "The Legacy of the Vietnam War." She writes the word *legacy* on the whiteboard and asks, "What does *legacy* mean?" Aden suggests, " I think legacy of war is the message from the soldiers who fought and sometimes died." Cristal adds, "And, it's what we've learned about heroism and sacrifice." Ms. Williams suggests that they create a legacy wall, and students work individually and with partners to create posters with sentences from the selections they read, well-known quotes about war, and their own expressions to place on the wall. Then Chase and Kelsey arrange some of the sentences to create this found poem:

> I salute the soldiers. They are true heroes.
>
> I will be a soldier; I will go proudly.
>
> When a soldier dies, his mother's heart breaks.
>
> You never should have been the one to die.
>
> Is war ever necessary?
>
> Without war, there will be no freedom.
>
> There's never been a good war or a bad peace.
>
> There is so much pain left from the Vietnam War.
>
> I hate war; I love peace.

Ms. Williams teaches two other seventh-grade language arts classes, and Joe visits both of them, too. One class is for students reading 2 to 3 years below grade level; she teaches the unit using the easier version of the textbook that was designed for struggling readers, with simplified language and shorter selections. The same literacy standards are addressed, and students participate in the same activities and assignments, but Ms. Williams provides more support.

Her other language arts class is for students reading more than 3 years below grade level; the reading levels of the 19 students in that class range from 2.5 to 3.8. Ms. Williams reads aloud *Cracker! The Best Dog in Vietnam* (Kadohata, 2008), a novel about a canine unit that helps soldiers sniff out booby traps, to build the students' background knowledge about the Vietnam War and interest them in the selections they'll read. Next, in **guided reading** groups the students read *The Wall* (Bunting, 1999), a picture-book story about a boy and his dad who visit the Vietnam Veterans Memorial, and *The Vietnam Veterans Memorial* (Schaefer, 2005), a nonfiction book about the Memorial Wall, The Three Servicemen, and the Vietnam Women's Memorial in Washington, DC. These books are written at the third-grade reading level, and the students can read them with Ms. Williams's assistance. She uses them to teach vocabulary, reading strategies, and the grade-level standards. Finally, she uses shared reading to expose students to the three selections in the *Language of Literature* textbook.

Textbook programs have been a staple of middle-grade literacy instruction for generations. These research-based instructional programs are tied to grade-level literacy standards. Fiction and nonfiction selections are presented in grade-level textbooks, and instruction on vocabulary, comprehension, grammar, literature, and writing topics is linked to each selection. Workbooks, online materials, and supplemental books are included, and sometimes separate textbooks for struggling readers and English learners are also available.

Teachers usually have strong feelings about textbooks: They either love or hate them. Advocates highlight these benefits:

- Instructional materials and lesson plans are supplied, which makes the teacher's job easier.
- The instructional program is closely aligned with grade-level reading and writing standards.
- Strategies and skills are clearly identified to make them easier to teach, test, and reteach.
- Students are prepared for high-stakes achievement tests because instruction focuses on grade-level standards.
- These programs are especially beneficial for inexperienced teachers who are less familiar with state standards and grade-level instructional materials and procedures.

What some people tout as benefits, however, others criticize as drawbacks. Detractors argue these points:

- The instructional materials in textbook programs are less authentic than trade books.
- Students aren't as engaged reading textbook selections as they are reading trade books.

- Textbook programs don't produce in-depth learning or an appreciation of literature.
- Instruction focuses on teaching isolated strategies and skills.
- Students often spend more time completing worksheets than reading.
- Textbooks aren't appropriate for all students.

Despite these criticisms, many teachers like Ms. Williams use textbooks as part of their literacy programs.

Basal Reading Programs

ommercial reading programs, commonly called *basal readers*, have been a staple in elementary-grade reading instruction for 150 years. Before 1850, William Holmes McGuffey wrote the McGuffey Readers, the first textbooks published with increasingly challenging reading materials designed for each grade level. The lessons featured literature selections that emphasized religious and patriotic values. Students applied phonics skills to decode words, studied vocabulary words in the context of stories, and practiced proper enunciation as they read aloud to the class. These books were widely used until the beginning of the 20th century. The Scott Foresman basal reading program, introduced in 1930 and used through the 1960s, is probably the most famous; the first-grade textbooks featured stories about two children named Dick and Jane; their little sister, Sally; their pets, Puff and Spot; and their parents. The first-grade books relied on the repetition of words through contrived sentences such as "See Jane. See Sally. See Jane and Sally." to teach words. Students were expected to memorize words rather than use phonics to decode them; this whole-word method was known as "look and say." The Scott Foresman program has been criticized for its lack of phonics instruction as well as for centering stories on an "ideal" middle-class white family.

Today's basal readers for kindergarten through sixth grade include more-authentic literature selections that celebrate diverse cultures, and emphasize an organized presentation of strategies and skills, especially phonics in the primary grades. Walsh (2003) reviewed five widely used series and found that they all provide visually stimulating artwork to engage students, similar methods of teaching decoding and comprehension, and teacher's guides with detailed lesson plans. She also uncovered a common problem: None of the programs provided for the sustained development of students' background knowledge, even though teachers know that beginning in fourth grade, if students don't develop a strong foundation of world and word knowledge, they have difficulty reading and understanding more conceptually demanding books. This drop in achievement is known as the "fourth-grade slump," and students from economically disadvantaged families are more likely to fall behind their classmates (Chall, Jacobs, & Baldwin, 1991).

Publishers of basal reading textbooks, including Harcourt, Houghton Mifflin, McGraw-Hill, and Scott Foresman, tout their products as complete literacy programs containing all the materials needed for literacy instruction. The accessibility of reading materials is one advantage: Teachers have copies of grade-level textbooks for every student. Another plus is that the instructional program is already planned; teachers follow step-by-step directions to teach strategies and skills and assign practice materials found in workbooks that accompany the textbook. It's unrealistic, however, to assume that any commercial reading program could be a complete literacy program. Students who read above or below grade level need reading materials at their level. In addition, students need many more opportunities to listen to books read aloud and to read and reread books than are provided in a basal reading program. In addition, a complete literacy program involves more than reading; students also need opportunities to learn the writing process, draft and refine compositions, and learn writing strategies and skills. An overview of basal reading programs is presented below.

Components of Basal Reading Programs

A number of commercial reading programs are available today, and most have these components:

- Selections in grade-level textbooks
- Instruction on word identification, vocabulary, comprehension, writing, grammar, and spelling

OVERVIEW OF THE INSTRUCTIONAL APPROACH

Basal Reading Programs

TOPIC	DESCRIPTION
Purpose	To teach the strategies and skills that successful readers need using an organized program that includes grade-level reading selections, workbook practice assignments, and frequent testing.
Components	Basal reading programs include selections in a grade-level textbook; instruction on strategies and skills aligned with state literacy standards; workbook assignments; related vocabulary, grammar, and spelling activities; supplemental books for independent reading; and a management plan that incorporates differentiation and ongoing assessment.
Theory Base	Basal reading programs are teacher centered and reflect behaviorism because teachers provide explicit instruction and students are typically passive rather than active learners.
Applications	Instruction is organized into units with weeklong lessons that include reading, strategy and skill instruction, and workbook activities. Basal readers should be used with other instructional approaches to ensure that students read books at their instructional levels and have opportunities to participate in authentic writing projects.
Strengths	• Textbooks are aligned with grade-level literacy standards. • Teachers teach strategies and skills in a sequential program. • The teacher's guide provides detailed instructions for teaching reading. • A variety of assessment tools are included in the program. • A lesson planner and other resources are available online.
Limitations	• Selections are too difficult for some students and too easy for others. • Many selections lack the authenticity of good literature. • Programs include too many workbook assignments. • Most instruction is presented to the whole class.

- Workbook assignments
- Materials for independent reading
- Assessment tools for monitoring student achievement

Basal readers are recognized for their strong skills component: Teachers teach skills in a predetermined sequence, and students apply the skills as they read textbook selections and complete workbook assignments.

Selections in Grade-Level Textbooks. Basal reading programs are organized into units on topics such as challenges and tall tales. A unit consists of four to six weeklong lessons, each with a featured selection. Many of the selections were originally published as picture books or chapters in novels. Everyone reads the same selections in the grade-level textbook, no matter their reading level. These commercial programs argue that it's important to expose all students to grade-level instruction because over the years, some students, especially those from minority groups, have been denied equal access to instruction. The teacher's guide provides suggestions for supporting struggling readers and English learners. Many programs also have audio and online resources. Audiotapes of the selections, which teachers often play as students follow along in their copies of the textbook, are an especially useful resource. After this shared reading experience, some less successful readers can then read the selection, but many teachers complain that a few students can't read the selections no matter how much support they provide.

Instruction. Teachers use basal reading programs to deliver explicit and systematic instruction that's aligned with state literacy standards. Most textbooks include instruction on word identification, vocabulary, comprehension, spelling, grammar, and writing mechanics (capitalization and punctuation). The programs also emphasize comprehension strategies, such as evaluating, monitoring, predicting, questioning, summarizing, and visualizing. These programs claim that it's their explicit, systematic instruction that ensures success.

Workbook Assignments. Students complete workbook pages before and after reading a selection to reinforce instruction; 10 to 12 workbook pages typically accompany each one. On these pages, students write words and sentences, match words and sentences, and complete graphic organizers as they apply the concepts, strategies, and skills they're learning. Teachers vary how they assign the workbook pages. Once students know how to complete a workbook page, such as the ones that focus on practicing spelling words, they work independently or with partners. However, for more-challenging assignments, such as those dealing with comprehension strategies or newly introduced skills, teachers guide students as the whole class works together. Teachers also devise various approaches for monitoring students' completion of workbook assignments: Sometimes students review their own work or have classmates check their work; at other times, teachers grade the assignments.

Materials for Independent Reading. Most basal reading programs include a collection of easy, grade-level, and advanced paperback books for students to read independently. The collections contain both fiction and nonfiction books that are related to unit themes, and they're intended to meet the needs of all students, but sometimes teachers still must supplement with much easier books for English learners or struggling readers.

Assessment Tools. Basal reading programs provide a battery of tests that are aligned with state literacy standards. The tests include selection tests, unit tests, skills tests, and spelling tests that teachers administer to track students' achievement, diagnose reading problems, and report to parents and administrators. Increasingly, basal reading programs are using Web-based testing and reporting systems where teachers retrieve tests from the program's online test library and generate customized tests. Students can take these tests online, and teachers receive immediate results pinpointing standards that students have mastered and those requiring reteaching.

Program Materials

At the center of a basal reading program is the student textbook. It's colorful and inviting, often featuring pictures of exciting adventures and fanciful locations on the cover. The selections are grouped into units, and each unit includes stories, poems, and nonfiction articles. Many multicultural selections have been added, and illustrations usually feature ethnically diverse people. Information about authors and illustrators is provided for many selections. Textbooks contain a table of contents and a glossary.

Commercial reading programs provide a wide variety of materials to support student learning. Consumable workbooks are well known; students write words and sentences in these books to practice word-identification, vocabulary, comprehension, writing, spelling, and test-taking skills. Black-line masters of parent letters are also available. Multimedia materials for students such as audio CDs, DVDs, and online resources are included, and some programs have online versions of their textbooks; teachers often use these materials at computer centers. Collections of paperback books coordinated with unit topics provide supplemental reading materials, and usually include books for grade-level readers as well as struggling and advanced students.

Teachers receive multiple management tools with basal reading programs. The teacher's guidebook is an oversize instructional manual that provides comprehensive information about how to plan lessons, teach the selections, differentiate instruction, and assess students' achievement. The selections are shown in reduced size in the guidebook, and background information about the selection, instructions for reading the selection, and ideas for coordinating skill and strategy instruction are included. Online lesson planners are available that teachers download and use to develop schedules, organize instruction, and coordinate their lessons with state standards. Most programs include a variety of handbooks to provide more in-depth information about differentiating instruction to meet students' needs, strengthening home–school connections, using literacy centers, teaching test-taking strategies and skills, and teaching and assessing writing. In addition, basal reading programs provide in-service training on how to teach with basal readers and other literacy topics. Figure 11–1 summarizes the materials usually available in basal reading programs.

Basal Readers and the Reading Process

Teachers employ the reading process when they implement basal reading textbooks, even though many activities are different than in trade book approaches:

Prereading. Teachers follow directions in the teacher's guide to activate and build students' background knowledge, introduce vocabulary, teach word-identification and comprehension strategies, and preview the selection.

FIGURE 11–1 ◆ Materials in Basal Reading Programs

Material	Description
Textbook	The student's grade-level book of thematically arranged fiction and nonfiction reading selections. Some of the selections were originally published as award-winning trade books.
Supplemental Books	Collections of paperback trade books for each grade level that are related to unit themes and include a variety of easy, grade-level, and advanced books.
Workbook	A consumable practice book with word-identification, vocabulary, comprehension, spelling, grammar, writing, and test-taking worksheets that are coordinated with reading selections and the strategies and skills being taught.
Teacher's Guide	An oversize book with comprehensive information about how to teach reading using the basal reading program. Suggestions for differentiating instruction, correlations with grade-level standards, and assessment options are provided.
Assessment System	An online testing and reporting system with a library of standards-based tests to monitor student achievement, diagnose problems, and report to parents and administrators.
Multimedia Resources	Audio, visual, and digital materials for students and teachers, including CDs of selections, information and updates on the textbook's website, Internet links, and online assessments.
Handbooks	Instructional guides for teachers on an assortment of topics, such as assessment, differentiation, home–school connections, literacy centers, test-taking strategies, and writing.
Lesson Planner	An online management tool that teachers download to use in planning for instruction and aligning lessons with state literacy standards.
Home–School Connections	Resources to strengthen home–school partnerships, including newsletters in English, Spanish, and several other languages.
Staff Development	In-service training to prepare teachers to use the basal reading program and special institutes on topics such as comprehension, rubrics, and literacy coaches.

Check the Compendium of Instructional Procedures, which follows Chapter 12, for more information on the highlighted terms.

Reading. Students read the selection independently, but if it's too difficult, teachers read it aloud or play an audiotape before students read it themselves.

Responding. Teachers follow directions in the teacher's guide to enhance students' comprehension by asking questions about the author's purpose, modeling **think-alouds**, encouraging students to draw inferences, and summarizing the selection. Students also complete workbook assignments that focus on comprehension.

Exploring. Teachers teach word analysis, spelling, and grammar skills, and students practice the skills by completing workbook assignments. They also teach students about authors, genres, and text structures.

Applying. Students read related selections in the basal reader or in supplemental books that accompany the program and participate in writing activities related to the selection or genre being studied.

One of the most striking differences is that students complete practice activities in workbooks during several of the stages rather than applying what they're learning in more-authentic ways.

Reality Check! Managing a Basal Reading Program

Teachers use online lesson planners to plan instruction and coordinate their lessons with grade-level literacy standards, and the teacher's guide offers suggestions for pacing for each unit, ideas for flexible grouping, and ongoing monitoring of student achievement. A variety of assessment tools, including end-of-lesson and end-of-unit tests and writing rubrics, are included. Teachers are encouraged to assess students' learning regularly to monitor their progress and to evaluate the effectiveness of the instructional program. Publishers also provide in-service training to show teachers how to use the basal reading program and special institutes and workshops on differentiation and other literacy topics.

Language Arts Textbooks

The literacy textbooks used in grades 6 through 8 are called *language arts textbooks* or, sometimes, *literature anthologies*. Publishers tout these textbooks as comprehensive programs containing a complete set of instructional materials. Prentice Hall, Holt, Glencoe, and other publishers of these programs advertise that their textbooks offer high-quality classic and contemporary literature selections and provide a solid foundation in grammar, reading, and writing strategies and skills that are aligned with grade-level standards. They assert that their textbooks reach all students, prepare them to do well on high-stakes achievement tests, and are easy to implement. The feature on the next page presents an overview of this instructional program.

Components of Language Arts Textbook Programs

Language arts textbook programs are similar to basal reading textbooks, and they usually include these components:

OVERVIEW OF THE INSTRUCTIONAL APPROACH

Language Arts Textbooks

TOPIC	DESCRIPTION
Purpose	To ensure sixth- through eighth-grade students' mastery of state literacy standards and to foster a love of literature using grade-level textbooks that contain short stories, excerpts from novels, feature articles and other nonfiction selections, and poems.
Components	Grade-level textbooks organized into units; instruction on literary analysis, writing, spelling, and grammar; and electronic and adapted textbooks available for struggling readers and English learners.
Theory Base	Like basal reading programs, language arts textbooks are teacher centered and represent behaviorism.
Applications	Instruction is organized into units with weeklong lessons that include reading literature and instruction on topics related to grade-level standards. Textbooks should be used with other instructional approaches so that students have opportunities to read literature at their own reading levels and to participate in authentic writing projects.
Strengths	• Instruction is aligned with grade-level standards. • Classic and contemporary literature selections are included in the textbook. • Differentiation is possible using alternative versions of the textbook for struggling readers and English learners. • The teacher's guide provides detailed instructions for reading selections and teaching strategies and skills. • Online lesson planner and assessment tools are provided.
Limitations	• Selections are too difficult for some students and too easy for others. • Programs overemphasize grammar and writing skills. • Most instruction is presented to the whole class. • Programs emphasize broad coverage of topics rather than in-depth learning.

- Literature selections in grade-level textbooks
- Instruction on literary analysis, grammar, and writing
- Online resources for students and teachers
- Assessment tools for monitoring student achievement

In addition, publishers claim that textbooks having these components will reduce teachers' workload and save valuable time.

Literature. Literature is the heart of middle school language arts textbook programs. The selections are organized into units and represent fiction, nonfiction, poetry, drama, and functional genres. The functional genre is new; students read "real world" texts such as recipes, nutrition labels, road maps, first aid instructions, and advertisements to follow directions, gain information, and use references. Figure 11–2 presents an overview of the genres. As students read and respond to these selections, they learn how to analyze and interpret literature and expand their knowledge about genres and other text factors.

Some literature selections were written by classic authors and others by contemporary writers. Classic authors include Edgar Allan Poe, Jack London, and Carl Sandburg, and their works have appeared in textbooks for generations. The contemporary authors are a distinguished group. Billy Collins, for example, was Poet Laureate of the United States; Christopher Paul Curtis received the Newbery Medal for his first novel, *The Watsons Go to Birmingham—1963* (2000); and Annie Dillard, N. Scott Momaday, and others have won the prestigious Pulitzer Prize. Some of the contemporary writers, such as Gary Paulsen and Karen Hesse, are known as writers for young adolescents, and others, including Annie Dillard and Dave Barry, are better known as writers for adults. Most of the classic authors were white men, but many contemporary authors are women. Today's authors also reflect America's diversity: Maya Angelou is African American, N. Scott Momaday is Native American, Gary Soto is Hispanic, and Amy Tan is Chinese American. Figure 11–3 presents a list of some of the authors whose work appears in sixth- through eighth-grade language arts textbooks.

Instruction. Language arts textbooks provide systematic instruction on vocabulary, literary analysis, grammar, writing, and test-taking skills that's tied to grade-level standards.

FIGURE 11–2 ◆ *Genres Featured in Language Arts Textbooks*

Genre	Description	Examples
Fiction	Students read and respond to stories, analyze story elements, examine how authors use narrative devices, and compare genres.	Folk tales Myths Novels Novellas Short stories
Nonfiction	Students read and comprehend informational accounts, learn about the genre, and analyze expository text structures.	Autobiographies Biographies Essays Feature articles News articles
Poetry	Students read and interpret poems, learn about poetic forms and devices, and analyze how language is used aesthetically to evoke emotional responses.	Haiku Limericks Narrative poems Odes Rhyming verse
Drama	Students read and perform drama scripts, learn about the genre and conventions used in scripts, and consider how fiction and nonfiction are represented in dramatic performances.	Comedies Historical dramas Radio plays Speeches Teleplays
Functional Texts	Students examine everyday reading materials and learn to locate and comprehend information presented in these texts.	Directions Nutrition labels Bus schedules Indexes Websites

FIGURE 11–3 ◆ Authors Featured in Language Arts Textbooks

Contemporary Authors for Young Adolescents	Contemporary Authors for Adults	Classic Authors
Avi	Maya Angelou	Basho
Christopher Paul Curtis	Isaac Asimov	Lewis Carroll
Paul Fleischman	James Baldwin	Charles Dickens
Karen Hesse	Dave Barry	Sir Arthur Conan Doyle
Walter Dean Myers	Peter Benchley	Robert Frost
Scott O'Dell	Sandra Cisneros	Langston Hughes
Gary Paulsen	Billy Collins	Jack London
Richard Peck	Annie Dillard	Henry Wadsworth Longfellow
Cynthia Rylant	Barbara Kingsolver	Edgar Allan Poe
Louis Sachar	N. Scott Momaday	Carl Sandburg
Gary Soto	Pablo Neruda	Mark Twain
Laurence Yep	Amy Tan	Walt Whitman

For each selection, teachers introduce academic vocabulary and have students practice the words by completing worksheets. Teachers reinforce students' application of comprehension strategies during reading, and they teach students how to do a close reading to interpret themes. They also teach grammar, writing, and test taking through additional worksheets or other assignments.

Online Resources. Interactive online versions of textbooks are becoming increasingly available, and students have access to a wealth of other resources at the publisher's website, including video clips about authors, information about grammar skills and writing conventions, practice activities, and self-checking quizzes. These digital materials, as you might imagine, are very appealing to young adolescents. Even more time-saving resources are available for teachers: instructional materials, an assessment and reporting system, lesson planners that coordinate instruction with state literacy standards, and staff-development materials.

Assessment Tools. Most publishers provide an online assessment system with a test bank, rubrics, and materials for managing and reporting students' achievement. The test bank includes tests to determine students' reading levels, selection and unit tests, tests on grammar and writing conventions, writing prompts, practice tests to use in preparation for high-stakes assessments, and end-of-year tests. Teachers can also customize many of the tests to match their instructional program or to meet their students' needs.

Program Materials

Language arts textbook programs provide a variety of instructional materials for students and support materials for teachers. The hardbound student textbook is the most familiar piece; it's a grade-level anthology of classic and contemporary literature with integrated instruction on literary analysis, grammar, and writing. There's also an online version of the textbook with many interactive features that appeals to students who typically aren't interested in reading and those who need additional support.

Alternative versions of the textbook for struggling readers and English learners are also available, often as consumable books. These books provide additional support; the selections have been adapted, but the instruction addresses the same grade-level standards. Some publishers offer a single version of the text for struggling readers at a reading level 2 to 3 years below grade level, but others offer multiple versions that are 2 years, 3 years, and 4 years below grade level. The version for English learners provides additional English language and vocabulary support. These alternative versions make it easier for teachers to differentiate instruction.

Instructional materials on grammar, study skills, writing, and test taking are also found in textbook programs. These materials are called *tool kits*, *handbooks*, or *guides*; they may be published in a separate book, as individual booklets, or as appendixes at the back of the student textbook:

- The grammar tool kit covers the parts of a sentence, parts of speech, sentence structure, subject–verb agreement, capitalization, punctuation, and diagramming sentences.
- The study skills tool kit reviews note taking, effective listening, building vocabulary, and reading content-area textbooks.
- The writing tool kit addresses the writing process, sentences, paragraphs, genres, word choice, and proofreading.
- The test-taking tool kit contains information on multiple-choice questions, short-answer questions, essay tests, online tests, test anxiety, and preparing for tests.

STRUGGLING READERS AND WRITERS

Textbooks

Students need textbooks at their reading levels.

Many publishers have developed one or more versions of their textbooks designed for students reading 2 or more years below grade level. The selections in these books are interesting and age-appropriate, and they're often coordinated with the grade-level textbooks so that teachers can differentiate instruction more easily. As with grade-level textbooks, the instruction provided in these books is aligned with state standards. Consumable workbooks often accompany these below-grade-level texts so students have numerous opportunities to practice the strategies and skills they're learning.

Increasingly, many publishers have developed interactive online versions of their below-grade-level textbooks. These versions are appealing, and students are more engaged when they're reading selections and doing practice activities online than in the traditional print format. Digital technology also supports struggling readers:

- Students can listen to the selection read aloud before reading it themselves.
- Students can highlight vocabulary words to hear them pronounced in English and Spanish or to check their definitions.
- Students can use electronic sticky notes to indicate their strategy use or respond to the text.
- Students can type responses in their online reading logs.
- Students can practice skills by completing electronic worksheets.
- Students can assess their progress by taking quizzes on vocabulary, comprehension, and grammar and immediately receiving their score.

The teacher's guide provides detailed information about teaching with these texts, including how to coordinate them with the grade-level version. In addition, staff-development materials show teachers how to help struggling readers. Handbooks provide suggestions for differentiating instruction and teaching word-identification and comprehension strategies. One textbook program features a video showing teachers how to work with struggling readers in a heterogeneous classroom and suggests solutions to common management problems.

Sometimes practice activities are also included in these tool kits.

The teacher's guide presents comprehensive information about how to teach reading and writing using the textbook program. Detailed directions for teaching the selections are provided along with guidelines for differentiating instruction and assessing student achievement. Teachers understand how the concepts they're teaching are aligned with grade-level standards because the standards being addressed are highlighted for each selection.

Textbook publishers have embraced technology! Online versions of textbooks are now available that incorporate interactive features to engage less motivated students and support struggling readers. Students can also complete assignments online and e-mail them to their teacher. Companion websites provide a wealth of resources for students and teachers. Materials for students include video clips about authors, tool kits with information about grammar and other skills, grammar and spelling quizzes, and rubrics. Website materials for teachers include an assessment system, a lesson planner, and updates about the textbook program. The online testing and reporting system consists of a test bank and tools to document students' achievement and create progress reports for students, parents, and administrators. There's a lesson planner, too. It's an online management tool that teachers use to create lesson plans and align instruction with grade-level standards.

Publishers provide in-service training to show teachers how to implement the language arts textbook program and online courses on special topics. Figure 11–4 reviews the materials available in language arts textbook programs.

Language Arts Textbooks and the Reading Process

Teachers involve students in activities representing each of the five stages of the reading process as they use language arts textbooks. The activities are similar to those that teachers use with basal reading programs, but they focus more on literary analysis:

Prereading. Teachers activate and build background knowledge, introduce academic vocabulary words, and preview the selection with students. They also teach new reading strategies and skills that students will use while they're reading.

Reading. Teachers guide students as they read the selection. Students read the first page or two of the text, and then they stop and discuss what they've read. Sometimes teachers identify a purpose for reading and at other times, students make predictions and then read to find out if they're right.

Responding. Reading and responding are often integrated, especially when students do close reading to analyze a novel. Students talk and write about the text to deepen their interpretation.

Exploring. Students complete graphic organizers related to the selection, do worksheets, and participate in activities to learn academic vocabulary from the selection. Teachers also provide explicit instruction on comprehension, grammar, test-taking skills, and writing.

Applying. Students often complete writing assignments related to the topic of the selection or unit, and they take selection and unit tests so teachers can monitor their achievement and reteach any concepts or skills they haven't learned.

FIGURE 11–4 ◆ Language Arts Textbook Materials

Material	Description
Textbook	A grade-level anthology of classic and contemporary literature that's organized into units with vocabulary, literary analysis, grammar, writing, and spelling instruction woven into the units.
Other Versions of the Textbook	Most programs offer correlated texts for struggling readers, an adapted book for English learners, and an online version for students who aren't motivated to read print materials or who need extra support.
Tool Kits	Grammar, study skills, writing, and test-taking "tool kits" for students. These instructional materials are sometimes packaged as separate handbooks, as workbooks, or as appendixes at the back of the textbook.
Teacher's Guide	An oversize manual that presents comprehensive information about how to teach the textbook program. Detailed directions for teaching the selections, alignment with grade-level standards, and ways to differentiate instruction and assess student achievement are provided.
Online Resources	An online version of the textbook and websites for students with author information, video clips, grammar and spelling quizzes, and rubrics; an assessment system, a lesson planner in-service training, and a website with information and updates for teachers.
Assessment System	An online testing and reporting system that includes a test bank and tools to document students' achievement and create progress reports for students, parents, and administrators.
Lesson Planner	An online management tool that teachers use to create lesson plans and align instruction with state literacy standards.
Staff Development	Publishers provide in-service training on implementing the language arts textbook program and online courses on special topics.

In this teacher-centered approach, teachers are actively teaching and guiding students in every stage of the reading process.

Scaffolding English Learners

Most programs have an alternative version of their textbook for English learners. A few EL texts are published as traditional textbooks, but most are consumable textbooks that contain both literature selections and workbook pages. Some selections from the grade-level text have been adapted for this text, and other fiction, nonfiction, drama, and functional selections written by acclaimed multicultural authors have been chosen specifically for this textbook. The selections have simplified vocabulary and sentence structures, but they deal with age-appropriate topics and are thematically related to the selections in the grade-level textbook.

The selections in EL textbooks are presented differently than in grade-level texts. For example, there's usually a preview page that presents an overview of the selection, introduces academic vocabulary, builds background knowledge, and helps students make connections to the topic. Each selection is divided into smaller parts, and a summary is placed at the end of each part. Vocabulary words are highlighted in the text, and several passages are marked for reading aloud or rereading because they're crucial to understanding the selection. Margin notes provide additional support for students. These are the most commonly used types of margin notes:

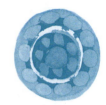

- Boxes that provide background knowledge about technical terms
- Notes about confusing words, phrases, and cultural references
- Reading tips, including suggestions about word-identification and comprehension strategies
- Reading checks to clarify big ideas
- Think-and-reflect boxes at the end of each part

Students are encouraged to write notes and mark up consumable books as they read.

Teachers provide instruction on the same literary analysis, grammar, test-taking, and writing topics using this version of text that are taught with the grade-level textbook. They're encouraged to create graphic organizers and other visual aids to clarify meaning, provide sufficient wait time while students formulate their answers in English, and involve students in interactive small-group activities.

Reality Check! Managing a Language Arts Textbook Program

One advantage of language arts textbooks is that all instructional and assessment materials are provided, but the list of skills teachers are expected to teach and the number of selections students are expected to read and practice activities they're expected to complete are overwhelming. It's essential that teachers make choices and adapt the textbook program to meet their instructional goals and their students' learning needs, as Ms. Williams did in the vignette. For example, the "Legacy of the Vietnam War" unit was designed for 1 week according to the textbook's schedule, but Ms. Williams devoted 2 weeks to it to build background knowledge, make personal connections, and deepen students' learning. One criticism of textbook programs is that they don't provide for in-depth learning, but by customizing their program, teachers can do that.

Textbook publishers tout the time-saving features of their programs, such as the online lesson planner that's aligned with state standards and the assessment system. Most teachers like these features and use them regularly. Even so, planning for instruction, grading papers, and keeping track of students' achievement is very time-consuming when teachers in departmentalized schools teach multiple sections with more than 30 students in each class.

Specialty Textbooks

eachers use a variety of specialty textbooks on grammar, vocabulary, spelling, writing, and other topics to supplement classroom instruction and meet students' needs. The content of these texts is often tied to state standards and described as "comprehensive" and "research based." Teachers can combine these add-on programs with either trade book and textbook programs or use them in intervention programs.

Skill-Review Programs

Grade-level skill-review programs provide 10-minute daily lessons. The skills presented at each grade level and in each program vary, but they generally incorporate comprehension, grammar, vocabulary, and writing topics; some programs also include test-preparation or study skills. Figure 11–5 lists many of the topics included these programs. Most programs can be purchased as consumable workbooks, e-books, and sets of transparencies to be used on an overhead projector.

Teachers implement these programs in several ways, depending on how much scaffolding students need:

Whole-Class Lessons. The teacher reviews the topics using an overhead transparency or page from the e-book projected on the whiteboard, and then the teacher and students work together to write the answers with an erasable pen.

Small-Group Activities. When students are already familiar with the topics, they work in small groups or with partners to complete the workbook page. Afterward, the teacher reviews the answers with the class, marking them on an overhead transparency or e-book page displayed on a whiteboard.

Independent Activities. The teacher reviews the topics orally, and then students work independently to complete the workbook page or copy made from the e-book.

FIGURE 11–5 ◆ Topics Included in Skill-Review Programs

Comprehension	Grammar	Writing Mechanics	Vocabulary
big ideas	possessive nouns	proper nouns and adjectives	affixes
narrative genre	comparative/superlative adjectives	abbreviations	root words
expository genre	prepositional phrases	dialogue	antonyms
fact and opinion	verb tenses	punctuation marks	synonyms
context clues	subject–verb agreement	quotation marks	homonyms
cause and effect	sentence types	correct spellings	idioms
sequencing	run-on sentences	syllabication	words often confused
summarizing			multiple meanings
drawing inferences			

Afterward, students check their answers together, with the teacher or a student writing the correct answers on an overhead transparency or e-book page.

It's essential that teachers take time to go over the answers so students hear peers and the teacher modeling the correct responses.

Daily Oral Language. Probably the best-known skill-review program is Daily Oral Language, published by Great Source, the supplemental textbook division of Houghton Mifflin. In this program, students review capitalization, punctuation, grammar, and writing skills while practicing proofreading skills. Each day, students proofread two sentences to locate and correct errors. This program is available in grade-level editions, either as consumable student books or as transparencies that teachers display using an overhead projector.

Daily Language Review. Evan-Moor's Daily Language Review teaches language arts topics through daily practice activities: Students write correct spellings, identify sentence types, choose synonyms, divide words into syllables, and match words with definitions. In addition to workbooks and transparencies, this grade-level program is available as an e-book that teachers download and project on a whiteboard. The company's website provides a correlation of the lessons with each state's literacy standards.

Standards.Plus. Standards Plus® is a supplemental program to review the topics addressed in grade-level literacy standards. Teachers provide instruction and practice with 10-minute minilessons. In addition to grammar and other topics, some lessons focus on test-taking strategies. The publisher recommends teaching these minilessons at either the beginning or the end of the instructional period. Standards Plus includes a teacher resource kit with lesson plans, scripted directions for teaching each lesson, and a reference CD with a pacing calendar.

Writing Textbooks

Write Source publishes two writing programs; one is a textbook and the other is a kit. Their textbook program is *Write Source* (Kemper, Sebranek, & Meyer, 2005). The writing process, writing genres, and the basic elements of writing (i.e., parts of speech, effective sentences, and strong paragraphs) are addressed in these grade-level texts, and mechanics are taught as a natural part of the writing process. The publisher's website has additional model compositions submitted by students, writing prompts, and rubrics for assessing students' writing. These writing textbooks are more authentic than skill-review programs, and they're organized into units with these features:

- Units are organized around the writing genres.
- The writing process is covered in every unit.
- The six traits are integrated into every unit.
- Suggestions for differentiating instruction to address students' needs are provided.
- Rubrics are provided for assessing writing.

Great Source also publishes Write Traits® Classroom Kits for each grade level. These popular kits contain student "traitbooks" with information about each trait, model compositions, and writing activities; a teacher's guide with lessons, revision guidelines, and rubrics; transparencies of student writing samples; posters about the six traits to hang in the classroom; and folders to hold student work.

Word-Study Textbooks

Bear and his colleagues revolutionized word-study instruction with *Words Their Way: Word Study for Phonics, Vocabulary, and Spelling Instruction* (Bear, Invernizzi, Templeton, & Johnston, 2008), a practical, research-based, and classroom-proven way to teach phonics, vocabulary, and spelling with **word-sort** activities. These authors have developed a series of supplemental activity books using their word-study approach. Teachers use *Words Their Way: Word Sorts for Syllables and Affixes Spellers* (2nd ed.) (Johnston, Invernizzi, & Bear, 2009) to teach about multisyllabic words in fourth through eighth grades; the lessons begin with consonant doubling and move through an investigation of prefixes and suffixes. To explore spelling–meaning relationships in sixth through eighth grades, teachers use *Words Their Way: Word Sorts for Derivational Relations Spellers* (Johnston, Bear, & Invernizzi, 2009); the lessons focus on the structure of written words and examine how the spelling visually represents meaningful units (e.g., *muscle–muscular, impede–impediment*). These books are collections of approximately 150 word-sort activities. Each lesson provides teachers with reproducible sorts and step-by-step directions. In addition, *Words Their Way With English Learners* (Bear, Helman, Templeton, Invernizzi, & Johnston, 2007) provides word-study lessons for English learners.

Reality Check! Using Specialty Textbooks

Specialty textbooks provide targeted instruction, but even though they serve a useful purpose in middle-grade classrooms, they can be time-consuming and difficult to integrate, despite publishers' claims. Skill-review programs may take only 5 to 10 minutes a day, but even that brief amount of time can hard to find in 45- to 55-minute instructional periods. The word-study and writing programs are more time-consuming because they involve authentic literacy activities. In addition, these supplemental programs are expensive, especially when students write in consumable workbooks and new copies must be purchased each year.

These supplemental programs are useful in differentiating instruction and for ensuring that their instruction addresses state literacy standards. It's not possible to implement every program, so teachers must choose carefully after analyzing their curriculum and their students' achievement levels to determine priorities. Teachers should take time to carefully examine the program they're considering and decide how they'll use it before making a purchase. It's also a good idea to talk to teachers in other schools with similar student populations to find out if they recommend the program and whether it's been effective.

CHAPTER 11

How Effective Teachers Teach With Textbooks

▶ Teachers use basal reading textbooks to teach reading in fourth through sixth grades.

▶ Teachers use language arts textbooks to teach reading and writing in sixth through eighth grades.

▶ Teachers recognize that even though textbooks often claim to be complete instructional programs, they aren't.

▶ Some teachers use specialty textbooks to address students' instructional needs or meet grade-level standards.

CHAPTER 12

Using Literacy in the Content Areas

Ms. Boland's Students Study Medieval Life

Ms. Boland's eighth graders are learning about medieval life in their integrated English/social studies class. These students are part of a special "laptop" project: Each student has a laptop computer to use at school and at home. They've learned keyboarding skills and how to use a variety of computer programs, and their classroom has wireless Internet access. Ms. Boland begins the unit by reading *Catherine, Called Birdy* (Cushman, 1994), a novel written in diary form. Catherine is a young noblewoman in 1290, and her diary entries provide fascinating glimpses into medieval life. The book's humorous tone makes it very popular. Tito explains, "This is one 'girl' book that I don't mind reading. It's laugh-out-loud funny!" Every few days, students meet in literature circles to talk about the book, and Ms. Boland sits in on many of the discussions to help students focus on both the story's events and the historical information they're learning. They also write **reading log** entries using a three-column chart for each chapter; they write a summary in the first column, historical notes in the second column, and a personal, historical, or literary connection in the third.

Once Ms. Boland is confident that her students have the background knowledge to read the chapter in their social studies textbook, she previews it. The students do a text walk together, reading the five main headings, the subheadings, and the end-of-chapter questions. They notice boldfaced words, such as *chivalry*, which they know, and others that are unfamiliar, including *Saracen*. Ms. Boland reads aloud sentences containing the words, and students use context clues whenever possible to figure out the words' meanings.

They check the glossary at the back of the textbook to see whether their definitions are correct. The students also examine the illustrations, maps, and diagrams in the chapter.

Next, students divide into five groups, and each group is responsible for reading and reporting back on one section of the chapter. Ms. Boland distributes copies of a study sheet to each group to focus their attention on the big ideas as they read and prepare to share what they've learned. During their presentations, she'll distribute copies of the study sheet to all students so they can take notes as they listen. The study sheet for the group reading about knights is shown in box on page 314.

Each group also adds academic vocabulary to "Ye Olde Word Wall," which is posted in the classroom, and students also make their own word walls on their laptops. Ms. Boland's students write the words in three colors to apply what they recently learned about words entering English from various languages: The English words (e.g., *knight, sword*) are written in black, the words from French and Latin (e.g., *plague, medieval*) in blue, and the Greek words (e.g., *pope, Saracen*) in red. The students are surprised that so many words come from French and Latin, such as *archer, castle, chivalry, feudal, moat, melee, pilgrimage, serf, siege, squire, troubadours,* and *villein,* so Ms. Boland teaches a mini-lesson about the Norman conquest and explains that English lords and ladies spoke French during the 12th and 13th centuries.

Ms. Boland has collected a text set with multiple copies of fiction, nonfiction, and poetry books, including *Crispin: The Cross of Lead* (Avi, 2004), *The Midwife's Apprentice* (Cushman, 1996b), *Castle Diary: The Journal of Tobias Burgess* (Platt, 2003), *Medieval Life* (Langley, 2004), *Castle* (Macaulay, 1977), *Knights and Castles* (Osborne, 2000), *Outrageous Women of the Middle Ages* (Leon, 1998), *A Medieval Feast* (Aliki, 1986), *When Plague Strikes* (Giblin, 1997), and *Good Masters! Sweet Ladies! Voices From a Medieval Village* (Schlitz, 2007). Most are written at the students' grade level, but several are easier reading. The eighth graders read these books independently during reading workshop and they search for information about medieval life; they'll use the results of their research to create an interactive museum to showcase their learning for other students, their parents, administrators, and school board members. They work individually, with partners, and in small groups to investigate the Crusades, heraldry, castles, jousts and tournaments, the King Arthur legends, women in the Middle Ages, food and feasts, knights and armor, plagues, chivalry, cathedrals, and other topics related to medieval life. The students identify research questions, consult books in the text set and websites to gather information, and organize what they learned for their museum displays.

Students' displays include visual, oral, and digital components. The visual component is a display using posters, charts, and artifacts that will be arranged on a table for visitors to view. Many students also create costumes to wear on Museum Day. The oral component is the talk students will present to visitors about their displays and computer applications. The digital component incorporates students' laptops—a PowerPoint presentation, a picture gallery, a webquest, or another computer application that's related to their topic.

On the day before Museum Day, students set up their displays in the library and rehearse their presentations in front of their classmates. Then on Museum Day, students dress up in their costumes and stand beside their displays to talk with visitors, sharing information, explaining artifacts, and using their computer application. Some students take on the "expert" role as they talk about their topic while others assume the "eyewitness" role and become a knight, midwife, monk, serf, Crusader, lord, or lady. The Middle Ages come to life as Jeremy and Connor talk about a knight's armor; Jacob, Tyler, and Zach trace the route of the Crusaders; Alyssa and Ruby describe the

A Study Sheet for a Section of a Textbook on Becoming a Knight

BECOMING A KNIGHT

Knights were the most important *fighting* men in the Middle Ages. With the invention of the *stirrups*, the mounted soldiers in the cavalry became the most important part of the army, and knights became more and more powerful off the battlefield, too.

LEARNING TO BE A KNIGHT

Step 1: A Page	Step 2: A Knight's Esquire	Step 3: A Knight
Age 7 — Live with a noble family. Serve meals and learn manners. Learn to ride horses and fight.	Age 14 — Dress a knight for battle. Serve a knight in battle.	Age 21 — Pray all night in a vigil. Dubbed in a ceremony. Receive a sword and spurs.

CODE OF BEHAVIOR

There was more to knighthood than fighting. Knights were expected to follow a code of behavior called *Chivalry*. At first the word just meant *horsemanship*, but it came to mean a way of life. The knights' four duties were:

1. *Be honorable.*
2. *Be brave.*
3. *Protect the weak.*
4. *Respect women.*

Unfortunately, many knights failed to live up to these high standards.

THE MAID OF ORLEANS

Although women could not become knights, a French woman named *Joan of Arc* dressed in armor and led the knights in an attack against the English in 1429. What happened to her? *She was burned at the stake.*

roles of women; Arturo explains the designs and colors on a coat of arms; Jade and Dori show how monks made illuminated manuscripts; Gabriel and Joe explicate the parts of a castle and their uses; Maya and Amy retell several of the King Arthur legends; and Luis and Marcus demonstrate jousting using toy knights on horseback while visitors move from one display to another and medieval music plays in the background.

The eighth graders receive grades on their museum displays. Ms. Boland and her students developed a 4-point rubric, which is shown here, to assess their work. They made the rubric before they got started so that they'd understand what's expected of them. The students use the rubric to self-assess their progress midway through the development of their display to be sure that they're on the right track and again several days before Museum Day so that they can make any needed adjustments. Then Ms. Boland uses the rubric to assess their displays on Museum Day.

Museum Rubric

	Excellent	Very Good	Good	Inadequate
Talk	Insightful talk about ideas and relationships.	Entertaining presentation focusing on the big ideas.	Useful presentation of information.	Presentation is very brief or unfocused.
Visuals	3–4 visuals extend visitors' knowledge.	3 visuals enrich the display.	1–2 visuals present information.	Visuals aren't used.
Artifacts	3–4 artifacts are used interactively.	3 artifacts are integrated into the display.	1–2 realistic artifacts can be examined.	Artifacts aren't available.
Technology	Computer is used in several ways.	Computer is integrated into the display.	Computer is used to review information.	A computer isn't used.
Overall Impression	Impressive display challenges visitors to think in new ways.	Inviting display engages visitors in hands-on activities.	Informative display enhances visitors' knowledge.	Display isn't useful.

ontent-area textbooks are important resources that students use to learn about social studies, science, and other content areas, but they aren't a complete instructional program. Students need to know how to read content-area textbooks because these books differ from other reading materials: They have unique conventions and structures that students use as aids in reading and remembering the big ideas. Because many students find textbooks more challenging to read than other books, teachers need to support their students' reading so that they'll be successful.

Connecting Reading and Writing

eading and writing are connected because reading has a powerful impact on writing, and vice versa (Tierney & Shanahan, 1996): When students read about a topic before writing, their writing is enhanced because of what they learn about the topic, and when they write about the ideas in a book they're reading, their comprehension is deepened because they're exploring big ideas and relationships among ideas. Making this connection is especially important when students are learning content-area information because of the added challenges that unfamiliar topics and academic vocabulary present. There are other reasons for connecting reading and writing, too. Making meaning is the goal of both reading and writing: Students activate background knowledge, set purposes, and use many of the same strategies for reading and writing. In addition, the reading and writing processes are remarkably similar.

Reading Trade Books

A wide variety of high-quality picture books and chapter books are available today for teachers to use in teaching thematic units. Two outstanding science-related trade books, for example, are *Team Moon: How 400,000 People Landed Apollo 11 on the Moon* (Thimmesh, 2006), a stunning book that highlights the contributions of the people working behind the scenes on that space mission, and *Oh, Rats! The Story of Rats and People* (Marrin, 2006), a riveting book of facts about a champion of survival. Two notable trade books on social studies topics are *Freedom Riders: John Lewis and Jim Zwerg on the Front Lines of the Civil Rights Movement* (Bausum, 2006), a powerful book that contrasts black America and white America in the 1960s by tracing the journeys of two young men, and *One Thousand Tracings: Healing the Wounds of World War II* (Judge, 2007), a poignant picture-book story of an American family who started a relief effort that reached 3,000 people in war-ravaged Europe. These books are entertaining and informative, and the authors' engaging writing styles and formats keep readers interested. They're relevant, too, because many students make connections to their own life experiences and background knowledge as they read them, and teachers use them to build students' background knowledge at the beginning of a thematic unit.

Teachers use varied procedures to share these trade books with students. They use **interactive read-alouds** to share some books that are too difficult for students to read on their own, and they feature others in literature focus units and thematic units. They choose related books at a range of reading levels for literature circles, and provide others for students to read independently during reading workshop. Because many books on social studies and science topics are available at a range of reading levels, teachers can find good books, many at their students' reading levels, to use in teaching in the content areas.

> Check the Compendium of Instructional Procedures, which follows this chapter, for more information on the highlighted terms.

Text Sets. Teachers collect text sets of books and other reading materials on topics to use in teaching thematic units, as Ms. Boland did in the vignette at the beginning of the chapter. Materials for text sets are carefully chosen to incorporate different genres, a range of reading levels to meet the needs of all students in the class, and multimedia resources that present a variety of perspectives. It's especially important to include plenty of books and other materials that English learners and struggling readers can read (Robb, 2002).

Teachers collect as many different types of materials as possible, for example:

atlases and maps	nonfiction books
biographies	novels
brochures and pamphlets	photographs
encyclopedias	picture books
films, DVDs, and videos	poems and songs
magazines	primary source materials
models and diagrams	reference books
newspaper articles	websites and webquests

FIGURE 12–1 ◆ *Magazines for Middle-Grade Students*

Format	Magazines
Print	*Appleseeds* (social studies) *Calliope* (history) *Cobblestone* (history) *Cricket* (stories) *Dig* (archeology) *Faces: People, Places, Cultures* (multicultural) *Kids Discover* (science and history) *Muse* (science and the arts) *National Geographic for Kids* (geography and culture) *Odyssey* (science) *OWL* (science) *Skipping Stones* (multicultural) *Sports Illustrated for Kids* (sports) *Time for Kids* (current events)
Online	*CobblestoneOnline.net,* at www.cobblestoneonline.net (history) *Dig,* at www.digonsite.com (archeology) *Kids Newsroom,* at www.kidsnewsroom.org (current events) *KidsPost,* at www.washingtonpost.com/wp-srv/kidspost/orbit/ kidspost.html (current events) *National Geographic for Kids,* at www.kids.nationalgeographic. com (geography and culture) *Odyssey,* at www.odysseymagazine.com (science) *OWL,* at owlkids.com/ (science) *Sports Illustrated for Kids,* at www.sikids.com/ (sports) *Time for Kids,* at www.timeforkids.com/ (current events)

They collect single copies of some books and multiple copies of others. Too often, teachers don't think about using magazines to teach social studies and science, but many excellent magazines are available, including *Cobblestone* and *Time for Kids*. Some magazines are also available online, such as *Time for Kids*. Figure 12–1 presents a list of print and online magazines for young adolescents.

Mentor Texts. Teachers model quality writing with stories, nonfiction books, and poems that students are familiar with (Dorfman & Cappelli, 2007). Picture books are especially useful mentor texts because they're short enough to be reread quickly. Teachers begin by rereading a mentor text and pointing out a specific feature such as adding vivid verbs, writing from a different perspective, or changing the tone by placing adjectives after nouns. Then students imitate the feature in brief collaborative compositions and in their own writing. Students have opportunities to experiment with literary devices, imitate sentence and text structures, try out new genres, or explore different page arrangements.

Nonfiction books are often used as mentor texts to teach students about new genres, organizational structures, and page formats. For example, *Gone Wild: An Endangered Animal Alphabet* (McLimans, 2006) is a graphic masterpiece where letters of the alphabet are transformed into vulnerable animals, and text boxes accompanying each letter provide information about the animal; students can use this format to write a class

Text Sets

These eighth graders are reading a novel as part of a text set about the Civil War. As they read, they enjoy the story and learn information at the same time. Other books in the text set include nonfiction books and their social studies textbook. After finishing the novel, the students will preview the unit in their textbook, read other books in the text set, and then return to the textbook to read it thoroughly. The text set helps students expand their knowledge base about the Civil War, prepares them to read the textbook, and extends their learning.

alphabet book during a science or social studies unit. Another excellent mentor text is *Good Masters! Sweet Ladies! Voices From a Medieval Village* (Schlitz, 2007), a collection of 23 first-person character sketches of young people living in an English village in 1255; each character has a distinct personality and societal role, and historical notes are included in the margins. This book was designed as a play or a **readers theatre** presentation. During a unit on ancient Rome or World War II, for example, students can imitate this mentor text to write their own collection of character sketches and present them for students in other classrooms or their parents.

Teachers use mentor texts in **minilessons** to teach students how to make their writing more powerful, and students use these books as springboards for writing as part of thematic units. Dorfman and Cappelli (2007) explain that "mentor texts serve as snapshots into the future. They help students envision the kind of writers they can become" (p. 3).

Writing as a Learning Tool

Students use writing as a tool for learning during thematic units to take notes, categorize ideas, draw graphic organizers, and write summaries. The focus is on using writing to help students think and learn, not on spelling every word correctly. Nevertheless, students should use classroom resources, such as word walls, to spell most words correctly and write as neatly as possible so that they can reread their own writing. Armbruster, McCarthey, and Cummins (2005) also point out that writing to learn serves two other purposes as well: When students write about what they're learning, it helps them become better writers, and teachers can use students' writing to assess their learning.

Learning Logs. Students use **learning logs** to record and react to what they're learning in social studies, science, or other content areas. Laura Robb (2003) explains that learning logs are "a place to think on paper" (p. 60). Students write in these journals to discover gaps in their knowledge and to explore relationships between what they're learning and their past experiences. Through these activities, students practice taking notes, writing descriptions and directions, and making graphic organizers.

Double-Entry Journals. **Double-entry journals** are just what the name suggests: Students divide their journal pages into two columns and write different types of information in each part (Daniels & Zemelman, 2004). They may write important facts in one column and their reactions to the facts in the other, or questions about the topic in the left column and answers in the right. Figure 12–2 shows a sixth grader's

FIGURE 12–2 ◆ *A Page From a Sixth Grader's Double-Entry Journal*

DRUGS

Take notes	Make Notes
pot affects your brain mariquania is a ilegal drug and does things to your lungs makes you forget things. affects your brain	How long does it take to affect your brain? how long does it last? Could it make you forget how to drive?
Crack and coacain is illegal a small pipeful can cause death. It can cause heart atachs. is very dangerous It doesent make you cool. It makes you a dummy. you and your friends might think so but others think your a dummy. people are stupid if they attemp to take drugs. The ansew is no, no, no, no.	Like basketball players? Why do people use drugs? How do people get the seeds to grow drugs?

double-entry journal written during a unit on drug prevention. In the left column, the student wrote information she was learning, and in the right column, she made personal connections to the information.

Simulated Journals.   In some stories, such as *Catherine, Called Birdy* (Cushman, 1994), the author assumes the role of a character and writes a series of diary entries from his or her point of view. Here is an excerpt from one of Birdy's entries, which describes life in the Middle Ages:

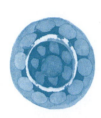

> 12th Day of October
>
> No more sewing and spinning and goose fat for me! Today my life is changed. How it came about is this:
>
> We arrived at the abbey soon after dinner, stopping just outside the entry gate at the guest-house next to the mill. The jouncing cart did my stomach no kindness after jellied eel and potted lamb, so I was most relieved to alight. (Cushman, 1994, p. 25)

These books can be called *simulated journals*. They're rich with historical details and feature examples of both the vocabulary and the sentence structure of the period. At the end of the book, authors often include information about how they researched the period and explanations about the liberties they took with the characters or events that are recorded.

Scholastic has created two series of historical journals; one is for girls, and the other is for boys. *I Walk in Dread: The Diary of Deliverance Trembly, Witness to the Salem Witch Trials* (Fraustino, 2004), *A Picture of Freedom: The Diary of Clotee, a Slave Girl* (McKissack, 1997), and *Survival in the Storm: The Dust Bowl Diary of Grace Edwards* (Janke, 2002) are from the Dear America series; each book provides a glimpse into American history from a girl's perspective. The My Name Is America series features books written from a boy's point of view; three examples are *The Journal of Patrick Seamus Flaherty: United States Marine Corps* (White, 2002), *The Journal of Ben Uchida: Citizen 13559, Mirror Lake Internment Camp* (Denenberg, 1999), and *The Journal of Jesse Smoke: A Cherokee Boy, Trail of Tears, 1838* (Bruchac, 2001). These books are handsomely bound to look like old journals with heavy paper rough cut around the edges.

Students, too, can write simulated journals by assuming the role of another person and writing from that person's perspective. They assume the role of a historical figure when they read biographies or as part of social studies units. As they read novels, students assume the role of a character in the story. In this way, they gain insight into other people's lives and into historical events. When students write from the viewpoint of a famous person, they begin by making a "life line," a time line of the person's life. Then they pick key dates in the person's life and write entries about those dates. A look at a series of diary entries written by a fifth grader who has assumed the role of Benjamin Franklin shows how the student chose the important dates for each entry and wove in factual information:

December 10, 1719

Dear Diary,
My brother James is so mad at me. He just figured out that I'm the one who wrote the articles for his newspaper and signed them Mistress Silence Dogood. He says I can't do any more of them. I don't understand why. My articles are funny. Everyone reads them. I bet he won't sell as many newspapers anymore. Now I have to just do the printing.

February 15, 1735

Dear Diary,

I have printed my third "Poor Richard's Almanack." It is the most popular book in America and now I am famous. Everyone reads it. I pretend that somebody named Richard Saunders writes it, but it's really me. I also put my wise sayings in it. My favorite wise saying is "Early to bed, early to rise, makes a man healthy, wealthy, and wise."

June 22, 1763

Dear Diary,

I've been an inventor for many years now. There are a lot of things I have invented like the Franklin stove (named after me) and bifocal glasses, and the lightning rod, and a long arm to get books off of the high shelves. That's how I work. I see something that we don't have and if it is needed, I figure out how to do it. I guess I just have the knack for inventing.

May 25, 1776

Dear Diary,

Tom Jefferson and I are working on the Declaration of Independence. The patriots at the Continental Congress chose us to do it but it is dangerous business. The Red Coats will call us traitors and kill us if they can. I like young Tom from Virginia. He'll make a good king of America some day.

April 16, 1790

Dear Diary,

I am dying. I only have a day or two to live. But it's OK because I am 84 years old. Not very many people live as long as I have or do so many things in a life. I was a printer by trade but I have also been a scientist, an inventor, a writer, and a statesman. I have lived to see the Philadelphia that I love so very much become part of a new country. Good-bye to my family and everyone who loves me.

Students can use simulated journals in two ways: as a journal or as a refined and polished composition—a demonstration-of-learning project. When students use simulated journals as a tool for learning, they write the entries as they're reading a book to get to know the character better, or during a thematic unit as they're learning about a historical period. In these entries, students are exploring concepts and making connections between what they're learning and what they already know. These journal entries are less polished than when students write a simulated journal as a culminating project for a unit. For a project, students plan out their journals carefully, choose important dates, and use the writing process to draft, revise, edit, and publish their journals. They often add covers typical of the historical period. For example, a simulated journal written as part of a unit on ancient Greece might be written on a long sheet of butcher paper and rolled like a scroll, or a pioneer journal might be backed with paper cut from a brown grocery bag to resemble an animal hide.

Quickwriting. Teachers use **quickwriting** to activate background knowledge and review big ideas (Readence, Moore, & Rickelman, 2000). Students write on a topic for 10 minutes, letting thoughts flow without focusing on mechanics or revisions. Toward the end of a thematic unit on the solar system, for example, fourth graders each chose a word from the **word wall** for a quickwrite, and then they shared their writing with classmates. This is one student's quickwrite on Mars:

 Mars is known as the red planet. Mars is Earth's neighbor. Mars is a lot like Earth. On Mars one day lasts 24 hours. It is the fourth planet in the solar system. Mars may have life forms. Two Viking ships landed on Mars. Mars has a dusty and rocky surface. The Viking ships found no life forms. Mars' surface shows signs of water long ago. Mars has no water now. Mars has no rings.

Quickwrites provide a good way of checking on what students are learning and an opportunity to clarify misconceptions. After students write, they usually share their quick-writes in small groups, and then one student in each group shares with the class. Sharing also takes about 10 minutes, so the entire activity can be completed in 20 minutes.

Writing to Demonstrate Learning

Students research topics and then use writing to demonstrate their learning. This writing is more formal, and students use the writing process to revise and edit their writing before making a final copy. Four types of writing to demonstrate learning are reports, essays, poems, and multigenre projects.

Reports. To demonstrate learning, students write many types of reports, ranging from posters to collaborative books and individual reports. Too often, students aren't exposed to report writing until they're faced with writing a term paper in high school, and then they're overwhelmed with figuring out how to take notes on note cards, organize information, write the paper, and compile a bibliography. There's no reason to postpone report writing; successful experiences with writing teach students about content-area topics as well as how to share information (Harvey, 1998; Tompkins, 2008). Here are five types of reports:

Posters. Students combine visual and verbal elements when they make posters (Moline, 1995). They draw pictures and diagrams and write labels and commentary. For example, students draw diagrams of the parts of a complex machine, label the clothing a Revolutionary War soldier wore and the supplies he carried, list important events of a person's life on a life line, or chart the explorers' voyages to America and around the world on a map. Students plan the information they want to include in the poster and consider how to devise an attention-getting display using headings, illustrations, captions, boxes, and rules. They prepare a rough draft of their posters, section by section, and then revise and edit each section. Then they make a final copy of each section, glue the sections onto a sheet of posterboard, and share their posters with classmates as they would share finished pieces of writing. As part of a reading and writing workshop focusing on nonfiction books, a fifth grader read *The Magic School Bus Inside a Beehive* (Cole, 1996) and created the poster shown in Figure 12–3 to share what he had learned.

Alphabet Books. Students use the letters of the alphabet to organize the information they want to share in an alphabet book. These collaborative books incorporate the sequence structure, because the pages are arranged in alphabetical order. Alphabet books such as *Z Is for Zamboni: A Hockey Alphabet* (Napier, 2002) and *The Queen's Progress: An Elizabethan Alphabet* (Mannis, 2003) can be used as models. Students begin by brainstorming information related to the topic being studied and identify a word or fact for each letter of the alphabet. Then they work individually, in pairs, or in small groups to compose pages for the book. The format for the pages is similar to

FIGURE 12–3 ◆ A Fifth Grader's Poster About Bees

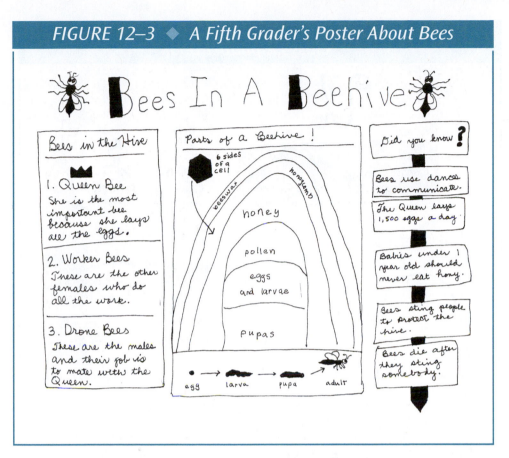

the one used in alphabet books written by professional authors: Students write the letter in one corner of the page, draw an illustration, and write a sentence or paragraph to describe the word or fact. The text usually begins "_____ is for _____," and then a sentence or paragraph description follows. The "U" page from a fourth-grade class's alphabet book on the California missions is shown in Figure 12–4.

Class Collaborations. Students work together to write collaborative books. Sometimes students each write one page, or they can work together in small groups to write chapters. Students create collaborative reports on almost any science or social studies topic. They write collaborative biographies; each student or small group writes about one event or accomplishment in the subject's life, and then the pages are assembled in chronological order. Or, students work in small groups to write chapters for a collaborative report on the properties of matter or the Oregon Trail.

Individual Reports. Students also write individual reports during thematic units. They do "authentic" research, in which they explore topics that interest them or hunt for answers to questions that puzzle them (Harvey, 1998). Students read books and interview people with special knowledge to learn about their topics, and increasingly they're turning to the Internet for information. After learning about their topics, students use the writing process to write reports to share their new knowledge.

Essays. Students write essays to explain, analyze, and persuade; sometimes their topics are personal, such as the death of a parent or adjusting to a new school, and at other times, they address national and international issues such as gun control, famine, and global warming. These compositions are short, usually no longer than

FIGURE 12–4   ◆   The "U" Page From a Fourth-Grade Class's Alphabet Book

Some of the Indians thought life was UNBEARABLE at the missions. They thought this because they couldn't hunt or do the things they were used to. Once they were at the missions they couldn't leave. They were sometimes beaten if they did.

two pages. They're classified as nonfiction but often include some story elements, especially in personal essays. Students write essays from their own viewpoints, and their voices should come clearly through the writing (Pryle, 2007). They learn to write personal essays, in which they recount an experience, shaping it to illustrate a theme or generalization; comparison essays, in which they compare two or more things to emphasize important differences and sometimes offer an opinion; and persuasive essays, in which they try to persuade readers to accept an idea, agree with an opinion, or follow a course of action.

Poetry. Students often write poems as projects after reading books and as part of thematic units. They write formula poems by beginning each line or stanza with a word or line, they create free-form poems, and they follow the structure of model poems as they create their own poems. Here are three poetry forms that students use to demonstrate content-area learning:

"I Am . . ." Poems. Students assume the role of a person and write a poem from that person's viewpoint. They begin and end the poem (or each stanza) with "I am ____" and begin all the other lines with "I." For example, an eighth grader wrote an

"I am . . ." poem from the viewpoint of John F. Kennedy after reading a biography about the 35th president:

I am John Fitzgerald Kennedy.
I commanded a PT boat in World War II.
I saved my crew after a Japanese ship hit us.
I became a politician because that's what my dad wanted me to do.
I was elected the 35th president of the United States.
I said, "Ask not what your country can do for you—ask what you can do for your country."
I believed in equal rights for blacks and whites.
I began the Peace Corps to help the world live free.
I cried the tears of assassination because
Lee Harvey Oswald shot me dead.
I left my young family in America's love.
I am John Fitzgerald Kennedy.

Poems for Two Voices. Students take on two, often contrasting, roles to write poems for two voices. This free-verse form is arranged in two columns, side by side. The columns are read by two readers: One reads the left column, and the other reads the right column. When both readers have words—either the same words or different words—written on the same line, they read them simultaneously so that the poem sounds like a duet. Two eighth graders wrote the following poem about Harriet Tubman and the Underground Railroad. The left column is from the slave's perspective, and the right column from the conductor's.

FREEDOM!	*FREEDOM!*
	I hide slaves in my house;
	It is my moral duty.
I dodge the law wherever I go;	
I follow the north star.	
	I feed them until they get
	to the next stop.
I hide in closets and cellars	
and sleep whenever I can.	
	It is a big risk.
I am in grave danger.	
BUT IT'S WORTH IT!	*BUT IT'S WORTH IT!*
Harriet Tubman is the Moses	
of our people.	
	I am a conductor,
	helping her and her passengers
	along the way.
Once we reach Canada,	
we're free.	
Will freedom be sweet?	
	Oh, yes it will.
FREE AT LAST!	*FREE AT LAST!*

Found Poems. Students create poems by culling words and phrases from a book they're reading and arranging the words and phrases into a free-form poem.

New Literacies

Webquests

Webquests are inquiry-oriented online projects that enhance students' learning by scaffolding their thinking and involving them in meaningful tasks. These projects also foster students' ability to use the Internet to search and retrieve information from websites and understand multimodal presentations (Ikpeze & Boyd, 2007). Too often, students waste time searching for Internet resources, but in webquests, the resources have been bookmarked so students can locate them easily. Webquests have these components:

- **Introduction.** An engaging scenario is presented with background information and descriptions of the roles that students will assume, such as botanist, superhero, or archaeologist.
- **Task.** A description of the creative activity that students will accomplish is provided, including open-ended questions to answer. Possible activities include making brochures, maps, or posters; writing poems, newspaper articles, letters, or songs; or creating board games or video-diaries.
- **Process.** The steps that students will follow to complete the task are presented.
- **Resources.** The bookmarked websites and any other resources that students will need are listed.
- **Evaluation.** A rubric is provided for students to self-assess their work. Teachers also use it to assess students' work.

- **Conclusion.** Opportunities are presented for students to share their experience, reflect on learning, and pursue extensions.

These online learning projects were invented by Bernie Dodge of San Diego State University in 1995. His website at http://webquest.org/ provides useful information about locating teacher-made webquests and creating your own.

Webquests are quickly becoming popular. Teachers have created hundreds on a wide range of literature, social studies, science, and literature topics that are available without charge on the Internet. For example, in one webquest, students who have read *Hatchet* (Paulsen, 2007) embark on a wilderness journey and answer scavenger-hunt questions as they learn survival skills, and in another, students who are studying ancient Egypt travel back to 1250 B.C. to find King Tut's burial mask and decode the message hidden inside it. Other webquest topics include biomes, voting, polygons, World War II, and hurricanes, as well as popular books, such as *The Outsiders* (Hinton, 2007).

Most online resources for webquests are informational websites that include graphics, photos, maps, video clips, and interactive activities. It's harder to locate good online resources for literature webquests, but they generally include websites about the author and topics related to the story's setting and social issues.

Webquests should include the components described here, and resource links must be active, or teachers need to replace them. In addition, teachers should consider whether the webquest will enhance students' understanding and promote higher-level thinking.

For example, fourth graders created this poem about a Saguaro cactus after reading *Cactus Hotel* (Guiberson, 2007):

> *A young cactus sprouts up.*
> *After 10 years only four inches high,*
> *after 25 years two feet tall,*
> *after 50 years 10 feet all.*
> *A welcoming signal across the desert.*
> *A Gila woodpecker,*
> *a white-winged dove,*
> *an elf owl*
> *decide to stay.*
> *After 60 years an arm grows,*
> *the cactus hotel is 18 feet tall.*
> *After 150 years 7 long branches*
> *and holes of every size*
> *in the cactus hotel.*

Multigenre Projects. Students combine content-area study with writing as they explore a science or social studies topic using several genres in a multigenre project (Allen, 2001). Romano (2000) explains that each genre offers ways of learning and understanding that the others don't; students gain different understandings, for example, by writing a simulated journal entry, an alphabet book, and a time line. Teachers or students identify a *repetend*, a common thread or unifying feature for the project, which helps students move beyond the level of remembering facts to a higher, more analytical level of understanding.

Depending on the information they want to present and their repetend, students use some of these genres for their projects:

acrostics	"I am . . ." poems	riddles
alphabet books	letters	simulated journals
biographical sketches	maps	songs
book boxes	photo galleries	time lines
cartoons	posters	Venn diagrams
double-entry journals	questions and answers	videos
essays	quotes	websites
found poems	reports	word sorts

Students generally use three or more genres in a multigenre project and include both textual and visual genres. What matters most is that the genres amplify and extend the repetend.

Not only can students create multigenre projects, but some authors use the technique in trade books; *The Magic School Bus and the Electric Field Trip* (Cole, 1999) and others in the Magic School Bus series are examples of multigenre books. Each book features a story about Ms. Frizzle and her students on a fantastic science adventure, and on the side panels of pages, explanations, charts, diagrams, and essays are presented. Together the story and informational side panels present an in-depth, multigenre presentation. Other multigenre books include *To Be a Slave* (Lester, 2005b), *Nothing But the Truth* (Avi, 2003), *Lemony Snicket: The Unauthorized Autobiography* (Snicket, 2003), *Middle School Is Worse Than Meatloaf* (Holms, 2007), and *Ernest L. Thayer's Casey at the Bat: A Ballad of the Republic Sung in the Year 1888* (Thayer, 2000).

Content-Area Textbooks

Textbooks have traditionally been the centerpiece of social studies and science classes, but these textbooks have shortcomings that limit their effectiveness. Too often, content-area textbooks are unappealing and too difficult for students to read and understand, and they cover too many topics superficially. It's up to teachers to make content-area textbooks more comprehensible and to supplement students' learning with other reading and writing activities during thematic units. A list of guidelines for using content-area textbooks is presented on page 328.

Features of Content-Area Textbooks

Content-area textbooks look different than other types of books and have unique conventions, such as the following:

- Headings and subheadings to direct readers' attention to the big ideas
- Photographs and drawings to illustrate the big ideas

Guidelines
for Using Content-Area Textbooks

▶ Teach students about the unique conventions of textbooks, and show how to use them as comprehension aids.

▶ Have students create questions before reading each section of a chapter and then read to find the answers.

▶ Introduce key terms before students read the textbook assignment.

▶ Have students focus on the big ideas instead of trying to remember lots of facts.

▶ Have students complete graphic organizers as they read because these visual representations emphasize the big ideas and the connections between them.

▶ Include small-group activities to make textbooks more comprehensible.

▶ Teach students to take notes about the big ideas as they read.

▶ Encourage students to be active readers, to ask themselves questions, and to monitor their reading.

▶ Use the listen-read-discuss format when textbook assignments are too difficult for students to read on their own.

▶ Collect text sets to supplement content-area textbooks.

- Charts and maps to provide detailed information visually
- Margin notes to provide supplemental information or to direct readers to additional information on a topic
- Highlighted words to identify key academic vocabulary
- An index for locating specific information
- A glossary to assist readers in pronouncing and defining technical words
- Study questions at the end of the chapter to check readers' comprehension

These features make the textbook easier to read. It's essential that students learn to use them to make reading content-area textbooks more effective and improve their comprehension (Harvey & Goudvis, 2007). Teachers teach **minilessons** about these features and demonstrate how to use them to read more effectively.

Making Textbooks More Comprehensible

Teachers use a variety of activities during each stage of the reading process to make content-area textbooks more "reader friendly" and to improve students' comprehension. Figure 12–5 lists ways teachers can make content-area textbooks more comprehensible at each stage of the reading process. Teachers choose one or more activities at each stage to support their students' reading but never try to do all of the activities listed in the figure during a single reading assignment.

Stage 1: Prereading. Teachers prepare students to read the chapter and nurture their interest in the topic. There are four purposes:

- Activate and build students' background knowledge about the topic
- Introduce big ideas and technical words

FIGURE 12–5 ◆ *Ways to Make Content-Area Textbooks More Comprehensible*		
Stage	**Activities**	
Prereading	K-W-L charts Text sets Websites, videos, and DVDs Anticipation guides Exclusion brainstorming	Possible sentences Prereading plan Question-Answer-Relationships Text walks Word walls
Reading	Interactive read-alouds Small-group read and share	Note taking Graphic organizers
Responding	Discussions Think-pair-square-share Graphic organizers	Learning logs Double-entry journals Quickwriting
Exploring	Word walls Word sorts Data charts	Semantic feature analysis Hot seat Tea party
Applying	Webquests PowerPoint presentations RAFT	Multigenre projects Oral reports Essays

- Set purposes for reading
- Preview the text

Prereading activities are crucial because they often determine whether students will be successful in reading and understanding the textbook chapter.

Teachers use a variety of activities to activate and build students' background knowledge about the topic, including developing **K-W-L charts**, reading aloud stories and non-fiction books, reading information on websites, and viewing videos and DVDs. They also use the gamelike formats of anticipation guides and exclusion brainstorming to heighten students' interest. In **anticipation guides**, teachers introduce a set of statements on the topic of the chapter; students agree or disagree with each statement, and then they read the assignment to see if they were right. In **exclusion brainstorming**, students examine a list of words and decide which ones they think are related to the textbook chapter and then read the chapter to check their predictions.

Teachers introduce the big ideas in a chapter when they create a **prereading plan** in which they present an idea discussed in the chapter and then have students brainstorm words and ideas related to it. They begin a **word wall** with some key words. Another activity is possible sentences, in which students compose sentences that might be in the textbook chapter using two or more vocabulary words from the chapter. Later, as they read the chapter, students check to see if their sentences are included or are accurate enough so that they could be used in the chapter.

Students are more successful when they have a purpose for reading. Teachers set the purpose through prereading activities, and they also can have students read the questions at the end of the chapter, assume responsibility for finding the answer to a specific question, and then read to find the answer. After reading, students share their answers with the class. To preview the chapter, teachers take students on a "text walk"

STRUGGLING READERS AND WRITERS

Content-Area Textbooks

Struggling readers need to know how to read content-area textbooks.

Struggling readers approach all reading assignments the same way—they open to the first page and read straight through—and afterward complain that they don't remember anything. This approach isn't successful because students aren't actively involved in the reading experience, and they're not taking advantage of the special features used in content-area textbooks, including headings, highlighted words, illustrations, end-of-chapter questions, and a glossary, that make the books easier to read.

Successful readers think about the text while they're reading, and the textbook features encourage students' active engagement. Before beginning to read, students activate their background knowledge by previewing the chapter. They read the introduction, the headings, the conclusion, and the end-of-chapter questions and examine photos and illustrations. They locate highlighted vocabulary words, use context clues to figure out the meaning of some words, and check the meaning of others in the glossary. Now they're thinking about the topic. As they read, students try to identify the big ideas and the relationships among them. They stop after reading each section to add information to a graphic organizer, take notes on small self-stick notes, or talk about the section with a classmate. After students finish reading the entire chapter, they make sure they can answer the end-of-chapter questions.

Teachers need to teach students how to read a content-area textbook, pointing out the special features and demonstrating how to use them. Next, students work in small groups or with partners as they practice using the features to engage their thinking and improve their comprehension. With guided practice and opportunities to work collaboratively with classmates, students can become more-successful readers.

page by page through the chapter, noting main headings, examining illustrations, and reading diagrams and charts. Sometimes students turn the main headings into questions and prepare to read to find the answers to the questions or check the questions at the end of the chapter to determine the **Question-Answer-Relationships**.

Stage 2: Reading. Students read the textbook chapter. There are three purposes:

- Ensure that students can read the assignment
- Assist students in identifying the big ideas
- Help students organize ideas and details

Students read efferently because their goal is to remember important information.

Sometimes the prereading activities provide enough scaffolding so that students can read the assignment successfully, but they may need more support. When students can't read the chapter, teachers have several options. They can read the chapter aloud before students read it independently, or students can read with partners. Teachers also can divide the chapter into sections and assign groups of students to read each section and report back to the class; in this way, the reading assignment is shorter, and students can read along with their group members. Students learn the material from the entire chapter as they listen to classmates share their sections. After this sharing experience, students may then be able to go back and read the chapter independently. Teachers also scaffold students as they identify and organize the big ideas. Taking notes and completing graphic organizers are two ways to help students focus on the big ideas as they read.

Stage 3: Responding. Teachers help students develop their understanding about the information they've read. There are three purposes:

- Clarify students' misunderstandings
- Help students summarize the big ideas
- Make connections to students' lives

Students use talk and writing as tools for learning during this stage.

Students discuss the big ideas, ask questions to clarify confusions, and make connections as they participate in discussions. One popular technique is think-pair-square-share, in which students think about a topic individually for several minutes, then they pair up with classmates to share their thoughts and hear other points of view. Next, each pair of students gets together with another pair, forming a square, to share their thinking. Finally, students come back together as a class to discuss the topic.

Writing is another way for students to respond: They do **quickwrites**, write in **learning logs**, or use **double-entry journals** to record quotes or important information from the chapter and make connections to their own lives. Students also write summaries in which they synthesize the big ideas and describe the relationships among them. Summary writing requires students to think strategically as they analyze what they've read to determine which ideas are the most important. The minilesson on page 332 shows how Mr. Surabian teaches his fourth graders to write summaries.

Stage 4: Exploring. Teachers guide students as they dig into the text to focus on academic vocabulary, examine the text, and analyze the big ideas. There are three purposes:

- Have students study vocabulary words
- Review the big ideas
- Help students connect the big ideas and details

In this "teaching" stage, students participate in activities to deepen their understanding of content-area topics.

As they study the academic vocabulary in the chapter, students post words on **word walls**, make posters to study their meaning, and do **word sorts** to emphasize the relationships among the big ideas. To focus on the big ideas, students make data charts to record important information or create a **semantic feature analysis** chart to classify details. Figure 12–6 shows an excerpt from a data chart that fourth graders made as they studied the regions of their state. Students often keep these charts and refer to them when writing reports or creating other projects. They also participate in **hot seat** and **tea party** to talk about what they're learning.

Stage 5: Applying. Teachers support students as they apply what they've learned by creating projects. There are three purposes:

- Expand students' knowledge about the topic
- Personalize students' learning
- Expect students to share their knowledge

As students create projects, they integrate their content-area knowledge and use writing to demonstrate knowledge.

Students participate in webquests, read books from the text set, conduct research online, and interview people to expand their knowledge, and then they share what they've learned by writing reports and essays, creating PowerPoint presentations and multigenre projects, presenting oral reports, and doing other projects.

Learning How to Study

Students are often asked to remember content-area material that they've read for a discussion, to take a test, or for an oral or written project. The traditional way to study is to memorize a list of facts, but it's more effective to use strategies that require

TOPIC: *Writing Summaries of Informational Articles*
GRADE: *Fourth Grade*
TIME: *Five 30-minute sessions*

Mr. Surabian plans to teach his students how to write a summary; only a few students are familiar with the term *summary writing*, and no one knows how to write one. Writing a summary is one of the state's fourth-grade standards. The teacher recognizes that his students need both instruction in how to write a summary and practice opportunities to be successful on high-stakes writing tests.

❶ Introduce the Topic

Mr. Surabian explains that a summary is a brief statement of the main points of an article. He presents a poster with these characteristics of a summary:

- ▶ A summary tells the big ideas.
- ▶ A summary is organized to show connections between the big ideas.
- ▶ A summary has a conclusion.
- ▶ A summary is written in a student's own words.
- ▶ A summary is brief.

❷ Share Examples

Mr. Surabian shares a one-page article about Wilbur and Orville Wright and the summary he's written about it, and the students check that the summary meets all of the characteristics on the poster. Next, he shares a second article about mummification, and the students pick out the big ideas and highlight them. Then he shares his summary, and the fourth graders check that he included the big ideas and that the summary meets all of the characteristics on the poster.

❸ Provide Information

The next day, Mr. Surabian reviews the characteristics of a summary and shares an article about motorcycles. The students read it, identify and highlight the big ideas, draw a diagram to illustrate the relationships among the ideas, and create a conclusion. After this preparation, they write a summary of the article, checking that it meets the characteristics listed on the classroom poster. On the third day, Mr. Surabian's students repeat the process with an article about rain forests.

❹ Guide Practice

On the fourth day, Mr. Surabian shares an article about the Mississippi River. The students read and discuss it, identifying the big ideas, relationships among them, and possible conclusions. Next, students work in small groups to write a summary. Afterward, they share their summaries. The class repeats this activity the next day; this time, they read about porpoises. Mr. Surabian shortens the time spent discussing the article and identifying the big ideas and conclusions so that students assume more responsibility for developing the summary.

❺ Assess Learning

Mr. Surabian assesses students' learning by monitoring them as they work in small groups. He identifies several students who need practice, and he plans additional minilessons with them.

FIGURE 12–6 ◆ *An Excerpt From a Data Chart on California*

REGION	VEGETATION	ANIMALS	PLACES	HISTORY	ECONOMY
North	Redwood tres	Grizzly Bears Salmon	Eureka Napa Valley	Sutter's Fort GOLD!	Logging Wine
North Coast	Redwood trees Giant Sequoia tres	seals Sea Otters Monarch Butterflies	San Francisco	Chinatown Cable Cars Earthquake	Computers Ghirardelli chocolate Levis
South Coast	Palm tres Orange tres	Gray whales Condors	Los Angeles Hollywood	El Camino Real missions O.J. Simpson Earthquake	Disneyland TV + movies airplanes
Central Valley	Poppies	Quail	Fresno Sacramento	capital Pony Express Railroad	grapes Peaches Cotton Almond
Sierra Nevada	Giant Sequoia Lupine	Mule Deer Golden eagles Black Baers	Yosemite	John Muir	skiing

students to think critically and to elaborate ideas. As they study, students need to do the following:

- Restate the big ideas in their own words
- Make connections between the big ideas
- Add details to each big idea
- Ask questions about the importance of the ideas
- Monitor whether they understand the ideas

Students use these strategies as they study class notes, complete graphic organizers to highlight the big ideas, and orally rehearse by explaining the big ideas to themselves.

Taking Notes. When students take notes, they identify what's most important and then restate it in their own words. They select and organize the big ideas, identify organizational patterns, paraphrase and summarize information, and use abbreviations and symbols to take notes more quickly. Copying information verbatim is less effective than restating it because students are less actively involved in understanding what they're reading.

Students take notes in different ways: They can make outlines or bulleted lists; draw flow charts, webs, and other graphic organizers; or make **double-entry journals** with notes in one column and interpretations in the other column. Or, if students can mark on the text they're reading, they underline or highlight the big ideas and write notes in the margin.

Too often, teachers encourage students to take notes without teaching them how to do it. It's important that teachers share copies of notes they've taken so students see different styles of note taking, and that they demonstrate note taking—identifying the big ideas, organizing them, and restating information in their own words—as students read an article or an excerpt from a content-area textbook. Once students understand how to identify the big ideas and to state them in their own words, they need opportunities to practice note taking. First, they work in small groups to take notes collaboratively, and then they work with a partner.

Teachers often use study guides to direct students toward the big ideas when they read content-area textbooks. They create the study guides using diagrams, charts, lists, and sentences, and students complete them as they read using information and vocabulary from the chapter. Afterward, the students review their completed study guides with partners, small groups, or the whole class and check that their work is correct.

It's also important that teachers teach students how to review notes to study for quizzes and tests. Too often, students think they're finished with notes once they've written them because they don't understand that the notes are a study tool.

Question-Answer-Relationships. Students use Raphael's **Question-Answer-Relationships** (QARs) technique (1986) to understand how to answer the questions at the end of content-area textbook chapters. The technique teaches students to notice whether they're likely to find the answer to a question "right there" on the page, between the lines, or beyond the information provided in the text. When students are aware of the requirements posed by a question, they're prepared to answer it correctly.

Why Aren't Content-Area Textbooks Enough?

Sometimes content-area textbooks are used as the complete instructional program in social studies or science, but that's not a good idea. Textbooks survey topics, and other instructional materials are needed to provide depth and understanding. Textbook-only programs are often limited to reading a textbook chapter together as a class and answering the questions at the end of the chapter; however, students need to read, write, and talk about topics they're learning. It's more effective to use the reading process and then extend students' learning with projects. In addition, content-area textbooks are one-size-fits-all, ignoring the reality of diversity in today's classrooms. It's more effective to develop thematic units with a variety of reading materials, instructional activities, and grouping patterns and use the textbook as one resource.

Thematic Units

A thematic unit is an in-depth study of a topic that integrates reading and writing with social studies, science, and other curricular areas. Students are often involved in planning thematic units and identifying some of the questions they want to explore and the activities that interest them. Textbooks are used as a resource, but only one of many. Students explore topics that interest them and research answers to questions they have posed and are genuinely interested in answering. They share their learning at the end of the unit, as Ms. Boland's students did in the vignette at the beginning of the chapter, and are assessed on what they've learned as well as on the processes they used in learning and working in the classroom.

How to Develop a Thematic Unit

To begin planning a thematic unit, teachers choose the general topic and determine the instructional focus using literacy and content-area standards. Next, teachers identify the resources they have available and develop their teaching plan, integrating content-area study with reading and writing activities. Here's an overview of the important considerations:

1. **Determine the focus.** Teachers identify three or four big ideas to emphasize in the unit because the goal isn't to teach a collection of facts but to help students grapple with big understandings. Teachers also choose the literacy and content-area standards to teach during the unit.

2. **Collect a text set of books.** Teachers collect picture books, novels, nonfiction books, and poems on topics related to the unit for the text set and place them in a special area in the classroom library. Teachers will read aloud some books, and students will read others independently or in small groups. Other books are used for minilessons or as mentor texts for writing projects.

3. **Coordinate content-area textbook readings.** Teachers review the content-area textbook chapters related to the unit and decide how to use them. For example, they might use one chapter as an introduction, have students read others during the unit, or read the chapters to review the big ideas. They also think about how to make the textbook more comprehensible, especially for English learners and struggling readers.

4. **Locate Internet and other multimedia materials.** Teachers locate websites, webquests, DVDs, maps, models, artifacts, and other materials for the unit; some materials are used to build students' background knowledge and others to teach the big ideas. Also, students create multimedia materials to display in the classroom.

5. **Design instructional activities.** Teachers think about ways to teach the unit using reading and writing as learning tools, brainstorm possible activities, and then develop a planning cluster incorporating the activities. They also make decisions about coordinating the thematic unit with a literature focus unit using one book related to the unit, literature circles featuring books from the text set, or reading and writing workshop.

6. **Identify topics for minilessons.** Teachers plan minilessons to teach strategies and skills related to reading and writing nonfiction as well as content-area topics related to the unit based on state standards and the needs teachers have identified from students' work.

7. **Consider ways to differentiate instruction.** Teachers plan to use flexible grouping to adjust instruction so that it meets students' achievement and language proficiency levels, provides appropriate books and other instructional materials for all students, and scaffolds struggling students and challenges high achievers with tiered activities and projects.

8. **Brainstorm possible projects.** Teachers think about projects students can pursue to apply and personalize their learning at the end of the unit. This planning enables teachers to collect supplies and have suggestions ready for students who need assistance in choosing a project.

9. **Plan for assessment.** Teachers consider how they'll monitor students' learning and evaluate learning at the end of the unit; this planning allows them to explain to students at the beginning of the unit how they'll be evaluated and check to see that their assessment emphasizes students' learning of the big ideas.

After considering unit goals, grade-level expectations, the available resources, and possible activities, teachers are prepared to develop a time schedule, write lesson plans, and create rubrics and other assessment tools.

Scaffolding English Learners

Teachers have two goals in mind as they consider how to accommodate English learners' instructional needs when they develop thematic units: They want to maximize students' opportunities to learn English and develop content-area knowledge, and they consider the instructional challenges facing their students and how to adjust instruction and assessment to meet their needs (Peregoy & Boyle, 2008).

Challenges in Learning Content-Area Information. English learners often have more difficulty learning during thematic units than during literacy instruction because of the additional language demands of unfamiliar topics, academic vocabulary, and nonfiction books (Rothenberg & Fisher, 2007). Here are the most important challenges facing many of these students:

English Language Proficiency. Students' ability to understand and communicate in English has an obvious effect on their learning. Teachers address this challenge by teaching English and content-area information together. They use realia and visual materials to support students' understanding of the topics they're teaching, and they simplify the language, when necessary, in their explanations of the big ideas. They consider the reading levels of the trade books and content-area textbooks they're using, and when students can't read these books themselves, they read them aloud. But if the books are still too difficult, they find others to use instead. Teachers also provide frequent opportunities for ELs to use the new vocabulary as they talk informally about the topics they're learning.

Background Knowledge. English learners often lack the necessary background knowledge about content-area topics, especially about American history, so teachers need to take time to expand students' knowledge base using artifacts, photos, models, picture books, videos, and field trips, and they need to make clear links between the topics and students' past experiences and previous thematic units; otherwise, the instruction won't be meaningful. Finding time to preteach this information isn't easy, but without it, English learners aren't likely to learn much during the unit. Teachers also involve all students, including ELs, in making **K-W-L charts**, doing **exclusion brainstorming**, and marking **anticipation guides** to activate their background knowledge.

Academic Vocabulary. English learners are often unfamiliar with content-area vocabulary because these words aren't used in everyday conversation; they're technical terms, such as *prairie schooner, democracy, scavenger,* and *photosynthesis.* Because some words, such as *democracy,* are cognates, students who speak Spanish or another Latin-based language at home may be familiar with them, but other terms have entered English from other languages. Teachers address this challenge by preteaching key vocabulary words, posting words (with picture clues, if needed) on **word walls**, and using realia, photos, and picture books to introduce the words. They also involve students in a variety of vocabulary activities, including doing **word sorts**, making a **semantic feature analysis**, and drawing diagrams and posters about the words.

Reading. Nonfiction books and content-area textbooks are different than stories: Authors organize information differently, incorporate special features, and use more-sophisticated sentence structures. In addition, nonfiction text is dense, packed with facts and academic vocabulary. Teachers address the challenge of an unfamiliar genre in three ways. First, they teach students about nonfiction books, including the expository text structures and the distinctive text features of this genre. Next, they teach the strategies that readers use to comprehend nonfiction books, including determining the big ideas and summarizing. Third, they teach ELs to make graphic organizers and take notes to highlight the big ideas and the relationships among them. Through this instruction, English learners are equipped with the necessary tools to read nonfiction books and textbooks more effectively.

Writing. Writing is difficult for English learners because it reflects their English proficiency, but it also supports their learning of content knowledge and English. All students should use writing as a tool for learning during thematic units. As they **quickwrite**, draw graphic organizers, make charts and diagrams, take notes, and write in **learning logs**, they're grappling with the big ideas and the vocabulary they're learning. Students also use writing to demonstrate learning. This more-formal type of writing is much more difficult for English learners because of increased language demands. Teachers address this challenge by choosing a project that requires less writing or by having students work with partners or in small groups.

These challenges are primarily the result of the students' limited knowledge of English, and when teachers address them, ELs are more likely to be successful in learning content-area information and developing English language proficiency.

Adjusting Instruction. Teachers address the challenges facing English learners as they differentiate instruction to maximize students' learning. They also find ways to increase students' participation in instructional activities because many ELs avoid interacting with mainstream classmates or fear asking questions in class (Peregoy & Boyle, 2008; Rothenberg & Fisher, 2007). These suggestions guide teachers in adjusting their instruction:

- Use visuals and manipulatives, including artifacts, videos, photographs, and models
- Preteach big ideas and academic vocabulary
- Teach students about expository text structures
- Practice taking notes with students
- Highlight relationships among big ideas with graphic organizers and other diagrams
- Organize students to work in small collaborative groups and with partners
- Include frequent opportunities for students to talk informally about big ideas
- Provide opportunities for students to use oral language, reading, and writing
- Collect text sets, including picture books and online resources
- Use a textbook as only one resource
- Review big ideas and key vocabulary

These suggestions take into account students' level of English development, their limited background knowledge and vocabulary about many unit topics, and their reading and writing levels.

Plans for a Fourth-Grade Unit on the Desert Ecosystem

UNIT INTRODUCTION

- Make a K-W-L chart about the desert ecosystem.
- Share one or more books from the text set.
- Have students participate in a tea party activity.
- Use the possible sentences activity to think about deserts.
- View a film about the fragile desert ecosystem.

NEW LITERACIES

- Visit theme-related websites, including Desert Biomes (www.desertusa.com) and A Virtual Museum of the Mojave Desert (http://score.rims. k12.ca.us/activity/mojave/index/html).
- Complete a webquest about the desert ecosystem.
- Use Inspiration software to create a graphic about the ecosystem.
- Create a virtual museum or website about deserts.

CONTENT-AREA TEXTBOOKS

- Preview the chapter, noticing reader-friendly features, before reading.
- Use picture books to introduce ideas before students read the chapter.
- Read sections of the chapter in small groups and report back to the class.
- Take notes immediately after reading using graphic organizers.
- Examine end-of-chapter questions using QARs.

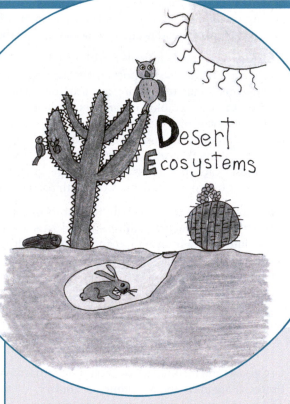

DIGGING INTO THE BIG IDEAS

- Create posters and graphic organizers about big ideas and relationships among them.
- Complete a semantic feature analysis comparing deserts to other ecosystems.
- Record information and explore ideas about deserts in learning logs.
- Research topics related to this ecosystem and share information in multigenre reports and other projects.

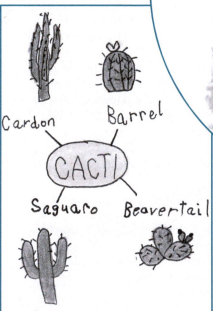

CENTERS

- **Data chart:** Record information about desert biomes on the ecosystem chart.
- **Listening:** Listen to a book from the text set.
- **Word sort:** Sort words from the word wall.
- **Visual literacy:** Create tabletop dioramas about various desert biomes.
- **Writing:** Prepare a page for the class alphabet book about deserts.

USING THE TEXT SET

- Use for interactive read-alouds.
- Read these books during reading workshop.
- Participate in literature circles using books from the text set.
- Use books in minilessons about genres, expository text structures, and nonfiction features.
- Use books as mentor texts for writing activities.

TEXT SET ON THE DESERT ECOSYSTEM

Bash, B. (2002). *Desert giant*. Boston: Little, Brown.
Baylor, B. (1993). *Desert voices*. New York: Scribner.
George, J. C. (1996). *One day in the desert*. New York: HarperTrophy.
Gibbons, G. (1999). *Deserts*. New York: Holiday House.
Guiberson, B. Z. (2007). *Cactus hotel*. New York: Holt.
Jablonsky, A. (1994). *100 questions about desert life*. Tucson, AZ: Southwest Parks and Monuments Association.
Mora, P. (2008). *The desert is my mother*. Houston: Piñata Books.
Pratt-Serafini, K. J. (2002). *Saguaro moon: A desert journal*. Nevada City, CA: Dawn Publications.
Siebert, D. (1992). *Mojave*. New York: HarperTrophy.
Simon, S. (1990). *Deserts*. New York: Morrow.
Taylor, B. (1998). *Desert life*. New York: Dorling Kindersley.
Wright-Frierson, V. (2002). *A desert scrapbook*. New York: Aladdin Books.

ACADEMIC VOCABULARY

- Post words on a word wall.
- Make posters and diagrams to learn about key Tier 3 vocabulary.
- Use quickwrites to explore meanings of words.
- Do a word sort using words from the world wall.
- Create a class alphabet book about the desert using words from the word wall.

AUTHOR STUDY

- Share information about author Byrd Baylor, who lives in the Arizona desert.
- Read Byrd Baylor's books about the desert, including *The Desert Is Theirs* (1987) and *Desert Voices* (1993).
- Write "I Am . . ." poems based on *Desert Voices*.
- Create a multigenre project about the author and her books.
- Write letters to Byrd Baylor.

DESERT WORD WALL

ABC	DEFGH	IJKL
biome	ecosystem	kangaroo rat
cactus	fragile	king snake
adaptation	gila monster	jackrabbit
coyote	dunes	Joshua tree
coral snake	endangered	lizard
camouflage	exoskeleton	javelina
burrow	hamster	
coyote	hawk	

MNO	PQRS	TVWXYZ
Mojave Desert	Sahara Desert	water
oasis	scorpion	tortoise
owl	Sonoran Desert	toad
	roadrunner	yucca
	sandgrouse	
	spiny	
	saguaro	
	sidewinder	

CULMINATING PROJECTS

- Create a class multigenre project on deserts.
- Write a collaborative report about the desert ecosystem.
- Research a desert animal or plant and give a PowerPoint presentation about it.
- Design a chart to compare the desert ecosystem with another ecosystem.
- Develop a website or virtual museum about this ecosystem.

Plans for a Sixth-Grade Unit on Ancient Egypt

UNIT INTRODUCTION

- Create a K-W-L chart about ancient Egypt.
- Read books from the text set about ancient Egypt.
- Use an anticipation guide.
- Participate in a webquest on ancient Egypt.
- Examine a collection of pictures or view a film.

CENTERS

- **Maps:** Compare ancient and modern Egyptian maps and draw a map of ancient Egypt.
- **Hieroglyphics:** Create a poster with a message written in hieroglyphics.
- **Word sort:** Do a word sort using words from the word wall.
- **Research:** Investigate an Egyptian god and share information in a poster.
- **Computer:** Do a webquest.

CONTENT-AREA TEXTBOOKS.

- Use QARs to examine end-of-chapter questions before reading.
- Read sections of text with partners or in small groups.
- Turn headings into questions, read to find answers, and answer questions in quickwrites.
- Use graphic organizers to highlight big ideas and relationships among them.
- Give small-group presentations to answer end-of-chapter questions.

ACADEMIC VOCABULARY

- Post vocabulary on a word wall.
- Make word maps and posters to analyze the root words and etymologies.
- Do a word sort related to the theme.
- Complete a semantic feature analysis chart using key vocabulary.
- Create a class alphabet book on ancient Egypt.

WORD WALL

ABCDE	FGH	IJKLM
craftsmen	fertile	mudbrick
embalming	Howard Carter	irrigation
canopic jars	harvest	lotus
Africa	Great Pyramid	linen
Champolion	Hatshepsut	Isis
Amun-Ra	harmony	Imhotep
dynasty	hieroglyphs	Luxor
Cleopatra	Horus	Memphis
Egyptologist	Geb	

NOP	QRS	TUVWXYZ
Nut	silt	temple
pharaoh	Ramses the	worship
Nile River	Great	Tutankhamun
Nefertiti	scarab beetle	Valley of the
natron	rituals	Kings
pyramid	Ra	Thoth
Old Kingdom	Seth	Tefnut
New Kingdom	Seshat	vizier
Ptah	Sekhmet	
Nephthys	Shu	
Oriris	Senet	
obelisk	scribes	
papyrus	Rosetta stone	

ORAL LANGUAGE

- Make a collection of objects and pictures related to the theme and share them with the class.
- Participate in a hot seat as an Egyptologist. King Tut, Cleopatra, an embalmer, or another personality.
- Research a topic related to the theme and give a PowerPoint presentation to share new knowledge.
- Present a choral reading related to the theme.

DIGGING INTO THE BIG IDEAS

- Add information to a data chart comparing ancient civilizations.
- Write a simulated journal or learning log.
- Create an open-mind portrait of a historical figure or another person.
- Make a Venn diagram to compare ancient Egypt to another ancient civilization or modern America.
- Research a topic related to the theme and prepare an oral or written report.

CULMINATING PROJECTS

- Write an essay about how this ancient civilization influenced ours.
- Create an artifact and share information about its importance in an oral or written report.
- Create a class multigenre project.
- Write an essay explaining how to mummify a person.
- Create a website or virtual museum about ancient Egypt.

NEW LITERACIES

- Visit websites about ancient Egypt, including the British Museum's website (www.ancientegypt.co.uk).
- Complete a webquest at (www.iwebquest.com/egypt/ancientegypt) and other quest sites.
- Create a multigenre project that includes a digital component.
- Create a virtual museum or website on ancient Egypt.

TEXT SET

Cole, J. (2003). *Ms. Frizzle's adventures: Ancient Egypt*. New York: Scholastic.

Der Manuelian, P. (1996). *Hieroglyphs from A to Z*. New York: Scholastic.

Edwards, R. (2006). *Who was King Tut?* New York: Grosset & Dunlap.

Gregory, K. (1999). *Cleopatra VII, daughter of the Nile*. New York: Scholastic.

Hart, G. (2008). *Ancient Egypt*. New York: DK Publishing.

Macaulay, D. (1982). *Pyramid*. Boston: Houghton Mifflin.

McGraw, E. J. (1985). *Mara, daughter of the Nile*. New York: Puffin Books.

Perl, L. (1990). *Mummies, tombs, and treasure: Secrets of ancient Egypt*. New York: Clarion Books.

Rubalcaba, J. (2007). *Ancient Egypt: Archaeology unlocks the secrets of Egypt's past*. Washington, DC: National Geographic Children's Books.

Sabuda, R. (1997). *Tutankhamen's gift*. New York: Aladdin Books.

Winters, K. (2003). *Voices of ancient Egypt*. Washington, DC: National Geographic Children's Books.

USING THE TEXT SET

- Do book talks to introduce the books.
- Use the interactive read-aloud procedure to share some books with the class.
- Teach nonfiction genre, expository text structures, or nonfiction features using these books.
- Participate in literature circles.
- Read text set books during reading workshop.

Choosing Alternative Assessments. Teachers monitor English learners' progress using a combination of observation and questioning. Too often, teachers ask ELs if they understand, but that usually isn't effective because they tend respond positively, even when they're confused. It's more productive to interact with students, talking with them about the activity they're involved in or asking questions about the book they're reading.

Teachers also devise alternative assessments to learn more about English learners' achievement when they have difficulty on regular evaluations (Rothenberg & Fisher, 2007). For example, instead of writing an essay, students can draw pictures or create graphic organizers about the big ideas and add words from the **word wall** to label them to demonstrate their learning, or they can talk about what they've learned in a conference with the teacher. Instead of giving written tests, teachers can simplify the wording of the test questions and have ELs answer them orally. When it's important to have English learners create written projects, they'll be more successful if they work collaboratively in small groups. Portfolios are especially useful in documenting ELs' achievement. Students also place work samples in their portfolios to show what they've learned about content-area topics and how their English proficiency has developed.

A Fourth-Grade Unit on the Desert Ecosystem

During this 3-week unit, students investigate the plants, animals, and people that live in the desert and learn how they support each other. They keep **learning logs** in which they take notes and write reactions to books they're reading. Students divide into book clubs during the first week to read books about the desert. During the second week of the unit, students participate in an author study of Byrd Baylor, a woman who lives in the desert and writes about desert life, and they read many of her books. During the third week, students participate in reading workshop to read other desert books and reread favorites. To extend their learning, students create projects, including writing desert riddles, making a chart of the desert ecosystem, and drawing a desert mural. Together as a class, students write a desert alphabet book. The plans for the unit are presented on pages 338 and 339.

A Sixth-Grade Unit on Ancient Egypt

Students learn about this great ancient civilization during a monthlong unit. Key concepts include the influence of the Nile River on Egyptian life, the contributions of this civilization to contemporary America, a comparison of ancient to modern Egypt, and the techniques Egyptologists use to locate tombs of the ancient rulers and decipher Egyptian hieroglyphics. Students read books in literature circles and read other books from the text set independently. They also consult online resources and complete a webquest about ancient Egypt. Teachers teach minilessons on map-reading skills, taking notes from content-area textbooks, Egyptian gods, and writing poems. At the end of the unit, students create projects and share them on Egypt day, when they assume the roles of ancient Egyptians, dressing as ancient people did and eating foods of the period. The plans for the unit are on pages 340 and 341.

CHAPTER 12

How Effective Teachers Use Reading and Writing in the Content Areas

▶ Teachers have students use reading and writing as learning tools.

▶ Teachers teach students about the features of content-area textbooks.

▶ Teachers use a variety of activities to make content-area textbooks more comprehensible.

▶ Teachers teach students how to take notes and study effectively.

▶ Teachers focus on big ideas in thematic units.

Compendium of Instructional Procedures

Anticipation Guides

Teachers use anticipation guides (Head & Readence, 1986) to activate students' background knowledge before they read content-area textbooks and nonfiction articles and books. Teachers prepare a list of statements about the topic for students to discuss; some statements are true, and others are incorrect or based on common misconceptions. Students discuss each statement and decide whether they agree with it. Then after reading the selection, students discuss the statements again and decide whether they agree with them. Usually students change some of their opinions, and they realize that they've refined their understanding of the subject through the activity.

An anticipation guide about immigration that eighth graders considered before reading a chapter in their social studies textbook included these statements:

> *There are more people immigrating to the United States today than ever before in history.*
> *The government sets a quota for the number of people allowed to enter the United States each year.*
> *Most people immigrate to the United States because they want to find better jobs and earn more money.*
> *Aliens are people who are in the United States illegally.*
> *Refugees are people who are forced to flee from their homeland because of war or other disasters.*
> *Many immigrants have difficulty adjusting to the new ways of life in America.*

You'd probably agree with some of these statements and disagree with others; perhaps you're unsure about a couple of them. These questions direct your attention to the big ideas, and as you read, you might find that your initial assessment of one or two statements wasn't accurate, so you'll make some changes when you repeat the assessment afterward.

The Procedure. Teachers follow these steps to develop and use anticipation guides:

1. ***Identify several major concepts related to the reading assignment.*** Teachers keep in mind students' knowledge about the topic and any misconceptions they might have about it.
2. ***Develop a list of four to six statements.*** Teachers compose statements that are general enough to stimulate discussion and are useful in clarifying misconceptions and make copies for students. The guide has space for students to mark whether they agree with each statement before and again after reading.

345

Anticipation Guide on Gangs

Before Reading		Gangs	After Reading	
Agree	Disagree		Agree	Disagree
		1. Gangs are bad.		
		2. Gangs are exciting.		
		3. It is safe to be a gang member.		
		4. Gangs make a difference in a gang member's life.		
		5. Gangs fill a need.		
		6. Once you join a gang, it is very difficult to get out.		

3. ***Discuss the anticipation guide.*** Teachers introduce the anticipation guide and have students respond to the statements. Working in small groups, with partners, or individually, students decide whether they agree with each statement. Then, as a class, students discuss their responses and defend their positions.

4. ***Read the text.*** Students read the selection and compare their responses to what's stated in the text.

5. ***Discuss the statements again.*** Students talk about each statement again, citing information from the text that supports or refutes it. Or, students can again respond to each of the statements and compare their answers before and after reading. Teachers can have them fold back their first set of responses on the left side of the paper and then respond to each item again on the right side of the paper.

Anticipation guides can also be used to explore complex issues in novels, including homelessness, crime and punishment, and immigration. An eighth-grade class, for example, studied gangs before reading *The Outsiders* (Hinton, 2007) and completed the anticipation guide shown above before and after reading the novel. The statements about gangs probe important points and lead to lively discussion and thoughtful responses.

Book Talks

Book talks are brief teasers that teachers give to introduce students to books. Teachers show the book, summarize it without giving away the ending, and read a short excerpt aloud to hook students' interest. Then they pass the book off to an interested reader or place it in the classroom library. Students use the same steps when they give book talks to share the books they've read during reading workshop.

The Procedure.   Here are the steps in conducting a book talk:

1. ***Select a book to share.*** Teachers choose a new book to introduce to students or one that students haven't shown much interest in. They familiarize themselves with the book by reading or rereading it.

2. ***Plan a brief presentation.*** Teachers plan how to present the book to interest students in reading it. They usually begin with the title and author of the book, and

they mention the genre or topic and briefly summarize the plot without giving away the ending. Teachers also think about why students might be interested in it. Sometimes they choose a short excerpt to read.

3. **Show the book and present the book talk.** Teachers present the book talk and show the book. Their comments are usually enough so that at least one student will ask to borrow the book to read.

Teachers use book talks to introduce students to books in the classroom library. At the beginning of the school year, teachers take time to introduce lots of books, and during the year, they introduce new books as they're added to the library. They also introduce the books for a literature circle, or a text set of books for a thematic unit.

Choral Reading

Students use choral reading to share poems orally. This activity provides students, especially dysfluent readers, with valuable oral reading practice in which they increase their reading speed and develop prosody (Rasinski & Padak, 2004). In addition, it's valuable for English learners: As they read with English-speaking classmates, ELs hear and practice English pronunciation of words, phrasing of words in a sentence, and intonation patterns.

Many arrangements for choral reading are possible: Students read the text together as a class or read stanzas in small groups. Or, individual students may read particular lines while the class reads the rest. Here are four arrangements:

Echo Reading. A leader reads each line and the group repeats it.

Leader and Chorus Reading. A leader reads the main part, and the group reads the refrain in unison.

Small-Group Reading. The class divides into two or more groups, and each group reads part of the poem.

Cumulative Reading. One student reads the first line or stanza, and another student joins in as each line or stanza is read to create a cumulative effect.

Students experiment with different arrangements until they decide which one conveys meaning most effectively.

The Procedure. Here are the steps in doing choral readings:

1. *Select a poem to use for choral reading.* Teachers choose a poem or other text and copy it onto a chart or make multiple copies for students to read.
2. *Arrange the text for choral reading.* Teachers work with students to decide how to arrange the text. They add marks to the chart, or they have students code individual copies so that they can follow the arrangement.
3. *Rehearse the poem.* Teachers practice reading the poem with students several times at a natural speed, pronouncing words carefully.
4. *Have students read the poem aloud.* Students read the poem aloud several times as teachers emphasize that they pronounce words clearly and read with expression. Sometimes teachers record students' choral readings so that they can hear themselves.

Choral reading makes students active participants in a collaborative reading experience. Many poems can be used for choral reading; poems with repetitions, echoes, refrains, or questions and answers work well. Poems written specifically for two readers are very effective, including Fleischman's collection of insect poems, *Joyful Noise: Poems for Two Voices* (2004). Teachers can also use speeches, songs, and longer poems; try, for example, *Brother Eagle, Sister Sky: A Message From Chief Seattle* (Jeffers, 1993) and *This Land Is Your Land* (Guthrie, 2002).

Cloze Procedure

The cloze procedure is a diagnostic assessment that teachers use to gather information about readers' abilities to deal with the content and structure of texts (Tierney & Readence, 2005). To construct a cloze passage, teachers choose an excerpt from a book—a story, a nonfiction book, or a content-area textbook—that students have read, and they delete every fifth word in the passage and replace them with blanks. Then students read the passage and fill in the missing words. Only the exact word is correct.

This cloze passage is about wolves:

> *The leaders of a wolf pack are called the alpha wolves. There is an _____ male and an alpha _____. They are usually the _____ and the strongest wolves _____ the pack. An alpha _____ fight any wolf that _____ to take over the _____. When the alpha looks _____ other wolf in the _____, the other wolf crouches _____ and tucks its tail _____ its hind legs. Sometimes _____ rolls over and licks _____ alpha wolf's face as _____ to say, "You are _____ boss."*

The missing words are *alpha, female, largest, in, will, tries, pack, the, eye, down, between, it, the, if,* and *the.*

The cloze procedure assesses sentence-level comprehension. It's a useful tool for determining which texts are at students' instructional levels and for monitoring students' comprehension. A caution, however: Cloze doesn't measure comprehension globally; it assesses only students' ability to use their knowledge of word meanings and sentence structure within individual sentences and paragraphs.

The Procedure. Teachers follow these steps to use the cloze procedure:

1. *Select a passage from a textbook or trade book.* Teachers select a passage and retype it. The first sentence is typed exactly as it appears in the original text, but beginning with the second sentence, one of the first five words is deleted and replaced with a blank. Then every fifth word in the remainder of the passage is deleted and replaced with a blank.
2. *Complete the cloze activity.* Students silently read the passage all the way through once and then reread it and predict or "guess" the word that goes in each blank. They write the deleted words in the blanks.
3. *Score students' work.* Teachers award one point for each correctly identified word. Next, they calculate the percentage of correct answers by dividing the number of points by the number of blanks and compare the percentage with this scale to determine the student's reading level:

61% or more correct replacements: independent level

41–60% correct replacements: instructional level

fewer than 40% correct replacements: frustration level

The cloze procedure can be used to assess students' reading level in unfamiliar books, or to measure their comprehension after reading a book. When teachers wish to check students' comprehension, they delete specific words, such as character names and facts related to key events, rather than every fifth word. This assessment procedure is also used to judge whether a book is appropriate for classroom instruction. Teachers prepare a cloze passage and have students predict the missing words. If students correctly predict more than 50% of the deleted words, it's easy reading, but if they predict fewer than 30%, it's too difficult. The instructional range is 30–50% correct predictions (Reutzel & Cooter, 2008).

Double-Entry Journals

A double-entry journal is a **reading log** in which the pages are divided into two columns, and students write different types of information in each column (Berthoff, 1981). In the left column, students write quotes from the book, and in the right column, they reflect on the quotes by making connections to their own lives or the world, asking questions, or making predictions. An excerpt from a fifth grader's double-entry journal about *The Lion, the Witch and the Wardrobe* (Lewis, 2005) is shown below. Double-entry journals help students structure their thinking about a text (Tovani, 2000). The quotes that students select indicate what they think is important, and the responses they make reveal their understanding of what they've read.

The Procedure. Students write double-entry journals independently after reading each chapter or two of a novel or nonfiction book, and they follow these steps:

1. *Design journal pages.* Students divide the pages in their reading logs into two columns. They may label the left column "Quotes" and the right column "Reflections."
2. *Write quotes in journals.* After reading, students copy one or more important or interesting quotes in the left column.

Excerpts From a Fifth Grader's Double-Entry Journal About The Lion, the Witch and the Wardrobe

Chapter	Quotes	Reflections
1	I will tell you this is the sort of house where no one is going to mind what we do.	I remember the time that I went to Beaumont, Texas to stay with my aunt. My aunt's house was very large. She had a piano and she let us play it. She told us that we could do whatever we wanted to.
5	"How do you know?" he asked, "that your sister's story is not true?"	It reminds me of when I was little and I had an imaginary place. I would go there in my mind. I made up all kinds of make-believe stories about myself in this imaginary place. One time I told my big brother about my imaginary place. He laughed at me and told me I was silly. But it didn't bother me because nobody can stop me from thinking what I want.
15	Still they could see the shape of the great lion lying dead in his bonds.	When Aslan died I thought about when my Uncle Carl died.
	They're nibbling at the cords.	This reminds me of the story where the lion lets the mouse go and the mouse helps the lion.

3. *Reflect on the quotes.* In the right column, students explain why they chose a quote, write connections, or make predictions. If students have difficulty writing reflections, it's helpful to have them talk about the quotes with partners first.

Students can use double-entry journals in other ways, too. For example, they can analyze a character, delve into a social issue, or compare viewpoints as they read a novel, and instead of writing quotes they make notes in the left column and reflect on them in the right column.

Exclusion Brainstorming

Teachers use exclusion brainstorming to activate students' background knowledge and expand their understanding about a topic before reading (Blachowicz, 1986). Teachers present a list of words, and students identify the ones that they think don't relate to the topic. Then after reading, students review the list and decide whether they chose correctly. Exclusion brainstorming is a useful prereading activity because as students talk about the words on the list, they refine their knowledge, expand their academic vocabulary, and set a purpose for reading.

The Procedure. Here are the steps in exclusion brainstorming:

1. *Prepare a word list.* Teachers identify words related to a nonfiction book or content-area textbook chapter and include a few unrelated words. They write the list on chart paper or make copies for students.
2. *Read the list of words.* Teachers read the list, and then, in small groups or together as a class, students decide which words aren't related and draw circles around them.
3. *Learn about the topic.* Students read the text, noticing whether the words in the exclusion brainstorming exercise are mentioned in the text.
4. *Review the list.* Students check their list and make corrections based on their reading: They put checkmarks by related words and cross out unrelated words, whether or not they circled them earlier.

Teachers use exclusion brainstorming as a prereading activity to familiarize students with academic vocabulary before they read nonfiction articles and books. An eighth-grade teacher prepared the list of words shown here before his students read

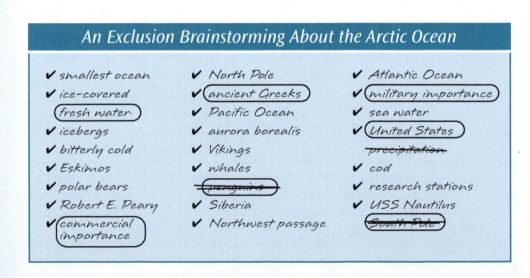

An Exclusion Brainstorming About the Arctic Ocean

✔ smallest ocean
✔ ice-covered
(fresh water)
✔ icebergs
✔ bitterly cold
✔ Eskimos
✔ polar bears
✔ Robert E. Peary
✔ (commercial importance)

✔ North Pole
✔ (ancient Greeks)
✔ Pacific Ocean
✔ aurora borealis
✔ Vikings
✔ whales
~~penguins~~
✔ Siberia
✔ Northwest passage

✔ Atlantic Ocean
✔ (military importance)
✔ sea water
✔ (United States)
~~precipitation~~
✔ cod
✔ research stations
✔ USS Nautilus
~~South Pole~~

an article on the Arctic Ocean; all of the words except *penguins*, *South Pole*, and *precipitation* are related to the topic. Students circled seven words as possibly unrelated, and after reading, they crossed out the three words that their teacher expected them to eliminate.

Grand Conversations

Grand conversations are discussions about stories in which students explore the big ideas and reflect on their feelings (Peterson & Eeds, 2007). They're different than traditional discussions because they're student centered. Students do most of the talking as they voice their opinions and support their views with examples from the story. They talk about what puzzles them, what they find interesting, their personal connections, connections to the world, and connections they've noticed between this story and others they've read. Students usually don't raise their hands to be called on by the teacher; instead, they take turns and speak when no one else is speaking, much as adults do when talking with friends. Students also encourage their classmates to contribute to the conversation. Even though teachers participate, the talk is primarily among the students.

Grand conversations have two parts. The first part is open ended: Students talk about their reactions to the book, and their comments direct the conversation; teachers ask questions and provide information. Later, teachers focus students' attention on one or two topics that they didn't talk about earlier. Grand conversations can be difficult for English learners unless they feel comfortable and safe in the group (Graves & Fitzgerald, 2003).

The Procedure. Teachers follow these steps in using this instructional procedure:

1. *Read the book.* Students read a story or part of a story or listen to the teacher read it aloud.
2. *Prepare for the grand conversation.* Students think about the story by drawing pictures or writing in **reading logs**. This step is especially important for students who don't talk much because with this preparation, they're more likely to have ideas to share.
3. *Have small-group conversations.* Students form small groups to talk about the story before getting together as a class. This step is optional and is generally used when students need more time to talk about the story.
4. *Begin the grand conversation.* Students form a circle so they can see each other. Teachers begin by asking, "Who would like to begin?" or "What are you thinking about?" One student makes a comment, and classmates take turns talking about the idea the first student introduced.
5. *Continue the conversation.* A student introduces a new idea, and classmates talk about it, expanding on the idea, asking questions, and reading excerpts to make a point. Students limit their comments to the idea being discussed, and then a new one is introduced. To ensure that everyone participates, teachers often ask students to make no more than three comments until everyone has spoken at least once.
6. *Ask questions.* Teachers ask questions to direct students to topics they've missed; for example, an element of story structure, a narrative device, or the author's craft.
7. *Conclude the conversation.* Teachers summarize their discussion and prepare students to continue reading the next chapter.
8. *Reflect on the conversation.* Students write (or write again) in reading logs to reflect on the ideas discussed in the grand conversation.

Both whole-class and small-group grand conversations are worthwhile. When students get together for a whole-class conversation during literature focus units, teachers scaffold the conversation and have opportunities to provide information. During literature circles, students hold grand conversations in small groups, and they have more opportunities to develop responsibility for their learning and to share their ideas.

Guided Reading

Guided reading is a small-group instructional procedure that teachers use to teach reading to a small group of students who read at approximately the same level. Teachers often use leveled books, and the books they select should be at students' instructional level, that is, books students can read with approximately 90% accuracy (Fountas & Pinnell, 1996). During a guided reading lesson, students read silently at their own pace through the entire book, and teachers support students' reading and their use of word-identification and comprehension strategies. Guided reading is often used in the primary grades, but many middle-grade teachers continue to use guided reading, especially with struggling readers. It's important to choose the right books for young adolescents—ones that are appropriate for their interests and their reading levels. Peregoy and Boyle (2008) add that guided reading is effective for ELs because they experience success as they read books in small, comfortable groups with teacher guidance.

The Procedure. Teachers adapt the guided reading procedure to address their students' needs, but they generally follow these steps:

1. *Choose an appropriate book.* Teachers choose a book that students in the small group can read with 90% accuracy and collect copies for each student.
2. *Introduce the book.* Teachers set the purpose for reading and show the book's cover, reading the title and the author's name. Next, they activate students' background knowledge on a topic related to the book, introducing academic vocabulary as they talk. Students preview the book, looking at the illustrations, talking about them, and making predictions. And finally, teachers review one or more reading strategies they've already taught and remind students to use them as they read.
3. *Have students read the book.* Students read an entire short book or a chapter or two in a longer book. They read silently, and teachers assist with word identification and comprehension as needed. Teachers move around the group, monitoring students' progress. They listen to individual students read a paragraph aloud and talk about what they've read.
4. *Talk about the book.* Students discuss the book, ask questions, and relate it to others they've read, as in a grand conversation. They reflect on their strategy use, and teachers compliment students on the strategies they used successfully.
5. *Have students revisit the text.* Teachers use the text that students have just read to demonstrate a comprehension strategy, teach a word-identification strategy, or review vocabulary words.
6. *Provide opportunities for independent reading.* Students reread the book independently after reading it with teacher supervision or continue reading the next chapter in a longer book.

Teachers teach guided reading lessons while the other students are involved in other literacy activities; classmates are often participating in literature circles, reading workshop, or writing workshop.

Hot Seat

Hot seat is a role-playing activity that builds students' comprehension. Students assume the persona of a character from a novel, the featured person from a biography, or an author whose books they've read, and they sit in a chair designated as the "hot seat" to be interviewed by classmates. It's called *hot seat* because students have to think quickly and respond to their peers' questions. Wilhelm (2002) explains that through this activity, students explore the characters, analyze story events, draw inferences, and try out different interpretations. Students aren't intimidated by performing for classmates; in fact, most students are eager for their turn to sit in the hot seat. They often wear a costume when they assume the character's persona and share artifacts they've made or collected.

The Procedure. Here are the steps in the hot seat activity:

1. *Learn about the character.* Students prepare for the hot seat activity by reading a story or a biography to learn about the character they will impersonate.
2. *Create a costume.* Students design a costume appropriate for their character. In addition, they often collect objects or create artifacts to use in their presentations.
3. *Prepare opening remarks.* Students think about the things they'd like to share and plan what they'll say at the beginning of the activity.
4. *Introduce the character.* One student sits in front of classmates in the "hot seat" chair, tells a little about the character he or she is role-playing using a first-person viewpoint (e.g., "I was the first person to step onto the moon's surface"), and shares artifacts.
5. *Ask questions and make comments.* Classmates ask thoughtful questions to learn more about the character and make comments, and the student remains in the role to respond to them.
6. *Summarize the ideas.* The student in the hot seat selects a classmate to summarize the important ideas that were presented about the character.

During literature focus units, students take turns role-playing characters and being interviewed. Students representing different characters can also come together for a conversation—a group hot seat activity. For example, during a literature focus unit on *The View From Saturday* (Kongisburg, 1998), about a championship sixth-grade Academic Bowl team that's told from the perspectives of the team members, students representing Noah, Nadia, Ethan, Julian, and their teacher, Mrs. Olinski, take turns sitting on the hot seat, or they come together to talk about the story.

Interactive Read-Alouds

Teachers use the interactive read-aloud procedure to share books with students. The focus is on enhancing students' comprehension by engaging them before, during, and after reading. Teachers introduce the book and activate students' background knowledge during prereading. Next, they engage students during reading through conversation and other activities. Afterward, they involve students in responding to the book. What's most important is how teachers engage students while they're reading aloud (Fisher, Flood, Lapp, & Frey, 2004).

Teachers often engage students by pausing periodically to talk about what's just been read. The timing is crucial: When reading stories, it's more effective to stop where students can make predictions and connections, after episodes that students might find confusing, and just before the ending becomes clear. When reading

Interactive Techniques	
Stories	• Make and revise predictions at pivotal points. • Share personal, world, and literary connections. • Draw a picture of a character or an event. • Assume the persona of a character and share the character's thoughts. • Reenact a scene from the story.
Nonfiction	• Ask questions or share information. • Raise hands when specific information is read. • Restate the headings as questions. • Take notes. • Complete graphic organizers.
Poetry	• Add sound effects. • Read along with the teacher. • Repeat lines after the teacher. • Clap when rhyming words, alliteration, or other poetic devices are heard.

nonfiction, teachers stop to talk about big ideas as they're presented, briefly explain technical terms, and emphasize connections among the ideas. Teachers often read a poem from beginning to end once, and then stop as they're rereading it for students to play with words, notice poetic devices, and repeat favorite words and lines. The box above lists interactive techniques. Deciding how often to pause and knowing when to continue reading develop through practice and vary from one group of students to another.

The Procedure. Teachers follow these steps to conduct interactive read-alouds:

1. *Pick a book.* Teachers choose award-winning and other high-quality books that are appropriate for students and that fit into their instructional programs.
2. *Prepare to share the book.* Teachers practice reading the book to ensure that they can read it fluently and to decide where to pause and engage students with the text; they write prompts on self-stick notes to mark these pages. Teachers also think about how they'll introduce the book and highlight academic vocabulary.
3. *Introduce the book.* Teachers activate students' background knowledge, set a purpose for listening, and preview the text.
4. *Read the book interactively.* Teachers read the book aloud, stop periodically to ask questions to focus students on specific points in the text, and involve them in other activities.
5. *Involve students in after-reading activities.* Students participate in discussions and other response activities.

Teachers use this instructional procedure whenever they're reading aloud, no matter whether it's an after-lunch read-aloud period or during a literature focus unit, reading workshop, or a thematic unit. Reading aloud has always been an important activity in primary-grade classrooms, and sometimes teachers think they should read to children only until they learn to read, but reading aloud to share the excitement of books, especially those that students can't read themselves, should remain an important part of the literacy program at all grade levels. Middle graders report that when they listen to the teacher read aloud, they get more interested in the book and understand it better, and the experience often makes them want to read it themselves (Ivey, 2003).

Interactive Writing

Teachers use interactive writing to create a message with students and write it on chart paper (Button, Johnson, & Furgerson, 1996). Students compose the text together, and the teacher guides them as they write it sentence by sentence. Students take turns writing the text on chart paper; at the same time, each student writes it on a small whiteboard. Interactive writing is a powerful instructional procedure to use with English learners and struggling writers, no matter whether they're first graders or young adolescents (Tompkins & Collom, 2004).

The Procedure. Teachers follow these steps to do interactive writing:

1. *Collect supplies.* Teachers collect chart paper, colored marking pens, white correction tape, and a pointer.
2. *Set a purpose.* Teachers set a purpose for the activity; for example, they might summarize a chapter they've read in a novel or review information they're learning in a thematic unit.
3. *Plan the writing.* Teachers and students brainstorm ideas and words and then organize them using a graphic organizer.
4. *Distribute writing supplies.* Teachers distribute small whiteboards, pens, and erasers for students to use to write the text individually as it's written collaboratively on chart paper. They periodically ask students to hold their boards up so they can see that the students are writing legibly.
5. *Write the first sentence or paragraph.* Depending on students' developmental level, they write the first sentence word by word or the first paragraph sentence by sentence. They refer to the graphic organizer for ideas and take turns doing the writing on chart paper. Teachers choose students to do the writing, and each student uses a different pen color. They use white correction tape to correct illegible writing and misspellings. Teachers use a black pen to write words students can't spell or to quickly write some of the text. After writing each sentence or paragraph, students reread what they've written. When appropriate, teachers point out capital letters, punctuation marks, and other conventions of print.
6. *Write additional sentences and paragraphs.* Teachers follow the procedure described in step 5 to finish the text.
7. *Display the completed text.* After completing the message, teachers post the chart in the classroom and refer to it during other activities.

Even though many teachers think of interactive writing as an instructional procedure used in the primary grades, middle-grade teachers often use this more-sophisticated version to create collaborative texts during minilessons. They also use interactive writing with struggling writers to demonstrate the writing process and teach writing strategies.

K-W-L Charts

Teachers use K-W-L charts during thematic units to activate students' background knowledge at the beginning of the unit and then organize the information they're learning (Ogle, 1986). They hang a large sheet of chart paper on a classroom wall, divide it into three columns, and label the columns *K*, *W*, and *L*; the letters stand for "What We

A K-W-L Chart About the Titanic

K	W	L
What We Know	**What We Wonder**	**What We Learned**
It sunk.	Why wasn't the crew watching for icebergs?	The Titanic sank on April 15, 1912.
It happened a long time ago.	Why did the ship sail so far north?	The ship sank 4 hours after hitting the iceberg.
The Titanic sailed from England.	How many people died?	Only 868 people survived.
The ship was supposed to be unsinkable.	Are any survivors alive today?	Most of the survivors were women and children.
It hit an iceberg.	Why weren't there enough lifeboats?	A passenger named Molly Brown became the famous "Unsinkable Molly Brown."
A lot of people died.	Why didn't the radio operator pay attention to the warning?	The Carpathia picked up most of the survivors.
The tragedy happened on its first voyage—its maiden voyage.	How long did it take to sink?	If the lifeboats didn't go far enough away from the ship, they could be sucked under with the ship.
There was a movie of it.	How could the survivors live with the terrible memories?	Today all ships have enough lifeboats for everyone on it.
	Could this happen today?	Tragedy brings out the best and worst of people.

Know," "What We **W**onder," and "What We **L**earned." At the beginning of the unit, students list what they know about the topic in the K column and ask questions that are written in the W column. Then, toward the end of the unit, students complete the L column, documenting what they've learned. A sixth-grade class K-W-L chart about the *Titanic* is shown on the preceding page.

The Procedure. Teachers follow these steps to develop a K-W-L chart:

1. *Post a K-W-L chart.* Teachers post a large chart on the classroom wall, divide it into three columns, and label the columns *K* (What We **K**now), *W* (What We **W**onder), and *L* (What We **L**earned).
2. *Complete the K column.* At the beginning of a thematic unit, teachers ask students to brainstorm what they know about the topic and write this information in the K column. Sometimes students suggest information that isn't correct; these statements are turned into questions and added to the W column.
3. *Complete the W column.* Teachers write the questions that students suggest in the W column. They continue to add questions to the W column during the unit.
4. *Complete the L column.* At the end of the unit, students reflect on what they've learned, and teachers record this information in the L column of the chart.

Sometimes teachers organize the information on the K-W-L chart into categories to highlight the big ideas and to help students remember more of what they're learning; this procedure is called K-W-L Plus (Carr & Ogle, 1987). Teachers either provide three to six big-idea categories when they introduce the chart, or they ask students to decide on categories after they brainstorm information about the topic for the K column. Students then focus on these categories as they complete the L column, classifying each piece of information according to one of the categories. When categories are used, it's easier to make sure students learn about each of the big ideas.

Learning Logs

Students write in learning logs as part of thematic units. Learning logs, like other journals, are booklets in which students record information, write questions, summarize big ideas, draw diagrams, and reflect on their learning. Their writing is impromptu, and the emphasis is on using writing as a learning tool rather than on creating polished products. Even so, students should be encouraged to work carefully, write legibly, and spell content-related words correctly, especially those posted on the **word wall**. Teachers monitor students' logs to quickly check that they understand what they're learning.

The Procedure. Here are the steps in making and using learning logs:

1. *Prepare learning logs.* At the beginning of a thematic unit, students construct learning logs by stapling a combination of lined and unlined paper into booklets with tagboard or laminated construction-paper covers.
2. *Have students use their learning logs.* Students take notes, draw diagrams, list vocabulary words, do **quickwrites**, and write summaries.
3. *Monitor students' entries.* Teachers read students' learning logs and answer their questions and clarify confusions.
4. *Have students write reflections.* Teachers have students review their entries at the end of the unit and write a reflection about what they've learned.

Students use learning logs during thematic units to record and respond to information they're learning as they read nonfiction articles and books, study content-area textbooks, view videos, and research information online. They make notes, draw diagrams, write academic vocabulary words, list information, make charts, and do quickwrites.

Making Words

Making words is a teacher-directed spelling activity in which students arrange letter cards to spell words (Cunningham & Cunningham, 1992). Teachers choose key words from books students are reading that exemplify particular spelling patterns for students to practice, and they prepare a set of letter cards that small groups of students or individual students use to spell words. The teacher leads students as they create a variety of words from the letters.

Teachers often use this activity with small groups of English learners to practice spelling strategies and skills. Sometimes teachers bring together a group of ELs to do a making words activity as a preview before doing it with the whole class (or afterward as a review), and sometimes a different word is used to reinforce a spelling pattern that they're learning.

The Procedure.   Here are the steps in making words:

1. *Make letter cards*. Teachers prepare a set of small letter cards with multiple copies of each letter, especially common letters such as *a, e, i, r, s,* and *t*. They package the cards letter by letter in small plastic bags or partitioned plastic boxes.

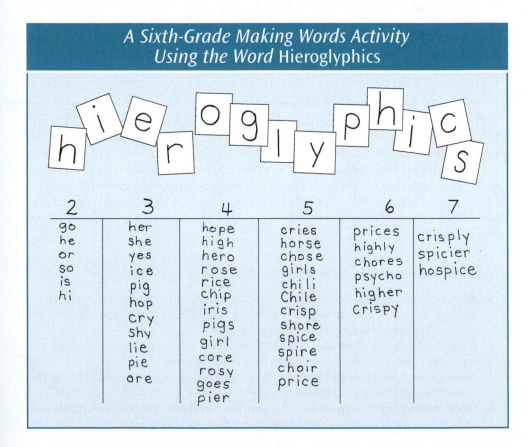

A Sixth-Grade Making Words Activity Using the Word Hieroglyphics

2	3	4	5	6	7
go	her	hope	cries	prices	crisply
he	she	high	horse	highly	spicier
or	yes	hero	chose	chores	hospice
so	ice	rose	girls	psycho	
is	pig	rice	chili	higher	
hi	hop	chip	Chile	crispy	
	cry	iris	crisp		
	shy	pigs	shore		
	lie	girl	spice		
	pie	core	spire		
	ore	rosy	choir		
		goes	price		
		pier			

2. ***Choose a word.*** Teachers choose a word to use in the word-making activity, and without disclosing it, have a student distribute the needed letter cards to classmates.

3. ***Arrange the letter cards.*** Teachers have students arrange the letter cards on their desks with consonants in one group and vowels in another.

4. ***Make words.*** Students use the letter cards to spell words containing two, three, four, five, six, or more letters, and they list the words they can spell on a chart. Teachers monitor students' work and help them fix misspelled words.

5. ***Share words.*** Teachers have students identify two-letter words they made with the letter cards and continue to report longer and longer words until they identify the chosen word made using every letter card. After students share, teachers suggest any words they missed and point out recently taught spelling patterns.

Teachers choose words for word-making lessons from books during literature focus units and from thematic units. While a sixth-grade class was studying ancient Egypt, they completed the making words activity shown on the preceding page using the word *hieroglyphics.* Teachers can get additional ideas for word-making activities from Cunningham and Hall's (1994) collection of making words activities.

Minilessons

Teachers teach brief, focused lessons called *minilessons* on literacy strategies and skills (Atwell, 1998; Hoyt, 2000). Topics include how to use commas in a series, draw inferences, and use sentence combining. In these lessons, teachers introduce a topic and connect it to the reading or writing students are involved in, provide information, and supervise during a practice activity. Minilessons usually last 15 to 30 minutes, and sometimes teachers extend a lesson over several days as students apply the topic in literacy activities. The best time to teach a minilesson is when students will have an immediate opportunity to apply what they're learning. It's not enough to simply explain a strategy or remind students to use it; in a minilesson, teachers actively engage students, encourage and scaffold them while they're learning, and then gradually withdraw their support (Dorn & Soffos, 2001).

The Procedure. Teachers follow these steps to present minilessons to small groups and to the whole class:

1. ***Introduce the topic.*** Teachers introduce the strategy or skill by naming it and making a connection between the topic and activities going on in the classroom.

2. ***Share examples.*** Teachers show how to use the topic with examples from students' own writing or from books students are reading.

3. ***Provide information.*** Teachers provide information, explaining and demonstrating the strategy or skill.

4. ***Supervise practice.*** Students practice using the strategy or skill with teacher supervision.

5. ***Assess learning.*** Teachers monitor students' progress and evaluate their use of newly learned strategies or skills.

Teachers teach minilessons on literacy strategies and skills as a part of literature focus units, reading and writing workshop, and other instructional approaches. Other minilessons focus on instructional procedures, such as how to use a dictionary or share writing from the author's chair, and concepts, such as homophones or adjectives.

Open-Mind Portraits

Students draw open-mind portraits to help them think more deeply about a character, reflect on story events from the character's viewpoint, and analyze the theme (McLaughlin & Allen, 2001). The portraits have two parts: the character's face on the top, "portrait" page, and several "thinking" pages revealing the character's thoughts at pivotal points in the story. The two pages from a fourth grader's open-mind portrait on Sarah, the mail-order bride in *Sarah, Plain and Tall* (MacLachlan, 2004), are shown below. The words and pictures on the "thinking" page represent her thoughts at the end of the story.

The Procedure. Students follow these steps to make open-mind portraits:

1. *Make a portrait of a character.* Students draw and color a large portrait of the head and neck of a character in a novel they're reading.
2. *Cut out the "portrait" and "thinking" pages.* Students cut out the portrait and attach it with a brad or staple to several more sheets of drawing paper. It's important that students place the brad or staple at the top of the portrait so that there's space available to draw and write on the "thinking" pages.
3. *Design the "thinking" pages.* Students lift the portrait page and draw and write about the character's thoughts at pivotal points in the story.
4. *Share the completed open-mind portraits.* Students share their portraits with peers and talk about the words and pictures included on their "thinking" pages.

An Open-Mind Portrait of Sarah From Sarah, Plain and Tall

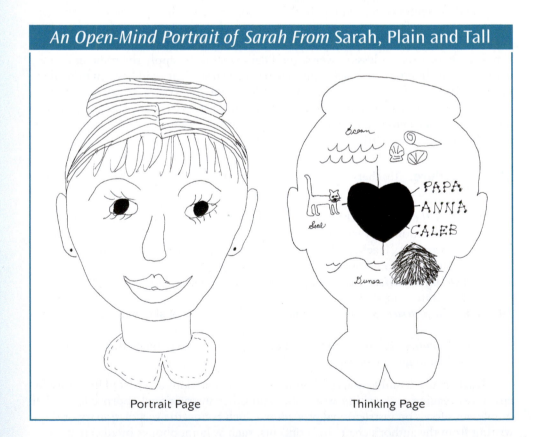

Portrait Page   Thinking Page

Students create open-mind portraits to think more deeply about a character. They often reread parts of the novel to recall specific details about the character's appearance before they draw the portrait, and they write several entries in a simulated journal to start thinking from that character's viewpoint before making the "thinking" pages. In addition, students can make open-mind portraits of historical figures as part of a thematic unit, and of featured personalities after reading a biography.

Teachers use the prereading plan (PReP) to diagnose and build necessary background knowledge before students read a chapter in a content-area textbook (Vacca & Vacca, 2008). Teachers introduce a key concept discussed in the reading assignment and ask students to brainstorm related ideas and words; then they talk about the key concept. This activity is especially useful in preparing English learners who have limited background knowledge and academic vocabulary to read a content-area textbook chapter. An added benefit is that students' engagement often increases as they participate in this activity.

Prereading Plan

The Procedure. Teachers follow these steps when they use this instructional procedure:

1. *Discuss a key concept.* Teachers introduce a key concept using a word, phrase, object, or picture to initiate a discussion.
2. *Brainstorm ideas.* Teachers ask students to brainstorm ideas about the topic and record them on a chart. They also help students make connections between the ideas.
3. *Introduce academic vocabulary.* Teachers present additional words that students need to read the assignment.
4. *Quickwrite about the topic.* Teachers have students quickwrite about the topic using words from the brainstormed list.
5. *Share the quickwrites.* Students share their quickwrites, and teachers ask questions to help them clarify and elaborate their thinking.
6. *Read the assignment.* Students read the assignment and relate what they're reading to what they learned before reading.

Teachers use this instructional procedure during thematic units. Before reading a social studies textbook chapter about the Bill of Rights, for example, an eighth-grade teacher used PReP to introduce the concept that citizens have freedoms and responsibilities. Students brainstormed this list during a discussion about the Bill of Rights:

guaranteed in the Constitution	*James Madison*
1791	*10 amendments*
citizens	*freedom of speech*
freedom of religion	*owning guns and pistols*
homes can't be searched without a search warrant	*act responsibly*
limits on these freedoms for everyone's good	*serve on juries*
"life, liberty, and the pursuit of happiness"	*right to a jury trial*
no cruel or unusual punishments	*vote intelligently*

Then before reading the chapter, students wrote quickwrites to make personal connections to the ideas they'd brainstormed. Here is one student's quickwrite:

I always knew America was a free country but I thought it was because of the Declaration of Independence. Now I know that the Bill of Rights is a list of our freedoms. There are 10 freedoms in the Bill of Rights. I have the freedom to go to any church I want, to own guns, to speak my mind, and to read newspapers. I never thought of serving on a jury as a freedom and my Mom didn't either. She was on a jury about a year ago and she didn't want to do it. It took a whole week. Her boss didn't like her missing work. The trial was about someone who robbed a store and shot a man but he didn't die. I'm going to tell her that it is important to do jury duty. When I am an adult, I hope I get to be on a jury of a murder trial. I want to protect my freedoms and I know it is a citizen's responsibility, too.

When the teacher read this student's quickwrite, she noticed that the student confused the number of amendments with the number of freedoms listed in the amendments, so she clarified the misunderstandings individually with her.

Question-Answer-Relationships

The Question-Answer-Relationships (QAR) procedure teaches students to be consciously aware of whether they are likely to find the answer to a question "right there" on the page, between the lines, or beyond the information provided in the text so they're better able to answer it (Raphael, Highfield, & Au, 2006). Students use the QAR procedure when they're reading both fiction and nonfiction texts and answering comprehension questions independently.

This procedure differentiates among the types of questions and the kinds of thinking required to answer them: Some questions require only literal thinking, but others demand higher levels of thinking. Here are the types of questions:

Right There Questions. Readers find the answer "right there" in the text, usually in the same sentence as words from the question. These are literal-level questions.

Think and Search Questions. The answer is in the text, but readers must search for it in different parts of the text and put the ideas together. These are inferential-level questions.

Author and Me Questions. Readers use a combination of the author's ideas and their own to answer the question. These questions combine inferential and application levels.

On My Own Questions. Readers use their own ideas to answer the question; sometimes they don't need to read the text to answer it. These are application- and evaluation-level questions.

The first two types of questions are known as "in the book" questions because the answers can be found in the book, and the last two types are "in the head" questions because they require information and ideas not presented in the book. An eighth grader's chart describing these types of questions is shown on the next page.

The Procedure. Here are the steps in the QAR procedure:

1. *Read the questions first.* Students read the questions as a preview before reading the text to give them an idea of what to think about as they read.

An Eighth Grader's QAR Chart

?UESTIONS

RIGHT THERE — The answer is easy to find in the book. It is near the Question.

THINK AND SEARCH — The answer is in the book but it isn't all in one place. I have to search for it and put the parts together.

AUTHOR AND ME — The answer is a combination of Ideas in the book and my own Ideas.

ON MY OWN — The answer is NOT in the book. I have to do my own thinking.

2. ***Predict how to answer the questions.*** Students consider which of the four types each question represents and the level of thinking required to answer it.
3. ***Read the text.*** Students read the text while thinking about the questions they will answer afterward.
4. ***Answer the questions.*** Students reread the questions, determine where to find the answers, locate the answers, and write them.
5. ***Share answers.*** Students read their answers aloud and explain how they answered the questions. Students should again refer to the type of question and whether the answer was "in the book" or "in the head."

Students use the QAR procedure whenever they're expected to answer questions after reading a story, nonfiction book, or content-area textbook. They can also write their own "in the book" and "in the head" questions. An eighth-grade teacher, for instance, asked his students to write questions representing the four levels in their **reading logs** as they were reading *The Giver* (Lowry, 2006b). Here are some of their questions:

Right There Questions
What was the first color Jonas could see?
What does a Receiver do?

Think and Search Questions
How is Jonas different than the other people?
Why did Rosemary ask to be released?

Author and Me Questions
What happened to Jonas and Gabe at the end of the book?
Was the Giver an honorable person?

On My Own Questions
What would you have done if you were Jonas?
Could this happen in the United States?

Students also write questions when reading nonfiction books and chapters in content-area textbooks.

Questioning the Author

Questioning the Author (QtA) teaches students how to construct meaning from a text. Beck and McKeown (2006) developed this procedure to encourage students to question texts, particularly content-area textbooks, as they read. Students learn to view texts as fallible products written by authors who make errors and sometimes don't write as clearly as they should. Once students understand this tenet of fallibility, they read differently. Too often, students assume that if they don't understand something, it's because they aren't smart or don't read well enough.

Teachers teach students to ask questions, called *queries*, and talk about the text with classmates while they're reading to make sense of it. Queries support students as they comprehend. Sometimes the focus is on a single sentence, and at other times, it's on a paragraph or longer chunk of text in these whole-class discussions. Teachers and students ask queries such as these:

What is the author trying to tell us here?

What is the author talking about here?

How does this fit with what the author told us before?

Why is the author telling us this?

As students respond to these questions, they share ideas and work together to construct meaning.

Teachers use these discussion moves as they orchestrate the discussion:

Marking. Teachers draw attention to particular ideas students have expressed.

Turning-Back. Teachers return responsibility for exploring the text to students and turn students' attention back to the text.

Revoicing. Teachers interpret and rephrase students' ideas that they're struggling to express.

Recapping. Teachers summarize the big ideas.

Modeling. Teachers make their thinking public as they talk about a point students may have missed.

Annotating. Teachers provide information during a discussion. (Beck & McKeown, 2006)

Although teachers prompt students to think more deeply, they should do less talking than the students do.

The Procedure. Teachers follow these steps as they teach QtA to the whole class:

1. *Analyze the text.* Teachers identify the big ideas that they want students to focus on and decide how to segment the text to facilitate students' comprehension.
2. *Develop queries.* Teachers brainstorm a list of queries to ask about the big ideas in each segment. For example: "What's the author trying to tell us?" and "Why did the author say _____?" These queries are used to encourage students to probe the ideas, facilitate their discussion, and extend their understanding. Teachers often jot them on self-stick notes that they place in their copy of the book students are reading.
3. *Have students read.* Students read the first segment of text, stopping at a predetermined point to talk about what they've read.
4. *Ask queries.* Teachers present a query to begin the discussion. Students respond by sharing their interpretations, reading excerpts from the text, questioning ideas, clarifying confusions, and talking together to deepen their understanding. Teachers orchestrate the discussion using marking, revoicing, modeling, and the other discussion moves, and they ask additional questions based on the students' comments, including "Do you agree with what _____ said?" and "How does this information connect with what you already know?"
5. *Repeat reading and asking queries.* Teachers repeat steps 3 and 4 as students read and discuss each segment of text.
6. *Discuss the text.* Teachers lead a discussion based on students' responses to the queries to bring closure to the reading experience. They raise issues of accuracy and viewpoint; invite students to make personal, world, and textual connections; and compare this text to others on the same topic or to others by the same author.

Teachers explain the central tenet of QtA, that authors and their texts are fallible, at the beginning of the school year to give students more confidence in their abilities to read and understand books. They also teach students how to ask questions and talk about a text so that they're ready to use QtA whenever they're reading difficult texts. Teachers can use this procedure during literature focus units or literature circles whenever students have difficulty understanding a particular passage, and they use it during thematic units when they're reading chapters in content-area textbooks and other nonfiction books.

Quickwriting

Quickwriting is an impromptu writing activity in which students explore a topic or respond to a question (Brozo & Simpson, 2007). They write for 5 to 10 minutes, letting their thoughts flow without stopping to make revisions or correct misspelled words; the focus is on generating ideas and developing writing fluency. Students think about ideas, reflect on what they know about a topic, ramble on paper, and make connections between ideas. Here's a series of quickwrites that a fifth grader wrote as she listened to her teacher read aloud *The Higher Power of Lucky* (Patron, 2006), an award-winning story of a plucky 10-year-old girl named Lucky who tries to surmount her problems and bring stability to her life:

Prompt: Why do you think the main character is named Lucky?
I don't know. At this point I don't think Lucky is lucky at all. Her mom died and her dad doesn't want her. She seems pretty unlucky. All that I can think is that Lucky is going to get

more lucky at the end of the book. I hope something really good happens to her because she deserves it.

Prompt: Do you think Brigitte will abandon Lucky?
Lucky is really afraid that Brigitte will go back home to Paris. I don't think Brigitte is going to leave. It would be a really mean thing to do and Brigitte is sort of a mom and moms don't do that. I also think it's bad for a girl to have to worry about being abandoned. That's really sad. I predict that Lucky will have a real family at the end of the book.

Prompt: What happened when Lucky hit bottom?
It happened when she ran away from home. There was a bad dust storm and Miles was lost and it was her fault that Miles was lost. She was wearing Brigitte's beautiful red dress and she probably ruined it. I thought she'd get in big trouble and maybe she'd even die and so would Miles and her dog but it didn't happen that way. Everybody in town drove their cars out to the caves to find her and they were so happy to see her and Miles that they didn't even get mad. Lots of good things happened. Best of all, she found out that Brigitte was going to adopt her and would always be her mom. I love this book.

Students wrote their quickwrites after the teacher finished reading each chapter or two, and the quickwrites helped them reflect on what was happening in the story and prepare for the **grand conversations**.

The Procedure. Here are the steps in this instructional procedure:

1. *Choose a topic.* Students choose a topic or question (or the teacher assigns one) for the quickwrite, and they write it at the top of their papers.
2. *Write about the topic.* Students write to explore the topic for 5 to 10 minutes. They focus on interesting ideas, make connections between the topic and their own lives, and reflect on their reading or learning. They rarely, if ever, stop writing to reread or correct errors in what they've written.
3. *Read quickwrites.* Students meet in small groups to read their quickwrites, and then one student in each group is chosen to share with the class. That student rereads his or her quickwrite in preparation for sharing with the whole class and adds any missing words and completes any unfinished thoughts.
4. *Share chosen quickwrites.* Students in each group who have been chosen to share their quickwrites with the whole class take turns reading them aloud.
5. *Write a second time.* Sometimes students write a second time on the same topic or on a new topic that emerged through writing and sharing; this second quickwrite is usually more focused than the first. Or students expand their first quickwrite after listening to peers or after learning more about the topic.

Teachers use quickwriting to promote thinking during literature focus units and thematic units. Quickwrites are used as a warm-up at the beginning of a lesson or to promote reflection at the end of a lesson. Sometimes students identify the topics or questions for the quickwrite, and at other times, the teacher provides them. Quickwrites are also an effective prewriting procedure (Routman, 2004). Students often do several quickwrites to explore what they know about a topic before beginning to write; they brainstorm ideas and vocabulary, play with language, and identify ideas they need to learn more about before moving on to the drafting stage.

RAFT

Teachers use RAFT to create projects and other assignments to enhance students' comprehension of novels they're reading and of information they're learning in thematic units (Holston & Santa, 1985). RAFT is an acronym for *role, audience, format,* and *topic,* and teachers consider these four dimensions as they design projects:

Role. The role is the person or people students become for this project. Sometimes they take on the role of a book character, historical figure, or contemporary personality, such as Oprah, and at other times, they are themselves.

Audience. The audience is the person or people who will read or view this project; they may include students, teachers, parents, or community members, as well as simulated audiences, such as book characters and historical personalities.

Format. The format is the genre or activity that students create; it might be a letter, brochure, cartoon, journal, poster, essay, newspaper article, speech, or digital scrapbook.

Topic. The topic is the subject of the project; it may be an issue related to the text, an essential question, or something of personal interest.

When students develop projects, they process ideas and information in different ways as they assume varied viewpoints and complete projects directed to specific audiences. Their thinking is imaginative and interpretive; in contrast, students' comprehension tends to be more literal when they do more-traditional assignments, such as writing answers to questions.

RAFT is an effective way to differentiate instruction by providing tiered activities: Projects on the same text or topic can be adjusted according to students' achievement levels, English proficiency, and interests. For example, a seventh-grade teacher developed the chart of RAFT ideas on page 368 for the Newbery Honor Book *The Wednesday Wars* (Schmidt, 2007); this coming-of-age novel chronicles the everyday trials of Holling Hoodhood, who is at odds with his seventh-grade English teacher, Mrs. Baker.

The Procedure. Teachers follow these steps to use RAFT after reading a book or studying a topic during a thematic unit:

1. *Establish the purpose.* Teachers reflect on what they want students to learn through this activity and consider how it can enhance their learning.
2. *Prepare a RAFT chart.* Teachers prepare a RAFT chart of possible projects by brainstorming roles, choosing audiences, identifying genres and other formats for projects, and listing topics.
3. *Read the book or study the topic.* Students read and discuss a book or learn about a topic before they create RAFT projects.
4. *Choose projects.* Sometimes teachers assign the same project for all students, but at other times, they vary the assignment for small groups or let students choose a project from the RAFT chart.
5. *Create projects.* Students create their projects and get feedback from the teacher as they work.
6. *Shared completed projects.* Students share their projects with small groups, the whole class, or other audiences.

RAFT is usually an applying-stage activity because students develop these projects after reading and discussing a novel or after studying a social studies or science topic,

RAFT Ideas for The Wednesday Wars

Role	Audience	Format	Topic
Holling and William Shakespeare	Our class	Interview	Explain "To thine own self be true" and other life lessons.
Mrs. Baker	Her son, a U.S. soldier in Vietnam	Letter	Tell why you took such an interest in Holling.
You	Our class	Poster	Describe the cultural and political uproar of the 1960s.
You	Newbery Award committee	Persuasive essay	Present reasons why this book should win the Newbery Award.
Bullies	Students at Camillo Junior High	Speech	Research bullying, and explain how to deal with bullies.
Mai Thi (Holling's classmate)	Our class	Digital scrapbook	Share information about Vietnam and the war's effect on you and your home country.
Holling	Mrs. Baker	Letter, written when Holling is 30 years old	Explain how you've followed Mrs. Baker's advice: "Learn everything you can—everything. And then use all that you have learned to be a wise and good man."

but it can also be used in preparation for **grand conversations** or literature circle discussions. In addition, many teachers use RAFT as a prewriting activity to help students understand the relationships among topics, formats or genres, authors, and readers.

Readers Theatre

Readers theatre is a dramatic performance of a script by a group of readers (Black & Stave, 2007). Students each assume a part, rehearse by reading and rereading their characters' lines, and then perform for their classmates. Students can read scripts in trade books and textbooks, or they can create their own. The box on the next page presents books of fiction and nonfiction scripts. Students interpret the story with their voices, without using much action. They may stand or sit, but they carry the whole communication of the plot, characterization, mood, and theme through their voices, gestures, and facial expressions.

There are many reasons to recommend readers theatre. Students have opportunities to read good literature, and through this procedure they engage with text and interpret the characters (Keehn, Martinez, & Roser, 2005). English learners and dysfluent readers, in particular, gain valuable oral reading practice in a relaxed, small-group setting. They increase their reading speed, learn how to phrase and chunk words in sentences, and read with more expression. In addition, readers theatre avoids many of the problems inherent in theatrical productions: Students don't memorize their parts; elaborate props and costumes aren't needed; and long, tedious hours aren't spent rehearsing.

The Procedure. Teachers follow these steps as they work with a small group or the whole class:

1. *Select a script.* Students select a script and then read and discuss it. Afterward, they volunteer to read each part.
2. *Rehearse the reading.* Students decide how to use their voice, gestures, and facial expressions to interpret the characters they're reading. They read the script several times, striving for accurate pronunciation, voice projection, and appropriate inflections.
3. *Stage the reading.* Readers theatre is presented in front of the classroom. Students stand or sit in a row and read their lines. They stay in position through the production. If readers are sitting, they stand to read their lines; if they're standing, they step forward to read. The emphasis isn't on production quality; rather, it's on the interpretive quality of readers' voices. Costumes and props aren't necessary; however, adding a few small props enhances interest as long as they don't interfere with the interpretive quality of the reading.

Students create their own scripts from books they've read and about topics related to thematic units (Flynn, 2007). When students are creating a script, it's important to choose a story with lots of conversation; any parts that don't include dialogue can become narrator parts. Depending on the number of narrator parts, one to four students can share the narrator duties. Teachers often make photocopies of the text for students to mark up or highlight as they develop the script. Sometimes students simply use their marked-up copies as the finished script, and at other times, they retype the script, omitting the unnecessary parts.

Readers Theatre Scripts

Barchers, S. I., & Kroll, J. L. (2002). *Classic readers theatre for young adults*. Portsmouth, NH: Teacher Ideas Press.

Black, A. N. (2008). *Readers theatre for middle school boys: Investigating the strange and mysterious*. Portsmouth, NH: Teacher Ideas Press.

Fredericks, A. D. (2001). *Readers theatre for American history*. Portsmouth, NH: Teacher Ideas Press.

Jenkins, D. R. (2004), *Just deal with it! Funny readers theatre for life's not-so-funny moments*. Portsmouth, NH: Teacher Ideas Press.

Laughlin, M. K., Black, P. T., & Loberg, M. K. (1991). *Social studies readers theatre for children: Scripts and script development*. Portsmouth, NH: Teacher Ideas Press.

Martin, J. M. (2002). *12 fabulously funny fairy tale plays*. New York: Scholastic.

Pugliano-Martin, C. (1999). *25 just-right plays for emergent readers*. New York: Scholastic.

Sanders, J., & Sanders, N. I. (2008). *Readers theatre for African American history*. Portsmouth, NH: Teacher Ideas Press.

Shepard, A. (2005). *Stories on stage: Children's plays for reader's theater with 15 play scripts from 15 authors*. Olympia, WA: Shepard.

Wolf, J. M. (2002). *Cinderella outgrows the glass slipper and other zany fractured fairy tale plays*. New York: Scholastic.

Wolfman, J. (2004). *How and why stories for readers theatre*. Portsmouth, NH: Teacher Ideas Press.

Reading Logs

Reading logs are journals in which students write their reactions and opinions about books they're reading or listening to the teacher read aloud. In these entries, students clarify misunderstandings, explore ideas, and deepen their comprehension (Hancock, 2008). They also list words from the **word wall**, draw diagrams about story elements, and write information about authors and genres. Sometimes students choose what they'll write about in entries, and at other times, they respond to questions or prompts that teachers have prepared. Both student-choice and teacher-directed entries are useful: When students choose topics, they delve into their own ideas and questions, sharing what's important to them, and when teachers prepare prompts, they direct students' thinking to topics they might otherwise miss. Teachers choose the best mix of student-choice and teacher-directed entries when they know their students well.

The Procedure. Students follow these steps as they write independently in reading logs:

1. *Prepare reading logs.* Students make reading logs by stapling paper into booklets, and they write the title of the book on the cover.
2. *Write entries.* Students write their reactions and reflections about the chapter. Sometimes they choose their own topics; at other times, teachers pose questions.
3. *Share entries.* Students share their reading logs with teachers so they can monitor students' work. Teachers also write comments back to students about their interpretations and reflections.

Students at all grade levels can write reading log entries to help them understand novels they're reading during literature focus units and literature circles (Daniels, 2001). As a sixth-grade class read *The Giver* (Lowry, 2006b), a Newbery Award–winning story of a not-so-perfect society, students discussed each chapter and brainstormed several possible chapter titles. Then they wrote entries in their reading logs and labeled each chapter with the number and the title they felt was most appropriate. These three entries show how a sixth grader grappled with the idea of "release":

Chapter 18: "Release"
I think release is very rude. People have a right to live where they want to. Just because they're different they have to go somewhere else. I think release is when you have to go and live elsewhere. If you're released you can't come back to the community.

Chapter 19: "Release—The Truth"
It is so mean to kill people that didn't do anything bad. They kill perfectly innocent people. Everyone has a right to live. The shot is even worse to give them. They should be able to die on their own. If I were Jonas I would probably go insane. The people who kill the people that are to be released don't know what they're doing.

Chapter 20: "Mortified"
I don't think that Jonas is going to be able to go home and face his father. What can he do? Now that he knows what release is he will probably stay with The Giver for the rest of his life until he is released.

After reading and discussing Chapter 18, this student doesn't understand that "release" means "killing," but he grasps the awful meaning of the word as he reads Chapter 19.

Rubrics

Rubrics are scoring guides that teachers use to assess students' writing (Spandel, 2009). These guides usually have 4, 5, or 6 levels, ranging from high to low, and assessment criteria are described at each level. Students receive a copy of the rubric as they begin writing so they understand what's expected and how they'll be assessed. Depending on the rubric's intricacy, teachers mark the assessment criteria either while they're reading the composition or immediately afterward and then determine the piece's overall score.

The assessment criteria on some rubrics describe general qualities of effective writing, such as ideas, organization, word choice, and mechanics, but others focus on genre characteristics. Teachers often use genre-specific rubrics to assess personal narratives, reports, and persuasive essays. No matter which assessment criteria are used, the same ones are addressed at each level. If a criterion addresses sentence fluency, for example, descriptors about sentence fluency are included at each level; the statement "contains short, choppy sentences" might be used at the lowest level and "uses sentences varying in length and style" at the highest level. Each level represents a one-step improvement in students' application of that criterion.

Rubrics can be constructed with any number of levels, but it's easier to show growth in students' writing when the rubric has more levels. Much more improvement is needed for students to move from one level to another if the rubric has 4 levels than if it has 6 levels. A rubric with 10 levels would be even more sensitive, but rubrics with more levels are harder to construct and very time-consuming to use. Researchers usually recommend that teachers use rubrics with either 4 or 6 levels so that there's no middle score—each level is either above or below the middle—because teachers are inclined to choose the middle-level score, when one is available.

Rubrics are used for determining proficiency levels and assigning grades. The level that is above the midpoint is usually designated as "proficient," "competent," or "passing"—that's a 3 on a 4-point rubric and a 4 on a 6-point rubric. The levels on a 6-point rubric can be described this way:

1 = minimal level	4 = proficient level
2 = beginning or limited level	5 = excellent level
3 = developing level	6 = superior level

These levels can also be equated to letter grades.

The Procedure. Teachers follow these steps as they use rubrics:

1. *Choose a rubric.* Teachers choose a rubric that's appropriate to the writing project or create one that reflects the assignment.
2. *Introduce the rubric.* Teachers distribute copies of the rubric to students and talk about the criteria used at each level, focusing on the requirements at the "proficient" level.
3. *Have students self-assess their writing.* Students use the rubric to self-assess their writing as part of the revising stage, highlighting phrases in the rubric that best describe their writing. Then they determine which level has the most highlighted words; that's the overall score.
4. *Assess students' writing.* Teachers assess students' writing by highlighting phrases in the rubric that best describe the composition. Then they assign the overall score by determining which level has the most highlighted words and circle it.
5. *Conference with students.* Teachers talk with students about the assessment, identifying strengths and weaknesses. Based on this assessment, students set goals for the next writing assignment.

Students use rubrics during writing workshop or whenever they're using the writing process to draft and refine a piece of writing. Many commercially prepared rubrics are available: State departments of education post rubrics for mandated writing tests on their websites, and school districts hire teams of teachers or consultants to develop writing rubrics for each grade level. Spandel (2009) provides rubrics that assess the six traits of writing. Other rubrics are provided with basal readers and other textbook programs, in professional books for teachers, and online.

Even though commercially prepared rubrics are convenient, they may not be appropriate for some students or for specific writing assignments: The rubrics may have only 4 levels when 6 would be better, they may have been designed for a different grade level, or they may not address a specific genre. Because of these limitations, teachers often develop their own or adapt commercial rubrics to meet their needs.

Running Records

In this reading-stage activity, teachers observe individual students as they read aloud and record information to analyze their reading fluency (Clay, 2000). They calculate the percentage of words the student reads correctly and then analyze the errors. Teachers make a checkmark on a copy of the text as the student reads each word correctly and use other marks to indicate words that the student doesn't know or mispronounces.

The Procedure. Teachers conduct running records with individual students using these steps:

1. *Choose a book.* Teachers have the student choose an excerpt for the assessment at least 100 words in length from a book he or she is reading.

How to Mark Errors		
Miscue	Explanation	Marking
Incorrect word	If the student reads a word incorrectly, the teacher writes the incorrect word and the correct word under it.	take / taken
Self-correction	If the student self-corrects an error, the teacher writes SC (for "self-correction") following the incorrect word.	for SC / from
Unsuccessful attempt	If the student attempts to pronounce a word, the teacher records each attempt and adds the correct text underneath.	be-bēf-before / before
Skipped word	If the student skips a word, the teacher marks the error with a dash.	— / the
Inserted word	If the student says words that are not in the text, the teacher records the inserted words and writes an insertion symbol (caret) underneath.	not / ^
Supplied word	If the student can't identify a word, the teacher supplies it and writes T above the word.	T / which
Repetition	If the student repeats a word or phrase, it isn't scored as an error, but the teacher notes it by making a checkmark for each repetition.	✓✓✓ / so

2. **Take the running record.** As the student reads the excerpt aloud, the teacher records information about the words read correctly as well as those misread. The teacher makes checkmarks on a copy of the text for each word read correctly and uses other marks for errors. The box on the preceding page shows how to mark errors.

3. **Calculate the percentage of errors.** Teachers calculate the percentage of errors by dividing the number of errors by the total number of words read. When the student makes 5% or fewer errors, the book is at the student's independent level. When there are 6–10% errors, the book is at the student's instructional level, and when there are more than 10% errors, the book is too difficult—at the student's frustration level.

4. **Analyze the errors.** Teachers look for patterns in the errors to determine how the student is growing as a reader and which strategies and skills should be taught next.

Middle-grade teachers conduct running records to monitor their struggling students' progress and diagnose reading problems. The box below shows a running record and analysis of sixth-grade Josh's oral reading. He read the beginning of *Bunnicula: A Rabbit-Tale of Mystery* (Howe & Howe, 2006), a hilarious story about a vampire bunny told from the viewpoint of a dog named Harold with an end-of-fourth-grade reading level. The results of the analysis indicate that the book is appropriate for Josh; it's at his instructional level.

Josh's Running Record and Analysis

Running Record	Analysis
✓ will/shall ✓✓✓✓✓✓✓ — tie-red/now tired ✓✓✓✓✓✓✓ T ✓✓✓✓✓✓ admonition ✓✓✓✓✓✓✓✓ ✓✓✓✓✓✓✓✓ ✓✓✓✓✓✓✓✓ ✓✓ wa-wash-watchdog/watchdog ✓✓✓✓ ✓✓✓✓✓✓✓✓✓ ✓✓✓✓✓✓✓✓✓✓ lay/lie ✓✓✓✓✓✓✓✓ — /And ✓✓✓✓ impo-impo-T/impolite ✓✓ ✓✓✓✓✓✓ scrap/scratch ✓✓✓✓✓✓✓✓ streaked/stretched ✓✓✓✓✓ ✓✓✓✓✓✓ radio/radiator	**SUMMARY** Total words 128 words Errors 11 Accuracy rate 92% (instructional level) **ERROR ANALYSIS** • Substitution will/shall streaked/stretched lay/lie radio/radiator scrap/scratch • Omission now and • Mispronounced tie-red/tired • Teacher pronounced admonition impolite • Prolonged decoding watchdog Most of the errors involve multisyllabic words. Josh couldn't break them into syllables. A series of minilessons on breaking apart multisyllabic words to decode them is recommended. The first 2 substitution errors didn't affect meaning, and the 2 omission errors didn't either. **OVERALL IMPRESSION** Josh read the text with interest, enthusiasm, and good expression. After reading, he was able to talk about what he'd read and make predictions about Harold's role in the story.

Semantic Feature Analysis

Teachers create a semantic feature analysis to help students examine the characteristics of content-area concepts and learn academic vocabulary (Pittelman, Heimlich, Berglund, & French, 1991). They draw a grid for the analysis with words listed on one axis and the characteristics listed on the other. Students reading a novel, for example, can do a semantic feature analysis with vocabulary words listed on one axis and the characters' names on the other; they decide which words relate to which characters and use pluses and minuses to mark the relationships on the grid. Teachers often do a semantic feature analysis with the whole class, but students can work in small groups or individually to complete the grid. The examination should be done as a whole-class activity, however, so that students can share their insights.

The Procedure. Here are the steps in doing a semantic feature analysis:

1. *Create a grid.* Teachers create a grid with words listed on the vertical axis and characteristics on the horizontal axis.
2. *Complete the grid.* Students complete the grid, cell by cell, by considering the relationship between each item on the vertical axis and the items on the horizontal axis. Then they mark each cell with a plus to indicate a relationship, a minus to indicate no relationship, and a question mark when they're unsure.
3. *Examine the grid.* Students and the teacher examine the grid for patterns and then draw conclusions based on the patterns.

Teachers have students do a semantic feature analysis as part of literature focus units and thematic units. In a thematic unit on immigration, for example, fifth-grade class did a semantic feature analysis, shown here, to review what they were learning about

Fifth Graders' Semantic Feature Analysis on Immigration										
	Arrived in the 1600s	Arrived in the 1700s	Arrived in the 1800s	Arrived in the 1900s	Came to to Ellis Island	Came for religious freedom	Came for safety	Came for opportunity	Were refugees	Experienced prejudice
English	+	+	–	–	–	+	–	+	–	–
Africans	+	+	+	–	–	–	–	–	–	+
Irish	–	–	+	–	–	–	+	+	+	+
Other Europeans	–	+	+	+	+	–	+	+	+	+
Jews	–	–	+	+	+	+	+	+	+	+
Chinese	–	–	+	–	–	–	–	–	–	+
Latinos	–	–	–	+	–	–	–	+	–	+
Southeast Asians	–	–	–	+	–	–	+	+	+	+

Code: + = yes
       – = no
       ? = don't know

America as a culturally pluralistic society. They listed the groups of people who immigrated to the United States on one axis and historical features on the other. Next, they completed the grid by marking each cell. Afterward, the students examined it for patterns and identified these big ideas:

Different peoples immigrated to America at different times.

The Africans who came as slaves were the only people who were brought to America against their will.

The English were the only immigrants who didn't suffer prejudice.

Sketch-to-Stretch

Sketch-to-stretch is a tool for helping students deepen their understanding of novels they've read (Short & Harste, 1996). Students work in small groups to draw pictures or diagrams that represent what a story means to them, not pictures of their favorite character or episode. In particular, they focus on theme and on symbols to represent the theme as they make sketch-to-stretch drawings (Dooley & Maloch, 2005). An added benefit is that students learn that stories rarely have only one interpretation and that by reflecting on the characters and events, they usually discover one or more themes.

Students need many opportunities to experiment with this activity before they learn to think symbolically. It's helpful to introduce this instructional procedure through a minilesson and to draw several sketches together as a class before students do their own. With practice, students learn that there isn't a single correct interpretation, and teachers help students focus on the interpretation rather than on their artistic talents. The box on page 376 shows a fourth grader's sketch-to-stretch made after reading *The Ballad of Lucy Whipple* (Cushman, 1996), a story set during the California gold rush. The sketch-to-stretch emphasizes two themes—you make your own happiness, and home is where you are.

The Procedure. Teachers follow these steps to implement this instructional procedure:

1. *Read and respond.* Students read a novel and respond to it in a grand conversation and in reading logs.
2. *Discuss the themes.* Students talk about the themes in the novel and ways to symbolize meanings. They learn that they can use lines, colors, shapes, symbols, and words to visually represent what a story means to them. They talk about possible meanings and ways they might visually represent these meanings.
3. *Draw the sketches.* Students work individually, with partners, or in small groups to draw sketches that reflect the story's meaning. Teachers emphasize that students should focus on their thinking about the meaning of the story, not on their favorite part, and that there's no single correct interpretation.
4. *Share the sketches.* Students meet in small groups to share their sketches and talk about the symbols they used. Teachers encourage classmates to study each student's sketch and explain what they think the student is conveying.
5. *Share some sketches with the class.* Each group chooses one sketch to share with the class.
6. *Revise sketches and make final copies.* Students add to their sketches based on feedback they received and ideas from classmates, and then they make the final copies.

A Fourth Grader's Sketch-to-Stretch About
The Ballad of Lucy Whipple

Students can use sketch-to-stretch whenever they're reading novels. In literature circles, for example, students create sketch-to-stretch drawings about themes and symbols that they share during group meetings (Whitin, 2002). Through this sharing, students gain insights about their classmates' thinking and clarify their own understanding. The same is true when students create and share sketch-to-stretch drawings during literature focus units.

Story Boards

Story boards are cards on which the illustrations and text from a picture book have been attached. Teachers make story boards by cutting apart two copies of a picture book and gluing the pages on pieces of tagboard. The most important use of story boards is to examine the elements of story structure, particularly plot, when only a few copies of a book are available. When students read novels, they create their own story boards. Partners work together to create a story board for one chapter: They make a poster with a detailed drawing illustrating events in the chapter and write a summary of it. Two eighth graders' story board summarizing Chapter 2 of *Dragonwings* (Yep, 2000) is shown on the next page.

The Procedure. Teachers generally use story boards with a small group of students or with the whole class, but individual students can reexamine them as part of center activities. Here are the steps:

1. *Collect two copies of a book.* Teachers use two copies of a picture book to make into story boards. In a few picture books, all the illustrations are on right-hand or left-hand pages, so only one copy is needed.

2. *Cut the books apart.* Teachers remove the covers and separate the pages, evening out the cut edges.

An Eighth-Grade Story Board From Dragonwings

Chapter 2
"The Company"

Moon Shadow meets his Uncle Bright Star. He had worked in the California Gold Rush and building the railroad. Then Windrider, Moon Shadow's dad, shows Moon Shadow around, to make him feel safe at home. They go past the Barbary Coast where the white demons live to his new home in Chinatown, the town of the Tang People. It looks like his old home in China. Moon Shadow's dad gave him a kite to fly. It was like a blue and green butterfly. Moon Shadow loved his new kite. Moon Shadow hasn't flown his kite yet, but I bet that he can't wait! They all go into a big house called the Company of the Peach Order Vow and then Uncle Bright Star's son named Black Dog comes. He is in a gang and he takes drugs. He tells everyone that the demons hate them and want to kill them. Then they heard the sound of a window shattering. So they went downstairs and they saw that a window was broken and the white demons were yelling and shouting at them. Moon Shadow is scared but Windrider protects him.

3. *Attach the pages to pieces of cardboard.* Teachers glue each page or double-page spread to a piece of cardboard, making sure that pages from each book are alternated so that each illustration is included.

4. *Laminate the cards.* Teachers laminate the cards so that they can withstand use by students.

5. *Use the cards in sequencing activities.* Teachers use the story board cards for a number of activities, including sequencing, story structure, rereading, and word-study activities.

Story boards are especially useful tools for English learners who use them to preview a story before reading or to review the events after reading. ELs also draw story boards because they can often share their understanding better through art than through language.

Sustained Silent Reading (SSR) is an independent reading time set aside during the school day for students in one class or the entire school to silently read self-selected books (Gardiner, 2005). In some schools, everyone—students, teachers, principals, secretaries, and custodians—stops to read, usually for a 15- to 30-minute period. Through numerous studies, SSR has been found to be beneficial in developing students' reading ability—fluency, vocabulary, and comprehension (Marshall, 2002; Pilgreen, 2000). In addition, it promotes a positive attitude toward reading and encourages the habit of daily reading.

Sustained Silent Reading

Teachers use SSR to increase the amount of reading students do every day and to develop their ability to read silently and without interruption. SSR follows these guidelines:

- Students choose the books they read.
- Students read silently.
- The teacher serves as a model by reading.
- Students choose one book or other reading material for the entire reading time.
- The teacher sets a timer for a predetermined, uninterrupted time period, usually 15–30 minutes.
- Everyone participates.
- The teacher doesn't keep records or evaluate students on their performance. (Pilgreen, 2000)

The Procedure. Teachers follow these steps in implementing this instructional procedure:

1. *Set aside a time for SSR.* Teachers allow 20 to 30 minutes every day for uninterrupted, independent reading. Teachers often begin with a 10-minute period and then extend the time as students build endurance and want to continue reading.
2. *Ensure that students have books to read.* Students read independently in self-selected books at their reading level.
3. *Set a timer for a predetermined time.* Teachers set a timer for the SSR reading period. To ensure that students aren't disturbed during SSR, some teachers place a "do not disturb" sign on the door.
4. *Read along with students.* Teachers read a book, magazine, or newspaper for pleasure while students read to model what capable readers do and to show that reading is a pleasurable activity.

Even though SSR was specifically developed without follow-up activities, many teachers have students give **book talks** to tell the class about their books. As students listen to one another, they get ideas about books that they might like to read. In some classrooms, students develop a ritual of passing on the books they've finished reading to interested classmates.

Tea Party

Students participate in a tea party to read or reread excerpts from a novel, nonfiction book, or content-area textbook. It's an active, participatory activity, with students moving around the classroom and socializing with classmates as they read short excerpts aloud to each other and talk about them (Beers, 2003). Teachers choose and make copies of excerpts, back them with tagboard, and laminate them. Then they distribute the excerpts to students, provide some rehearsal time, and have students participate in the tea party activity.

Teachers often use tea party as a prereading activity to introduce a new chapter in a content-area textbook. They usually select the excerpts to introduce big ideas and academic vocabulary and build background knowledge. At other times, teachers invite students to reread favorite excerpts to celebrate a book they've finished reading. When tea party is used as a postreading activity, students review big ideas, summarize the events, or focus on an element of story structure. Students can also create vocabulary cards, each featuring a word from the **word wall**, its definition, and an illustration. After making the cards, students participate in a tea party to share their word cards and explain them to classmates.

This instructional procedure is especially valuable for English learners because students have opportunities to build background knowledge before reading and review texts after reading in a supportive classroom environment (Rea & Mercuri, 2006). It's important that teachers choose excerpts that are written at English learners' reading levels or adapt them so that these students can read them fluently.

The Procedure. Teachers follow these steps as they implement tea party:

1. *Make the cards.* Teachers make cards with excerpts from a novel, nonfiction book, or content-area textbook and laminate them.
2. *Practice reading.* Students practice reading the excerpts to themselves until they can read them fluently.
3. *Share excerpts.* Students move around the classroom, stopping to read their excerpts to classmates. When students pair up, they take turns reading their excerpts. After the first student reads, both students discuss the text; then the other student reads and both students comment on the second student's text. Then students move apart and read their cards to other classmates.
4. *Share excerpts with the class.* Students return to their desks after 10 to 15 minutes, and teachers invite several students to read their excerpts to the class or talk about what they learned through the tea party activity.

The box below shows six tea party cards that a fifth-grade teacher used to introduce a unit on ecology. She collected some of the sentences and paragraphs from nonfiction books and a textbook chapter that students would read, and she wrote other selections herself. Students read and discussed the excerpts and began a **word wall** with these academic vocabulary words: *acid rain, biodegrade, landfills, ozone layer, pollution, recycle,* and *smog.*

Tea Party Cards With Information About Ecology

Recycling means using materials over and over or making them into new things instead of throwing them away.

Acid rain happens when poisonous gases from factories and cars get into rain clouds. Then the gases mix with rain and fall back to earth. It is harmful to our environment and to the people and animals on earth.

Plastic bottles, plastic forks, and plastic bags last forever! A big problem with plastic is that it doesn't biodegrade. Instead of filling landfills with plastic, it should be recycled.

Many cities have air filled with pollution called smog. This pollution is so bad that the sky looks brown, not blue.

The ozone layer around the earth protects us from the harmful rays of the sun. This layer is being damaged by gases called chlorofluorocarbons or CFCs. These gases are used in air conditioners, fire extinguishers, and styrofoam.

Americans cut down 850 million trees last year to make paper products. Sound like a lot of trees? Consider this: One tree can be made into approximately 700 grocery bags, and a large grocery store uses about that many bags in an hour!

Think-Alouds

Teachers use the think-aloud procedure to teach students to monitor their thinking during reading (Wilhelm, 2001). By making their thinking explicit, they're demonstrating what capable readers do implicitly (Keene & Zimmermann, 2007). After they watch teachers think aloud, students practice the procedure by thinking aloud about the literacy strategies they're learning. This procedure is valuable because students learn to be more-active readers. They learn to think metacognitively and regulate their own cognitive processes (Baker, 2002).

The Procedure. Teachers use these steps to teach students to think aloud:

1. *Choose a book.* Teachers make copies of an excerpt from a book they're reading aloud to the class to demonstrate how to think aloud.
2. *Plan the think-aloud.* Teachers decide which strategies to demonstrate, where they'll pause, and the kinds of thinking they want to share.
3. *Demonstrate a think-aloud.* Teachers read the text, pausing to think aloud, explaining what they're thinking and how they're using a strategy or solving a reading problem. They often use these "I" sentence starters to talk about their thinking:

   I wondered if . . .

   I was confused by . . .

   I didn't understand why . . .

   I think the big idea is . . .

   I reread this part because . . .

4. *Annotate the text.* Teachers write a small self-stick note about their thinking and attach it next to the text that prompted the think-aloud. They often use a word or phrase, such as *picture in my mind*, *context clues*, or *reread*, to quickly document their thinking.
5. *Continue thinking aloud.* Teachers continue reading the book, pausing to think aloud again and annotate the text with additional notes about their thinking.
6. *Reflect on the procedure.* Teachers review their annotations, talk about their strategy use, and reflect on the usefulness of think-alouds as a tool for comprehending what they're reading.
7. *Repeat the procedure.* Teachers read another book and have students take turns thinking aloud and annotating the text. Once students are familiar with the procedure, they practice doing think-alouds in small groups and with partners.

Once students know how to think aloud, teachers can use this procedure as an assessment tool. During student–teacher conferences, students reflect on their reading and evaluate how well they use particular strategies, and they think about what they could do to comprehend more effectively.

Word Ladders

Word ladders are spelling games where students change one word into another by altering letters using as few steps as possible to change the first word into the last one. This type of puzzle was invented by Lewis Carroll, author of *Alice in Wonderland*. Typically, the first and last words are related in some way, such as *fall–down*, *slow–fast*, and *trick–treat*,

A Cat–Dog *Word Ladder*

The teacher says:	Students write:
Begin with the word *cat*.	cat
Change the vowel to form another word for *bed*, sometimes the kind of bed you use when you're camping.	cot
Change one letter to form a word that means "a tiny, round mark."	dot
Finally, change the final consonant to make a word that goes with the first word, *cat*.	dog

and all the words in between must be real words. A well-known word ladder is *cat–dog*, which can be solved in three steps: *cat–cot–dot–dog*. It's shown above.

Teachers make word ladders to reinforce the spelling patterns their students are learning; in this case, it's not necessary to ensure that the first and last words are related as in traditional word ladders. A word ladder to practice words with the short and long sounds of /oo/ is shown below.

An / oo / *Word Ladder*

The teacher says:	Students write:
Write the word *good*. We're practicing words with *oo* today.	good
Change the beginning sound to write the past tense of *stand*. The word is *stood*.	stood
Change the ending sound to write a word that means "a seat without arms or a back."	stool
Change the beginning sound to write a word that means the opposite of *warm*.	cool
Add two letters—one before and one after the *c*—to spell where we are right now.	school
Change the beginning sound to spell *tool*.	tool
Drop a letter to make a word that means *also*.	too
Change the first letter to write a word that means "a place where people can go to see wild animals."	zoo
Add a letter to *zoo* to spell the sound a car makes.	zoom
Change the beginning sound—use two letters for this blend—to spell something we use for sweeping.	broom
Change one letter to spell a word that means *creek*.	brook
Change the beginning sound to make a word that means "a dishonest person."	crook

The Procedure. Here's the procedure for using word ladders:

1. *Create the word ladder.* Teachers create a word ladder with 5 to 15 words, choosing words from spelling lists, and they write clues for each word, trying to incorporate a combination of spelling and meaning clues.
2. *Pass out supplies.* Teachers generally have students use whiteboards and marking pens for this activity, but they can also use blank paper or paper with word ladders already drawn on them.
3. *Do the word ladder.* Teachers read the clues they've prepared and have students write the words. Students take turns identifying the words and spelling them correctly. When necessary, teachers provide additional clues and explain any unfamiliar words or spelling patterns.
4. *Review the word ladder.* Once students complete the word ladder, they reread the words and talk about any words they had difficulty writing.

Word ladders are a fun way for students to practice the spelling skills they're learning and, at the same time, think about the meanings of words. The activity's gamelike format makes it engaging for both students and teachers. To see more word ladders, check Rasinski's (2005a, 2005b) books of easy-to-use word ladder games; other word ladder games are available online.

Word Sorts

Students use word sorts to categorize words according to their meanings or spelling patterns (Bear, Invernizzi, Templeton, & Johnston, 2008). The purpose is to help students focus on spelling features of words and identify recurring patterns. Teachers choose categories for word sorts, depending on instructional goals or students' developmental levels:

◆ Spelling patterns
◆ Root words and affixes
◆ Parts of speech and other grammar concepts
◆ Conceptual relationships

Many of the words chosen for word sorts come from books students are reading or from thematic units. The boxes on the next page show two word sorts using words from *Holes* (Sachar, 2008); the first is a conceptual sort and the second is a grammar sort.

Word sorts are effective for English learners because students learn how English differs from their native language, and they develop knowledge to help them predict meaning through spelling (Bear, Helman, Invernizzi, & Templeton, 2007). Because word sorts can be done in small groups, teachers can choose words that are appropriate for students' developmental levels.

The Procedure. Here are the steps for conducting a word sort:

1. *Choose a topic.* Teachers choose a spelling skill or content-area topic for the word sort and decide whether it will be an open or closed sort. In an open sort, students determine the categories based on the words they're sorting. In a closed sort, teachers present the categories as they introduce the sorting activity.
2. *Compile a list of words.* Teachers compile a list of 15 to 30 words, depending on grade level, that exemplify particular categories, and they write the words on small cards.
3. *Introduce the sorting activity.* Teachers present the categories and have students sort word cards into these categories, if it's a closed sort; but if it's an open sort, students identify the words and think about possible categories. Students arrange and rearrange the cards until they're satisfied with the sorting. Then they add category labels.

A Concept Sort Using Words From Holes

Stanley	Zero	Camp Green Lake	Mr. Sir	The Warden	The Escape
unlucky	nobody	wasteland	grotesque	Ms. Walker	miracle
sneakers	Hector Zeroni	guards	cowboy hat	holes	sploosh
Caveman	confession	investigation	swollen	venom	thumbs-up sign
overweight	homeless	yellow-spotted lizard	tattoo	miserable	impossible
callused	Clyde Livingston's shoes	scorpions	sunflower seeds	fingernail polish	ledges
million dollars	digger	girl scout camp	guard	make-up kit	Big Thumb
suitcase	frail	temperature	tougher	freckles	happiness

A Grammar Sort Using Words From Holes

Adjectives	Nouns	Verbs	Adverbs
half-opened	wasteland	chewing	surely
scratchy	curiosity	waits	previously
tougher	fossil	howled	quickly
desolate	allergies	startled	well
throbbing	pitchfork	watches	intently
metallic	warden	gazes	supposedly
shriveled	sneakers	wiggled	always

4. *Make a permanent record.* Students glue the word cards onto a large sheet of construction paper or write the words in columns on a sheet of paper.
5. *Share word sorts.* Students share their word sorts with peers, explaining the categories they used (for open sorts).

Teachers use word sorts to teach spelling and vocabulary. During literature focus units, students sort vocabulary words according to the beginning, middle, or end of the story or according to character. During thematic units, students sort vocabulary words according to big ideas.

Word Walls

Word walls are collections of words posted in the classroom that students use for word-study activities and refer to when they're writing (Wagstaff, 1999). Teachers make word walls using construction-paper squares or sheets of butcher paper that have been divided into alphabetized sections. Students and the teacher write academic vocabulary from novels and other books they're reading on the word wall. Usually students choose the words to write on the word wall, and they may even do the writing themselves, but teachers add any important words—especially Tier 2 words—that students have missed.

The Procedure. Teachers create word walls with the whole class, and they follow these steps:

1. *Prepare the word wall.* Teachers prepare a blank word wall in the classroom from sheets of construction paper or butcher paper, dividing it into 12 to 24 boxes and labeling the boxes with letters of the alphabet.
2. *Introduce the word wall.* Teachers introduce the word wall and write several words on it before beginning to read.
3. *Add words to the word wall.* Students suggest "important" words for the word wall as they read a novel. Students and the teacher write the words in the alphabetized blocks, making sure to write large enough so that most students can see the words. If a word is misspelled, it's corrected because students will be using the words in various activities. Sometimes the teacher writes a synonym for a difficult word, puts a box around the root word, or writes related words nearby.
4. *Use the word wall.* Teachers use the word wall for a variety of word-study activities, and students refer to it when they're writing.

Teachers post a second word wall to use during thematic units to highlight academic vocabulary, and students refer to these words when they're writing and use them for semantic feature analysis, tea party, word sorts, and other word-study activities.

Writing Groups

During the revising stage of the writing process, students meet in writing groups to share their rough drafts and get feedback on how well they're communicating. Writing group members offer compliments about things writers have done well and make suggestions for improvement. Their comments reflect these topics and other aspects of the author's craft:

leads	word choice	voice
dialogue	sentences	metaphors
endings	organization	ideas
description	point of view	flashbacks

These topics are used for both compliments and suggestions. When students are offering a compliment, they might say, "I liked your lead. It grabbed me and made me keep listening," and when they're making a suggestion, they say, "I wonder if you could start with a question to make your lead more interesting. Maybe you could say, 'Have you ever ridden in a police car? Well, that's what happened to me!'"

Teaching students how to share their rough drafts in a writing group and offer constructive feedback isn't easy. When teachers introduce revision, they model appropriate responses because students may not know how to offer specific and meaningful comments tactfully. Teachers and students can brainstorm a list of appropriate compliments and suggestions and post it in the classroom to refer to. Comments should usually begin with "I," not "you." Notice the difference in tone in these two sentence stems: "I wonder if . . ." versus "You need to . . ." Here are some ways to begin compliments:

I like the part where . . .

I learned how . . .

I like the way you described . . .

I like how you organized the information because . . .

Students also offer suggestions about how classmates can revise their writing. It's important that students phrase what they say in helpful ways. Here are some suggestions:

I got confused in the part about . . .

I wonder if you need a closing . . .

I'd like you to add more about . . .

I wonder if these paragraphs are in the right order . . .

I think you might want to combine these sentences . . .

Student-writers also ask classmates for help with specific problems they've identified. Looking to classmates for feedback is a big step in learning to revise. Here are some questions writers can ask:

What do you want to know more about?

Is there a part that I should throw away?

What details can I add?

What do you think is the best part of my writing?

Are there some words I need to change?

Writing groups work effectively once students understand how to support and help their classmates by offering compliments, making suggestions, and asking questions.

Revising is the most difficult part of the writing process because it's hard for students to stand back and assess their writing objectively in order to communicate more effectively. As students participate in writing groups, they learn how to accept compliments and suggestions and to provide useful feedback to classmates.

The Procedure. Teachers teach students to use this instructional procedure so that they can work in small groups to get feedback about their writing. Here are the steps:

1. *Read drafts aloud.* Students take turns reading their rough drafts aloud to the group. Everyone listens politely, thinking about compliments and suggestions they'll make after the writer finishes reading. Only the writer looks at the composition because when classmates look at it, they quickly notice and comment on mechanical errors, even though the emphasis during revising is on content. Listening keeps the focus on content.

2. *Offer compliments.* Students in the writing group tell the writer what they liked about the composition. These positive comments should be specific, focusing on strengths, rather than the often-heard "I liked it" or "It was good"; even though these are positive comments, they don't provide effective feedback.

3. *Ask clarifying questions.* Writers ask for assistance with trouble spots they identified earlier when rereading their writing, or they may ask questions that reflect more-general concerns about how well they're communicating.

4. *Offer other revision suggestions.* Members of the writing group ask questions about things that were unclear to them and make suggestions about how to revise the rough draft.

5. *Repeat the process.* Members of the writing group repeat the process so that all students can share their rough drafts. The first four steps are repeated for each student's composition.

6. *Make plans for revision.* Students each make a commitment to revise their writing based on the comments and suggestions of the group members. The final decision on what to revise always rests with the writers themselves, but with the understanding that their rough drafts aren't perfect comes the realization that some revision will be necessary. When students verbalize their planned revisions, they're more likely to complete the revision stage.

Students meet in writing groups whenever they're using the writing process. Once they've written a rough draft, students are ready to share their writing and get some feedback from classmates. They often meet with the same writing group throughout the school year, or students can form groups when they're ready to meet. Many teachers have students sign up on the chalkboard; this way, whenever four students are ready, they can form a group. Both established and spontaneously formed groups can be effective. What matters most is that students get feedback about their writing when they need it.

GLOSSARY

Aesthetic reading Reading for pleasure.

Affix A syllable added to the beginning (prefix) or end (suffix) of a word to change the word's meaning (e.g., *il-* in *illiterate* and *-al* in *national*).

Alphabetic principle The assumption underlying alphabetical language systems that each sound has a corresponding graphic representation (or letter).

Applying The fifth stage of the reading process, in which readers use what they've learned in another literacy experience, often by making a project.

Authentic Activities and materials related to real-world reading and writing.

Automaticity Identifying words accurately and quickly.

Basal reading program A collection of student textbooks, workbooks, teacher's manuals, and other materials and resources for reading instruction.

Bound morpheme A morpheme that is not a word and cannot stand alone (e.g., *-s, tri-*).

Cloze An activity in which students replace words that have been deleted from a text.

Close reading A procedure for interpreting literature.

Comprehension The process of constructing meaning using both the author's text and the reader's background knowledge for a specific purpose.

Consonant A speech sound characterized by friction or stoppage of the airflow as it passes through the vocal tract; usually any letter except *a, e, i, o,* and *u*.

Content-area literacy Reading and writing in social studies, science, and other areas of the curriculum.

Context clue Information from the words or sentences surrounding a word that helps to clarify the word's meaning.

Decoding Using word-identification strategies to pronounce and attach meaning to an unfamiliar word.

Diagnosis Determining specific problems readers are having, generally using a test.

Differentiated instruction Procedures for assisting students in learning, providing options, challenging students, and matching books to students to maximize their learning.

Drafting The second stage of the writing process, in which writers pour out ideas in a rough draft.

Editing The fourth stage of the writing process, in which writers proofread to identify and correct spelling, capitalization, punctuation, and grammar errors.

Efferent reading Reading for information.

Etymology The origin and history of words; the etymological information is enclosed in brackets in dictionary entries.

Explicit instruction Systematic instruction of concepts, strategies, and skills that builds from simple to complex.

Exploring The fourth stage of the reading process, in which readers reread the text, study vocabulary words, and learn strategies and skills.

Fluency Reading smoothly, quickly, and with expression.

Free morpheme A morpheme that can stand alone as a word (e.g., *book, cycle*).

Frustration level Reading material that is too difficult for a student to read successfully.

Genre A category of literature such as science fiction, biography, or historical fiction, or a writing form.

Goldilocks principle A strategy for choosing "just right" books.

Grand conversation A small-group or whole-class discussion about literature.

Grapheme A written representation of a sound using one or more letters.

Graphic organizers Diagrams that provide organized visual representations of information from texts.

Guided reading Students read leveled books in small-group lessons with teacher support.

Homonyms Words that sound alike but are spelled differently (e.g., *sea–see, there–their–they're*); also called *homophones*.

Hyperbole A stylistic device involving obvious exaggerations.

Imagery The use of words and figurative language to create an impression.

Independent reading level Reading material that a student can read independently.

Inflectional endings Suffixes that express plurality or possession when added to a noun (e.g., *girls, girl's*), tense when added to a verb (e.g., *walked, walking*), or comparison when added to an adjective (e.g., *happier, happiest*).

Informal reading inventory (IRI) An individually administered reading test that's used to determine students' independent, instructional, and frustration levels.

Instructional reading level Reading material that a student can read with teacher support.

Intervention Intense, individualized instruction for struggling readers to solve reading problems and accelerate their growth.

Leveling books A method of estimating the difficulty level of a text.

Lexile scores A method of estimating the difficulty level of a text.

Listening capacity level The highest level of graded passage that can be comprehended well when read aloud to the student.

Literacy The ability to read and write.

Literal comprehension The understanding of what is explicitly stated in a text.

Literature circle An instructional approach in which students meet in small groups to read and respond to a book.

Literature focus unit An instructional approach in which the class reads and responds to a piece of literature.

Metacognition Students' awareness of their own thought and learning processes.

Metaphor A comparison expressed directly, without using *like* or *as*.

Miscue analysis A strategy for categorizing and analyzing a student's oral reading errors.

Morpheme The smallest meaningful part of a word; sometimes it's a word (e.g., *cup*, *hope*), sometimes not (e.g., *-ly*, *bi-*).

New literacies The ability to use digital and multimodal technologies to communicate and learn effectively.

Orthography The spelling system.

Personification Figurative language in which things are represented as having human qualities.

Phoneme A sound; it is represented in print with slashes (e.g., /s/ and /th/).

Phoneme-grapheme correspondence The relationship between a sound and the letter that represents it.

Phonics Predictable relationships between phonemes and graphemes.

Prefix A syllable added to the beginning of a word to change the word's meaning (e.g., *re-* in *reread*).

Prereading The first stage of the reading process, in which readers activate background knowledge, set purposes, and make plans for reading.

Prewriting The first stage of the writing process, in which writers gather and organize ideas for writing.

Proofreading Reading a composition to identify spelling and other mechanical errors.

Prosody The ability to orally read sentences expressively, with appropriate phrasing and intonation.

Publishing The fifth stage of the writing process, in which writers make the final copy of their writing and share it with an audience.

Readability formula A method of estimating the difficulty level of a text.

Reading The second stage of the reading process, in which readers read the text for the first time.

Reading process Students use prereading, reading, responding, exploring, and applying to comprehend a text.

Reading speed Reading rate, usually reported as the average number of words read correctly in 1 minute (wcpm).

Reading workshop An approach in which students read self-selected texts independently.

Responding The third stage of the reading process, in which readers respond to the text, often through grand conversations and by writing in reading logs.

Revising The third stage of the writing process, in which writers clarify meaning in the rough draft.

Scaffolding The support a teacher provides to students as they read and write.

Simile A comparison expressed using *like* or *as*.

Skill An automatic processing behavior that students use in reading and writing, such as distinguishing fact from opinion and capitalizing proper nouns.

Strategy A problem-solving behavior that students use in reading and writing, such as predicting, monitoring, and summarizing.

Struggling reader or writer A student who isn't meeting grade-level standards in reading or writing.

Suffix A syllable added to the end of a word to change the word's meaning (e.g., *-y* in *hairy*, *-ful* in *careful*).

Syllable An uninterrupted segment of speech that includes a vowel sound (e.g., *get*, *a-bout*, *but-ter-fly*, *con-sti-tu-tion*).

Symbol The author's use of an object to represent something else.

Text Words appearing in print.

Trade book A published book that is not a textbook; the type of books in bookstores and libraries.

Vowel A voiced speech sound made without friction or stoppage of the airflow as it passes through the vocal tract; the letters *a, e, i, o, u,* and sometimes *w* and *y.*

Word identification Strategies that students use to decode words, such as phonic analysis, analogies, syllabic analysis, and morphemic analysis.

Writing process Students use prewriting, drafting, revising, editing, and publishing to develop and refine a composition.

Writing workshop An approach in which students use the writing process to write compositions, often on self-selected topics.

Zone of proximal development The distance between a student's actual developmental level and his or her potential developmental level that can be reached with scaffolding.

REFERENCES

Aardema, V. (2004). *Why mosquitoes buzz in people's ears.* New York: Puffin Books.

Ada, A. F. (1998), *Under the royal palms: A childhood in Cuba.* New York: Scholastic.

Afflerbach, P. (2007a). Best practices in literacy assessment. In L. B. Gambrell, L. M. Morrow, & M. Pressley (Eds.), *Best practices in literacy instruction* (3rd ed., pp. 264–282). New York: Guilford Press.

Afflerbach, P. (2007b). *Understanding and using reading assessment, K–12.* Newark, DE: International Reading Association.

Afflerbach, P., Pearson, P. D., & Paris, S. G. (2008). Clarifying differences between reading skills and reading strategies. *The Reading Teacher, 61,* 364–373.

Alderman, M. K. (1999). *Motivation for achievement: Possibilities for teaching and learning.* Mahwah, NJ: Erlbaum.

Aliki. (1986). *A medieval feast.* New York: HarperCollins.

Allen, C. A. (2001). *The multigenre research paper: Voice, passion, and discovery in grades 4–6.* Portsmouth, NH: Heinemann.

Allen, J. (1999). *Words, words, words.* Portsmouth, NH: Heinemann.

Allen, J. (2000). *Yellow brick road: Shared and guided paths to independent reading, 4–12.* Portland, ME: Stenhouse.

Allen, J. (2002). *On the same page: Shared reading beyond the primary grades.* Portland, ME: Stenhouse.

Allen, J. (2007). *Inside words: Tools for teaching academic vocabulary, grades 4–12.* Portland, ME: Stenhouse.

Allington, R. L. (2006). *What really matters for struggling readers: Designing research-based programs* (2nd ed.). Boston: Allyn & Bacon/Pearson.

Allington, R. L. (2009a). *What really matters in fluency: Research-based practices across the curriculum.* Boston: Allyn & Bacon/Pearson.

Allington, R. L. (2009b). *What really matters in Response to Intervention.* Boston: Allyn & Bacon/Pearson.

Allington, R. L., & Johnston, P. H. (Eds.). (2002). *Reading to learn: Lessons from exemplary fourth-grade classrooms.* New York: Guilford Press.

Almond, D. (2001). *Skellig.* New York: Laurel Leaf.

Almond, D. (2007). *My dad's a birdman.* Cambridge, MA: Candlewick Press.

Angelillo, J. (2005). *Writing to the prompt: When students don't have a choice.* Portsmouth, NH: Heinemann.

Angelillo, J. (2008). *Whole-class teaching: Minilessons and more.* Portsmouth, NH: Heinemann.

Applegate, M. D., Quinn, K. B., & Applegate, A. J. (2008). *The critical reading inventory: Assessing students' reading and thinking* (2nd ed.). Upper Saddle River, NJ: Merrill/Prentice Hall.

Armbruster, B. B., McCarthey, S. J., & Cummins, S. (2005). Writing to learn in elementary classrooms. In R. Indrisano & J. R. Paratore (Eds.), *Learning to write, writing to learn: Theory and research in practice* (pp. 71–96). Newark, DE: International Reading Association.

Arnold, C., & Comora, M. (2007). *Taj Mahal.* Minneapolis: Carolrhoda.

Atwell, N. (1998). *In the middle: New understandings about writing, reading, and learning* (2nd ed.). Portsmouth, NH: Heinemann/Boynton/Cook.

Atwell, N. (2007). *The reading zone: How to help kids become skilled, passionate, habitual, critical readers.* New York: Scholastic.

Avi. (1994). *The fighting ground.* New York: HarperCollins.

Avi. (2003). *Nothing but the truth.* New York: HarperTrophy.

Avi. (2004). *Crispin: The cross of lead.* New York: Hyperion Books.

Avi. (2005). *Poppy.* New York: HarperTrophy.

Baker, L. (2002). Metacognition in comprehension instruction. In C. C. Block & M. Pressley (Eds.), *Comprehension instruction: Research-based best practices* (pp. 77–95). New York: Guilford Press.

Baker, L., & Brown, A. (1984). Metacognitive skills of reading. In P. D. Pearson, M. Kamil, P. B. Mosenthal, & R. Barr (Eds.), *Handbook of reading research* (pp. 353–394). New York: Longman.

Bandura, A. (1997). *Self-efficacy: The exercise of control.* New York: W. H. Freeman.

Barretta, G. (2007). *Dear deer: A book of homophones.* New York: Holt.

Baumann, J. F., Edwards, E. C., Font, G., Tereshinski, C. A., Kame'enui, E. J., & Olejnik, S. (2002). Teaching morphemic and contextual analysis to fifth grade students. *Reading Research Quarterly, 37,* 150–176.

Baumann, J. F., Font, G., Edwards, E. C., & Boland, E. (2005). Strategies for teaching middle-grade students to use word-part and context clues to expand reading vocabulary. In E. Hiebert & M. L. Kamil (Eds.), *Teaching and learning vocabulary: Bringing research to practice* (pp. 179–205). Mahwah, NJ: Erlbaum.

Baumann, J. F., Kame'enui, E. J., & Ash, G. (2003). Research on vocabulary instruction: Voltaire redux. In J. Flood, D. Lapp, J. R. Squire, & J. M. Jensen (Eds.), *Handbook of research on teaching the English language arts* (2nd ed., pp. 752–785). Mahwah, NJ: Erlbaum.

Bausum, A. (2006). *Freedom riders: John Lewis and Jim Zwerg on the front lines of the civil rights movement.* Washington, DC: National Geographic Children's Books.

Baylor, B. (1987). *The desert is theirs.* New York: Aladdin Books.

Baylor, B. (1993). *Desert voices.* New York: Scribner.

Bean, R. M., & Swan, A. (2006). Vocabulary assessment: A key to planning vocabulary instruction. In C. C. Block & J. N. Mangieri (Eds.), *The vocabulary-enriched classroom: Practices for improving the reading performance of all students in grades 3 and up* (pp. 164–187). New York: Scholastic.

Bear, D. R., Helman, L., Templeton, S., Invernizzi, M., & Johnston, F. (2007). *Words their way with English learners: Word study for spelling, phonics, and vocabulary instruction.* Upper Saddle River, NJ: Merrill/Prentice Hall.

Bear, D. R., Invernizzi, M., Templeton, S., & Johnston, F. (2008). *Words their way: Word study for phonics, vocabulary, and spelling instruction* (4th ed.). Upper Saddle River, NJ: Merrill/Prentice Hall.

Beaver, J., & Carter, M. (2005). *Developmental reading assessment* (2nd ed.). Upper Saddle River, NJ: Celebration Press/Pearson.

Beck, I. L., & McKeown, M. G. (2006). *Improving comprehension with questioning the author: A fresh and expanded view of a powerful approach.* New York: Scholastic.

Beck, I. L., McKeown, M. G., & Kucan, L. (2002). *Bringing words to life: Robust vocabulary instruction.* New York: Guilford Press.

Beers, K. (2003). *When kids can't read, what teachers can do.* Portsmouth, NH: Heinemann.

Bender, W. N., & Shores, C. (2007). *Response to Intervention: A practical guide for every teacher.* Thousand Oaks, CA: Corwin Press and the Council for Exceptional Children.

Berthoff, A. E. (1981). *The making of meaning.* Montclair, NJ: Boynton/Cook.

Blachowicz, C. L. Z. (1986). Making connections: Alternatives to the vocabulary notebook. *Journal of Reading 29,* 643–649.

Blachowicz, C. L. Z., & Fisher, P. J. (2007). Best practices in vocabulary instruction. In L. B. Gambrell, L. M. Morrow, & M. Pressley (Eds.), *Best practices in literacy instruction* (3rd ed., pp. 178–203). New York: Guilford Press.

Black, A., & Stave, A. M. (2007). *A comprehensive guide to readers theatre: Enhancing fluency and comprehension in middle school and beyond.* Newark, DE: International Reading Association.

Blanton, W. E., Wood, K. D., & Moorman, G. B. (1990). The role of purpose in reading instruction. *The Reading Teacher, 43,* 486–493.

Blasingame, J., & Bushman, J. H. (2005) *Teaching writing in middle and secondary schools.* Upper Saddle River, NJ: Pearson/Merrill/Prentice Hall.

Block, C. C., & Pressley, M. (2007). Best practices in teaching comprehension. In L. B. Gambrell, L. M. Morrow, & M. Pressley (Eds.), *Best practices in literacy instruction* (3rd ed., pp. 220–242). New York: Guilford Press.

Block, C., Oakar, M., & Hurt, N. (2002). The expertise of literacy teachers: A continuum from preschool–grade 5. *Reading Research Quarterly, 37,* 178–206.

Blume, J. (2007). *Tales of a fourth grade nothing.* New York: Puffin Books.

Bollard, J. K. (2006). *Scholastic children's thesaurus.* New York: Scholastic.

Bottomley, D. M., Henk, W. A., & Melnick, S. A. (1997/1998). Assessing children's views about themselves as writers using the Writer Self-Perception Scale. *The Reading Teacher, 51,* 286–296.

Bouchard, M. (2005). *Comprehension strategies for English language learners*. New York: Scholastic.

Boyd-Batstone, P. (2004). Focused anecdotal records assessment: A tool for standards-based, authentic assessment. *The Reading Teacher, 58,* 230–239.

Bracey, G. W. (2004). *Setting the record straight: Responses to misconceptions about public education in the United States*. Portsmouth, NH: Heinemann.

Braunger, J., & Lewis, J. P. (2006). *Building a knowledge base in reading* (2nd ed.). Newark, DE: International Reading Association/National Council of Teachers of English.

Brennan-Nelson, D. (2004), *My teacher likes to say*. Chelsea, MI: Sleeping Bear Press.

Brett, J. (2003). *Town mouse, country mouse*. New York: Putnam.

Brewster, H. (1997). *Inside the Titanic*. Boston: Little, Brown.

Broach, E. (2007). *Shakespeare's secret*. New York: Square Fish.

Brock, C. H., & Raphael, T. E. (2005). *Windows to language, literacy, and culture: Insights from an English-language learner*. Newark, DE: International Reading Association.

Brophy, J. (2004). *Motivating students to learn* (2nd ed.). Mahwah, NJ: Erlbaum.

Brown, D. F., & Knowles, T. (2007). *What every middle school teacher should know* (2nd ed.). Portsmouth, NH: Heinemann/National Middle School Association.

Brown, J. S., Collins, A., & Duguid, S. (1989). Situated cognition and the culture of learning. *Educational Researcher, 18*(1), 32–42.

Brozo, W. G., & Simpson, M. L. (2007). *Content literacy for today's adolescents: Honoring diversity and building competence* (5th ed.). Upper Saddle River, NJ: Merrill/Prentice Hall.

Bruchac, J. (2001). *The journal of Jesse Smoke: A Cherokee boy, Trail of Tears, 1838*. New York: Scholastic.

Bunting, E. (1992). *The wall*. New York: Aladdin Books.

Bunting, E. (1998). *So far from the sea*. Boston: Houghton Mifflin.

Burke, J. (2007). *The English teacher's companion: A complete guide to classroom, curriculum, and the profession* (3rd ed.). Portsmouth, NH: Heinemann.

Buss, K., & Karnowski, L. (2000). *Reading and writing literary genres*. Newark, DE: International Reading Association.

Butler, A., & Turbill, J. (1984). *Towards a reading-writing classroom*. Portsmouth, NH: Heinemann.

Button, K., Johnson, M. J., & Furgerson, P. (1996). Interactive writing in a primary classroom. *The Reading Teacher, 49,* 446–454.

Calderon, M. (2007). *Teaching reading to English language learners, grades 6–12*. Thousand Oaks, CA: Corwin Press.

Caldwell, J. S., & Leslie, L. (2005). *Intervention strategies to follow informal reading inventory assessment: So what do I do now?* Boston: Allyn & Bacon/Pearson.

Calkins, L. M. (1994). *Teaching writing* (rev. ed.). Portsmouth, NH: Heinemann.

Calkins, L., Montgomery, K., & Santman, D. (1998). *A teacher's guide to standardized reading tests: Knowledge is power*. Portsmouth, NH: Heinemann.

Cappellini, M. (2005). *Balancing reading and language learning: A resource for teaching English language learners, K–5*. York, ME: Stenhouse.

Caputo, P. (2005). *10,000 days of thunder: A history of the Vietnam War*. New York: Atheneum.

Carr, E., & Ogle, D. (1987). K-W-L Plus: A strategy for comprehension and summarization. *Journal of Reading, 31,* 626–631.

Casbarro, J. (2005, February). The politics of high-stakes testing. *Education Digest, 70*(6), 20–23.

Casey, K. (2006). *Literacy coaching: The essentials*. Portsmouth, NH: Heinemann.

Castek, J., Bevans-Mangelson, J., & Goldstone, B. (2006). Reading adventures online: Five ways to introduce the new literacies of the Internet through children's literature. *The Reading Teacher, 59,* 714–728.

Chall, J. S., & Jacobs, V. A. (2003). Poor children's fourth-grade slump. *American Educator, 27*(1), 14–15, 44.

Chall, J. S., Jacobs, V. A., & Baldwin, L. E. (1991). *The reading crisis: Why poor children fall behind*. Cambridge, MA: Harvard University Press.

Chiseri-Strater, E., & Sunstein, B. S. (2006). *What works? A practical guide for teacher research*. Portsmouth, NH: Heinemann.

Christensen, B. (2001). *Woody Guthrie: Poet of the people*. New York: Knopf.

Christenson, T. A. (2002). *Supporting struggling writers in the elementary classroom*. Newark, DE: International Reading Association.

Clarke, B. (1990). *Amazing frogs and toads*. New York: Knopf.

Clarke, L. W., & Holwadel, J. (2007). "Help! What is wrong with these literature circles and how can we fix them?" *The Reading Teacher, 61,* 20–29.

Clay, M. M. (2000). *Running records for classroom teachers*. Portsmouth, NH: Heinemann.

Clay, M. M. (2007). *An observation survey of early literacy achievement* (rev. ed.). Portsmouth. NH: Heinemann.

Clements, A. (2007). *Dogku*. New York: Simon & Schuster.

Coiro, J. (2003). Reading comprehension on the Internet: Expanding our understanding of reading comprehension to encompass new literacies. *The Reading Teacher, 56,* 458–464.

Coiro, J., & Dobler, E. (2007). Exploring the online reading comprehension strategies used by sixth-grade skilled readers to search for and locate information on the Internet. *Reading Research Quarterly, 42,* 214–257.

Cole, J. (1996). *The magic school bus inside a beehive*. New York: Scholastic.

Cole, J. (1999). *The magic school bus and the electric field trip*. New York: Scholastic.

Cole, J. (2006). *The magic school bus and the science fair expedition*. New York: Scholastic.

Colman, P. (1998). *Rosie the riveter: Women working on the home front during World War II*. New York: Crown.

Cooper, J. D., Chard, D. J., & Kiger, N. D. (2006). *The struggling reader: Interventions that work*. New York: Scholastic.

Cooter, R. B., Jr., Flynt, E. S., & Cooter, K. S. (2007). *Comprehensive reading inventory*. Upper Saddle River. NJ: Merrill/Prentice Hall.

Craft, K. Y. (2002). *Sleeping beauty*. New York: SeaStar Books.

Creech, S. (2001). *Love that dog*. New York: HarperCollins.

Creech, S. (2005). *Granny Torrelli makes soup*. New York: HarperTrophy.

Culham, R. (2003). *6 + 1 traits of writing*. New York: Scholastic.

Cunningham, P. (1990). The Names Test: A quick assessment of decoding ability. *The Reading Teacher, 44,* 124–129.

Cunningham, P. M. (2008). *Phonics they use: Words for reading and writing* (5th ed.). Boston: Allyn & Bacon.

Cunningham, P. M. (2009). *What really matters in vocabulary: Research-based practices across the curriculum*. Boston: Allyn & Bacon/Pearson.

Cunningham, P. M., & Allington, R. L. (2007). *Classrooms that work: They can all read and write* (4th ed.). Boston: Allyn & Bacon/Pearson.

Cunningham, P. M., & Cunningham, J. W. (1992). Making words: Enhancing the invented spelling-decoding connection. *The Reading Teacher, 46,* 106–115.

Cunningham, P. M., & Cunningham, J. W. (2002). What we know about how to teach phonics. In A. E. Farstrup & S. J. Samuels (Eds.), *What research has to say about reading instruction* (3rd ed., pp. 87–109). Newark, DE: International Reading Association.

Cunningham, P. M., & Hall, D. P. (1994). *Making big words*. Parsippany, NJ: Good Apple.

Curtis, C. P. (1999). *Bud, not Buddy*. New York: Delacorte.

Curtis, C. P. (2000). *The Watsons go to Birmingham—1963*. New York: Lourel Leaf.

Curtis, M. E. (2004). Adolescents who struggle with world identification: Research and practice. In T. L. Jetton & J. A. Dole (Eds.), *Adolescent literacy research and practice* (pp. 119–134). New York: Guilford Press.

Cushman, K. (1994). *Catherine, called Birdy*. New York: HarperCollins.

Cushman, K. (1996a). *The ballad of Lucy Whipple*. New York: Clarion Books.

Cushman, K. (1996b). *The midwife's apprentice*. New York: HarperCollins.

D'Aoust, C. (1992). Portfolios: Process for students and teachers. In K. B. Yancy (Ed.), *Portfolios in the writing classroom* (pp. 39–48). Urbana, IL: National Council of Teachers of English.

Dahl, R. (2007). *Charlie and the chocolate factory*. New York: Puffin Books.

Daniels, H. (2001). *Literature circles: Voice and choice in book clubs and reading groups*. York, ME: Stenhouse.

Daniels, H., & Bizar, M. (1998). *Methods that matter: Six structures for best practice classrooms*. York, ME: Stenhouse.

Daniels, H., & Steineke, N. (2004). *Mini-lessons for literature circles*. Portsmouth, NH: Heinemann.

Daniels, H., & Zemelman, S. (2004). *Subjects matter: Every teacher's guide to content-area reading*. Portsmouth, NH: Heinemann.

David, L., & Gordon, C. (2007). *The down-to-earth guide to global warming*. New York: Orchard/Scholastic.

Dean, D. (2006). *Strategic writing: The writing process and beyond in the secondary English classroom*. Urbana, IL: National Council of Teachers of English.

Delano, M. F. (2005). *American heroes*. Washington, DC: National Geographic Society.

Demi. (2002). *King Midas: The golden touch*. New York: McElderry.

Demi. (2003). *Muhammad*. New York: McElderry.

Denenberg, B. (1999). *The journal of Ben Uchida: Citizen 13559, Mirror Lake Internment Camp*. New York: Scholastic.

Denenberg, B. (2008). *Lincoln shot: A president's life remembered*. New York: Feiwel and Friends.

Dewey, J. (1997). *Experience and education*. New York: Free Press.

DiCamillo, K. (2003). *The tale of Despereaux*. Cambridge, MA: Candlewick Press.

DiCamillo, K. (2008). *The miraculous journey of Edward Tulane*. New York: Walker.

Donovan, C. A., & Smolkin, L. B. (2002). Children's genre knowledge: An examination of K–5 students' performance on multiple tasks providing differing levels of scaffolding. *Reading Research Quarterly, 37*, 428–465.

Dooley, C. M., & Maloch, B. (2005). Exploring characters through visual representations. In N. L. Roser & M. G. Martinez (Eds.), *What a character! Character study as a guide to literary meaning making in grades K–8* (pp. 111–123). Newark, DE: International Reading Association.

Dorfman, L. R., & Cappelli, R. (2007). *Mentor texts: Teaching writing through children's literature, K–6*. Portland, ME: Stenhouse.

Dorn, L. J., & Soffos, C. (2001). *Shaping literate minds: Developing self-regulated learners*. York, ME: Stenhouse.

Dowhower, S. L. (1989). Repeated reading: Research into practice. *The Reading Teacher, 42*, 502–507.

Dowhower, S. L. (1991). Speaking of prosody: Fluency's unattended bedfellow. *Theory Into Practice, 30*, 165–173.

Duffelmeyer, F. A., Kruse, A. E., Merkley, D. J., & Fyfe, S. A. (1994). Further validation and enhancement of the Names Test. *The Reading Teacher, 48*, 118–128.

Duke, N. K., & Pearson, P. D. (2002). Effective practices for developing reading comprehension. In A. E. Farstrup & S. J. Samuels (Eds.), *What research has to say about reading instruction* (3rd ed., pp. 205–242). Newark, DE: International Reading Association.

Editors of the American Heritage Dictionary. (2004). *100 words every high school freshman should know*. Boston: Houghton Mifflin.

Edwards, P. A. (2004). *Children's literacy development: Making it happen through school, family, and community involvement*. Boston: Allyn & Bacon/Pearson.

Ehrlich, A. (2004). *Cinderella*. New York: Dutton.

Elbow, P. (1998). *Writing without teachers* (2nd ed.). New York: Oxford University Press.

Eldredge, J. L. (2005). *Teach decoding: How and why* (2nd ed.). Upper Saddle River, NJ: Merrill/Prentice Hall.

Elkind, D. (1970). *Children and adolescents: Interpretive essays on Jean Piaget*. New York: Oxford University Press.

Ellis, D. (2001). *The breadwinner*. Toronto, Ontario, Canada: Groundwood Books.

Ellis, D. (2008). *Off to war: Voices of soldiers' children*. Toronto, Ontario, Canada: Groundwood Books.

Erickson, J. R. (1998). *The original adventures of Hank the cowdog*. New York: Puffin Books.

Erlich, A. (2006). *The snow queen*. New York: Dutton.

Faigley, L., Cherry, R. D., Jolliffe, D. A., & Skinner, A. M. (1985). *Assessing writers' knowledge and processes of composing*. Norwood, NJ: Ablex.

Faigley, L., & Witte, S. (1981). Analyzing revision. *College Composition and Communication, 32*, 400–410.

Falk, B., & Blumenreich, M. (2005). *The power of questions: A guide to teacher and student research*. Portsmouth, NH: Heinemann.

Farmer, N. (2002). *The house of the scorpion*. New York: Atheneum.

Farr, R., & Tone, B. (1994). *Portfolio and performance assessment*. Orlando: Harcourt Brace.

Fay, K., & Whaley, S. (2004). *Becoming one community: Reading and writing with English language learners*. Portland, ME: Stenhouse.

Fisher, D., Flood, J., Lapp, D., & Frey, N. (2004). Interactive read-alouds: Is there a common set of implementation practices? *The Reading Teacher, 58*, 8–17.

Fisher, D., Frey, N., & Lapp, D. (2008). Shared readings: Modeling comprehension, vocabulary, text structures, and text features for older readers. *The Reading Teacher, 61*, 548–556.

Fitzgerald, J. (1989). Enhancing two related thought processes: Revision in writing and critical thinking. *The Reading Teacher, 43*, 42–48.

Flake, S. (2007). *The skin I'm in*. New York: Hyperion Books.

Fleischman, P. (2004a). *Joyful noise: Poems for two voices*. New York: HarperCollins.

Fleischman, P. (2004b). *Seedfolks*. New York: Harper Trophy.

Fleischman, S. (2006). *Escape! The story of the Great Houdini*. New York: Greenwillow.

Fletcher, R. (2007). *Reflections*. Katonah, NY: Richard C. Owen.

Fletcher, R., & Portalupi, J. (2001). *Writing workshop: The essential guide*. Portsmouth, NH: Heinemann.

Fletcher, R., & Portalupi, J. (2007). *Craft lessons: Teaching writing K–8* (2nd ed.). York, ME: Stenhouse.

Flower, L. (1989). Taking thought: The role of conscious processing in the making of meaning. In E. P. Maimon, B. F. Nodine, & F. W. O'Connor (Eds.), *Thinking, reasoning, and writing* (pp. 185–212). New York: Longman.

Flynn, R. M. (2007). *Dramatizing the content with curriculum-based readers theatre, grades 6–12*. Newark, DE: International Reading Association.

Fountas, I. C., & Pinnell, G. S. (1996). *Guided reading: Good first teaching for all children*. Portsmouth, NH: Heinemann.

Fountas, I. C., & Pinnell, G. S. (2001). *Guiding readers and writers, grades 3–6*. Portsmouth, NH: Heinemann.

Fountas, I. C., & Pinnell, G. S. (2006a). *The Fountas and Pinnell leveled book list, K–8* (2006–2008 ed.). Portsmouth, NH: Heinemann.

Fountas, I. C., & Pinnell, G. S. (2006b). *Leveled books, K–8: Matching texts to readers for effective teaching*. Portsmouth, NH: Heinemann.

Fountas, I. C., & Pinnell, G. S. (2006c). *Teaching for comprehending and fluency: Thinking, talking, and writing about reading, K–8*. Portsmouth, NH: Heinemann.

Fountas, I. C., & Pinnell, G. S. (2007). *The Fountas and Pinnell benchmark assessment system*. Portsmouth, NH: Heinemann.

Fox, P. (2001). *Slave dancer*. New York: Atheneum.

Frasier, D. (2007). *Miss Alaineus: A vocabulary disaster*. New York: HarperCollins/Voyager.

Fraustino, L. R. (2004). *I walk in dread: The diary of Deliverance Trembly, witness to the Salem witch trials*. New York: Scholastic.

Freedman, R. (1997). *Eleanor Roosevelt: A life of discovery*. New York: Clarion Books.

Freire, P. (2000). *Pedagogy of the oppressed* (30th anniversary ed.). New York: Continuum.

Friedland, E. S., & Truesdell, K. S. (2004). Kids reading together. *The Reading Teacher, 58*, 76–83.

Fry, E. (1968). A readability formula that saves time. *Journal of Reading, 11*, 587.

Funke, C. (2003). *Inkheart*. New York: Scholastic.

Gallagher, K. (2006). *Teaching adolescent writers*. Portland, ME: Stenhouse.

Gambrell, L. B., Malloy, J. A., & Mazzoni, S. A. (2007). Evidence-based best practices for comprehensive literacy instruction. In L. B. Gambrell, L. M. Morrow, & M. Pressley (Eds.), *Best practices in literacy instruction* (3rd ed., pp. 11–29). New York: Guilford Press.

Gambrell, L. B., Palmer, B. M., Codling, R. M., & Mazzoni, S. A. (1996). Assessing motivation to read. *The Reading Teacher, 49*, 518–533.

Ganskey, K. (2000). *Word journeys: Assessment-guided phonics, spelling, and vocabulary instruction*. New York: Guilford Press.

Gantos, J. (2005). *Joey Pigza loses control*. New York: HarperCollins.

Gantos, J. (2007). *I am not Joey Pigza*. New York: Farrar, Straus & Giroux.

Garcia, G. E. (2000). Bilingual children's reading. In M. Kamil, P. B. Mosenthal, P. D. Pearson, & R. Barr (Eds.), *Handbook of reading research* (Vol. 3, pp. 813–834). Newark, DE: International Reading Association.

Garcia, G. E., & Godina, H. (2004). Addressing the literacy needs of adolescent English language learners. In T. L. Jetton & J. A. Dole (Eds.), *Adolescent literacy research and practice* (pp. 304–320): New York: Guilford Press.

Gardiner, S. (2005). *Building students' literacy through SSR*. Alexandria, VA: Association for Supervision and Curriculum Development.

Gaskins, R. W., Gaskins, J. W., & Gaskins, I. W. (1991). A decoding program for poor readers—and the rest of the class, too! *Language Arts, 68,* 213–225.

Gay, G. (2000). *Culturally responsive teaching: Theory, research, and practice.* New York: Teachers College Press.

Genesee, F., & Riches, C. (2006). Literacy: Instructional issues. In F. Genesee, K. Lindholm-Leary, W. M. Saunders, & D. Christian (Eds.), *Educating English language learners: A synthesis of research evidence* (pp. 109–175). New York: Cambridge University Press.

Gentry, J. R., & Gillet, J. W. (1993). *Teaching kids to spell.* Portsmouth, NH: Heinemann.

George, J. C. (2005). *Julie of the wolves.* New York: HarperTrophy.

George-Warren, H. (2006). *Honky-tonk heroes and hillbilly angels: The pioneers of country and western music.* Boston: Houghton Mifflin.

Giblin, J. C. (1997). *When plague strikes.* New York: HarperCollins.

Gill, S. R. (2007). Learning about word parts with Kidspiration. *The Reading Teacher, 61,* 79–84.

Gilles, C. (1998). Collaborative literacy strategies: "We don't need a circle to have a group." In K. G. Short & K. M. Pierce (Eds.), *Talking about books: Literature discussion groups in K–8 classrooms* (pp. 55–68). Portsmouth, NH: Heinemann.

Gillet, J. W., & Beverly, L. (2001). *Directing the writing workshop: An elementary teacher's handbook.* New York: Guilford Press.

Gollub, M. (2004). *Cool melons—turn to frogs! The life and poems of Issa.* New York: Lee & Low.

Goodman, Y. M. (1978). Kid watching: An alternative to testing. *The National Elementary Principal, 57,* 41–45.

Graham, S., & Perin, D. (2007). *Writing next: Effective strategies to improve writing of adolescents in middle and high schools—A report to Carnegie Corporation of New York.* Washington, DC: Alliance for Excellent Education.

Graham, S., MacArthur, C. A., & Fitzgerald, J. (2007). Introduction: Best practices in writing instruction. In S. Graham, C. A. McArthur, & J. Fitzgerald (Eds.), *Best practices in writing instruction* (pp. 1–9). New York: Guilford Press.

Graham, S., Weintraub, N., & Berninger, V. W. (1998). The relationship between handwriting style and speed and legibility. *Journal of Educational Research, 91,* 290–296.

Grandits, J. (2007). *Blue lipstick: Concrete poems.* New York: Clarion Books.

Graves, M. F. (2006). *The vocabulary book: Learning and instruction.* New York: Teachers College Press.

Graves, M. F., & Fitzgerald, J. (2003). Scaffolding reading experiences for multilingual classrooms. In G. G. Garcia (Ed.), *English learners: Reaching the highest level of English literacy* (pp. 96–124). Newark, DE: International Reading Association.

Graves, M. F., & Watts-Taffe, S. M. (2002). The place of word consciousness in a research-based vocabulary program. In S. J. Samuels & A. E. Farstrup (Eds.), *What research has to say about reading instruction* (3rd ed., pp. 140–165). Newark, DE: International Reading Association.

Greenburg, D. (2000). *How I went from bad to verse.* New York: Grosset & Dunlap.

Greene, A. H., & Melton, G. D. (2007). *Test talk: Integrating test preparation into reading workshop.* Portsmouth, ME: Stenhouse.

Griffith, L. W., & Rasinski, T. V. (2004). A focus on fluency: How one teacher incorporated fluency with her reading curriculum. *The Reading Teacher, 58,* 126–137.

Gruber, B. (2006). *Ancient Inca.* Washington, DC: National Geographic Children's Books.

Guiberson, B. Z. (2007). *Cactus hotel.* New York: Henry Holt.

Guthrie, J. T. (2004). Teaching for literacy engagement. *Journal of Literacy Research, 36*(1), 1–28.

Guthrie, J. T., & Wigfield, A. (2000). Engagement and motivation in reading. In M. L. Kamil, P. B. Mosenthal, P. D. Pearson, & R. Barr (Eds.), *Handbook of reading research* (Vol. 3, pp. 403–422). Mahwah, NJ: Erlbaum.

Guthrie, W. (2002). *This land is your land.* Boston: Little, Brown.

Gutman, D. (2006). *The get rich quick club.* New York: HarperCollins.

Gwynne, F. (2005). *A chocolate moose for dinner.* New York: Aladdin Books.

Gwynne, F. (2006). *The king who rained.* New York: Aladdin Books.

Hamilton, V. (2000). *The girl who spun gold.* New York: Blue Sky Press.

Hancock, M. R. (2007). *Language arts: Extending the possibilities.* Upper Saddle River, NJ: Merrill/Pearson.

Hancock, M. R. (2008). *A celebration of literature and response: Children, books, and teachers in K–8 classrooms* (3rd ed.). Upper Saddle River, NJ: Merrill/Prentice Hall.

Harvey, S. (1998). *Nonfiction matters: Reading, writing, and research in grades 3–8*. York, ME: Stenhouse.

Harvey, S., & Goudvis, A. (2007). *Strategies that work: Teaching comprehension for understanding and engagement* (2nd ed.). Portland, ME: Stenhouse.

Haskins, J. (2006). *Delivering justice: W. W. Law and the fight for civil rights*. Cambridge, MA: Candlewick Press.

Hayes, J. R. (2004). A new framework for understanding cognition and affect in writing. In R. B. Ruddell & N. J. Unrau (Eds.), *Theoretical models and processes of reading* (5th ed., pp. 1399–1430). Newark, DE: International Reading Association.

Heacox, D. (2002). *Differentiating instruction in the regular classroom: How to reach and teach all learners, grades 3–12*. Minneapolis, MN: Free Sprit Publishing.

Head, M. H., & Readence, J. E. (1986). Anticipation guides: Meaning through prediction. In E. K. Dishner, T. W. Bean, J. E. Readence, & D. W. Moore (Eds.), *Reading in the content areas* (2nd ed., pp. 229–234). Dubuque, IA: Kendall/Hunt.

Hebert, E. A. (2001). *The power of portfolios: What children can teach us about learning and assessment*. San Francisco: Jossey-Bass.

Heller, M. F. (2006). Telling stories and talking facts: First graders' engagement in a nonfiction book club. *The Reading Teacher, 60*, 358–369.

Hellweg, P. (2006). *The American Heritage children's thesaurus*. Boston: Houghton Mifflin.

Henk, W. A., & Melnick, S. A. (1995). The Reader Self-Perception Scale (RSPS): A new tool for measuring how children feel about themselves as readers. *The Reading Teacher, 48*, 470–482.

Hennessy, B. G. (2006). *The boy who cried wolf*. New York: Simon & Schuster.

Hesse, K. (1999). *Out of the dust*. New York: Scholastic.

Hesse, K. (2001). *Witness*. New York: Scholastic.

Hinton, S. E. (2007). *The outsiders*. New York: Viking.

Hoffman, J. V., Assaf, L. C., & Paris, S. G. (2005). High-stakes testing in reading: Today in Texas, tomorrow? In S. J. Barrentine & S. M. Stokes (Eds.), *Reading assessment: Principles and practices for elementary teachers* (2nd ed., pp. 108–120). Newark, DE: International Reading Association.

Hollingworth, L. (2007). Five ways to prepare for standardized tests without sacrificing best practice. *The Reading Teacher, 61*, 339–342.

Holm, J. L. (2005). *Babymouse: Queen of the world*. New York: Random House.

Holm, J. L. (2007). *Middle school is worse than meatloaf: A year told through stuff*. New York: Atheneum.

Holmes, C. T., & Brown, C. L. (2003). *A controlled evaluation of a total school improvement process, School Renaissance* (Technical report). Athens: University of Georgia.

Holston, V., & Santa, C. (1985). RAFT: A method of writing across the curriculum that works. *Journal of Reading, 28*, 456–457.

Howe, D., & Howe, J. (2006). *Bunnicula: A rabbit-tale of mystery*. New York: Aladdin Books.

Hoyt, L. (2000). *Snapshots*. Portsmouth, NH: Heinemann.

Hubbard, R. S., & Power, B. M. (2003). *The art of classroom inquiry: A handbook for teacher-researchers* (rev. ed.). Portsmouth, NH: Heinemann.

Huerta-Macías, A. (1995). Alternative assessment: Responses to commonly asked questions. *TESOL Journal, 5*, 8–10.

Ikpeze, C. H., & Boyd, F. B. (2007). Web-based inquiry learning: Facilitating thoughtful literacy with webquests. *The Reading Teacher, 60*, 644–654.

International Reading Association (IRA). (1999). *High-stakes assessments in reading: A position statement*. Newark, DE: Author.

Irwin, J. W. (1991). *Teaching reading comprehension processes* (2nd ed). Boston: Allyn & Bacon.

Ivey, G. (2003). "The teacher makes it more explainable" and other reasons to read aloud in the intermediate grades. *The Reading Teacher, 56*, 812–814.

Ivey, G. (2008). Intervening when older youth struggle with reading. In K. A. Hinchman H. K. Sheridan-Thomas (Eds.), *Best practices in adolescent literacy instruction* (pp. 247–260). New York: Guilford Press.

Ivey, G., & Baker, M. I. (2004). Phonics instruction for older students? Just say no. *Educational Leadership, 61*(6), 35–39.

Ivey, G., & Broaddus, K. (2001). "Just plain reading": A survey of what makes students want to read in middle school classrooms. *Reading Research Quarterly, 36*, 350–377.

Jacobson, J., Lapp, D., & Flood, J. (2007). A seven-step instructional plan for teaching English-language learners to comprehend and use homonyms, homophones, and homographs. *Journal of Adolescent and Adult Literacy, 51*, 98–111.

Janeczko, P. B. (2003). *Opening a door: Reading poetry in the middle school classroom.* New York: Scholastic.

Janeczko, P. B. (2005). *A poke in the I: A collection of concrete poems.* Cambridge, MA: Candlewick Press.

Janeczko, P. B. (2009). *A kick in the head: An everyday guide to poetic forms.* Cambridge, MA: Candlewick Press.

Janke, K. (2002). *Survival in the storm: The dust bowl diary of Grace Edwards.* New York: Scholastic.

Jeffers, S. (1993). *Brother eagle, sister sky: A message from Chief Seattle.* New York: Puffin Books.

Jenkins, S. (2007). *Dogs and cats.* Boston: Houghton Mifflin.

Jiménez, F. (1998). *La mariposa.* Boston: Houghton Mifflin.

Jiménez, F. (1999). *The circuit.* Boston: Houghton Mifflin.

Joftus, S., & Maddox-Dolan, B. (2003). *Left out and left behind: NCLB and the American high school.* Washington, DC: Alliance for Excellent Education.

Johns, J. L., & Berglund, R. L. (2006). *Fluency: Strategies and assessments* (3rd ed.). Newark, DE: International Reading Association and Kendall/Hunt.

Johnson, H., & Freedman, L. (2005). *Developing critical awareness at the middle level.* Newark, DE: International Reading Association.

Johnston, F., Bear, D. R., & Invernizzi, M. (2009). *Words their way: Word sorts for derivational relations spellers* (2nd ed.). Upper Saddle River, NJ: Merrill/Prentice Hall.

Johnston, F., Invernizzi, M., & Bear, D. R. (2009). *Words their way: Word sorts for syllables and affixes spellers* (2nd ed.). Upper Saddle River, NJ: Merrill/Prentice Hall.

Judge, L. (2007). *One thousand tracings: Healing the wounds of World War II.* New York: Hyperion Books.

Kadohata, C. (2008). *Cracker! The best dog in Vietnam.* New York: Aladdin Books.

Kame'enui, E., Simmons, D., & Cornachione, C. (2000). *A practical guide to reading assessments.* Newark, DE: International Reading Association.

Karchmer, R. A., Mallette, M. H., Kara-Soteriou, J., & Leu, D. (Eds.). (2005). *Innovative approaches to literacy education: Using the Internet to support new literacies.* Newark, DE: International Reading Association.

Karchmer-Klein, R. (2007). Best practices in using the Internet to support writing. In S. Graham, C. A. McArthur, & J. Fitzgerald (Eds.), *Best practices in writing instruction* (pp. 222–241). New York: Guilford Press.

Kear, D. J., Coffman, G. A., McKenna, M. C., & Ambrosio, A. L. (2000). Measuring attitude toward writing: A new tool for teachers. *The Reading Teacher, 54*, 10–23.

Keehn, S., Martinez, M. G., & Roser, N. L. (2005). Exploring character through readers theatre. In N. L. Roser & M. G. Martinez (Eds.), *What a character! Character study as a guide to literary meaning making in grades K–8* (pp. 96–110). Newark, DE: International Reading Association.

Keene, E. (2006). *Assessing comprehension thinking strategies.* Huntington Beach, CA: Shell Education.

Keene, E. O., & Zimmermann, S. (2007). *Mosaic of thought: The power of comprehension strategy instruction* (2nd ed.). Portsmouth, NH: Heinemann.

Kemper, D., Sebranek, P., & Meyer, V. (2005.) *Write Source.* Wilmington, MA: Write Source/Houghton Mifflin.

Kentley, E. (2001). *Story of the Titanic.* London: Dorling Kindersley.

Kiefer, B. Z., Price-Dennis, D., & Ryan, C. L. (2006). Children's books in a multimodal age. *Language Arts, 84*, 92–98.

Kiester, J. B. (2006a). *Blowing away the state writing assessment test* (3rd ed.). Gainsville, FL: Maupin House.

Kiester, J. B. (2006b). *Giggles in the middle: Caught'ya! Grammar with a giggle for middle school.* Gainesville, FL: Maupin House.

Killgallon, D. (1997). *Sentence composing for middle school: A worktext on sentence variety and maturity.* Portsmouth, NH: Heinemann/Boynton/Cook.

Killgallon, D. (2000). *Sentence composing for elementary school: A worktext to build better sentences.* Portsmouth, NH: Heinemann.

King-Smith, D. (2005). *Babe: The gallant pig.* New York: Knopf.

Kinney, J. (2007). *Diary of a wimpy kid.* New York: Abrams.

Kintsch, W. (2004). The construction-integration model and its implications for instruction. In R. B. Ruddell

& N. J. Unrau (Eds.), *Theoretical models and processes of reading* (5th ed., pp. 1270–1328). Newark, DE: International Reading Association.

Kist, W. (2005). *New literacies in action: Teaching and learning in multiple media.* New York: Teachers College Press.

Koch, K. (1990). *Ross, where did you get that red?* New York: Vintage Books.

Kohn, A. (2001). *Punished by rewards: The trouble with gold stars, incentive plans, A's, praise, and other bribes.* Boston: Houghton Mifflin.

Konigsburg, E. L. (1998). *The view from Saturday.* New York: Aladdin Books.

Korman, G. (2000). *No more dead dogs.* New York: Hyperion Books.

Krulik, N. E. (2008). *P.S. I really like you.* New York: Scholastic.

Krull, K. (2006). *Isaac Newton.* New York: Viking.

Kuhn, M. R., & Rasinski, T. (2007). Best practices in fluency instruction. In L. B. Gambrell, L. M. Morrow, & M. Pressley (Eds.), *Best practices in literacy instruction* (3rd ed., pp. 204–219). New York: Guilford Press.

Kuhn, M. R., & Stahl, S. A. (2004). Fluency: A review of developmental and remedial practices. In R. B. Ruddell & N. J. Unrau (Eds.), *Theoretical models and processes of reading* (5th ed., pp. 412–453). Newark, DE: International Reading Association.

Kuhs, T. M., Johnson, R. L., Agruso, S. A., & Monrad, D. M. (2001). *Put to the test: Tools and techniques for classroom assessment.* Portsmouth, NH: Heinemann.

Labbo, L. D. (2005). Fundamental qualities of effective Internet literacy instruction: An exploration of worthwhile classroom practices. In R. A. Karchmer, M. H. Mallette, J. Kara-Soteriou, & D. J. Leu, Jr. (Eds.), *Innovative approaches to literacy education: Using the Internet to support new literacies* (pp. 165–179). Newark, DE: International Reading Association.

Langley, A. (2004). *Medieval life.* New York: DK Children's Books.

Language of literature, grade 7. (2009). Geneva, IL: Holt McDougal.

Lapp, D., & Flood, J. (2003). Understanding the learner: Using portable assessment. In R. L. McCormack & J. R. Paratore (Eds.), *After early intervention, then what? Teaching struggling readers in grades 3 and beyond* (pp.

10–24). Newark, DE: International Reading Association.

Lattimer, H. (2003). *Thinking through genre.* Portland, ME: Stenhouse.

Lave, J., & Wenger, E. (1991). *Situated learning: Legitimate, peripheral participation.* Cambridge, England: Cambridge University Press.

Lee, H. (2006). *To kill a mockingbird.* New York: HarperCollins.

Leedy, L. (2003). *There's a frog in my throat! 440 animal sayings a little bird told me.* New York: Holiday House.

Leon, V. (1998). *Outrageous women of the middle ages.* New York: Wiley.

Leslie, L., & Caldwell, J. (2006). *Qualitative reading inventory* (4th ed.). Boston: Allyn & Bacon/Pearson.

Lester, J. (1999). *John Henry.* New York: Puffin Books.

Lester, J. (2005a). *Day of tears: A novel in dialogue.* New York: Hyperion Books.

Lester, J. (2005b). *To be a slave.* New York: Puffin Books.

Leu, D. J., Jr., Kinzer, C. K., Coiro, J., & Cammack, D. W. (2004). Toward a theory of new literacies emerging from the Internet and other communication technologies. In R. Ruddell & N. Unrau (Eds.), *Theoretical models and processes of reading* (5th ed., pp. 1570–1613). Newark, DE: International Reading Association.

Lewis, C. S. (2005). *The lion, the witch and the wardrobe.* New York: HarperCollins.

Lewis, J. P. (2002). *Doodle dandies! Poems that take shape.* New York: Aladdin Books.

Lewison, M., Leland, C., & Harste, J. C. (2008). *Creating critical classrooms: K–8 reading and writing with an edge.* New York: Erlbaum.

Lindholm-Leary, K., & Borsato, G. (2006). Academic achievement. In F. Genesee, K. Lindholm-Leary, W. M. Saunders, & D. Christian (Eds.), *Educating English language learners: A synthesis of research evidence* (pp. 176–222). New York: Cambridge University Press.

Longfellow, H. W. (2001). *The midnight ride of Paul Revere* (C. Bing, Illus.). Brooklyn, NY: Handprint Books.

Lowry, L. (1998). *Number the stars.* New York: Laurel Leaf.

Lowry, L. (2006a). *Gathering blue.* New York: Delacorte.

Lowry, L. (2006b). *The giver.* New York: Delacorte.

Lowry, L. (2006c). *The messenger.* New York: Delacorte.

Lukens, R. J. (2006). *A critical handbook of children's literature* (8th ed.). Boston: Allyn & Bacon/Pearson.

Macaulay, D. (1977). *Castle*. Boston: Houghton Mifflin.

Macaulay, D. (2008). *The way we work: Getting to know the amazing human body*. Boston: Houghton Mifflin.

MacLachlan, P. (2004). *Sarah, plain and tall*. New York: HarperTrophy.

Mannis, C. D. (2003). *The queen's progress: An Elizabethan alphabet*. New York: Viking.

Mariotti, A. S., & Homan, S. P. (2005). *Linking reading assessment to instruction*. London: Routledge.

Marrin, A. (2006). *Oh, rats! The story of rats and people*. New York: Dutton.

Marshall, J. C. (2002). *Are they really reading? Expanding SSR in the middle grades*. Portland, ME: Stenhouse.

Martin, S., & Chast, R. (2007). *The alphabet from A to Y with bonus letter Z!* New York: Flying Dolphin Press.

Martinez, M., Roser, N. L., & Strecker, S. (1998/1999). "I never thought I could be a star": A readers theatre ticket to fluency. *The Reading Teacher, 52*, 326–334.

Marzano, R. J., & Pickering, D. J. (2005). *Building academic vocabulary: Teacher's manual*. Alexandria, VA: Association for Supervision and Curriculum Development.

Mather, N., Sammons, J., & Schwartz, J. (2006). Adaptations of the Names Test: Easy to use phonics assessments. *The Reading Teacher, 60*, 114–122.

McCabe, P. P. (2003). Enhancing self-efficacy for high-stakes reading tests. *The Reading Teacher, 57*, 12–20.

McDaniel, L. (1999). *Reach for tomorrow*. New York: Laurel Leaf.

McDermott, G. (2001). *Raven*. San Diego: Voyager.

McGee, L. M., & Richgels, D. J. (1985). Teaching expository text structures to elementary students. *The Reading Teacher, 38*, 739–745.

McKenna, M. C. (2002). *Help for struggling readers: Strategies for grades 3–8*. New York: Guilford Press.

McKenna, M. C., & Kear, D. J. (1990). Measuring attitudes toward reading: A new tool for teachers. *The Reading Teacher, 43*, 626–639.

McKenna, M. C., & Stahl, S. A. (2003). *Assessment for reading instruction*. New York: Guilford Press.

McKeown, M. G., & Beck, I. L. (2004). Direct and rich vocabulary instruction. In J. F. Baumann & E. J. Kame'enui (Eds.), *Vocabulary instruction: Research to practice* (pp. 13–27). New York: Guilford Press.

McKissack, P. C. (1997). *A picture of freedom: The diary of Clotee, a slave girl*. New York: Scholastic.

McLaughlin, M., & Allen, M. B. (2001). *Guided comprehension: A teaching model for grades 3–8*. Newark, DE: International Reading Association.

McLeod, B. (2006). *Superhero ABC*. New York: HarperCollins.

McLimans, D. (2006). *Gone wild: An endangered animal alphabet*. New York: Walker.

McNabb, M. L. (2006). *Literacy learning in networked classrooms: Using the Internet with middle-level students*. Newark, DE: International Reading Association.

McQuillan, J. (1998). *The literacy crisis: False claims, real solutions*. Portsmouth, NH: Heinemann.

Mellard, D. F., & Johnson, E. (2008). *RTI: A practitioner's guide to implementing Response to Intervention*. Thousand Oaks, CA: Corwin Press and the National Association of Elementary School Principals.

Mermelstein, L. (2007). *Don't forget to share: The crucial last step in the writing workshop*. Portsmouth, NH: Heinemann.

Meyer, B. J. F., & Poon, L. W. (2004). Effects of structure strategy training and signaling on recall of text. In R. B. Ruddell & N. J. Unrau (Eds.), *Theoretical models and processes of reading* (5th ed., pp. 810–850). Newark, DE: International Reading Association.

Mitchell, S. (2007). *The ugly duckling*. Cambridge, MA: Candlewick Press.

Moline, S. (1995). *I see what you mean: Children at work with visual information*. York, ME: Stenhouse.

Moll, L. (1994). Literacy research in community and classrooms: A sociocultural approach. In R. R. Ruddell, M. R. Ruddell, & H. Singer (Eds.), *Theoretical models and processes of reading* (4th ed., pp. 197–207). Newark, DE: International Reading Association.

Moll, L. C., & Gonzales, N. (2004). Engaging life: A funds of knowledge approach to multicultural education. In J. A. Banks & C. A. M. Banks (Eds.), *Handbook of research on multicultural education* (2nd ed., pp. 699–715). San Francisco: Jossey-Bass.

Mortenson, G., & Relin, D. O. (2007). *Three cups of tea: One man's mission to promote peace . . . one school at a time*. New York: Penguin.

Murray, D. M. (1982). *Learning by teaching*. Montclair, NJ: Boynton/Cook.

Murray, D. M. (2003). *A writer teaches writing* (2nd ed.). Belmont, CA: Wadsworth.

Myers, W. D. (2005). *Patrol*. New York: HarperCollins.

Myers, W. D. (2008). *Fallen angels*. New York: Scholastic.

Nagy, W. E. (1988). *Teaching vocabulary to improve reading comprehension*. Urbana, IL: ERIC Clearinghouse on Reading and Communication Skills and the National Council of Teachers of English and the International Reading Association.

Nagy, W. E., Anderson, R. C., & Herman, P. A. (1987). Learning word meanings from context during normal reading. *American Educational Research Journal, 24*, 237–270.

Napier, M. (2002). *Z is for Zamboni: A hockey alphabet*. Chelsea, MI: Sleeping Bear Press.

National Commission on Excellence in Education. (1983). *A nation at risk: The imperative for educational reform*. Washington, DC: U.S. Government Printing Office.

National Governors Association. (2005). *Reading to achieve: A governor's guide to literacy*. Washington DC: National Governors Association for Best Practices.

National Middle School Association. (2003). *This we believe: Successful schools for young adolescents*. Westerville, OH: Author.

National Reading Panel. (2000). *Teaching children to read: An evidence-based assessment of the scientific research literature on reading and its implications for reading instruction*. Washington, DC: National Institute of Child Health and Human Development.

Naylor, P. R. (1998). *Sang spell*. New York: Atheneum.

Nelson, K. (2008). *We are the ship: The story of Negro League baseball*. New York: Hyperion Books.

Neruda, P. (2000). *Selected odes of Pablo Neruda*. Berkeley: University of California Press.

Nilsson, N. L. (2008). A critical analysis of eight informal reading inventories. *The Reading Teacher, 61*, 526–536.

Nye, N. S. (Compiler). (2002a). *The flag of childhood: Poems from the Middle East*. New York: Aladdin Books.

Nye, N. S. (2002b). *19 varieties of gazelle: Poems of the Middle East*. New York: Greenwillow.

O'Brien, T. (1998). *The things they carried*. New York: Broadway.

O'Donohue, W., & Kitchener, R. F. (Eds.). (1998). *Handbook of behaviorism*. New York: Academic Press.

Ogle, D. M. (1986). K-W-L: A teaching model that develops active reading of expository text. *The Reading Teacher, 39*, 564–570.

Ohlhausen, M. M., & Jepsen, M. (1992). Lessons from Goldilocks: "Somebody's been choosing my books but I can make my own choices now!" *The New Advocate*, 5, 31–46.

Oldfather, P. (1995). Commentary: What's needed to maintain and extend motivation for literacy in the middle grades. *Journal of Reading, 38*, 420–422.

Olson, C. B., & Land, R. (2007). A cognitive strategies approach to reading and writing instruction for English language learners in secondary school. *Research in the Teaching of English, 41*, 269–303.

O'Malley, J. M., & Pierce, L. V. (1996). *Authentic assessment for English language learners: Practical approaches for teachers*. Boston: Addison-Wesley.

O'Neill, M. (1990). *Hailstones and halibut bones*. New York: Doubleday.

Opitz, M. F., & Ford, M. P. (2008). *Do-able differentiation: Varying groups, texts, and supports to reach readers*. Portsmouth, NH: Heinemann.

Opitz, M. F., Ford, M. P., & Zbaracki, M. D. (2006). *Books and beyond: New ways to reach readers*. Portsmouth, NH: Heinemann.

Opitz, M. F., & Rasinski, T. V. (1998). *Good-bye round robin: Twenty-five effective oral reading strategies*. Portsmouth, NH: Heinemann.

Osborne, M. P. (1998). *Hour of the Olympics*. New York: Random House.

Osborne, M. P. (2000). *Knights and castles*. New York: Random House.

Osborne, M. P., & Boyce, N. P. (2004). *Olympics of Ancient Greece*. New York: Random House.

Osborne, W., & Osborne, M. P. (1995). *Tonight on the Titanic*. New York: Random House.

Osborne, W., & Osborne, M. P. (2002). *Titanic: A nonfiction companion to Tonight on the Titanic*. New York: Random House.

Padgett, R. (2007). *Handbook of poetic forms* (2nd ed.). New York: Teachers & Writers Collaborative.

Palinscar, A. S., & Brown, A. L. (1986). Interactive teaching to promote independent learning from text. *The Reading Teacher, 39*, 771–777.

Palmer, B. C., Shackelford, V. S., Miller, S. C., & Leclere, J. T. (2006/2007). Bridging two worlds: Reading comprehension, figurative language instruction, and the English-language learner. *Journal of Adolescent and Adult Literacy, 50*, 258–267.

Paris, S. G., Wasik, D. A., & Turner, J. C. (1991). The development of strategic readers. In R. Barr, M. L.

Kamil, P. B. Mosenthal, & P. D. Pearson (Eds.), *Handbook of reading research* (Vol. 2, pp. 609–640). Mahwah, NJ: Erlbaum.

Park, B. (1997). *Junie B. Jones is a party animal*. New York: Random House.

Park, L. S. (2007). *Project mulberry*. New York: Yearling.

Patent, D. H. (2004). *Right dog for the job: Ira's path from service dog to guide dog*. New York: Walker.

Paterson, K. (2005). *Bridge to Terabithia*. New York: HarperTrophy.

Patron, S. (2006). *The higher power of Lucky*. New York: Atheneum.

Paulsen, G. (2007). *Hatchet*. New York: Simon & Schuster.

Pearson, P. D., Raphael, T. E., Benson, V. L., & Madda, C. L. (2007). Balance in comprehensive literacy instruction: Then and now. In L. B. Gambrell, L. M. Morrow, & M. Pressley (Eds.), *Best practices in literacy instruction* (3rd ed., pp. 31–54). New York: Guilford Press.

Peregoy, S. F., & Boyle, O. F. (2008). *Reading, writing, and learning in ESL: A resource book for teaching K–12 English learners* (5th ed.). Boston: Allyn & Bacon/Pearson.

Persky, H. R., Daane, M. C., & Jin, Y. (2003). *The nation's report card: Writing 2002*. Washington, DC: U.S. Department of Education.

Peterson, R., & Eeds, M. (2007). *Grand conversations: Literature groups in action* (updated ed.). New York: Scholastic.

Philbrick, R. (2001). *Freak the mighty*. New York: Scholastic.

Piaget, J. (1969). *The psychology of intelligence*. Paterson, NJ: Littlefield, Adams.

Pikulski, J. J., & Chard, D. J. (2005). Fluency: Bridge between decoding and reading comprehension. *The Reading Teacher, 58*, 510–519.

Pilgreen, J. L. (2000). *The SSR handbook: How to organize and manage a sustained silent reading program*. Portsmouth, NH: Boynton/Cook/Heinemann.

Pittelman, S. D., Heimlich, J. E., Berglund, R. L., & French, M. P. (1991). *Semantic feature analysis: Classroom applications*. Newark, DE: International Reading Association.

Platt, R. (2003). *Castle diary: The journal of Tobias Burgess*. Cambridge, MA: Candlewick Press.

Porter, C., & Cleland, J. (1995). *The portfolio as a learning strategy*. Portsmouth, NH: Heinemann.

Pratt-Serafini, K. J. (2002). *Saguaro moon: A desert journal*. Nevada City, CA: Dawn.

Prelutsky, J. (1993). *Nightmares: Poems to trouble your sleep*. New York: Mulberry Books.

Prelutsky, J. (1996). *A pizza the size of the sun*. New York: Greenwillow.

Prelutsky, J. (Sel.). (2000). *The Random House book of poetry for children*. New York: Random House.

Prelutsky, J. (2007). *My parents think I'm sleeping*. New York: Greenwillow.

Pressley, M. (2000). What should comprehension instruction be instruction of? In M. L. Kamil, P. B. Mosenthal, P. D. Pearson, & R. Barr (Eds.), *Handbook of reading research* (Vol. 3, pp. 545–561). Mahwah, NJ: Erlbaum.

Pressley, M. (2002a). Comprehension strategies instruction: A turn-of-the-century status report. In C. C. Block & M. Pressley (Eds.), *Comprehension instruction: Research-based best practices* (pp. 11–27). New York: Guilford Press.

Pressley, M. (2002b). Metacognition and self-regulated comprehension. In A. E. Farstrup & S. J. Samuels (Eds.), *What research has to say about reading instruction* (3rd ed., pp. 291–309). Newark, DE: International Reading Association.

Pressley, M., Dolezal, S. E., Raphael, L. M., Mohan, L., Roehrig, A. D., & Bogner, K. (2003). *Motivating primary-grade students*. New York: Guilford Press.

Pryle, M. (2007). *Teaching students to write effective essays*. New York: Scholastic.

Raphael, T. E. (1986). Teaching question-answer relationships, revisited. *The Reading Teacher, 39*, 516–523.

Raphael, T. E., Highfield, K., & Au, K. H. (2006). *QAR now: A powerful and practical framework that develops comprehension and higher-level thinking in all students*. New York: Scholastic.

Rasinski, T. (2003). *The fluent reader*. New York: Scholastic.

Rasinski, T. (2005a). *Daily word ladders: Grades 2–3*. New York: Scholastic.

Rasinski, T. (2005b). *Daily word ladders: Grades 4–6*. New York: Scholastic.

Rasinski, T., & Padak, N. (2004). *Effective reading strategies: Teaching children who find reading difficult*. Upper Saddle River, NJ: Merrill/Prentice Hall.

Rasinski, T., & Padak, N. (2005a). *3-minute reading assessments: Word recognition, fluency, and comprehension for grades 1–4*. New York: Scholastic.

Rasinski, T., & Padak, N. (2005b). *3-minute reading assessments: Word recognition, fluency, and comprehension for grades 5–8*. New York: Scholastic.

Rasinski, T., & Padak, N. (2008). *From phonics to fluency: Effective teaching of decoding and reading fluency in the elementary school* (2nd ed.). Boston: Allyn & Bacon/Pearson.

Rea, D. M., & Mercuri, S. P. (2006). *Research-based strategies for English language learners: How to teach goals and meet standards, K–8*. Portsmouth, NH: Heinemann.

Readence, J. E., Moore, D. W., & Rickelman, R. J. (2000). *Prereading activities for content area reading and learning* (3rd ed.). Newark, DE: International Reading Association.

Reutzel, D. R., & Cooter, R. B., Jr. (2008). *Teaching children to read: From basals to books* (5th ed.). Upper Saddle River, NJ: Merrill/Prentice Hall.

Riches, C., & Genesee, F. (2006). Literacy: Crosslinguistic and crossmodal issues. In F. Genesee, K. Lindholm-Leary, W. M. Saunders, & D. Christian (Eds.), *Educating English language learners: A synthesis of research evidence* (pp. 64–108). New York: Cambridge University Press.

Rickelman, R. J., & Taylor, D. B. (2006). Teaching vocabulary and learning content-area words. In C. C. Block & J. N. Mangieri (Eds.), *The vocabulary-enriched classroom: Practices for improving the reading performance of all students in grades 3 and up* (pp. 54–73). New York: Scholastic.

Robb, L. (2002). Multiple texts: Multiple opportunities for teaching and learning. *Voices From the Middle, 9*(4), 28–32.

Robb, L. (2003). *Teaching reading in social studies, science, and math*. New York: Scholastic.

Robb, L. (2008). *Differentiating reading instruction: How to teach reading to meet the needs of each student*. New York: Scholastic.

Romano, T. (2000). *Blending genre, alternating style: Writing multiple genre papers*. Portsmouth, NH: Heinemann/Boynton/Cook.

Rosenblatt, L. (2005). *Making meaning with texts: Selected essays*. Portsmouth, NH: Heinemann.

Rosenblatt, L. M. (2004). The transactional theory of reading and writing. In R. B. Ruddell & N. J. Unrau (Eds.), *Theoretical models and processes of reading* (5th ed., pp. 1363–1398). Newark, DE: International Reading Association.

Rothenberg, C., & Fisher, D. (2007). *Teaching English language learners: A differentiated approach*. Upper Saddle River, NJ: Merrill/Prentice Hall.

Routman, R. (2004). *Writing essentials: Raising expectations and results while simplifying teaching*. Portsmouth, NH: Heinemann.

Rowling, J. K. (1999). *Harry Potter and the chamber of secrets*. New York: Scholastic.

Ruddell, D. (2007). *Today at the Bluebird Café: A branchful of birds*. New York: McElderry.

Ruddell, R. B., & Unrau, N. J. (2004). Reading as a meaning-construction process: The reader, the text, and the teacher. In R. B. Ruddell & N. J. Unrau (Eds.), *Theoretical models and processes of reading* (5th ed., pp. 1462–1521). Newark, DE: International Reading Association.

Rumelhart, D. E. (2004). Toward an interactive model of reading. In R. B. Ruddell & N. J. Unrau (Eds.), *Theoretical models and processes of reading* (5th ed., pp. 1149–1179). Newark, DE: International Reading Association.

Ryan, P. M. (1998). *Riding Freedom*. New York: Scholastic.

Ryan, P. M. (2002). *Esperanza rising*. New York: Scholastic.

Rylant, C. (1988). *Every living thing*. New York: Aladdin Books.

Sachar, L. (2008). *Holes*. New York: Farrar, Straus & Giroux.

Samuels, S. J. (1979). The method of repeated readings. *The Reading Teacher, 32,* 403–408.

Samway, K. D., & Whang, G. (1996). *Literature study circles in a multicultural classroom*. York, ME: Stenhouse.

Santoro, L. E., Chard, D. J., Howard, L., & Baker, S. K. (2008). Making the *very* most of classroom read-alouds to promote comprehension and vocabulary. *The Reading Teacher, 61,* 396–408.

Schaefer, T. (2005). *The Vietnam Veterans Memorial*. Portsmouth, NH: Heinemann.

Schlitz, L. A. (2007). *Good masters! Sweet ladies! Voices from a medieval village*. Cambridge, MA: Candlewick Press.

Schmidt, G. D. (2007). *The Wednesday wars*. New York: Clarion Books.

Schmidt, R. (2008). Really reading: What does Accelerated Reader teach adults and children? *Language Arts, 85,* 202–211.

Schreider, P. A. (1991). Understanding prosody's role in reading acquisition. *Theory Into Practice, 30,* 158–164.

Schwartz, D. M. (2001). *Q is for quark: A science alphabet book.* Berkeley, CA: Tricycle Press.

Scieszka, J. (1996). *The true story of the 3 little pigs!* New York: Puffin Books.

Scieszka, J. (2004a). *Knights of the kitchen table.* New York: Puffin Books.

Scieszka, J. (2004b). *Tut tut.* New York: Puffin Books.

Scieszka, J. (2004c). *Your mother was a Neanderthal.* New York: Puffin Books.

Scieszka, J. (2005). *Baloney (Henry P.).* New York: Puffin Books.

Scott, J. A., & Nagy, W. E. (2004). Developing word consciousness. In J. F. Baumann & E. J. Kame'enui (Eds.), *Vocabulary instruction: Research to practice* (pp. 210–217). New York: Guilford Press.

Selznick, B. (2007). *The invention of Hugo Cabret.* New York: Scholastic.

Seuling, B. (2003). *Flick a switch: How electricity gets to your home.* New York: Holiday House.

Shanahan, T. (1988). The reading-writing relationship: Seven instructional principles. *The Reading Teacher, 41,* 636–647.

Shanahan, T. (2004). Overcoming the dominance of communication: Writing to think and to learn. In T. L. Jettson & J. A. Dole (Eds.), *Adolescent literacy research and practice* (pp. 59–73). New York: Guilford Press.

Shanahan, T., & Beck, I. (2006). Effective literacy teaching for English-language learners. In D. August & T. Shanahan (Eds.), *Developing literacy in second-language learners: Report of the National Literacy Panel on Language-Minority Children and Youth* (pp. 415–488). Mahwah, NJ: Erlbaum.

Shanker, J. L., & Cockrum, W. (2009). *Locating and correcting reading difficulties* (9th ed.). Boston: Allyn & Bacon/Pearson.

Shannon, P. (1995). *Text, lies, & videotape: Stories about life, literacy, & learning.* Portsmouth, NH: Heinemann.

Shea, M. (2006). *Where's the glitch? How to use running records with older readers, grades 5–8.* Portsmouth, NH: Heinemann.

Shelton, N. R., & Fu, D. (2004). Creating space for teaching writing and for test preparation. *Language Arts, 82,* 120–128.

Short, K. G., & Harste, J. (1996). *Creating classrooms for authors and inquirers.* Portsmouth, NH: Heinemann.

Shulman, M. (2006). *Mom and dad are palindromes.* San Francisco: Chronicle Books.

Sidman, J. (2007). *This is just to say: Poems of apology and forgiveness.* Boston: Houghton Mifflin.

Siebert, D. (2006). *Tour America: A journey through poems and art.* San Francisco: Chronicle Books.

Silverman, S. (2005). Getting connected: My experience as a collaborative Internet project coordinator. In R. A. Karchmer, M. H. Mallette, J. Kara-Soteriou, & D. J. Leu, Jr. (Eds.), *Innovative approaches to literacy education: Using the Internet to support new literacies* (pp. 103–120). Newark, DE: International Reading Association.

Silvernail, D. L., & Gritter, A. K. (2007). *Maine's middle school laptop program: Creating better writers.* Gorham, ME: University of Southern Maine, Maine Education Policy Research Institute.

Simon, L. (2005). *Write as an expert: Explicit teaching of genres.* Portsmouth, NH: Heinemann.

Simon, S. (2006). *The brain: Our nervous system.* New York: HarperCollins.

Sipe, R. B., & Rosewarne, T. (2006). *Purposeful writing: Genre study in the secondary writing workshop.* Portsmouth, NH: Heinemann.

Skillings, M. J., & Ferrell, R. (2000). Student-generated rubrics: Bringing students into the assessment process. *The Reading Teacher, 53,* 452–455.

Skinner, B. F. (1974). *About behaviorism.* New York: Random House.

Slavin, R. E., Cheung, A., Groff, C., & Lake, C. (2008). Effective reading programs for middle and high schools: A best-evidence synthesis. *Reading Research Quarterly, 43,* 290–322.

Smith, J. (2005). *Bone: Out of Boneville.* New York: Scholastic/Graphix.

Smith, K. (1998). Entertaining a text: A reciprocal process. In K. G. Short & K. M. Pierce (Eds.), *Talking about books: Literature discussion groups in K–8 classrooms* (pp. 17–31). Portsmouth, NH: Heinemann.

Snicket, L. (2003). *Lemony Snicket: The unauthorized autobiography.* New York: HarperCollins.

Soto, G. (2005). *Neighborhood odes.* San Diego: Harcourt.

Soto, G. (2007). *Canto familiar.* San Diego: Harcourt.

Spandel, V. (2001). *Books, lessons, ideas for teaching the six traits*. Wilmington, MA: Great Source.

Spandel, V. (2009). *Creating writers through 6-trait writing assessment and instruction* (5th ed.). Boston: Allyn & Bacon/Pearson.

Speare, E. G. (2001). *The witch of Blackbird Pond*. Boston: Houghton Mifflin.

Spinelli, J. (2002). *Loser*. New York: HarperCollins.

Spinelli, J. (2004). *Stargirl*. New York: Laurel Leaf.

Spivey, N. (1997). *The constructivist metaphor: Reading, writing, and the making of meaning*. New York: Academic Press.

Stahl, S. A. (1999). *Vocabulary development*. Cambridge, MA: Brookline Books.

Stahl, S. A., & Kapinus, B. (1991). Possible sentences: Predicting word meanings to teach content area vocabulary. *The Reading Teacher, 45*, 36–43.

Stahl, S. A., & Nagy, W. E. (2006). *Teaching word meanings*. Mahwah, NJ: Erlbaum.

Stahl, S. A., Richek, M. G., & Vandevier, R. (1991). Learning word meanings through listening: A sixth grade replication. In J. Zutell & S. McCormick (Eds.), *Learning factors/teacher factors: Issues in literacy research. Fortieth yearbook of the National Reading Conference* (pp. 185–192). Chicago: National Reading Conference.

Stanovich, K. E. (1986). Matthew effects in reading: Some consequences of individual differences in the acquisition of literacy. *Reading Research Quarterly, 21*, 360–406.

Stanovich, K. E. (1992). Speculations on the causes and consequences of individual differences in early reading acquisition. In P. B. Gough, L. C. Ehri, & R. Treiman (Eds.), *Reading acquisition* (pp. 307–342). Hillsdale, NJ: Erlbaum.

Steig, W. (1990). *Doctor De Soto*. New York: Farrar, Straus & Giroux.

Steig, W. (2006). *Sylvester and the magic pebble*. New York: Aladdin Books.

Stien, D., & Beed, P. L. (2004). Bridging the gap between fiction and nonfiction in the literature circle setting. *The Reading Teacher, 57*, 510–518.

Stipek, D. J. (2002). *Motivation to learn: Integrating theory and practice* (4th ed.). Boston: Allyn & Bacon.

Stires, S. (1991). Thinking through the process: Self-evaluation in writing. In B. M. Power & R. Hubbard (Eds.), *The Heinemann reader: Literacy in process* (pp. 295–310). Portsmouth, NH: Heinemann.

Swanborn, M. S. W., & de Glopper, K. (1999). Incidental word learning while reading: A meta-analysis. *Review of Educational Research, 69*, 261–285.

Sweet, A. P., & Snow, C. E. (2003). Reading for comprehension. In A. P. Sweet & C. E. Snow (Eds.), *Rethinking reading comprehension* (pp. 1–11). New York: Guilford Press.

Swift, K. (1993). Try reading workshop in your classroom. *The Reading Teacher, 46*, 366–371.

Tan, S. (2007). *The arrival*. New York: Arthur A. Levine/Scholastic.

Tanaka, S. (1996). *On board the Titanic: What it was like when the great liner sank*. New York: Hyperion Books.

Taylor, M. D. (2001). *Roll of thunder, hear my cry*. New York: Dial Books.

Taylor, T. (2003), *The cay*. New York: Laurel Leaf.

Terban, M. (1992). *The dove dove: Funny homograph riddles*. New York: Clarion Books.

Terban, M. (2006a). *Scholastic dictionary of idioms*. New York: Scholastic.

Terban, M. (2006b). *Scholastic dictionary of spelling*. New York: Scholastic.

Terban, M. (2007a). *Eight ate: A feast of homonym riddles*. New York: Clarion Books.

Terban, M. (2007b). *In a pickle and other funny idioms*. New York: Clarion Books.

Terban, M. (2007c). *Mad as a wet hen! And other funny idioms*. New York: Clarion Books.

Testa, M. (2005). *Becoming Joe Di Maggio*. Cambridge, MA: Candlewick Press.

Thayer, E. L. (2000). *Ernest L. Thayer's Casey at the Bat: A ballad of the republic sung in the year 1888* (C. Bing, Illus.) Brooklyn, NY: Handprint Books.

Thayer, E. L. (2006). *Casey at the bat*. Tonawanda, NY: Kids Can Press.

Thimmesh, C. (2006). *Team moon: How 400,000 people landed Apollo 11 on the moon*. Boston: Houghton Mifflin.

Tierney, R. J. (1983). Writer-reader transactions: Defining the dimensions of negotiation. In P. L. Stock (Ed.), *Forum: Essays on theory and practice in the teaching of writing* (pp. 147–151). Upper Montclair, NJ: Boynton/Cook.

Tierney, R., & Pearson, P. D. (1983). Toward a composing model of reading. *Language Arts, 60*, 568–580.

Tierney, R. J. (1990). Redefining reading comprehension. *Educational Leadership, 47,* 37–42.

Tierney, R. J., & Readence, J. E. (2005). *Reading strategies and practices: A compendium* (6th ed.). Boston: Allyn & Bacon.

Tierney, R. J., & Shanahan, T. (1996). Research on the reading-writing relationship: Interactions, transactions, and outcomes. In R. Barr, M. L. Kamil, P. Mosenthal, & P. D. Pearson (Eds.), *Handbook of reading research* (Vol. 2, pp. 246–280). Mahwah, NJ: Erlbaum.

Toll, C. A. (2005). *The literacy coach's survival guide: Essential questions and practical answers.* Newark, DE: International Reading Association.

Tomlinson, C. A. (2001). *The differentiated classroom: Responding to the needs of all learners* (2nd ed.). Alexandria, VA: Association for Supervision and Curriculum Development.

Tomlinson, C. A. (2004). *How to differentiate instruction in mixed-ability classrooms* (2nd ed.). Alexandria, VA: Association for Supervision and Curriculum Development.

Tompkins, G. E. (2008). *Teaching writing: Balancing process and product* (5th ed.). Upper Saddle River, NJ: Merrill/Prentice Hall.

Tompkins, G. E., & Collom, S. (Eds.). (2004). *Sharing the pen: Interactive writing with young children.* Upper Saddle River, NJ: Merrill/Prentice Hall.

Tompkins, G. E., & Yaden, D. B., Jr. (1986). *Answering students' questions about words.* Urbana, IL: ERIC Clearinghouse on Reading and Communication Skills and the National Council of Teachers of English.

Topping, K. J., & Paul, T. D. (1999). Computer-assisted assessment of practice at reading: A large scale survey using Accelerated Reader data. *Reading & Writing Quarterly, 15,* 213–231.

Tovani, C. (2000). *I read it, but I don't get it: Comprehension strategies for adolescent readers.* Portland, ME: Stenhouse.

Tracey, D. H., & Morrow, L. M. (2006). *Lenses on reading: An introduction to theories and models.* New York: Guilford Press.

Turner, J., & Paris, S. G. (1995). How literacy tasks influence children's motivation for literacy. *The Reading Teacher, 48,* 662–673.

Unrau, N. (2004). *Content area reading and writing: Fostering literacies in middle and high school cultures.* Upper Saddle River, NJ: Merrill/Prentice Hall.

Vacca, R. T., & Vacca, J. L. (2008). *Content area reading: Literacy and learning across the curriculum* (9th ed.). Boston: Allyn & Bacon/Pearson.

Van Allsburg, C. (1982). *Jumanji.* Boston: Houghton Mifflin.

Van Allsburg, C. (1983). *Wreck of the Zephyr.* Boston: Houghton Mifflin.

Van Allsburg, C. (1986). *The stranger.* Boston: Houghton Mifflin.

Van Allsburg, C. (1988). *Two bad ants.* Boston: Houghton Mifflin.

Van Allsburg, C. (1990). *Just a dream.* Boston: Houghton Mifflin.

Van Allsburg, C. (1991). *The wretched stone.* Boston: Houghton Mifflin.

Van Allsburg, C. (1993a). *The garden of Abdul Gasazi.* Boston: Houghton Mifflin.

Van Allsburg, C. (1993b). *The sweetest fig.* Boston: Houghton Mifflin.

Van Allsburg, C. (1996). *The mysteries of Harris Burdick.* Boston: Houghton Mifflin.

Van Allsburg, C. (2002). *Zathura.* Boston: Houghton Mifflin.

Van Allsburg, C. (2005). *The polar express.* Boston: Houghton Mifflin.

Van Allsburg, C. (2006). *Probuditi.* Boston: Houghton Mifflin.

Van Den Broek, P., & Kremer, K. E. (2000). The mind in action: What it means to comprehend during reading. In B. M. Taylor, M. F. Graves, & P. Van Den Broek (Eds.), *Reading for meaning: Fostering comprehension in the middle grades* (pp. 1–31). New York: Teachers College Press.

Venezky, R. L. (1999). *The American way of spelling: The structure and origins of American English orthography.* New York: Guilford Press.

Vietnam War. (2005). New York: DK Publishing.

Vygotsky, L. S. (1978). *Mind in society.* Cambridge, MA: Harvard University Press.

Vygotsky, L. S. (1986). *Thought and language.* Cambridge, MA: MIT Press.

Wagstaff, J. (1999). *Teaching reading and writing with word walls.* New York: Scholastic.

Walsh, K. (2003, Spring). Basal readers: The lost opportunity to build the knowledge that propels comprehension. *American Educator, 27,* 24–27.

Ward, C. C. (2006). *How writers grow: A guide for middle school teachers*. Portsmouth, NH: Heinemann.

Warren, A. (2008). *Escape from Saigon: How a Vietnam War orphan became an American boy*. New York: Farrar, Straus & Giroux.

Weber, C. (2002). *Publishing with students: A comprehensive guide*. Portsmouth, NH: Heinemann.

Whelan, G. (2001). *Homeless bird*. New York: HarperCollins.

White, E. B. (2006). *Charlotte's web*. New York: HarperCollins.

White, E. E. (1998). *Voyage on the great Titanic: The diary of Margaret Ann Brady*. New York: Scholastic.

White, T. G., Sowell, J., & Yanagihara, A. (1989). Teaching elementary students to use word-part clues. *The Reading Teacher, 42*, 302–308.

Whitin, P. E. (2002). Leading into literature circles through the sketch-to-stretch strategy. *The Reading Teacher, 55*, 444–450.

Wilhelm, J. D. (2001). *Improving comprehension with think-aloud strategies*. New York: Scholastic.

Wilhelm, J. D. (2002). *Action strategies for deepening comprehension*. New York: Scholastic.

Williams, M. (2007). *The adventures of Robin Hood*. New York: Walker.

Winograd, P., & Arrington, H. J. (1999). Best practices in literacy assessment. In L. B. Gambrell, L. M. Morrow, S. B. Neuman, & M. Pressley (Eds.), *Best practices in literacy instruction* (pp. 210–241). New York: Guilford Press.

Wong, J. S. (2006). *Before it wriggles away*. Katonah, NY: Richard C. Owen.

Wood-Ellem, E. (2001). *Queen Salote of Tonga*. Honolulu: University of Hawai'i Press.

Woods, M. L., & Moe, A. J. (2007). *Analytical reading inventory* (8th ed.). Upper Saddle River. NJ: Merrill/Prentice Hall.

Woodson, J. (2002). *Hush*. New York: Scholastic.

Woodson, J. (2004). *Locomotion*. New York: Puffin Books.

Woodson, J. (2007). *Feathers*. New York: Putnam.

Woodson, J. (2008). *After Tupac & D Foster*. New York: Putnam.

Wormeli, R. (2001). *Meet me in the middle: Becoming an accomplished middle-level teacher*. Portland, ME: Stenhouse/National Middle School Association.

Yatvin, J. (2004). *A room with a differentiated view: How to serve ALL children as individual learners*. Portsmouth, NH: Heinemann.

Yep, L. (2000). *Dragonwings*. New York: HarperTrophy.

Ysseldyke, J. E., & Taylor, B. M. (2007). Understanding the factors that allegedly contribute to students' reading difficulties. In B. M. Taylor & J. E. Ysseldyke (Eds.), *Effective instruction for struggling readers, K–6* (pp. 1–16). New York: Teachers College Press.

Zelinsky, P. O. (1996). *Rumpelstiltskin*. New York: Puffin Books.

Zimmermann, S., & Hutchins, C. (2003). *7 keys to comprehension: How to help your kids read it and get it!* New York: Three Rivers Press.

INDEX